PROBLEMS
AND PERSPECTIVES
IN THE PHILOSOPHY OF RELIGION

edited by

George I. Mavrodes,   *The University of Michigan*

Stuart C. Hackett,   *Wheaton College*

ALLYN AND BACON

BOSTON

Frontispiece and cover: the sign   "AH" on a lotus supported by a Vajra.
(Courtesy, Museum of Fine Arts, Boston)
Gift of Edward W. Forbes

PREFACE

The present volume attempts to introduce the reader to the principal questions of the philosophy of religion. It does so by confronting him with the work of some of the historical and contemporary thinkers who have made significant contributions in dealing with the varied perplexities involved in such issues.

We have wanted to acquaint the reader with the major topics that have been discussed, with the range of the viewpoints that have been expressed, and with the variety of styles of argument that have been and are being used. In addition, and perhaps most important, we have wanted the selections to provide a stimulus for the reader to enter the philosophic arena himself, by way of his own discussion of, reaction against, or development of the views presented.

Some special features of the book may require a few words of explanation. The questions of this branch of philosophic study have usually been discussed in one or other of two ways: first, by a consideration of particular problems—e.g., the meaning of religious language, the nature of revelation, the existence and characteristics of the Divine Reality; second, by a development of total perspectives which constitute more or less complete approaches within each of which all the various problems are given attention. Therefore the materials of the volume have been arranged in two ways to exhibit both the problems approach and the approach in terms of inclusive viewpoints.

The first table of contents groups the selections under six different topics: (1) Reason, Faith, and Philosophy, (2) Arguments for the Divine Reality, (3) Religious Experience and Revelation, (4)

Religion and Ethics, (5) The Meaning of Religious Statements, and (6) God, Man and the World. In the text the selections appear in the order in which this table of contents lists them. The second table of contents groups the same selections under four different philosophical traditions or styles: (1) Rationalism-Idealism, (2) Empiricism, (3) Existentialism, and (4) Analysis.

There is a brief introduction to each major topic immediately preceding the selections on that topic. An introduction to the major divisions of the second arrangement immediately follows the second table of contents.

Finally, the questions treated here have often been discussed in the Western world with very little consideration of the contributions of oriental philosophies of religion; here, however, an attempt has been made to include a few selections which represent those relatively neglected (but very extensive) contributions.

The authors wish to express their appreciation to the publishers, Allyn and Bacon, Inc., for their constant cooperation and many helpful suggestions. Grateful acknowledgment is also made to the following secretarial assistants who did much of the mechanical work involved in preparing the manuscript:

> Miss Ximena de Gumucio
> Miss Judy Freeborn
> Miss Carole Kaplan
> Miss Nancy Kubany
> Miss Cecilie Sewejkis
> Miss Carol Silvers

It is, of course, impossible to acknowledge all the influences that have guided the authors in their selection of materials; yet, while the responsibility for both comments and selections is theirs, they wish to pay tribute to all those who have provoked their thought and interest about these questions.

George I. Mavrodes
Stuart Cornelius Hackett

CONTENTS ❋ *topical*

INTRODUCTION / *1*

PART I Reason, Faith and Philosophy / 8

1 ST. THOMAS AQUINAS, *Reason and Faith* / *10*
2 WILLIAM K. CLIFFORD, *The Ethics of Belief* / *20*
3 WILLIAM JAMES, *The Will to Believe* / *27*
4 JOSIAH ROYCE, *Religion and Philosophy* / *47*
5 CHARLES A. CAMPBELL, *Reason and Revelation* / *61*
6 EMIL BRUNNER, *Philosophy and Theology* / *73*
7 PAUL TILLICH, *Philosophy and Religion* / *80*

PART II Arguments for the Divine Reality / 92

A Priori Arguments

1 ST. ANSELM, *The Ontological Argument* / *95*
2 IMMANUEL KANT, *The Impossibility of an Ontological Proof* / *97*

A Posteriori Arguments

3 ST. THOMAS AQUINAS, *Five Proofs of God's Existence* / *103*
4 A. E. TAYLOR, *The Moral Argument* / *113*
5 RICHARD TAYLOR, *From the Senses to God* / *121*
6 DAVID HUME, *Difficulties of the Teleological Argument* / *128*
7 AUROBINDO GHOSE, *Difficulties of Both Naturalism and Theism* / *143*
8 SOREN KIERKEGAARD, *The Uselessness of Proofs* / *151*

PART III Religious Experience and Revelation / 158

1 LAO TZU, *Mystical Union,* / *161*
2 PAUL TOURNIER, *A Religious Experience* / *165*

3   F. SCHLEIERMACHER, *Religion as the Feeling of Absolute Dependence* / 167

4   C. D. BROAD, *The Argument from Religious Experience* / 180

5   HERBERT FARMER, *Revelation* / 192

6   EMIL BRUNNER, *The Bible and Revelation* / 203

7   NINIAN SMART, *Revelation, Reason and Religions* / 215

8   D. T. SUZUKI, *Satori* / 226

PART IV   Religion and Ethics / 240

1   ST. AUGUSTINE, *Good and Evil* / 242

2   DAVID HUME, *The Problem of Evil* / 250

3   AUROBINDO GHOSE, *A Vedanta Solution of the Problem of Evil* / 262

4   J. L. MACKIE, *Evil and Omnipotence* / 280

5   ALVIN PLANTINGA, *The Free Will Defense* / 293

6   WANG YANG-MING, *The Ideal of Love* / 309

7   JOSEPH BUTLER, *Moral Conscience and Divine Law* / 318

8   PAUL TILLICH, *The Religious Dimension of the Moral Imperative* / 332

PART V   Meaning and Meaningfulness / 344

1   ST. THOMAS AQUINAS, *Analogy* / 346

2   E. L. MASCALL, *Analogy* / 356

3   A. J. AYER, *Religion as Nonsense* / 377

4   F. C. COPLESTON, *Positivism and Religion* / 385

5   IAN RAMSEY, *The Possibiilty of Theology* / 390

PART VI   God, Man, and the World / 412

1   A. N. WHITEHEAD, *God and the World* / 415

2   KARL JASPERS, *The Encompassing* / 421

3   VASUBANDHU, *The Mind-Only Doctrine* / 435

4   HSUANG-TSANG, *Answers to Objections* / 440

5   FUNG YU-LAN, *Human Life and the Transcendent* / 447

6   LUDWIG FEUERBACH, *God as a Projection* / 463

7   A. E. TAYLOR, *Immortality* / 473

8   NICOLAS BERDYAEV, *Human Destiny* / 485

INDEX / 493

CONTENTS ❈ *systematic*

I. *RATIONALISM-IDEALISM* / 2

1 ST. ANSELM, *The Ontological Argument* / 95
2 ST. AUGUSTINE, *Good and Evil* / 242
3 AUROBINDO GHOSE, *Difficulties of Both Naturalism and Theism* / 143
4 AUROBINDO GHOSE, *A Vedanta Solution of the Problem of Evil* / 262
5 JOSEPH BUTLER, *Moral Conscience and Divine Law* / 318
6 CHARLES A. CAMPBELL, *Reason and Revelation* / 61
7 LUDWIG FEUERBACH, *God as a Projection* / 463
8 FUNG YU-LAN, *Human Life and the Transcendent* / 447
9 HSUANG-TSANG, *Answers to Objections* / 440
10 IMMANUEL KANT, *The Impossibility of an Ontological Proof* / 97
11 JOSIAH ROYCE, *Religion and Philosophy* / 47
12 A. E. TAYLOR, *The Moral Argument* / 113
13 A. E. TAYLOR, *Immortality* / 473
14 VASUBANDHU, *The Mind-Only Doctrine* / 435
15 WANG YANG-MING, *The Ideal of Love* / 309
16 A. N. WHITEHEAD, *God and the World* / 415

II. *EMPIRICISM* / 3

1 C. D. BROAD, *The Argument from Religious Experience* / 180
2 WILLIAM K. CLIFFORD, *The Ethics of Belief* / 20
3 FREDERICK C. COPLESTON, *Positivism and Religion* / 385
4 HERBERT FARMER, *Revelation* / 192
5 DAVID HUME, *Difficulties of the Teleological Argument* / 128
6 DAVID HUME, *The Problem of Evil* / 250
7 WILLIAM JAMES, *The Will to Believe* / 27
8 LAO TZU, *Mystical Union* / 161
9 E. L. MASCALL, *Analogy* / 356
10 F. SCHLEIERMACHER, *Religion as the Feeling of Absolute Dependence* / 167

| vii

11 D. T. SUZUKI, *Satori* / *226*

12 RICHARD TAYLOR, *From the Senses to God* / *121*

13 ST. THOMAS AQUINAS, *Five Proofs of God's Existence* / *103*

14 ST. THOMAS AQUINAS, *Reason and Faith* / *10*

15 ST. THOMAS AQUINAS, *Analogy* / *346*

16 PAUL TOURNIER, *A Religious Experience* / *165*

III. EXISTENTIALISM / 4

1 NICOLAS BERDYAEV, *Human Destiny* / *485*

2 EMIL BRUNNER, *Philosophy and Theology* / *73*

3 EMIL BRUNNER, *The Bible and Revelation* / *203*

4 KARL JASPERS, *The Encompassing* / *421*

5 SOREN KIERKEGAARD, *The Uselessness of Proofs* / *151*

6 PAUL TILLICH, *Philosophy and Religion* / *80*

7 PAUL TILLICH, *The Religious Dimension of the Moral Imperative* / *352*

IV. ANALYSIS / 5

1 A. J. AYER, *Religion as Nonsense* / *377*

2 J. L. MACKIE, *Evil and Omnipotence* / *280*

3 ALVIN PLANTINGA, *The Free Will Defense* / *293*

4 IAN RAMSEY, *The Possibility of Theology* / *390*

5 NINIAN SMART, *Revelation, Reason and Religions* / *215*

Introduction

One result that emerges from an analysis of the particular problems with which philosophy of religion is concerned is the impression that conclusions about these questions are not achieved in isolation from one another. They tend rather to form clusters which become the nuclei for clearly distinguishable total approaches to the more restricted special problems of religious philosophy. Proposed solutions about any one problem involve assumptions and conclusions about all the other principal problems (a general position on the relation between faith and reason, for example, is reflected in conclusions about the meaning of each, the nature of the Divine reality, and the validity of rational arguments for that Reality). Furthermore, an individual thinker's solutions to these problems is expressive of a basic and total commitment which has reverberations all along the line of religious-philosophical thought.

In view of these considerations, it seems plausible to view philosophy of religion from the standpoint of inclusive perspectives, as well as from that of the separate problems involved. Perhaps a suitable term for describing these pervasive differences is the word *system*. By a *system* here is meant a broad general approach which provides an integrating framework for the understanding of more specific questions. For some thinkers this framework involves a closely-knit network of conceptions whose deductive relations are characterized by rationally necessary connections; for others, the general approach involves simply an all-inclusive world-view whose parts are far more loosely related through a variety of principles other than deductive logical connection; and for still others, such a perspective embraces no more than a basic methodology for considering and resolving particular problems. When such an inclusive concept of system is employed in relation to the alternatives in the philosophy of religion, a number of such distinguishable perspectives appear. In most cases, the perspectives themselves are defined with such breadth that each general approach contains within itself important contrasts, while at the same time the approach as a whole is not sharply divided from other approaches. There is considerable overlapping among the positions, and there are important individual thinkers whose systematic affinities are so diverse that their views seem to resist classification in any schematism of perspectives.

While systematic classification is therefore to some extent arbitrary and the choice of different systems is partly relative, one method of bringing out significant positions in religious philosophy consists in distinguishing four different approaches: rationalism-idealism, empiricism, existentialism, and analysis.

I. Rationalism-Idealism

THE first and in many ways the most traditional approach may be termed *idealism*. Idealism emphasizes the basic thesis that reality is ultimately to be explained in terms of the primacy of mind and purpose in the universe, and that man finds his place in the scheme of things by adjusting himself to this ultimate factor. Such a monistic explanation (i.e., explanation in terms of a single fundamental principle), aims at an all-inclusive, total explanation of existence. In such an explanation every particular problem of religious philosophy ideally finds a plausible solution. Finally, in most cases idealism emphasizes the validity and importance of objective principles of value and of moral obligations that can be satisfactorily explained only through their dependence on the ultimate principle.

Metaphysical views of this sort have often been associated with what might be called a broadly *rationalist* epistemology, which holds that some important truths about the nature of reality can be known independently of experience. We have here combined these two traditions in a single section. But some thinkers emphasize one of these traditions much more than the other, or they may even reject one entirely while accepting the other. Here, as elsewhere in philosophy, the use of broad labels is of only limited use. The student, therefore, should not be surprised to find an empiricist accepting parts of the idealist metaphysic or a rationalist rejecting parts of it. We must emphasize again that there is constant intellectual traffic across the borders of these systematic divisions.

Within this general perspective, however, some significant contrasts appear —two of which are perhaps deserving of special notice. The first is the distinction between those views which hold that the principles of rational and discursive intellect (concepts, propositions, logical laws) are adequate at every level for the achievement of a total explanation of reality, and those which maintain that the ultimate reality is by its very nature beyond understanding in terms of intellectual concepts, so that such concepts have at best no more than symbolical significance at this highest level of reality. Thinkers like Josiah Royce, Anselm of Canterbury, Alfred North Whitehead, and Fung Yu Lan tend to stand with the first of these alternatives; while such philosophers as Immanuel Kant, C. A. Campbell, Aurobindo Ghose, and Vasubandhu take the opposite stand. On the other hand, an important thinker like Augustine seems to express elements of both approaches.

A second contrast is that between personalism and impersonalism in the understanding of the ultimate reality. While all the thinkers included under idealism agree that the ultimate cannot be less than absolute mind in some sense, there is a deep rift between those who believe (notably in the Christian tradition) that categories of personal being are clearly applicable to the ultimate, and those who feel that, for one reason or another, the application of these categories would involve an inappropriate restriction or limitation. Such thinkers as Augustine, Anselm, and A. E. Taylor seem clearly to stand on the first side of this line, while absolute idealists (like Campbell and Royce) and oriental philosophers generally are on the other side. Whitehead, with his distinction between God's unconscious primordial nature and his conscious consequent nature, seems to stand, consistently or not, on both sides of this issue.

II. Empiricism

A SECOND systematic approach may be called *empiricism* because of its emphasis on particular facts of experience as the basis for arriving at an adequate apprehension of religious truth. Generally speaking, thinkers of this tradition decline any appeal to *a priori* truths of reason and seek to lay the foundation for their conclusions on the elements provided by experience. Presupposed principles are replaced by insights growing out of the flow of conscious experiences. As a result, while some thinkers in this tradition achieve a total view as inclusive as any found in idealism (Thomas Aquinas, for example), they are generally less concerned with achieving a speculatively constructed all-inclusive explanation.

Possibly the contrasts within empiricism are even more striking than those within idealism. There is, for example, the distinction between sensory empiricism and non-sensory or mystical empiricism. The first of these takes sense experience as its principal point of departure and asks what conclusions about religious philosophy, if any, follow from taking such sense facts as the basis and the ultimate test of truth. Even if attention is directed inward (e.g., to psychic phenomena or mystical states), these facts are regarded as data for a descriptive analysis from which generalizations can be drawn. For non-sensory empiricism, on the other hand, the crucial and decisive experiences are not objectively available sensory or intro-spective facts, but rather those distinctive, perhaps even supranormal, private states of awareness which, to the one who experiences them, are a self-accrediting manifestation of the ultimate reality of spiritual life. From the standpoint of this basic contrast, thinkers like David Hume, W. K. Clif-ford, and C. D. Broad are sensory empiricists, while Lao-tzu, Friedrich Schleiermacher, and H. H. Farmer all have an emphasis that is appropri-ately described as non-sensory or mystical empiricism. Thomas Aquinas and William James, finally, have positions that incorporate both of these emphases as supplementary to one another.

A further contrast appears between agnostics like Hume and Clifford who conclude that no objectively valid truth about the ultimate reality and about human destiny can be achieved on the basis of empirical facts, and those who maintain that an empirical foundation (whether sensory or non-sensory) leads to positive truths about the ultimate reality and human destiny. These last may emphasize mystical experiences, inferences from sense facts, or practical consequences as bases for such a positive view; but they seem agreed that experiences of one sort or another provide a solid foundation for ultimate explanations. From this standpoint, mysticism, natural theology (as in Thomas, for example, with his empirically grounded rational arguments for the existence of God), and the pragmatism of James stand united.

III. Existentialism

WHILE the roots of idealism and religious empiricism lie deeply imbedded in long-standing traditions, *existentialism* finds expression significantly for the first time in the nineteenth-century Danish philosopher, Soren Kierke-gaard. The perspective he initiated may be defined generally as that philo-sophical attitude which is characterized by concern about human destiny in the face of the apparent absurdity of life, and by the thesis that it is through personal encounter and responsible personal decision that man comes in contact with reality as it is and achieves for himself authentic self-significance. This general attitude may be more clearly understood by re-garding it as a reaction against the ideal of rational objectivity (the "spectator" theory of knowledge), which is emphasized by many thinkers in the idealistic tradition. In contrast, existentialism holds that "truth is subjectivity"—that is, that all understanding of reality by an existing individual is relative to his own involvement in the very world that philosophy purports to explain, so that such objectivity is an impossible achievement for man. As a consequence of this drift toward subjectivism and irrationalism, existentialists tend to dwell on man's anxious and despairing perplexity about the meaning of human life. They assert that precisely through such a preoccupation, and the resultant responsive decisions that emerge from it, man can achieve authentic existence in a way that is impossible for the "rational man" of the traditional approaches.

While Kierkegaard found in these attitudes the basis for a distinctly religious view of the world, a non-religious or even atheistic view has in our century emerged from thinkers like Martin Heidegger and Jean-Paul Sartre. But even if we limit our attention to philosophers who follow Kierkegaard in constructing a religious world view on an existential foundation, here again significant contrasts emerge within the general perspective. One such distinction divides those whose orientation is based primarily on presuppositions of a theological nature and who emphasize the thesis that religious truth must begin by assuming divine revelation interpreted as personal encounter, from those who believe that an existential analysis of human life can provide the speculative framework within which revelation itself must be interpreted. Kierkegaard, Nicolas Berdyaev, and Emil Brunner would represent the former emphasis, while the latter is exemplified by Paul Tillich. Thinkers of the second type understandably display much less distrust for speculative reason than the first group, but the differences on this point are primarily of degree and both groups are opposed in principle to the traditional emphasis on thoroughgoing rational objectivity.

IV. Analysis

THE historically most recent general approach may be appropriately designated as *analysis*. For many thinkers (but not all) this perspective is associated with a variety of sensory empiricism which tends, on the one hand, to deny that there are any universal and necessary rational principles with which the mind is disposed to understand reality, and, on the other hand, to affirm that our only factual knowledge about the world is based ultimately on particular sense observations. For this view, if there are any logically necessary truths, they are necessary by conventionally adopted axioms and definitions (like the "necessary truth" that there are three feet in a yard), so that they provide in themselves no information about the world, but merely information about our definitions of terms. The further feature that distinguishes this view from traditional empiricism is its thesis that one of philosophy's most important tasks (if not indeed its only one), is the logical analysis of terms, statements, and arguments with a view to eliminating many serious misconceptions of traditional philosophy—mistakes that originated precisely from inattention to this task.

Now it is only in terms of this emphasis on an empirical, analytic methodology that this perspective can be called a systematic approach. Generally speaking, thinkers of this sort are comparatively disinterested in the construction of all-inclusive metaphysical world-views; indeed, some members of this tradition are in principle opposed to any such comprehensive task. Thus it is typical for these philosophers to attack one narrowly defined problem after another in such a way that often the only interconnectedness of the various proposed solutions is found in the common methodology that is employed. In relation to questions of religious philosophy, for the most part these thinkers do not attempt to develop a constructive religious world view. Instead, they try to characterize the logic and significance of religious statements and arguments to determine what sort of truth and validity they possess, if any.

But as with the other approaches, so here important contrasts emerge within the over-all perspective. Perhaps the religiously most significant distinction is that between cognitivism and non-cognitivism. Cognitivism regards religious statements, rightly interpreted, as in some sense genuine assertions that are either true or false, although the relevant tests here are often regarded as quite distinct from those employed in empirical science. Non-cognitivism, on the contrary, maintains that genuinely religious statements make no actual assertions at all but must be interpreted as having some other sort of significance. Hence these statements are neither true nor false, although they may be appropriate or inappropriate in the emotional or expressive role they fill.

This first contrast leads to two others closely connected with it. First, those who accept a cognitive view of religious statements tend to construct a religious world view, while noncognitivists are precluded in principle from any such task and are involved instead in a kind of destructive analysis that purports to show that a religious metaphysic is impossible. Finally, both of the above contrasts seem to rest on the distinction, within the perspective of linguistic analysis, between logical positivism and ordinary language empiricism. According to logical positivism, the only cognitively significant statements are either those of formal logic (based on conventionally adopted axioms), or statements of empirical fact which constitute the basis of one or another of the empirical sciences. For ordinary language empiricism, however, no such rigid criterion of cognitive meaningfulness can be adopted; any statement that has a genuine function in communication has a genuine meaning even if it falls outside the areas of formal logic and empirical science. It should be obvious that for positivism religious statements are non-cognitive and the task of constructing a testable religious world view is eliminated; while for ordinary language empiricism it seems possible to provide some basis at least for constructing precisely such a religious metaphysic. Among the writers represented in this volume, A. J. Ayer (in his early period) represents the non-cognitive, positivist approach, while Ian Ramsey and Ninian Smart stand in the more constructive cognitivist tradition.

PART I

REASON, FAITH

and PHILOSOPHY

O ne of the things about which philosophers of religion disagree is the contribution it is reasonable to expect of philosophy in understanding or evaluating religious beliefs. Nor do they seem to agree about the conditions under which it is proper to adopt a belief (religious or otherwise), or the proper role of "reason" in such an adoption.

The essays by James and Clifford discuss the role of evidence in the acceptance of belief. Clifford argues strongly that it is immoral to accept a belief without adequate evidence. James appears to say that such an acceptance is sometimes justifiable. But they may not disagree as much as they appear to, or their disagreement may not be about the role of evidence but about something else. James is interested in a special case, one in which we *must* believe one way or the other, rather than remain undecided. Clifford does not seem to discuss this case at all. And if there were such a case, it is not clear how his advice could differ substantially from that of James. On the other hand, Clifford may not believe there are any such cases. But neither he nor James appears to argue this point at length. It is possible that they themselves were not clear about the crucial point of their difference.

This sort of situation is by no means uncommon in philosophy. Many apparent disagreements are either not disagreements at all, or else their crux is not where it is made out to be. (The same is true, of course, for many cases of apparent *agreement*.) This is one of the main difficulties hindering the resolution of philosophical problems.

The remaining selections in this section discuss more broadly the relation of reason to various aspects of religious experience. Here we will encounter key terms whose meaning varies from writer to writer. St. Thomas, for example, says that some religious truths can be attained by reason while others exceed the competence of reason. Campbell, on the other hand, seems to assign reason a competence with respect to every religious claim. St. Thomas, however, seems to mean by "reason" a combination of logic and sense-perception, while by this term, Campbell refers to some standard for judging the relevancy of any sort of evidence whatever. It is possible, therefore, that Campbell might agree with St. Thomas that logic and sense-perception are not sufficient to lead one to all religious truths, and that St. Thomas might not object greatly to Campbell's application of "thought's internal standards." Similar comments might be made about the concept of "philosophy" as it is used by Royce, Brunner, and Tillich.

The positions and arguments of these writers, therefore, can be neither compared nor evaluated without careful attention to the meaning they assign to key terms. This is not, however, a purely academic exercise or one relevant only to the discussion of philosophical writers. The student himself probably uses the term "reason." Does he use it in St. Thomas' sense? Campbell's? Or in some other? And can he presume that the friends with whom he discusses these questions use it in the same sense? To distinguish some of the senses terms may bear and to see the consequences of these senses are indispensable for developing one's own thinking and understanding the thought of others.

I

REASON

AND FAITH*

St. Thomas Aquinas *Thomas Aquinas (1226–1274) was a scholar and university teacher of the Dominican Order whose Christianized version of Aristotelianism has become virtually the official philosophy of the Roman Catholic Church and the classical expression of the philosophic tradition which bears his name. His principal works are:* Summa Theologica *and* Summa Contra Gentiles *in which he expounds and defends his philosophical theology.*

SINCE, however, not every truth is to be made known in the same way, *and it is the part of an educated man to seek for conviction in each subject, only so far as the nature of the subject allows,*[1] as the Philosopher most rightly observes as quoted by Boethius,[2] it is necessary to show first of all in what way it is possible to make known the aforesaid truth.

Now in those things which we hold about God there is truth in two ways. For certain things that are true about God wholly surpass the capability of human reason, for instance that God is three and one: while there are certain things to which even natural reason can attain, for instance that God is, that God is one, and others like these, which even the philosophers proved demonstratively of God, being guided by the light of natural reason.

That certain divine truths wholly surpass the capability of human reason, is most clearly evident. For since the principle of all the knowledge which the reason acquires about a thing, is the understanding of that thing's essence, because according to the

* From St. Thomas Aquinas, *Summa Contra Gentiles,* tr. by The English Dominican Fathers. Reprinted by permission of the English Dominicans and Burns, Oates, & Washbourne, Ltd.

1 1 *Ethic.* iii. 4.

2 *De Trin.* ii.

Philosopher's teaching[1] the principle of a demonstration is *what a thing is*, it follows that our knowledge about a thing will be in proportion to our understanding of its essence. Wherefore, if the human intellect comprehends the essence of a particular thing, for instance a stone or a triangle, no truth about that thing will surpass the capability of human reason. But this does not happen to us in relation to God, because the human intellect is incapable by its natural power of attaining to the comprehension of His essence: since our intellect's knowledge, according to the mode of the present life, originates from the senses: so that things which are not objects of sense cannot be comprehended by the human intellect, except in so far as knowledge of them is gathered from sensibles. Now sensibles cannot lead our intellect to see in them what God is, because they are effects unequal to the power of their cause. And yet our intellect is led by sensibles to the divine knowledge so as to know about God that He is, and other such truths, which need to be ascribed to the first principle. Accordingly some divine truths are attainable by human reason, while others altogether surpass the power of human reason.

Again. The same is easy to see from the degrees of intellects. For if one of two men perceives a thing with his intellect with greater subtlety, the one whose intellect is of a higher degree understands many things which the other is altogether unable to grasp; as instanced in a yokel who is utterly incapable of grasping the subtleties of philosophy. Now the angelic intellect surpasses the human intellect more than the intellect of the cleverest philosopher surpasses that of the most uncultured. For an angel knows God through a more excellent effect than does man, for as much as the angel's essence, through which he is led to know God by natural knowledge, is more excellent than sensible things, even than the soul itself, by which the human intellect mounts to the knowledge of God. And the divine intellect surpasses the angelic intellect much more than the angelic surpasses the human. For the divine intellect by its capacity equals the divine essence, wherefore God perfectly understands of Himself what He is, and He knows all things that can be understood about Him: whereas the angel knows not what God is by his natural knowledge, because the angel's essence, by which he is led to the knowledge of God, is an effect unequal to the power of its cause. Consequently an angel is unable by his natural knowledge to grasp all that God understands about Himself: nor again is human reason capable of grasping all that an angel understands by his natural power. Accordingly just as a man would show himself to be a most insane fool if he declared the

[1] 2 *Anal. Post.* iii. 9.

assertions of a philosopher to be false because he was unable to understand them, so, and much more, a man would be exceedingly foolish, were he to suspect of falsehood the things revealed by God through the ministry of His angels, because they cannot be the object of reason's investigations.

Furthermore. The same is made abundantly clear by the deficiency which every day we experience in our knowledge of things. For we are ignorant of many of the properties of sensible things, and in many cases, we are unable to discover the nature of these properties which we perceive by our senses. Much less therefore is human reason capable of investigating all the truths about that most sublime essence.

With this the saying of the Philosopher is in accord (2 *Metaph.*)[1] where he says that *our intellect in relation to those primary things which are most evident in nature is like the eye of a bat in relation to the sun.*

To this truth Holy Writ also bears witness. For it is written (Job xi. 7): *Peradventure thou wilt comprehend the steps of God and wilt find out the Almighty perfectly?* and (xxxvi. 26): *Behold God is great, exceeding our knowledge,* and (1 Cor. xiii. 9): *We know in part.*

Therefore all that is said about God, though it cannot be investigated by reason, must not be forthwith rejected as false, as the Manicheans and many unbelievers have thought.[2]

. . .

THAT THE TRUTH ABOUT DIVINE THINGS WHICH IS ATTAINABLE BY REASON IS FITTINGLY PROPOSED TO MAN AS AN OBJECT OF BELIEF

WHILE then the truth of the intelligible things of God is twofold, one to which the inquiry of reason can attain, the other which surpasses the whole range of human reason, both are fittingly proposed by God to man as an object of belief. We must first show this with regard to that truth which is attainable by the inquiry of reason, lest it appears to some, that since it can be attained by reason, it was useless to make it an object of faith by supernatural inspiration. Now three disadvantages would result if this truth were left solely to the inquiry of reason. One is that few men would have knowledge of God: because very many are hindered from gathering the fruit of diligent inquiry, which is the discovery of truth, for

---

[1] D. 1a. 1, 2. In future references D. stands for the Didot edition of Aristotle's and Plato's works.

[2] S. Aug., *De utilit. credendi* i, 2; *Retract.* xiv. 1.

three reasons. Some indeed on account of an indisposition of temperament, by reason of which many are naturally indisposed to knowledge: so that no efforts of theirs would enable them to reach to the attainment of the highest degree of human knowledge, which consists in knowing God. Some are hindered by the needs of household affairs. For there must needs be among men some that devote themselves to the conduct of temporal affairs, who would be unable to devote so much time to the leisure of contemplative research as to reach the summit of human inquiry, namely the knowledge of God. And some are hindered by laziness. For in order to acquire the knowledge of God in those things which reason is able to investigate, it is necessary to have a previous knowledge of many things: since almost the entire consideration of philosophy is directed to the knowledge of God: for which reason metaphysics, which is about divine things, is the last of the parts of philosophy to be studied. Wherefore it is not possible to arrive at the inquiry about the aforesaid truth except after a most laborious study: and few are willing to take upon themselves this labour for the love of a knowledge, the natural desire for which has nevertheless been instilled into the mind of man by God.

The second disadvantage is that those who would arrive at the discovery of the aforesaid truth would scarcely succeed in doing so after a long time. First, because this truth is so profound, that it is only after long practice that the human intellect is enabled to grasp it by means of reason. Secondly, because many things are required beforehand, as stated above. Thirdly, because at the time of youth, the mind, when tossed about by the various movements of the passions, is not fit for the knowledge of so sublime a truth, whereas *calm gives prudence and knowledge,* as stated in 7 *Phys.*[1] Hence mankind would remain in the deepest darkness of ignorance, if the path of reason were the only available way to the knowledge of God: because the knowledge of God which especially makes men perfect and good, would be acquired only by the few, and by these only after a long time.

The third disadvantage is that much falsehood is mingled with the investigations of human reason, on account of the weakness of our intellect in forming its judgments, and by reason of the admixture of phantasms. Consequently many would remain in doubt about those things even which are most truly demonstrated, through ignoring the force of the demonstration: especially when they perceive that different things are taught by the various men who are called wise. Moreover among the many demonstrated truths, there is sometimes a mixture of falsehood that is not

[1] iii. 7.

demonstrated, but assumed for some probable or sophistical reason which at times is mistaken for a demonstration. Therefore it was necessary that definite certainty and pure truth about divine things should be offered to man by the way of faith.

Accordingly the divine clemency has made this salutary commandment, that even some things which reason is able to investigate must be held by faith: so that all may share in the knowledge of God easily, and without doubt or error.

Hence it is written (Eph. iv. 17, 18) : That *henceforward you walk not as also the Gentiles walk in the vanity of their mind, having their understanding darkened;* and (Isa. liv. 13) : *All thy children shall be taught of the Lord.*

.   .   .

THAT THOSE THINGS WHICH CANNOT BE INVESTIGATED BY REASON ARE FITTINGLY PROPOSED TO MAN AS AN OBJECT OF FAITH

IT may appear to some that those things which cannot be investigated by reason ought not to be proposed to man as an object of faith: because divine wisdom provides for each thing according to the mode of its nature. We must therefore prove that it is necessary also for those things which surpass reason to be proposed by God to man as an object of faith.

For no man tends to do a thing by his desire and endeavour unless it be previously known to him. Wherefore since man is directed by divine providence to a higher good than human frailty can attain in the present life, as we shall show in the sequel,[1] it was necessary for his mind to be bidden to something higher than those things to which our reason can reach in the present life, so that he might learn to aspire, and by his endeavours to tend to something surpassing the whole state of the present life. And this is especially competent to the Christian religion, which alone promises goods spiritual and eternal: for which reason it proposes many things surpassing the thought of man: whereas the old law which contained promises of temporal things, proposed few things that are above human inquiry. It was with this motive that the philosophers, in order to wean men from sensible pleasures to virtue, took care to show that there are other goods of greater account than those which appeal to the senses, the taste of which things affords much greater delight to those who devote themselves to active or contemplative virtues.

[1] Bk. III.

Again it is necessary for this truth to be proposed to man as an object of faith in order that he may have truer knowledge of God. For then alone do we know God truly, when we believe that He is far above all that man can possibly think of God, because the divine essence surpasses man's natural knowledge, as stated above.[1] Hence by the fact that certain things about God are proposed to man, which surpass his reason, he is strengthened in his opinion that God is far above what he is able to think.

There results also another advantage from this, namely, the checking of presumption which is the mother of error. For some there are who presume so far on their wits that they think themselves capable of measuring the whole nature of things by their intellect, in that they esteem all things true which they see, and false which they see not. Accordingly, in order that man's mind might be freed from this presumption, and seek the truth humbly, it was necessary that certain things far surpassing his intellect should be proposed to man by God.

Yet another advantage is made apparent by the words of the Philosopher (10 *Ethic.*).[2] For when a certain Simonides maintained that man should neglect the knowledge of God, and apply his mind to human affairs, and declared that *a man ought to relish human things, and a mortal, mortal things:* the Philosopher contradicted him, saying that *a man ought to devote himself to immortal and divine things as much as he can.* Hence he says (II *De Animal.*)[3] that though it is but little that we preceive of higher substances, yet that little is more loved and desired than all the knowledge we have of lower substances. He says also (2 *De Cœlo et Mundo*)[4] that when questions about the heavenly bodies can be answered by a short and probable solution, it happens that the hearer is very much rejoiced. All this shows that however imperfect the knowledge of the highest things may be, it bestows very great perfection on the soul: and consequently, although human reason is unable to grasp fully things that are above reason, it nevertheless acquires much perfection, if at least it holds things, in any way whatever, by faith.

Wherefore it is written (Ecclus. iii. 25): *Many things are shown to thee above the understanding of men,* and (I Cor. ii. 10, 11): *The things . . . that are of God no man knoweth, but the Spirit of God: but to us God hath revealed them by His Spirit.*

.   .   .

---

[1] Ch. iii.   [2] vii. 8.   [3] *De Part. Animal.* i. 5.   [4] xii. 1.

THAT IT IS NOT A MARK OF LEVITY TO ASSENT TO THE THINGS
THAT ARE OF FAITH, ALTHOUGH THEY ARE ABOVE REASON

Now those who believe this truth, of *which reason affords a proof*,[1] believe not lightly, as though *following foolish*[2] *fables* (2 Pet. i. 16). For divine Wisdom Himself, Who knows all things most fully, deigned to reveal to man *the secrets of God's wisdom*:[3] and by suitable arguments proves His presence, and the truth of His doctrine and inspiration, by performing works surpassing the capa-. bility of the whole of nature, namely, the wondrous healing of the sick, the raising of the dead to life, a marvellous control over the heavenly bodies, and what excites yet more wonder, the inspiration of human minds, so that unlettered and simple persons are filled with the Holy Ghost, and in one instant are endowed with the most sublime wisdom and eloquence. And after considering these argu- ments, convinced by the strength of the proof, and not by the force of arms, nor by the promise of delights, but—and this is the greatest marvel of all—amidst the tyranny of persecutions, a countless crowd of not only simple but also of the wisest men, embraced the Chris- tian faith, which inculcates things surpassing all human under- standing, curbs the pleasures of the flesh, and teaches contempt of all worldly things. That the minds of mortal beings should assent to such things, is both the greatest of miracles, and the evident work of divine inspiration, seeing that they despise visible things and desire only those that are invisible. And that this happened not suddenly nor by chance, but by the disposition of God, is shown by the fact that God foretold that He would do so by the manifold oracles of the prophets, whose books we hold in veneration as bearing witness to our faith. This particular kind of proof is alluded to in the words of Heb. ii. 3, 4: *Which,* namely the salvation of mankind, *having begun to be declared by the Lord, was confirmed with us by them that heard Him, God also bearing witness by signs and wonders, and divers*[4] . . . *distributions of the Holy Ghost.*

Now such a wondrous conversion of the world to the Chris- tian faith is a most indubitable proof that such signs did take place, so that there is no need to repeat them, seeing that there is evidence of them in their result. For it would be the most wondrous sign of all if without any wondrous signs the world were persuaded by simple and lowly men to believe things so arduous, to accomplish

1 S. Greg. the Great: *Hom. in Ev.* ii. 26.
2 Vulg., *cunningly devised (doctas.* S. Thomas read *indoctas.*) .
3 Job xi. 6.
4 Vulg., *divers miracles and distributions* . . .

things so difficult, and to hope for things so sublime. Although God ceases not even in our time to work miracles through His saints in confirmation of the faith.

On the other hand those who introduced the errors of the sects proceeded in contrary fashion, as instanced by Mohammed, who enticed peoples with the promise of carnal pleasures, to the desire of which the concupiscence of the flesh instigates. He also delivered commandments in keeping with his promises, by giving the reins to carnal pleasure, wherein it is easy for carnal men to obey: and the lessons of truth which he inculcated were only such as can be easily known to any man of average wisdom by his natural powers: yea rather the truths which he taught were mingled by him with many fables and most false doctrines. Nor did he add any signs of supernatural agency, which alone are a fitting witness to divine inspiration, since a visible work that can be from God alone, proves the teacher of truth to be invisibly inspired: but he asserted that he was sent in the power of arms, a sign that is not lacking even to robbers and tyrants. Again, those who believed in him from the outset were not wise men practised in things divine and human, but beastlike men who dwelt in the wilds, utterly ignorant of all divine teaching; and it was by a multitude of such men and the force of arms that he compelled others to submit to his law.

Lastly, no divine oracles of prophets in a previous age bore witness to him; rather did he corrupt almost all the teaching of the Old and New Testaments by a narrative replete with fables, as one may see by a perusal of his law. Hence by a cunning device, he did not commit the reading of the Old and New Testament Books to his followers, lest he should thereby be convicted of falsehood. Thus it is evident that those who believe his words believe lightly.

. . .

THAT THE TRUTH OF REASON IS NOT IN OPPOSITION TO THE TRUTH OF THE CHRISTIAN FAITH

Now though the aforesaid truth of the Christian faith surpasses the ability of human reason, nevertheless those things which are naturally instilled in human reason cannot be opposed to this truth. For it is clear that those things which are implanted in reason by nature, are most true, so much so that it is impossible to think them to be false. Nor is it lawful to deem false that which is held by faith, since it is so evidently confirmed by God. Seeing then that the false alone is opposed to the true, as evidently appears if we examine their definitions, it is impossible for the aforesaid truth of faith to be contrary to those principles which reason knows naturally.

Again. The same thing which the disciple's mind receives from its teacher is contained in the knowledge of the teacher, unless he teach insincerely, which it were wicked to say of God. Now the knowledge of naturally known principles is instilled into us by God, since God Himself is the author of our nature. Therefore the divine Wisdom also contains these principles. Consequently whatever is contrary to these principles, is contrary to the divine Wisdom; wherefore it cannot be from God. Therefore those things which are received by faith from divine revelation cannot be contrary to our natural knowledge.

Moreover. Our intellect is stayed by contrary arguments, so that it cannot advance to the knowledge of truth. Wherefore if conflicting knowledges were instilled into us by God, our intellect would thereby be hindered from knowing the truth. And this cannot be ascribed to God.

Furthermore. Things that are natural are unchangeable so long as nature remains. Now contrary opinions cannot be together in the same subject. Therefore God does not instil into man any opinion or belief contrary to natural knowledge.

Hence the Apostle says (Rom. x. 8) : *The word is nigh thee even in thy heart and in thy mouth. This is the word of faith which we preach.* Yet because it surpasses reason some look upon it as though it were contrary thereto; which is impossible.

This is confirmed also by the authority of Augustine who says (*Gen. ad lit.* ii) :[1] *That which truth shall make known can nowise be in opposition to the holy books whether of the Old or of the New Testament.*

From this we may evidently conclude that whatever arguments are alleged against the teachings of faith, they do not rightly proceed from the first self-evident principles instilled by nature. Wherefore they lack the force of demonstration, and are either probable or sophistical arguments, and consequently it is possible to solve them.

· · ·

IN WHAT RELATION HUMAN REASON STANDS TO THE TRUTH OF FAITH

IT would also seem well to observe that sensible things from which human reason derives the source of its knowledge, retain a certain trace of likeness to God, but so imperfect that it proves altogether inadequate to manifest the substance itself of God. For effects resemble their causes according to their own mode, since like action

[1] Ch. xviii.

proceeds from like agent; and yet the effect does not always reach to a perfect likeness to the agent. Accordingly human reason is adapted to the knowledge of the truth of faith, which can be known in the highest degree only by those who see the divine substance, in so far as it is able to put together certain probable arguments in support thereof, which nevertheless are insufficient to enable us to understand the aforesaid truth as though it were demonstrated to us or understood by us in itself. And yet however weak these arguments may be, it is useful for the human mind to be practised therein, so long as it does not pride itself on having comprehended or demonstrated: since although our view of the sublimest things is limited and weak, it is most pleasant to be able to catch but a glimpse of them, as appears from what has been said.[1]

The authority of Hilary is in agreement with this statement: for he says (*De Trin.*)[2] while speaking of this same truth: *Begin by believing these things, advance and persevere; and though I know thou wilt not arrive, I shall rejoice at thy advance. For he who devoutly follows in pursuit of the infinite, though he never come up with it, will always advance by setting forth. Yet pry not into that secret, and meddle not in the mystery of the birth of the infinite,*[3] *nor presume to grasp that which is the summit of understanding: but understand that there are things thou canst not grasp.*

[1] Ch. v.

[2] ii. 10, 11.

[3] *Interminibilis.* S. Hilary wrote *inopinabilis*—i.e., *of that which surpasses our ken.*

THE ETHICS

OF BELIEF*

William K. Clifford *William K. Clifford (1845–1879), who taught at University College, London, was primarily a mathematician. Of philosophical interest are his* Lectures and Essays, Seeing and Thinking, *and* Common Sense of the Exact Sciences.

I. The Duty of Inquiry

A SHIPOWNER was about to send to sea an emigrant-ship. He knew that she was old, and not over-well built at the first; that she had seen many seas and climes, and often had needed repairs. Doubts had been suggested to him that possibly she was not seaworthy. These doubts preyed upon his mind, and made him unhappy; he thought that perhaps he ought to have her thoroughly overhauled and refitted, even though this should put him to great expense. Before the ship sailed, however, he succeeded in overcoming these melancholy reflections. He said to himself that she had gone safely through so many voyages and weathered so many storms that it was idle to suppose she would not come safely home from this trip also. He would put his trust in Providence, which could hardly fail to protect all these unhappy families that were leaving their father-land to seek for better times elsewhere. He would dismiss from his mind all ungenerous suspicions about the honesty of builders and contractors. In such ways he acquired a sincere and comfortable conviction that his vessel was thoroughly safe and seaworthy; he watched her departure with a light heart, and benevolent wishes for the success of the exiles in their strange new home that was to be; and he got his insurance-money when she went down in mid-ocean and told no tales.

What shall we say of him? Surely this, that he was verily guilty of the death of those men. It is admitted that he did sincerely believe in the soundness of his ship; but the sincerity of his convic-tion can in no wise help him, because *he had no right to believe on*

* From William K. Clifford, *Lectures and Essays.*

such evidence as was before him. He had acquired his belief not by honestly earning it in patient investigation, but by stifling his doubts. And although in the end he may have felt so sure about it that he could not think otherwise, yet inasmuch as he had knowingly and willingly worked himself into that frame of mind, he must be held responsible for it.

Let us alter the case a little, and suppose that the ship was not unsound after all; that she made her voyage safely, and many others after it. Will that diminish the guilt of her owner? Not one jot. When an action is once done, it is right or wrong for ever; no accidental failure of its good or evil fruits can possibly alter that. The man would not have been innocent, he would only have been not found out. The question of right or wrong has to do with the origin of his belief, not the matter of it; not what it was, but how he got it; not whether it turned out to be true or false, but whether he had a right to believe on such evidence as was before him.

There was once an island in which some of the inhabitants professed a religion teaching neither the doctrine of original sin nor that of eternal punishment. A suspicion got abroad that the professors of this religion had made use of unfair means to get their doctrines taught to children. They were accused of wresting the laws of their country in such a way as to remove children from the care of their natural and legal guardians; and even of stealing them away and keeping them concealed from their friends and relations. A certain number of men formed themselves into a society for the purpose of agitating the public about this matter. They published grave accusations against individual citizens of the highest position and character, and did all in their power to injure these citizens in the exercise of their professions. So great was the noise they made, that a Commission was appointed to investigate the facts; but after the Commission had carefully inquired into all the evidence that could be got, it appeared that the accused were innocent. Not only had they been accused on insufficient evidence, but the evidence of their innocence was such as the agitators might easily have obtained, if they had attempted a fair inquiry. After these disclosures the inhabitants of that country looked upon the members of the agitating society, not only as persons whose judgment was to be distrusted, but also as no longer to be counted honourable men. For although they had sincerely and conscientiously believed in the charges they had made, yet *they had no right to believe on such evidence as was before them.* Their sincere convictions, instead of being honestly earned by patient inquiring, were stolen by listening to the voice of prejudice and passion.

Let us vary this case also, and suppose, other things remaining as before, that a still more accurate investigation proved the accused to have been really guilty. Would this make any difference in the guilt of the accusers? Clearly not; the question is not whether their belief was true or false, but whether they entertained it on wrong grounds. They would no doubt say, "Now you see that we were right after all; next time perhaps you will believe us." And they might be believed, but they would not thereby become honourable men. They would not be innocent, they would only be not found out. Every one of them, if he chose to examine himself *in foro conscientiae*, would know that he had acquired and nourished a belief, when he had no right to believe on such evidence as was before him; and therein he would know that he had done a wrong thing.

It may be said, however, that in both of these supposed cases it is not the belief which is judged to be wrong, but the action following upon it. The shipowner might say, "I am perfectly certain that my ship is sound, but still I feel it my duty to have her examined, before trusting the lives of so many people to her." And it might be said to the agitator, "However convinced you were of the justice of your cause and the truth of your convictions, you ought not to have made a public attack upon any man's character until you had examined the evidence on both sides with the utmost patience and care."

In the first place, let us admit that, so far as it goes, this view of the case is right and necessary; right, because even when a man's belief is so fixed that he cannot think otherwise, he still has a choice in regard to the action suggested by it, and so cannot escape the duty of investigating on the ground of the strength of his convictions; and necessary, because those who are not yet capable of controlling their feelings and thoughts must have a plain rule dealing with overt acts.

But this being premised as necessary, it becomes clear that it is not sufficient, and that our previous judgment is required to supplement it. For it is not possible so to sever the belief from the action it suggests as to condemn the one without condemning the other. No man holding a strong belief on one side of a question, or even wishing to hold a belief on one side, can investigate it with such fairness and completeness as if he were really in doubt and unbiased; so that the existence of a belief not founded on fair inquiry unfits a man for the performance of this necessary duty.

Nor is that truly a belief at all which has not some influence upon the actions of him who holds it. He who truly believes that which prompts him to an action has looked upon the action to lust after it, he has committed it already in his heart. If a belief is not realized immediately in open deeds, it is stored up for the guidance of the future. It goes to make a part of that aggregate of beliefs which is the link between sensation and action at every moment of all our lives, and which is so organized and compacted together that no part of it can be isolated from the rest, but every new addition modifies the structure of the whole. No real belief, however trifling and fragmentary it may seem, is ever truly insignificant; it prepares us to receive more of its like, confirms those which resembled it before, and weakens others; and so gradually it lays a stealthy train in our inmost thoughts, which may some day explode into overt action, and leave its stamp upon our character for ever.

And no one man's belief is in any case a private matter which concerns himself alone. Our lives are guided by that general conception of the course of things which has been created by society for social purposes. Our words, our phrases, our forms and processes and modes of thought, are common property, fashioned and perfected from age to age; an heirloom which every succeeding generation inherits as a precious deposit and a sacred trust to be handed on to the next one, not unchanged but enlarged and purified, with some clear marks of its proper handiwork. Into this, for good or ill, is woven every belief of every man who has speech of his fellows. An awful privilege, and an awful responsibility, that we should help to create the world in which posterity will live.

In the two supposed cases which have been considered, it has been judged wrong to believe on insufficient evidence, or to nourish belief by suppressing doubts and avoiding investigation. The reason of this judgment is not far to seek: it is that in both these cases the belief held by one man was of great importance to other men. But forasmuch as no belief held by one man, however seemingly trivial the belief, and however obscure the believer, is ever actually insignificant or without its effect on the fate of mankind, we have no choice but to extend our judgment to all cases of belief whatever. Belief, that sacred faculty which prompts the decisions of our will, and knits into harmonious working all the compacted energies of our being, is ours not for ourselves, but for humanity. It is rightly used on truths which have been established by long experience and waiting toil, and which have stood in the fierce light of free and fearless questioning. Then it helps to bind men together, and to strengthen and direct their common action. It is desecrated when given to unproved and unquestioned statements, for the solace and private pleasure of the believer; to add a tinsel splendour to the plain straight road of our life and display a bright mirage beyond it; or even to drown the common sorrows of our kind by a self-deception which allows them not only to cast down, but also to degrade us. Whoso would deserve well of his fellows in this matter will guard the purity of his belief with a very fanaticism of jealous care, lest at any time it should rest on an unworthy object, and catch a stain which can never be wiped away.

It is not only the leader of men, statesman, philosopher, or poet, that owes this bounden duty to mankind. Every rustic who delivers in the village alehouse his slow, infrequent sentences, may help to kill or keep alive the fatal superstitions which clog his race. Every hard-worked wife of an artisan may transmit to her children beliefs which shall knit society together, or rend it in pieces. No simplicity of mind, no obscurity of station, can escape the universal duty of questioning all that we believe.

It is true that this duty is a hard one, and the doubt which comes out of it is often a very bitter thing. It leaves us bare and powerless where we thought that we were safe and strong. To know all about anything is to know how to deal with it under all circumstances. We feel much happier and more secure when we think we know precisely what to do, no matter what happens, than when we have lost our way and do not know where to turn. And if we have supposed ourselves to know all about anything, and to be capable of doing what is fit in regard to it, we naturally do not like to find that we are really ignorant and powerless, that we have to begin again at the beginning, and try to learn what the thing is and how it is to be dealt with—if indeed anything can be learnt about it. It is the sense of power attached to a sense of knowledge that makes men desirous of believing, and afraid of doubting.

This sense of power is the highest and best of pleasures when the belief on which it is founded is a true belief, and has been fairly earned by investigation. For then we may justly feel that it is common property, and hold good for others as well as for ourselves. Then we may be glad, not that *I* have learned secrets by which I am safer and stronger, but that *we men* have got mastery over more of the world; and we shall be strong, not for ourselves, but in the name of Man and in his strength. But if the belief has been accepted on insufficient evidence, the pleasure is a stolen one. Not only does it deceive ourselves by giving us a sense of power which we do not really possess, but it is sinful, because it is stolen in defiance of our duty to mankind. That duty is to guard ourselves from such beliefs as from a pestilence, which may shortly master our own body and then spread to the rest of the town. What would be thought of one who, for the sake of a sweet fruit, should deliberately run the risk of bringing a plague upon his family and his neighbours?

And, as in other such cases, it is not the risk only which has to be considered; for a bad action is always bad at the time when it is done, no matter what happens afterwards. Every time we let ourselves believe for unworthy reasons, we weaken our powers of self-control, of doubting, of judicially and fairly weighing evidence. We all suffer severely enough from the maintenance and support of false beliefs and the fatally wrong actions which they lead to, and the evil born when one such belief is entertained is great and wide. But a greater and wider evil arises when the credulous character is maintained and supported, when a habit of believing for unworthy reasons is fostered and made permanent. If I steal money from any person, there may be no harm done by the mere transfer of possession; he may not feel the loss, or it may prevent him from using the money badly. But I cannot help doing this great wrong towards Man, that I make myself dishonest. What hurts society is not that it should lose its property, but that it should become a den of thieves; for then it must cease to be society. This is why we ought not to do evil that good may come; for at any rate this great evil has come, that we have done evil and are made wicked thereby. In like manner, if I let myself believe anything on insufficient evidence, there may be no great harm done by the mere belief; it may be true after all, or I may never have occasion to exhibit it in outward acts. But I cannot help doing this great wrong towards Man, that I make myself credulous. The danger to society is not merely that it should believe wrong things, though that is great enough; but that it should become credulous, and lose the habit of testing things and inquiring into them; for then it must sink back into savagery.

The harm which is done by credulity in a man is not confined to the fostering of a credulous character in others, and consequent support of false beliefs. Habitual want of care about what I believe leads to habitual want of care in others about the truth of what is told to me. Men speak the truth to one another when each reveres the truth in his own mind and in the other's mind; but how shall my friend revere the truth in my mind when I myself am careless about it, when I believe things because I want to believe them, and because they are comforting and pleasant? Will he not learn to cry, "Peace," to me, when there is no peace? By such a course I shall surround myself with a thick atmosphere of falsehood and fraud, and in that I must live. It may matter little to me, in my cloud-castle of sweet illusions and darling lies; but it matters much to Man that I have made my neighbours ready to deceive. The credulous man is father to the liar and the cheat; he lives in the bosom of this his family, and it is no marvel if he should become even as they are. So closely are our duties knit together, that whoso shall keep the whole law, and yet offend in one point, he is guilty of all.

To sum up: it is wrong always, everywhere, and for anyone, to believe anything upon insufficient evidence.

If a man, holding a belief which he was taught in childhood or persuaded of afterwards, keeps down and pushes away any doubts which arise about it in his mind, purposely avoids the reading of books and the company of men that call in question or discuss it, and regards as impious those questions which cannot easily be asked without disturbing it—the life of that man is one long sin against mankind.

If this judgment seems harsh when applied to those simple souls who have never known better, who have been brought up from the cradle with a horror of doubt, and taught that their eternal welfare depends on *what* they believe, then it leads to the very serious question, *Who hath made Israel to sin?*

It may be permitted me to fortify this judgment with the sentence of Milton[1]—

"A man may be a heretic in the truth; and if he believe things only because his pastor says so, or the assembly so determine, without knowing other reason, though his belief be true, yet the very truth he holds becomes his heresy."

And with this famous aphorism of Coleridge[2]—

"He who begins by loving Christianity better than Truth, will proceed by loving his own sect or Church better than Christianity, and end in loving himself better than all."

Inquiry into the evidence of a doctrine is not to be made once for all, and then taken as finally settled. It is never lawful to stifle a doubt; for either it can be honestly answered by means of the inquiry already made, or else it proves that the inquiry was not complete.

"But," says one, "I am a busy man; I have no time for the long course of study which would be necessary to make me in any degree a competent judge of certain questions, or even able to understand the nature of the arguments." Then he should have no time to believe.

---

[1] *Areopagitica.*
[2] *Aids to Reflection.*

3

THE WILL
TO BELIEVE*

 William James

William James (1842–1910), a leading exponent of pragmatism, has been one of the most influential American philosophers. Some of his major works are: Principles of Psychology, Varieties of Religious Experience, *and* Pragmatism: A New Name for Some Old Ways of Thinking.

IN THE recently published Life by Leslie Stephen of his brother, Fitz-James, there is an account of a school to which the latter went when he was a boy. The teacher, a certain Mr. Guest, used to converse with his pupils in this wise: "Gurney, what is the difference between justification and sanctification?—Stephen, prove the omnipotence of God!" etc. In the midst of our Harvard freethinking and indifference we are prone to imagine that here at your good old orthodox College conversation continues to be somewhat upon this order; and to show you that we at Harvard have not lost all interest in these vital subjects, I have brought with me to-night something like a sermon on justification by faith to read to you,—I mean an essay in justification *of* faith, a defence of our right to adopt a believing attitude in religious matters, in spite of the fact that our merely logical intellect may not have been coerced. 'The Will to Believe,' accordingly, is the title of my paper.

I have long defended to my own students the lawfulness of voluntarily adopted faith; but as soon as they have got well imbued with the logical spirit, they have as a rule refused to admit my contention to be lawful philosophically, even though in point of fact they were personally all the time chock-full of some faith or other themselves. I am all the while, however, so profoundly convinced that my own position is correct, that your invitation has seemed to me a good occasion to make my statements more clear.

* From William James, *The Will to Believe and Other Essays.*
* An Address to the Philosophical Clubs of Yale and Brown Universities. Published in the New World, June, 1896.

Perhaps your minds will be more open than those with which I have hitherto had to deal. I will be as little technical as I can, though I must begin by setting up some technical distinctions that will help us in the end.

I

LET US give the name of *hypothesis* to anything that may be proposed to our belief; and just as the electricians speak of live and dead wires, let us speak of any hypothesis as either *live* or *dead*. A live hypothesis is one which appeals as a real possibility to him to whom it is proposed. If I ask you to believe in the Mahdi, the notion makes no electric connection with your nature,—it refuses to scintillate with any credibility at all. As an hypothesis it is completely dead. To an Arab, however (even if he be not one of the Mahdi's followers), the hypothesis is among the mind's possibilities: it is alive. This shows that deadness and liveness in an hypothesis are not intrinsic properties, but relations to the individual thinker. They are measured by his willingness to act. The maximum of liveness in an hypothesis means willingness to act irrevocably. Practically, that means belief; but there is some believing tendency wherever there is willingness to act at all.

Next, let us call the decision between two hypotheses an *option*. Options may be of several kinds. They may be—1, *living* or *dead;* 2, *forced* or *avoidable;* 3, *momentous* or *trivial;* and for our purposes we may call an option a *genuine* option when it is of the forced, living, and momentous kind.

1. A living option is one in which both hypotheses are live ones. If I say to you: "Be a theosophist or be a Mohammedan," it is probably a dead option, because for you neither hypothesis is likely to be alive. But if I say: "Be an agnostic or be a Christian," it is otherwise: trained as you are, each hypothesis makes some appeal, however small, to your belief.

2. Next, if I say to you: "Choose between going out with your umbrella or without it," I do not offer you a genuine option, for it is not forced. You can easily avoid it by not going out at all. Similarly, if I say, "Either love me or hate me," "Either call my theory true or call it false," your option is avoidable. You may remain indifferent to me, neither loving nor hating, and you may decline to offer any judgment as to my theory. But if I say, "Either accept this truth or go without it," I put on you a forced option, for there is no standing place outside of the alternative. Every dilemma

based on a complete logical disjunction, with no possibility of not choosing, is an option of this forced kind.

3. Finally, if I were Dr. Nansen and proposed to you to join my North Pole expedition, your option would be momentous; for this would probably be your only similar opportunity, and your choice now would either exclude you from the North Pole sort of immortality altogether or put at least the chance of it into your hands. He who refuses to embrace a unique opportunity loses the prize as surely as if he tried and failed. *Per contra*, the option is trivial when the opportunity is not unique, when the stake is insignificant, or when the decision is reversible if it later prove unwise. Such trivial options abound in the scientific life. A chemist finds an hypothesis live enough to spend a year in its verification: he believes in it to that extent. But if his experiments prove inconclusive either way, he is quit for his loss of time, no vital harm being done.

It will facilitate our discussion if we keep all these distinctions well in mind.

II

THE next matter to consider is the actual psychology of human opinion. When we look at certain facts, it seems as if our passional and volitional nature lay at the root of all our convictions. When we look at others, it seems as if they could do nothing when the intellect had once said its say. Let us take the latter facts up first.

Does it not seem preposterous on the very face of it to talk of our opinions being modifiable at will? Can our will either help or hinder our intellect in its perceptions of truth? Can we, by just willing it, believe that Abraham Lincoln's existence is a myth, and that the portraits of him in McClure's Magazine are all of some one else? Can we, by any effort of our will, or by any strength of wish that it were true, believe ourselves well and about when we are roaring with rheumatism in bed, or feel certain that the sum of the two one-dollar bills in our pocket must be a hundred dollars? We can *say* any of these things, but we are absolutely impotent to believe them; and of just such things is the whole fabric of the truths that we do believe in made up,—matters of fact, immediate or remote, as Hume said, and relations between ideas, which are either there or not there for us if we see them so, and which if not there cannot be put there by any action of our own.

In Pascal's Thoughts there is a celebrated passage known in literature as Pascal's wager. In it he tries to force us into Christianity by reasoning as if our concern with truth resembled our concern with the stakes in a game of chance. Translated freely his words are these: You must either believe or not believe that God is—which will you do? Your human reason cannot say. A game is going on between you and the nature of things which at the day of judgment will bring out either heads or tails. Weigh what your gains and your losses would be if you should stake all you have on heads, or God's existence: if you win in such case, you gain eternal beatitude; if you lose, you lose nothing at all. If there were an infinity of chances, and only one for God in this wager, still you ought to stake your all on God; for though you surely risk a finite loss by this procedure, any finite loss is reasonable, even a certain one is reasonable, if there is but the possibility of infinite gain. Go, then, and take holy water, and have masses said; belief will come and stupefy your scruples,—*Cela vous fera croire et vous abêtira.* Why should you not? At bottom, what have you to lose?

You probably feel that when religious faith expresses itself thus, in the language of the gaming-table, it is put to its last trumps. Surely Pascal's own personal belief in masses and holy water had far other springs; and this celebrated page of his is but an argument for others, a last desperate snatch at a weapon against the hardness of the unbelieving heart. We feel that a faith in masses and holy water adopted wilfully after such a mechanical calculation would lack the inner soul of faith's reality; and if we were ourselves in the place of the Deity, we should probably take particular pleasure in cutting off believers of this pattern from their infinite reward. It is evident that unless there be some pre-existing tendency to believe in masses and holy water, the option offered to the will by Pascal is not a living option. Certainly no Turk ever took to masses and holy water on its account; and even to us Protestants these means of salvation seem such foregone impossibilities that Pascal's logic, invoked for them specifically, leaves us unmoved. As well might the Mahdi write to us, saying, "I am the Expected One whom God has created in his effulgence. You shall be infinitely happy if you confess me; otherwise you shall be cut off from the light of the sun. Weigh, then, your infinite gain if I am genuine against your finite sacrifice if I am not!" His logic would be that of Pascal; but he would vainly use it on us, for the hypothesis he offers us is dead. No tendency to act on it exists in us to any degree.

The talk of believing by our volition seems, then, from one point of view, simply silly. From another point of view it is worse than silly, it is vile. When one turns to the magnificent edifice of the physical sciences, and sees how it was reared; what thousands of disinterested moral lives of men lie buried in its mere foundations;

what patience and postponement, what choking down of preference, what submission to the icy laws of outer fact are wrought into
its very stones and mortar; how absolutely impersonal it stands in
its vast augustness,—then how besotted and contemptible seems
every little sentimentalist who comes blowing his voluntary smoke-
wreaths, and pretending to decide things from out of his private
dream! Can we wonder if those bred in the rugged and manly
school of science should feel like spewing such subjectivism out of
their mouths? The whole system of loyalties which grow up in the
schools of science go dead against its toleration; so that it is only
natural that those who have caught the scientific fever should pass
over to the opposite extreme, and write sometimes as if the incor-
ruptibly truthful intellect ought positively to prefer bitterness and
unacceptableness to the heart in its cup.

It fortifies my soul to know
That, though I perish, Truth is so—

sings Clough, while Huxley exclaims: "My only consolation lies in
the reflection that, however bad our posterity may become, so far as
they hold by the plain rule of not pretending to believe what they
have no reason to believe, because it may be to their advantage so to
pretend [the word 'pretend' is surely here redundant], they will
not have reached the lowest depth of immorality." And that deli-
cious *enfant terrible* Clifford writes: "Belief is desecrated when
given to unproved and unquestioned statements for the solace and
private pleasure of the believer. . . . Whoso would deserve well of
his fellows in this matter will guard the purity of his belief with a
very fanaticism of jealous care, lest at any time it should rest on an
unworthy object, and catch a stain which can never be wiped
away. . . . If [a] belief has been accepted on insufficient evidence
[even though the belief be true, as Clifford on the same page
explains] the pleasure is a stolen one. . . . It is sinful because it is
stolen in defiance of our duty to mankind. That duty is to guard
ourselves from such beliefs as from a pestilence which may shortly
master our own body and then spread to the rest of the town. . . .
It is wrong always, everywhere, and for every one, to believe
anything upon insufficient evidence."

III

ALL this strikes one as healthy, even when expressed, as by Clifford,
with somewhat too much of robustious pathos in the voice. Free-will
and simple wishing do seem, in the matter of our credences, to be

only fifth wheels to the coach. Yet if any one should thereupon assume that intellectual insight is what remains after wish and will and sentimental preference have taken wing, or that pure reason is what then settles our opinions, he would fly quite as directly in the teeth of the facts.

It is only our already dead hypotheses that our willing nature is unable to bring to life again. But what has made them dead for us is for the most part a previous action of our willing nature of an antagonistic kind. When I say 'willing nature,' I do not mean only such deliberate volitions as may have set up habits of belief that we cannot now escape from,—I mean all such factors of belief as fear and hope, prejudice and passion, imitation and partisanship, the circumpressure of our caste and set. As a matter of fact we find ourselves believing, we hardly know how or why. Mr. Balfour gives the name of 'authority' to all those influences, born of the intellectual climate, that make hypotheses possible or impossible for us, alive or dead. Here in this room, we all of us believe in molecules and the conservation of energy, in democracy and necessary progress, in Protestant Christianity and the duty of fighting for 'the doctrine of the immortal Monroe,' all for no reasons worthy of the name. We see into these matters with no more inner clearness, and probably with much less, than any disbeliever in them might possess. His unconventionality would probably have some grounds to show for its conclusions; but for us, not insight, but the *prestige* of the opinions, is what makes the spark shoot from them and light up our sleeping magazines of faith. Our reason is quite satisfied, in nine hundred and ninety-nine cases out of every thousand of us, if it can find a few arguments that will do to recite in case our credulity is criticised by some one else. Our faith is faith in some one else's faith, and in the greatest matters this is most the case. Our belief in truth itself, for instance, that there is a truth, and that our minds and it are made for each other,—what is it but a passionate affirmation of desire, in which our social system backs us up? We want to have a truth; we want to believe that our experiments and studies and discussions must put us in a continually better and better position towards it; and on this line we agree to fight out our thinking lives. But if a pyrrhonistic sceptic asks us *how we know* all this, can our logic find a reply? No! certainly it cannot. It is just one volition against another,—we willing to go in for life upon a trust or assumption which he, for his part, does not care to make.*

As a rule we disbelieve all facts and theories for which we have no use. Clifford's cosmic emotions find no use for Christian

* Compare the admirable page 310 in S. H. Hodgson's "Time and Space," London, 1865.

feelings. Huxley belabors the bishops because there is no use for sacerdotalism in his scheme of life. Newman, on the contrary, goes over to Romanism, and finds all sorts of reasons good for staying there, because a priestly system is for him an organic need and delight. Why do so few 'scientists' even look at the evidence for telepathy, so called? Because they think, as a leading biologist, now dead, once said to me, that even if such a thing were true, scientists ought to band together to keep it suppressed and concealed. It would undo the uniformity of Nature and all sorts of other things without which scientists cannot carry on their pursuits. But if this very man had been shown something which as a scientist he might *do* with telepathy, he might not only have examined the evidence, but even have found it good enough. This very law which the logicians would impose upon us—if I may give the name of logicians to those who would rule out our willing nature here—is based on nothing but their own natural wish to exclude all elements for which they, in their professional quality of logicians, can find no use.

Evidently, then, our non-intellectual nature does influence our convictions. There are passional tendencies and volitions which run before and others which come after belief, and it is only the latter that are too late for the fair; and they are not too late when the previous passional work has been already in their own direction. Pascal's argument, instead of being powerless, then seems a regular clincher, and is the last stroke needed to make our faith in masses and holy water complete. The state of things is evidently far from simple; and pure insight and logic, whatever they might do ideally, are not the only things that really do produce our creeds.

IV

OUR next duty, having recognized this mixed-up state of affairs, is to ask whether it be simply reprehensible and pathological, or whether, on the contrary, we must treat it as a normal element in making up our minds. The thesis I defend is, briefly stated, this: *Our passional nature not only lawfully may, but must, decide an option between propositions, whenever it is a genuine option that cannot by its nature be decided on intellectual grounds; for to say, under such circumstances, "Do not decide, but leave the question open," is itself a passional decision,—just like deciding yes or no,—and is attended with the same risk of losing the truth.* The thesis thus abstractly expressed will, I trust, soon become quite clear. But I must first indulge in a bit more of preliminary work.

V

IT WILL be observed that for the purposes of this discussion we are on 'dogmatic' ground,—ground, I mean, which leaves systematic philosophical scepticism altogether out of account. The postulate that there is truth, and that it is the destiny of our minds to attain it, we are deliberately resolving to make, though the sceptic will not make it. We part company with him, therefore, absolutely, at this point. But the faith that truth exists, and that our minds can find it, may be held in two ways. We may talk of the *empiricist* way and of the *absolutist* way of believing in truth. The absolutists in this matter say that we not only can attain to knowing truth, but we can *know when* we have attained to knowing it; while the empiricists think that although we may attain it, we cannot infallibly know when. To *know* is one thing, and to know for certain *that* we know is another. One may hold to the first being possible without the second; hence the empiricists and the absolutists, although neither of them is a sceptic in the usual philosophic sense of the term, show very different degrees of dogmatism in their lives.

If we look at the history of opinions, we see that the empiricist tendency has largely prevailed in science, while in philosophy the absolutist tendency has had everything its own way. The characteristic sort of happiness, indeed, which philosophies yield has mainly consisted in the conviction felt by each successive school or system that by it bottom-certitude had been attained. "Other philosophies are collections of opinions mostly false; *my* philosophy gives standing-ground forever,"—who does not recognize in this the key note of every system worthy of the name? A system, to be a system at all, must come as a *closed* system, reversible in this or that detail, perchance, but in its essential features never!

Scholastic orthodoxy, to which one must always go when one wishes to find perfectly clear statement, has beautifully elaborated this absolutist conviction in a doctrine which it calls that of 'objective evidence.' If, for example, I am unable to doubt that I now exist before you, that two is less than three, or that if all men are mortal than I am mortal too, it is because these things illumine my intellect irresistibly. The final ground of this objective evidence possessed by certain propositions is the *adæquatio intellectus nostri cum ré.* The certitude it brings involves an *aptitudinem ad extorquendum certum assensum* on the part of the truth envisaged, and on the side of the subject a *quietem in cognitione,* when once the object is mentally received, that leaves no possibility of doubt behind; and in the whole transaction nothing operates but the *entitas ipsa* of the object and the *entitas ipsa* of the mind. We slouchy modern thinkers dislike to talk in Latin,—indeed, we dislike to talk in set terms at all; but at bottom our own state of mind is very much like this whenever we uncritically abandon ourselves: You believe in objective evidence, and I do. Of some things we feel that we are certain: we know, and we know that we do know. There is something that gives a click inside of us, a bell that strikes twelve, when the hands of our mental clock have swept the dial and meet over the meridian hour. The greatest empiricists among us are only empiricists on reflection: when left to their instincts, they dogmatize like infallible popes. When the Cliffords tell us how sinful it is to be Christians on such 'insufficient evidence,' insufficiency is really the last thing they have in mind. For them the evidence is absolutely sufficient, only it makes the other way. They believe so completely in an anti-christian order of the universe that there is no living option: Christianity is a dead hypothesis from the start.

VI

BUT now, since we are all such absolutists by instinct, what in our quality of students of philosophy ought we to do about the fact? Shall we espouse and indorse it? Or shall we treat it as a weakness of our nature from which we must free ourselves, if we can?

I sincerely believe that the latter course is the only one we can follow as reflective men. Objective evidence and certitude are doubtless very fine ideals to play with, but where on this moonlit and dream-visited planet are they found? I am, therefore, myself a complete empiricist so far as my theory of human knowledge goes. I live, to be sure, by the practical faith that we must go on experiencing and thinking over our experience, for only thus can our opinions grow more true; but to hold any one of them—I absolutely do not care which—as if it never could be reinterpretable or corrigible, I believe to be a tremendously mistaken attitude, and I think that the whole history of philosophy will bear me out. There is but one indefectibly certain truth, and that is the truth that pyrrhonistic scepticism itself leaves standing,—the truth that the present phenomenon of consciousness exists. That, however, is the bare starting-point of knowledge, the mere admission of a stuff to be philosophized about. The various philosophies are but so many attempts at expressing what this stuff really is. And if we repair to our libraries what disagreement do we discover! Where is a certainly true answer found? Apart from abstract propositions of comparison (such as two and two are the same as four), propositions which tell us nothing by themselves about concrete reality, we find no proposition ever regarded by any one as evidently certain, that has not either been called a falsehood, or at least had its truth sincerely questioned by some one else. The transcending of the axioms of geometry, not in play but in earnest, by certain of our contemporaries (as Zöllner and Charles H. Hinton), and the rejection of the whole Aristotelian logic by the Hegelians, are striking instances in point.

No concrete test of what is really true has ever been agreed upon. Some make the criterion external to the moment or perception, putting it either in revelation, the *consensus gentium,* the instincts of the heart, or the systematized experience of the race. Others make the perceptive moment its own test,—Descartes, for instance, with his clear and distinct ideas guaranteed by the veracity of God; Reid with his 'common-sense;' and Kant with his forms of synthetic judgment *a priori.* The inconceivability of the opposite; the capacity to be verified by sense; the possession of complete organic unity or self-relation, realized when a thing is its own other,—are standards which, in turn, have been used. The much lauded objective evidence is never triumphantly there; it is a mere aspiration or *Grenzbegriff,* marking the infinitely remote ideal of our thinking life. To claim that certain truths now possess it, is simply to say that when you think them true and they *are* true, then their evidence is objective, otherwise it is not. But practically one's conviction that the evidence one goes by is of the real objective brand, is only one more subjective opinion added to the lot. For what a contradictory array of opinions have objective evidence and absolute certitude been claimed! The world is rational through and through,—its existence is an ultimate brute fact; there is a personal God,—a personal God is inconceivable; there is an extra-mental physical world immediately known,—the mind can only know its own ideas; a moral imperative exists,—obligation is only the resultant of desires; a permanent spiritual principle is in every one,—there are only shifting states of mind; there is an endless chain of causes,—there is an absolute first cause; an eternal necessity,—a freedom; a purpose,—no purpose; a primal One,—a primal Many; a universal continuity,—an essential discontinuity in things; an infinity—no infinity. There is this,—there is that; there is indeed nothing which some one has not thought absolutely true, while his neighbor deemed it absolutely false; and not an absolutist among them seems ever to have considered that the trouble may all the time be essential, and that the intellect, even with truth directly in its grasp, may have no infallible signal for knowing whether it be truth or no. When, indeed, one remembers that the most striking practical application to life of the doctrine of objective certitude has been the conscientious labors of the Holy Office of the Inquisition, one feels less tempted than ever to lend the doctrine a respectful ear.

But please observe, now, that when as empiricists we give up the doctrine of objective certitude, we do not thereby give up the quest or hope of truth itself. We still pin our faith on its existence, and still believe that we gain an ever better position towards it by systematically continuing to roll up experiences and think. Our great difference from the scholastic lies in the way we face. The strength of his system lies in the principles, the origin, the *terminus a quo* of his thought; for us the strength is in the outcome, the upshot, the *terminus ad quem*. Not where it comes from but what it leads to is to decide. It matters not to an empiricist from what quarter an hypothesis may come to him: he may have acquired it by fair means or by foul; passion may have whispered or accident suggested it; but if the total drift of thinking continues to confirm it, that is what he means by its being true.

VII

ONE more point, small but important, and our preliminaries are done. There are two ways of looking at our duty in the matter of opinion,—ways entirely different, and yet ways about whose difference the theory of knowledge seems hitherto to have shown very little concern. *We must know the truth;* and *we must avoid error,*— these are our first and great commandments as would-be knowers; but they are not two ways of stating an identical commandment, they are two separable laws. Although it may indeed happen that when we believe the truth *A,* we escape as an incidental consequence from believing the falsehood *B,* it hardly ever happens that by merely disbelieving *B* we necessarily believe *A.* We may in escaping *B* fall into believing other falsehoods, *C* or *D,* just as bad as *B;* or we may escape *B* by not believing anything at all, not even *A.*

Believe truth! Shun error!—these, we see, are two materially different laws; and by choosing between them we may end by coloring differently our whole intellectual life. We may regard the chase for truth as paramount, and the avoidance of error as secondary; or we may, on the other hand, treat the avoidance of error as more imperative, and let truth take its chance. Clifford, in the instructive passage which I have quoted, exhorts us to the latter course. Believe nothing, he tells us, keep your mind in suspense forever, rather than by closing it on insufficient evidence incur the awful risk of believing lies. You, on the other hand, may think that the risk of being in error is a very small matter when compared with the blessings of real knowledge, and be ready to be duped many times in your investigation rather than postpone indefinitely the chance of guessing true. I myself find it impossible to go with Clifford. We must remember that these feelings of our duty about either truth or error are in any case only expressions of our passional life. Biologically considered, our minds are as ready to grind out falsehood as veracity, and he who says, "Better go without belief forever than believe a lie!" merely shows his own preponderant private horror of becoming a dupe. He may be critical of many of his desires and fears, but this fear he slavishly obeys. He cannot imagine any one questioning its binding force. For my own part, I have also a horror of being duped; but I can believe that worse things than being duped may happen to a man in this world: so Clifford's exhortation has to my ears a thoroughly fantastic sound. It is like a general informing his soldiers that it is better to keep out of battle forever than to risk a single wound. Not so are victories either over enemies or over nature gained. Our errors are surely not such awfully solemn things. In a world where we are so certain to incur them in spite of all our caution, a certain lightness of heart seems healthier than this excessive nervousness on their behalf. At any rate, it seems the fittest thing for the empiricist philosopher.

VIII

AND now, after all this introduction, let us go straight at our question. I have said, and now repeat it, that not only as a matter of fact do we find our passional nature influencing us in our opinions, but that there are some options between opinions in which this influence must be regarded both as an evitable and as a lawful determinant of our choice.

I fear here that some of you my hearers will begin to scent danger, and lend an inhospitable ear. Two first steps of passion you have indeed had to admit as necessary,—we must think so as to avoid dupery, and we must think so as to gain truth; but the surest path to those ideal consummations, you will probably consider, is from now onwards to take no further passional step.

Well, of course, I agree as far as the facts will allow. Wherever the option between losing truth and gaining it is not momentous, we can throw the chance of *gaining truth* away, and at any rate save ourselves from any chance of *believing falsehood,* by not making up our minds at all till objective evidence has come. In scientific questions, this is almost always the case; and even in human affairs in general, the need of acting is seldom so urgent that a false belief to act on is better than no belief at all. Law courts, indeed, have to decide on the best evidence attainable for the moment, because a judge's duty is to make law as well as to ascertain it, and (as a learned judge once said to me) few cases are worth spending much time over: the great thing is to have them decided on *any* acceptable principle, and got out of the way. But in our dealings with objective nature we obviously are recorders, not makers, of the truth; and decisions for the mere sake of deciding promptly and getting on to the next business would be wholly out of place. Throughout the breadth of physical nature facts are what they are quite independently of us, and seldom is there any such hurry about them that the risks of being duped by believing a premature theory need be faced. The questions here are always trivial options, the hypotheses are hardly living (at any rate not living for us spectators), the choice between believing truth or falsehood is seldom forced. The attitude of sceptical balance is therefore the absolutely wise one if we would escape mistakes. What difference, indeed, does it make to most of us whether we have or have not a theory of the Röntgen rays, whether we believe or not in mind-stuff, or have a conviction about the causality of conscious states? It makes no difference. Such options are not forced on us. On every account it is better not to make them, but still keep weighing reasons *pro et contra* with an indifferent hand.

I speak, of course, here of the purely judging mind. For purposes of discovery such indifference is to be less highly recommended, and science would be far less advanced than she is if the passionate desires of individuals to get their own faiths confirmed had been kept out of the game. See for example the sagacity which Spencer and Weismann now display. On the other hand, if you want an absolute duffer in an investigation, you must, after all, take the man who has no interest whatever in its results: he is the warranted incapable, the positive fool. The most useful investigator, because the most sensitive observer, is always he whose eager interest in one side of the question is balanced by an equally keen nervousness lest he become deceived.* Science has organized this nervousness into a regular *technique,* her so-called method of verification; and she has fallen so deeply in love with the method

* Compare Wilfrid Ward's Essay, "The Wish to Believe," in his *Witnesses to the Unseen,* Macmillan & Co., 1893.

that one may even say she has ceased to care for truth by itself at all. It is only truth as technically verified that interests her. The truth of truths might come in merely affirmative form, and she would decline to touch it. Such truth as that, she might repeat with Clifford, would be stolen in defiance of her duty to mankind. Human passions, however, are stronger than technical rules. "Le cœur a ses raisons," as Pascal says, "que la raison ne connaît pas;" and however indifferent to all but the bare rules of the game the umpire, the abstract intellect, may be, the concrete players who furnish him the materials to judge of are usually, each one of them, in love with some pet 'live hypothesis' of his own. Let us agree, however, that wherever there is no forced option, the dispassionately judicial intellect with no pet hypothesis, saving us, as it does, from dupery at any rate, ought to be our ideal.

The question next arises: Are there not somewhere forced options in our speculative questions, and can we (as men who may be interested at least as much in positively gaining truth as in merely escaping dupery) always wait with impunity till the coercive evidence shall have arrived? It seems *a priori* improbable that the truth should be so nicely adjusted to our needs and powers as that. In the great boarding-house of nature, the cakes and the butter and the syrup seldom come out so even and leave the plates so clean. Indeed, we should view them with scientific suspicion if they did.

IX

Moral questions immediately present themselves as questions whose solution cannot wait for sensible proof. A moral question is a question not of what sensibly exists, but of what is good, or would be good if it did exist. Science can tell us what exists; but to compare the *worths,* both of what exists and of what does not exist, we must consult not science, but what Pascal calls our heart. Science herself consults her heart when she lays it down that the infinite ascertainment of fact and correction of false belief are the supreme goods for man. Challenge the statement, and science can only repeat it oracularly, or else prove it by showing that such ascertainment and correction bring men all sorts of other goods which man's heart in turn declares. The question of having moral beliefs at all or not having them is decided by our will. Are our moral preferences true or false, or are they only odd biological phenomena, making things good or bad for *us,* but in themselves indifferent? How can your pure intellect decide? If your heart does not *want* a world of moral reality, your head will assuredly never make you believe in one.

Mephistophelian scepticism, indeed, will satisfy the head's play-instincts much better than any rigorous idealism can. Some men (even at the student age) are so naturally cool-hearted that the moralistic hypothesis never has for them any pungent life, and in their supercilious presence the hot young moralist always feels strangely ill at ease. The appearance of knowingness is on their side, of *naiveté* and gullibility on his. Yet, in the inarticulate heart of him, he clings to it that he is not a dupe, and that there is a realm in which (as Emerson says) all their wit and intellectual superiority is no better than the cunning of a fox. Moral scepticism can no more be refuted or proved by logic than intellectual scepticism can. When we stick to it that there *is* truth (be it of either kind), we do so with our whole nature, and resolve to stand or fall by the results. The sceptic with his whole nature adopts the doubting attitude; but which of us is the wiser, Omniscience only knows.

Turn now from these wide questions of good to a certain class of questions of fact, questions concerning personal relations, states of mind between one man and another. *Do you like me or not?*—for example. Whether you do or not depends, in countless instances, on whether I meet you half-way, am willing to assume that you must like me, and show you trust and expectation. The previous faith on my part in your liking's existence is in such cases what makes your liking come. But if I stand aloof, and refuse to budge an inch until I have objective evidence, until you shall have done something apt, as the absolutists say, *ad extorquendum assensum meum,* ten to one your liking never comes. How many women's hearts are vanquished by the mere sanguine insistence of some man that they *must* love him! he will not consent to the hypothesis that they cannot. The desire for a certain kind of truth here brings about that special truth's existence; and so it is in innumerable cases of other sorts. Who gains promotions, boons, appointments, but the man in whose life they are seen to play the part of live hypotheses, who discounts them, sacrifices other things for their sake before they have come, and takes risks for them in advance? His faith acts on the powers above him as a claim, and creates its own verification.

A social organism of any sort whatever, large or small, is what it is because each member proceeds to his own duty with a trust that the other members will simultaneously do theirs. Wherever a desired result is achieved by the co-operation of many independent persons, its existence as a fact is a pure consequence of the precursive faith in one another of those immediately concerned. A government, an army, a commercial system, a ship, a college, an athletic team, all exist on this condition, without which not only is nothing achieved, but nothing is even attempted. A whole train of passengers (individually brave enough) will be looted by a few highwaymen, simply because the latter can count on one another, while each passenger fears that if he makes a movement of resistance, he will be shot before any one else backs him up. If we believed that the whole car-full would rise at once with us, we should each severally rise, and train-robbing would never even be attempted. There are, then, cases where a fact cannot come at all unless a preliminary faith exists in its coming. *And where faith in a fact can help create the fact,* that would be an insane logic which should say that faith running ahead of scientific evidence is the 'lowest kind of immorality' into which a thinking being can fall. Yet such is the logic by which our scientific absolutists pretend to regulate our lives!

X

IN TRUTHS dependent on our personal action, then, faith based on desire is certainly a lawful and possibly an indispensable thing.

But now, it will be said, these are all childish human cases, and have nothing to do with great cosmical matters, like the question of religious faith. Let us then pass on to that. Religions differ so much in their accidents that in discussing the religious question we must make it very generic and broad. What then do we now mean by the religious hypothesis? Science says things are; morality says some things are better than other things; and religion says essentially two things.

First, she says that the best things are the more eternal things, the overlapping things, the things in the universe that throw the last stone, so to speak, and say the final word. "Perfection is eternal,"—this phrase of Charles Secrétan seems a good way of putting this first affirmation of religion, an affirmation which obviously cannot yet be verified scientifically at all.

The second affirmation of religion is that we are better off even now if we believe her first affirmation to be true.

Now, let us consider what the logical elements of this situation are *in case the religious hypothesis in both its branches be really true.* (Of course, we must admit that possibility at the outset. If we are to discuss the question at all, it must involve a living option. If for any of you religion be a hypothesis that cannot, by any living possibility be true, then you need go no farther. I speak to the 'saving remnant' alone.) So proceeding, we see, first that religion offers itself as a *momentous* option. We are supposed to gain, even now, by our belief, and to lose by our nonbelief, a certain vital good. Secondly, religion is a *forced* option, so far as that good goes. We cannot escape the issue by remaining sceptical and waiting for more light, because, although we do avoid error in that way *if religion be untrue,* we lose the good, *if it be true,* just as certainly as if we positively chose to disbelieve. It is as if a man should hesitate indefinitely to ask a certain woman to marry him because he was not perfectly sure that she would prove an angel after he brought her home. Would he not cut himself off from that particular angel-possibility as decisively as if he went and married some one else? Scepticism, then, is not avoidance of option; it is option of a certain particular kind of risk. *Better risk loss of truth than chance of error,*—that is your faith-vetoer's exact position. He is actively playing his stake as much as the believer is; he is backing the field against the religious hypothesis, just as the believer is backing the religious hypothesis against the field. To preach scepticism to us as a duty until 'sufficient evidence' for religion be found, is tantamount therefore to telling us, when in presence of the religious hypothesis, that to yield to our fear of its being error is wiser and better than to yield to our hope that it may be true. It is not intellect against all passions, then; it is only intellect with one passion laying down its law. And by what, forsooth, is the supreme wisdom of this passion warranted? Dupery for dupery, what proof is there that dupery through hope is so much worse than dupery through fear? I, for one, can see no proof; and I simply refuse obedience to the scientist's command to imitate his kind of option, in a case where my own stake is important enough to give me the right to choose my own form of risk. If religion be true and the evidence for it be still insufficient, I do not wish, by putting your extinguisher upon my nature (which feels to me as if it had after all some business in this matter), to forfeit my sole chance in life of getting upon the winning side,—that chance depending, of course, on my willingness to run the risk of acting as if my passional need of taking the world religiously might be prophetic and right.

All this is on the supposition that it really may be prophetic and right, and that, even to us who are discussing the matter, religion is a live hypothesis which may be true. Now, to most of us religion comes in a still further way that makes a veto on our active faith even more illogical. The more perfect and more eternal aspect of the universe is represented in our religions as having personal form. The universe is no longer a mere *It* to us, but a *Thou,* if we are religious; and any relation that may be possible from person to person might be possible here. For instance, although in one sense we are passive portions of the universe, in another we show a curious autonomy, as if we were small active centres on our own account. We feel, too, as if the appeal of religion to us were made to our own active good-will, as if evidence might be forever withheld from us unless we met the hypothesis half-way. To take a trivial illustration: just as a man who in a company of gentlemen made no advances, asked a warrant for every concession, and believed no one's word without proof, would cut himself off by such churlishness from all the social rewards that a more trusting spirit would earn,—so here, one who should shut himself up in snarling logicality and try to make the gods extort his recognition willy-nilly, or not get it at all, might cut himself off forever from his only opportunity of making the gods' acquaintance. This feeling, forced on us we know not whence, that by obstinately believing that there are gods (although not to do so would be so easy both for our logic and our life) we are doing the universe the deepest service we can, seems part of the living essence of the religious hypothesis. If the hypothesis *were* true in all its parts, including this one, then pure intellectualism, with its veto on our making willing advances, would be an absurdity; and some participation of our sympathetic nature would be logically required. I, therefore, for one, cannot see my way to accepting the agnostic rules for truth-seeking, or wilfully agree to keep my willing nature out of the game. I cannot do so for this plain reason, that *a rule of thinking which would absolutely prevent me from acknowledging certain kinds of truth if those kinds of truth were really there, would be an irrational rule.* That for me is the long and short of the formal logic of the situation, no matter what the kinds of truth might materially be.

I confess I do not see how this logic can be escaped. But sad experience makes me fear that some of you may still shrink from radically saying with me, *in abstracto,* that we have the right to believe at our own risk any hypothesis that is live enough to tempt our will. I suspect, however, that if this is so, it is because you have got away from the abstract logical point of view altogether, and are thinking (perhaps without realizing it) of some particular religious hypothesis which for you is dead. The freedom to 'believe what we will' you apply to the case of some patent superstition; and the faith you think of is the faith defined by the schoolboy when he said, "Faith is when you believe something that you know ain't true." I can only repeat that this is misapprehension. *In concreto,* the freedom to believe can only cover living options which the intellect of the individual cannot by itself resolve; and living options never seem absurdities to him who has them to consider. When I look at the religious question as it really puts itself to concrete men, and when I think of all the possibilities which both practically and theoretically it involves, then this command that we shall put a stopper on our heart, instincts, and courage, and *wait*—acting of course meanwhile more or less as if religion were *not* true*—till doomsday, or till such time as our intellect and senses working together may have raked in evidence enough,—this command, I say, seems to me the queerest idol ever manufactured in the philosophic cave. Were we scholastic absolutists, there might be more excuse. If we had an infallible intellect with its objective certitudes, we might feel ourselves disloyal to such a perfect organ of knowledge in not trusting to it exclusively, in not waiting for its releasing word. But if we are empiricists, if we believe that no bell in us tolls to let us know for certain when truth is in our grasp, then it seems a piece of idle fantasticality to preach so solemnly our duty of waiting for the bell. Indeed we *may* wait if we will,—I hope you do not think that I am denying that,—but if we do so, we do so at our peril as much as if we believed. In either case we *act*, taking our life in our hands. No one of us ought to issue vetoes to the other, nor should we bandy words of abuse. We ought, on the contrary, delicately and profoundly to respect one another's mental freedom: then only shall we bring about the intellectual republic; then only shall we have that spirit of inner tolerance without which all our outer tolerance is soulless, and which is empiricism's glory; then only shall we live and let live, in speculative as well as in practical things.

I began by a reference to Fitz-James Stephen; let me end by a quotation from him. "What do you think of yourself? What do you think of the world? . . . These are questions with which all must deal as it seems good to them. They are riddles of the Sphinx, and in some way or other we must deal with them. . . . In all important transactions of life we have to take a leap in the dark. . . . If we decide to leave the riddles unanswered, that is a choice; if we waver in our answer, that, too, is a choice: but whatever choice we make, we make it at our peril. If a man chooses to turn his back altogether on God and the future, no one can prevent him; no one can show beyond reasonable doubt that he is mistaken. If a man

---

* Since belief is measured by action, he who forbids us to believe religion to be true, necessarily also forbids us to act as we should if we did believe it to be true. The whole defence of religious faith hinges upon action. If the action required or inspired by the religious hypothesis is in no way different from that dictated by the naturalistic hypothesis, then religious faith is a pure superfluity, better pruned away, and controversy about its legitimacy is a piece of idle trifling, unworthy of serious minds. I myself believe, of course, that the religious hypothesis gives to the world an expression which specifically determines our reactions, and makes them in a large part unlike what they might be on a purely naturalistic scheme of belief.

thinks otherwise and acts as he thinks, I do not see that any one can prove that *he* is mistaken. Each must act as he thinks best; and if he is wrong, so much the worse for him. We stand on a mountain pass in the midst of whirling snow and blinding mist, through which we get glimpses now and then of paths which may be deceptive. If we stand still we shall be frozen to death. If we take the wrong road we shall be dashed to pieces. We do not certainly know whether there is any right one. What must we do? 'Be strong and of a good courage.' Act for the best, hope for the best, and take what comes. . . . If death ends all, we cannot meet death better."*

* Liberty, Equality, Fraternity, p. 353, 2d edition. London, 1874.

4
_____

RELIGION
AND PHILOSOPHY*

Josiah Royce (1855–1916) was professor
of philosophy at Harvard University
and perhaps the most brilliant American
representative of Neo-Hegelian ideal-
ism. His principal works are: The
Religious Aspect of Philosophy, The
Spirit of Modern Philosophy, The World
and the Individual *(perhaps his greatest*
work), *and* Lectures on Modern Idealism.

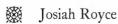 Josiah Royce

WE speak commonly of religious feelings and of religious beliefs;
but we find difficulty in agreeing about what makes either beliefs or
feelings religious. A feeling is not religious merely because it is
strong, nor yet because it is also morally valuable, nor yet because it
is elevated. If the strength and the moral value of a feeling made it
religious, patriotism would be religion. If elevation of feeling were
enough, all higher artistic emotion would be religious. But such
views would seem to most persons very inadequate. As for belief, it
is not religious merely because it is a belief in the supernatural. Not
merely is superstition as such very different from religion, but even
a belief in God as the highest of beings need not be a religious
belief. If La Place had needed what he called "that hypothesis," the
Deity, when introduced into his celestial mechanics, would have
been but a mathematical symbol, or a formula like Taylor's the-
orem,—no true object of religious veneration. On the other hand,
Spinoza's impersonal Substance, or the Nirvâna of the Buddhists, or
any one of many like notions, may have, either as doctrines about
the world or as ideals of human conduct, immense religious value.
Very much that we associate with religion is therefore non-essential
to religion. Yet religion is something unique in human belief and
emotion, and must not be dissolved into any lower or more commonplace elements. What then is religion?

* From Josiah Royce, *The Religious Aspect of Philosophy*. Reprinted by permission of Houghton, Mifflin & Company.

So MUCH at all events seems sure about religion. It has to do with action. It is impossible without some appearance of moral purpose. A totally immoral religion may exist; but it is like a totally unseaworthy ship at sea, or like a rotten bank, or like a wild-cat mine. It deceives its followers. It pretends to guide them into morality of some sort. If it is blind or wicked, not its error makes it religious, but the faith of its followers in its worth. A religion may teach the men of one tribe to torture and kill men of another tribe. But even such a religion would pretend to teach right conduct. Religion, however, gives us more than a moral code. A moral code alone, with its "Thou shalt," would be no more religious than is the civil code. A religion adds something to the moral code. And what it adds is, first, enthusiasm. Somehow it makes the faithful regard the moral law with devotion, reverence, love. By history, by parable, by myth, by ceremony, by song, by whatever means you will, the religion gives to the mere code life and warmth. A religion not only commands the faithful, but gives them something that they are glad to live for, and if need be to die for.

But not yet have we mentioned the element of religion that makes it especially interesting to a student of theoretical philosophy. So far as we have gone, ethical philosophy would criticise the codes of various religions, while theoretical philosophy would have no part in the work. But, in fact, religion always adds another element. Not only does religion teach devotion to a moral code, but the means that it uses to this end include a more or less complete theory of things. Religion says not merely *do and feel,* but also *believe.* A religion tells us about the things that it declares to exist, and most especially it tells us about their relations to the moral code and to the religious feeling. There may be a religion without a supernatural, but there cannot be a religion without a theoretical element, without a statement of some supposed matter of fact, as part of the religious doctrine.

These three elements, then, go to constitute any religion. A religion must teach some moral code, must in some way inspire a strong feeling of devotion to that code, and in so doing must show something in the nature of things that answers to the code or that serves to reinforce the feeling. A religion is therefore practical, emotional, and theoretical; it teaches us to do, to feel, and to believe, and it teaches the belief as a means to its teaching of the action and of the feeling.

WE MAY NOW see how philosophy is related to religion. Philosophy is not directly concerned with feeling, but both action and belief are direct objects of philosophical criticism. And on the other hand, in so far as philosophy suggests general rules for conduct, or discusses the theories about the world, philosophy must have a religious aspect. Religion invites the scrutiny of philosophy, and philosophy may not neglect the problems of religion. Kant's fundamental problems: *What do I know?* and *What ought I to do?* are of religious interest no less than of philosophic interest. They ask how the highest thought of man stands related to his highest needs, and what in things answers to our best ideals. Surely no one ought to fear such questions, nor ought any philosophic student to hesitate to suggest in answer to them whatever after due reflection he honestly can suggest, poor and tentative though it may be. In fact there is no defense for one as sincere thinker if, undertaking to pay attention to philosophy as such, he willfully or thoughtlessly neglects such problems on the ground that he has no time for them. Surely he has time to be not merely a student of philosophy, but also a man, and these things are among the essentials of humanity, which the non-philosophic treat in their way, and which philosophic students must treat in theirs.

When, however, we say that the thinker must study and revere these questions, we must not fancy that because of their importance he may prejudge them. Assumptions, postulates, *a priori* demands, these indeed are in all thinking, and no thinker is without such. But prejudice, *i.e.* foregone conclusions in questionable matters, deliberate unwillingness to let the light shine upon our beliefs, all this is foreign to true thought. Thinking is for us just the clarifying of our minds, and because clearness is necessary to the unity of thought, necessary to lessen the strife of sects and the bitterness of doubt, necessary to save our minds from hopeless, everlasting wandering, therefore to resist the clarifying process, even while we undertake it, is to sin against what is best in us, and is also to sin against humanity. Deliberately insincere, dishonest thinking is downright blasphemy. And so, if we take any interest in these things, our duty is plain. Here are questions of tremendous importance to us and to the world. We are sluggards or cowards if, pretending to be philosophic students and genuine seekers of truth, we do not attempt to do something with these questions. We are worse than cowards if, attempting to consider them, we do so otherwise than reverently, fearlessly, and honestly.

The religious thought of our time has reached a position that arouses the anxiety of all serious thinkers, and the interest of many who are not serious. We are not content with what we learned from our fathers; we want to correct their dogmas, to prove what they held fast without proof, to work out our own salvation by our own efforts. But we know not yet what form our coming faith will take. We are not yet agreed even about the kind of question that we shall put to ourselves when we begin any specific religious inquiry. People suggest very various facts or aspects of facts in the world as having a religious value. The variety of the suggestions shows the vagueness of the questions that people have in mind when they talk of religion. One man wants to worship Natural Law, or even Nature in general. Another finds Humanity to be his ideal object of religious veneration. Yet another gravely insists that the Unknowable satisfies his religious longings. Now it is something to be plain in expressing a question, even if you cannot give an answer. We shall do something if we only find out what it is that we ought to seek. And the foregoing considerations may help us in this way, even if what follows should be wholly ineffective. For we have tried to give a definition that shall express, not merely what a Buddhist or a Catholic or a Comtist or an Hegelian means by his religion, but what all men everywhere mean by religion. They all want religion to define for them their duty, to give them the heart to do it, and to point out to them such things in the real world as shall help them to be steadfast in their devotion to duty. When people pray that they may be made happy, they still desire to learn what they are to do in order to become happy. When saints of any creed look up to their God as their only good, they are seeking for guidance in the right way. The savages of whom we hear so much nowadays have indeed low forms of religion, but these religions of theirs still require them to do something, and tell them why it is worth while to do this, and make them more or less enthusiastic in doing it. Among ourselves, the poor and the lonely, the desolate and the afflicted, when they demand religious comfort, want something that shall tell them what to do with life, and how to take up once more the burdens of their broken existence. And the religious philosophers must submit to the same test that humanity everywhere proposes to its religions. If one tries to regulate our diet by his theories, he must have the one object, whatever his theory, since he wants to tell us what is healthful for us. If he tells us to eat nothing but snow, that is his fault. The true object of the theory of diet remains the same. And so if men have expressed all sorts of one-sided, disheartening, inadequate views of religion, that does not make the object of religious theory less catholic, less comprehensive, less definitely human. A man who propounds a religious system must have a moral code, an emotional life, and some theory of things to offer us. With less we cannot be content. He need not, indeed, know or pretend to know very much about our wonderful world, but he must know something, and that something must be of definite value.

To state the whole otherwise. Purely theoretic philosophy tries to find out what it can about the real world. When it makes this effort, it has to be perfectly indifferent to consequences. It may not shudder or murmur if it comes upon unspeakably dreadful truths. If it finds nothing in the world but evil, it must still accept the truth, and must calmly state it without praise and without condemnation. Theoretic philosophy knows no passion save the passion for truth, has no fear save the fear of error, cherishes no hope save the hope of theoretic success. But religious philosophy has other objects in addition to these. Religious philosophy is indeed neither the foe nor the mistress of theoretic philosophy. Religious philosophy dare not be in opposition to the truths that theory may have established. But over and above these truths it seeks something else. It seeks to know their value. It comes to the world with other interests, in addition to the purely theoretic ones. It wants to know what in the world is worthy of worship as the good. It seeks not merely the truth, but the inspiring truth. It defines for itself goodness, moral worth, and then it asks, *What in this world is worth anything?* Its demands in this regard are boundless. It will be content only with the best it can find. Having formulated for itself its ideal of worth, it asks at the outset: *Is there then, anywhere in the universe, any real thing of Infinite Worth?* If this cannot be found, then and then only will religious philosophy be content with less. Then it will still ask: *What in this world is worth most?* It cannot make realities, but it is determined to judge them. It cannot be content with blind faith, and demands the actual truth as much as theoretic philosophy demands it; but religious philosophy treats this truth only as the material for its ideal judgments. It seeks the ideal among the realities.

Upon such a quest as this, we ask the reader to accompany us in the following pages. We have not space to be exhaustive, nor in fact to offer much more than suggestions; but we want the suggestions to be explicit, and we hope that they may stimulate some reader, and may perhaps help him in completing his own trains of thought.

PEOPLE come to such questions as these with certain prejudices about the method and spirit of inquiry; and all their work may be hampered by these prejudices. Let us say yet a little more of what we think as to this matter. There are two extremes to fear in religious philosophy: indifference that arises from a dogmatic disposition to deny, and timidity that arises from an excessive show of reverence for the objects of religious faith. Both of these extreme moods have their defective methods in dealing with religious philosophy. The over-skeptical man looks with impatience on all lengthy discussions of these topics. There can be nothing in it all, he says; nothing but what Hume, in an eloquent passage, called sophistry and delusion. Why spend time to puzzle over these insoluble mysteries? Hence his method is: swift work, clear statement of known difficulties, keen ridicule of hasty assumptions, and then a burning of the old deserted Moscow of theology, and a bewildering flight into the inaccessible wintry wastes, where no army of religious philosophers shall follow him. Now for our part we want to be as skeptical as anybody; and we personally always admire the freedom of motion that pure skepticism gives. Our trouble with it all, however, is that, after we have enjoyed the freedom and the frosty air of pure philosophic skepticism for a while, we find ourselves unexpectedly in the midst of philosophic truth that needs closer examination. The short and easy agnostic method is not enough. You must supplement skepticism by philosophy; and when you do so, you find yourself forced to accept, not indeed the old theology of your childhood, but something that satisfies, oddly enough, certain religious longings, that, as skeptic, you had carefully tried to forget. Then you find yourself with what you may have to call a religious doctrine; and then you may have to state it as we are here going to do, not in an easy or fascinating way, such as the pure skeptic can so well follow, but at all events with some approach to a serious and sustained effort to consider hard questions from many sides. The skeptical method is not only a good, but also a necessary beginning of religious philosophy. But we are bound to go deeper than mere superficial agnosticism. If, however, any reader is already sure that we cannot go deeper, and that modern popular agnosticism has exhausted all that can be said on religious questions, then we bid him an immediate and joyous farewell. If we had not something to say in this book that seems to us both foreign to the popular modern agnostic range of discussion, and deeper than the insight of popular modern skepticism, we should say nothing. The undertaking of this book is not to wrangle in the old way over the well-known ordinary debates of to-day, but to turn the flank of the common popular thought on these topics altogether, by going back to a type of philosophic investigation, that is nowadays familiar indeed to a certain school of specialists, but forgotten by the general public. In this type of investigation, we have furthermore something to offer that seems to us no mere repetition of the views of other thinkers, but an effort to make at least one little step in advance of the thoughts that the great masters of philosophy have given to us. Yet we know indeed that the range of any useful independent thought in philosophy must be, in case of any one individual, very narrow.

The other mood and its method remain. It is the mood of excessive reverence. It wastes capital letters on all the pronouns and adjectives that have to do with the objects of religious faith; but it fears to do these objects the honor to get clear ideas about them. Now we respect this mood when it appears in men who do well their life-work, who need their religious faith for their work, and who do not feel any calling as truth-seekers. No man has any business to set up his vocation as the highest one; and the man for whom truth is useful in his actual life-work as an inspiration, revealed to him only in feeling, is welcome to his feelings, is worthy of all regard from those whose vocation is philosophy, and shall not be tormented by our speculations. He is careful and troubled about many things; the world needs him, and philosophy does not. We only lay claim to our own rights, and do not want to interfere with his. Our right to clear thought, we must insist upon. For looked at philosophically, and apart from the necessary limitations of the hard worker, all this dumb reverence, this vague use of vague names, has its serious dangers. You are reverent, we may say to the man who regards philosophic criticism as a dangerous trifling with stupendous truths; you are reverent, but what do you reverence? Have a care lest what you reverence shall turn out to be your own vague and confused notions, and not the real divine Truth at all. Take heed lest your object of worship be only your own little pet infinite, that is sublime to you mainly because it is yours, and that is in truth about as divine and infinite as your hat. For this is the danger that besets these vague and lofty sentiments. Unreflected upon, uncriticised, dumbly experienced, dumbly dreaded, these, your religious objects, may become mere feelings, mere visceral sensations of yours, that you have on Sunday mornings, or when you pray. Of course, if you are a worker, you may actually realize these vague ideas, in so far as they inspire you to work. If they do, they shall be judged by their fruits. Otherwise, do not trust too confidently their religious value. You, individually regarded, are but a mass of thought and feeling. What is only yours and in you, is not divine at all. Unless you lift it up into the light of thought and examine it often, how do you know into what your cherished religious ideal may not have rotted in the darkness of your emotions? Once in a while, there does come to a man some terrible revelation of himself in a great sorrow. Then in the tumult of anguish he looks for his religious faith to clothe his nakedness against the tempest; and he finds perhaps some moth-eaten old garment that profits him nothing, so that his soul miserably perishes in the frost of doubt. Such a man has expected God to come to his help in every time of need; but the only god he has actually and consciously had, has been his own little contemptible, private notion and dim feeling of a god, which he has never dared fairly to look at. Any respectable wooden idol would have done him better service; for then a man could know where and what his idol is. Such is only too apt to be the real state of the man who regards it as profanity to think clearly and sensibly on religious topics.

We claim, then, the right to criticise as fearlessly, as thoroughly, and as skeptically as may be, the foundations of conduct and faith. For what we criticise are, at the outset, our own notions, which we want to have conform to the truth, if so be that there is any truth. As for doubt on religious questions, that is for a truth-seeker not only a privilege but a duty; and, as we shall experience all through this study, doubt has a curious and very valuable place in philosophy. Philosophic truth, as such, comes to us first under the form of doubt; and we never can be very near it in our search unless, for a longer or shorter time, we have come to despair of it altogether. First, then, the despair of a thorough-going doubt, and then the discovery that this doubt contains in its bosom the truth that we are sworn to discover, however we can,—this is the typical philosophic experience. May the memory of this suggestion support the failing patience of the kindly disposed reader through some of the longer and more wearisome stretches of dry skeptical analysis over which we must try to journey together. Whatever may be the truth, it must lie beyond those deserts.

. . .

WE are in a new world of Divine Life. The dark world of the powers has passed away from our thought. Here is the Eternal, for which all these powers exist, in which they dwell. Here we are in the presence of the Ideal Judge who knows all Good and Evil. From the other side the world as we approached it had seemed so restless, so disheartening, so deaf. The world of our postulates was a brighter one only because we determined to make it so. But there was something lonesome in the thought that the postulates got, as answer from the real world, only their own echo, and not always that. Their world was rather their own creation than an external something that gave them independent support. Sometimes there seemed to be nothing solid that could echo back anything at all. Now we seem to look upon a truth that satisfies indeed no selfish longings of ours, no whims of theological tradition, no demands of our personal narrow lives. We shall not learn in this way who is first in the kindgom of heaven, nor how the dead are raised, nor any answer to any other special demand of any set of men. We learn, however, this at least: *All truth is known to One Thought, and that Infinite.* What does that imply? Let us see.

Our argument is somewhat near to the thought that partially satisfied St. Augustine when he found it in his Plato. That there should be a truth at all implies, we have seen, that there should be an Infinite Truth, known to an Infinite Thought; or, in other words, that all is for thought, and without thought is nothing that is. We also are a part of this infinite thought. We know not yet more of the nature of this thought, save that it must be eternal, all-embracing, and One. What then shall we be able further to say about it?

To answer would be to expound a system of philosophy. But we must limit ourselves here to the necessary. And so, for the first, we shall try to point out what this ideal and infinite life of thought that we have found as the eternal truth of things *cannot* be expected to accomplish for the purposes of our religion, and then to consider what we may nevertheless dare to hope from it.

It cannot be expected to furnish us an *a priori* knowledge of any fact of experience, of any particular law of nature, of the destiny of any one finite being. All that remains just as dark as it was before. We neither rejoice in this result, nor lament it. Nobody who wanders into the ideal world may expect to find it ordered for his individual advantage; nor need he try to find there good investments for his money. The Infinite does not wait for his individual approval; although morally speaking he may do well to get the approval of the Infinite. The Infinite was not elected to office by his vote, and he may not impeach it for disregard of his humble petitions for good things, nor threaten it with want of confidence because it does not secure passage for his private bills. In so far as to say this is to condemn the Real, we unhesitatingly do so. But then, as we saw in our ethical discussion, the moral insight is not so much concerned with private bills, as with certain greater matters. If the moral insight wants religious support, possibly the failure of all these personal concerns of ours to find any hint of response from the Absolute, may not render impossible the ethical undertakings of the human spirit. If as individuals we must hear the dreadful words from the spirit of nature: *Du gleichst dem Geist den du begreifst, nicht mir;* still it is possible that with a higher insight, looking upon this same spirit in its eternal and inmost nature, we may yet come with full reason at last to say: *Erhabner Geist, du gabst mir, gabst mir alles, warum ich bat.* For there are demands and demands. Man, as lover, demands success in love, and the course of the world may thwart him; as toiler, he demands for himself personal immortality, and the course of the world may care naught for his individual life; as bereaved, as mourner over his dead, he may demand for his loved ones also this immortality, and the course of the world may leave the fate of all his loved ones mysterious forever; as lover of mankind, he may demand an infinite future of blessed progress for his race, and the law of the dissipation of energy may give him the only discoverable physical answer to his demand; as just man, he may cry aloud that evil shall cease from among men, and the wicked may still laugh in triumph unpunished. And yet for all this he may find some higher compensation. Agnostic as he will remain about all the powers of this world, about the outcome of all finite processes, he will take comfort in the assurance that an Infinite Reason is above all and through all, embracing everything, judging everything, infallible, perfect.

.　　.　　.

BUT if we leave these limitations of our view, and pass to its positive religious value, our first sense is one of joy and freedom to find that our long sought ideal of a perfect unity of life is here attained. Let us look away for a moment from our finite existence, with its doubts and its problems, to the conception of that infinite life. In that life is all truth, fully present in the unity of one eternal moment. The world is no mass of separate facts, stuck one to another in an external way, but, for the infinite, each fact is what it is only by reason of its place in the infinite unity. The world of life is then what we desired it to be, an organic total; and the individual selves are drops in this ocean of the absolute truth.

Thus then, seen in the light of this our result, the human

tasks that we sketched in our ethical discussion find their place in the objective world. Now, and in fact for the first time, we can see what we were really trying to accomplish through our ideal. We were trying in a practical way to realize what we now perceive to be the fullness of the life of God. So that the one highest activity, in which all human activities were to join, is known to us now as the *progressive realization by men of the eternal life of an Infinite Spirit.* So whereas we formerly had to say to men: Devote yourselves to art, to science, to the state, or to any like work that does tend to organize your lives into one life, we may now substitute one absolute expression for all those accidental expressions, and may say: *Devote yourselves to losing your lives in the divine life.* For all these special aims that we have mentioned are but means of accomplishing the knowledge of the fullness of the truth. And Truth is God.

Now this precept is no barren abstraction. It means to take hold of every act of life, however humble and simple. "Where art thou, O man?" our ideal says to us. "Art thou not in God? To whom dost thou speak? With whom dost thou walk? What life is this in whose midst thou livest? What are all these things that thou seemest to touch? Whose is all this beauty that thou enjoyest in art, this unity that thou seekest to produce in thy state, this truth that thou pursuest in thy thought? All this is in God and of God. Thou has never seen, or heard, or touched, or handled, or loved anything but God. Know this truth, and thy life must be transformed to thee in all its significance. Serve the whole God, not the irrationally separate part that thy delusions have made thee suppose to be an independent thing. Live out thy life in its full meaning; for behold, it is God's life."

So, as it seems, the best that we could have wished from the purely moral side is attained. The Divine Thought it is that actually accomplishes what we imperfectly sought to attain, when we defined for ourselves Duty. In the Divine Thought is perfectly and finally realized the Moral Insight and the Universal Will of our ethical discussion. And this insight and will are not realized as by some Power, that then should set about to accomplish their fulfillment externally. But in the infinite, where all is eternally complete, the insight is both present and fulfilled; the universal will gets what it seeks. There is no lack there, nor hesitation, nor striving, nor doubt, nor weariness; but all is eternally perfect triumph.

Now this, though it sounds mystical enough to our untrained common sense, is no mere poetry of thought. It is the direct philosophical outcome of what we have found by a purely logical process. The driest thought, the simplest fragment of rationality, involves this absolute, infinite, and perfect thought. And this it involves because it involves the possibility of error, and because, as separate from the infinite, this possibility of error in a single thought becomes unintelligible and contradictory. We did all that we could to escape this conclusion. We wandered in the thickets of confusion and contradiction, until there was no chance of finding there a further pathway. And then we turned to see, and behold, God was in this place, though we had known it not. The genuine God that we thus found was no incomplete, struggling God, whom we might pity in his conflict with evil, but the all-embracing thought, in which the truth is eternally finished. And this God it is that we now see as the complete realization of our own ideal, as of all worthy ideals.

For consider if you will this element in our conception of this Thought. Can this infinite know itself as imperfect, or as not possessing some object that it knows to be good? This is impossible, and doubly so. Not only does the conception of an Infinite, in which and for which are all things, wholly exclude the possibility of any good thing beyond the Infinite itself, but also in still another way does the same truth appear. For if you suppose that this infinite thought desires some perfection G, that it has not, then either it is right in supposing this perfection to be truly desirable, or it is wrong. In either case the previous argument of Chapter XI. shows us that the truth or the falsity of this judgment of desire about G must exist as known truth or falsity for a higher thought, which, including the thought that desires, and itself actually having this desired good thing, compares the desired object with the conception of the thought that desires it, and judges of them both. Above the desire, then, must in every case exist the satisfaction of the desire in a higher thought. So that for the Infinite there can be no unsatisfied desire. Unsatisfied desire exists only in the finite beings, not in the inclusive Infinite.

The world then, as a whole, is and must be absolutely good, since the infinite thought must know what is desirable, and knowing it, must have present in itself the true objects of desire. The existence of any amount of pain or of other evil, of crime or of baseness in the world as we see it, is, thus viewed, no evidence against the absolute goodness of things, rather a guaranty thereof. For all evil viewed externally is just an evidence to us finite beings that there exists something desirable, which we have not, and which we just now cannot get. However stubborn this evil is for us, that has naught to do with the perfection of the Infinite. For the infinite did not make this evil, but the evil, *together with the making of it,* which indeed was also in its separateness evil,—all this is a phenomenon for the infinite thought, which, in knowing this evil, merely knows the absolute desirableness of that which it also possesses, namely, the absolutely good.

We have used here an argument that could not be used in our study of the "World of Doubt." When we there thought evil to be possible for the world as a whole, we conceived that a being who knew all the world would yet desire something better. But what would this imply? It implies that this being would desire a state of things different from the existing one, and would do so believing that state to be better than the existing one. But would he truly know this desired state to be better, or would he only hope so? Who truly knows the value of a state save the one that possesses it? Knowledge is of the present. Therefore this being would not really know the better state, unless it were already actual for him. But in that case he would include not only the present world, but the perfect world, and his total state could not be one of discontent. So the other alternative remains. Our supposed being would only hope the desired state to be better than what was real already for him. But would his hope be a true one? If so, then it could only be true in case this perfection is already realized in a higher thought. For the Infinite then the question, "Is there anything better than what exists?" must be nonsense. For him the actual and the possible fall together in one truth; and this one truth cannot be evil.

On another side, our conception gives us religious support. The imperfection of the purely moral view lay in part in the fact that there was an inner incompleteness about the very definition of our ideal, as well as a doubt about its attainability. This inner incompleteness must however be removed in and for the Infinite Mind. In dealing with the work of life, we came to a point where we said, thus far we can see our way, but beyond that our ideal remains incomplete. We must have faith, so we implied, that if we attained so much of the ideal social condition, the way from that point onward would become clear. But now we see why the way would of necessity become clear to one whose knowledge of life were broad enough and deep enough. For in the Infinite that includes all life, that rests above all finite strife in the absolute attainment of the ideal, there can be no incompleteness, no torso of an ideal, but a perfect knowledge of what is most excellent. Those faint fore-shadowings of a perfect life that art and science and social work show to us, must be for the Infinite no faint foreshadowings, but absolute certainty and perfect clearness. Hence by our religious doctrine we get not merely the assurance that such ideals as we have are realized for the Infinite; but, better than this, we get our first full assurance that our incomplete ideals have an actual completion as ideals. For we thus get our first full assurance that there is in the highest sense any definite ideal at all. Pessimism, as we have seen, implies either doubt about what the ideal state is, or unavoidable lack of that state. And the Infinite can be no Pessimist in either sense.

The religious comfort that a man can get from contemplating all this truth is indeed very different from the consolation of the separate individual as such that many people want their religion to give them. And this very fact furnishes us a good test of moral sincerity. The religious comfort that we find is no comfort save to the truly religious spirit in us. It says to us: "You that have declared your willingness to serve moral ideals because they are such, does this help you to know, not of a goodly place where you personally and individually shall live without tears forever as a reward for your services, but of an eternal Judge that respects in no whit your person, before whom and in whom you are quite open and perfectly known, who now and for all eternity sees your good and your evil, and estimates you with absolute justice? This blaze of infinite light in which you stand, does it cheer you? If it does, then you are glad to learn that above all your struggles there is the eternal Victory, amid all your doubts there is the eternal Insight, and that your highest triumph, your highest conception, is just an atom of the infinite truth that all the time is there. But if all this is true of you, then you do love the ideal for its own sake. Then it is not your triumph that you seek, but the triumph of the Highest. And so it is that you rejoice to learn how this that is best in the world not only will triumph, but always has triumphed, since, as you now learn, for God the highest good is thus a matter of direct experience."

5

REASON
AND REVELATION*

*Charles A. Campbell (1897–   ) was
professor of logic and rhetoric at
Glasgow University from 1938 to 1961.
His philosophical position lies generally
within the idealist tradition. Besides*
On Selfhood and Godhood, *his major
writings include* Defense of Free Will
and Moral Intuition and the Principle
of Self Realisation.

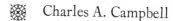 Charles A. Campbell

OUR FIRST STEP—and it is not quite so simple as it looks—is to try to get clear about the precise nature of the claim which the philosopher, *qua* philosopher, actually makes for the competence of reason. For it seems to me that the attack from the side of religion upon philosophy's alleged aggrandisement of reason is very often in practice an attack upon the (no doubt) overweening claims which *certain philosophers* (or schools of philosophy) have made for reason—not upon any claim that can be said to be inherent in the character of philosophy as such. The real point that is at issue, which is important, thus tends to be befogged for the ordinary religious enquirer not widely versed in philosophical literature. Persuaded, for example (as he very well may be), of the unanswerable force of such criticisms as those which Kierkegaard brings against the claims for reason implicit in the Hegelian philosophy, he is apt to imagine, and he is sometimes encouraged to believe, that it is the pretensions of philosophy itself that have been exposed and annihilated. I think there is great need, therefore, that the claim for reason inherent in philosophy itself be set out with care. When that is done, objection will, without a doubt, still be taken to the claim in some religious quarters. But it will no longer seem plausible, I think, to dismiss the claim as preposterous.

We need not linger long over a definition of reason sufficient for the purpose in hand. Within the framework of the dispute

* From Charles A. Campbell, *On Selfhood and Godhood.* Reprinted by permission of George Allen & Unwin, Ltd., publishers.

about the competence of reason in religion, reason can, I think, be taken with fair safety as denoting for all parties the kind of thinking which is directed to the attainment of truth under the sole guidance and control of thought's own internal standards. That is 'reason' in the sense in which reason is the characteristic instrument of philosophy. And obviously the philosopher *qua* philosopher must make *some* claim for the competence of his instrument. Our immediate question is, just how much must the philosopher claim for it, if he is not to stultify his very choice of it *as* his instrument?

Now it is clear at once that the competence claimed for it is not *omni*-competence; that is to say, it is certainly not the ability of reason to develop from its own internal resources the whole system of truths about the universe. So much *has*, of course, on occasion been claimed; in a downright way by some seventeenth-century Rationalists, and in a more qualified way by Hegelians. But there are no Rationalists today; and even those who believe—rightly in my view—that Hegel has at least as much to teach contemporary philosophy as contemporary philosophy has to teach him are not, as a rule, prepared to follow him closely in his constructive Panlogism. Today almost all philosophers are agreed that data for reason's search after truth, data for the construction of a philosophy, come from many sides of experience that cannot possibly be identified (even in 'the last resort') with reason. Almost all, e.g. acknowledge sense experience as an indispensable source of data: the vast majority would add introspection: a great many would add moral experience; and at least some important philosophers would add either aesthetic experience or religious experience or both.[1] Moreover, even those philosophers who, because they favour a subjectivist interpretation of moral or aesthetic or religious experience, do not regard such modes of experience as contributing positively to a theory of the nature of objective reality, would certainly allow that they are all of them 'data' for the philosopher, in the sense that they have at least got to be taken account of by reason in the course of any serious attempt at philosophical construction. Evidently, then, any criticism of the 'reason' of the philosophers on the ground that it ignores sides of experience other than the purely rational has no substance whatever in relation to philosophy of the present age.

But there is a more important, if perhaps less obvious, concession which can willingly be made to the critic of reason's powers without in any way prejudicing the claim for reason that is inherent in philosophy. The philosopher is not committed by his occupational loyalty to reason to the position that God can be

---

[1] I do not, of course, suggest that this list of 'data' is exhaustive.

known only if He can be apprehended as an 'object' of reason. A philosopher might come (and some philosophers have come) to the considered conclusion that reality is supra-rational, that it is not in its ultimate nature amenable to conceptual understanding: and he might combine with this the view, also on evidence that approves itself to his reason, that *putative* religious insights are, *sometimes*, authentic religious insights, i.e. genuine revelations of the ultimate reality that is God. In that case he would in effect be contending that God is known, but is known only in the immediacy of religious experience and not as an object of reason. Such a philosophical position may or may not be finally tenable. But that is not the point at present. The point is that it *is* a *philosophical* position, and is so regarded even by those who reject it. It follows that the very significant limitation of the competence of reason which this position entails is not taken by philosophers to be inconsistent with the claims for reason that are inherent in philosophy as such.

Now I have little doubt that a good deal of the animus towards philosophy which one remarks in so many religious circles today rests on the erroneous assumption that the philosopher does, *qua* philosopher, conceive of his instrument reason as an organ competent to apprehend God, if any God there be: and I should agree that against such a claim for reason it is possible to bring very formidable arguments indeed. On the other hand, it is certain that some of the religious critics of philosophy, and these not the least influential nor the least articulate, know perfectly well that this is not a claim that is intrinsic to philosophy, and that there are many philosophers who would not make it. Presumably, therefore, these critics must have in mind some *other* claim for reason which, rightly or wrongly, they ascribe to the philosopher, and which they feel to be offensive to religious faith. What is this claim?

I think it is as follows. And I think the critics are right in believing that it belongs to philosophy as such, but wrong in believing that it is an invalid claim, and wrong also in believing it to be somehow derogatory to religion.

The philosopher *must* claim, I think, that wherever the question of objective truth arises, whether it be the truth of religion or of anything else, it is for reason, and for reason *alone*, to carry out the assessment of the evidence, and to make the final adjudication upon it. The evidence may come from quarters, including, unquestionably, what is called 'religious experience'. But how far, e.g. (if at all) a putative instance of religious experience can be regarded as an authentic instance of religious experience, involving the actual revelation of Deity that it is taken by the experiencing subject to involve; and how far, accordingly, (if at all) weight is to be attached to it in the construction of a theory about the ultimate nature of things—these are surely not matters that settle themselves. They are matters to be reflectively determined in the light of a variety of relevant considerations. And what is there save *reason*, the philosopher asks, to perform this office? That reason is the ultimate arbiter in the sphere of truth: that no proposition, no matter whence it springs, has in the end a valid title to acceptance except in so far as it approves itself to reason; such is the claim for reason which, it seems to me, the philosopher is bound to make if he is not to betray his own calling. He is not bound as a philosopher, I think, to claim anything more. But he is, I think, defaulting as a philosopher if he claims anything less.

Is this, then, the claim for reason inherent in philosophy which induces so many religious thinkers to repudiate and disparage philosophy? I believe that it is. To exalt philosophy, or its organ reason, to the status of supreme judge in matters even of *religious* truth seems to them shocking; an irreligious assault upon the supremacy of faith. 'If philosophy must make this claim or perish', they would say, 'then so much the worse for philosophy'.

Nevertheless, it does seem to me that the validity of this 'philosophic' claim for reason is, in the end, inescapable. And I think we can best see that it is so by directing our attention to a simple, but surely very significant, fact. No one, so far as I am aware, is prepared to admit that his own religious beliefs are unreasonable. If that were imputed against him, on the ground, perhaps, that he is putting his trust in some non-rational mode of apprehension, he is ready to argue in defence of his so doing. He will say, perhaps, that 'mere reason' is out of its depth in the realm of religion, and that a God who is truly God can be apprehended only through His own Self-revelation, not by any processes initiated and controlled by the human reason. But then, notice well, he *is arguing*. He is contending that it is reasonable, in view of certain relevant considerations, to put one's trust in a non-rational (or supra-rational) mode of apprehension. And what can this appeal to reason mean save the acceptance of reason as the ultimate court of appeal, even in matters of religion, which is just what the philosopher claims it to be?

Incidentally, it should be observed that the believer's argument is not self-contradictory in thus tacitly appealing to reason to show that it is not by reason that we can apprehend God. For his appeal is to reason as ultimate arbiter, not to show that reason is not the *ultimate arbiter,* but to show that reason is not an appropriate organ for the apprehension of God.

On the other hand, it *is* self-contradictory to appeal to reason as ultimate arbiter to show that reason is not the ultimate arbiter. And that, I am suggesting, is precisely what the religious critic of philosophy's claim for reason is committed to doing, if he is going to try to justify his attitude at all. He may, of course, simply *assert* that not reason, but Authority, or the Inner Light, or what you will, is the ultimate arbiter: but as soon as he commits himself to *defending* the proposition, to arguing in its support, he presupposes the truth of the very proposition he is aiming to disprove. 'Argument' has no meaning if it does not invite decision in accordance with the evidence as it approves itself to *reason*.

I cannot persuade myself, therefore, that there is any real alternative to acknowledging reason as the ultimate arbiter in the field of truth—religious truth or any other sort of truth—except silence, a dogged refusal even to begin to argue in defence of one's beliefs. It need hardly be pointed out that this alternative is not one that has much commended itself to the leading apostles of anti-reason in the religious world of today.

· · ·

LET US ASSUME, however, that reason's examination of ostensibly revelational experience in general leaves it as at least an open question whether or not some instances of it are authentic revelations, disclosures of the nature of an objectively real being. The task remains for reason as arbiter to discriminate, with the highest measure of probability that the nature of the case permits, between the authentic and the spurious among the ostensible revelations. What, then, are the criteria which it is proper for reason to adopt in the execution of this task? I make no claim in what follows to be listing the criteria exhaustively, much less to be saying all that requires to be said about any one of them. But I shall deal in some detail with those criteria which seem to me to be the most important.

The criteria may be conveniently divided into (*a*) psychological criteria and (*b*) logical criteria. First, then, as to the psychological criteria.

THESE are applicable, of course, only where we have a good deal of information about the individual who claims the revelational experience. We require to know something of his personality, of his mental history, of his mode of life, and of the circumstances immediately preceding the alleged revelation. Sometimes we are not in a position to learn much about these matters; but where, as is not infrequent, fairly detailed knowledge is available, it can, I think, give legitimate aid in determining the authenticity or objectivity of the experience. For example, religious revelation, if it is anything, is revelation *of* a spirit *to* a spirit. We should therefore expect it to occur only in persons whose normal lives indicate that they are, in some measure, 'spiritually oriented'. *Some* degree of spiritual preparedness, we presume, must precede spiritual discernment. It seems unlikely that—to take an extreme case—a drunken profligate engrossed throughout most of his waking hours in fleshly pleasures should have the capacity for attaining exalted visions of the Divine nature. In a similar way it offends our sense of the fitness of things to suppose that the taking of drugs, e.g. the inhalation of nitrous oxide, can yield, as it does sometimes seem to the person concerned to be yielding, profound insights into the very heart of being (the 'anaesthetic revelation', as it has been called). We cannot, of course, rule out *a priori* the possibility of God revealing Himself for purposes of His own through what may appear to us rather surprising and improbable media. Nevertheless we do seem justified in taking it as evidence, so far, for the authenticity of an ostensible revelation that it occurs in a person whom we have reason to believe to be attuned to things of the spirit, and as evidence against where the experiencing subject is notoriously preoccupied with material concerns.

In the second place, in view of the virtual certainty that some ostensible revelations are fantasies unconsciously produced by the subject himself, psychological study of the experiencing subject can usefully be directed to ascertaining whether he appears to be the kind of inhibited and generally maladjusted person from whom, in accordance with the teachings of psychopathology, one might expect fantasy-projection as a means of effecting substitute satisfactions for unfulfilled desires; and more particularly to ascertaining whether, if a maladjustment *is* diagnosed, its specific character bears a discernible relationship to the specific content of the 'revelation'. The excesses in the way of forced interpretations which we find in over-enthusiastic practitioners of depth psychology may reasonably incline one to observe special caution in this line of enquiry; but few, I think, who have any considerable acquaintance with the strange forms which 'revelational' experience often takes would wish to discount the usefulness of such psychological techniques in discriminating the spurious from the authentic.

FROM these perhaps too cursory observations upon the psychological criteria I pass on to a somewhat closer consideration of the logical criteria.

By the 'logical' criteria I understand criteria relating directly to the *content* of the ostensible revelation; to the actual doctrines it incorporates or implies concerning God's nature and His relation to the world and to the human soul. Reason requires that the propositions affirmed explicitly or implicitly in the 'revelation' be propositions which reason can accept as true. This does *not* mean, be it noted, that they must be propositions which reason can see to be logically self-evident, or to be necessary implications of propositions that are logically self-evident. To require that would be to insist that reason is, after all, not merely the arbiter but also the organ of religious truth. What it does mean is that the propositions in question must, at the very least, not violate the principle of self-consistency. So understood, the logical criterion takes two main forms. We require that the propositions inherent in the revelation be consistent with one another. And we require also—although this is a condition which must be elaborated and in some degree qualified—that they be consistent with well-accredited propositions about reality got through other channels.

So far as the first form of the logical criterion is concerned—internal self-consistency—the demand of reason is absolute. If the content of the 'revelation' contains a definite self-contradiction, it cannot be a revelation of the truth. There are really only the two alternatives before reason. Either it declines the task of appraising ostensible revelations altogether; in which case the question arises—as unanswerable as it is inevitable—how then *are* we to distinguish between the authentic and the spurious? Or, accepting the task, reason proceeds in accordance with its own inherent principles; in which case it must reject as untrue whatever contains a self-contradiction.

But there is an important *caveat* to be entered here. The criterion of internal self-consistency is absolute. But its application to religious utterances is very far from being always a simple matter. It must be remembered that religious utterances abound in deliberate paradox; in statements which at first glance are self-contradictions, and which if interpreted in a literal, everyday sense *are* self-contradictions, but which, in the meaning the words bear for the person uttering them, are not self-contradictory at all.

.   .   .

TURNING now to the second form of the logical criterion—consistency of the content of ostensible revelation with well-accredited knowledge got through other media—the great difficulty here is to decide when a piece of knowledge got through other media is *sufficiently* well-accredited to justify the rejection of a 'revelational' content inconsistent with it. Ideally, these other propositions should be so well-accredited as to be completely certain. If not, it is always possible that it is these other propositions that are in error, and that the religious utterances may be true. But most of us would agree that propositions about objective reality, got through ordinary channels, for which anything like complete certainty can be claimed, are very few indeed.

Nevertheless one is bound to hold, I think, that where an ostensible revelation is in conflict with a rationally grounded proposition for which the competent judges in the appropriate field claim a very high degree of probability, the likelihood that the ostensible revelation is authentic is, at the very least, sensibly weakened. It would be foolish to pretend, e.g. that confidence in a 'revelation', in terms of the Book of Genesis, about the historical origin of living things—as in George Fox's celebrated vision of the Creation—can remain unaffected by its contradiction of a biological proposition so amply evidenced as that which affirms the evolution of species. There are probably few professional biologists who would not regard a denial of the theory of evolution (as distinct, of course, from a denial of some theory concerning the mechanism by which evolution proceeds) as almost tantamount to a vote of 'no confidence' in the capacity of reason to achieve any sort of systematic knowledge about the natural world. And while there is a case for the view that reason is not a competent organ for the knowledge of the supernatural, the power over nature which science has enabled man to acquire seems sufficient answer to any suggestion that reason is not competent to deal even with the natural. The least that one could demand before agreeing that a 'revelation' of the simultaneous creation of all species should be taken seriously is a tolerably plausible alternative explanation of the vast multitude of facts enumerated by the biologist in support of his evolution theory. Of such plausible alternatives there seem to be none. I do not feel called upon to explain why I do not accept as 'tolerably plausible' the hypothesis that the facts upon which the biologist relies—fossil remains and the like—are deliberately deceitful evidence planted by God in order to test the firmness of man's faith when it comes into conflict with even the best founded deliverances of his reason. I suppose it is in a sense inevitable that man should construe God after the image of man; but there seems no need to construe Him after the image of a rather disagreeable kind of man.

It is well to bear in mind, however, that the just claims of scientific knowledge *vis à vis* the claims of religious revelation are only its claims *as* scientific knowledge. The task of natural science is to discover uniformities of sequence and coexistence between physical events in the space-time order. Success in that undertaking entitles the scientist to make, with varying degrees of confidence, retrospective judgments about the past course of events in that order, and prospective judgments about the future course of events. There is nothing whatever in his specialised scientific training which qualifies him to talk about the *universe;* which, at the lowest estimate, is something much more than a space-time order of physical events. That the expert scientist is somehow possessed of such qualifications is a myth which the greater among them discourage by precept, and the less great by awful example. Yet the myth dies hard. Presumably its rational basis is the belief, plausible but quite untrue, that the scientist has acquired an exceptional competence in the assessment of evidence. He hasn't. He has probably acquired exceptional competence in assessing a special kind of evidence—that relating to his own and allied fields of specialist study. But competence in the assessment of evidence is not transferable directly from one field to a quite different field. Indeed it is hardly possible to know even what constitutes evidence in a field markedly different from one's own without the arduous preliminary of prolonged personal immersion in its subject-matter. One may know very well what kind of evidence to look for in order to evaluate the scientific proposition that the mosquito *Anopheles* is a carrier of malaria, and yet have not the faintest notion how to set about evaluating the philosophic proposition that a unitary self-consciousness is a condition of the possibility of significant experience. The singular naïveté which so many eminent scientists display in their *obiter dicta* upon social, economic, and political principles ought to be sufficient warning that their pronouncements in the spheres of religion and metaphysics—where the relevant evidence is usually still less familiar to them than the relevant evidence for social, economic and political theory—are, to say the least of it, unlikely to be instructive.

Actually, since the primary concern of religion is with the ultimate ground of all being, and since this is in no way science's concern, it is not immediately obvious why the two should ever come into conflict at all. Conflicts do arise, however, and they are not wholly due to misunderstanding of the respective provinces of religion and science. The most important reason for this is, I think, that what goes on in the Space-Time world of Nature cannot be irrelevant to the view we take of Nature's ultimate ground. Conflict will occur—not necessarily, of course, irresolvable conflict—if science, in pursuit of her proper avocation, presents us with a picture of Nature which is, in some of its phases not easy to reconcile with the character which religion typically ascribes to Nature's ultimate ground; not easy to interpret in terms of an all-wise, all-powerful and supremely good Creator. Again, religious 'revelations' often enough extend (as we have seen in the case of George Fox's vision) to the manifestations of God's Will in the order of Nature, and may purport to give a comparatively detailed historical account of the course of events in certain important aspects. In so far as that is the case, a direct collision with science is in principle possible. I am inclined to think, however, that collisions induced in the latter manner are for the most part on the periphery of religion rather than at its centre. That is to say, not much of real consequence would be lost to religion if it were frankly to disavow all 'revelations' about the historical order that are clearly inconsistent with established scientific knowledge. For those 'revelations' whose religious significance is manifestly profound do not as a rule relate to occurrences about which there is well-accredited scientific knowledge. It could not be maintained, e.g. that the momentous religious proposition, founded upon revelation, that God was incarnated in the historical figure of Christ, conflicts with well-accredited scientific knowledge in the decisive way in which, e.g. the 'revelation' of the simultaneous creation of animal species does. I fancy that few of those who have arrived at a considered rejection of the proposition that God was incarnated in Christ, and hence of the authenticity of the 'revelation' on which it is based, would wish to support their denial by calling in evidence anything that would normally go by the name of 'scientific' knowledge at all.

But that very fact serves to remind us that the well-accredited knowledge from other sources with which reason demands that 'revelation' be consistent need not be confined to scientific knowledge. What, e.g. of the propositions of philosophy? It is obvious that where collision between philosophy and religion does occur, it must be of a peculiarly crucial character. For philosophy and religion are aiming, in their different ways, to do the same thing. Each of them, unlike science, aspires to apprehend the real in its *ultimate* nature, and in its *totality*. Potentially, therefore, religion would seem to have a great deal more to fear from philosophy than from science.

In actual practice, nevertheless, I think most religious people feel that they have a great deal less to fear from philosophy than from science; or at any rate from philosophy in its constructive, as distinct from its purely critical, manifestations. And the reason is not far to seek. It is simply that there are so very few, if indeed there be any, propositions of constructive philosophy which constitute 'well-accredited knowledge' in the sense in which a great many scientific propositions can claim that title, viz. as enjoying the assent of all competent judges. This lack of concord among the philosophers should not greatly surprise anyone who has reflected upon the nature of the philosopher's task and the kind of evidence that is appropriate to it. Still, the result is to leave the way open for a very obvious riposte from the defender of a religious view of the universe, if that should be challenged by some philosophical view. He can always say, with evident point, 'But aren't there any number of *philosophers* who reject this philosophical view? And if so, why should religion trouble itself over-much about it?'

At the same time it is easy to make too much, in the religious context, of these mutual disagreements of the philosophers. After all, are there so very many *religious* propositions that command the assent of all competent judges in the field of *religion?* We cannot deduce from the differences of opinion in philosophical theory that constructive philosophy is incapable in principle of achieving a metaphysic of reality, and may therefore be justly ignored by religion. Propositions of constructive philosophy that are opposed to an ostensible revelation *may* be true, even although they have behind them no solid consensus of philosophic opinion. And it remains the case that, from the standpoint of the individual person reflecting upon the claim to validity of some ostensible revelation, that revelation must be accounted at least suspect if it contradicts any proposition which the individual himself is, on philosophical grounds, strongly disposed to believe. Awareness of the extent to which philosophers disagree among themselves in their constructive thinking ought certainly to discourage sharply any tendency to dogmatism on the part of the individual thinker. But it need not, and it clearly does not, prevent him from feeling at least considerable confidence about the truth of some philosophical propositions. This confidence is probably more often felt with regard to propositions in *moral* philosophy that have metaphysical bearings, than with regard to what are ordinarily called 'metaphysical' propositions. Many thinkers by no means inclined to dogmatism have arrived on grounds of reason at strong convictions about the truth of propositions concerning, e.g. the objective reality of duty, or the objective reality of moral responsibility. Where that is so, the individual thinker has no option but to require, with a degree of stringency proportionate to the degree of his certainty, that revelation be consistent with the proposition or propositions in question. Thus if reflection upon moral experience induces in a man a strong conviction of the reality of personal freedom in moral choice, he will rightly feel doubt about the authenticity of some 'revelation' which proclaims or implies that human choices are all preordained from the beginning of time.

There is, indeed, one alternative (if such it can be called) in which refuge may be sought by those who are fearful of letting their philosophical beliefs bear upon their religion. There is always the 'double-truth' hypothesis, according to which a proposition may be 'true for reason', and a proposition which directly contradicts it be 'true for religion'. I am afraid I can find nothing to commend in this endeavour to run with the hare and hunt with the hounds. To say that we can accept a proposition as true *qua* religious being, while rejecting it as false *qua* rational being, is to ignore the plain fact that we are for ourselves not two beings but one. We can acquiesce in our own self-diremption only if we fail to notice it. Admittedly this schizophrenic condition is not altogether rare. But where a man does notice his own 'double-think', where he does realise that he is subscribing to two mutually contradictory 'truths', the question surely forces itself upon him 'But which of the "truths" is really true?' And since it is the 'really true' that 'really matters', the 'not *really* true' must simply give way before it.

THIS lecture has been (so far) an attempt to reinforce the thesis of its predecessor by illustrating what I take to be the legitimate rôle of reason *vis à vis* the claims of revelation. In some measure, I confess, I have seemed to myself to be labouring the obvious. I do not find it easy to understand how anyone who has even a nodding acquaintance with comparative religion and modern psychology can seriously suppose an ostensible revelation—even where he is himself the experient—to be self-sufficient, in no need of support from any other quarter. On the other hand, it is hard not to interpret the anti-rational trend in much religious writing today as a direct encouragement to men to rest content with a faith that neither knows nor seeks any justification beyond itself. Perhaps, therefore, there may still be something to be gained by reasserting the ancient truth that the only faith that is fitting in a rational being is a faith that is buttressed by reason. As Socrates almost said, 'An unexamined faith is not worth having'. 'Childlike' faith is undoubtedly a beautiful thing; but only, I would suggest, in a child.

6

PHILOSOPHY
AND THEOLOGY*

Emil Brunner (1889–   ), for many years professor at Zurich, is a Swiss Protestant theologian whose views fall within the tradition usually called neo-orthodoxy with its emphasis on revelation as personal encounter. Among his principal works are: Revelation and Reason, The Mediator, The Divine Imperative, The Christian Doctrine of God, *and* The Christian Doctrine of Creation and Redemption.

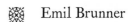   Emil Brunner

PHILOSOPHY consists in reflection on the connection between all particular facts, and the means it employs to this end is thought investigating the way in which the facts are intellectually founded. But we shall need first to supply the ground for the inquiry into connection by showing that the latter has intelligible meaning. Hence we must define the problem of philosophy more closely and say that it inquires how far a mental ground is discoverable for the connection between particular facts. By this means we shall become convinced of the necessity, and therefore of the justification, of the inquiry in itself irrespective of its subject matter. Such an inquiry, again, will include that into the meaning of all science, all civilization and indeed human life in general. But when any school of philosophy surveys the more significant expressions of human life, it will discover among them a form of life which on the one hand is in the closest connection with the set of problems peculiar to philosophy, while on the other it has characteristic differences from every school of philosophy, or is even actually opposed to philosophy. This form of life is religion. The kinship between the two rests on the fact that religion as well as philosophy has in view the whole of existence and life; the opposition between them consists in the fact

* From Emil Brunner, *The Philosophy of Religion from the Standpoint of Protestant Theology*, tr. by A. J. D. Farrer and Bertram L. Woolf. Reprinted by permission of James Clarke & Co., Ltd.

that religion itself claims to supply an answer to the crucial question about reality. It gives this answer in the shape of revelation, and not as the result of the methodical reflection of the intellect, i.e. of an activity within the bounds of reason. Thus philosophy is brought face to face with a most difficult problem, that of showing the meaning and justification of religion within the mental ground known to philosophy. In this way philosophy of religion arises as a part, and perhaps indeed as the culminating point, of philosophy in general.

Provided, however, that the philosopher is serious in his concern about the truth of religion, he cannot avoid listening in the first place to the affirmations of religion about itself—and this always means the affirmations of some specific form of religion. It might of course be the case that religion will have to reject altogether any such classification under philosophy on the plea that it would involve a misinterpretation of religion. In that case the relation between the two would have to be determined conversely, i.e. by starting from religion. Then religion would not have its basis assigned within the bounds of philosophy, but conversely, viz. philosophy, being a special department of man's activity as a reasonable creature, would take its place within the bounds of revealed truth. If such an assertion is not meant to forego every connection with the mind of science, civilization, and philosophy, we must of course make several requirements: that religion should find in her own presuppositions the grounds for thus inverting the relationship between ground and consequence; that it should also report on its mode of supplying these grounds; and once more, that, on the second presupposition, it should make plain the possibility of science, civilization, and philosophy. That would be the way in which, starting from the side of religion, the discussion would have to be carried on with a philosophy originating in the general cultural consciousness. But such an undertaking could be called philosophy of religion only in a secondary sense, and the name as just defined could merely serve to designate the sphere of the discussion.

The state of the case only becomes really clear when, as is incumbent upon us, we look from the stand-point of general possibilities at the special situation that faces us. There are two reasons why we can speak only in a secondary sense of a Christian, and more particularly of a Protestant, philosophy of religion. First, Christian faith, especially in the particular form given to it in Protestant theology, is a fundamentally different thing from every philosophy. To philosophize is to reflect on the mental grounds, with the assumption that ultimate validity belongs to the complex of grounds and consequences developed by natural reason. Christian faith on the other hand involves recognizing that this complex has been broken into by revelation. It is on this revelation that the affirmations of Christian faith are grounded. Theology, which is Christian faith in scientific form, could only lay claim to a scientific character provided it gave clear and exact expression to the fact that its complex of grounds and consequences differs from that of all other sciences as to the final authority it recognizes; provided further that it developed all its affirmations purely out of its own presuppositions and thus founded them on that complex; and provided finally, that on this basis it investigated the relations, whether positive or negative, between revealed faith and rational knowledge. Thus theology is on common ground with philosophy in showing the existence of an intelligible connection embracing all things; but this is not, as it is for philosophy, the logos of the natural reasoning process, but the logos of revelation. Hence Christian theology can never be required to make faith rational by giving it scientific form; on the contrary, it has to keep revelation and religion duly apart by means of clearly defined concepts.

It would be to weaken, or rather to do away with, the opposition were we to equate the relation between reason and revelation with that between rational and irrational. Revelation in the Christian sense stands in the same two-fold relation to the irrational as it does to the rational. The irrational (feeling, intuition, etc.) has not more but, on the contrary, less to do with the paradox of revelation than has the logos of reason. In the modern irrationalist philosophies of religion, the irrational is in every case grafted on a rational system (e.g. in the case of Otto and Scholz on an idealistic, and in that of James, on a naturalistic rationalism) .

Neither can there be philosophy of religion in the strict sense of the term in the realm of Christian theology, for the further reason that theology has to do not with religion but with revelation. Whatever else religion may be, it is a mode of human life, whereas revelation is a self-disclosure of God. While the philosopher of religion is concerned with historical phenomena, i.e. with the historical religions and their "nature", the theologian is concerned with the ground of all phenomena.

To the philosopher as to the theologian, religion is not the ultimate fact but something that roots in the ultimate. In the former case it is reason that supplies the ultimate ground, while in the latter it is revelation. The aim of theology is thus something quite different from religion, and at bottom is no more closely related to religion than it is to any other department of human life. This conclusion, moreover, follows directly from the fundamental presupposition of theology: its ground, its content, and its standard alike are found not in any consciousness of man's, but in God's self-disclosure.

Christian faith, to which theology gives the form of scientific conceptions, is the knowledge and acknowledgment of God's self-revelation in Jesus Christ. He, the incarnate logos, is the ground, content, and standard of all the affirmations of faith. That is where faith differs from every religion as well as from every philosophy. By Christian faith is meant, not some universal truth, nor yet some universal religious experience, but a definite fact which as such is opposed to every universal, be it religion or philosophy. Not that it denies the existence of a certain universal knowledge of God, religious as well as philosophical: rather it presupposes this. But it does deny that the personal and living God can be generally known from possibilities that lie either in the world or in man's spirit as such. It contends that the living and personal God can be known only by a personal meeting, through His personal word, through that special event to which the Bible, and the Bible alone, bears witness, and the content of which is Jesus Christ. Hence this definite fact is not to be understood merely as an illustration, or an embodiment, or even a symbol where such language is used concerning this matter it is not Christian faith with which we have to do. On the contrary, the definite fact of revelation takes the place of what is universal, of truth in general, or of the final criterion of valid assertions; the incarnate logos here occupies the position otherwise held by the logos of reason, the essential idea of truth. This is the case because the personal God, who is the ground of all truth, cannot be known as personal by means of idea, but only by personal, concrete revelation; only when He no longer hides Himself, but issues forth and discloses Himself as the ground of all being, all values, and all thought.

This particular fact, this miracle of divine revelation, which by its very particularity is a stumbling block to thinking in universals, is the presupposition of Christian theology. Christian faith consists precisely in taking this peculiar view of ultimate truth. It would cease to be faith, it would indeed give the lie to its own affirmation, if it wanted to ground the truth of this affirmation on a universal truth. Either revelation supplies its own grounds or else it is not revelation. The only man who can look for some other foundation beside the *Deus dixit* is the man who withholds belief from the *Deus dixit* and wants secretly to replace revelation by symbol. Hence theology cannot substantiate its scientific character by such a change in the class of ground and consequent as falsifies faith, but on the contrary, only by giving a logically exact expression to this special, nonuniversal quality in all its uniqueness. But this means that theology is not a free science void of presuppositions, but one that is closely tied. It is tied to the definite fact of the revelation of God in Jesus Christ. How tied it is appears most clearly in the fact that theology is only possible within the borders of the Christian community or church, and has its definite content and its definite standard in the Bible. Only by perceiving in Scripture the utterance of God does a man become a believer; and only as such, i.e. as a member of the community of believers, is the thinker in a position to think theologically. Theology is in place only in the church, just as in the same way its ground and content are to be found only in the Scriptural revelation.

This again is the starting point for a Protestant philosophy of religion, using this term now in the modified or secondary sense. Such a philosophy must come from theology and, further back still, from faith. It is not the case that it leads towards faith. It is a part of Christian theology as such, i.e. that part in which it carries on the discussion with the common consciousness of truth, i.e. with philosophy; it is that chapter of Christian theology whose business is to start from definitely Christian presuppositions, and give a well-founded description of the relations between revelation and rational knowledge on the one hand, and between revelation and religion on the other. Hence it is not a universal science, of which Christian theology would form a subdivision as being the doctrine of a particular religion. This erroneous view was largely followed in the nineteenth century. The very nature of revealed faith involves reversing the classification of universal and special in this case, because here a particular, viz. revelation, is regarded as ranking above every universal.

Despite the fact then that for us philosophy of religion can be only a branch of theology in general, we have good reason for separating it as a special science from theology; the reason lies in the need of the times, which demands very special attention to this problem; and the need of the times always has determined and always should determine the perspective of theology. Unlike the rest of theology, philosophy of religion is concerned with the formal and general problems of Christian faith, i.e. specifically with the complex of grounds and consequences set forth in the affirmations of faith as distinct from all other affirmations, in other words, with the problem of revelation. Nowhere, however, is it less possible than here to keep form and content apart: what is to be the Christian conception of revelation can only be made clear in connection with the content of that revelation. But is at least possible to distinguish between form and content. On this distinction will depend the possibility of discussing the problems of philosophy of religion apart from those of theology proper. Such separation involves the further condition that, to a greater extent than in theology as such, philosophy of religion must have its being in the realm of abstract concepts, despite the fact that the conceptions have here just the same wholly concrete and personal basis as they have in the simplest confession of faith ever made by an unlettered man. At bottom, the philosopher of religion knows no more than any plain Christian: he merely knows it in the more exact form of abstract conceptions and in connection with the rational knowledge of his age. The reverse side of this advantage is that the abstract nature of his knowledge imperils the personal character of his faith—which ought to penetrate the said knowledge—even more than does the abstract nature of theology in general.

There is no fundamental difference between a theological and a non-theological expression of Christian faith. All utterance about God, no matter how much of personal earnestness it may have, has always the abstractness of theology. Even the parables of Jesus are theology. And conversely, the very earnestness of a personal, vital faith may lead it in certain circumstances, e.g. in its discussion and contention with the thought of one's age, to avail itself of the most abstract forms conceivable. Yet the primary interest of Christianity is not systematic knowledge, but the relation of a personal faith to revelation. Hence of course faith is constantly directed towards overcoming abstract concepts as completely as possible; and therefore the philosophy of religion must be judged as lying at best on the edge of Christian doctrine and never at its centre.

Revelation meets and fits human consciousness. It is not a matter of indifference that this consciousness should be defined as human, although on the other hand it is not essential to know in what more specific way it is so defined. Faith is indeed bound up with humanity but not with any particular grade of humanity. Of course it presupposes man as man, but not a particular type of humanity, nor yet any particular feature in man. It takes man in his totality, not in some special locus that can be fixed by psychology. The locus in which revelation and the spirit of man meet each other cannot be assigned positively but only negatively: it consists in receptivity. If in place of this we would rather put a particular form of consciousness, we might say that it is "inquiry" when this has assumed the form of a vital need. But although this is a presupposition for faith, it does not designate a particular psychological quality, but, on the contrary, what is universally human. In fact, we can indicate the locus yet more definitely without thereby abandoning what is universally human: the negative point of contact is a consciousness of vital need which is at the same time a consciousness of guilt. Therefore we might fittingly express our meaning as follows: any account of the faith evoked by revelation should be preceded by another account giving the results of man's investigation of universal mental characteristics, which investigation would lead up to the afore-mentioned point of contact. Lack of space obliges us to omit such an account. Ultimately, however, this makes no difference because in every case faith appropriate to revelation must be understood entirely by itself and not by means of any common consciousness of man's. Faith appropriate to revelation can be understood only by revelation, just in the same way as any rational thought can only be understood by its ground in reason, or a sensation of light only by the light-stimulus. Therefore it is necessary to start from revelation as known to faith; in doing so we have only to bear in mind that revelation is always the answer to a question on man's part. But whether man's question, and indeed humanity itself, have their ground in revelation, and only in it can attain their proper meaning; and therefore whether man's question has not its *prius* in God's address to him—these are matters that can be discussed only in connection with the knowledge appropriate to revelation. At all events faith is certain that revelation alone enables us rightly to apprehend that need, that vital incapacity, which is the presupposition of faith; and that thereby revelation itself begets its own presupposition in the crucial sense.

7

PHILOSOPHY

AND RELIGION*

Paul Tillich ⬡

Paul Tillich (1886–1965) was a German philosophical theologian who spent most of his academic years at Union Theological Seminary in New York, and later taught at both Harvard and Chicago. Widely known as an interpreter of Christianity through the categories of both Hegelian idealism and existentialism, Tillich wrote Systematic Theology, The Courage to Be, *and* Dynamics of Faith.

Theology and Philosophy: A Question

THEOLOGY claims that it constitutes a special realm of knowledge, that it deals with a special object and employs a special method. This claim places the theologian under the obligation of giving an account of the way in which he relates theology to other forms of knowledge. He must answer two questions: What is the relationship of theology to the special sciences (*Wissenschaften*) and what is its relationship to philosophy? The first question has been answered implicitly by the preceding statement of the formal criteria of theology. If nothing is an object of theology which does not concern us ultimately, theology is unconcerned about scientific procedures and results and vice versa. Theology has no right and no obligation to prejudice a physical or historical, sociological or psychological, inquiry. And no result of such an inquiry can be directly productive or disastrous for theology. The point of contact between scientific research and theology lies in the philosophical element of both, the sciences and theology. Therefore, the question of the relation of theology to the special sciences merges into the question of the relation between theology and philosophy.

The difficulty of this question lies partly in the fact that there is no generally accepted definition of philosophy. Every

---

* From *Dynamics of Faith* by Paul Tillich. Copyright © 1957 by Paul Tillich. Reprinted by permission of Harper & Row, Publishers.

philosophy proposes a definition which agrees with the interest, purpose, and method of the philosopher. Under these circumstances the theologian can only suggest a definition of philosophy which is broad enough to cover most of the important philosophies which have appeared in what usually is called the history of philosophy. The suggestion made here is to call philosophy *that cognitive approach to reality in which reality as such is the object.* Reality as such, or reality as a whole, is not the whole of reality; it is the structure which makes reality a whole and therefore a potential object of knowledge. Inquiring into the nature of reality as such means inquiring into those structures, categories, and concepts which are presupposed in the cognitive encounter with every realm of reality. From this point of view philosophy is by definition critical. It separates the multifarious materials of experience from those structures which make experience possible. There is no difference in this respect between constructive idealism and empirical realism. The question regarding the character of the general structures that make experience possible is always the same. It is *the* philosophical question.

The critical definition of philosophy is more modest than those philosophical enterprises which try to present a complete system of reality, including the results of all the special sciences as well as the general structures of prescientific experience. Such an attempt can be made from "above" or from "below." Hegel worked from "above" when he filled the categorical forms, developed in his *Logic,* with the available material of the scientific knowledge of his time and adjusted the material to the categories. Wundt worked from "below" when he abstracted general and metaphysical principles from the available scientific material of his time, with the help of which the entire sum of empirical knowledge could be organized. Aristotle worked from both "above" and "below" when he carried through metaphysical and scientific studies in interdependence. This also was the ideal of Leibniz when he sketched a universal calculus capable of subjecting all of reality to mathematical analysis and synthesis. But in all these cases the limits of the human mind, the finitude which prevents it from grasping the whole, became visible. No sooner was the system finished than scientific research trespassed its boundaries and disrupted it in all directions. Only the general principles were left, always discussed, questioned, changed, but never destroyed, shining through the centuries, reinterpreted by every generation, inexhaustible, never antiquated or obsolete. These principles are the material of philosophy.

This understanding of philosophy is, in the other hand, less modest than the attempt to reduce philosophy to epistemology and ethics, which was the goal of the Neo-Kantian and related schools in the nineteenth century, and less modest also than the attempt to reduce it to logical calculus, which has been the goal of logical positivism and related schools in the twentieth century. Both attempts to avoid the ontological question have been unsuccessful. The later adherents of the Neo-Kantian philosophy recognized that every epistemology contains an implicit ontology. It cannot be otherwise. Since knowing is an act which participates in being or, more precisely, in an "ontic relation," every analysis of the act of knowing must refer to an interpretation of being (cf. Nicolai Hartmann). At the same time the problem of values pointed toward an ontological foundation of the validity of value-judgments. If values have no *fundamentum in re* (cf. Plato's identification of the good with the essential structures, the ideas of being), they float in the air of a transcendent validity, or else they are subjected to pragmatic tests which are arbitrary and accidental unless they introduce an ontology of essences surreptitiously. It is not necessary to discuss the pragmatic-naturalistic line of philosophical thought, for, in spite of the antimetaphysical statements of some of its adherents, it has expressed itself in definite ontological terms such as life, growth, process, experience, being (understood in an all-embracing sense), etc. But it is necessary to compare the ontological definition of philosophy, suggested above, with the radical attempts to reduce philosophy to scientific logic. The question is whether the elimination of almost all traditional philosophical problems by logical positivism is a successful escape from ontology. One's first reaction is the feeling that such an attitude pays too high a price, namely, the price of making philosophy irrelevant. But, beyond this impression, the following argument can be put forward. If the restriction of philosophy to the logic of the sciences is a matter of taste, it need not be taken seriously. If it is based on an analysis of the limits of human knowledge, it is based, like every epistemology, on ontological assumptions. There is always at least one problem about which logical positivism, like all semantic philosophies, must make a decision. What is the relation of signs, symbols, or logical operations to reality? Every answer to this question says something about the structure of being. It is ontological. And a philosophy which is so radically critical of all other philosophies should be sufficiently self-critical to see and to reveal its own ontological assumptions.

Philosophy asks the question of reality as a whole; it asks the question of the structure of being. And it answers in terms of categories, structural laws, and universal concepts. It must answer in ontological terms. Ontology is not a speculative-fantastic attempt to establish a world behind the world; it is an analysis of those structures of being which we encounter in every meeting with reality. This was also the original meaning of metaphysics; but the preposition *meta* now has the irremediable connotation of pointing to a duplication of this world by a transcendent realm of beings. Therefore, it is perhaps less misleading to speak of ontology instead of metaphysics.

Philosophy necessarily asks the question of reality as a whole, the question of the structure of being. Theology necessarily asks the same question, for that which concerns us ultimately must belong to reality as a whole; it must belong to being. Otherwise we could not encounter it, and it could not concern us. Of course, it cannot be one being among others; then it would not concern us infinitely. It must be the ground of our being, that which determines our being or not-being, the ultimate and unconditional power of being. But the power of being, its infinite ground or "being-itself," expresses itself in and through the structure of being. Therefore, we can encounter it, be grasped by it, know it, and act toward it. Theology, when dealing with our ultimate concern, presupposes in every sentence the structure of being, its categories, laws, and concepts. Theology, therefore, cannot escape the question of being any more easily than can philosophy. The attempt of biblicism to avoid nonbiblical, ontological terms is doomed to failure as surely as are the corresponding philosophical attempts. The Bible itself always uses the categories and concepts which describe the structure of experience. On every page of every religious or theological text these concepts appear: time, space, cause, thing, subject, nature, movement, freedom, necessity, life, value, knowledge, experience, being and not-being. Biblicism may try to preserve their popular meaning, but then it ceases to be theology. It must neglect the fact that a philosophical understanding of these categories has influenced ordinary language for many centuries. It is surprising how casually theological biblicists use a term like "history" when speaking of Christianity as a historical religion or of God as the "Lord of history." They forget that the meaning they connect with the word "history" has been formed by thousands of years of historiography and philosophy of history. They forget that historical being is one kind of being in addition to others and that, in order to distinguish it from the word "nature," for instance, a general vision of the structure of being is presupposed. They forget that the problem of history is tied up with the problems of time, freedom, accident, purpose, etc., and that each of these concepts has had a development similar to the concept of history. The theologian must take seriously the meaning of the terms he uses. They must be known to him in the whole depth and breadth of their meaning. Therefore, the systematic theologian must be a philosopher in critical understanding even if not in creative power.

The structure of being and the categories and concepts describing this structure are an implicit or explicit concern of every philosopher and of every theologian. Neither of them can avoid the ontological question. Attempts from both sides to avoid it have proved abortive. If this is the situation, the question becomes the more urgent: What is the relation between the ontological question asked by the philosopher and the ontological question asked by the theologian?

Theology and Philosophy: An Answer

PHILOSOPHY and theology ask the question of being. But they ask it from different perspectives. Philosophy deals with the structure of being in itself; theology deals with the meaning of being for us. From this difference convergent and divergent trends emerge in the relation of theology and philosophy.

The first point of divergence is a difference in the cognitive attitude of the philosopher and the theologian. Although driven by the philosophical *erōs,* the philosopher tries to maintain a detached objectivity toward being and its structures. He tries to exclude the personal, social, and historical conditions which might distort an objective vision of reality. His passion is the passion for a truth which is open to general approach, subject to general criticism, changeable in accordance with every new insight, open and communicable. In all these respects he feels no different from the scientist, historian, psychologist, etc. He collaborates with them. The material for his critical analysis is largely supplied by empirical research. Just as all sciences have their origin in philosophy, so they contribute in turn to philosophy by giving to the philosopher new and exactly defined material far beyond anything he could get from a prescientific approach to reality. Of course, the philosopher, as a philosopher, neither criticizes nor augments the knowledge provided by the sciences. This knowledge forms the basis of his description of the categories, structural laws, and concepts which constitute the structure of being. In this respect the philosopher is as dependent on the scientist as he is dependent on his own prescientific observation of reality—often more dependent. This relation to the sciences (in the broad sense of *Wissenschaften*) strengthens the detached, objective attitude of the philosopher. Even in the intuitive-synthetic side of his procedure he tries to exclude influences which are not purely determined by his object.[1]

The theologian, quite differently, is not detached from his object but is involved in it. He looks at his object (which transcends the character of being an object) with passion, fear, and love. This is not the *erōs* of the philosopher or his passion for objective truth; it is the love which accepts saving, and therefore personal, truth. The basic attitude of the theologian is commitment to the content he expounds. Detachment would be a denial of the very nature of this content. The attitude of the theologian is "existential." He is involved—with the whole of his existence, with his finitude and his anxiety, with his self-contradictions and his despair, with the healing forces in him and in his social situation. Every theological statement derives its seriousness from these elements of existence. The theologian, in short, is determined by his faith. Every theology presupposes that the theologian is in the theological circle. This contradicts the open, infinite, and changeable character of philosophical truth. It also differs from the way in which the philosopher is dependent on scientific research. The theologian has no direct relation to the scientist (including the historian, sociologist, psychologist). He deals with him only in so far as philosophical implications are at stake. If he abandons the existential attitude, as some of the "empirical" theologians have done, he is driven to statements the reality of which will not be acknowledged by anybody who does not share the existential presuppositions of the assumedly empirical theologian. Theology is necessarily existential, and no theology can escape the theological circle.

The second point of divergence between the theologian and the philosopher is the difference in their sources. The philosopher looks at the whole of reality to discover within it the structure of reality as a whole. He tries to penetrate into the structures of being by means of the power of his cognitive function and its structures. He assumes—and science continuously confirms this assumption—that there is an identity, or at least an analogy, between objective and subjective reason, between the *logos* of reality as a whole and the *logos* working in him. Therefore, this *logos* is common; every reasonable being participates in it, uses it in asking questions and criticizing the answers received. There is no particular place to discover the structure of being; there is no particular place to stand to discover the categories of experience. The place to look is all places; the place to stand is no place at all; it is pure reason.

[1] The concept of a "philosophical faith" appears questionable from this point of view (see Karl Jaspers, *The Perennial Scope of Philosophy* [New York: Philosophical Library, 1949]).

The theologian, on the other hand, must look where that which concerns him ultimately is manifest, and he must stand where its manifestation reaches and grasps him. The source of his knowledge is not the universal *logos* but the Logos "who became flesh," that is, the *logos* manifesting itself in a particular historical event. And the medium through which he receives the manifestation of the *logos* is not common rationality but the church, its traditions and its present reality. He speaks in the church about the foundation of the church. And he speaks because he is grasped by the power of this foundation and by the community built upon it. The concrete *logos* which he sees is received through believing commitment and not, like the universal *logos* at which the philosopher looks, through rational detachment.

The third point of divergence between philosophy and theology is the difference in their content. Even when they speak about the same object, they speak about something different. The philosopher deals with the categories of being in relation to the material which is structured by them. He deals with causality as it appears in physics or psychology; he analyzes biological or historical time; he discusses astronomical as well as microcosmic space. He describes the epistemological subject and the relation of person and community. He presents the characteristics of life and spirit in their dependence on, and independence of, each other. He defines nature and history in their mutual limits and tries to penetrate into ontology and logic of being and nonbeing. Innumerable other examples could be given. They all reflect the cosmological structure of the philosophical assertions. The theologian, on the other hand, relates the same categories and concepts to the quest for a "new being." His assertions have a soteriological character. He discusses causality in relation to a *prima causa,* the ground of the whole series of causes and effects; he deals with time in relation to eternity, with space in relation to man's existential homelessness. He speaks of the self-estrangement of the subject, about the spiritual center of personal life, and about community as a possible embodiment of the "New Being." He relates the structures of life to the creative ground of life and the structures of spirit to the divine Spirit. He speaks of the participation of nature in the "history of salvation," about the victory of being over nonbeing. Here also the examples could be increased indefinitely; they show the sharp divergence of theology from philosophy with respect to their content.

The divergence between philosophy and theology is counterbalanced by an equally obvious convergence. From both sides converging trends are at work. The philosopher, like the theologian, "exists," and he cannot jump over the concreteness of his existence and his implicit theology. He is conditioned by his psychological, sociological, and historical situation. And, like every human being, he exists in the power of an ultimate concern, whether or not he is fully conscious of it, whether or not he admits it to himself and to others. There is no reason why even the most scientific philosopher should not admit it, for without an ultimate concern his philosophy would be lacking in passion, seriousness, and creativity. Wherever we look in the history of philosophy, we find ideas and systems which claim to be ultimately relevant for human existence. Occasionally the philosophy of religion openly expresses the ultimate concern behind a system. More often it is the character of the ontological principles, or a special section of a system, such as epistemology, philosophy of nature, politics and ethics, philosophy of history, etc., which is most revealing for the discovery of the ultimate concern and the hidden theology within it. Every creative philosopher is a hidden theologian (sometimes even a declared theologian). He is a theologian in the degree to which his existential situation and his ultimate concern shape his philosophical vision. He is a theologian in the degree to which his intuition of the universal *logos* of the structure of reality as a whole is formed by a particular *logos* which appears to him on his particular place and reveals to him the meaning of the whole. And he is a theologian in the degree to which the particular *logos* is a matter of active commitment within a special community. There is hardly a historically significant philosopher who does not show these marks of a theologian. But the philosopher does not intend to be a theologian. He wants to serve the universal *logos*. He tries to turn away from his existential situation, including his ultimate concern, toward a place above all particular places, toward pure reality. The conflict between the intention of becoming universal and the destiny of remaining particular characterizes every philosophical existence. It is its burden and its greatness.

The theologian carries an analogous burden. Instead of turning away from his existential situation, including his ultimate concern, he turns toward it. He turns toward it, not in order to make a confession of it, but in order to make clear the universal validity, the *logos* structure, of what concerns him ultimately. And he can do this only in an attitude of detachment from his existential situation and in obedience to the universal *logos*. This obligates him to be critical of every special expression of his ultimate concern. He cannot affirm any tradition and any authority except through a "No" and a "Yes." And it is always possible that he may not be able to go all the way from the "No" to the "Yes." He cannot join the chorus of those who live in unbroken assertions. He must take the risk of being driven beyond the boundary line of the theological circle. Therefore, the pious and powerful in the church are suspicious of him, although they live in dependence upon the work of the former theologians who were in the same situation. Theology, since it serves not only the concrete but also the universal *logos*, can become a stumbling block for the church and a demonic temptation for the theologian. The detachment required in honest theological work can destroy the necessary involvement of faith. This tension is the burden and the greatness of every theological work.

The duality of divergence and convergence in the relation between theology and philosophy leads to the double question: Is there a necessary conflict between the two and is there a possible synthesis between them? Both questions must be answered negatively. Neither is a conflict between theology and philosophy necessary, nor is a synthesis between them possible.

A conflict presupposes a common basis on which to fight. But there is no common basis between theology and philosophy. If the theologian and the philosopher fight, they do so either on a philosophical or on a theological basis. The philosophical basis is the ontological analysis of the structure of being. If the theologian needs this analysis, either he must take it from a philosopher or he must himself become a philosopher. Usually he does both. If he enters the philosophical arena, conflicts as well as alliances with other philosophers are unavoidable. But all this happens on the philosophical level. The theologian has no right whatsoever to argue for a philosophical opinion in the name of his ultimate concern or on the basis of the theological circle. He is obliged to argue for a philosophical decision in the name of the universal *logos* and from the place which is no place: pure reason. It is a disgrace for the theologian and intolerable for the philosopher if in a philosophical discussion the theologian suddenly claims an authority other than pure reason. Conflicts on the philosophical level are conflicts between two philosophers, one of whom happens to be a theologian, but they are not conflicts between theology and philosophy.

Often, however, the conflict is fought on the theological level. The hidden theologian in the philosopher fights with the professed theologian. This situation is more frequent than most philosophers realize. Since they have developed their concepts with the honest intention of obeying the universal *logos*, they are reluctant to recognize the existentially conditioned elements in their systems. They feel that such elements, while they give color and direction to their creative work, diminish its truth value. In such a situation the theologian must break the resistance of the philosopher against a theological analysis of his ideas. He can do this by pointing to the history of philosophy, which discloses that in every significant philosopher existential passion (ultimate concern) and rational power (obedience to the universal *logos*) are united and that the truth value of a philosophy is dependent on the amalgamation of these two elements in every concept. The insight into this situation is, at the same time, an insight into the fact that two philosophers, one of whom happens to be a theologian, can fight with each other and that two theologians, one of whom happens to be a philosopher, can fight with each other; but there is no possible conflict between theology and philosophy because there is no common basis for such a conflict. The philosopher may or may not convince the philosopher-theologian. And the theologian may or may not convert the theologian-philosopher. In no case does the theologian as such stand against the philosopher as such and vice versa.

Thus there is no conflict between theology and philosophy, and there is no synthesis either—for exactly the same reason which insures that there will be no conflict. A common basis is lacking. The idea of a synthesis between theology and philosophy has led to the dream of a "Christian philosophy." The term is ambiguous. It can mean a philosophy whose existential basis is historical Christianity. In this sense all modern philosophy is Christian, even if it is humanistic, atheistic, and intentionally anti-Christian. No philosopher living within Western Christian culture can deny his dependence on it, as no Greek philosopher could have hidden his dependence on an Apollonian-Dionysian culture, even if he was a radical critic of the gods of Homer. The modern vision of reality and its philosophical analysis is different from that of pre-Christian times, whether one is or is not existentially determined by the God of Mount Zion and the Christ of Mount Golgotha. Reality is encountered differently; experience has different dimensions and directions than in the cultural climate of Greece. No one is able to jump out of this "magic" circle. Nietzsche, who tried to do so, announced the coming of the Anti-Christ. But the Anti-Christ is dependent on the Christ against whom he arises. The early Greeks, for whose culture Nietzsche was longing, did not have to fight the Christ; indeed, they unconsciously prepared his coming by elaborating the questions to which he gave the answer and the categories in which the answer could be expressed. Modern philosophy is not pagan. Atheism and anti-Christianity are not pagan. They are anti-Christian in Christian terms. The scars of the Christian tradition cannot be erased; they are a *character indelebilis.* Even the paganism of naziism was not really a relapse to paganism (just as bestiality is not a relapse to the beast) .

But the term "Christian philosophy" is often meant in a different sense. It is used to denote a philosophy which does not look at the universal *logos* but at the assumed or actual demands of a Christian theology. This can be done in two ways: either the church authorities or its theological interpreters nominate one of the past philosophers to be their "philosophical saint" or they demand that contemporary philosophers should develop a philosophy under special conditions and with a special aim. In both cases the philosophical *erōs* is killed. If Thomas Aquinas is officially named *the* philosopher of the Roman Catholic church, he has ceased to be for Catholic philosophers a genuine partner in the philosophical dialogue which goes on through the centuries. And if present-day Protestant philosophers are asked to accept the idea of personality as their highest ontological principle because it is the principle most congenial to the spirit of the Reformation, the work of these philosophers is mutilated. There is nothing in heaven and earth, or beyond them, to which the philosopher must subject himself except the universal *logos* of being as it gives itself to him in experience. Therefore, the idea of a "Christian philosophy" in the narrower sense of a philosophy which is intentionally Christian must be rejected. The fact that every modern philosophy has grown on Christian soil and shows traces of the Christian culture in which it lives has nothing to do with the self-contradicting ideal of a "Christian philosophy."

Christianity does not need a "Christian philosophy" in the narrower sense of the word. The Christian claim that the *logos* who has become concrete in Jesus as the Christ is at the same time the universal *logos* includes the claim that wherever the *logos* is at work it agrees with the Christian message. No philosophy which is obedient to the universal *logos* can contradict the concrete *logos,* the Logos "who became flesh."

Additional Readings

BARTH, KARL, *The Knowledge of God and the Service of God.*

BRUNNER, EMIL, *Revelation and Reason.*

BUTLER, JOSEPH, *The Analogy of Religion.*

DEWEY, JOHN, *A Common Faith.*

FREUD, SIGMUND, *The Future of an Illusion.*

JASPERS, KARL, *Truth and Symbol.*

KIERKEGAARD, S., *Concluding Unscientific Postscript.*

LOCKE, JOHN, *Essay Concerning Human Understanding,* Book IV, Chap. 17, 18.

MACINTOSH, D. C., *The Problem of Religious Knowledge.*

MACQUARRIE, JOHN, *Twentieth Century Religious Thought.*

PLANTINGA, A. (ed.), *Faith and Philosophy* (an anthology of contemporary discussions of several topics in the philosophy of religion).

SANTAYANA, G., *Scepticism and Animal Faith.*

PART II

ARGUMENTS

FOR THE

DIVINE REALITY

One of the most crucial questions provoked by the problems concerning reason, faith, and philosophy is whether, on the basis of some assumed theory of knowledge, there are adequate grounds for belief in a transcendent Divine Reality, and if so, what these grounds are. By an argument for the Divine Reality therefore we mean one based on a set of premises which, adequately understood, involve the conclusion that such a Reality does in fact exist.

To make the role of such arguments in religious philosophy clear, a number of considerations must be explained. First, not all those who believe in such a basis for a religious world view agree about the sort of argument that is adequate for this purpose or about the sort of Divine Reality implied by such arguments. Secondly, not all those who reject such an approach are opposed to the existence of a Divine Reality. While some critics do indeed regard the existence of such a Reality as either impossible or improbable, others reject the arguments because they are confident that some alternative way of knowing God is possible—a way involving an appeal to special revelation, or mystical experience, for example.

Traditionally, arguments for the Divine Reality have often been classified as either *a priori* or *a posteriori*. *A priori* arguments rest an analysis of concepts without any appeal to particular facts of experience. *A posteriori* arguments, while sometimes partly based on *a priori* principles, appeal decisively to certain facts of experience as their principal foundation. Nearly all arguments of an *a priori* nature are called ontological arguments and involve the contention that the concept of an Absolute Divine Reality, when adequately analyzed, logically implies the necessary existence of precisely that Reality. The form of this argument given by Anselm of Canterbury is perhaps the classical expression of this thesis and has provoked the most extensive discussion of it.

A posteriori arguments, on the other hand, are of several different sorts, nearly all of which have been given classical expression in the five proofs of the existence of God by Thomas Aquinas. Three basic types of argument may be distinguished: cosmological, teleological and moral. The first type urges, in various ways illustrated by the first three Thomistic proofs, that the existence of anything at all ultimately implies an absolutely necessary being whose existence is independent of the natural order. Teleological arguments, on the other hand, argue from the special characteristics of the universe, as we experience it, to the reality of God as the only plausible explanation of these characteristics. The most widely emphasized qualities of this sort are, on the one hand, the order exhibited in the universe, and on the other hand, the presence of mind in the universe. The fifth Thomistic argument, for example, contains both elements. Richard Taylor's formulation should probably also be considered a version of the teleological argument. Finally, a typical moral argument for God would attempt to show that morality is adequately understood only when regarded as founded upon objective principles of value whose authority is inexplicable apart from the Divine Reality. The analysis of A. E. Taylor illustrates this type of approach.

Criticisms of an argumentative approach to a religious world view commonly embody one or another of three basic orientations. First, an empirical criticism—exemplified by David Hume and Immanuel Kant—urges that the limitation of our knowledge of reality to statements verifiable through sense experience makes speculative knowledge of the Divine Reality either improbable or impossible. Such arguments invariably involve either logical fallacies or an appeal to *a priori* principles whose application to reality is unjustified on the basis of empirical knowledge. Again, thinkers whose orientation is basically existential—illustrated here by Soren

Kierkegaard—maintain that all such arguments presuppose a kind of objective, speculative detachment from historical existence. No existing human individual can achieve such a standpoint. Finally, a mystically-oriented philosopher like Aurobindo Ghose maintains that intellectually-based world views, whether theistic (implying a transcendent God), or naturalistic (in which nature requires no such explanation), are rendered implausible by logical difficulties that can be exposed by the very intellectual principles to which such views appeal for support. For Ghose, the ultimate reality is known rather through an experience of conscious identity.

THE ONTOLOGICAL

ARGUMENT*

Anselm of Canterbury (1033–1109) was a member of the Benedictine Order. His views attempt a defense of Christian doctrines through a philosophic framework heavily influenced by Platonism. Best known for his classical expression of the ontological argument for the existence of God, Anselm wrote principally: Monologium, Proslogium, *and* Cur Deus Homo.

 St. Anselm

TRULY THERE IS A GOD, ALTHOUGH THE FOOL HATH SAID IN HIS HEART, THERE IS NO GOD.

AND SO, Lord, do thou, who dost give understanding to faith, give me, so far as thou knowest it to be profitable, to understand that thou art as we believe; and that thou art that which we believe. And, indeed, we believe that thou art a being than which nothing greater can be conceived. Or is there no such nature, since the fool hath said in his heart, there is no God? (Psalms xiv. 1) . But, at any rate, this very fool, when he hears of this being of which I speak—a being than which nothing greater can be conceived—understands what he hears, and what he understands is in his understanding; although he does not understand it to exist.

For, it is one thing for an object to be in the understanding, and another to understand that the object exists. When a painter first conceives of what he will afterwards perform, he has it in his understanding, but he does not yet understand it to be, because he has not yet performed it. But after he has made the painting, he both has it in his understanding, and he understands that it exists, because he has made it.

Hence, even the fool is convinced that something exists in the understanding, at least, than which nothing greater can be

* From *St. Anselm: Basic Writings,* tr. by S. N. Deane, with an introduction by Charles Hartshorne, La Salle, Illinois, 1961. Reprinted by permission of The Open Court Publishing Company, La Salle, Illinois.

conceived. For, when he hears of this, he understands it. And whatever is understood, exists in the understanding. And assuredly that, than which nothing greater can be conceived, cannot exist in the understanding alone. For, suppose it exists in the understanding alone: then it can be conceived to exist in reality; which is greater.

Therefore, if that, than which nothing greater can be conceived, exists in the understanding alone, the very being, than which nothing greater can be conceived, is one, than which a greater can be conceived. But obviously this is impossible. Hence, there is no doubt that there exists a being, than which nothing greater can be conceived, and it exists both in the understanding and in reality.

GOD CANNOT BE CONCEIVED NOT TO EXIST.—GOD IS THAT, THAN WHICH NOTHING GREATER CAN BE CONCEIVED.—THAT WHICH CAN BE CONCEIVED NOT TO EXIST IS NOT GOD.

And it assuredly exists so truly, that it cannot be conceived not to exist. For, it is possible to conceive of a being which cannot be conceived not to exist; and this is greater than one which can be conceived not to exist. Hence, if that, than which nothing greater can be conceived, can be conceived not to exist, it is not that, than which nothing greater can be conceived. But this is an irreconcilable contradiction. There is, then, so truly a being than which nothing greater can be conceived to exist, that it cannot even be conceived not to exist; and this being thou art, O Lord, our God.

So truly, therefore, dost thou exist, O Lord, my God, that thou canst not be conceived not to exist; and rightly. For, if a mind could conceive of a being better than thee, the creature would rise above the Creator; and this is most absurd. And, indeed, whatever else there is, except thee alone, can be conceived not to exist. To thee alone, therefore, it belongs to exist more truly than all other beings, and hence in a higher degree than all others. For, whatever else exists does not exist so truly, and hence in a less degree it belongs to it to exist. Why, then, has the fool said in his heart, there is no God (Psalms xiv. 1), since it is so evident, to a rational mind, that thou dost exist in the highest degree of all? Why, except that he is dull and a fool?

2

THE IMPOSSIBILITY OF
AN ONTOLOGICAL PROOF*

*Immanuel Kant (1724–1804) is one of
the greatest of all occidental philosophers,
standing in the tradition of German
idealism and emphasizing a theory of
knowledge that combines rationalism
and empiricism. He exerted an incalculable influence on the whole of modern
philosophy primarily through his writings, the best known of which are:*
Critique of Pure Reason, Critique of
Practical Reason, Critique of Judgment,
and Fundamental Principles of the
Metaphysic of Morals.

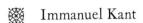 Immanuel Kant

IT IS EVIDENT from what has been said, that the conception of an
absolutely necessary being is a mere idea, the objective reality of
which is far from being established by the mere fact that it is a need
of reason. On the contrary, this idea serves merely to indicate a
certain unattainable perfection, and rather limits the operations
than, by the presentation of new objects, extends the sphere of the
understanding. But a strange anomaly meets us at the very thresh-
old; for the inference from a given existence in general to an
absolutely necessary existence, seems to be correct and unavoidable,
while the conditions of the *understanding* refuse to aid us in
forming any conception of such a being.

Philosophers have always talked of an *absolutely necessary*
being, and have nevertheless declined to take the trouble of conceiving, whether—and how—a being of this nature is even cogi-
table, not to mention that its existence is actually demonstrable. A
verbal definition of the conception is certainly easy enough; it is
something, the non-existence of which is impossible. But does this
definition throw any light upon the conditions which render it
impossible to cogitate the non-existence of a thing—conditions

* From Immanuel Kant, *Critique of Pure Reason*, tr. by J. M. D. Meiklejohn
(rev. ed.).

which we wish to ascertain, that we may discover whether we think anything in the conception of such a being or not? For the mere fact that I throw away, by means of the word *Unconditioned,* all the conditions which the understanding habitually requires in order to regard anything as necessary, is very far from making clear whether by means of the conception of the unconditionally necessary I think of something, or really of nothing at all.

Nay, more, this chance-conception, now become so current, many have endeavored to explain by examples, which seemed to render any inquiries regarding its intelligibility quite needless. Every geometrical proposition—a triangle has three angles—it was said, is absolutely necessary; and thus people talked of an object which lay out of the sphere of our understanding as if it were perfectly plain what the conception of such a being meant.

All the examples adduced have been drawn, without exception, from *judgments,* and not from *things.* But the unconditioned necessity of a judgment does not form the absolute necessity of a thing. On the contrary, the absolute necessity of a judgment is only a conditioned necessity of a thing, or of the predicate in a judgment. The proposition above-mentioned, does not enounce that three angles necessarily exist, but, upon condition that a triangle exists, three angles must necessarily exist—in it. And thus this logical necessity has been the source of the greatest delusions. Having formed an *à priori* conception of a thing, the content of which was made to embrace existence, we believed ourselves safe in concluding that, because existence belongs necessarily to the object of the conception (that is, under the condition of my positing this thing as given), the existence of the thing is also posited necessarily, and that it is therefore absolutely necessary—merely because its existence has been cogitated in the conception.

If, in an identical judgment, I annihilate the predicate in thought, and retain the subject, a contradiction is the result; and hence I say, the former belongs necessarily to the latter. But if I suppress both subject and predicate in thought, no contradiction arises; for there *is nothing* at all, and therefore no means of forming a contradiction. To suppose the existence of a triangle and not that of its three angles, is self-contradictory; but to suppose the non-existence of both triangle and angles is perfectly admissible. And so is it with the conception of an absolutely necessary being. Annihilate its existence in thought, and you annihilate the thing itself with all its predicates; how then can there be any room for contradiction? Externally, there is nothing to give rise to a contradiction, for a thing cannot be necessary externally; nor internally, for, by the annihilation or suppression of the thing itself, its internal properties are also annihilated. God is omnipotent—that is a necessary judgment. His omnipotence cannot be denied, if the existence of a Deity is posited—the existence, that is, of an infinite being, the two conceptions being identical. But when you say, *God does not exist*, neither omnipotence nor any other predicate is affirmed; they must all disappear with the subject, and in this judgment there cannot exist the least self-contradiction.

You have thus seen, that when the predicate of a judgment is annihilated in thought along with the subject, no internal contradiction can arise, be the predicate what it may. There is no possibility of evading the conclusion—you find yourselves compelled to declare: There are certain subjects which cannot be annihilated in thought. But this is nothing more than saying: There exist subjects which are absolutely necessary—the very hypothesis which you are called upon to establish. For I find myself unable to form the slightest conception of a thing which, when annihilated in thought with all its predicates, leaves behind a contradiction; and contradiction is the only criterion of impossibility, in the sphere of pure *à priori* conceptions.

Against these general considerations, the justice of which no one can dispute, one argument is adduced, which is regarded as furnishing a satisfactory demonstration from the fact. It is affirmed, that there is one and only one conception, in which the non-being or annihilation of the object is self-contradictory, and this is the conception of an *ens realissimum*. It possesses, you say, all reality, and you feel yourselves justified in admitting the possibility of such a being. (This I am willing to grant for the present, although the existence of a conception which is not self-contradictory, is far from being sufficient to prove the possibility of an object.*) Now the notion of all reality embraces in it that of existence; the notion of existence lies, therefore, in the conception of this possible thing. If this thing is annihilated in thought, the internal possibility of the thing is also annihilated, which is self-contradictory.

I answer: It is absurd to introduce—under whatever term disguised—into the conception of a thing, which is to be cogitated solely in reference to its possibility, the conception of its existence. If this is admitted, you will have apparently gained the day, but in

---

* A conception is always possible, if it is not self-contradictory. This is the logical criterion of possibility, distinguishing the object of such a conception from the *nihil negativum*. But it may be, notwithstanding, an empty conception, unless the objective reality of this synthesis, by which it is generated, is demonstrated; and a proof of this kind must be based upon principles of possible experience, and not upon the principle of analysis or contradiction. This remark may be serviceable as a warning against concluding, from the possibility of a conception —which is logical, the possibility of a thing—which is real.

reality have enounced nothing but a mere tautology. I ask, is the proposition, *this or that thing* (which I am admitting to be possible) *exists,* an analytical or a synthetical proposition? If the former, there is no addition made to the subject of your thought by the affirmation of its existence; but then the conception in your minds is identical with the thing itself, or you have supposed the existence of a thing to be possible, and then inferred its existence from its internal possibility—which is but a miserable tautology. The word *reality* in the conception of the thing, and the word *existence* in the conception of the predicate, will not help you out of the difficulty. For, supposing you were to term all positing of a thing, reality, you have thereby posited the thing with all its predicates in the conception of the subject and assumed its actual existence, and this you merely repeat in the predicate. But if you confess, as every reasonable person must, that every existential proposition is synthetical, how can it be maintained that the predicate of existence cannot be denied without contradiction—a property which is the characteristic of analytical propositions, alone.

I should have a reasonable hope of putting an end forever to this sophistical mode of argumentation, by a strict definition of the conception of existence, did not my own experience teach me that the illusion arising from our confounding a logical with a real predicate (a predicate which aids in the determination of a thing) resists almost all the endeavors of explanation and illustration. A *logical predicate* may be what you please, even the subject may be predicated of itself; for logic pays no regard to the content of a judgment. But the determination of a conception is a predicate, which adds to and enlarges the conception. It must not, therefore, be contained in the conception.

Being is evidently not a real predicate, that is, a conception of something which is added to the conception of some other thing. It is merely the positing of a thing, or of certain determinations in it. Logically, it is merely the copula of a judgment. The proposition, *God is omnipotent,* contains two conceptions, which have a certain object or content; the word *is,* is no additional predicate—it merely indicates the relation of the predicate to the subject. Now, if I take the subject (God) with all its predicates (omnipotence being one), and say, *God is,* or, *There is a God,* I add no new predicate to the conception of God, I merely posit or affirm the existence of the subject with all its predicates—I posit the *object* in relation to my *conception.* The content of both is the same; and there is no addition made to the conception, which expresses merely the possibility of the object, by my cogitating the object—in the expression, it *is*—as absolutely given or existing. Thus the real contains no more than the possible. A hundred real dollars contain no more than a hundred possible dollars. For, as the latter indicate the conception, and the former the object, on the supposition that the content of the former was greater than that of the latter, my conception would not be an expression of the whole object, and would consequently be an inadequate conception of it. But in reckoning my wealth there may be said to be more in a hundred real dollars, than in a hundred possible dollars—that is, in the mere conception of them. For the real object—the dollars—is not analytically contained in my conception, but forms a synthetical addition to my conception (which is merely a determination of my mental state), although this objective reality—this existence—apart from my conception, does not in the least degree increase the aforesaid hundred dollars.

By whatever and by whatever number of predicates—even to the complete determination of it—I may cogitate a thing I do not in the least augment the object of my conception by the addition of the statement, this thing exists. Otherwise, not exactly the same, but something more than what was cogitated in my conception, would exist, and I could not affirm that the exact object of my conception had real existence. If I cogitate a thing as containing all modes of reality except one, the mode of reality which is absent is not added to the conception of the thing by the affirmation that the thing exists; on the contrary, the thing exists—if it exist at all—with the same defect as that cogitated in its conception; otherwise not that which was cogitated, but something different, exists. Now, if I cogitate a being as the highest reality, without defect or imperfection, the question still remains—whether this being exists or not? For although no element is wanting in the possible real content of my conception, there is a defect in its relation to my mental state, that is, I am ignorant whether the cognition of the object indicated by the conception is possible à *posteriori*. And here the cause of the present difficulty becomes apparent. If the question regarded an object of sense merely, it would be impossible for me to confound the conception with the existence of a thing. For the conception merely enables me to cogitate an object as according with the general conditions of experience; while the existence of the object permits me to cogitate it as contained in the sphere of actual experience. At the same time, this connection with the world of experience does not in the least augment the conception, although a possible perception has been added to the experience of the mind. But if we cogitate existence by the pure category alone, it is not to be wondered at, that we should find ourselves unable to present any criterion sufficient to distinguish it from mere possibility.

Whatever be the content of our conception of an object, it is necessary to go beyond it, if we wish to predicate existence of the object. In the case of sensuous objects, this is attained by their connection according to empirical laws with some one of my perceptions; but there is no means of cognizing the existence of objects of pure thought, because it must be cognized completely *à priori*. But all our knowledge of existence (be it immediately by perception, or by inferences connecting some object with a perception) belongs entirely to the sphere of experience—which is in perfect unity with itself—and although an existence out of this sphere cannot be absolutely declared to be impossible, it is a hypothesis the truth of which we have no means of ascertaining.

The notion of a supreme being is in many respects a highly useful idea; but for the very reason that it is an idea, it is incapable of enlarging our cognition with regard to the existence of things. It is not even sufficient to instruct us as to the possibility of a being which we do not know to exist. The analytical criterion of possibility, which consists in the absence of contradiction in propositions, cannot be denied it. But the connection of real properties in a thing is a synthesis of the possibility of which an *à priori* judgment cannot be formed, because these realities are not presented to us specifically; and even if this were to happen, a judgment would still be impossible, because the criterion of the possibility of synthetical cognitions must be sought for in the world of experience, to which the object of an idea cannot belong. And thus the celebrated Leibnitz has utterly failed in his attempt to establish upon *à priori* grounds the possibility of this sublime ideal being.

The celebrated ontological or Cartesian argument for the existence of a Supreme Being is therefore insufficient; and we may as well hope to increase our stock of knowledge by the aid of mere ideas, as the merchant to augment his wealth by the addition of noughts to his cash-account.

3

FIVE PROOFS OF
GOD'S EXISTENCE*

*Thomas Aquinas (1226–1274) was a
scholar and university teacher of the
Dominican order whose Christianized
version of Aristotelianism has become
virtually the official philosophy of the
Roman Catholic Church and the classical
expression of the philosophic tradition
which bears his name. His principal
works are:* Summa Theologica *and*
Summa Contra Gentiles *in which he
expounds and defends his philosophical theology.*

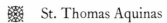 St. Thomas Aquinas

THE EXISTENCE OF GOD CAN BE PROVED IN FIVE WAYS

THE first and more manifest way is the argument from motion. It is
certain, and evident to our senses, that in the world some things are
in motion. Now whatever is moved is moved by another, for
nothing can be moved except it is in potentiality to that towards
which it is moved; whereas a thing moves inasmuch as it is in act.
For motion is nothing else than the reduction of something from
potentiality to actuality. But nothing can be reduced from potentiality to actuality, except by something in a state of actuality. Thus
that which is actually hot, as fire, makes wood, which is potentially
hot, to be actually hot, and thereby moves and changes it. Now it is
not possible that the same thing should be at once in actuality and
potentiality in the same respect, but only in different respects. For
what is actually hot cannot simultaneously be potentially hot; but
it is simultaneously potentially cold. It is therefore impossible that
in the same respect and in the same way a thing should be both
mover and moved, *i.e.*, that it should move itself. Therefore,

* From *Basic Writings of St. Thomas Aquinas*, ed. by Anton C. Pegis, copyright
1945 by Random House, Inc., and St. Thomas Aquinas, *Summa Contra Gentiles*,
tr. by the English Dominican Fathers. Reprinted by permission of Random
House, Inc., and The English Dominicans, and Burns, Oates & Washbourne, Ltd.

whatever is moved must be moved by another. If that by which it is moved be itself moved, then this also must needs be moved by another, and that by another again. But this cannot go on to infinity, because then there would be no first mover, and, consequently, no other mover, seeing that subsequent movers move only inasmuch as they are moved by the first mover; as the staff moves only because it is moved by the hand. Therefore it is necessary to arrive at a first mover, moved by no other; and this everyone understands to be God.

The second way is from the nature of efficient cause. In the world of sensible things we find there is an order of efficient causes. There is no case known (neither is it, indeed, possible) in which a thing is found to be the efficient cause of itself; for so it would be prior to itself, which is impossible. Now in efficient causes it is not possible to go on to infinity, because in all efficient causes following in order, the first is the cause of the intermediate cause, and the intermediate is the cause of the ultimate cause, whether the intermediate cause be several, or one only. Now to take away the cause is to take away the effect. Therefore, if there be no first cause among efficient causes, there will be no ultimate, nor any intermediate, cause. But if in efficient causes it is possible to go on to infinity, there will be no first efficient cause, neither will there be an ultimate effect, nor any intermediate efficient causes; all of which is plainly false. Therefore it is necessary to admit a first efficient cause, to which everyone gives the name of God.

The third way is taken from possibility and necessity, and runs thus. We find in nature things that are possible to be and not to be, since they are found to be generated, and to be corrupted, and consequently, it is possible for them to be and not to be. But it is impossible for these always to exist, for that which can not-be at some time is not. Therefore, if everything can not-be, then at one time there was nothing in existence. Now if this were true, even now there would be nothing in existence, because that which does not exist begins to exist only through something already existing. Therefore, if at one time nothing was in existence, it would have been impossible for anything to have begun to exist; and thus even now nothing would be in existence—which is absurd. Therefore, not all beings are merely possible, but there must exist something the existence of which is necessary. But every necessary thing either has its necessity caused by another, or not. Now it is impossible to go on to infinity in necessary things which have their necessity caused by another, as has been already proved in regard to efficient causes. Therefore we cannot but admit the existence of some being having of itself its own necessity, and not receiving it from another, but rather causing in others their necessity. This all men speak of as God.

The fourth way is taken from the gradation to be found in things. Among beings there are some more and some less good, true, noble, and the like. But *more* and *less* are predicated of different things according as they resemble in their different ways something which is the maximum, as a thing is said to be hotter according as it more nearly resembles that which is hottest; so that there is something which is truest, something best, something noblest, and, consequently, something which is most being, for those things that are greatest in truth are greatest in being, as it is written in *Metaph.* ii.[1] Now the maximum in any genus is the cause of all in that genus, as fire, which is the maximum of heat, is the cause of all hot things, as is said in the same book.[2] Therefore there must also be something which is to all beings the cause of their being, goodness, and every other perfection; and this we call God.

The fifth way is taken from the governance of the world. We see that things which lack knowledge, such as natural bodies, act for an end, and this is evident from their acting always, or nearly always, in the same way, so as to obtain the best result. Hence it is plain that they achieve their end, not fortuitously, but designedly. Now whatever lacks knowledge cannot move towards an end, unless it be directed by some being endowed with knowledge and intelligence; as the arrow is directed by the archer. Therefore some intelligent being exists by whom all natural things are directed to their end; and this being we call God.

· · ·

HAVING shown then that it is not futile to endeavour to prove the existence of God, we may proceed to set forth the reasons whereby both philosophers and Catholic doctors have proved that there is a God. In the first place we shall give the arguments by which Aristotle sets out to prove God's existence: and he aims at proving this from the point of view of movement, in two ways.

The *first way* is as follows.[3] Whatever is in motion is moved by another: and it is clear to the sense that something, the sun for instance, is in motion. Therefore it is set in motion by something else moving it. Now that which moves it is itself either moved or not. If it be not moved, then the point is proved that we must needs postulate an immovable mover: and this we call God. If, however, it be moved, it is moved by another mover. Either, therefore, we must proceed to infinity, or we must come to an immovable mover. But it

1 *Metaph.* Ia, 1 (993b 30) .   2 *Ibid.* (993b 25) .   3 7 *Phys.* i.

is not possible to proceed to infinity. Therefore it is necessary to postulate an immovable mover.

This argument contains two propositions that need to be proved: namely that *whatever is in motion is moved by another,* and that *it is not possible to proceed to infinity in movers and things moved.*

The first of these is proved by the Philosopher in *three ways. First,* thus. If a thing moves itself, it must needs have the principle of its movement in itself, else it would clearly be moved by another. Again it must be *moved primarily,* that is, it must be moved by reason of itself and not by reason of its part, as an animal is moved by the movement of its foot, for in the latter way not the whole but the part would be moved by itself, and one part by another. Again it must be divisible and have parts, since whatever is moved is divisible, as is proved in 6 *Phys.*[1]

These things being supposed, he argues as follows. That which is stated to be moved by itself is moved primarily. Therefore if one of its parts is at rest, it follows that the whole is at rest. For if, while one part is at rest, another of its parts were in motion, the whole itself would not be moved primarily, but its part which is in motion while another is at rest. Now nothing that is at rest while another is at rest, is moved by itself: For that which is at rest as a result of another thing being at rest must needs be in motion as a result of the other's motion, and hence it is not moved by itself. Hence that which was stated to be moved by itself, is not moved by itself. Therefore whatever is in motion must needs be moved by another.

Nor is this argument traversed by the statement that might be made, that supposing a thing moves itself, it is impossible for a part thereof to be at rest, or again by the statement that to be at rest or in motion does not belong to a part except accidentally, as Avicenna quibbles.[2] Because the force of the argument lies in this, that if a thing moves itself primarily and of itself, not by reason of its parts, it follows that its being moved does not depend on some thing; whereas with a divisible thing, being moved, like being, depends on its parts, so that it cannot move itself primarily and of itself. Therefore the truth of the conclusion drawn does not require that we suppose as an absolute truth that a part of that which moves itself is at rest, but that this conditional statement be true that *if a part were at rest,* the whole would be at rest. Which statement can be true even if the antecedent be false, even as this conditional proposition is true: *If a man is an ass he is irrational.*

[1] Ch. iv.   [2] 2 *Suffic.* i.

Secondly,[1] he proves it by induction, thus. A thing is not moved by itself if it is moved accidentally, since its motion is occasioned by the motion of something else. Nor again if it is moved by force, as is manifest. Nor if it is moved by its nature like those things whose movement proceeds from themselves, such as animals, which clearly are moved by their souls. Nor if it is moved by nature, as heavy and light things are, since these are moved by their generating cause and by that which removes the obstacle to their movement. Now whatsoever things are in motion are moved either *per se* or accidentally; and if *per se,* either by force or by nature: and if the latter, either by something in them, as in the case of animals, or not by something in them, as in the case of heavy and light bodies. Therefore whatever is in motion is moved by another.

Thirdly,[2] he proves his point thus. Nothing is at the same time in act and in potentiality in respect of the same thing. Now whatever is in motion, as such, is in potentiality, because motion is *the act of that which is in potentiality, as such*.[3] Whereas whatever moves, as such, is in act, for nothing acts except in so far as it is in act. Therefore nothing is both mover and moved in respect of the same movement. Hence nothing moves itself.

We must observe, however, that Plato,[4] who asserted that every mover is moved, employed the term *movement* in a more general sense than Aristotle. For Aristotle took movement in its strict sense, for the act of a thing that is in potentiality as such, in which sense it applies only to divisible things and bodies, as is proved in 6 *Phys.*[5] Whereas according to Plato that which moves itself is not a body; for he took movement for any operation, so that to understand or to think is a kind of movement, to which manner of speaking Aristotle alludes in 3 *De Anima.*[6] In this sense, then, he said that the first mover moves itself, in as much as it understands, desires and loves itself. This, in a certain respect, is not in contradiction with the arguments of Aristotle; for it makes no difference whether with Plato we come to a first mover that moves itself, or with Aristotle to something first which is altogether immovable.

He proves the other proposition, namely that *it is impossible to proceed to infinity in movers and things moved,* by three arguments.

The *first*[7] of these is as follows. If one were to proceed to infinity in movers and things moved, all this infinite number of things would necessarily be bodies, since whatever is moved is divisible and corporeal, as is proved in 6 *Phys.*[8] Now every body

---

1 8 *Phys.* iv.   2 8 *Phys.* v. 8.   3 3 *Phys.* i. 6.   4 *Phædrus* § xxiv. (D.).
5 *L.c.*   6 Ch. vii.   7 7 *Phys., l.c.*   8 *L.c.*

that moves through being moved is moved at the same time as it moves. Therefore all this infinite number of things are moved at the same time as one of them is moved. But one of them, since it is finite, is moved in a finite time. Therefore all this infinite number of things are moved in a finite time. But this is impossible. Therefore it is impossible to proceed to infinity in movers and things moved.

That it is impossible for the aforesaid infinite number of things to be moved in a finite time, he proves thus.[1] Mover and moved must needs be simultaneous; and he proves this by induction from each species of movement. But bodies cannot be simultaneous except by continuity or contact. Wherefore since all the aforesaid movers and things moved are bodies, as proved, they must needs be as one movable thing through their continuity or contact. And thus one infinite thing would be moved in a finite time, which is shown to be impossible in 6 *Phys.*[2]

The *second argument*[3] in proof of the same statement is as follows. In an ordinate series of movers and things moved, where namely throughout the series one is moved by the other, we must needs find that if the first mover be taken away or cease to move, none of the others will move or be moved: because the first is the cause of movement in all the others. Now if an ordinate series of movers and things moved proceed to infinity, there will be no first mover, but all will be intermediate movers as it were. Therefore it will be impossible for any of them to be moved: and thus nothing in the world will be moved.

The *third argument*[4] amounts to the same, except that it proceeds in the reverse order, namely by beginning from above: and it is as follows. That which moves instrumentally, cannot move unless there be something that moves principally. But if we proceed to infinity in movers and things moved, they will all be like instrumental movers, because they will be alleged to be moved movers, and there will be nothing by way of principal mover. Therefore nothing will be moved.

We have thus clearly proved both statements which were supposed in the first process of demonstration whereby Aristotle proved the existence of a *first immovable mover.*

The *second*[5] *way* is as follows. If every mover is moved, this statement is true either in itself or accidentally. If accidentally, it follows that it is not necessary: for that which is accidentally true is not necessary. Therefore it is a contingent proposition that no mover is moved. But if a mover be not moved, it does not move, as the opponent asserts. Therefore it is contingent that nothing is

---

[1] 7 *Phys.* i. ii. [2] Ch. vii. [3] 8 *Phys.* v. [4] *Ibid.* [5] *Ibid.*

moved, since, if nothing moves, nothing is moved. Now Aristotle holds this to be impossible,[1] namely, that at any time there be no movement. Therefore the first proposition was not contingent, because a false impossibility does not follow from a false contingency. And therefore this proposition, *Every mover is moved by another*, was not accidentally true.

Again, if any two things are found accidentally united in a certain subject, and one of them is to be found without the other, it is probable that the latter can be found without the former: thus if *white* and *musical* are found in Socrates, and *musical* without *white* is found in Plato, it is probable that it is possible to find *white* without *musical* in some subject. Accordingly if mover and moved be united together in some subject accidentally, and it be found that a certain thing is moved without its being a mover, it is probable that a mover is to be found that is not moved. Nor can one urge against this the case of two things one of which depends on the other; because those in question are united not *per se* but accidentally. If, however, the aforesaid proposition is true in itself, again there follows something impossible or unfitting. For the mover must needs be moved either by the same kind of movement or by another kind. If by the same kind, it follows that whatever causes alteration must itself be altered, and furthermore that the healer must be healed, that the teacher must be taught, and in respect of the same science. But this is impossible: for the teacher must needs have science, while the learner must needs not have it, and thus the same will be both possessed and not possessed by the same, which is impossible. And if it be moved by another kind of movement, so that, to wit, that which causes alteration be moved in respect of place, and that which moves in respect of place be increased, and so on, it will follow that we cannot go on indefinitely, since the genera and species of movement are finite in number. And thus there will be some first mover that is not moved by another. Unless, perchance, someone say that a recurrence takes place, in this way, that when all the genera and species of movement have been exhausted, a return must be made to the first; for instance, if that which moves in respect of place be altered, and that which causes alteration be increased, then again that which is increased be moved in respect of place. But the consequence of this will be the same as before; namely, that which moves by one kind of movement is itself moved by the same kind, not immediately indeed but mediately. It remains therefore that *we must needs postulate some first mover that is not moved by anything outside itself*.

Since however, given that there is a first mover that is not moved by anything outside itself, it does not follow that it is

[1] 8 *Phys.* i.

absolutely immovable, Aristotle proceeds further, saying that this may happen in two ways. First, so that this first mover is absolutely immovable. And if this be granted, our point is established, namely that there is a first immovable mover. Secondly, that this first mover is moved by itself. And this seems probable: because what is of itself is always prior to what is of another: wherefore also in things moved, it is logical that what is moved first is moved by itself and not by another.

But, if this be granted, the same consequence follows.[1] For it cannot be said that the whole of that which moves itself is moved by its whole self, because then the absurd consequences mentioned above would follow, namely that a person might teach and be taught at the same time, and in like manner as to other kinds of movement; and again that a thing would be at the same time in act and in potentiality, since a mover, as such, is in act, while that which is moved is in potentiality. It remains, therefore, that one part thereof is mover only, and the other part moved. And thus we have the same conclusion as before, namely that there is something that moves and is itself immovable.

And it cannot be said that both parts are moved, so that one is moved by the other; nor that one part moves both itself and the other; nor that the whole moves a part; nor that part moves the whole, since the above absurdities would follow, namely that something would both move and be moved by the same kind of movement, and that it would be at the same time in potentiality and in act, and moreover that the whole would move itself not primarily but by reason of its part. It remains, therefore, that in that which moves itself, one part must be immovable, and must move the other part.

Since, however, in those things among us which move themselves, namely animals, the part which moves, namely the soul, though immovable of itself, is nevertheless moved accidentally, he goes on to show that in the first mover, the part which moves is not moved neither of itself nor accidentally.[2]

For in those things which among us move themselves, namely animals, since they are corruptible, the part which moves is moved accidentally. Now those corruptible things which move themselves must needs be reducible to some first self-mover that is everlasting. Therefore that which moves itself must have a mover, which is moved neither of itself nor accidentally.

It is clear that, in accordance with his hypothesis, some self-mover must be everlasting. For if, as he supposes, movement is everlasting, the production of these self-movers that are subject to generation and corruption must be everlasting. But no one of these

---

[1] 8 *Phys., l.c.*   [2] 8 *Phys.* vi.

self-movers, since it does not always exist, can be the cause of this everlastingness. Nor can all of them together, both because they would be infinite, and because they do not exist all together. It follows therefore that there must be an everlasting self-mover, that causes the everlastingness of generation in these lower self-movers. And thus its mover is not moved, neither of itself nor accidentally. Again, we observe that in self-movers some begin to be moved anew on account of some movement whereby the animal is not moved by itself, for instance by the digestion of food or a change in the atmosphere: by which movement the mover that moves itself is moved accidentally. Whence we may gather that no self-mover, whose mover is moved *per se* or accidentally, is always moved. But the first self-mover is always in motion, else movement could not be everlasting, since every other movement is caused by the movement of the first self-mover. It follows therefore that the first self-mover is moved by a mover who is not moved, neither *per se* nor accidentally.

Nor is this argument rebutted by the fact that the movers of the lower spheres cause an everlasting movement, and yet are said to be moved accidentally. For they are said to be moved accidentally not by reason of themselves, but by reason of the things subject to their motion, which follow the motion of the higher sphere.

Since, however, God is not part of a self-mover, Aristotle goes on in his *Metaphysics*[1] to trace from this motor that is part of a self-mover, another mover altogether separate, which is God. For since every self-mover is moved through its appetite, it follows that the motor that is part of a self-mover, moves on account of the appetite for some appetible object. And this object is above the motor in moving, because the appetent is a moved mover, whereas the appetible is a mover altogether unmoved. Therefore *there must needs be a first mover separate and altogether immovable,* and this is God.

Now two things would seem to weaken the above arguments. The *first* of these is that they proceed from the supposition of the eternity of movement, and among Catholics this is supposed to be false. To this we reply that the most effective way to prove God's existence is from the supposition of the eternity of the world, which being supposed, it seems less manifest that God exists. For if the world and movement had a beginning, it is clear that we must suppose some cause to have produced the world and movement, because whatever becomes anew must take its origin from some cause of its becoming, since nothing evolves itself from potentiality to act, or from non-being to being.

The *second* is that the aforesaid arguments suppose that the

[1] D. 11. vii.

first moved thing, namely the heavenly body, has its motive principle in itself, whence it follows that it is animated: and by many this is not granted.

To this we reply that if the first mover is not supposed to have its motive principle in itself, it follows that it is immediately moved by something altogether immovable. Hence also Aristotle draws this conclusion with an alternative, namely that either we must come at once to a first mover immovable and separate, or to a self-mover from which again we come to a first mover immovable and separate.[1]

The Philosopher proceeds in a *different way* in 2 *Metaph.* to show that it is impossible to proceed to infinity in efficient causes, and that we must come to one first cause, and this we call God. This is how he proceeds. In all efficient causes following in order, the first is the cause of the intermediate cause, and the intermediate is the cause of the ultimate, whether the intermediate be one or several. Now if the cause be removed, that which it causes is removed. Therefore if we remove the first the intermediate cannot be a cause. But if we go on to infinity in efficient causes, no cause will be first. Therefore all the others which are intermediate will be removed. Now this is clearly false. Therefore we must suppose *the existence of a first efficient cause:* and this is God.

Another reason can be drawn from the words of Aristotle. For in 2 *Metaph.*[2] he shows that those things which excel as true excel as beings: and in 4 *Metaph.*[3] he shows that there is something supremely true, from the fact that we see that of two false things one is falser than the other, wherefore it follows that one also is truer than the other. Now this is by reason of approximation to that which is simply and supremely true. Wherefore we may further conclude that *there is something that is supremely being.* And this we call God.

Another argument in support of this conclusion is adduced by Damascene[4] from the government of things: and the same reasoning is indicated by the Commentator in 2 *Phys.*[5] It runs as follows. It is impossible for contrary and discordant things to accord in one order always or frequently except by someone's governance, whereby each and all are made to tend to a definite end. Now we see that in the world things of different natures accord in one order, not seldom and fortuitously, but always or for the most part. Therefore it follows that there is *someone by whose providence the world is governed.* And this we call God.

---

[1] 8 *Phys.* v. 12.   [2] D. 1*a.* i. 5.   [3] D. 3. iv. 27, 28.   [4] *De Fide Orth.* i. 3.
[5] Text 75.

4

THE MORAL ARGUMENT*

Alfred E. Taylor (1869–1945) was Professor of Moral Philosophy in Edinburgh University from 1924 to 1941. He was a well-known Platonic scholar whose own philosophical leanings were toward idealism. His major writings include several works on Plato and Aristotle as well as The Faith of a Moralist, Does God Exist? *and* The Christian Hope of Immorality.

※ A. E. Taylor

As FAR as I can see, the systematic disregard of all "moral" arguments would only be possible to one who frankly takes the line that there *are* no moral facts, that is, that right and wrong are pure illusions; there are no such differences *in rerum natura*. But even those who in theory profess to hold this view always reveal to a little inspection that, being human, they do not really mean what they say. The denial that our accepted moral distinctions have any "objective validity" is alleged as a reason why we *ought* to be tolerant of violation of the current model code. I am told that I *ought* to make no complaint of a wife's infidelity because it is a baseless "superstition" to fancy that adultery—or anything else—is *wrong;* so *because* nothing whatever is wrong, *therefore* something— my moral disapproval of adultery, or untruthfulness, or ingratitude —*is* wrong. On the face of it this is self-contradictory—the man who says it really believes all the time in the existence of the distinction between right and wrong. Where he differs from the rest of us is only in holding that we put many things which are right in the class of wrong things, and put the thing he regards as particularly wrong—moral disapproval of conduct which he himself thinks right—in the class of right things. On his own showing there is at

* From A. E. Taylor, *Does God Exist?* Reprinted by permission of Macmillan & Co., Ltd.

least one genuine moral fact, the fact that "intolerance" is wrong.[1]

We may safely take it, then, that there are moral facts. They can be left out of account for the special purposes of the biologist, just as the fact that there are living organisms may be left unmentioned in a work on mechanics or physics. But life is as much a fact as gravitation, though the physicist cannot avoid talking about gravitation but need never mention life. Similarly the biologist is concerned with the fact that there is a distinction between the living and the lifeless, but never need refer to any distinction between right and wrong. Yet the two facts are equally facts, and any general theory about the universe which is to do justice to the "facts" must take both into account. It is as much the "nature of man" to be conscious of a difference between right and wrong as it is to be alive to a difference between male and female.[2]

Now what does this consciousness of a difference between right and wrong imply whenever it is felt? Plainly it implies that there is a way of living—the doing of the things we ought to do and the refusal to do the things we ought not to do—which is, in its own nature, the life we ought to lead, or the life which it is good to lead, as distinguished from other ways of life which are those which ought not to be followed, or which are bad. And in the end there is no reason why we ought to lead the life we ought to lead, or why it is good to lead that kind of life other than that this *is* how we ought to live, or how it *is* good to live. We cannot say "the reason why we ought to live thus, or why this kind of life is good is that it is a *means* to something else", because to say this raises the question "And why ought I to take the means to this result, or why is it good

[1] It would be no real reply to say that when the professed disbeliever in the reality of moral distinctions calls intolerance *wrong*, he is using the word *wrong* in a non-ethical sense of his own, and only means *e.g.* "not conducive to survival." The intolerance of a group with the will and the power to "eliminate" all who disagree with it may be highly conducive to the survival of the group, and the propagandist methods of our totalitarian dictators show that they are alive to the fact. Alternately the immoralist who calls intolerance *wrong* might conceivably only mean that it is a thing which he personally dislikes. But if he means no more than this, it is ridiculous in him to call on the rest of us to agree with him that it is wrong, that is, that *we* also dislike it. It will always be a complete answer to him to say "but *I* like intolerance quite well, and *de gustibus non est disputandum.*"

[2] It may be said that the first difference is perhaps only imagined, whereas the other is manifest to sight and touch. This would not be wholly true. The differences between man and woman are not confined to those glaring differences in configuration which can be directly detected by the senses; they extend to characteristic ways of thinking and feeling which do not disclose themselves thus grossly to the senses. We should rightly find fault with the "psychology" of a novelist whose women, though having the outward appearance of women, were made to feel and think like so many unbearded "men in women's clothes."

to take those means, rather than to take the quite different means to a quite different result?" Thus we are back again at the point from which we started, that there is something which ought to be done, or which it is good to do, *because* it ought to be done or is good to do. There is no getting away from "you ought simply because you ought".

This is just as true on a utilitarian theory of morality as on any other. If a man has persuaded himself that the only reason why he ought to be honest, truthful, chaste is that honesty, veracity, chastity are means to the promotion of human happiness, and that they have no value except as means to this result, the question still recurs, "But why ought I to promote human happiness, when I perhaps should prefer to go as I please without bothering about the effects of my conduct on the general happiness?" and to that question the Utilitarian can really only reply, "You ought to promote the general happiness because you ought, because it is the highest good." Even a *morality* of pure self-seeking is faced by the same problem. If you tell me that in the end the only reason why it is right for me to do some things and to avoid doing others is that by acting thus I shall secure my own happiness, it is open to me to retort that I do not set all this store by my own happiness—as R. L. Stevenson wrote, that mankind are partial to happiness is a statement which may be doubted—and that I do not see why I should. My egoistic Mentor could only give me the answer, "If you do not care about your own happiness, you *ought* to care about it." Kant's own account of the principle of morality may be open to criticism on more grounds than one, but on one fundamental point he is clearly right; any coherent theory of morality must presuppose what he calls a categorical imperative. It must assume that there is *something* which ought to be done for no other reason than that it ought to be done. To deny this would be tantamount to denying that there is any distinction whatever between right and wrong, and if you deny this, you can no longer have any theory of morality good or bad; you can only have a theory about the way in which the illusion that there is such a thing as morality has arisen. (Just as a man who denies that there can be such a thing as a witch can have no theory of witchcraft, or as one who denied that there is any sun or planets could have no theory of the solar system, though either might have theories about the way in which men have been deluded into fancying that there are witches or that there is a sun.)

What the sense of the difference between right and wrong implies, then, unless it is a pure delusion, is that there is something—the existence of persons living the life they ought to lead—which is of absolute worth, a good in itself and on its own account, and not merely as conducive to some further result whereto it is a mere means. And if this is true, an answer is suggested to our question whether there is anything to which the whole course of nature may stand as means to end. It would be a rational way of thinking to conceive of the whole system of nature as the means to a single end, the development and maintenance of intelligent and moral personalities, the only things known to us which have a worth which is both inherent and absolute.[1] If we can think thus of nature rightly, the singleness of the end to which the whole infinite complex of nature's processes are directed will be proof of the singleness of the directing intelligence they presuppose, and the coincidence of that end with the end of all moral action will be our warrant for ascribing goodness to that intelligence. We shall have replaced the plurality of possibly competing "departmental deities", which is perhaps all that the argument for "design in nature", taken by itself, would permit us to assert, by the "one God" of the great monotheistic religions.

To set the matter in the clearest light, let us consider two of the distinctive characteristics of our sense of right and wrong. (1) In the first place, the distinction between right and wrong is—if it exists at all—what the moralists of the seventeenth and eighteenth centuries called it—*immutable and eternal*. This does not mean that it may not be wrong for one man in one set of circumstances to do what it would be equally wrong for another man in different circumstances not to do; it may be wrong for *A,* who has a family to support by his own exertions, to contribute to public charities sums it would be wrong in *B,* who has ample "private means" and only himself to support, not to contribute; it may be wrong for the magistrate dealing with a rebellion against his necessary and legitimate authority, to treat the principal instigator of trouble with a lenience which it is no more than a duty to show to the rank and file of those whom the "rebel" has led astray. There may perhaps be no hard-and-fast rule which we can trust unreservedly to show us what line of action would certainly be right in the particular case; it is at least possible that *every* case may have unique features which

---

[1] It might be asked whether life itself, or at least sentient life, apart from intelligence or moral character, may not be the thing of inherent and absolute value, and the end of nature, if nature has an end. But the answer must pretty clearly be, NO. We are not destroying a thing of absolute value when we make a region of the earth a safe home for human beings by exterminating wild beasts and other "pests." To clear the country of wolves is no crime, though it would be a crime to make room for the civilized population by clearing the district in the same way of "savages." It is a crime to have extirpated the Tasmanians: it would not be one to have extinguished the "Tasmanian devil." It is one thing to treat rattlesnakes as "pizun," quite another to treat "Injuns" in the same fashion.

make it necessary to consider it on "its own merits". At least, we may concede so much for the purposes of our present argument. But when all this has been granted, it remains an integral part of what we mean by distinction between right and wrong, that the distinction is valid independently of the thoughts and wishes of any of us. If a man asks me now—I having the resources I have, and the claims on me being what they are, and he being in the situation in which he actually is and intending to apply the gift as he does intend—for a gift of a certain sum of money, it may be right to grant his request, or it may not; but if it is right, then it remains right whether I happen to think it so or not. If it is wrong for me to do a certain act, I may be a morally indifferent person and so never reflect that the act is wrong, or I may be mistaken and actually believe that the act in question is right, but my ignorance or my error makes no difference to the fact that what I am doing is really wrong. Still less do my wishes affect the moral character of the act. If it is right, no wish of mine to the contrary could make it wrong; and if it is wrong, no wishing that it were not wrong will make it anything but wrong. Just so, if a certain line is crooked, it is crooked, and though I may very possibly not remark this, or may even think that the line is straight, or may wish that it were straight, it is none the less crooked for all that.

(2) Again, it is universally characteristic of the sense of right and wrong that it is attended, as Butler puts it, with a consciousness of good or ill *desert*, merit or demerit. There are, indeed, difficult problems connected with this notion of *desert* which I must be content here merely to indicate without any attempt to solve them. It is hard sometimes to say of the "deserving" exactly what they deserve and at whose hands they deserve it. We commonly say that a man who is in business and is habitually industrious, honest and obliging "deserves to get on". Yet an undertaker carrying on business in a district where the inhabitants are healthy and long-lived may be "deserving" on all these grounds, but is not likely to make much of a living by his profession, and we should hesitate to say that he "deserves" a rise in the local mortality from disease or accident, though it may well be that his prosperity depends on it. No degree of honesty, industry, ability is likely to make the legal profession a source of prosperity anywhere where the public at large are so honest that neighbours make no attempt to take advantage of one another, so intelligent that when conflicts of interest arise, they readily see for themselves what arrangement will be fair to all parties, and so fraternal that they prefer amicable settlement of disputes, even with some personal loss, to resort to the courts. Yet we can hardly suggest that the deserving man of law deserves that

his neighbours shall be stupid, grasping and litigious. I could not with a straight face tell a healthy and peaceable man, "A. B. the undertaker deserves that you should die this winter," or "C. D. the barrister that you should start a long and expensive suit against E. F." If a man is deserving, there must be something in particular which he deserves and someone at whose hands he deserves it, and yet it seems plain that it would often be hard to say what is that *something* or who is that *somebody*.

Yet these difficulties do not affect the main point which Butler has in mind in what he says about desert.[1] It is true, as he says, that in our judgements upon ourselves we do pronounce ourselves to have in some way deserved ill when we have done ill. If the consequences of our misdeeds are calamitous, we recognize that we are not entitled to complain, or to look for the same sympathy we might reasonably expect if the same misfortune had befallen us without any contributory fault of our own. To expand one of Butler's own remarks, if one man is disinherited by some senile freak of the relative who had encouraged him to expect an inheritance, and a second as the consequence of folly, dissipation or ingratitude persisted in after due warning, the same pinch of need may be equally felt by both, but only the second has the added and peculiar bitterness of knowing that he has brought the need on himself by his own misdoing. Nor, as it is important to add, is there any necessary connection between this "sense of ill-desert" which attends conscious wrong-doing and the spirit of vindictiveness towards themselves, but it is just in the case of my own misdeeds that my sense of ill-desert is keenest: it is much easier to persuade myself about some other offender that he does not deserve all that his misconduct has brought upon him. At bottom what we all feel is, I take it, this: there is one source of pain of which we can always say that it is merited by a morally evil will; the man who wills evil always deserves that his evil will should be in the end frustrated, whereas the man who wills what is morally right, though he may

---

1 "This approbation and disapprobation are altogether different from mere desire of our own, or of their happiness, and from sorrow upon missing it. For the object or occasion of this last kind of perception is satisfaction or uneasiness, whereas the object of the first is active behaviour. In one case, what our thoughts fix upon is our own condition; in the other, our conduct." ". . . men often say of themselves with remorse, and of others with some indignation, that they deserve to suffer for such calamities, because they brought them upon themselves, and would not take warning. Particularly when persons come to poverty and distress by a long course of extravagance . . . we plainly do not regard such people as a like object of compassion with those, who are brought into the same condition by unavoidable accident."—"Dissertation upon the Nature of Virtue" appended to the *Analogy*.

not deserve to be rewarded with length of days or wealth, always deserves that his rightful will, because it is rightful, shall in the end take effect. It would not, so far as I can see, offend our moral sense that the course of history is not so controlled that every morally evil volition shall "get its due" in the shape of so much torture by fire and brimstone, or the like; indeed, we may perhaps think that the whole conception of an equivalence of so much discomfort to just such-and-such a degree of moral obliquity is preposterous. But it would, I believe, shock any man's moral sense to find that the world is so constituted that the man who wills evil in the end "gets his wicked will". What is "due" to the morally bad will is frustration, and frustration more or less complete as the volition itself is more or less perverted. And similarly, what is due to the good will is fulfil-ment more or less complete as the volition is itself more or less good. And these are the purposes which we should count on finding fulfilled in the history of the universe, if nature itself has an end, and that end is the personal good life.

If so much is true, consider what follows. The law of right, we say, is eternally valid, unless our moral convictions are founded on mere illusion. But can a law be valid except by reference to an intelligence which recognizes and upholds it? Yet the human intel-ligences which are the only intelligences with which we are directly acquainted have taken a long time to reach such apprehension of the moral law as they possess; its leading principles have only dawned upon them very gradually and are still far from being universally recognized, and even those of us who admit them in theory in moments of calm are constantly disregarding them in practice, when our passions are stirred, or what we think to be our interest is at stake. As we know that there are many moral obliga-tions to which our own society has only become alive in our own lifetime, so I suppose, we all hope that our successors will be con-scious of obligations which have not yet dawned on ourselves, and sensible of faults which we perpetrate to-day without any conscious-ness that they are faults. Yet those demands of the law of right which we have not yet discovered are none the less requirements and our neglect of them none the less a fault because of our blindness. And a law cannot hold *in vacuo*. There could be no law of gravitation and no laws of motion if there were nothing which gravitated or moved, no laws of chemical combination if there were not a plurality of chemical elements. So there could be no law for the right direction of the will if there were no wills to direct. But were there no will in existence except the wills of human beings, who are so often ignorant of the law of right and so often defy it, it is not apparent what the *validity* of the law could mean. Recognition of the validity of the law thus seems to carry with it a reference to an intelligence which has not, like our own, to make acquaintance with it piecemeal, slowly and with difficulty, but has always been in full and clear possession of it, and a will which does not, like our own, often set it at nought, but is guided by it in all its operations.[1]

Consider again that if reflection on the character of the moral law leads us to believe that nature as a whole serves a moral purpose (the development of moral personalities) and that purpose is one that is attained, we may fairly draw some important conclusions about the knowledge and power of the intelligence whose purpose this is. It, or He, as you will, must from the first know the whole system of nature in its minutest detail, so that nothing can take Him by surprise, and He must also, since the end is the fulfilment or frustration of every volition of every one of us according to its moral worth, be able directly to read the inmost secrets of all hearts; He must know not only what I do or say, but what I will, or even wish, to do or say, even though the actual speech or deed does not follow. And He must have such sovereign control of all that happens in nature that every detail contributes to the realization of the supreme purpose. There must be no possibility that anything in nature can deflect the achievement of this purpose by a hair's breadth; so much follows at once from the admission that this is *the* purpose for which nature exists. It follows, does it not, that the supreme moral intelligence must be not merely in sovereign control of the course of nature, but must be the actual originator of nature and everything that nature contains, author, as the scholastic phrase ran, of form and matter alike? For to say less than this amounts to saying not that nature *exists* for this end, but only that it is an end to which a nature which exists for some other end, or for none at all, has been put. Hence if the implications of the moral law are what Kant, and though less explicitly Butler, take them to be, consideration of it leads us not merely to an acknowledgement of "one God" but of "one God . . . almighty, creator of heaven and earth and of all things visible and invisible".

[1] See the fuller elaboration of this thought in W. R. Sorley, *Moral Values and the Idea of God* (ch. 13, "The Moral Argument"), to which I am deeply indebted here. I do not think the force of Professor Sorley's (and my own) contention is seriously affected by anything that is contained in Professor Laird's *Mind and Deity* (chs. 7 and 8), though I should wish my reader to weigh what is said there carefully.

5

FROM THE SENSES
TO GOD*

*Richard Taylor (1919–   ) is Professor
of Philosophy at Brown University. He
is the author of several articles on metaphysics as well as the book,* Metaphysics,
from which this selection is taken.

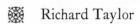   Richard Taylor

CHANCE AND EVIDENCE

THE idea we want to develop here is not easy to grasp without
misunderstanding, so it will be best to approach it stepwise by
considering first an example or two that should make it quite
obvious.

Suppose, then, that you are riding in a railway coach and
glancing from the window at one of the stops, you see numerous
white stones scattered about on a small hillside near the train in a
pattern resembling these letters: THE BRITISH RAILWAYS WELCOMES YOU
TO WALES. Now you could scarcely doubt that theses stones do not
just accidentally happen to exhibit that pattern. You would, in fact,
feel quite certain that they were purposefully *arranged* that way to
convey an intelligible message. At the same time, however, you
could not prove, just from a consideration of their arrangement
alone, that they were arranged by a purposeful being. It is possible—at least logically so—that there was no guiding hand at all in
back of this pattern, that it is simply the result of the operations of
inanimate nature. It is possible that the stones, one by one, rolled
down the hill and, over the course of centuries, finally ended up in
that interesting arrangement, or that they came in some other
accidental way to be so related to each other. For surely the mere
fact that something has an interesting or striking shape or pattern,
and thus *seems* purposefully arranged, is no proof that it is. There
might always be some other explanation. Snowflakes, viewed under
magnification, exhibit symmetrical, interesting and often beautiful

shapes, and yet we know that these are not designed but can be explained simply in terms of the physics of crystallization. We find *apparently* purposeful arrangements and contrivances around us all the time, but we cannot always conclude that these are in fact the expressions of any purpose. Our own bodies and their organs seem purposeful not only in their individual structures but in their relationships to each other, and yet there are well known theories, resting on such nonpurposeful concepts as chance variation, natural selection, and so on, which are able, at least in the opinion of many learned men, to explain these structures without introducing any ideas of purpose and design at all.

Here, however, is the important point which it is easy to overlook; namely, that *if,* upon seeing from the train window a group of stones arranged as described, you were to conclude that you were entering Wales, and *if* your sole reason for thinking this, whether it was in fact good evidence or not, was that the stones were so arranged, *then* you could not, consistently with that, suppose that the arrangement of the stones was accidental. You would, in fact, be presupposing that they were arranged that way by an intelligent and purposeful being or beings, for the purpose of conveying a certain message having nothing to do with the stones themselves. Another way of expressing the same point is, that it would be *irrational* for you to regard the arrangement of the stones as evidence that you were entering Wales, and at the same time to suppose that they might have come to have that arrangement accidentally, that is, as the result of the ordinary interactions of natural or physical forces. If, for instance, they came to be so arranged over the course of time, simply by rolling down the hill, one by one, and finally just happening to end up that way, or if they were strewn upon the ground that way by the forces of an earthquake or storm or whatnot, then their arrangement would in no sense constitute evidence that you were entering Wales, or for anything whatever unconnected with themselves.

Consider another example. Suppose a stone were dug up and found to be covered with interesting marks, all more or less the same size and more or less in rows. Now there is nothing very remarkable about that. Glaciers and volcanoes have produced stones no less interesting, in abundance. They may at first sight seem purposefully fabricated, but a geologist who knows how they came to be there can usually explain their interesting shapes and properties. Suppose further, however, that the marks on this stone are found to resemble the characters of an ancient alphabet. This, too, does not prove that they were purposefully inscribed, for natural forces can leave such marks as these on stones, and over the course of millions of years it is entirely possible that this should occasionally happen. There are places where one can, at will, pick up stones that are almost perfect rectangles and look exactly as though they were hewn by stonecutters, though in fact they resulted from glaciation. But now suppose that these marks are recognized by a scholar having a knowledge of that alphabet, and that with considerable uncertainty due to the obscurity of some of the marks and the obliteration of others, he renders a translation of them as follows: HERE KIMON FELL LEADING A BAND OF ATHENIANS AGAINST THE FORCES OF XERXES. Now one can, to be sure, still maintain that the marks are accidental, that they are only scratches left by volcanic activity, and that it is only a singular coincidence that they resemble, more or less, some intelligible message. Nature sometimes produces effects hardly less interesting and arresting than this. The point to make again, however, is this: if anyone having a knowledge of this stone concludes, solely on the basis of it, that there was someone named Kimon who died in battle near where this stone was found, then he cannot, rationally, suppose that the marks on the stone are the result of the chance or purposeless operations of the forces of nature. He must, on the contrary, assume that they were inscribed there by someone whose purpose was to record an historical fact. If the marks had a purposeless origin, as from volcanic activity or whatnot, then they cannot reveal any fact whatever except, perhaps, certain facts about themselves or their origin. It would, accordingly, be irrational for anyone to suppose *both* that what is seemingly expressed by the marks is true, and *also* that they appeared as the result of nonpurposeful forces, provided the marks are his *sole* evidence for believing that what they seem to say is true.

SENSATION AND EVIDENCE

OUR own organs of sense, to say nothing of our brains and nervous systems, are things of the most amazing and bewildering complexity and delicacy. No matter how far and minutely psychologists and physiologists press their studies of these organs, they seem hardly any closer to a real understanding of them, and how they enable us to *perceive* the world around us. At best they discover only how they convey stimuli and impress physical changes upon the brain. Theories of perception, drawing upon all the scientific and physiological knowledge accumulated to date, are hardly less crude than the speculations of the Greeks.

Some of these organs, moreover, strikingly resemble things purposefully designed and fabricated by men, though they greatly exceed in their delicacy and versatility anything men have invented. The parts and structure of the eye, for example, closely resemble those of a camera. Yet the comparison of these, however striking, is superficial, for the eye does not take pictures. Unlike a camera, it somehow enables its possessor to perceive and thereby to understand. Things like this can be more or less imitated by men, but they are usually crude and makeshift in comparison. It is sometimes almost irresistible, when considering such a thing as the eye, to suppose that, however it may have originated, it is constructed in that manner *in order* to enable its possessor to see. Many persons quite naturally think in these terms, without at all realizing the implications of such purposeful or teleological conceptions.

It must be noted, however, that just as it is possible for a collection of stones to present a novel and interesting arrangement on the side of a hill, and for marks to appear on a stone in a manner closely resembling some human artifact, and for these things still to be the accidental results of natural, nonpurposeful forces, so also it is possible for such things as our own organs of sense to be the accidental and unintended results, over ages of time, of perfectly impersonal, nonpurposeful forces. In fact, ever so many biologists believe that this is precisely what has happened, that our organs of sense are in no real sense purposeful things, but only appear so because of our failure to consider how they might have arisen through the normal workings of nature. It is supposed, for example, that if we apply the conceptions of chance mutations and variations, natural selection, and so on, then we can see how it is at least possible—perhaps even almost inevitable—that things of this sort should finally emerge, without any purpose behind them at all.

It would be astonishing indeed if a quantity of stones were hurled into the air and fell to earth in a pattern spelling out some intelligible message. Any man would feel, quite irresistibly, that it had been somehow *arranged* that they should fall that way. It would be less astonishing, however, if those stones were thrown a million times, and sooner or later fell to earth in such a pattern. Our astonishment would be still less if we found some perfectly natural, nonpurposeful explanation why they might sooner or later fall in that manner and, having so fallen, be thus preserved. If, for instance, we found that the stones were of slightly different weights, sizes and shapes, that these influenced how they were thrown and how they rolled upon landing, that these slight differences tended to favor the likelihood that certain ones would come to rest in the striking manner in which they do come to rest, and that certain obstructions on the ground would tend to preserve them in this arrangement, and so on, then we might find it entirely plausible how they might fall as they do without the intervention of any purposeful being at all. If our explanation were of this kind, however, then, as noted before, their arrangement would constitute no evidence whatever for anything not causally connected with themselves.

The mere complexity, refinement and seemingly purposeful arrangement of our sense organs do not, accordingly, constitute any conclusive reason for supposing that they are the outcome of any purposeful activity. A natural, nonpurposeful explanation of them is possible, and has been attempted—successfully, in the opinion of many.

The important point, however, and one that is rarely considered is that we do not simply *marvel* at these structures, and wonder how they came to be that way. We do not simply view them as amazing and striking things, and speculate upon their origins. We, in fact, whether justifiably or not, *rely* on them for the discovery of things that we suppose to be true and which we suppose to exist quite independently of those organs themselves. We suppose, without even thinking about it, that they reveal to us things that have nothing to do with themselves, their structures, or their origins. Just as we supposed that the stones on the hill told us that we were entering Wales—a fact having nothing to do with the stones themselves—so also we suppose that our senses in some manner "tell us" what is true, at least sometimes. The stones on the hill could, to be sure, have been an accident, in which case we cannot suppose that they really tell us anything at all. So also, our senses and all our faculties could be accidental in their origins, and in that case they do not really tell us anything either. But the fact remains, that we do trust them, without the slightest reflection on the matter. Our seeing something is often thought to be, quite by itself, a good reason for believing that the thing exists, and it would be absurd to suggest that we *infer* this from the structure of our eyes or speculations upon their evolutionary origins. And so it is with our other faculties. Our remembering something is often considered to be, quite by itself, a good reason for believing that the thing remembered did happen. Our hearing a sound is often considered, quite by itself, a good reason for believing that a sound exists; and so on.

We are not here suggesting that our senses are infallible, nor even, that we ought to rely upon their testimony. The point is that we do rely upon them. We do not believe merely that our senses are remarkably interesting things. We do not believe merely that they produce interesting effects within us, nor merely that they produce beliefs in us. We assume, rightly or wrongly, that they are *trust-worthy* guides with respect to what is true, and what exists independently of our senses and their origins; and we still assume this, even when they are our only guides.

We saw that it would be irrational for anyone to say *both* that the marks he found on a stone had a natural, nonpurposeful origin and *also* that they reveal some truth with respect to something other than themselves, something that is not merely inferred from them. One cannot rationally believe both of these things. So also, it is now suggested, it would be irrational for one to say *both* that his sensory and cognitive faculties had a natural, nonpurposeful origin and *also* that they reveal some truth with respect to something other than themselves, something that is not merely inferred from them. *If* their origin can be entirely accounted for in terms of chance variations, natural selection, and so on, without supposing that they somehow embody and express the purposes of some creative being, then the most we can say of them is that they exist, that they are complex and wondrous in their construction, and are perhaps in other respects interesting and remarkable. We cannot say that they are, entirely by themselves, reliable guides to any truth whatever, save only what can be inferred from their own structure and arrangement. If, on the other hand, we do assume that they are guides to some truths having nothing to do with themselves, then it is difficult to see how we can, consistently with that supposition, believe them to have arisen by accident, or by the ordinary workings of purposeless forces, even over ages of time.

At this point persons who have a deep suspicion of all such arguments as this, and particularly persons who are hostile to any of the claims of religion, are likely to seize upon numberless objections of a sort that it would hardly occur to anyone to apply to our first two examples, involving the stones. Thus, it is apt to be said that our cognitive faculties are not so reliable as some would suppose, which is irrelevant; or that arguments from analogy prove nothing, which is also irrelevant, since none of the foregoing is an argument from analogy. Or it is claimed that we rely on our cognitive faculties only because we have found them reliable in the past, and thus have a sound inductive basis for our trust, which is absurd, if not question-begging. The reason I believe there is a world around me is, quite simply, that I see it, feel it, hear it, and am in fact perpetually in cognitive contact with it, or at least assume myself to be, without even considering the matter. To suggest that I *infer* its existence from the effects that it has within me, and that I find the inference justified on the ground that such inner effects have, in the past, been accompanied by external causes, is not only a ridiculous caricature, but begs the question of how, without relying upon my faculties, I could ever confirm such an idea in the first place. Again, it is sometimes said that the capacity to grasp truths has a decided value to the survival of an organism, and that our cognitive faculties have evolved, quite naturally, through the operation of this principle. This appears farfetched, however, even if for no other reason than that man's capacity to understand what is true, through reliance upon his senses and cognitive faculties, far exceeds what is needed for survival. One might as well say that the sign on the hill welcoming tourists to Wales originated over the course of ages purely by accident, and has been preserved by the utility it was then found to possess. This is of course possible, but also immensely implausible.

THE SIGNIFICANCE OF THESE ARGUMENTS

IT would be extravagant indeed to suppose that these reflections amount to any sort of confirmation of religion, or even, that they have much tc do with religion. They are purely metaphysical and philosophical considerations having implications of only a purely speculative kind. Even if they are utterly probative, which is of course controversial, it can still be pointed out, correctly, that they are consistent with ever so many views which are radically inconsistent with religion. They imply almost nothing with respect to any divine attributes, such as benevolence, and one could insist with some justification that even the word God, which is supposed to be the proper name of a personal being and not just a label to be attached to metaphysically inferred things, is out of place in them.

No more is claimed for these arguments, however, than that they are good arguments, and that they seem to yield the conclusions derived from them. If they are defective, the defects are not gross or obvious. The reader may suit himself whether they yield those conclusions, and if so, what their human significance might be.

6

DIFFICULTIES OF THE
TELEOLOGICAL ARGUMENT*

David Hume ▒

*David Hume (1711–1776) is one of the
most influential philosophers of modern
times. He continued and developed the
tradition of empiricism initiated in
Britain by John Locke and George Berkeley. His major works include* A Treatise
of Human Nature, Inquiry Concerning
the Human Understanding, *and* Dialogues on Natural Religion.

NOT to lose any time in circumlocutions, said Cleanthes, addressing
himself to Demea, much less in replying to the pious declamations
of Philo; I shall briefly explain how I conceive this matter. Look
round the world: contemplate the whole and every part of it: you
will find it to be nothing but one great machine, subdivided into an
infinite number of lesser machines, which again admit of subdivi-
sions to a degree beyond what human senses and faculties can trace
and explain. All these various machines, and even their most
minute parts, are adjusted to each other with an accuracy which
ravishes into admiration all men who have ever contemplated them.
The curious adapting of means to ends, throughout all nature,
resembles exactly, though it much exceeds, the productions of
human contrivance; of human designs, thought, wisdom, and intelligence. Since, therefore, the effects resemble each other, we are
led to infer, by all the rules of analogy, that the causes also
resemble; and that the Author of Nature is somewhat similar to the
mind of man, though possessed of much larger faculties, propor-
tioned to the grandeur of the work which he has executed. By this
argument *a posteriori,* and by this argument alone, do we prove at
once the existence of a Deity, and his similarity to human mind and
intelligence.

I shall be so free, Cleanthes, said Demea, as to tell you, that
from the beginning, I could not approve of your conclusion con-

* From David Hume, *Dialogues Concerning Natural Religion.*

cerning the similarity of the Deity to men; still less can I approve of the mediums by which you endeavor to establish it. What! No demonstration of the Being of God! No abstract arguments! No proofs *a priori!* Are these, which have hitherto been so much insisted on by philosophers, all fallacy, all sophism? Can we reach no further in this subject than experience and probability? I will not say that this is betraying the cause of a Deity: but surely, by this affected candor, you give advantages to Atheists, which they never could obtain by the mere dint of argument and reasoning.

What I chiefly scruple in this subject, said Philo, is not so much that all religious arguments are by Cleanthes reduced to experience, as that they appear not to be even the most certain and irrefragable of that inferior kind. That a stone will fall, that fire will burn, that the earth has solidity, we have observed a thousand and a thousand times; and when any new instance of this nature is presented, we draw without hesitation the accustomed inference. The exact similarity of the cases gives us a perfect assurance of a similar event; and a stronger evidence is never desired nor sought after. But wherever you depart, in the least, from the similarity of the cases, you diminish proportionably the evidence; and may at last bring it to a very weak *analogy,* which is confessedly liable to error and uncertainty. After having experienced the circulation of the blood in human creatures, we make no doubt that it takes place in Titius and Mævius. But from its circulation in frogs and fishes, it is only a presumption, though a strong one, from analogy, that it takes place in men and other animals. The analogical reasoning is much weaker, when we infer the circulation of the sap in vegetables from our experience that the blood circulates in animals; and those, who hastily followed that imperfect analogy, are found, by more accurate experiments, to have been mistaken.

If we see a house, Cleanthes, we conclude, with the greatest certainty, that it had an architect or builder; because this is precisely that species of effect which we have experienced to proceed from that species of cause. But surely you will not affirm, that the universe bears such a resemblance to a house, that we can with the same certainty infer a similar cause, or that the analogy is here entire and perfect. The dissimilitude is so striking, that the utmost you can here pretend to is a guess, a conjecture, a presumption concerning a similar cause; and how that pretension will be received in the world, I leave you to consider.

It would surely be very ill received, replied Cleanthes; and I should be deservedly blamed and detested, did I allow, that the proofs of a Deity amounted to no more than a guess or conjecture. But is the whole adjustment of means to ends in a house and in the universe so slight a resemblance? The economy of final causes? The order, proportion, and arrangement of every part? Steps of a stair are plainly contrived, that human legs may use them in mounting; and this inference is certain and infallible. Human legs are also contrived for walking and mounting; and this inference, I allow, is not altogether so certain, because of the dissimilarity which you remark; but does it, therefore, deserve the name only of presumption or conjecture?

Good God! cried Demea, interrupting him, where are we? Zealous defenders of religion allow, that the proofs of a Deity fall short of perfect evidence! And you, Philo, on whose assistance I depended in proving the adorable mysteriousness of the Divine Nature, do you assent to all these extravagant opinions of Cleanthes? For what other name can I give them? or, why spare my censure, when such principles are advanced, supported by such an authority, before so young a man as Pamphilus?

You seem not to apprehend, replied Philo, that I argue with Cleanthes in his own way; and, by showing him the dangerous consequences of his tenets, hope at last to reduce him to our opinion. But what sticks most with you, I observe, is the representation which Cleanthes has made of the argument *a posteriori;* and finding that that argument is likely to escape your hold and vanish into air, you think it so disguised, that you can scarcely believe it to be set in its true light. Now, however much I may dissent, in other respects, from the dangerous principles of Cleanthes, I must allow that he has fairly represented that argument; and I shall endeavor so to state the matter to you, that you will entertain no further scruples with regard to it.

Were a man to abstract from every thing which he knows or has seen, he would be altogether incapable, merely from his own ideas, to determine what kind of scene the universe must be, or to give the preference to one state or situation of things above another. For as nothing which he clearly conceives could be esteemed impossible or implying a contradiction, every chimera of his fancy would be upon an equal footing; nor could he assign any just reason why he adheres to one idea or system, and rejects the others which are equally possible.

Again; after he opens his eyes, and contemplates the world as it really is, it would be impossible for him at first to assign the cause of any one event, much less of the whole of things, or of the universe. He might set his fancy a rambling; and she might bring him in an infinite variety of reports and representations. These would all be possible; but being all equally possible, he would never of himself give a satisfactory account for his preferring one of them to the rest. Experience alone can point out to him the true cause of any phenomenon.

Now, according to this method of reasoning, Demea, it follows, (and is, indeed, tacitly allowed by Cleanthes himself,) that order, arrangement, or the adjustment of final causes, is not of itself any proof of design; but only so far as it has been experienced to proceed from that principle. For aught we can know *a priori*, matter may contain the source or spring of order originally within itself as well as mind does; and there is no more difficulty in conceiving, that the several elements, from an internal unknown cause, may fall into the most exquisite arrangement, than to conceive that their ideas, in the great universal mind, from a like internal unknown cause, fall into that arrangement. The equal possibility of both these suppositions is allowed. But, by experience, we find, (according to Cleanthes,) that there is a difference between them. Throw several pieces of steel together, without shape or form; they will never arrange themselves so as to compose a watch. Stone, and mortar, and wood, without an architect, never erect a house. But the ideas in a human mind, we see, by an unknown, inexplicable economy, arrange themselves so as to form the plan of a watch or house. Experience, therefore, proves, that there is an original principle of order in mind, not in matter. From similar effects we infer similar causes. The adjustment of means to ends is alike in the universe, as in a machine of human contrivance. The causes, therefore, must be resembling.

I was from the beginning scandalized, I must own, with this resemblance, which is asserted, between the Deity and human creatures; and must conceive it to imply such a degradation of the Supreme Being as no sound Theist could endure. With your assistance, therefore, Demea, I shall endeavor to defend what you justly call the adorable mysteriousness of the Divine Nature, and shall refute this reasoning of Cleanthes, provided he allows that I have made a fair representation of it.

When Cleanthes had assented, Philo, after a short pause, proceeded in the following manner.

That all inferences, Cleanthes, concerning fact, are founded on experience; and that all experimental reasonings are founded on the supposition that similar causes prove similar effects, and similar effects similar causes; I shall not at present much dispute with you. But observe, I entreat you, with what extreme caution all just reasoners proceed in the transferring of experiments to similar cases. Unless the cases be exactly similar, they repose no perfect confidence in applying their past observation to any particular phenomenon. Every alteration of circumstances occasions a doubt concerning the event; and it requires new experiments to prove certainly, that the new circumstances are of no moment or importance. A change in bulk, situation, arrangement, age, disposition of the air, or surrounding bodies; any of these particulars may be attended with the most unexpected consequences: and unless the objects be quite familiar to us, it is the highest temerity to expect with assurance, after any of these changes, an event similar to that which before fell under our observation. The slow and deliberate steps of philosophers here, if anywhere, are distinguished from the precipitate march of the vulgar, who, hurried on by the smallest similitude, are incapable of all discernment or consideration.

But can you think, Cleanthes, that your usual phlegm and philosophy have been preserved in so wide a step as you have taken, when you compared to the universe houses, ships, furniture, machines, and, from their similarity in some circumstances, inferred a similarity in their causes? Thought, design, intelligence, such as we discover in men and other animals, is no more than one of the springs and principles of the universe, as well as heat or cold, attraction or repulsion, and a hundred others, which fall under daily observation. It is an active cause, by which some particular parts of nature, we find, produce alterations on other parts. But can a conclusion, with any propriety, be transferred from parts to the whole? Does not the great disproportion bar all comparison and inference? From observing the growth of a hair, can we learn any thing concerning the generation of a man? Would the manner of a leaf's blowing, even though perfectly known, afford us any instruction concerning the vegetation of a tree?

But, allowing that we were to take the *operations* of one part of nature upon another, for the foundation of our judgment concerning the *origin* of the whole, (which never can be admitted,) yet why select so minute, so weak, so bounded a principle, as the reason and design of animals is found to be upon this planet? What peculiar privilege has this little agitation of the brain which we call *thought,* that we must thus make it the model of the whole universe? Our partiality in our own favor does indeed present it on all occasions; but sound philosophy ought carefully to guard against so natural an illusion.

So far from admitting, continued Philo, that the operations of a part can afford us any just conclusion concerning the origin of the whole, I will not allow any one part to form a rule for another part, if the latter be very remote from the former. Is there any reasonable ground to conclude, that the inhabitants of other planets possess thoughts, intelligence, reason, or any thing similar to these faculties in men? When nature has so extremely diversified her manner of operation in this small globe, can we imagine that she incessantly copies herself throughout so immense a universe? And if thought, as we may well suppose, be confined merely to this narrow corner, and has even there so limited a sphere of action, with what propriety can we assign it for the original cause of all things? The narrow views of a peasant, who makes his domestic economy the rule for the government of kingdoms, is in comparison a pardonable sophism.

But were we ever so much assured, that a thought and reason, resembling the human, were to be found throughout the whole universe, and were its activity elsewhere vastly greater and more commanding than it appears in this globe; yet I cannot see, why the operations of a world constituted, arranged, adjusted, can with any propriety be extended to a world which is in its embryo state, and is advancing towards that constitution and arrangement. By observation, we know somewhat of the economy, action, and nourishment of a finished animal; but we must transfer with great caution that observation to the growth of the fœtus in the womb, and still more in the formation of an animalcule in the loins of its male parent. Nature, we find, even from our limited experience, possesses an infinite number of springs and principles, which incessantly discover themselves on every change of her position and situation. And what new and unknown principles would actuate her in so new and unknown a situation as that of the formation of a universe, we cannot, without the utmost temerity, pretend to determine.

A very small part of this great system, during a very short time, is very imperfectly discovered to us; and do we then pronounce decisively concerning the origin of the whole?

Admirable conclusion! Stone, wood, brick, iron, brass, have not, at this time, in this minute globe of earth, an order or arrangement without human art and contrivance; therefore the universe could not originally attain its order and arrangement, without something similar to human art. But is a part of nature a rule for another part very wide of the former? Is it a rule for the whole? Is a very small part a rule for the universe? Is nature in one situation, a certain rule for nature in another situation vastly different from the former?

And can you blame me, Cleanthes, if I here imitate the prudent reserve of Simonides, who, according to the noted story, being asked by Hiero, *What God was?* desired a day to think of it, and then two days more; and after that manner continually prolonged the term, without ever bringing in his definition or description? Could you even blame me, if I answered at first, *that I did not know,* and was sensible that this subject lay vastly beyond the reach of my faculties? You might cry out sceptic and railer, as much as you pleased: but having found, in so many other subjects much more familiar, the imperfections and even contradictions of human reason, I never should expect any success from its feeble conjectures, in a subject so sublime, and so remote from the sphere of our observation. When two *species* of objects have always been observed to be conjoined together, I can *infer,* by custom, the existence of one wherever I *see* the existence of the other; and this I call an argument from experience. But how this argument can have place, where the objects, as in the present case, are single, individual, without parallel, or specific resemblance, may be difficult to explain. And will any man tell me with a serious countenance, that an orderly universe must arise from some thought and art like the human, because we have experience of it? To ascertain this reasoning, it were requisite that we had experience of the origin of worlds.

· · ·

I shall endeavor to show you, a little more distinctly, the inconveniences of that Anthropomorphism, which you have embraced; and shall prove, that there is no ground to suppose a plan of the world to be formed in the Divine mind, consisting of distinct ideas, differently arranged, in the same manner as an architect forms in his head the plan of a house which he intends to execute.

It is not easy, I own, to see what is gained by this supposition, whether we judge of the matter by *Reason* or by *Experience.* We are still obliged to mount higher, in order to find the cause of this cause, which you had assigned as satisfactory and conclusive.

If *Reason* (I mean abstract reason, derived from inquiries *a priori*) be not alike mute with regard to all questions concerning cause and effect, this sentence at least it will venture to pronounce. That a mental world, or universe of ideas, requires a cause as much, as does a material world, or universe of objects: and, if similar in its arrangement, must require a similar cause. For what is there in this subject, which should occasion a different conclusion or inference? In an abstract view, they are entirely alike; and no difficulty attends the one supposition, which is not common to both of them.

Again, when we will needs force *Experience* to pronounce some sentence, even on these subjects which lie beyond her sphere, neither can she perceive any material difference in this particular, between these two kinds of worlds; but finds them to be governed by similar principles, and to depend upon an equal variety of causes in their operations. We have specimens in miniature of both of them. Our own mind resembles the one; a vegetable or animal body the other. Let experience, therefore, judge from these samples. Nothing seems more delicate, with regard to its causes, than thought; and as these causes never operate in two persons after the same manner, so we never find two persons who think exactly alike. Nor indeed does the same person think exactly alike at any two different periods of time. A difference of age, of the disposition of his body, of weather, of food, of company, of books, of passions; any of these particulars, or others more minute, are sufficient to alter the curious machinery of thought, and communicate to it very different movements and operations. As far as we can judge, vegetables and animal bodies are not more delicate in their motions, nor depend upon a greater variety or more curious adjustment of springs and principles.

How, therefore, shall we satisfy ourselves concerning the cause of that Being whom you suppose the Author of Nature, or, according to your system of Anthropomorphism, the ideal world, into which you trace the material? Have we not the same reason to trace that ideal world into another ideal world, or new intelligent principle? But if we stop, and go no further; why go so far? why not stop at the material world? How can we satisfy ourselves without going on *in infinitum?* And, after all, what satisfaction is there in that infinite progression? Let us remember the story of the Indian philosopher and his elephant. It was never more applicable than to the present subject. If the material world rests upon a similar ideal world, this ideal world must rest upon some other; and so on, without end. It were better, therefore, never to look beyond the present material world. By supposing it to contain the principle of its order within itself, we really assert it to be God; and the sooner we arrive at that Divine Being, so much the better. When you go one step beyond the mundane system, you only excite an inquisitive humor which it is impossible ever to satisfy.

To say, that the different ideas which compose the reason of the Supreme Being, fall into order of themselves, and by their own nature, is really to talk without any precise meaning. If it has a meaning, I would fain know, why it is not as good sense to say, that the parts of the material world fall into order of themselves and by their own nature. Can the one opinion be intelligible, while the other is not so?

We have, indeed, experience of ideas which fall into order of themselves, and without any *known* cause. But, I am sure, we have a much larger experience of matter which does the same; as, in all instances of generation and vegetation, where the accurate analysis of the cause exceeds all human comprehension. We have also experience of particular systems of thought and of matter which have no order; of the first in madness, of the second in corruption. Why, then, should we think, that order is more essential to one than the other? And if it requires a cause in both, what do we gain by your system, in tracing the universe of objects into a similar universe of ideas? The first step which we make leads us on for ever. It were, therefore, wise in us to limit all our inquiries to the present world, without looking further. No satisfaction can ever be attained by these speculations, which so far exceed the narrow bounds of human understanding.

It was usual with the Peripatetics, you know, Cleanthes, when the cause of any phenomenon was demanded, to have recourse to their *faculties* or *occult qualities;* and to say, for instance, that bread, nourished by its nutritive faculty, and senna purged by its purgative. But it has been discovered, that this subterfuge was nothing but the disguise of ignorance; and that these philosophers, though less ingenuous, really said the same thing with the sceptics or the vulgar, who fairly confessed that they knew not the cause of these phenomena. In like manner, when it is asked, what cause produces order in the ideas of the Supreme Being; can any other reason be assigned by you, Anthropomorphites, than that it is a *rational* faculty, and that such is the nature of the Deity? But why a similar answer will not be equally satisfactory in accounting for the order of the world, without having recourse to any such intelligent creator as you insist on, may be difficult to determine. It is only to say, that *such* is the nature of material objects, and that they are all originally possessed of a *faculty* of order and proportion. These are only more learned and elaborate ways of confessing our ignorance; nor has the one hypothesis any real advantage above the other, except in its greater conformity to vulgar prejudices.

You have displayed this argument with great emphasis, replied Cleanthes. You seem not sensible how easy it is to answer it. Even in common life, if I assign a cause for any event, is it any objection, Philo, that I cannot assign the cause of that cause, and answer every new question which may incessantly be started? And what philosophers could possibly submit to so rigid a rule? philosophers, who confess ultimate causes to be totally unknown; and are sensible, that the most refined principles into which they trace the phenomena, are still to them as inexplicable as these phenomena themselves are to the vulgar. The order and arrangement of nature, the curious adjustment of final causes, the plain use and intention of every part and organ; all these bespeak in the clearest language an intelligent cause or author. The heavens and the earth join in the same testimony: the whole chorus of Nature raises one hymn to the praises of its Creator. You alone, or almost alone, disturb this general harmony. You start abstruse doubts, cavils, and objections: you ask me, what is the cause of this cause? I know not; I care not; that concerns not me. I have found a Deity; and here I stop my inquiry. Let those go further, who are wiser or more enterprising.

I pretend to be neither, replied Philo: and for that very reason, I should never perhaps have attempted to go so far; especially when I am sensible, that I must at last be contented to sit down with the same answer, which, without further trouble, might have satisfied me from the beginning. If I am still to remain in utter ignorance of causes, and can absolutely give an explication of nothing, I shall never esteem it any advantage to shove off for a moment a difficulty, which, you acknowledge, must immediately, in its full force, recur upon me. Naturalists indeed very justly explain particular effects by more general causes, though these general causes themselves should remain in the end totally inexplicable; but they never surely thought it satisfactory to explain a particular effect by a particular cause, which was no more to be accounted for than the effect itself. An ideal system, arranged of itself, without a precedent design, is not a whit more explicable than a material one, which attains its order in a like manner; nor is there any more difficulty in the latter supposition than in the former.

．　　．　　．

To render it still more unsatisfactory, said Philo, there occurs to me another hypothesis, which must acquire an air of probability from the method of reasoning so much insisted on by Cleanthes. That like effects arise from like causes: this principle he supposes the foundation of all religion. But there is another principle of the same kind, no less certain, and derived from the same source of experience; that where several known circumstances are observed to be similar, the unknown will also be found similar. Thus, if we see the limbs of a human body, we conclude that it is also attended with a human head, though hid from us. Thus, if we see, through a chink in a wall, a small part of the sun, we conclude, that, were the wall removed, we should see the whole body. In short, this method of reasoning is so obvious and familiar, that no scruple can ever be made with regard to its solidity.

Now, if we survey the universe, so far as it falls under our knowledge, it bears a great resemblance to an animal or organized body, and seems actuated with a like principle of life and motion. A continual circulation of matter in it produces no disorder: a continual waste in every part is incessantly repaired: the closest sympathy is perceived throughout the entire system: and each part or member, in performing its proper offices, operates both to its own preservation and to that of the whole. The world, therefore, I infer, is an animal; and the Deity is the SOUL of the world, actuating it, and actuated by it.

You have too much learning, Cleanthes, to be at all surprised at this opinion, which, you know, was maintained by almost all the Theists of antiquity, and chiefly prevails in their discourses and reasonings. For though, sometimes, the ancient philosophers reason from final causes, as if they thought the world the workmanship of God; yet it appears rather their favorite notion to consider it as his body, whose organization renders it subservient to him. And it must be confessed, that, as the universe resembles more a human body than it does the works of human art and contrivance, if our limited analogy could ever, with any propriety, be extended to the whole of nature, the inference seems juster in favor of the ancient than the modern theory.

There are many other advantages, too, in the former theory, which recommended it to the ancient theologians. Nothing more repugnant to all their notions, because nothing more repugnant to common experience, than mind without body; a mere spiritual substance, which fell not under their senses nor comprehension, and of which they had not observed one single instance throughout all nature. Mind and body they knew, because they felt both: an order, arrangement, organization, or internal machinery, in both, they likewise knew, after the same manner: and it could not but seem reasonable to transfer this experience to the universe; and to suppose the divine mind and body to be also coeval, and to have, both of them, order and arrangement naturally inherent in them, and inseparable from them.

Here, therefore, is a new species of *Anthropomorphism,* Cleanthes, on which you may deliberate; and a theory which seems not liable to any considerable difficulties. You are too much superior, surely, to *systematical prejudices,* to find any more difficulty in supposing an animal body to be, originally, of itself, or from unknown causes, possessed of order and organization, than in supposing a similar order to belong to mind. But the *vulgar prejudice,* that body and mind ought always to accompany each other, ought not, one should think, to be entirely neglected; since it is founded on *vulgar experience,* the only guide which you profess to follow in all these theological inquiries. And if you assert, that our limited experience is an unequal standard, by which to judge of the unlimited extent of nature; you entirely abandon your own hypothesis, and must thenceforward adopt our Mysticism, as you call it, and admit of the absolute incomprehensibility of the Divine Nature.

.   .   .

IF THE universe bears a greater likeness to animal bodies and to vegetables, than to the works of human art, it is more probable that its cause resembles the cause of the former than that of the latter, and its origin ought rather to be ascribed to generation or vegetation, than to reason or design. Your conclusion, even according to your own principles, is therefore lame and defective.

Pray open up this argument a little further, said Demea, for I do not rightly apprehend it in that concise manner in which you have expressed it.

Our friend Cleanthes, replied Philo, as you have heard, asserts, that since no question of fact can be proved otherwise than by experience, the existence of a Deity admits not of proof from any other medium. The world, says he, resembles the works of human contrivance; therefore its cause must also resemble that of the other. Here we may remark, that the operation of one very small part of nature, to wit man, upon another very small part, to wit that inanimate matter lying within his reach, is the rule by which Cleanthes judges of the origin of the whole; and he measures objects, so widely disproportioned, by the same individual standard. But to waive all objections drawn from this topic, I affirm, that there are other parts of the universe (besides the machines of human invention) which bear still a greater resemblance to the fabric of the world, and which, therefore, afford a better conjecture concerning the universal origin of this system. These parts are animals and vegetables. The world plainly resembles more an animal or a vegetable, than it does a watch or a knitting-loom. Its cause, therefore, it is more probable, resembles the cause of the former. The cause of the former is generation or vegetation. The cause, therefore, of the world, we may infer to be something similar or analogous to generation or vegetation.

But how is it conceivable, said Demea, that the world can arise from any thing similar to vegetation or generation?

Very easily, replied Philo. In like manner as a tree sheds its seeds into the neighboring fields, and produces other trees; so the great vegetable, the world, or this planetary system, produces within itself certain seeds, which, being scattered into the surrounding chaos, vegetate into new worlds. A comet, for instance, is the seed of a world; and after it has been fully ripened, by passing from sun to sun, and star to star, it is at last tossed into the unformed elements which everywhere surround this universe, and immediately sprouts up into a new system.

Or, if, for the sake of variety (for I see no other advantage), we should suppose this world to be an animal; a comet is the egg of this animal: and in like manner as an ostrich lays its egg in the sand, which, without any further care, hatches the egg, and produces a new animal; so . . . I understand you, says Demea: but what wild, arbitrary suppositions are these! What *data* have you for such extraordinary conclusions? And is the slight, imaginary resemblance of the world to a vegetable or an animal sufficient to establish the same inference with regard to both? Objects, which are in general so widely different, ought they to be a standard for each other?

Right, cries Philo: this is the topic on which I have all along insisted. I have still asserted, that we have no *data* to establish any system of cosmogony. Our experience, so imperfect in itself, and so limited both in extent and duration, can afford us no probable conjecture concerning the whole of things. But if we must needs fix on some hypothesis; by what rule, pray, ought we to determine our choice? Is there any other rule than the greater similarity of the objects compared? And does not a plant or an animal, which springs from vegetation or generation, bear a stronger resemblance to the world, than does any artificial machine, which arises from reason and design?

But what is this vegetation and generation of which you talk? said Demea. Can you explain their operations, and anatomize that fine internal structure on which they depend?

As much, at least, replied Philo, as Cleanthes can explain the operations of reason, or anatomize that internal structure on which *it* depends. But without any such elaborate disquisitions, when I see an animal, I infer, that it sprang from generation; and that with as great certainty as you conclude a house to have been reared by design. These words, *generation, reason,* mark only certain powers and energies in nature, whose effects are known, but whose essence is incomprehensible; and one of these principles, more than the other, has no privilege for being made a standard to the whole of nature.

In reality, Demea, it may reasonably be expected, that the larger the views are which we take of things, the better will they conduct us in our conclusions concerning such extraordinary and such magnificent subjects. In this little corner of the world alone, there are four principles, *reason, instinct, generation, vegetation,* which are similar to each other, and are the causes of similar effects. What a number of other principles may we naturally suppose in the immense extent and variety of the universe, could we travel from planet to planet, and from system to system, in order to examine each part of this mighty fabric? Any one of these four principles above mentioned, (and a hundred others which lie open to our conjecture,) may afford us a theory by which to judge of the origin of the world; and it is a palpable and egregious partiality to confine our view entirely to that principle by which our own minds operate. Were this principle more intelligible on that account, such a partiality might be somewhat excusable: but reason, in its internal fabric and structure, is really as little known to us as instinct or vegetation; and, perhaps, even that vague, undeterminate word, *Nature,* to which the vulgar refer every thing, is not at the bottom more inexplicable. The effects of these principles are all known to us from experience; but the principles themselves, and their manner of operation, are totally unknown; nor is it less intelligible, or less comformable to experience, to say, that the world arose by vegetation, from a seed shed by another world, than to say that it arose from a divine reason or contrivance, according to the sense in which Cleanthes understands it.

But methinks, said Demea, if the world had a vegetative quality, and could sow the seeds of new worlds into the infinite chaos, this power would be still an additional argument for design in its author. For whence could arise so wonderful a faculty but from design? Or how can order spring from any thing which perceives not that order which it bestows?

You need only look around you, replied Philo, to satisfy yourself with regard to this question. A tree bestows order and organization on that tree which springs from it, without knowing the order; an animal in the same manner on its offspring; a bird on its nest; and instances of this kind are even more frequent in the world than those of order, which arise from reason and contrivance. To say, that all this order in animals and vegetables proceeds ultimately from design, is begging the question; nor can that great point be ascertained otherwise than by proving, a priori, both that order is, from its nature, inseparably attached to thought; and that it can never of itself, or from original unknown principles, belong to matter.

But further, Demea; this objection which you urge can never be made use of by Cleanthes, without renouncing a defence which he has already made against one of my objections. When I inquired concerning the cause of that supreme reason and intelligence into which he resolves every thing; he told me, that the impossibility of satisfying such inquiries could never be admitted as an objection in any species of philosophy. *We must stop somewhere,* says he; *nor is it ever within the reach of human capacity to explain ultimate causes, or show the last connections of any objects. It is sufficient, if any steps, so far as we go, are supported by experience and observation.* Now, that vegetation and generation, as well as reason, are experienced to be principles of order in nature, is undeniable. If I rest my system of cosmogony on the former, preferably to the latter, it is at my choice. The matter seems entirely arbitrary. And when Cleanthes asks me what is the cause of my great vegetative or generative faculty, I am equally entitled to ask him the cause of his great reasoning principle. These questions we have agreed to forbear on both sides; and it is chiefly his interest on the present occasion to stick to this agreement. Judging by our limited and imperfect experience, generation has some privileges above reason: for we see every day the latter arise from the former, never the former from the latter.

Compare, I beseech you, the consequences on both sides. The world, say I, resembles an animal; therefore it is an animal, therefore it arose from generation. The steps, I confess, are wide; yet there is some small appearance of analogy in each step. The world, says Cleanthes, resembles a machine; therefore it is a machine, therefore it arose from design. The steps are here equally wide, and the analogy less striking. And if he pretends to carry on *my* hypothesis a step further, and to infer design or reason from the great principle of generation, on which I insist; I may, with better authority, use the same freedom to push further *his* hypothesis, and infer a divine generation or theogony from his principle of reason. I have at least some faint shadow of experience, which is the utmost that can ever be attained in the present subject. Reason, in innumerable instances, is observed to arise from the principle of generation, and never to arise from any other principle.

7

DIFFICULTIES OF BOTH
NATURALISM AND THEISM*

Aurobindo Ghose (1872–1950) was perhaps the greatest contemporary exponent of the Vedanta philosophy of Hinduism, although he modified the classical view of Sankara by reinterpreting the latter's cosmic illusionism. Mystic philosopher, early leader of Indian nationalism, and founder of a noted Ashram at Pondicherry, Aurobindo's main works are: The Life Divine, The Synthesis of Yoga, The Ideal of Human Unity, *and* The Human Cycle.

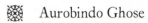 Aurobindo Ghose

IT IS possible indeed to question the need of positing an Infinite which contains our formed universe, although this conception is imperatively demanded by our mind as a necessary basis to its conceptions,—for it is unable to fix or assign a limit whether in Space or Time or essential existence beyond which there is nothing or before or after which there is nothing,—although too the alternative is a Void or Nihil which can be only an abyss of the Infinite into which we refuse to look; an infinite mystic zero of Non-Existence would replace an infinite x as a necessary postulate, a basis for our seeing of all that is to us existence. But even if we refuse to recognise anything as real except the limitless expanding finite of the material universe and its teeming determinations, the enigma remains the same. Infinite existence, infinite non-being or boundless finite, all are to us original indeterminates or indeterminables; we can assign to them no distinct characters or features, nothing which would predetermine their determinations. To describe the fundamental character of the universe as Space or Time or Space-Time does not help us; for even if these are not abstractions of our intelligence which we impose by our mental view on the cosmos, the mind's necessary perspective of its picture, these too are indetermi-

* From Sri Aurobindo Ghose, *The Life Divine*. Reprinted by permission of Sri Aurobindo Ashram Press.

nates and carry in themselves no clue to the origin of the determinations that take place in them; there is still no explanation of the strange process by which things are determined or of their powers, qualities and properties, no revelation of their true nature, origin and significance.

Actually to our Science this infinite or indeterminate Existence reveals itself as an Energy, known not by itself but by its works, which throws up in its motion waves of energism and in them a multitude of infinitesimals; these, grouping themselves to form larger infinitesimals, become a basis for all the creations of the Energy, even those farthest away from the material basis, for the emergence of a world of organised Matter, for the emergence of Life, for the emergence of Consciousness, for all the still unexplained activities of evolutionary Nature. On the original process are erected a multitude of processes which we can observe, follow, can take advantage of many of them, utilise; but they are none of them, fundamentally, explicable. We know now that different groupings and a varying number of electric infinitesimals can produce or serve as the constituent occasion—miscalled the cause, for here there seems to be only a necessary antecedent condition—for the appearance of larger atomic infinitesimals of different natures, qualities, powers; but we fail to discover how these different dispositions can come to constitute these different atoms,—how the differentiæ in the constituent occasion or cause necessitate the differentiæ in the constituted outcome or result. We know also that certain combinations of certain visible atomic infinitesimals produce or occasion new and visible determinations quite different in nature, quality and power from the constituent infinitesimals; but we fail to discover, for instance, how a fixed formula for the combination of oxygen and hydrogen comes to determine the appearance of water which is evidently something more than a combination of gases, a new creation, a new form of substance, a material manifestation of a quite new character. We see that a seed develops into a tree, we follow the line of the process of production and we utilise it; but we do not discover how a tree can grow out of a seed, how the life and form of the tree come to be implied in the substance or energy of the seed or, if that be rather the fact, how the seed can develop into a tree. We know that genes and chromosomes are the cause of hereditary transmissions, not only of physical but of psychological variations; but we do not discover how psychological characteristics can be contained and transmitted in this inconscient material vehicle. We do not see or know, but it is expounded to us as a cogent account of Nature-process, that a play of electrons, of atoms and their resultant molecules, of cells, glands, chemical secretions and physiological processes manages by their activity on the nerves and brain of a Shakespeare or a Plato to produce or could be perhaps the dynamic occasion for the production of a *Hamlet* or a *Symposium* or a *Republic;* but we fail to discover or appreciate how such material movements could have composed or necessitated the composition of these highest points of thought and literature: the divergence here of the determinants and the determination becomes so wide that we are no longer able to follow the process, much less understand or utilise. These formulæ of Science may be pragmatically correct and infallible, they may govern the practical how of Nature's processes, but they do not disclose the intrinsic how or why; rather they have the air of the formulæ of a cosmic Magician, precise, irresistible, automatically successful each in its field, but their rationale is fundamentally unintelligible.

There is more to perplex us; for we see the original indeterminate Energy throwing out general determinates of itself,—we might equally in their relation to the variety of their products call them generic indeterminates,—with their appropriate states of substance and determined forms of that substance: the latter are numerous, sometimes innumerable variations on the substance-energy which is their base: but none of these variations seems to be predetermined by anything in the nature of the general indeterminate. An electric Energy produces positive, negative, neutral forms of itself, forms that are at once waves and particles; a gaseous state of energy-substance produces a considerable number of different gases; a solid state of energy-substance from which results the earth principle develops into different forms of earth and rock of many kinds and numerous minerals and metals; a life principle produces its vegetable kingdom teeming with a countless foison of quite different plants, trees, flowers; a principle of animal life produces an enormous variety of genus, species, individual variations: so it proceeds into human life and mind and its mind-types towards the still unwritten end or perhaps the yet occult sequel of that unfinished evolutionary chapter. Throughout there is the constant rule of a general sameness in the original determinate and, subject to this substantial sameness of basic substance and nature, a profuse variation in the generic and individual determinates; an identical law obtains of sameness or similarity in the genus or species with numerous variations often meticulously minute in the individual. But we do not find anything at any general or generic determinate necessitating the variant determinations that result from it. A necessity of immutable sameness at the base, of free and unaccountable variations on the surface seems to be the law; but who or what necessitates or determines? What is the rationale of the determination, what is its original truth or its significance? What compels or impels this exuberant play of varying possibilities which seem to have no aim or meaning unless it be the beauty or delight of creation? A Mind, a seeking and curious inventive Thought, a hidden determining Will might be there, but there is no trace of it in the first and fundamental appearance of material Nature.

A first possible explanation points to a self-organising dynamic Chance that is at work,—a paradox necessitated by the appearance of inevitable order on one side, of unaccountable freak and fantasy on the other side of the cosmic phenomenon we call Nature. An inconscient and inconsequent Force, we may say, that acts at random and creates this or that by a general chance without any determining principle,—determinations coming in only as the result of a persistent repetition of the same rhythm of action and succeeding because only this repetitive rhythm could succeed in keeping things in being,—this is the energy of Nature. But this implies that somewhere in the origin of things there is a boundless Possibility or a womb of innumerable possibilities that are manifested out of it by the original Energy,—an incalculable Inconscient which we find some embarrassment in calling either an Existence or a Non-Existence; for without some such origin and basis the appearance and the action of the Energy is unintelligible. Yet an opposite aspect of the nature of the cosmic phenomenon as we see it appears to forbid the theory of a random action generating a persistent order. There is too much of an iron insistence on order, on a law basing the possibilities. One would be justified rather in supposing that there is an inherent imperative Truth of things unseen by us, but a Truth capable of manifold manifestation, throwing out a multitude of possibilities and variants of itself which the creative Energy by its action turns into so many realised actualities. This brings us to a second explanation—a mechanical necessity in things, its workings recognisable by us as so many mechanical laws of Nature;—the necessity, we might say, of some such secret inherent Truth of things as we have supposed, governing automatically the processes we observe in action in the universe. But a theory of mechanical Necessity by itself does not elucidate the free play of the endless unaccountable variations which are visible in the evolution: there must be behind the Necessity or in it a law of unity associated with a coexistent but dependent law of multiplicity, both insisting on manifestation; but the unity of what, the multiplicy of what? Mechanical Necessity can give no answer. Again the emergence of consciousness out of the Inconscient is a stumbling-block in the way of this theory; for it is a phenomenon which can have no place in an all-pervading truth of inconscient mechanical

Necessity. If there is a necessity which compels to emergence, it can be only this, that there is already a consciousness concealed in the Inconscient, waiting for evolution and when all is ready breaking out from its prison of apparent Nescience. We may indeed get rid of the difficulty of the imperative order of things by supposing that it does not exist, that determinism in Nature is imposed on it by our thought which needs such an imperative order to enable it to deal with its surroundings, but in reality there is no such thing; there is only a Force experimenting in a random action of infinitesimals which build up in their general results different determinations by a repetitive persistence operative in the sum of their action; thus we go back from Necessity to Chance as the basis of our existence. But what then is this Mind, this Consciousness which differs so radically from the Energy that produced it that for its action it has to impose its idea and need of order on the world she has made and in which it is obliged to live? There would then be the double contradiction of consciousness emerging from a fundamental Inconscience and of a Mind of order and reason manifesting as the brilliant final consequence of a world created by inconscient Chance. These things may be possible, but they need a better explanation than any yet given before we can accord to them our acceptance.

This opens the way for other explanations which make Consciousness the creator of this world out of an apparent original Inconscience. A Mind, a Will seems to have imagined and organised the universe, but it has veiled itself behind its creation; its first erection has been this screen of an inconscient Energy and a material form of substance, at once a disguise of its presence and a plastic creative basis on which it could work as an artisan uses for his production of forms and patterns a dumb and obedient material. All these things we see around us are then the thoughts of an extra-cosmic Divinity, a Being with an omnipotent and omniscient Mind and Will, who is responsible for the mathematical law of the physical universe, for its artistry of beauty, for its strange play of samenesses and variations, of concordances and discords, of combining and intermingling opposites, for the drama of consciousness struggling to exist and seeking to affirm itself in an inconscient universal order. The fact that this Divinity is invisible to us, undiscoverable by our mind and senses, offers no difficulty, since self-evidence or direct sign of an extra-cosmic Creator could not be expected in a cosmos which is void of his presence: the patent signals everywhere of the works of an Intelligence, of law, design, formula, adaptation of means to end, constant and inexhaustible invention, fantasy even but restrained by an ordering Reason might be considered sufficient proof of this origin of things. Or if this

Creator is not entirely supracosmic, but is also immanent in his works, even then there need be no other sign of him,—except indeed to some consciousness evolving in this inconscient world, but only when its evolution reached a point at which it could become aware of the indwelling Presence. The intervention of this evolving consciousness would not be a difficulty, since there would be no contradiction of the basic nature of things in its appearance; an omnipotent Mind could easily infuse something of itself into its creatures. One difficulty remains; it is the arbitrary nature of the creation, the incomprehensibility of its purpose, the crude meaninglessness of its law of unnecessary ignorance, strife and suffering, its ending without denouement or issue. A play? But why this stamp of so many undivine elements and characters in the play of One whose nature must be supposed to be divine? To the suggestion that what we see worked out in the world is the thoughts of God, the retort can be made that God could well have had better thoughts and the best thought of all would have been to refrain from the creation of an unhappy and unintelligible universe. All theistic explanations of existence starting from an extra-cosmic Deity stumble over this difficulty and can only evade it; it would disappear only if the creator were, even though exceeding the creation, yet immanent in it, himself in some sort both the player and the play, an Infinite casting infinite possibilities into the set form of an evolutionary cosmic order.

On that hypothesis, there must be behind the action of the material Energy a secret involved Consciousness, cosmic, infinite, building up through the action of that frontal Energy its means of an evolutionary manifestation, a creation out of itself in the boundless finite of the material universe. The apparent inconscience of the material Energy would be an indispensable condition for the structure of the material world-substance in which this Consciousness intends to involve itself so that it may grow by evolution out of its apparent opposite; for without some such device a complete involution would be impossible. If there is such a creation by the Infinite out of itself, it must be the manifestation, in a material disguise, of truths or powers of its own being: the forms or vehicles of these truths or powers would be the basic general or fundamental determinates we see in Nature; the particular determinates, which otherwise are unaccountable variations that have emerged from the vague general stuff in which they originate, would be the appropriate forms or vehicles of the possibilities that the truths or powers residing in these fundamentals bore within them. The principle of free variation of possibilities natural to an infinite Consciousness would be the explanation of the aspect of inconscient Chance of which we are aware in the workings of Nature,—inconscient only in appearance and so appearing because of the complete involution in Matter, because of the veil with which the secret Consciousness has disguised its presence. The principle of truths, real powers of the Infinite imperatively fulfilling themselves would be the explanation of the opposite aspect of a mechanical Necessity which we see in Nature,—mechanical in appearance only and so appearing because of the same veil of Inconscience. It would then be perfectly intelligible why the Inconscient does its works with a constant principle of mathematical architecture, of design, of effective arrangement of numbers, of adaptation of means to ends, of inexhaustible device and invention, one might almost say, a constant experimental skill and an automatism of purpose. The appearance of consciousness out of an apparent Inconscience would also be no longer inexplicable.

All the unexplained processes of Nature would find their meaning and their place if this hypothesis proved to be tenable. Energy seems to create substance, but, in reality, as existence is inherent in Consciousness-Force, so also substance would be inherent in Energy,—the Energy a manifestation of the Force, substance a manifestation of the secret Existence. But as it is a spiritual substance, it would not be apprehended by the material sense until it is given by Energy the forms of Matter seizable by that sense. One begins to understand also how arrangement of design, quantity and number can be a base for the manifestation of quality and property; for design, quantity and number are powers of existence-substance, quality and property are powers of the consciousness and its force that reside in the existence; they can then be made manifest and operative by a rhythm and process of substance.

. . .

BUT an approach from the material end of Existence cannot give us any certitude of validity for this hypothesis or for that matter for any other explanation of Nature and her procedure: the veil cast by the original Inconscience is too thick for the Mind to pierce and it is behind this veil that is hidden the secret origination of what is manifested; there are seated the truths and powers underlying the phenomena and processes that appear to us in the material front of Nature. To know with greater certitude we must follow the curve of evolving consciousness until it arrives at a height and largeness of self-enlightenment in which the primal secret is self-discovered; for presumably it must evolve, must eventually bring out what was held from the beginning by the occult original Consciousness in things of which it is a gradual manifestation.

. . .

A SUPRAMENTAL Truth-consciousness is at once the self-awareness of the Infinite and Eternal and a power of self-determination inherent in that self-awareness; the first is its foundation and status, the second is its power of being, the dynamis of its self-existence. All that a timeless eternity of self-awareness sees in itself as truth of being, the conscious power of its being manifests in Time-eternity. To Supermind therefore the Supreme is not a rigid Indeterminable, an all-negating Absolute; an infinite of being complete to itself in its own immutable purity of existence, its sole power a pure consciousness able only to dwell on the being's changeless eternity, on the immobile delight of its sheer self-existence, is not the whole Reality. The Infinite of Being must also be an Infinite of Power; containing in itself an eternal repose and quiescence, it must also be capable of an eternal action and creation: but this too must be an action in itself, a creation out of its own self eternal and infinite, since there could be nothing else out of which it could create; any basis of creation seeming to be other than itself must be still really in itself and of itself and could not be something foreign to its existence.

8

THE USELESSNESS
OF PROOFS*

Soren Kierkegaard (1813–1855), Danish philosopher and theologian, and pincipal founder of the philosophical movement called existentialism, has achieved wide recognition as an important thinker only in the last two generations. His philosophy combines an acceptance of Christian concepts and an extensive rejection of speculative philosophy as represented by Hegelian idealism. His principal philosophical works are: Concluding Unscientific Postscript, Philosophical Fragments, *and* Either-Or.

 Soren Kierkegaard

BUT what is this unknown something with which the Reason collides when inspired by its paradoxical passion, with the result of unsettling even man's knowledge of himself? It is the Unknown. It is not a human being, in so far as we know what man is; nor is it any other known thing. So let us call this unknown something: *the God.* It is nothing more than a name we assign to it. The idea of demonstrating that this unknown something (the God) exists, could scarcely suggest iself to the Reason. For if the God does not exist it would of course be impossible to prove it; and if he does exist it would be folly to attempt it. For at the very outset, in beginning my proof, I would have presupposed it, not as doubtful but as certain (a presupposition is never doubtful, for the very reason that it is a presupposition), since otherwise I would not begin, readily understanding that the whole would be impossible if he did not exist. But if when I speak of proving the God's existence I mean that I propose to prove that the Unknown, which exists, is the God, then I express myself unfortunately. For in that case I do not prove anything, least of all an existence, but merely develop the content of a conception. Generally speaking, it is a difficult matter

* Reprinted from *Philosophical Fragments* by Soren Kierkegaard by permission of Princeton University Press. Copyright 1936, 1962 by Princeton University Press.

to prove that anything exists; and what is still worse for the intrepid souls who undertake the venture, the difficulty is such that fame scarcely awaits those who concern themselves with it. The entire demonstration always turns into something very different and becomes an additional development of the consequences that flow from my having assumed that the object in question exists. Thus I always reason from existence, not toward existence, whether I move in the sphere of palpable sensible fact or in the realm of thought. I do not for example prove that a stone exists, but that some existing thing is a stone. The procedure in a court of justice does not prove that a criminal exists, but that the accused, whose existence is given, is a criminal. Whether we call existence an *accessorium* or the eternal *prius*, it is never subject to demonstration. Let us take ample time for consideration. We have no such reason for haste as have those who from concern for themselves or for the God or for some other thing, must make haste to get existence demonstrated. Under such circumstances there may indeed be need for haste, especially if the prover sincerely seeks to appreciate the danger that he himself, or the thing in question, may be non-existent unless the proof is finished and does not surreptitiously entertain the thought that it exists whether he succeeds in proving it or not.

If it were proposed to prove Napoleon's existence from Napoleon's deeds, would it not be a most curious proceeding? His existence does indeed explain his deeds, but the deeds do not prove *his* existence, unless I have already understood the word "his" so as thereby to have assumed his existence. But Napoleon is only an individual, and in so far there exists no absolute relationship between him and his deeds; some other person might have performed the same deeds. Perhaps this is the reason why I cannot pass from the deeds to existence. If I call these deeds the deeds of Napoleon the proof becomes superfluous, since I have already named him; if I ignore this, I can never prove from the deeds that they are Napoleon's, but only in a purely ideal manner that such deeds are the deeds of a great general, and so forth. But between the God and his works there is an absolute relationship; God is not a name but a concept. Is this perhaps the reason that his *essentia involvit existentiam?*[1] The works of the God are such that only the

---

[1] So Spinoza, who probes the depths of the God-idea in order to bring being out of it by way of thought, but not, it should be noted, as if being were an accidental characteristic, but rather as if it constituted an essential determination of content. Here lies Spinoza's profundity, but let us examine his reasoning. In *principia philosophiae Cartesianae, pars I, propositio VII, lemma I*, he says: "*quo res sua natura perfectior est, eo majorem existentiam et magis necessariam involvit; et contra, quo magis necessariam existentiam res sua natura involvit, eo*

God can perform them. Just so, but where then are the works of the God? The works from which I would deduce his existence are not directly and immediately given. The wisdom in nature, the goodness, the wisdom in the governance of the world—are all these manifest, perhaps, upon the very face of things? Are we not here confronted with the most terrible temptations to doubt, and is it not impossible finally to dispose of all these doubts? But from such an order of things I will surely not attempt to prove God's existence; and even if I began I would never finish, and would in addition have to live constantly in suspense, lest something so terrible should suddenly happen that my bit of proof would be demolished. From what works then do I propose to derive the proof? From the works as apprehended through an ideal interpretation, i.e., such as they do not immediately reveal themselves. But in that case it is not from the works that I make the proof; I merely develop the ideality I have presupposed, and because of my confidence in *this* I make so bold as to defy all objections, even those that

---

perfectior." The more perfect therefore a thing is, the more being it has; the more being it has, the more perfect it is. This is however a tautology, which becomes still more evident in a note, *nota II: "quod hic non loquimur de pulchritudine et aliis perfectionibus, quas homines ex superstitione et ignorantia perfectiones vocare voluerunt. Sed per perfectionem intelligo tantum realitatem sive esse."* He explains *perfectio* by *realitas, esse;* so that the more perfect a thing is, the more it is; but its perfection consists in having more *esse* in itself; that is to say, the more a thing is, the more it is. So much for the tautology, but now further. What is lacking here is a distinction between factual being and ideal being. The terminology which permits us to speak of more or less of being, and consequently of degrees of reality or being, is in itself lacking in clearness, and becomes still more confusing when the above distinction is neglected—in other words, when Spinoza does indeed speak profoundly but fails first to consider the difficulty. In the case of factual being it is meaningless to speak of more or less of being. A fly, when it is, has as much being as God; with respect to factual being the stupid remark I here set down has as much being as Spinoza's profundity, for factual being is subject to the dialectic of Hamlet: to be or not to be. Factual being is wholly indifferent to any and all variations in essence, and everything that exists participates without petty jealousy in being, and participates in the same degree. Ideally, to be sure, the case is quite different. *But the moment I speak of being in the ideal sense I no longer speak of being, but of essence.* Highest ideality has this necessity and therefore it is. But this its being is identical with its essence; such being does not involve it dialectically in the determinations of factual being, since it is; nor can it be said to have more or less of being in relation to other things. In the old days this used to be expressed, if somewhat imperfectly, by saying that if God is possible, he is *eo ipso* necessary (Leibniz). Spinoza's principle is thus quite correct and his tautology in order; but it is also certain that he altogether evades the difficulty. For the difficulty is to lay hold of God's factual being and to introduce God's ideal essence dialectically into the sphere of factual being.

have not yet been made. In beginning my proof I presuppose the ideal interpretation, and also that I will be successful in carrying it through; but what else is this but to presuppose that the God exists, so that I really begin by virtue of confidence in him?

And how does the God's existence emerge from the proof? Does it follow straightway, without any breach of continuity? Or have we not here an analogy to the behaviour of the little Cartesian dolls? As soon as I let go of the doll it stands on its head. As soon as I let it go—I must therefore let it go. So also with the proof. As long as I keep my hold on the proof, i.e., continue to demonstrate, the existence does not come out, if for no other reason than that I am engaged in proving it; but when I let the proof go, the existence is there. But this act of letting go is surely also something; it is indeed a contribution of mine. Must not this also be taken into the account, this little moment, brief as it may be—it need not be long, for it is a *leap*. However brief this moment, if only an instantaneous now, this "now" must be included in the reckoning. If anyone wishes to have it ignored, I will use it to tell a little anecdote, in order to show that it nevertheless does exist. Chrysippus was experimenting with a sorites to see if he could not bring about a break in its quality, either progressively or retrogressively. But Carneades could not get it in his head when the new quality actually emerged. Then Chrysippus told him to try making a little pause in the reckoning, and so—so it would be easier to understand. Carneades replied: With the greatest pleasure, please do not hesitate on my account; you may not only pause, but even lie down to sleep, and it will help you just as little; for when you awake we will begin again where you left off. Just so; it boots as little to try to get rid of something by sleeping as to try to come into the possession of something in the same manner.

Whoever therefore attempts to demonstrate the existence of God (except in the sense of clarifying the concept, and without the *reservatio finalis* noted above, that the existence emerges from the demonstration by a leap) proves in lieu thereof something else, something which at times perhaps does not need a proof, and in any case needs none better; for the fool says in his heart that there is no God, but whoever says in his heart or to men: Wait just a little and I will prove it—what a rare man of wisdom is he![1] If in the moment of beginning his proof it is not absolutely undetermined whether the God exists or not, he does not prove it; and if it is thus undetermined in the beginning he will never come to begin, partly from fear of failure, since the God perhaps does not exist, and

[1] What an excellent subject for a comedy of the higher lunacy!

partly because he has nothing with which to begin.—A project of this kind would scarcely have been undertaken by the ancients. Socrates at least, who is credited with having put forth the physico-teleological proof for God's existence, did not go about it in any such manner. He always presupposes the God's existence, and under this presupposition seeks to interpenetrate nature with the idea of purpose. Had he been asked why he pursued this method, he would doubtless have explained that he lacked the courage to venture out upon so perilous a voyage of discovery without having made sure of the God's existence behind him. At the word of the God he casts his net as if to catch the idea of purpose; for nature herself finds many means of frightening the inquirer, and distracts him by many a digression.

The paradoxical passion of the Reason thus comes repeatedly into collision with this Unknown, which does indeed exist, but is unknown, and in so far does not exist. The Reason cannot advance beyond this point, and yet it cannot refrain in its paradoxicalness from arriving at this limit and occupying itself therewith. It will not serve to dismiss its relation to it simply by asserting that the Unknown does not exist, since this itself involves a relationship. But what then is the Unknown, since the designation of it as the God merely signifies for us that it is unknown? To say that it is the Unknown because it cannot be known, and even if it were capable of being known, it could not be expressed, does not satisfy the demands of passion, though it correctly interprets the Unknown as a limit; but a limit is precisely a torment for passion, though it also serves as an incitement. And yet the Reason can come no further, whether it risks an issue *via negationis* or *via eminentia*.

What then is the Unknown? It is the limit to which the Reason repeatedly comes, and in so far, substituting a static form of conception for the dynamic, it is the different, the absolutely different. But because it is absolutely different, there is no mark by which it could be distinguished. When qualified as absolutely different it seems on the verge of disclosure, but this is not the case; for the Reason cannot even conceive an absolute unlikeness. The Reason cannot negate itself absolutely, but uses itself for the purpose, and thus conceives only such an unlikeness within itself as it can conceive by means of itself; it cannot absolutely transcend itself, and hence conceives only such a superiority over itself as it can conceive by means of itself. Unless the Unknown (the God) remains a mere limiting conception, the single idea of difference will be thrown into a state of confusion, and become many ideas of many differences. The Unknown is then in a condition of dispersion (διασπορά), and the Reason may choose at pleasure from what is at hand and the imagination may suggest (the monstrous, the ludicrous, etc.) .

But it is impossible to hold fast to a difference of this nature. Every time this is done it is essentially an arbitrary act, and deepest down in the heart of piety lurks the mad caprice which knows that it has itself produced the God. If no specific determination of difference can be held fast, because there is no distinguishing mark, like and unlike finally become identified with one another, thus sharing the fate of all such dialectical opposites. The unlikeness clings to the Reason and confounds it, so that the Reason no longer knows itself and quite consistently confuses itself with the unlikeness. On this point paganism has been sufficiently prolific in fantastic inventions. As for the last named supposition, the self-irony of the Reason, I shall attempt to delineate it merely by a stroke or two, without raising any question of its being historical. There exists an individual whose appearance is precisely like that of other men; he grows up to manhood like others, he marries, he has an occupation by which he earns his livelihood, and he makes provision for the future as befits a man. For though it may be beautiful to live like the birds of the air, it is not lawful, and may lead to the sorriest of consequences: either starvation if one has enough persistence, or dependence on the bounty of others. This man is also the God. How do I know? I cannot know it, for in order to know it I would have to know the God, and the nature of the difference between the God and man; and this I cannot know, because the Reason has reduced it to likeness with that from which it was unlike. Thus the God becomes the most terrible of deceivers, because the Reason has deceived itself. The Reason has brought the God as near as possible, and yet he is as far away as ever.

Additional Readings

CAMPBELL, C. A., On Selfhood and Godhood.

GILSON, E., God and Philosophy.

HARTSHORNE, CHARLES, Man's Vision of God.

HICK, JOHN (ed.) , The Existence of God (an anthology of classical and contemporary discussions) .

LEWIS, C. S., Mere Christianity.

———, Miracles.

MARCEL, GABRIEL, Creative Fidelity, Ch. IX.

MARITAIN, JACQUES, *Approaches to God.*

PLANTINGA, A. (ed.), *The Ontological Argument* (an anthology of classical and contemporary discussions).

TEMPLE, WM., *Nature, Man and God.*

TENNANT, F. R., *Philosophical Theology,* Vol. II.

PART III

RELIGIOUS

EXPERIENCE

AND REVELATION

This group of selections deals with the claim of some people that their knowledge of God (or other religious knowledge) is derived from direct experience rather than from inference or argument. The difference is the same as that which separates the knowledge of the witness who saw a crime being committed from that of the detective who later pieces together a picture of the crime by drawing conclusions from a set of clues. They may possibly agree about the event, but the position of the witness is based more directly upon his own experience than is that of the detective, which is mediated by an inference.

Three further distinctions may be useful here. The first is that between religious experience in general and revelation in particular. A revelation would presumably be, or at least would depend upon, an experience. But some thinkers might wish to claim that the concept of revelation is more restricted, and perhaps more useful and informative, than that of religious experience. To make this distinction clear, of course, would require a specification of just what is meant by "revelation," i.e., a specification of just what features distinguish a revelatory experience from other sorts of experience.

Roughly, we might suppose that the notion of revelation is closely related to that of communication. If so, then religious revelatory experiences will be construed as sharing some special features with those experiences in which we say that one person "reveals himself" to another, especially in speech. These features seem mostly to involve things like intention and purpose on the part of the person who reveals himself. His own initiative plays a large part in bringing about the special revelatory experience. most often by speech or some other communicative activity. On the other hand, we may "experience" a person, without any initiative or intention on his part, in much the same way as we might see an animal or a stone. Thinkers who believe that any encounter with God will involve a large measure of God's activity may be expected to move toward the revelation terminology, and religions which view God as a person (or as very much like a person), with attributes such as will and purpose, will find it appropriate. Religious thinkers who construe God in an impersonal way, on the other hand, will probably find the concept of revelation unsuitable, and are likely to use more general terms, such as "experience," in their discussions.

The second distinction is that between one's own experience (whether revelatory or not], and the experience of someone else. A person might maintain that his religious knowledge is derived from his own experience of the divine reality, or that it is derived from reports of others, e.g., from the Bible, or the accounts of mystics. Many philosophical inquiries into religious experience seem to be limited to a discussion of such reports of experience. (Notice, for example, how Broad's discussion is carried on.) Such discussions will have to be evaluated within their self-imposed limits. But the student should also ask himself whether the problems which arise with respect to his own experience are not in some ways different from those which arise with respect to the reports of others. In judging whether his own seeing of a dog on the sidewalk is veridical, does he not in fact (and justifiably) follow some different method from that which he employs in determining whether his friend's report of seeing a dog is true? One might note, as a start, that a person could resolve to ignore all reports as unreliable and to rely only upon his own experience. While this would be very restrictive, it seems to be a possible course of action. A person could not, however, rely upon reports while rejecting all of his own experience as unreliable. For he cannot get the reports except through some experience of his own. One's own experience, then, seems to be in some way more fundamental than the reports of other people's experience, and a judgment as to the reliability of some of one's own experience is prior to analogous judgments about the testimony of others.

A third distinction is the rather vague one between mysticism and other sorts of religious experience. Mysticism is a very vague term, but we might use it to cover religious experiences which may be accompanied by unusual and extreme physiological or psychological states, and are largely, if not totally, independent of the experience of ordinary objects. We include in this section an excerpt from an oriental mystic, Lao Tzu, and a discussion of the Zen experience of Satori. Many western mystical writings (such as the works of St. Teresa cited in the list of additional readings) also seem to fit this description. Some religious experiences seem to be rather different from these, however. They are not independent of the experience of ordinary objects, but claim to reach the divine reality *through* the experience of the world or of some part of it. The short selection from Paul Tournier embodies such a claim. In the face of such claims, it is important not to assume uncritically that religious experiences must be either rare or highly dramatic.

MYSTICAL UNION*

Lao Tzu (6th century B.C.), an ancient Chinese sage, is reputed to be the founder of philosophical Taoism and traditionally believed to be the author of the Tao Te Ching (Classic of the Way and Virtue)*, in which the main theses of Taoist philosophy are given poetic expression.*

 Lao Tzu

The Tao that can be expressed is not the eternal Tao;
The name that can be defined is not the unchanging name.
Non-existence is called the antecedent of heaven and earth;
Existence is the mother of all things.
From eternal non-existence, therefore, we serenely observe the mysterious beginning of the Universe;
From eternal existence we clearly see the apparent distinctions.
These two are the same in source and become different when manifested.
This sameness is called profundity. Infinite profundity is the gate whence comes the beginning of all parts of the Universe.

When all in the world understand beauty to be beautiful, then ugliness exists.
When all understand goodness to be good, then evil exists.
Thus existence suggests non-existence;
Easy gives rise to difficult;
Short is derived from long by comparison;
Low is distinguished from high by positions;
Resonance harmonizes sound;
After follows before.
Therefore, the Sage carries on his business without action, and gives his teaching without words.

* From Lao Tzu, *Tao Te Ching,* tr. by Chu Ta-Kao. Reprinted by permission of George Allen & Unwin, Ltd., publishers.

Heaven is lasting and earth enduring.
The reason why they are lasting and enduring is that they do not
live for themselves;
Therefore they live long.
In the same way the Sage keeps himself behind and he is in the
front;
He forgets himself and he is preserved.
Is it not because he is not self-interested
That his self-interest is established?

Can you keep the soul always concentrated from straying?
Can you regulate the breath and become soft and pliant like an
infant?
Can you clear and get rid of the unforeseen and be free from
fault?
Can you love the people and govern the state by non-action?
Can you open and shut the gates of nature like a female?
Can you become enlightened and penetrate everywhere without
knowledge?

Thirty spokes unite in one nave,
And because of the part where nothing exists we have the use of a
carriage wheel.
Clay is moulded into vessels,
And because of the space where nothing exists we are able to use
them as vessels.
Doors and windows are cut out in the walls of a house,
And because they are empty spaces, we are able to use them.
Therefore, on the one hand we have the benefit of existence, and on
the other, we make use of non-existence.

That which we look at and cannot see is called plainness.
That which we listen to and cannot hear is called rareness.
That which we grope for and cannot get is called minuteness.
These three cannot be closely examined;
So they blend into One.

Revealed, it is not dazzling;
Hidden, it is not dark.
Infinite, it cannot be defined.
It goes back to non-existence.
It is called the form of the formless,
And the image of non-existence.
It is called mystery.
Meet it, you cannot see its face;
Follow it, you cannot see its back.

By adhering to the Tao of the past
You will master the existence of the present
And be able to know the origin of the past.
This is called the clue of Tao.

Attain to the goal of absolute vacuity;
Keep to the state of perfect peace.
All things come into existence,
And thence we see them return.
Look at the things that have been flourishing;
Each goes back to its origin.
Going back to the origin is called peace;
It means reversion to destiny.
Reversion to destiny is called eternity.
He who knows eternity is called enlightened.
He who does not know eternity is running blindly into miseries.
Knowing eternity he is all-embracing.
Being all-embracing he can attain magnanimity.
Being magnanimous he can attain omnipresence.
Being omnipresent he can attain supremacy.
Being supreme he can attain Tao.
He who attains Tao is everlasting.
Though his body may decay he never perishes.

The great virtue as manifested is but following Tao.
Tao is a thing that is both invisible and intangible.
Intangible and invisible, yet there are forms in it;
Invisible and intangible, yet there is substance in it;
Subtle and obscure, there is essence in it;
This essence being invariably true, there is faith in it.

From of old till now, it has never lost its (nameless) name,
Through which the origin of all things has passed.
How do I know that it is so with the origin of all things?
By this (Tao).

To be sparing of words is natural.

A violent wind cannot last a whole morning; pelting rain cannot last a whole day. Who have made these things but heaven and earth? Inasmuch as heaven and earth cannot last for ever, how can man? He who engages himself in Tao is identified with Tao. He who engages himself in virtue is identified with virtue. He who engages himself in abandonment is identified with abandonment. Identified with Tao he will be well received by Tao. Identified with virtue he will be well received by virtue. Identified with abandonment he will be well received by abandonment.

The great Tao pervades everywhere, both on the left and on the right.
By it all things came into being, and it does not reject them.
Merits accomplished, it does not possess them.
It loves and nourishes all things but does not dominate over them.
It is always non-existent; therefore it can be named as small.
All things return home to it, and it does not claim mastery over them; therefore it can be named as great.
Because it never assumes greatness, therefore it can accomplish greatness.

Not knowing that one knows is best;
Thinking that one knows when one does not know is sickness.
Only when one becomes sick of this sickness can one be free from sickness.
The Sage is never sick; because he is sick of this sickness, therefore he is not sick.

2

A RELIGIOUS

EXPERIENCE*

Paul Tournier (1898–) is a contemporary Swiss psychiatrist who has attempted to view the field of psychiatry from a Christian perspective. Some of his more important non-technical writings are The Meaning of Persons, The Healing of Persons, *and* Guilt and Grace.

 Paul Tournier

WE may hear the voice of God in a biblical passage which comes home to us personally, in the remembrance of a remark made by a friend, in a question which we put to ourselves, in a thought which comes to us when in his presence, sometimes when we least expect it.

I always remember one New Year's Eve. I had left my wife at home in order to spend the moment of midnight, in accordance with tradition, standing in the Cathedral square with the uncle who had brought me up. When I got back I found my wife overwhelmed and transformed.

'I have suddenly realized for the first time the greatness of God!' she told me.

As the bells rang out, telling of the inexorable and endless march of time, it had been borne in upon her that God was infinitely greater than she had ever imagined. The voice of God had spoken to her through the voice of the bells, and she had answered. Her answer could be read in her radiant face. It was a reply so clear and true that I in my turn was touched by it.

The greatest event in life had taken place: the personal encounter of Creator and creature, the dialogue between the voice of God, so great that it makes itself heard in every earthly sound, without any one of them ever sufficing completely to express it, and the voice of man, so weak that nothing he can say is adequate to the reply. It is an incredible dialogue, so disproportionate are the participants—and yet they are like, for God willed man to be 'in his

* From Paul Tournier, *The Meaning of Persons,* tr. by Edwin Hudson. Reprinted by permission of Harper & Row, Publishers.

image' (Gen. 1.27) ; they are both persons, capable of engaging together in dialogue.

We were very weary, my wife and I, at the time. For years I had devoted myself energetically to church work, where as everyone knows, one is always coming up against problems which seem trivial indeed compared with the task to be accomplished. And now, of a sudden, God was showing us his greatness, calling us out of the tangle of sterile arguments in which I had let myself be caught. During the year that followed he led us from experience to experience, to a renewing of our whole personal and professional life, calling us from ecclesiastical activity to a spiritual ministry.

3

RELIGION AS THE FEELING

OF ABSOLUTE DEPENDENCE*

*Friedrich Schleiermacher (1768–1834)
was professor at the University of Berlin
and is regarded widely as the classical
founder and exponent of protestant liberalism. His theology reinterprets traditional Christian concepts as constructions
of subjective religious experience. His
best known works are:* Addresses on Religion, *and* The Christian Faith.

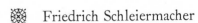 Friedrich Schleiermacher

3. THE PIETY WHICH FORMS THE BASIS OF ALL ECCLESIASTICAL COMMUNIONS IS, CONSIDERED PURELY IN ITSELF, NEITHER A KNOWING NOR A DOING, BUT A MODIFICATION OF FEELING, OR OF IMMEDIATE SELF-CONSCIOUSNESS.

NOTE.—Cf. the *Speeches on Religion* (Eng. trans.) , pp. 28 ff.

1. That a Church is nothing but a communion or association relating to religion or piety, is beyond all doubt for us Evangelical (Protestant) Christians, since we regard it as equivalent to degeneration in a Church when it begins to occupy itself with other matters as well, whether the affairs of science or of outward organization; just as we also always oppose any attempt on the part of the leaders of State or of science, as such, to order the affairs of religion. But, at the same time, we have no desire to keep the leaders of science from scrutinizing and passing judgment from their own point of view upon both piety itself and the communion relating to it, and determining their proper place in the total field of human life; since piety and Church, like other things, are material for scientific knowledge. Indeed, we ourselves are here entering upon such a scrutiny. And, similarly, we would not keep the leaders of State from fixing the outward relations of the religious communions according to the principles of civil organization—which, however, by no means implies that the religious communion is a product of the State or a component part of it.

* From Friedrich Schleiermacher, *The Christian Faith*, ed. by H. R. Mackintosh and J. S. Stewart. Reprinted by permission of T. & T. Clark.

However, not only we, but even those Churches which are not so clear about keeping apart Church and State, or ecclesiastical and scientific association, must assent to what we have laid down. For they cannot assign to the Church more than an indirect influence upon these other associations; and it is only the maintenance, regulation, and advancement of piety which they can regard as the essential business of the Church.

2. When Feeling and Self-consciousness are here put side by side as equivalent, it is by no means intended to introduce generally a manner of speech in which the two expressions would be simply synonymous. The term 'feeling' has in the language of common life been long current in this religious connexion; but for scientific usage it needs to be more precisely defined; and it is to do this that the other word is added. So that if anyone takes the word 'feeling' in a sense so wide as to include unconscious states, he will by the other word be reminded that such is not the usage we are here maintaining. Again, to the term 'self-consciousness' is added the determining epithet 'immediate,' lest anyone should think of a kind of self-consciousness which is not feeling at all; as, *e.g.*, when the name of self-consciousness is given to that consciousness of self which is more like an objective consciousness, being a representation of oneself, and thus mediated by self-contemplation. Even when such a representation of ourselves, as we exist in a given portion of time, in thinking, *e.g.*, or in willing, moves quite close to, or even interpenetrates, the individual moments of the mental state, this kind of self-consciousness does appear simply as an *accompaniment* of the state itself. But the real immediate self-consciousness, which is not representation but in the proper sense feeling, is by no means always simply an accompaniment. It may rather be presumed that in this respect everyone has a twofold experience. In the first place, it is everybody's experience that there are moments in which all thinking and willing retreat behind a self-consciousness of one form or another; but, in the second place, that at times this same form of self-consciousness persists unaltered during a series of diverse acts of thinking and willing, taking up no relation to these, and thus not being in the proper sense even an accompaniment of them. Thus joy and sorrow—those mental phases which are always so important in the realm of religion—are genuine states of feeling, in the proper sense explained above; whereas self-approval and self-reproach, apart from their subsequently passing into joy and sorrow, belong in themselves rather to the objective consciousness of self, as results of an analytic contemplation. Nowhere, perhaps, do the two forms

stand nearer to each other than here, but just for that reason this comparison puts the difference in the clearest light.

NOTE.—Steffen's account of feeling is closely akin to mine, and the passage from it to mine is easy (*Falsche Theologie,* pp. 99, 100). 'The immediate presence of whole undivided Being, etc.' On the other hand, the account given by Baumgarten-Crusius (*Einleitung in das Studium der Dogmatik,* p. 56), apart from its antithesis between feeling and self-consciousness, (*a*) does not comprehend the whole, but only the higher regions, of feeling, and (*b*) seems to transfer feeling into the realm of the objective consciousness by using the word 'perception' (*Wahrnehmung*).

3. Our proposition seems to assume that in addition to Knowing, Doing, and Feeling, there is no fourth. This is not done, however, in the sense which would be required for an apagogic proof; but those other two are placed alongside of Feeling simply in order that, with the exposition of our own view, we may at the same time take up and discuss those divergent views which are actually in existence. So that we might leave the question entirely aside whether there is a fourth such element in the soul, but for two reasons: namely, in the first place, that it is our duty to convince ourselves as to whether there is still another region to which piety might be assigned; and, in the second place, that we must set ourselves to grasp clearly the relation which subsists between Christian piety in itself, on the one hand, and both Christian belief (so far as it can be brought into the form of knowledge) and Christian action, on the other. Now, if the relation of the three elements above-mentioned were anywhere set forth in a universally recognized way, we could simply appeal to that. But, as things are, we must in this place say what is necessary on the subject; though this is to be regarded as simply borrowed from Psychology, and it should be well noted that the truth of the matter (namely, that piety is feeling) remains entirely independent of the correctness of the following discussion. Life, then, is to be conceived as an alternation between an abiding-in-self (*Insichbleiben*) and a passing-beyond-self (*Aussichheraustreten*) on the part of the subject. The two forms of consciousness (Knowing and Feeling) constitute the abiding-in-self, while Doing proper is the passing-beyond-self. Thus far, then, Knowing and Feeling stand together in antithesis to Doing. But while Knowing, in the sense of possessing knowledge, is an abiding-in-self on the part of the subject, nevertheless as the act of knowing, it only becomes real by a passing-beyond-self of the subject, and in this sense it is a Doing. As regards Feeling, on the other hand, it is not only in its duration as a result of stimulation that it is an abiding-in-self: even as the process of being stimulated,

it is not effected by the subject, but simply takes place in the subject, and thus, since it belongs altogether to the realm of receptivity, it is entirely an abiding-in-self; and in this sense it stands alone in antithesis to the other two—Knowing and Doing.

As regards the question whether there is a fourth to these three, Feeling, Knowing, and Doing; or a third to these two, abiding-in-self and passing-beyond-self: the unity of these is indeed not one of the two or the three themselves; but no one can place this unity alongside of these others as a co-ordinate third or fourth entity. The unity rather is the essence of the subject itself, which manifests itself in those severally distinct forms, and is thus, to give it a name which in this particular connexion is permissible, their common foundation. Similarly, on the other hand, every actual moment of life is, in its total content, a complex of these two or these three, though two of them may be present only in vestige or in germ. But a third to those two (one of which is again divided into two) will scarcely be found.

4. But now (these three, Feeling, Knowing, and Doing being granted) while we here set forth once more the oft-asserted view that, of the three, Feeling is the one to which piety belongs, it is not in any wise meant, as indeed the above discussion shows, that piety is excluded from all connexion with Knowing and Doing. For, indeed, it is the case in general that the immediate self-consciousness is always the mediating link in the transition between moments in which Knowing predominates and those in which Doing predominates, so that a different Doing may proceed from the same Knowing in different people according as a different determination of self-consciousness enters in. And thus it will fall to piety to stimulate Knowing and Doing, and every moment in which piety has a predominant place will contain within itself one or both of these in germs. But just this is the very truth represented by our proposition, and is in no wise an objection to it; for were it otherwise the religious moments could not combine with the others to form a single life, but piety would be something isolated and without any influence upon the other mental functions of our lives. However, in representing this truth, and thus securing to piety its own peculiar province in its connexion with all other provinces, our proposition is opposing the assertions from other quarters that piety is a Knowing, or a Doing, or both, or a state made up of Feeling, Knowing, and Doing; and in this polemical connexion our proposition must now be still more closely considered.

If, then, piety did consist in Knowing, it would have to be, above all, that knowledge, in its entirety or in its essence, which is here set up as the content of Dogmatics (*Glaubenslehre*) : otherwise it must be a complete mistake for us here to investigate the nature of piety in the interests of our study of Dogmatics. But if piety *is* that knowledge, then the amount of such knowledge in a man must be the measure of his piety. For anything which, in its rise and fall, is not the measure of the perfection of a given object cannot constitute the essence of that object. Accordingly, on the hypothesis in question, the most perfect master of Christian Dogmatics would always be likewise the most pious Christian. And no one will admit this to be the case, even if we premise that the most perfect master is only he who keeps most to what is essential and does not forget it in accessories and side-issues; but all will agree rather that the same degree of perfection in that knowledge may be accompanied by very different degrees of piety, and the same degree of piety by very different degrees of knowledge. It may, however, be objected that the assertion that piety is a matter of Knowing refers not so much to the content of that knowledge as to the certainty which characterizes its representations; so that the knowledge of doctrines is piety only in virtue of the certainty attached to them, and thus only in virtue of the strength of the conviction, while a possession of the doctrines without conviction is not piety at all. Then the strength of the conviction would be the measure of the piety; and this is undoubtedly what those people have chiefly in mind who so love to paraphrase the word *Faith* as 'fidelity to one's convictions.' But in all other more typical fields of knowledge the only measure of conviction is the clearness and completeness of the thinking itself. Now if it is to be the same with *this* conviction, then we should simply be back at our old point, that he who thinks the religious propositions most clearly and completely, individually and in their connexions, must likewise be the most pious man. If, then, this conclusion is still to be rejected, but the hypothesis is to be retained (namely, that conviction is the measure of piety) , the conviction in this case must be of a different kind and must have a different measure. However closely, then, piety may be connected with this conviction, it does not follow that it is connected in the same way with that knowledge. And if, nevertheless, the knowledge which forms Dogmatics has to relate itself to piety, the explanation of this is that while piety is, of course, the object of this knowledge, the knowledge can only be explicated in virtue of a certainty which inheres in the determinations of self-consciousness.

If, on the other hand, piety consists in Doing, it is manifest that the Doing which constitutes it cannot be defined by its content; for experience teaches that not only the most admirable but also the most abominable, not only the most useful but also the most inane and meaningless things, are done as pious and out of piety. Thus we are thrown back simply upon the form, upon the method and manner in which the thing comes to be done. But this can only be understood from the two *termini,* the underlying motive as the starting-point, and the intended result as the goal. Now no one will pronounce an action more or less pious because of the greater or less degree of completeness with which the intended result is achieved. Suppose we then are thrown back upon the motive. It is manifest that underlying every motive there is a certain determination of self-consciousness, be it pleasure or pain, and that it is by these that one motive can most clearly be distinguished from another. Accordingly an action (a Doing) will be pious in so far as the determination of self-consciousness, the feeling which had become affective and had passed into a motive impulse, is a pious one.

Thus both hypotheses lead to the same point: that there are both a Knowing and a Doing which pertain to piety, but neither of these constitutes the essence of piety: they only pertain to it inasmuch as the stirred-up Feeling sometimes comes to rest in a thinking which fixes it. sometimes discharges itself in an action which expresses it.

Finally, no one will deny that there are states of Feeling, such as penitence, contrition, confidence, and joy in God, which we pronounce pious in themselves, without regard to any Knowing or Doing that proceeds from them, though, of course, we expect both that they will work themselves out in actions which are otherwise obligatory, and that the reflective impulse will turn its attention to them.

5. From what we have now said it is already clear how we must judge the assertion that piety is a state in which Knowing, Feeling, and Doing are combined. Of course we reject it if it means that the Feeling is derived from the Knowing and the Doing from the Feeling. But if no subordination is intended, then the assertion might just as well be the description of any other quite clear and living moment as of a religious one. For though the idea of the goal of an action precedes the action itself, at the same time it continues to accompany the action, and the relation between the two expresses itself simultaneously in the self-consciousness through a greater or less degree of satisfaction and assurance; so that even here all three elements are combined in the total content of the state. A similar situation exists in the case of Knowing. For the thinking activity, as a successfully accomplished operation, expresses itself in the self-consciousness as a confident certainty. But simultaneously it becomes also an endeavour to connect the apprehended truth with other truths or to seek out cases for its application, and thus there is

always present simultaneously the commencement of a Doing, which develops fully when the opportunity offers; and so here also we find Knowing, Feeling, and Doing all together in the total state. But now, just as the first-described state remains, notwithstanding, essentially a Doing, and the second a Knowing, so piety in its diverse expressions remains essentially a state of Feeling. This state is subsequently caught up into the region of thinking, but only in so far as each religious man is at the same time inclined towards thinking and exercised therein; and only in the same way and according to the same measure does this inner piety emerge in living movement and representative action. It also follows from this account of the matter that Feeling is not to be thought of as something either confused or inactive; since, on the one hand, it is strongest in our most vivid moments, and either directly or indirectly lies at the root of every expression of our wills, and, on the other hand, it can be grasped by thought and conceived of in its own nature.

But suppose there are other people who would exclude Feeling altogether from our field, and therefore describe piety simply as a Knowledge which begets actions or as a Doing which proceeds from a Knowing: these people not only would have to settle first among themselves whether piety is a Knowing or a Doing, but would also have to show us how a Doing can arise from a Knowing except as mediated by a determination of self-consciousness. And if they have eventually to admit this point, then they will also be convinced by the above discussion that if such a complex does bear the character of piety, nevertheless the element of Knowing in it has not in itself got the length of being piety, and the element of Doing is in itself no longer piety, but the piety is just the determination of self-consciousness which comes in between the two. But that relationship can always hold in the reverse order also: the Doing has not got the length of being piety in those cases in which a determinate self-consciousness only results from an accomplished action; and the Knowing is in itself no longer piety when it has no other content than that determination of self-consciousness caught up into thought.

4. THE COMMON ELEMENT IN ALL HOWSOEVER DIVERSE EXPRESSIONS OF PIETY, BY WHICH THESE ARE CONJOINTLY DISTINGUISHED FROM ALL OTHER FEELINGS, OR, IN OTHER WORDS, THE SELF-IDENTICAL ESSENCE OF PIETY, IS THIS: THE CONSCIOUSNESS OF BEING ABSOLUTELY DEPENDENT, OR, WHICH IS THE SAME THING, OF BEING IN RELATION WITH GOD.

NOTE.—For the word *schlechthinig* [translated 'absolute'], which occurs frequently in the following exposition, I am indebted to Professor Delbrück. I was unwilling to venture upon its use, and I am not aware that it has occurred anywhere else. But now that he has given it me, I find it very convenient to follow his lead in using it.

1. IN any actual state of consciousness, no matter whether it merely accompanies a thought or action or occupies a moment for itself, we are never simply conscious of our Selves in their unchanging identity, but are always at the same time conscious of a changing determination of them. The Ego in itself can be represented objectively; but every consciousness of self is at the same time the consciousness of a variable state of being. But in this distinction of the latter from the former, it is implied that the variable does not proceed purely from the self-identical, for in that case it could not be distinguished from it. Thus in every self-consciousness there are two elements, which we might call respectively a self-caused element (*ein Sichselbstsetzen*) and a non-self-caused element (*ein Sichselbstnichtsogesetzthaben*) ; or a Being and a Having-by-some-means-come-to-be (*ein Sein und ein Irgendwiegewordensein*). The latter of these presupposes for every self-consciousness another factor besides the Ego, a factor which is the source of the particular determination, and without which the self-consciousness would not be precisely what it is. But this Other is not objectively presented in the immediate self-consciousness with which alone we are here concerned. For though, of course, the double constitution of self-consciousness causes us always to look objectively for an Other to which we can trace the origin of our particular state, yet this search is a separate act with which we are not at present concerned. In self-consciousness there are only two elements: the one expresses the existence of the subject for itself, the other its co-existence with an Other.

Now to these two elements, as they exist together in the temporal self-consciousness, correspond in the subject its *Receptivity* and its (spontaneous) *Activity*. If we could think away the co-existence with an Other, but otherwise think ourselves as we are, then a self-consciousness which predominantly expressed an affective condition of receptivity would be impossible, and any self-consciousness could then express only activity—an activity, however, which, not being directed to any object, would be merely an urge outwards, an indefinite 'agility' without form or colour. But as we never do exist except along with an Other, so even in every outward-tending self-consciousness the element of receptivity, in some way or other affected, is the primary one; and even the self-consciousness which accompanies an action (acts of knowing included), while it predominantly expresses spontaneous movement and activity, is always related (though the relation is often a quite indefinite one) to a prior moment of affective receptivity, through which the original 'agility' received its direction. To these propositions assent can be unconditionally demanded; and no one will deny them who is capable of a little introspection and can find interest in the real subject of our present inquiries.

2. The common element in all those determinations of self-consciousness which predominantly express a receptivity affected from some outside quarter is the *feeling of Dependence*. On the other hand, the common element in all those determinations which predominantly express spontaneous movement and activity is the *feeling of Freedom*. The former is the case not only because it is by an influence from some other quarter that we have come to such a state, but particularly because we *could* not so become except by means of an Other. The latter is the case because in these instances an Other is determined by us, and without our spontaneous activity could not be so determined. These two definitions may, indeed, seem to be still incomplete, inasmuch as there is also a mobility of the subject which is not connected with an Other at all, but which seems to be subject to the same antithesis as that just explained. But when we become such-and-such from within outwards, for ourselves, without any Other being involved, that is the simple situation of the temporal development of a being which remains essentially self-identical, and it is only very improperly that this can be referred to the concept 'Freedom.' And when we cannot ourselves, from within outwards, become such-and-such, this only indicates the limits which belong to the nature of the subject itself as regards spontaneous activity, and this could only very improperly be called 'Dependence.'

Further, this antithesis must on no account be confused with the antithesis between gloomy or depressing and elevating or joyful feelings, of which we shall speak later. For a feeling of dependence may be elevating, if the 'having-become-such-and-such' which it expresses is complete; and similarly a feeling of freedom may be dejecting, if the moment of predominating receptivity to which the action can be traced was of a dejecting nature, or again if the manner and method of the activity prove to be a disadvantageous combination.

Let us now think of the feeling of dependence and the feeling of freedom as *one,* in the sense that not only the subject but the corresponding Other is the same for both. Then the total self-consciousness made up of both together is one of *Reciprocity* between the subject and the corresponding Other. Now let us suppose the totality of all moments of feeling, of both kinds, as one whole: then the corresponding Other is also to be supposed as a totality or as one, and then that term 'reciprocity' is the right one for our self-consciousness in general, inasmuch as it expresses our connexion with everything which either appeals to our receptivity or is subjected to our activity. And this is true not only when we particularize this Other and ascribe to each of its elements a different degree of relation to the twofold consciousness within us, but also when we think of the total 'outside' as one, and moreover (since it contains other receptivities and activities to which we have a relation) as one together with ourselves, that is, as a *World*. Accordingly our self-consciousness, as a consciousness of our existence in the world or of our co-existence with the world, is a series in which the feeling of freedom and the feeling of dependence are divided. But neither an absolute feeling of dependence, *i.e.* without any feeling of freedom in relation to the co-determinant, nor an absolute feeling of freedom, *i.e.* without any feeling of dependence in relation to the co-determinant, is to be found in this whole realm. If we consider our relations to Nature, or those which exist in human society, there we shall find a large number of objects in regard to which freedom and dependence maintain very much of an equipoise: these constitute the field of equal reciprocity. There are other objects which exercise a far greater influence upon our receptivity than our activity exercises upon them, and also *vice versa*, so that one of the two may diminish until it is imperceptible. But neither of the two members will ever completely disappear. The feeling of dependence predominates in the relation of children to their parents, or of citizens to their fatherland; and yet individuals can, without losing their relationship, exercise upon their fatherland not only a directive influence, but even a counter-influence. And the dependence of children on their parents, which very soon comes to be felt as a gradually diminishing and fading quantity, is never from the start free from the admixture of an element of spontaneous activity towards the parents: just as even in the most absolute autocracy the ruler is not without some slight feeling of dependence. It is the same in the case of Nature: towards all the forces of Nature—even, we may say, towards the heavenly bodies—we ourselves do, in the same sense in which they influence us, exercise a counter-influence, however minute. So that our whole self-consciousness in relation to the World or its individual parts remains enclosed within these limits.

3. There can, accordingly, be for us no such thing as a feeling of absolute freedom. He who asserts that he has such a feeling is either deceiving himself or separating things which essentially belong together. For if the feeling of freedom expresses a forth-going activity, this activity must have an object which has been somehow given to us, and this could not have taken place without

an influence of the object upon our receptivity. Therefore in every such case there is involved a feeling of dependence which goes along with the feeling of freedom, and thus limits it. The contrary could only be possible if the object altogether came into existence through our activity, which is never the case absolutely, but only relatively. But if, on the other hand, the feeling of freedom expresses only an inward movement of activity, not only is every such individual movement bound up with the state of our stimulated receptivity at the moment, but, further, the totality of our free inward movements, considered as a unity, cannot be represented as a feeling of absolute freedom, because our whole existence does not present itself to our consciousness as having proceeded from our own spontaneous activity. Therefore in any temporal existence a feeling of absolute freedom can have no place. As regards the feeling of absolute dependence which, on the other hand, our proposition does postulate: for just the same reason, this feeling cannot in any wise arise from the influence of an object which has in some way to be *given* to us; for upon such an object there would always be a counter-influence, and even a voluntary renunciation of this would always involve a feeling of freedom. Hence a feeling of absolute dependence, strictly speaking, cannot exist in a single moment as such, because such a moment is always determined, as regards its total content, by what is *given,* and thus by objects towards which we have a feeling of freedom. But the self-consciousness which accompanies all our activity, and therefore, since that is never zero, accompanies our whole existence, and negatives absolute freedom, is itself precisely a consciousness of absolute dependence; for it is the consciousness that the whole of our spontaneous activity comes from a source outside of us in just the same sense in which anything towards which we should have a feeling of absolute freedom must have proceeded entirely from ourselves. But without any feeling of freedom a feeling of absolute dependence would not be possible.

4. As regards the identification of absolute dependence with 'relation to God' in our proposition: this is to be understood in the sense that the *Whence* of our receptive and active existence, as implied in this self-consciousness, is to be designated by the word 'God,' and that this is for us the really original signification of that word. In this connexion we have first of all to remind ourselves that, as we have seen in the foregoing discussion, this 'Whence' is not the world, in the sense of the totality of temporal existence, and still less is it any single part of the world. For we have a feeling of freedom (though, indeed, a limited one) in relation to the world, since we are complementary parts of it, and also since we are

continually exercising an influence on its individual parts; and, moreover, there is the possibility of our exercising influence on all its parts; and while this does permit a limited feeling of dependence, it excludes the absolute feeling. In the next place, we have to note that our proposition is intended to oppose the view that this feeling of dependence is itself conditioned by some previous knowledge about God. And this may indeed be the more necessary since many people claim to be in the sure possession of a concept of God, altogether a matter of conception and original, *i.e.* independent of any feeling; and in the strength of this higher self-consciousness, which indeed may come pretty near to being a feeling of absolute freedom, they put far from them, as something almost infra-human, that very feeling which for us is the basic type of all piety. Now our proposition is in no wise intended to dispute the existence of such an original knowledge, but simply to set it aside as something with which, in a system of Christian doctrine, we could never have any concern, because plainly enough it has itself nothing to do directly with piety. If, however, word and idea are always originally one, and the term 'God' therefore presupposes an idea, then we shall simply say that this idea, which is nothing more than the expression of the feeling of absolute dependence, is the most direct reflection upon it and the most original idea with which we are here concerned, and is quite independent of that original knowledge (properly so called), and conditioned only by our feeling of absolute dependence. So that in the first instance God signifies for us simply that which is the co-determinant in this feeling and to which we trace our being in such a state; and any further content of the idea must be evolved out of this fundamental import assigned to it. Now this is just what is principally meant by the formula which says that to feel oneself absolutely dependent and to be conscious of being in relation with God are one and the same thing; and the reason is that absolute dependence is the fundamental relation which must include all others in itself. This last expression includes the God-consciousness in the self-consciousness in such a way that, quite in accordance with the above analysis, the two cannot be separated from each other. The feeling of absolute dependence becomes a clear self-consciousness only as this idea comes simultaneously into being. In this sense it can indeed be said that God is given to us in feeling in an original way; and if we speak of an original revelation of God to man or in man, the meaning will always be just this, that, along with the absolute dependence which characterizes not only man but all temporal existence, there is given to man also the immediate self-consciousness of it, which becomes a consciousness of God. In whatever measure this actually takes place during the course of a personality through time, in just that measure do we ascribe piety to the individual. On the other hand, any possibility of God being in any way *given* is entirely excluded, because anything that is outwardly given must be given as an object exposed to our counter-influence, however slight this may be. The transference of the idea of God to any perceptible object, unless one is all the time conscious that it is a piece of purely arbitrary symbolism, is always a corruption, whether it be a temporary transference, *i.e.* a theophany, or a constitutive transference, in which God is represented as permanently a particular perceptible existence.

4

THE ARGUMENT FROM
RELIGIOUS EXPERIENCE*

C. D. Broad 🌐

*C. D. Broad (1887–　) was Knight-
bridge Professor of Moral Philosophy at
Cambridge University from 1933 to 1953.
His philosophical writing is especially
noted for its painstaking consideration of
a variety of possible alternatives. Some of
his major books are* Scientific Thought,
Mind and Its Place in Nature, *and* Five
Types of Ethical Theory.

THIS argument differs in the following important respect from the
other two empirical types of argument. The Argument from Design
and the arguments from ethical premises start from facts which are
common to every one. But some people seem to be almost wholly
devoid of any specifically religious experience; and among those
who have it the differences of kind and degree are enormous.
Founders of religions and saints, e.g., often claim to have been in
direct contact with God, to have seen and spoken with Him, and so
on. An ordinary religious man would certainly not make any such
claim, though he might say that he had had experiences which
assured him of the existence and presence of God. So the first thing
that we have to notice is that capacity for religious experience is in
certain respects like an ear for music. There are a few people who
are unable to recognize and distinguish the simplest tune. But they
are in a minority, like the people who have absolutely no kind of
religious experience. Most people have some slight appreciation of
music. But the differences of degree in this respect are enormous,
and those who have not much gift for music have to take the
statements of accomplished musicians very largely on trust. Let us,
then, compare tone-deaf persons to those who have no recognizable
religious experience at all; the ordinary followers of a religion to
men who have some taste for music but can neither appreciate the
more difficult kinds nor compose; highly religious men and saints to

* From C. D. Broad, *Religion, Philosophy and Psychical Research.* Reprinted by
permission of Humanities Press, Inc.

persons with an exceptionally fine ear for music who may yet be unable to compose it; and the founders of religions to great musical composers, such as Bach and Beethoven.

This analogy is, of course, incomplete in certain important respects. Religious experience raises three problems, which are different though closely interconnected. (i) What is the *psychological analysis* of religious experience? Does it contain factors which are present also in certain experiences which are not religious? Does it contain any factor which never occurs in any other kind of experience? If it contains no such factor, but is a blend of elements each of which can occur separately or in non-religious experiences, its psychological peculiarity must consist in the characteristic way in which these elements are blended in it. Can this peculiar structural feature of religious experience be indicated and described? (ii) What are the *genetic and causal conditions* of the existence of religious experience? Can we trace the origin and development of the disposition to have religious experiences (*a*) in the human race, and (*b*) in each individual? Granted that the disposition is present in nearly all individuals at the present time, can we discover and state the variable conditions which call it into activity on certain occasions and leave it in abeyance on others? (iii) Part of the content of religious experience is alleged knowledge or well-founded belief about the nature of reality, e.g., that we are dependent on a being who loves us and whom we ought to worship, that values are somehow conserved in spite of the chances and changes of the material world at the mercy of which they seem *prima facie* to be, and so on. Therefore there is a third problem. Granted that religious experience exists, that it has such-and-such a history and conditions, that it seems vitally important to those who have it, and that it produces all kinds of effects which would not otherwise happen, is it *veridical*? Are the claims to knowledge or well-founded belief about the nature of reality, which are an integral part of the experience, *true or probable*? Now, in the case of musical experience, there are analogies to the psychological problem and to the genetic or causal problem, but there is no analogy to the epistemological problem of validity. For, so far as I am aware, no part of the content of musical experience is alleged knowledge about the nature of reality; and therefore no question of its being veridical or delusive can arise.

Since both musical experience and religious experience certainly exist, any theory of the universe which was incompatible with their existence would be false, and any theory which failed to show the connexion between their existence and the other facts about reality would be inadequate. So far the two kinds of experience are in exactly the same position. But a theory which answers to the condition that it allows of the *existence* of religious experience and indicates the *connexion* between its existence and other facts about reality may leave the question as to its *validity* quite unanswered. Or, alternatively, it may throw grave doubt on its cognitive claims, or else it may tend to support them. Suppose, e.g., that it could be shown that religious experience contains no elements which are not factors in other kinds of experience. Suppose further it could be shown that this particular combination of factors tends to originate and to be activated only under certain conditions which are known to be very commonly productive of false beliefs held with strong conviction. Then a satisfactory answer to the questions of psychological analysis and causal antecedents would have tended to answer the epistemological question of validity in the negative. On the other hand, it might be that the only theory which would satisfactorily account for the origin of the religious disposition and for the occurrence of actual religious experiences under certain conditions was a theory which allowed some of the cognitive claims made by religious experience to be true or probable. Thus the three problems, though entirely distinct from each other, may be very closely connected; and it is the existence of the third problem in connexion with religious experience which puts it, for the present purpose, in a different category from musical experience.

In spite of this essential difference the analogy is not to be despised, for it brings out at least one important point. If a man who had no ear for music were to give himself airs on that account, and were to talk *de haut en bas* about those who can appreciate music and think it highly important, we should regard him, not as an advanced thinker, but as a self-satisfied Philistine. And, even if he did not do this but only propounded theories about the nature and causation of musical experience, we might think it reasonable to feel very doubtful whether his theories would be adequate or correct. In the same way, when persons without religious experience regard themselves as being *on that ground* superior to those who have it, their attitude must be treated as merely silly and offensive. Similarly, any theories about religious experience constructed by persons who have little or none of their own should be regarded with grave suspicion. (For that reason it would be unwise to attach very much weight to anything that the present writer may say on this subject.)

On the other hand, we must remember that the possession of a great capacity for religious experience, like the possession of a great capacity for musical appreciation and composition, is no guarantee of high general intelligence. A man may be a saint or a magnificent musician and yet have very little common sense, very little power of accurate introspection or of seeing causal connexions, and scarcely any capacity for logical criticism. He may also be almost as ignorant about other aspects of reality as the non-musical or non-religious man is about musical or religious experience. If such a man starts to theorize about music or religion, his theories may be quite as absurd, though in a different way, as those made by persons who are devoid of musical or religious experience. Fortunately it happens that some religious mystics of a high order have been extremely good at introspecting and describing their own experiences. And some highly religious persons have had very great critical and philosophical abilities. St. Teresa is an example of the first, and St. Thomas Aquinas of the second.

Now I think it must be admitted that, if we compare and contrast the statements made by religious mystics of various times, races, and religions, we find a common nucleus combined with very great differences of detail. Of course the interpretations which they have put on their experiences are much more varied than the experiences themselves. It is obvious that the interpretations will depend in a large measure on the traditional religious beliefs in which various mystics have been brought up. I think that such traditions probably act in two different ways.

(i) The tradition no doubt affects the theoretical interpretation of experiences which would have taken place even if the mystic had been brought up in a different tradition. A feeling of unity with the rest of the universe will be interpreted very differently by a Christian who has been brought up to believe in a personal God and by a Hindu mystic who has been trained in a quite different metaphysical tradition.

(ii) The traditional beliefs, on the other hand, probably determine many of the details of the experience itself. A Roman Catholic mystic may have visions of the Virgin and the saints, whilst a Protestant mystic pretty certainly will not.

Thus the relations between the experiences and the traditional beliefs are highly complex. Presumably the outlines of the belief are determined by the experience. Then the details of the belief are fixed for a certain place and period by the special peculiarities of the experiences had by the founder of a certain religion. These beliefs then become traditional in that religion. Thenceforth they in part determine the details of the experiences had by subsequent mystics of that religion, and still more do they determine the interpretations which these mystics will put upon their experiences. Therefore, when a set of religious beliefs has once been established, it no doubt tends to produce experiences which can plausibly be taken as evidence for it. If it is a tradition in a certain religion that one can communicate with saints, mystics of that religion will seem to see and to talk with saints in their mystical visions; and this fact will be taken as further evidence for the belief that one can communicate with saints.

Much the same double process of causation takes place in sense-perception. On the one hand, the beliefs and expectations which we have at any moment largely determine what *interpretation* we shall put on a certain sensation which we should in any case have had then. On the other hand, our beliefs and expectations do to some extent determine and modify some of the sensible characteristics of the *sensa themselves*. When I am thinking only of diagrams a certain visual stimulus may produce a sensation of a sensibly flat sensum; but a precisely similar stimulus may produce a sensation of a sensibly solid sensum when I am thinking of solid objects.

Such explanations, however, plainly do not account for the first origin of religious beliefs, or for the features which are common to the religious experiences of persons of widely different times, races, and traditions.

Now, when we find that there are certain experiences which, though never very frequent in a high degree of intensity, have happened in a high degree among a few men at all times and places; and when we find that, in spite of differences in detail which we can explain, they involve certain fundamental conditions which are common and peculiar to them; two alternatives are open to us. (i) We may suppose that these men are in contact with an aspect of reality which is not revealed to ordinary persons in their everyday experience. And we may suppose that the characteristics which they agree in ascribing to reality on the basis of these experiences probably do belong to it. Or (ii) we may suppose that they are all subject to a delusion from which other men are free. In order to illustrate these alternatives it will be useful to consider three partly analogous cases, two of which are real and the third imaginary.

(*a*) Most of the detailed facts which biologists tell us about the minute structure and changes in cells can be perceived only by persons who have had a long training in the use of the microscope. In this case we believe that the agreement among trained microscopists really does correspond to facts which untrained persons cannot perceive. (*b*) Persons of all races who habitually drink alcohol to excess eventually have perceptual experiences in which they seem to themselves to see snakes or rats crawling about their rooms or beds. In this case we believe that this agreement among drunkards is merely a uniform hallucination. (*c*) Let us now imagine a race of beings who can walk about and touch things but cannot see. Suppose that eventually a few of them developed the power of sight. All that they might tell their still blind friends about colour would be wholly unintelligible to and unverifiable by the latter. But they would also be able to tell their blind friends a great deal about what the latter would feel if they were to walk in certain directions. These statements would be verified. This would not, of course, *prove* to the blind ones that the unintelligible statements about colour correspond to certain aspects of the world which they cannot perceive. But it would show that the seeing persons had a source of additional information about matters which the blind ones could understand and test for themselves. It would not be unreasonable then for the blind ones to believe that probably the seeing ones are also able to perceive other aspects of reality which they are describing correctly when they make their unintelligible statements containing colour-names. The question then is whether it is reasonable to regard the agreement between the experiences of religious mystics as more like the agreement among trained microscopists about the minute structure of cells, or as more like the agreement among habitual drunkards about the infestation of their rooms by pink rats or snakes, or as more like the agreement about colours which the seeing men would express in their statements to the blind men.

Why do we commonly believe that habitual excess of alcohol is a cause of a uniform delusion and not a source of additional information? The main reason is as follows. The things which drunkards claim to perceive are not fundamentally different in kind from the things that other people perceive. We have all seen rats and snakes, though the rats have generally been grey or brown and not pink. Moreover the drunkard claims that the rats and snakes which he sees are literally present in his room and on his bed, in the same sense in which his bed is in his room and his quilt is on his bed. Now we may fairly argue as follows. Since these are the sort of things which we could see if they were there, the fact that we cannot see them makes it highly probable that they are not there. Again, we know what kinds of perceptible effect would generally follow from the presence in a room of such things as rats or snakes. We should expect fox-terriers or mongooses to show traces of excitement, cheese to be nibbled, corn to disappear from bins, and so on. We find that no such effects are observed in the bedrooms of persons suffering from *delirium tremens*. It therefore seems reasonable to conclude that the agreement among drunkards is a sign, not of a revelation, but of a delusion.

Now the assertions in which religious mystics agree are not

such that they conflict with what we can perceive with our senses. They are about the structure and organization of the world as a whole and about the relations of men to the rest of it. And they have so little in common with the facts of daily life that there is not much chance of direct collision. I think that there is only one important point on which there is conflict. Nearly all mystics seem to be agreed that time and change and unchanging duration are unreal or extremely superficial, whilst these seem to plain men to be the most fundamental features of the world. But we must admit, on the one hand, that these temporal characteristics present very great philosophical difficulties and puzzles when we reflect upon them. On the other hand, we may well suppose that the mystic finds it impossible to state clearly in ordinary language what it is that he experiences about the facts which underlie the appearance of time and change and duration. Therefore it is not difficult to allow that what we experience as the temporal aspect of reality corresponds in some sense to certain facts, and yet that these facts appear to us in so distorted a form in our ordinary experience that a person who sees them more accurately and directly might refuse to apply temporal names to them.

Let us next consider why we feel fairly certain that the agreement among trained microscopists about the minute structure of cells expresses an objective fact, although we cannot get similar experiences. One reason is that we have learned enough, from simpler cases of visual perception, about the laws of optics to know that the arrangement of lenses in a microscope is such that it will reveal minute structure, which is otherwise invisible, and will not simply create optical delusions. Another reason is that we know of other cases in which trained persons can detect things which untrained people will overlook, and that in many cases the existence of these things can be verified by indirect methods. Probably most of us have experienced such results of training in our own lives.

Now religious experience is not in nearly such a strong position as this. We do not know much about the laws which govern its occurrence and determine its variations. No doubt there are certain standard methods of training and meditation which tend to produce mystical experiences. These have been elaborated to some extent by certain Western mystics and to a very much greater extent by Eastern Yogis. But I do not think that we can see here, as we can in the case of microscopes and the training which is required to make the best use of them, any conclusive reason why these methods should produce veridical rather than delusive experiences. Uniform methods of training and meditation would be likely to produce more or less similar experiences, whether these experiences were largely veridical or wholly delusive.

Is there any analogy between the facts about religious experience and the fable about the blind men some of whom gained the power of sight? It might be said that many ideals of conduct and ways of life, which we can all recognize now to be good and useful, have been introduced into human history by the founders of religions. These persons have made actual ethical discoveries which others can afterwards recognize to be true. It might be said that this is at least roughly analogous to the case of the seeing men telling the still blind men of facts which the latter could and did verify for themselves. And it might be said that this makes it reasonable for us to attach some weight to what founders of religions tell us about things which we cannot understand or verify for ourselves; just as it would have been reasonable for the blind men to attach some weight to the unintelligible statements which the seeing men made to them about colours.

I think that this argument deserves a certain amount of respect, though I should find it hard to estimate how much weight to attach to it. I should be inclined to sum up as follows. When there is a nucleus of agreement between the experiences of men in different places, times, and traditions, and when they all tend to put much the same kind of interpretation on the cognitive content of these experiences, it is reasonable to ascribe this agreement to their all being in contact with a certain objective aspect of reality *unless* there be some positive reason to think otherwise. The practical postulate which we go upon everywhere else is to treat cognitive claims as veridical unless there be some positive reason to think them delusive. This, after all, is our only guarantee for believing that ordinary sense-perception is veridical. We cannot *prove* that what people agree in perceiving really exists independently of them; but we do always assume that ordinary waking sense-perception is veridical unless we can produce some positive ground for thinking that it is delusive in any given case. I think it would be inconsistent to treat the experiences of religious mystics on different principles. So far as they agree they should be provisionally accepted as veridical unless there be some positive ground for thinking that they are not. So the next question is whether there is any positive ground for holding that they are delusive.

There are two circumstances which have been commonly held to cast doubt on the cognitive claims of religious and mystical experience. (i) It is alleged that founders of religions and saints have nearly always had certain neuropathic symptoms or certain bodily weaknesses, and that these would be likely to produce delusions. Even if we accept the premises, I do not think that this is a very strong argument. (*a*) It is equally true that many founders of religions and saints have exhibited great endurance and great power of organization and business capacity which would have made them extremely successful and competent in secular affairs. There are very few offices in the cabinet or in the highest branches of the civil service which St. Thomas Aquinas could not have held with conspicuous success. I do not, of course, regard this as a positive reason *for* accepting the metaphysical doctrines which saints and founders of religions have based on their experiences; but it is relevant as a *rebuttal* of the argument which we are considering. (*b*) Probably very few people of extreme genius in science or art are perfectly normal mentally or physically, and some of them are very crazy and eccentric indeed. Therefore it would be rather surprising if persons of religious genius were completely normal, whether their experiences be veridical or delusive. (*c*) Suppose, for the sake of argument, that there is an aspect of the world which remains altogether outside the ken of ordinary persons in their daily life. Then it seems very likely that some degree of mental and physical abnormality would be a necessary condition for getting sufficiently loosened from the objects of ordinary sense-perception to come into cognitive contact with this aspect of reality. Therefore the fact that those persons who claim to have this peculiar kind of cognition generally exhibit certain mental and physical abnormalities is rather what might be anticipated if their claims were true. One might need to be slightly 'cracked' in order to have some peep-holes into the super-sensible world. (*d*) If mystical experience were veridical, it seems quite likely that it would *produce* abnormalities of behaviour in those who had it strongly. Let us suppose, for the sake of argument, that those who have religious experience are in frequent contact with an aspect of reality of which most men get only rare and faint glimpses. Then such persons are, as it were, living in two worlds, while the ordinary man is living in only one of them. Or, again, they might be compared to a man who has to conduct his life with one ordinary eye and another of a telescopic kind. Their behaviour may be appropriate to the aspect of reality which they alone perceive and think all-important; but, for that very reason, it may be inappropriate to those other aspects of reality which are all that most men perceive or judge to be important and on which all our social institutions and conventions are built.

(ii) A second reason which is commonly alleged for doubt about the claims of religious experience is the following. It is said that such experience always originates from and remains mixed with certain other factors, e.g., sexual emotion, which are such that experiences and beliefs that arise from them are very likely to be delusive. I think that there are a good many confusions on this point, and it will be worth while to begin by indicating some of them.

When people say that B 'originated from' A, they are liable to confuse at least three different kinds of connexion between A and B. (i) It might be that A is a necessary but insufficient condition of the existence of B. (ii) It might be that A is a necessary and sufficient condition of the existence of B. Or (iii) it might be that B simply *is* A in a more complex and disguised form. Now, when there is in fact evidence only for the first kind of connexion, people are very liable to jump to the conclusion that there is the third kind of connexion. It may well be the case, e.g., that no one who was incapable of strong sexual desires and emotions could have anything worth calling religious experience. But it is plain that the possession of a strong capacity for sexual experience is not a *sufficient* condition of having religious experience; for we know that the former quite often exists in persons who show hardly any trace of the latter. But, even if it could be shown that a strong capacity for sexual desire and emotion is *both* necessary and sufficient to produce religious experience, it would not follow that the latter is just the former in disguise. In the first place, it is not at all easy to discover the exact meaning of this metaphorical phrase when it is applied to psychological topics. And, if we make use of physical analogies, we are not much helped. A mixture of oxygen and hydrogen in presence of a spark is necessary and sufficient to produce water accompanied by an explosion. But water accompanied by an explosion is not a mixture of oxygen and hydrogen and a spark 'in a disguised form', whatever that may mean.

Now I think that the present rather vaguely formulated objection to the validity of the claims of religious experience might be stated somewhat as follows. 'In the individual religious experience originates from, and always remains mixed with, sexual desires and emotions. The other generative factor of it is the religious tradition of the society in which he lives, the teachings of his parents, nurses, schoolmasters, etc. In the race religious experience originated from a mixture of false beliefs about nature and man, irrational fears, sexual and other impulses, and so on. Thus the religious tradition arose from beliefs which we now recognize to have been false and from emotions which we now recognize to have been irrelevant and misleading. It is now drilled into children by those who are in authority over them at a time of life when they are intellectually and emotionally at much the same stage as the primitive savages among whom it originated. It is, therefore, readily accepted, and it determines beliefs and emotional dispositions which persist long after the child has grown up and acquired more adequate knowledge of nature and of himself.'

Persons who use this argument might admit that it does not definitely *prove* that religious beliefs are false and groundless. False beliefs and irrational fears in our remote ancestors *might* conceivably be the origin of true beliefs and of an appropriate feeling of awe and reverence in ourselves. And, if sexual desires and emotions be an essential condition and constituent of religious experience, the experience *may* nevertheless be veridical in important respects. We might merely have to rewrite one of the beatitudes and say 'Blessed are the *im*pure in heart, for they shall see God'. But, although it is logically possible that such causes should produce such effects, it would be said that they are most unlikely to do so. They seem much more likely to produce false beliefs and misplaced emotions.

It is plain that this argument has considerable plausibility. But it is worth while to remember that modern science has almost as humble an ancestry as contemporary religion. If the primitive witch-smeller is the spiritual progenitor of the Archbishop of Canterbury, the primitive rain-maker is equally the spiritual progenitor of the Cavendish Professor of Physics. There has obviously been a gradual refinement and purification of religious beliefs and concepts in the course of history, just as there has been in the beliefs and concepts of science. Certain persons of religious genius, such as some of the Hebrew prophets and the founders of Christianity and of Buddhism, do seem to have introduced new ethico-religious concepts and beliefs which have won wide acceptance, just as certain men of scientific genius, such as Galileo, Newton, and Einstein, have done in the sphere of science. It seems somewhat arbitrary to count this process as a continual approximation to true knowledge of the material aspect of the world in the case of science, and to refuse to regard it as at all similar in the case of religion. Lastly, we must remember that all of us have accepted the current common-sense and scientific view of the material world on the authority of our parents, nurses, masters, and companions at a time when we had neither the power nor the inclination to criticize it. And most of us accept, without even understanding, the more recondite doctrines of contemporary physics simply on the authority of those whom we have been taught to regard as experts.

On the whole, then, I do not think that what we know of the conditions under which religious beliefs and emotions have arisen in the life of the individual and the race makes it reasonable to think that they are *specially* likely to be delusive or misdirected. At any rate any argument which starts from that basis and claims to reach such a conclusion will need to be very carefully handled if its destructive effects are to be confined within the range contemplated by its users. It is reasonable to think that the concepts and beliefs of even the most perfect religions known to us are extremely inadequate to the facts which they express; that they are highly confused and are mixed up with a great deal of positive error and sheer nonsense; and that, if the human race goes on and continues to have religious experiences and to reflect on them, they will be altered and improved almost out of recognition. But all this could be said, *mutatis mutandis,* of scientific concepts and theories. The claim of any particular religion or sect to have complete or final truth on these subjects seems to me to be too ridiculous to be worth a moment's consideration. But the opposite extreme of holding that the whole religious experience of mankind is a gigantic system of pure delusion seems to me to be almost (though not quite) as far-fetched.

5

REVELATION*

Herbert Farmer   ✻

Herbert H. Farmer (1892–   ) was for many years Barbour Professor of Systematic Theology at Westminster College, Cambridge. His writings include Experience of God, The World and God, *and* Revelation and Religion.

IN nothing does the essentially personal quality of the religious apprehension of God come to clearer expression than in the fact that belief in revelation, in one form or another, seems to be characteristic of all religion. Yet the closeness, and the precise nature, of the connection between the awareness of God as personal and the idea of revelation are not always clearly understood.

We may start with the distinction between *revelation* and *discovery*. These two words, though in common speech not always properly and consistently differentiated from one another, certainly do not at bottom mean the same thing even for the undiscriminating popular mind. There are occasions when we instinctively and naturally speak of revelation and avoid the term discovery, as there are when we instinctively and naturally speak of discovery and avoid the term revelation. The distinction was recently well illustrated in the newspaper. The police had arrested a man of whose complicity in a crime they had much evidence. It was said in the paper that they had *discovered* certain facts about the man which pointed to his implication in the alleged crime. There was not, however, sufficient evidence to fasten it finally upon him. So they went to work upon him with several hours of continuous questioning, until at last he broke down and confessed. In his confession, said the paper, he *revealed* to the police certain things which they had not *discovered*, which, indeed, almost certainly they could never, without the suspect's aid, have laid bare at all.

So used, the distinction between the words leaps to the eye. Both words refer to the apprehension of truths, facts of our world. But in discovery there is activity on the one side only; the facts are there, static, quiescent, unknown, and they remain unknown until

* From *The World and God* by Professor H. H. Farmer (London: James Nisbet & Company, Limited. New York: Harper and Row). By permission of James Nisbet & Company, Limited.

someone searches them out; they never do anything to present themselves to the enquirer. But where there is activity on the other side, an activity *of* impartation directed *to* impartation, another word is required, the word revelation. All of which is obvious. Pursuing the analysis further, however, it becomes clear that an activity directed to, and not merely incidentally involving, impartation of truth to our minds, implies and presupposes as the source of the activity a person who in one way or another, through some sort of medium, enters into rapport with us and conveys to us what we have not discovered, and in some cases could not discover, by our own unaided activity. When the detective is seeking clues, it never enters his head that they will rise up and call attention to themselves; but when he is seeking a confession, he knows that unless this object which he calls the prisoner chooses to speak, he will probably never get to know what perhaps he most wants to know; hence his technique of enquiry is entirely different. In the one case he is out for a discovery which depends on his own activity alone, in the other case he is out for a revelation which in the end depends on the activity of another person capable of speaking a language he can understand. In the one case he is working in an impersonal medium, in the other in a personal.

In popular speech, of course, words seldom retain precise meanings, especially when they refer to the same general class of facts. Thus a detective might say: "I have *discovered* a clue which *reveals* to me so-and-so"; or he might come away from the prisoner's confession and say: "We have discovered so-and-so", when what he means is that the prisoner revealed it to him. But aside from the uncertain fringes, the distinction is in general clear and unmistakable. Pre-eminently the word revelation, even in popular speech, is appropriate to a two-term personal relationship where one actively imparts to another through a medium of communication, through speech; pre-eminently the word discovery is appropriate to our dealing with impersonal objects which do not in that sense actively convey themselves to us at all.

The relation of this to what was said earlier concerning the basic elements in the awareness of others as personal is obvious. The sense of the other as an inaccessible source of activity which is potentially co-operative in its resistance and potentially resistant in its co-operation is clearly at a maximum in the relation of active self-communication through speech or through some other medium. In some way the other has to speak, else he remains an impenetrable mystery, if indeed he can be recognised as personal at all. Much information, useful in its own sphere, might doubtless be gathered by examining his psycho-physical reactions with the same detached, impersonal methods as are used in researching into the ways of frogs or beetles; but it is not possible to know *him*, as personal, unless he chooses to unveil his inner life, to reveal himself to *you*, as personal, by talking to you, and that not as a mere echo of your words and thoughts, but himself taking the initiative, thrusting his mind communicatively and resistantly into yours, his values and purposes amongst yours, in respect of what is in some degree a common life-situation.

It is important, however, before we proceed and for reasons which will appear later, to note that though popular usage thus often clearly indicates the personal reference of the idea of revelation, none the less the word is sometimes used without the clear sense of a personal activity on the other side. Two such usages must be mentioned. First, the word revelation is often used of any acquirement of knowledge which is, or seems to be, disconnected with our own efforts of research and discovery. Usually also an element of suddenness or unexpectedness is included in this usage of the term. Thus a man may ponder long over a problem and when he is doing, or thinking of, something else, the solution flashes into his mind. Its coming appears to be unconnected with his mental processes, though, of course, there is in fact some relationship. In such circumstances he will often say that it came to him like a revelation, or even that it was a revelation.[1] Second, there is a use of the word which has nothing to do with the manner of acquiring knowledge, but arises from the fact that man's mental constitution impels him to try to get below the flux of merely surface impressions which his world makes upon him to what he conceives to be a deeper, more permanent and more orderly underlying reality. Thus a philosopher might say that the ultimate reality of the universe is revealed in the phenomena of time and sense; or a scientist might say that the law of gravitation is revealed in falling apples and stones, and like phenomena. Or it might be said, as it has been recently said, that the essential law-abidingness of a people is revealed only at times of economic tension and stress; at other times it cannot be known with certainty, being hidden behind the merely surface appearances of conventional behaviour. There is much to be said for the view that both these usages are derived from the religious usage of the term, with, however, the sense of an activity on the other side so attenuated as almost completely to have disappeared.

[1] An advertisement in *The Times* recently exhorted the reader to try a certain article and "the result will be a revelation to you."

When we turn to the religious usage of the term revelation, we find that quite central in it is the living sense of God as entering into personal rapport with the soul, the living sense, that is to say, of God as active personal will approaching the individual in his own immediate situation in absolute demand and final succour. The religious man, at the moment of living awareness of God, does not feel that he has happened upon God, as upon another object in his environment which it would be interesting to investigate further: rather he apprehends God as actively approaching him, as entering, of His own initiative, resistantly and savingly into his personal life. The only possible word to express this is revelation, the word discovery, with its predominant connotation of activity in man and quiescence on the other side, being woefully inadequate.

It is, indeed, sometimes said that in the last resort, in respect of religion, "no valid distinction can be drawn between discovery and revelation."[1] But this leaves unexplained the fact that such a distinction has been persistently made all down the history of religion. It is a truism that a revelation, in order to be received, must be actively attended to, and no truly religious mind ever overlooks the fact that he must seek God with his whole heart. What comes to expression in the distinction between discovery and revelation is not so much a difference between activity and passivity on the part of man, but a difference in the kind of reality, which, whether sought or unsought, presents itself to his apprehension in the religious awareness, and in the kind of relationship with him which it initiates. It is precisely the difference already indicated, namely that between a reality and a relationship which are not personal and a reality and a relationship which are. Doubtless, also, it may be argued by a theistic philosophy that all human activities, even the activity of exploring and discovering the truth about atoms, are rooted in, and, for their success, presuppose an ultimate reality of a personal kind, that the effort to attain truth in any sphere would not be successful "unless the one Source of truth were willing to reward it."[2] Yet the fact is, the thought of the ultimate as personal only became available for philosophy through religion, and in religion it is not discovered by argument, but is given by what is felt to be a direct encounter of a personal kind with an ultimate holy and succouring purpose. To overlook this fact is to confuse, as is so often done, the philosophy of religion, or rather a religious philosophy, with religion itself.

[1] So H. L. Goudge, article "Revelation," *Encyclopedia of Religion and Ethics,* Vol. X, p. 746.
[2] H. L. Goudge, *op. cit.*

It is, indeed, fresh evidence of the loss of the sense of God as personal in these days, and the obsession of men's minds with what is in reality a monistic system of thought, that even when the word revelation is used in respect of the knowledge of God, the thought of God's personal activity is often not present, or, if present, is so in such an attenuated form that the word discovery would be just as appropriate. The two popular non-religious uses of the term, noted above, in which the sense of an activity on the other side is omitted, seem, in fact, to have worked back into religious thought with very unfortunate results.

Thus first, in respect of the use of the word revelation in connexion with any sudden and apparently unconnected increment of knowledge, we have many consciously or unconsciously echoing Schleiermacher when he says, in effect, that the bearers of revelation in religion are simply the great men of religious history, who by a unique gift perceive something new and introduce it into man's religious outlook, so that all thereafter are enabled, in greater or less degree, to share in it. Revelation in religion thus becomes merely the high moments of religious discovery, the great revealers, so called, in religion being compared, in fact, by Schleiermacher to the great pioneers in science and art. It need not be denied that the facts warrant to some extent this way of looking at things. There are outstanding, critical figures in the history of religion on whose soul some new awareness of God's demanding and succouring dealings with men breaks, and through whom, as part of the historical process, God speaks to others. But this way of putting things is unfortunate for at least three reasons. First, by attaching the word revelation exclusively to moments when something original and touched with genius occurs in religion, the fact is obscured that all religious experience, if it is living and formative, has the quality of revelation in it, has within it the sense that the divine Thou makes Himself known to man in his own personal situation. Second, it tends to obscure the fact, to quote Häring, that "the believer has quite a different sort of earnestness about the reality of God" from that which the artist or the scientist has when dealing with that aspect of the world which interests him. And, third, it is apt to give the ordinary believer a wrong estimate of his own religious life. Instead of realising it to be a continuous intercourse with a living, revealing, divine purpose he is apt to regard it as something merely parasitic to the insights of others, or, at most, as a matter of merely occasional, and all too rare, exalted feelings. It is often said: "Oh, I have had no revelations"; yet, if week by week, in the worship of the Christian fellowship, ordinary folk apprehend anew, in relation to their own individual situation, the challenge and the forgiveness of God, that is every bit as much revelation as ever came to the most gifted prophet or seer in history.[1]

Second, in respect of the use of the word revelation which refers to an order underlying, and being known through, the phenomena of nature and history. Here, even more clearly there is something akin to the specifically religious usage of the word, for the religious awareness of God is an awareness of an ultimate reality which is above and beyond and within the immediate environment by which man is surrounded. Religion is nothing if it is not an apprehension of a reality underlying, and more permanent than, the mere flux of changing and evanescent events; yet always it is an apprehension of something which is felt as purposive and personal and addressing the soul in and through such events. When, however, the scientist or philosopher speaks of an underlying order being revealed in the events of nature and history, he consciously or unconsciously leaves out the religious thought of an activity on the other side. This, perhaps, is of no moment in itself, but it becomes of moment when the usage works back into theology and into men's whole approach to religion. Thus it is common to hear people say, in a general way, that they believe in a revelation of God in nature and history, and when questioned it appears they mean one of three things: either that there is an underlying unity or order of some sort, about which we may expect to know more as human knowledge and human faculties expand; or that they have occasionally felt mystical feelings of unity with this underlying, inclusive order, which they then proceed to describe, in vaguely idealistic and very abstract terms, as an order of absolute values, such as truth, beauty, and goodness; or, finally, if they do picture this ultimate reality to themselves as in any sense personal, that is explained away as being due to the inevitable anthropomorphism of human thinking and not to be taken as a report of it as it actually is. Seldom do the words appear to express a pungent and living sense of divine purpose or will actively dealing with them so insistently and directly that they can no more disregard it than they can someone hammering at the door.

It is not unimportant to realise that to speak of a general revelation of God in *all* nature and history is, from the point of view of the truth on which we are insisting, almost a contradiction in terms. For revelation, properly understood, is, as we have said, a category of personal relationship; but God cannot be related to a man personally through *all* nature and history. A personal relationship between God and man means God meeting the individual with

[1] See Häring, *The Christian Faith* (Eng. Trans.), Vol. I, p. 52 f.; also Titius, *Natur und Gott*, 2. Aufl. p. 738.

an immediately relevant insistency of value and proffer of succour, demanding here and now obedience and trust, and that could only be in and through the man's own concrete, personal situation, which so far from being general, is peculiar to him and sets an immediate responsibility of action upon him alone. All nature and history cannot be such a real, existential situation to anyone, being, in fact, a highly generalised and abstract idea. If we speak of a general revelation of God in nature and history, the most we can mean is, positively, that God may make any situation, into which any man may come at any time, the medium of His revealing word to the soul; and, negatively, that even those situations where He does not appear thus to speak to the soul are not apart from Him and do not separate from His overshadowing wisdom and love. But these convictions are not given through the contemplation of all nature and all history, which in the nature of the case is impossible; they are judgements of faith evoked by God's revealing Himself in the particularities of the individual's personal life. The content of the revelation, inasmuch as it concerns God, of necessity concerns all nature and all history in principle: but the medium of it is the soul's own immediate situation as part of its own unique life history.

It will be clear from this discussion why the religious mind has always tended to insist that the knowledge of God has fundamentally a different character, and depends on different conditions, from some other sorts of knowledge. Thus it is not a species of artistic feeling, whereby the mind merely contemplatively grasps the all-embracing unity of all things with one another and with itself; for the religious awareness has an incurable dualism in it, God and the soul being apprehended as standing over against one another in that tension of independent wills without which a personal relationship could not exist. Doubtless the religious awareness has a monistic element in it, in the sense that it sees all things as living and moving and having their being in God, and therefore the aesthetic sense of the unity of all things need not be excluded from the religious life; but concerning human personalities at least the religious mind is bound to assert, paradox though it be, that they have a measure of apartness from and independence of God, just because they are personalities and have been set by God in a personal dimension with Himself. Nor, again, is the knowledge of God an affirming of postulates to make sense of the categorical imperatives of the moral life. The awareness of absolute demand is, indeed, as we have insisted, right at the heart of the awareness of God, and if the validity of the latter be denied it is certainly difficult rationally to justify complete obedience to the former.

None the less it is not by such a process of postulation that the idea of God is given, for how could that be postulated of which otherwise there is no experience? The awareness of God and the awareness of absolute demand are given together in that ultimate and primordial rapport between God and man in a personal order, behind which we cannot go. Nor, finally, is the knowledge of God given through the merely intellectual processes.

In this connexion it may be noted the the age-long discussion of the relation between reason and revelation has derived in part from an ambiguity in the meaning of the word reason. Reason *per se* is an abstract idea to which nothing corresponds in the existential world; there are only rational personalities, though the phrase "rational personality" is almost a tautology, for personality is inconceivable apart from rationality or rationality apart from personality. If then we mean by reason what the Greeks meant by νοῦς as distinct from διάνοια, namely man's whole personality considered as functioning self-consciously in its highest awareness of the world, then it is by reason and reason alone that man is able to become aware of God's approach to the soul, that is, of revelation in the sense in which we are using the term. In the second chapter we said that the awareness of God is a functioning of the whole personality, and reason in the sense of νοῦς is the personality realising itself in awareness of, and response to, its world. If, however, by reason we mean something narrower, namely the ratiocinative processes whereby the mind temporarily withdraws from the personal situation, with its urgencies of action and decision, and substitutes for it an abstract pattern of logical or cause-effect relationships, then it cannot, so defined, apprehend that personal impact of God which is revelation and which is given only in personal situations unique to each individual, and not capable, as such, of being made the subject of generalisation at all. The statement that "if a man will do his will, he shall know of the doctrine" might be taken to express the same truth; for will is the mysterious, unifying centre of active reason (or personality), and in the tension of wills a personal reality is apprehended. Yet will cannot be apprehended or obeyed in the abstract, but only in relation to particular situations in respect of which a man must make a personal decision and act.

Our position is, then, that wheresoever and whensoever God declares Himself to the individual soul in such wise that He is apprehended as holy will actively present within the immediate situation, asking obedience at all costs and guaranteeing in and through such asking the soul's ultimate succour, there is revelation. The essential content of revelation is, therefore, rightly said to be God Himself, and not general truths about God or the universe or immortality or the way of duty; though such truths are implicit in the divine self-giving, as this is mediated ever more richly to the responsive soul in the changing situations of life, and are capable of reflective formulation. And the proper response to revelation is rightly said to be faith, faith being not an intellectual assent to general truths, but the decisive commitment of the whole person in active obedience to, and quiet trust in, the divine will apprehended as rightfully sovereign and utterly trustworthy at one and the same time. Faith, like revelation, to which it is correlative, is therefore also a category of personal relationship and presupposes the duality of personal relationship; it cannot be "pumped up", if such a phrase may be permitted, by the isolated self from within itself, but must be evoked by the other presenting itself as trustworthy. Hence faith, while always man's deed, always sees in God its giver. The same is true of human relationships. A child's trust in his parents is their greatest gift to him, for it is evoked and sustained in him only by their continually presenting themselves, revealing themselves, as trustworthy.

It follows from this conception of revelation that not all situations are equally calculated to be a medium of it, though any situation may become such, owing to a peculiar relevancy to the individual's life-history, which it may at any moment assume. Unless a situation is such that it calls for decision and obedience, and for a new self-commitment to the divine overshadowing providence in that obedience, it can hardly mediate that vivid awareness of personal rapport with God which is what revelation is. Revelations in this sense are always points of tension in the soul's history, and therefore points of crisis, where the soul must take either a step forward or a step backward in understanding of God and in stature as a child of God.[1] We do not mean by this that the living awareness of God as personal can only arise in situations of unusual stress and conflict. That would be palpably false. It may take possession of the soul through the solemn beauty of a summer evening, or in the quietness of worship and prayer, or in the sense of the wonder and responsibility of a first-born child. Yet in so far as the living awareness of God as personal does enter into even such situations, it always introduces an element of challenge and tension which would not otherwise be there, for such awareness is not possible unless and until the individual is confronted, in some meas-

[1] This is apparently what Herrmann means when he insists throughout his *Offenbarung und Wunder* that a genuine experience of revelation involves that the individual should not merely hear about new ranges of spiritual reality and experience, but should himself begin to live in them and so move forward to a new level of being himself.

ure, by the absolute demands as well as the bounty and benediction
of God. If such an element is not introduced, it is doubtful whether
the living awareness of God is present at all; at best there is only a
reflective superimposition on the situation of a quasi-philosophic or
poetic idea that all good things are from above. Every situation in
which God reveals Himself to the soul is a crisis calling for obedience and trust; it may begin or end by being such, but such at some
point and in some degree it must be. The relative prominence of
the element of demand and the element of succour in the total
awareness of God may, however, vary considerably according to the
situation. Sometimes the soul at its crisis needs more the sense of the
comforts of God than of His demands, but even then the latter is
only in the background. *Alle Gabe ist Aufgabe.*[1]

The notion that faith should be able to discern the active
presence of God in all events and all situations is merely pietistic; it
is neither supported by experience nor necessitated by the thought
of God and His intercourse with man. Rather the reverse would
seem to be true. Much of man's life of necessity runs in a routine of
daily tasks which are the better done for receiving undivided attention undisturbed by the explicit awareness of God; and there are
many decisions to be made and acts done which involve nothing of
crisis in the soul's life, but require only some experience and
common-sense. And even in those situations where the soul cries out
for an assurance of the living God, the revelation may not be
immediately given. Hunzinger suggests that when this happens it is
the result of sin,[2] and it cannot be questioned that this is a vitally
important factor, as we shall see; yet it may also be due to the
relative weakness and immaturity of a growing personal life, which
will be more truly succoured by God's withholding a present
revelation and requiring rather a steadfast walking forward in the
faith that the divine love and power, which have assuredly at other
times spoken to the soul, are also present now. Thus in a sense the
silence itself becomes a divine, challenging word. As we shall
maintain in the discussion of providence, in God's education of the
human spirit into a rich personal sonship to Himself there is a place
for darkness and mystery. What is required is not that God should
reveal Himself *in* all situations, but sufficiently *for* all situations,
and that we may believe He does.

Yet to distinguish between situations in which God reveals

1 Cf. 2 Cor. i. 4: "Who comforteth us . . . that we may be able to comfort them
which are in any trouble"; 1 John iii. 1–3: "Behold what manner of love the
Father hath bestowed upon us . . . every man that hath this hope purifieth himself even as he is pure."

2 *Das Wunder,* p. 60.

Himself in a direct and living rapport with the soul and situations where the mind is rightly preoccupied with other things is not to reduce life to a disjointed alternation of religious and irreligious moods. The living awareness of God given in the moments of revelation abides in the whole set and direction of the life, and in the soul's capacity in any situation, by a moment of recollection, to become again aware of the living God.[1]

[1] A word may be added concerning the Bible considered as the revelation of God. In the light of the principles set forth in this chapter it is clear that the Bible *per se,* i.e. considered simply as a written text is not, and never can be, a revelation of God. It becomes revelation only as God speaks through it relevantly to my situation, and it becomes unique revelation only as He speaks through it relevantly to something unique in my situation. It is as mediating Christ the Reconciler to my basic need of reconciliation in my present historical circumstance that the Bible becomes a unique source of God's revealing word to the soul. But I, or someone, has to bring it into my present situation, make it part of it, before God can speak livingly through it. Thus if we used the term "the Word" in the sense of God's living speech with the soul, it is true to say that the Bible is not the Word of God, but the Word of God is in the Bible, or—in the categories of this chapter—the Bible is not the Revelation of God, but the Revelation of God is in the Bible.

6

THE BIBLE
AND REVELATION*

Emil Brunner (1889–1965), for many years professor at Zurich, was a Swiss Protestant theologian whose views fall within the tradition usually called neo-orthodoxy with its emphasis on revelation as personal encounter. Among his principal works are: Revelation and Reason, The Mediator, The Divine Imperative, The Christian Doctrine of God, *and* The Christian Doctrine of Creation and Redemption.

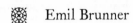 Emil Brunner

WHEN we inquire into the Biblical idea of revelation,[1] we must first of all make it clear to ourselves that there is no single word—in either the Old Testament or the New—that corresponds to our theological idea of revelation.[2] The Holy Scriptures as a whole are concerned with the divine revelation, even where there is no explicit mention of revelation. There is a great variety of words that point to the process of revelation; above all, there is a great variety

* From Emil Brunner, *Revelation and Reason*, tr. by Olive Wyon. Reprinted by permission of the Westminster Press. Copyright 1946.

[1] Cf. Köhler, *Theologie des Alten Testamentes*, pars. 34–40, *"Die Offenbarung Gottes"*; Eichrodt, *Theologie des Alten Testamentes*, Index, under *"Offenbarung"*; Bultmann, *Der Begriff der Offenbarung im Neuen Testament;* Scott, *The New Testament Idea of Revelation.*

[2] Neither in the O.T. nor in the N.T. is there a word that corresponds to our theological idea of "revelation." The O.T. has a number of words for this: God allows Himself to be seen, to be known, to be discovered; above all, God speaks; revelation is also meant where the event is described purely from its subjective human aspect: a seeing, a hearing, a beholding, a knowing, a perceiving (cf. Köhler, *ibid.*, pp. 82 ff.) . The same is true of the N.T.; not only ἀποκαλύπτειν and φανεροῦν but a number of other words describe that which we gather up under the one heading of "revelation": δηλοῦν, γνωρίζειν, λαλεῖν, φωτίζειν, and also nouns like λόγος, φῶς, ἀλήθεια. But even the preaching which "maketh manifest the savour of His knowledge," the Spirit of God who unveils to us the face of Christ and glorifies us, the message of salvation which "has shined in our hearts, to give the light of the knowledge of the glory of God," et cetera. A comprehensive treatment of the whole subject has not yet been made.

of facts and processes that have the significance of revelation. God reveals Himself through theophanies, through angels, through dreams, through oracles (such as Urim and Thummim), through visions and locutions, through natural phenomena and through historical events, through wonderful guidance given to human beings, and through the words and deeds of the Prophets. Above all the New Testament understands the person, the life, the sufferings, death, and resurrection of Jesus Christ, the Son of God, as the final self-manifestation of God, but again, not only Himself in His historical form, but also the witness given to Him by the Holy Spirit in the hearts of believers, the proclamation of Christ by His chosen Apostles, and through the believing community, and finally the fixing of this witness in written form in the Bible of the Old and New Testaments. Holy Scripture therefore does not only speak of the revelation; it is itself the revelation.

Because of this multiplicity it might seem impossible to speak of "the" view of revelation in the Bible. And yet this can, and must, be possible. For these varied forms of revelation are not so many disconnected phenomena, but they form a connected whole. It is when we look at them all *together,* from the right point of view, that we begin to perceive what the Bible means by revelation. It is indeed characteristic of the Biblical idea of revelation that it is not expressed in a unified formula, that it cannot be expressed as an abstract idea. The Biblical idea of revelation cannot be separated from the historical facts; it can only be grasped in them and with them. The revelation in the Old Testament differs from that in the New; but only in the connection between the two can we understand the Biblical revelation, and only as we look at them *both together* can we recognize the Biblical understanding of revelation. It is true, of course, that not all the ways in which events and ideas are presented in the Bible, to which "revealed" significance is ascribed, are of the same organic importance within the whole; but they are all related to the whole; none is without significance for the understanding of the whole. Our first task, in a preliminary survey, is to try to discover the one constant element which persists under these different forms.

Just as the God who reveals Himself in the Holy Scriptures is wholly different from the gods and divinities of the non-Biblical religions, so also the Biblical understanding of revelation is completely different. This, however, does not exclude the fact that certain characteristics which, within the various religions, differentiate the process of revelation from other processes and are thus described, are also present in the Biblical idea of revelation—otherwise how could the same word "revelation" be used? But in the Biblical understanding of revelation these characteristics are not only different in degree; they are changed in principle; and it is precisely this fundamentally different element which is the decisively Biblical element. In all religions "revelation" means a process through which something that had previously been hidden from man is disclosed, a mystery is mysteriously manifested, a knowledge that comes from outside the normal sphere of knowledge, which cannot be achieved by man, but must be given to him, enters suddenly and unexpectedly into his life, and not only increases his knowledge, but has significance for his life, for good or ill. These characteristics are also represented in the Biblical idea of revelation, but they are provided with a double signature, which gives them a completely new meaning. This double signature is absoluteness, and personal character. For this very reason, however, as we shall see, an abstract definition of revelation is impossible; its meaning can be grasped only through the historically "given." Let us look into this a little more closely, in the light of the elements that have already been mentioned.

1. Revelation always means that something hidden is made known, that a mystery is unveiled. But the Biblical revelation is the absolute manifestation of something that had been absolutely concealed. Hence it is a way of acquiring knowledge that is absolutely and essentially—and not only relatively—opposite to the usual human method of acquiring knowledge, by means of observation, research, and thought. Revelation means a supernatural kind of knowledge—given in a marvelous way—of something that man, of himself, could never know. Thus revelation issues from a region which, as such, is not accessible to man. The absolutely Mysterious is not only partially hidden from the natural knowledge of man; it is wholly inaccessible to man's natural faculties for research and discovery.

The sum total of all that in principle is accessible to man is called the "world." Man, it is true, never knows the world as a whole; much in it remains enigmatic or unknown. But these riddles can be solved in principle, in so far as they are *world* enigmas. The unconditioned mystery does not belong to this world; it is supramundane. To say that it is supramundane, and that it can only be known through revelation, really means the same thing. *Because* it is supramundane it can be known only through revelation; the very fact that we cannot perceive it of ourselves, but that we can receive tidings of it only through revelation,[1] shows that it is something altogether above and beyond this world.

---

1 "Eye hath not seen, nor ear heard, neither have entered into the heart of man" —thus that which is not the object of sense perception or of intellectual reflection, that "God hath revealed unto us by His Spirit" (I Cor. 2:9).

In the Bible, however, we are not confronted by an impersonal supernatural Absolute, but by One who transcends this earthly life; God, the Creator and Lord, is the absolute Mystery. In the Bible God and revelation are so intimately connected that there is no other revelation than that which comes to us from God, and there is no other knowledge of God than that which is given to us through revelation. The absolute, mysterious "It," *the* Absolute, is a cosmic abstraction. We arrive at this idea from our own cosmology.[1] This neutral, impersonal Absolute is an object of our own thought. Hence it does not need to be revealed; we are able to conceive it by our own processes of thought. But God is not the "Object" of our thought; this is because He, as the *Lord,* is precisely the absolute Subject, unconditioned Person. *He* is absolute Mystery until He reveals Himself; in so doing, He makes Himself known as the absolute Mystery, as the *Lord.* We have an analogy to this in our relation to persons. We can ourselves find the clue to *things;* they are objects, which confront us not in their own self-activity— making themselves known--but as entities which, by processes of research and thought, we can learn to understand. But *persons* are not enigmas of this kind; a person is a mystery which can be disclosed only through self-manifestation. In this self-disclosure alone do we meet this person as person; previously he or she is an "object," a "something." But God is not *a* Person, but Person, absolutely; not *a* Subject but absolute Subject, "I Yahweh, and none else." He can be known as absolute Subject only through the fact that He Himself makes Himself known through His own action: He is not at our disposal as an object of knowledge. He proves Himself as Lord in the fact that He, He alone, gives the knowledge of Himself, and that man has no power at his own disposal to enable him to acquire this knowledge. Both these statements are correlated: (*a*) that God is absolute Person and the absolute Mystery; and (*b*) that He can be known through revelation alone. In His very Being He is the absolute One who transcends the world. He is—so the Bible expresses it—Lord and Creator.[2] The Creator alone stands supreme above this world; the merely logical Absolute, by its very nature, belongs to this world; the Absolute does not stand above the world but is its immanent presupposition. The Absolute of thought is not truly mysterious, because it can be thought. But God cannot be found by thought; He can only be known through His own manifestation of Himself, and in this He shows Himself to be

---

[1] W. Herrmann has brought this out very clearly in his work *Die Religion im Verhältnis zum Welterkennen und zur Sittlichkeit.*

[2] Isa., chs. 40 ff., especially Isa. 46:8 ff.: the unity of God's sovereignty and His self-manifestation.

the absolute Mystery,[1] who can be understood only through His own self-revelation.

Finally, all that has been said leads up to this point: The real content of revelation in the Bible is not "something," but *God* Himself. Revelation is the self-manifestation of God. The real revelation, that is, the revelation with which the whole Bible is concerned, is God's self-manifestation. The "unreal" revelation is that which attempts to manifest "something" in mysterious "occult" ways; for instance,[2] where lost asses have to be found; and thus something which, in the nature of the case, could also be experienced in purely natural ways. The Bible is only remotely concerned with "unreal" revelations of this kind; its central message is always concerned with the revelation of God Himself, His nature and His will.[3]

2. Revelation everywhere includes within itself a negative presupposition; without it man is always in some way or other in a kind of darkness or bondage. In the Bible this darkness or bondage is always absolute, and it is always personal in character. This means that apart from revelation man does not merely feel that he lacks some knowledge which it would be useful or pleasant for him to possess. It is an absolute, a desperately serious darkness. Hence it does not affect the outside of his life, but himself, in the very core of his being. He himself is dark and fettered; he "walks in darkness";[4] he is "lost." This bondage is a negative personal quality, a negative relation to God; it is *sin*. The Biblical revelation is always and everywhere related to sin. Through the idea of sin man is characterized as not only, so to say, empty of God, but as one who is separated from God, as one who has closed the door between himself and God. Already the contrast between Creator and creature sets an infinite distance between God and man, the distance between Him whose Being is unconditioned and independent, and him whose being is conditioned and dependent. Through the concept "sinner" that which is merely negative becomes a negation.

1 This is the meaning of the prophetic expression, "The Holy One of Israel." "To whom then will ye liken me, or shall I be equal? saith the Holy One" (Isa. 40:25); the "incomparable" element is His Uniqueness, Sublimity, and Holiness. Cf. Ps. 99:2 ff.; Isa. 5:16; I Sam. 2:2. Cf. Kittel, *lib.* III, p. 574: "He is the God of mystery, who only discloses Himself when He wills to do so."

2 I Sam. 9:20.

3 In the Bible this means the concern with the revelation of the "name" of God or of His decree.

4 John 8:12; the contrast between darkness and light is the same as that between being "in" Christ and "outside of" Christ, I John 1:7.

From this conception, however, there springs a remarkable dialectic, very characteristic of the Bible. This negation, sin, presupposes a positive element, of which it is the negation. Sin is never the beginning; it always comes second. Sin always has a history behind it. It means turning away; it is a break with the originally positive element. Turning away from God presupposes an original positive relation with God, and thus an original revelation. The sinner is not merely blind; he has *become* blind; he has been blinded. He is not merely one who is shut up in himself; he has shut himself up and is therefore shut out. Thus the revelation that is given to the sinner is not the first one; it presupposes a previous revelation, apart from which man could not be a sinner. Sin is not a state of absence of relation, but it is a negative relation, the negative of an original positive relation to God. Sin therefore presupposes an original revelation.[1] As the darkness or bondage of man, the negative presupposition, is raised to its highest power by the concept of sin, so the revelation to the sinner is raised to its highest power because it points back to an original revelation. The "second" revelation is revelation in a quite different sense from the first; in an intensified sense it is personal and unconditioned.

3. Revelation means everywhere the communication of unusual knowledge, of something particular. In the Biblical revelation the particular character of this knowledge is not only one of degree, but it is fundamental and unconditioned, to such an extent that one hesitates to call it "knowledge" at all. This radical "otherness" of the Biblical revealed knowledge comes out clearly in three characteristics.

(*a*) Natural acquisition of secular knowledge makes us masters of that which we know. The knowing subject is superior to each object, because a subject is much more than an object. The "I" can have something in knowledge; but the "something" cannot have the "I." So long as the "I" asserts itself in knowing, so long as it is not insane or possessed, the "I" remains master of the object of that which is known. It stands above that which it knows in the act of knowing. But in revelation the opposite is the case. God, through His revelation, becomes Lord over me; He makes me His property;[2] but this does not mean that I become insane or "possessed"; by this very fact I become free, and indeed only then do I develop my true "I." Revelation is therefore fundamentally different from

---

1 See Chapter 6.

2 Because "knowledge puffeth up," the right knowledge of God means being known by Him (I Cor. 8:1 ff.) .

all other forms of knowledge, because it is not the knowledge of "something," but the meeting of the Unconditioned with the conditioned subject, the self-manifestation of the Absolute to the relative person. In revelation God makes Himself my Lord, and in so doing He makes me "truly free."[1]

(b) Ordinary knowledge has the effect of enlarging me, or, more exactly, my "sphere," but it does not transform me, myself. It enriches me, but it does not change me. It is like the enlargement of a house which the master of the house undertakes, but which leaves *him* unchanged. In revelation the exact opposite is the case. The knowledge of revelation does not add to my knowledge; it does not make me "educated"; it does not enlarge my "sphere," but it transforms *me myself;* it changes the one who receives it. For this process of transformation the Bible uses the strongest expression possible: rebirth, the death of the old, and the resurrection of the new man.[2]

(c) Ordinary knowledge, which is always knowledge of an object, for this very reason always means that I remain alone with my knowledge. The process of learning is an isolated one. It is so even when human beings, whether one or a thousand, are the objects of this knowledge. There could indeed be another kind of knowledge between human beings, namely, that in which the other confronts me not as object but as subject, where he is no longer an "It" but a "Thou." But *this* kind of knowledge is not at our disposal. "Natural" knowledge which we can acquire for ourselves does not create any form of community.

In revelation, however, the exact opposite takes place: since God makes Himself known to me, I am no longer solitary; the knowledge of God creates community, and indeed community is precisely the aim of the divine revelation. Hence frequently, in the Bible, when the knowledge given through revelation is mentioned, the one who knows and that which is known change places; the one who receives the revelation is one "who is known by God," and to be "known by God" means to have communion with Him. This process of being made known takes place in "love"—the revealing, generous, self-giving love of God. But because it is this love—the generous love of God and the receptive love in return of the man to whom the gift has been given—it is also connected with that relation between human beings, of which we said just now that it is not at our own disposal, namely, that "knowledge" of the other, where the other confronts me not as an "object" but as "Thou." This

1 John 8:36.
2 This connection between knowledge of revelation and transformation comes out most clearly in II Cor. 3:18.

transformation from the objective kind of knowledge of the other to the Thou-relationship is simply the "love of my neighbor," which becomes possible and actual in the fact that I receive the love of God. This love of my neighbor therefore is the natural effect of the reception of revelation. Hence "if any man loveth God, the same is known of Him," and "every one that loveth is begotten of God, and knoweth God."[1]

4. Hence in the Biblical revelation the concern is not only— as in other religions—with the communication of some knowledge which is important for life, but with life itself. The darkness of which the revelation makes an end is death, disaster, ruin, destruction; the light which it brings is salvation and life. Revelation is the communication of life, not merely an intensification of the life that already exists; nor is it merely an enrichment of knowledge, but it is the transformation of that which is evil and destructive into saving, eternal life. That is why, as we have already said, the history of revelation is the history of salvation, and the history of salvation is the history of revelation. Since God gives Himself to be known, He gives communion with Himself; and since He gives communion with Himself He gives us a share in His own eternal Life. Revelation is not concerned with "something," but with me myself, and with God Himself, namely, with my salvation and with His dominion over me and His communion with me. God Himself in His love gives Himself to me, and in so doing He does away with the darkness, the godlessness and lovelessness, the bondage and misery, which constitute the "lost state" of mankind without God.

Here we must note the change which has taken place, which the idea of revelation experiences through its relation to the negation. The darkness which fades before the Light is here—in contrast to physical darkness—not merely the absence of light, not a vacuum which is ultimately filled, the merely negative which now becomes positive; rather, the darkness which is called sin is a positive negative, an active negation; not an empty place, but a false attitude. Thus the communication of this knowledge is a struggle, in which the usurper is thrown out and the rightful owner comes in. The usurping "I," which has made itself master of its own existence, is dethroned, and in its place there stands the rightful Lord. The "I" renounces its dominant position in the center, and God becomes the Center, but the "I" takes its rightful, second place; it becomes the self which has been created in the image of God, which may "reign" with God and under His rule, in the fact that it serves God. In so doing man finds his original, divinely intended position, and in this regains his true freedom, and yet in this he finds more

[1] I Cor. 8:3; I John 4:7.

than he has lost. He finds the God who not only loves His creature, but loves His rebellious creature, and that with a depth of love which he would not otherwise have known.

Here we have already approached the decisive point, the heart of the Bible—the justification of the sinner, the forgiveness of guilt.

5. Revelation means always and everywhere a knowledge that is unexpected, something that has not been gained by our own efforts but, in one way or another, is always a gift, a "disclosure," which we could not have expected. The Biblical revelation, however, means the unexpected in unconditional form—indeed, that which could never have been expected. It does not mean that which could not have been expected, but that which one would not even dare to expect, because it is the very opposite of that which could be expected along any rational line whatever: that God should love, and give His love to one who has broken faith with Him and has been disobedient to Him. That which is absolutely unexpected, and never could have been expected, is God's forgiving grace.

The unexpected is that which we cannot fathom. All genuine love is unfathomable; God does not owe love to His creatures.[1] His love is always and everywhere a free gift. He loves one from whose love He gains nothing; His love is *agape,* not *eros,*[2] a "giving," and not a "grasping" love, a Love which does not seek a reason for loving the other, but which loves him simply because He wills to do so. He does not love the lovable, but He makes the unlovable lovable. He *gives* to him, He does not desire anything from him. But *agape* has this character in a highly intensified sense where the love of enemies is concerned. That God loved us "while we were yet sinners,"[3] that the Father loves His prodigal son—that is the grace which we would not expect, but not only so, we would not have dared to expect it. It is not only unexpected; it is contrary to all expectation. The most insolent words that have ever been spoken are those of the mocking cynic who said, *"Dieu pardonnera, c'est son métier."*

In the twofold concept of guilt and forgiveness, however, the personal character of man and of God is taken more seriously than in any other human expression. In the judgment "guilty" the responsible person is summoned, and his "lost estate" consists in the loss

[1] "I will proclaim the name of the Lord before thee; and will be gracious to whom I will be gracious, and will shew mercy on whom I will shew mercy" (Ex. 33:19) .

[2] In Nygren's book *Agape und Eros* this contrast between *agape* and *eros* has been well worked out as the contrast between Christianity and antiquity.

[3] Rom. 5:8.

of man's original communion with God; the guilty one is the one who is separated from God, the one who is banished from His presence; between him and the original presence of God there stands the angel with the flaming sword. Over him there broods the wrath and not the love of God. But forgiveness is the restoration of the original relationship purely from God's side, from the love which is all-giving, the προσαγωγή, the fact of being allowed once more to "draw near," the fact of being once more united with God. Hence on God's side too forgiveness is unconditionally personal, the absolute freedom of God, which reaches out beyond all that is rightful, all that is morally and legally required, and creates "purely by grace" a new righteousness of a paradoxical nature, the "justification of the sinner." This is more than anything we could ever imagine, παρὰ δόξαν, and this paradox is the center of the Biblical message of revelation.[1] But there is still one final point which, though it is not different, emphasizes what has just been said.

6. Revelation has always and everywhere the character of a sudden event. It stands out from all ordinary happenings, from the "normal" course of development, and is a kind of "incursion from another dimension." But in the Bible alone is this sudden happening understood in an absolute sense, as the unique, as that which can never be repeated. The world of natural development, as well as that of abstract truth, is more or less timeless. We can always see the world; it is always at our disposal. We can always think; the truths which the intellect can perceive are in principle always at our disposal. Through a methodical process of acquiring knowledge we can master the world and intellectual knowledge. This is true both of the sphere of the individual and of humanity as a whole. The history of knowledge is the story of a gradual, more or less continuous process of mastery. With "this" here, "that" there is always connected through the continuum of cause and effect, and through similarity or analogy. This continuum is broken through by revelation. Not all Biblical revelation has this unique and unconditional character. Every prophet is indeed unique in his way, it is true, and his message is, at least in part, unique. And yet none of the Prophets is *the* Unique One, but the later Prophets repeat and carry farther the teaching of the earlier ones. *The* unique and unrepeatable revelation is that event to which prophecy points as its real meaning, in which He Himself is here, "God with us," the Christ. Here there takes place that which, in its very nature, happens once for all, and is therefore unconditioned.

[1] Paul describes this as the heart of the message of *revelation:* Rom. 3:21; ch. 1:17. Cf. also I Peter 1:13.

Atonement, redemption, can, if it really takes place, happen only once for all. If Jesus Christ be really the Redeemer, then it is evident that "in no other is there salvation,"[1] that "in His name every knee shall bow."[2] Only this unconditionally personal event, the fact that God the Creator comes to man, can be the absolute and unique event; all other happenings are by their very nature repeatable, capable of intensification and variation; but this is not.

It is, however, no accident that in the passages in the New Testament where this uniqueness is expressed in logical terms, in actual words, we are directed to an actual event, at an actual spot on the earth, and at an actual time in history, to the Cross, to the sacrificial death of the Son of God, as the decisive event of redemption.[3] Here, on the very border line between death and life, between this world and the other, in death, but in this one death, the death of the Son of God, everything is concentrated with which this One, all His life, was concerned. Toward this point the whole life of Jesus Christ is directed, to this turning point in the absolute, utterly incomparable meaning of this word. On this unconditioned unique event hangs forgiveness, which is the central point in all the happenings of revelation. Here, in the close of the earthly story of Jesus, in the decline of His human powers, in the death of the God-man, there takes place something which could never take place anywhere else, not even approximately. Here, in *the* history which is in the strictest sense of the word on the very border line of historical happenings, there takes place that which all other history seeks in vain: salvation, the rescue from the powers of destruction. Here therefore the real revelation takes place, the revelation of the holiness and the mercy of God, of His nature and His will, of His plan for humanity and for the world.[4] Here takes places that which is the fulfillment of all history, and which at the same time bursts the framework of all history: the absolute Event.

The Reception of Revelation: Faith

1. REVELATION is a divine action; it is a movement which does not proceed *from* man, but one which comes *to* him. Thus it seems to be an objective phenomenon, independent of the subjective act of

1 Acts 4:12.　　2 Phil. 2:10.

3 Rom. 6:10; I Peter 3:18; Heb. 7:4; 9:12, 26, 28; 10:2, 10. The fact that the Epistle to the Hebrews brings out this uniqueness so plainly is all the more striking, since the author lays great stress on the variety of the revelation at the beginning of the Epistle.

4 Col. 1:20.

receiving, just as the things of the external world exist apart from our perception of them. It seems therefore as though we might set the objective nature of revelation over against the subjective character of the reception of revelation. The "Word" of the Prophets, the Person of Jesus Christ, the teaching of the Apostles in the Holy Scriptures are "the revelation"; they are what they are, quite apart from what we men think about them, whether we believe them to be the revelation or not.

It is, however, evident that the Bible itself does not make this distinction; indeed, it is the Bible that draws a definite subjective process into the sphere of revelation, and then describes it simply as "revelation." "When it was the good pleasure of God . . . to reveal His Son in me."[1] "He that loveth Me shall be loved of My Father, and I will love him, and will manifest [reveal] Myself to him."[2] If we reflect upon the original meaning of the words "revelation" and "reveal," this fact will cause us no surprise. Revelation is indeed that which becomes manifest to *us* through a definite action of God; it means that we, whose eyes were formerly closed, have now opened them to a certain light; that upon us, who were in darkness, the light has shone. Thus revelation only reaches its goal in the subject, man. Revelation is not a fact in itself, but it is this fact, plus an illumination, a disclosure, which makes the "fact" known. The fact of the illumination is therefore an integral part of the process of revelation; without this an event is no more a revelation than light is light without the seeing, illuminated, eye. Revelation is a transitive event which proceeds from God and ends in man, a light ray with these two poles. There is therefore no point in setting the objective fact of revelation over against the subjective act of receiving the revelation, because the revelation actually consists in the meeting of two subjects, the divine and the human, the self-communication of God to man. Jesus Christ is not "revelation" when He is not recognized by anyone as the Christ, just as He is not the Redeemer if He does not redeem anyone. The Biblical doctrine of revelation means this transition from the divine to the human subject.

[1] Gal. 1:15, 16.　　[2] John 14:21.

7

REVELATION, REASON
AND RELIGIONS*

Roderick Ninian Smart (1927–) has been H. G. Wood Professor of Theology at the University of Birmingham since 1961. He has written a number of articles and books on the philosophy of religion and on Eastern religions, including: Reasons and Faiths, *and* Doctrine and Argument in Indian Philosophy.

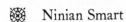 Ninian Smart

NATURAL theology is the Sick Man of Europe. In view of the subtle and exhaustive objections adduced by Hume, Kant and modern empiricists against the traditional arguments for God's existence, it is no longer reasonable to rely upon these particular supports for theistic belief. But the alternative is not irrationalism, for this can give us no guidance as to what we should choose: why be Christian rather than Hindu, or religious rather than atheistical? But if we can rely neither on metaphysical reasoning nor on unreasoning, we might feel tempted to write off religion altogether. Yet its truth-suggesting fascination in daily life and the testimony of many profound and holy men is not lightly to be disregarded. It is not my present task, however, to produce the theologian's stone, the long-searched-for argument that will convince the outsider. Rather I wish to consider whether there is a middle way between traditional natural theology and some simple appeal to revelation (or to any other authority). I wish, in effect, to adumbrate the religious reasons for holding doctrines. For I believe on the one hand, with the revelationists, that one cannot excogitate religious truth: one has to judge what is given, in the form of revelations and teachings —since ordinary philosophers and theologians are neither prophets nor Buddhas. But I believe on the other hand, with the rationalistically inclined, that one can still detect considerations favouring one position rather than another.

* From Ninian Smart, "Revelation, Reason, and Religions" in Ian Ramsey (ed.), *Prospect for Metaphysics.* Reprinted by permission of Philosophical Library, publishers.

But first a word about philosophical analysis. I take it that the job of the philosopher here is to elucidate, as far as possible, the manner in which religious propositions[1] have meaning. This involves connecting up doctrines and experience. Now of course there is no special reason for philosophers to confine themselves to Christian doctrines and life; indeed, to be fair it is necessary to consider other luminous teachings, such as those of Buddhism. Nor can it be pretended that all the great religions are saying the same thing—even if sometimes their doctrines overlap. But in a way this is fortunate, since contrasts help us to see the reasons for them, and in the comparative study of religions one is not merely enabled to view religious teachings (especially one's own) afresh, but one is also offered the chance to gain some further insight into the relation between beliefs and experiences. In brief, if one regards philosophical analysis here as a rather specialized branch of the comparative study of religion, one can acquire a little more clarity about the religious reasons implicit in revelation. But so far, the philosopher is being a neutral in the conflict of faiths. There is no absolute taboo, however, upon his descending into the dusty arena of general apologetic. I propose here to illustrate what can be done in this way in general defence of Christian doctrine. Admittedly, this need not be the job for a philosopher. But on the other hand, the purism of thinking that philosophical analysis is the only proper employment for philosophers is excessive. Intellectual compartmentalization, though often good at the start, may be sterile at the finish.

Thus, one job a philosopher may do is general apologetic. And so the above remarks can be placed in a different context. One way of refurbishing traditional metaphysics is to claim that it expresses, or even evokes, intuitions or disclosures of the divine Being. Now an appeal to such notions must lead in the direction along which I have already pointed. For if the intuition is utterly bare, it can guarantee nothing which can be formulated in words, and is therefore of no use in supporting doctrines. It must at least lead more naturally to one's saying certain things rather than others, and must therefore (albeit in a weak sense) be expressible. On the other hand, it is scarcely realistic to suppose that such an intuition bears a label containing a detailed and legible inscription. If it did, intuitionism would be with difficulty distinguished from, and hardly more plausible than, fundamentalism. It seems, then, to follow that if there are such intuitions, they are dimly suggestive of certain doctrines rather than others; but only *dimly* suggestive. But

[1] I use the word 'proposition' here as a generic term to cover statements, commands, etc.

further, if we appeal to metaphysical intuitions and disclosures we are already indulging in phenomenology; and there seems to be no good reason for confining ourselves to certain intuitions which may or may not arise in certain intellectual (or allegedly intellectual) [1] contexts, but rather ought to contemplate the whole field of religious phenomenology. If, for instance, we are speaking about God, it is reasonable to consider those experiences or disclosures which occur in specifically religious contexts, and which, though considerably ineffable, are dim pointers to certain forms of divine discourse rather than to others.

It might be objected that phenomenology involves merely the description of the psychological content of states of mind, whereas the whole point about an intuition is that it is cognitive, and thus cannot be considered merely as a psychological item. Consequently, it may be argued, an appeal to intuitions does not involve indulging in phenomenology (just as, when we are judging the report of an eyewitness, we are not dragged into a discussion of the psychology of perception). Nevertheless, the contrast seems unrealistic, in the present instance, for a number of reasons. First, to say that an intuition is cognitive is to say that one knows (or claims to know) something in virtue of it; but the same would be true of many numinous experiences (although it must be confessed that more needs to be done to make the notion of 'knowing' in religious contexts perspicuous). Second, intuitions of God only become plausible if they chime in with what is yielded in revelations and disclosures of God (for otherwise why talk of them as 'of God'?) ; but this already suggests at least some resemblance between revelations and intuitions. Third, even though one can draw a contrast between epistemology and the psychology of perception, the facts pertaining to the latter are by no means irrelevant to the former. Fourth, where rules of reasoning are not clear (and they are not clear in religion) the distinction between what is to count as cognitive and what counts as merely an item in psychology (or social history, etc.) becomes quite blurred. Fifth, it seems more in accord with common sense to discuss religious truth not merely in the context of supposed intuitions but also in the milieu of those experiences and activities which give religion its living power. I therefore turn to consider specifically religious experiences and disclosures.

For example, the numinous experience analysed by Otto,

---

[1] It may be wondered whether an intuition arising through an argument (such as one of the Five Ways) which can no longer be treated as valid in any straightforward way can properly be described as intellectual; but in any case, it is rather artificial to distinguish between different faculties of the mind.

though hardly definitive in its pronouncements, nevertheless provides the impulse to speak about gods or God. And again, rather
differently, mystical experience (by which I mean the interior and
imageless visions of the great Western mystics, the *samādhi* attained
by the *yogin*, and so on, and which must be distinguished from those
experiences mainly discussed by Otto),[1] though various in its
flavours and interpretations, does have certain formal characteristics which suggest certain ways of speaking about that which is
realized. In the ensuing, I am necessarily crude in my phenomenology, for this kind of task as I have set myself here cannot too well
be attempted in so brief a compass.[2]

There is one further preliminary point before I proceed,
namely that a defence of religion by appeal to intuitions or
disclosures (the merits of different terms here have to be canvassed)
need not entail that *all* people have such experiences. I am inclined
to feel that there may be some intimation of divinity which every
man may have; but such intimations *may* not occur to all, and in
any case may well be of less evidential value than certain profounder revelations to the comparatively few.

Christianity presents an ideologically significant picture of
the world which is not derivable from scientific investigations. The
elaboration, systematization and general defence of this view of the
world can not unreasonably be called an exercise in metaphysics.
There does not appear to me to be any clear line between theology
and speculation: for both are concerned with the kind of cosmos we
live in. And at least it makes for explicitness to count Christian
metaphysics as not an eassy in the exercise of pure reason (which
happens to be on the side of the angels), but a defence of a position
which cannot be worked out by reason alone. Moreover, this is (in a
broad, very broad, sense) an empirical approach, since we consider
what is given rather than legislate for reality.

Christianity claims to be monotheistic. Of course, the doctrine of the Trinity seems at first sight to belie this fact, and it is a
common accusation by Muslims that the belief in the Incarnation,
by identifying God with a visible person, is setting up another God
beside God. However, we shall return to this *prima facie* blasphemous and polytheistic character of Christianity in a moment.
Meanwhile let us consider the reasons for preferring monotheism to
polytheism. People may simply say, of course, that the truth just is

[1] For a discussion of Otto's term 'numinous' and the distinct characters of the
numinous and the mystical, see my 'Numen, Nirvana and the Definition of Religion' in *Church Quarterly Review*, April–June 1959, pp. 216–25.

[2] At least, however, I have the excuse of having treated these matters more fully
in my *Reasons and Faiths* (London, 1958).

that there is one God and that polytheists are heathens. But bad names get us nowhere. Perhaps certain intimations or intuitions tell men that there is something divine which glimmers in the world. But why one divine Being rather than many?

Can we not gain some insight into this matter? Perhaps the following considerations may help. First, monotheism gives us a more exalted view of the divine. But what if the divine is not that much exalted? All we can say here, maybe, is that the more profound and tremendous experiences of the numinous point in this direction. For the notion of discrete divinities, often clashing, hardly matches up to the overwhelming character of certain theophanies. Second, monotheism is simpler, and other things being equal we prefer the simpler hypothesis. Third, polytheism is more attached to local legend and therefore is less adaptable to those living outside the magic circle; and it is hard to believe that the experiences on which beliefs in the gods are based are so various in such distinct detail. Fourth, whether or not primeval religion was monotheistic, early religion is polytheistic, but shows a tendency to evolve towards monotheism or monism. Fifth, monotheism integrates better with moral insights (universal in nature) than does fragmentary polytheism, especially as the chaotic legends clustering around the gods may be far from edifying. Sixth, the mysterious and overwhelming presence can be linked aesthetically to the cosmological unease, the sense of the aweful contingency of the world. Seventh, monotheism, as we shall observe, chimes in, to some degree, with mystical experience.

It will be apparent that these comments on the religions of worship are somewhat aesthetic in character—rather formal explications of considerations which can be employed to back judgement. But if anything is to count as the adducing of reasons in religion, this is, I think, where we have to start.

But what of pantheism or monism? Do not all the above arguments favour such views as much as they do monotheism? And certainly the dividing line between pantheism and monotheism is shadowy. For example, how do we distinguish sharply between a picture of the divine Being concealed *within* all things and that of the divine Being as *beyond* them? It is not a matter simply of whether you have a three- or two-dimensional model (both admittedly not literal). All, I think, that can be said is that again the monotheistic picture is more intensely numinous. It expresses more strongly and vividly the gulf fixed between worshipper and the object of worship, and thus gives more intense expression to that which is met with in theophany. Again, the astonishment incorporated in the cosmological argument, namely that it is not the case that nothing exists, fits in better with a monotheistic picture than with the pantheistic; for divine fiat links with contingency, whereas emanation hints at necessity.

Yet all these points might well pass the Buddhist by. For in Theravāda Buddhism (not to mention the original teachings of Gautama) there is no doctrine of a divine Creator, no worship of a Supreme Being. Instead there is the interior mystical quest culminating in the attainment of *nirvāṇa*. Mystical quest, you may say? But is not mysticism a union with God? But that is looking at the matter theistically. And assuredly this is not the Buddhist notion, that there is a union between persons. Nevertheless, there are certain loose resemblances between the mystical goal (even in Buddhism) and the object of worship. These resemblances, while not necessitating a theistic interpretation, make it in some degree plausible. For in the mystical state, even on an agnostic interpretation, there is a timelessness reminiscent of divine immortality, a transcendence over mundane experience reminiscent of the otherness of the Supreme Being, a bliss which links up with the fascination of the numinous and with the notion of a divine *summum bonum*, a lack of ordinary perceptions which hints at the invisibility of the Creator, a power suggestive of grace—and so on. It is true that the lack of distinction btween subject and object in the mystical state leads to doctrines of deification and union with God which may be thought to be blasphemous by the ordinary worshipper. And not unconnectedly, pantheism chimes in with the mystical quest: for if God be within all things, it is not absurd to look within ourselves. Still, though there are such difficulties, certainly mysticism can be suggestively interpreted by the theist as a kind of vision of God (and incidentally is less amenable to a polytheistic interpretation, since the comparatively 'this-worldly' aspect of the gods is less in accord with the imperceptibility and transcendence of the mystical goal, etc.).

Nevertheless, the Theravāda is splendid in its doctrinal simplicity. It eschews metaphysical speculations about Creation and immortality, but concentrates almost exclusively upon inner insight and peace and is not complicated by divine ritual. If we praise monotheism for its simplicity, why not praise this form of Buddhism likewise? Why not indeed? Let us do so. But the later history of Buddhism is instructive. The austere simplicity is replaced in the Mahāyāna by the proliferation of a doctrinally complex faith—one where many of the concepts of theism show themselves: the worship of Avalokiteśvara, doctrines of grace (or the transfer of merit), the Three-Body doctrine (so reminiscent of Christianity), and so on. The intimations of the numinous were perhaps not to be denied. If the Lesser Vehicle, like early Islām in a different way, is glorious in its single-mindedness, it is thereby less rich. The Advaita Vedānta, Sūfism and mystical Christianity, as well as the Mahāyāna, are, though complex in welding together different religious insights, more accommodating. Maybe this will be thought to be no great gain. But we can only judge from the experience of spiritual men; and at least in these teachings there is a fairly convincing weaving together of diverse strands of religious language and experience. The outer God who is concealed from our gaze by the visible cosmos reappears at the depths of the soul. The unspeakably majestic object of worship is found in the ineffability of interior insight. Where directions are not literal, we may perchance attain the same place by transcending the world outwards and inwards.

Admittedly it is hard to argue against such a doctrine as that of the Advaita, where the picture of God is relegated firmly to second place, and where the Godhead is described somewhat impersonally in accordance, *prima facie,* with the insights of the mystical vision. (Not for nothing was Śaṅkara called a crypto-Buddhist.) Here the picture of the personal Lord is itself implicated in the grand illusion of *māyā.* And one must note that this kind of illusionist idealism is naturally generated by mystical withdrawal. The Christian apologist can appeal merely to three points here. First, the strength and vividness of numinous experience may not warrant the relegation of the personal picture of the Lord to second place. Second, realism about the cosmos fits in better with moral insight; for the promptings of conscience and the sentiments of justice and love fade somewhat where all things are illusory. And third, transcendence of the unreal has less merit than transcendence of the real.[1]

So far, then, I have adduced what may be called religious reasons for a monotheism which can, so to speak, accommodate the mystical vision. Thereby two main insights of religion are blended appropriately.

But theism generates a problem. For the exalted view of the divine holiness is reflected in reverse among the devotees. Who can confront this almighty splendour without feeling the converse of holiness? The worshipper so confronted repents in self-debasement. He recognizes not merely holiness in God, but unholiness in himself. The purity of the Godhead reveals the sinfulness of men. And this the more so because in theism morals and religion come together in a most intimate manner, so that religious impurity and moral defect coalesce. Thus the very glory of theism is liable to bring in its train a particular view of man, as sinful and removed from God's face by a great gulf fixed. How to bridge it?

Men have tried sacrifice, and even a broken spirit. But is it

1 I owe this point to Mr T. S. Gregory, in discussion.

in accord with the supreme blinding majesty of God that puny men should pretend to proffer an adequate expiation, whether by good works or otherwise? The worshipper here must feel that salvation or holiness can only come from the supreme source of holiness. Only God is holy, and so only God can bring holiness. So Allah is said, for all his terror, to be merciful; and here is a deep insight. But is it enough that men should merely live in hope of the divine compassion? Man still feels that it is he that must make expiation for his sins; while on the other hand he supposes that only God can bridge the gulf.

Theism thus brings a religious problem. Yet this is, so to speak, solved by Christianity. For Christ by being both man and God can achieve, through his solidarity with mankind, the expiation for mankind, and, through his Godhood, bridge the gulf. The two requirements are met. Hence too the reaction of the Church against docetism. For though doctrines such as the latter seem to preserve monotheism better they destroy the whole point of Christianity.

But Gāndhi said that the uniqueness of the Incarnation was a great stumbling-block to his acceptance of Christ. Why only one Incarnation? Why the scandal of particularity? First, the Christian doctrine, though it involves a seeming blasphemy, is the simplest of its kind. It is hard, perhaps, for the monotheist to accept what at first sight seems an abrogation of his belief; and it would be blasphemous to do it lightly. Second, multiple incarnations, as in Vaisṇavism, seem ill in accord with the majesty of God, especially where animal manifestations are produced through legend. Third, they tend in the direction of docetism, for a person who appears in many forms cannot be thought to *be* one of those forms in the full sense: they are likely to be regarded more as appearances than as realities. Thus the need for atonement will not easily be met by multiple incarnations. Fourth, historical data may be relevant, though I do not propose to examine these directly here.

But history reminds us of a problem. Even supposing that the doctrine of Incarnation strikes a deep chord, how do we recognize the divine human? What are the grounds, for instance, for calling Jesus God? True, we would only here be being wise after the event; but there are certain suggestive things to which we can point. Miracle-working is an intimation of omnipotence; signs of sinlessness correspond to the purity of the Holy One; the actions of an apparent Saviour chime in with the thought that only God can save; and the claim to divinity supervenes rather startingly on all these. Not only so but, looking further afield, the pattern of history fits in with the Messianic life.

Moreover, just as monotheism itself harmonizes more easily with the moral insights of men than does polytheism, so the Incarnation has a moral significance but dimly adumbrated in pure monotheism of the Jewish or Muslim variety: for Christ in making himself a sacrifice not merely fulfils, as it were, a profound religious function, but illuminates the field of morality by his example. The Suffering Servant helps us to understand the significance of love blended with humility. This is not to deny that elsewhere there are similar conceptions, as in Buddhist compassion; but it may well be claimed that in Christianity there is a striking tragic realism which weaves together the insights of numinous religion, mysticism and morality.

Perhaps all this balancing of insights is precarious and indeed flavoured with subjective preferences. I concede that the basic points, namely the superior richness of Christianity, the emphasis on theism and the religion of worship, the need for atonement and the attractiveness of *agapē*, constitute no knockdown arguments. And there are certainly counter-arguments, such as the imperilling of pure monotheism in Christianity and, perhaps, its Judaic dogmatism whereby little credit is given to the intuitions of the polytheist. Nevertheless, a sympathetic Buddhist or Hindu would, I suggest, regard the arguments as at least relevant. Maybe one can gain no more certainty in such matters than in, say, literary or artistic criticism. But one would not for this reason deny that there are relevant insights (or reasons) in regard to revelations. In any event, it is incumbent upon us to try to give such reasons, for they make explicit our religious value-judgements. The trouble about a great deal of comparative apologetic is that it is not thus explicit.

So much, albeit briefly, for what I mean by religious reasons. There are, however, other tasks for the apologist. Revelations, for various reasons, give different pictures of this world. And some of these apply more easily than others. Or at any rate there are problems about their application which must concern us. I use the term 'application' here for the following reason. On the view here presented, certain revelations or revelatory experiences are basically what are appealed to in defence of a religious position. I do not myself believe that one can gain a knowledge of God simply by observing the physical world. Nevertheless the doctrines themselves present a picture of the cosmos which has to square with reality. That is, we do not see that a daffodil is divine (save perhaps in peculiar contemplations) and thus come to believe in God. But our belief gives us the notion that the daffodil has a divine flavour. (A like remark applies to morality too.) Regarding problems of application, the purposive view of history, for example, implicit in Christianity can be contrasted with the cyclical and repetitive picture provided in Indian religion. More importantly, cosmology poses difficulties of application.

We find that there are billions of stars in countless galaxies. Some of these stars are suns; and some of these will perhaps have planets like ours. The theory of evolution and the possibility of the synthesis of organic from inorganic matter may suggest that it is not incredible (and perhaps even probable) that there is life elsewhere in the universe and that there are in other places reasoning organisms. Such speculations would create acute difficulties about the scandal of particularity: the scandal might indeed seem an outrage. Hinduism and Buddhism, with their florid imaginings of beings of all sorts in all kinds of worlds, find the task of applying themselves to this vast universe less difficult. For the Trinity Doctrine, as a final expression of truth about the Godhead, may suffer if there are men elsewhere to be saved through Incarnation. Agreed, all this is highly speculative, but it is a matter for the philosopher, *qua* metaphysical apologist, to discuss.

Again, there are certain more traditional metaphysical problems concerned with the application of doctrines to the world which ought to be discussed. Notably, there is the problem of free will, which links up with the truth or otherwise of scientific materialism. More precisely, it connects not only with the conceptual problem of whether one could adapt language in such a way as to remove the dualistic ontology which seems implicit in current usage, but also with informed speculation as to the possibility of a unified scientific theory of human behaviour. To this latter recent advances in cybernetics, brain physiology and so forth are obviously relevant.

What then is the situation? First, there is philosophical analysis, which helps to illuminate the structure and epistemology of doctrines, East and West. As such it is best regarded as a peculiar way of doing the comparative study of religions. Then there is general apologetics, the giving (in the present instance) of religious reasons for a certain view of the cosmos; and this might as well be done by the sympathetic philosopher as by anyone else. Here historical facts may enter in, but these already have to be interpreted by reference to certain religious insights. Then there arise questions of a general nature, which though not pure exercises in the *a priori* nevertheless ought to engage philosophers' attention, regarding the application of doctrines to the cosmos as we know it. And all this, save neutral philosophical analysis, can be termed 'metaphysics'. Or it is a sort of natural theology—it is natural, since it does not merely expound revelation but attempts to give reasons on behalf of a revelation; and it is theology because it involves religious beliefs and ways of speaking. But perhaps I am here being a Pickwick, for this is not natural theology in the old sense. It is a soft, rather than the old hard, variety.

Yet what of the glimmering abstractions of yesteryear? What of the Five Ways and the superb claims of reason? Here, I can only feel that the hard metaphysics of the old days, where Aristotle and others conspire with faith, has to be left on one side. It is true that there are uneasinesses about the cosmos which the traditional arguments for God's existence enshrine—in particular the cosmological worry of why anything exists at all. But the rules of argument in this connexion are so debatable that it is absurd to pretend that we have either strong inductions or deductions here. In short, traditional natural theology can supply hunches which perhaps reinforce the insights of religious phenomenology, but it cannot stand on its own.[1]

The main point of this paper may be put in another way by saying that any appeal to religious experience (whether intuitive or otherwise) must inevitably lead to a consideration of the experience not merely of Christians but of Buddhists and others, and thereby to an examination of the way experience is linked to different sorts of doctrines. Through this investigation one is bound to ask what the criteria are for choosing between different formulations of religious belief. And from the apologetic point of view it is necessary to give reasons for accepting one's own faith rather than some other. Since natural theology in the old form appears to me to be gravely suspect, and since an irrationalist appeal to revelation alone (whether fundamentalist or not) is utterly self-defeating, our only choice is to work with the notion of religious reasons of the kind which I have sketched.

All this may seem somewhat programmatic. But even programmes are sometimes useful, and I have tried to illustrate part of the programme of Christian metaphysics. I said at the outset that natural theology is the Sick Man of Europe. I do not profess to have cured him. But at least I have tried to give advice on how to live with one's coronary.

[1] This same point about the traditional proofs is made with a rather different emphasis in Ch. X, pp. 172-3.—Ed.

8

SATORI*

D. T. Suzuki   ▨

Daisetz Teitaro Suzuki (1870–1965) was one of the most important and influential recent philosophers within the Zen tradition. His works include: Zen and Japanese Culture *and* Essays on Zen.

STRANGE though it may seem, the fact is that Buddhist scholars are engrossed too much in the study of what they regard as the Buddha's teaching and his disciples' exposition of the Dharma, so called, while they neglect altogether the study of the Buddha's spiritual experience itself. According to my view, however, the first thing we have to do in the elucidation of Buddhist thought is to inquire into the nature of this personal experience of the Buddha, which is recorded to have presented itself to his inmost consciousness at the time of Enlightenment (*sambodhi*). What the Buddha taught his disciples was the conscious outcome of his intellectual elaboration to make them see and realize what he himself had seen and realized. This intellectual outcome, however philosophically presented, does not necessarily enter into the inner essence of Enlightenment experienced by the Buddha. When we want, therefore, to grasp the spirit of Buddhism, which essentially develops from the content of Enlightenment, we have to get acquainted with the signification of the experience of the founder—experience by virtue of which he is indeed the Buddha and the founder of the religious system which goes under his name.

. . .

THERE is no doubt that it was this spiritual experience that converted the Bodhisattva into the Buddha, the Perfectly Wise, the Bhagavat, the Arhat, the King of the Dharma, the Tathagata, the All-knowing One, and the Conqueror. In this, all the records we have, Hinayāna and Mahāyāna agree.

Here, then, arises the most significant question in the history of Buddhism. What was it in this experience that made the Buddha conquer Ignorance (*avijjā, avidyā*) and freed him from the Defile-

---

* From Daisetz Teitaro Suzuki, *Essays in Zen Buddhism* (first series). Published by Grove Press, Inc. Reprinted by permission of Grove Press, Inc.

ments (*āsava, āśrava*) ? What was the insight or vision he had into things, which had never before been presented to his mind? Was it his doctrine of universal suffering due to Thirst (*taṇhâ, tṛishṇā*) and Grasping (*upādāna*) ? Was it his causation theory by which he traced the source of pain and suffering to Ignorance?

It is quite evident that his intellectual activity was not the efficient cause of Enlightenment. 'Not to be grasped by mere logic' (*atakkāvacara*) is the phrase we constantly encounter in Buddhist literature, Pāli and Sanskrit. The satisfaction the Buddha experienced in this case was altogether too deep, too penetrating, and too far-reaching in result to be a matter of mere logic. The intellectual solution of a problem is satisfying enough as far as the blockage has been removed, but it is not sufficiently fundamental to enter into the depths of our soul-life. All scholars are not saints and all saints are by no means scholarly. The Buddha's intellectual survey of the Law of Origination (*paticca-samuppāda*), however perfect and thoroughgoing, could not make him so completely sure of his conquest over Ignorance, Pain, Birth, and Defilements. Tracing things to their origin or subjecting them to a scheme of concatenation is one thing, but to subdue them, to bring them to subjection in the actuality of life, is quite another thing. In the one the intellect alone is active, but in the other there is the operation of the will—and the will is the man. The Buddha was not the mere discoverer of the Twelvefold Chain of Causation, he took hold of the chain itself in his hands and broke it into pieces so that it would never again bind him to slavery.

His insight reached the bottom of his being and saw it really as it was, and the seeing was like the seeing of your own hand with your own eyes—there was no reflection, no inference, no judgment, no comparison, no moving either backward or forward step by step, the thing was seen and that was the end of it, there was nothing to talk about, nothing to argue, or to explain. The seeing was something complete in itself—it did not lead on to anything inside or outside, within or beyond. And it was this completeness, this finality, that was so entirely satisfying to the Buddha, who now knew that the chain was found broken and that he was a liberated man. The Buddha's experience of Enlightenment therefore could not be understood by referring it to the intellect which tantalizes but fails to fulfil and satisfy.

The Buddha's psychological experience of life as pain and suffering was intensely real and moved him to the very depths of his being, and in consequence the emotional reaction he experienced at the time of Enlightenment was in proportion to this intensity of feeling. All the more evident, therefore, it is that he could not rest satisfied with an intellectual glancing or surveying of the facts of life. In order to bring a perfect state of tranquillity over the waves of turmoil surging in his heart, he had to have recourse to something more deeply and vitally concerned with his inmost being. For all we can say of it, the intellect is after all a spectator, and when it does some work it is as a hireling for better or for worse. Alone it cannot bring about the state of mind designated as enlightenment. The feeling of perfect freedom, the feeling that 'aham hi araha loke, aham sattha anuttaro', could not issue from the consciousness of an intellectual superiority alone. There must have been in the mind of the Buddha a consciousness far more fundamental which could only accompany one's deepest spiritual experience.

To account for this spiritual experience the Buddhist writers exhaust their knowledge of words relating to the understanding, logical or otherwise. 'Knowledge' (*vijjā*), 'understanding' (*pajānanā*), 'reason' (*ñāṇa*), 'wisdom' (*paññā*), 'penetration' (*abhisameta*), 'realization' (*abhisambuddha*), 'perception' (*sañjā-nanam*), and 'insight' (*dassana*),[1] are some of the terms they use. In truth, so long as we confine ourselves to intellection, however deep, subtle, sublime, and enlightening, we fail to see into the gist of the matter. This is the reason why even the so-called primitive Buddhists who are by some considered positivists, rationalists, and agnostics, were obliged to assume some faculty dealing with things far above relative knowledge, things that do not appeal to our empirical ego.

The Mahāyāna account of Enlightenment as is found in the *Lalita-vistara* (chapter on 'Abhisambodhana') is more explicit as to the kind of mental activity or wisdom which converted the Bodhisattva into the Buddha. For it was through '*ekacittekshaṇa-sam-yukta-prajñā*' that supreme perfect knowledge was realized (*abhisambodha*) by the Buddha. What is this Prajñā? It is the understanding of a higher order than that which is habitually exercised in acquiring relative knowledge. It is a faculty both intellectual and spiritual, through the operation of which the soul is enabled to break the fetters of intellection. The latter is always dualistic inasmuch as it is cognizant of subject and object, but in the Prajñā which is exercised 'in unison with one-thought-viewing' there is no separation between knower and known, these are all viewed (*ikshaṇa*) in one thought (*ekacitta*), and enlightenment is the outcome of this. By thus specifying the operation of Prajñā, the Mahāyānists have achieved an advance in making clearer the

---

[1] *The Mahāvyutpatti*, CXLII, gives a list of thirteen terms denoting the act of comprehending with more or less definite shades of meaning: buddhi, mati, gati, matam, drishtam, abhisamitāvī, samyagavabodha, supratividdha, abhilakshita, gātimgata, avabodha, pratyabhijñā, and menire.

nature of sambodhi: for when the mind reverses its usual course of working and, instead of dividing itself externally, goes back to its original inner abode of oneness, it begins to realize the state of 'one-thought-viewing' where Ignorance ceases to scheme and the Defilements do not obtain.

Enlightenment we can thus see is an absolute state of mind in which no 'discrimination' (*parikalpana* or *vikalpa*), so called, takes place, and it requires a great mental effort to realize this state of viewing all things 'in one thought'. In fact, our logical as well as practical consciousness is too given up to analysis and ideation; that is to say, we cut up realities into elements in order to understand them; but when they are put together to make the original whole, its elements stand out too conspicuously defined, and we do not view the whole 'in one thought'. And as it is only when 'one thought' is reached that we have enlightenment, an effort is to be made to go beyond our relative empirical consciousness, which attaches itself to the multitudinosity and not to the unity of things. The most important fact that lies behind the experience of Enlightenment, therefore, is that the Buddha made the most strenuous attempt to solve the problem of Ignorance and his utmost will-power was brought forth to bear upon a successful issue of the struggle.

We read in the *Katha-Upanishad:* 'As rain water that has fallen on a mountain ridge runs down on all sides, thus does he who sees a difference between qualities run after them on all sides. As pure water poured into pure water remains the same, thus, O Gautama, is the self of a thinker who knows.' This pouring pure water into pure water is, as we have it here, the 'viewing all qualities in one thought' which finally cuts off the hopelessly entangling logical mesh by merging all differences and likenesses into the absolute oneness of the knower (*jñānin*) and the known (*jñeya*). This, however, in our practical dualistic life, is a reversion, a twisting, and a readjustment.

Eckhart, the great German mystic, is singularly one with the 'one-thought-viewing' of things as done by Buddhists when he expresses his view thus: 'Das Auge darin ich Gott sehe, ist dasselbe Auge, darin Gott mich sieht. Mein Auge und Gottes Auge ist ein Auge und ein Gesicht und ein Erkennen und eine Liebe.'[1] The idea of reversion is more clearly expressed in Jacob Boehme's simile of the 'umgewandtes Auge' with which God is recognized.

Enlightenment, therefore, must involve the will as well as the intellect. It is an act of intuition born of the will. The will wants to know itself as it is in itself, *yathābhūtam dassana,* free

[1] Franz Pfeiffer, p. 312, Martensen, p. 29.

from all its cognitive conditions. The Buddha attained this end when a new insight came upon him at the end of his ever-circulatory reasoning from decay and death to Ignorance and from Ignorance to decay and death, through the twelve links of the Paticca-samuppāda. The Buddha had to go over the same ground again and again, because he was in an intellectual *impasse* through which he could not move further on. He did not repeat the process, as is originally imagined, for his own philosophical edification.

The fact was that he did not know how to escape this endless rotation of ideas; at this end there was birth, there was decay and death, and at the other end there was Ignorance. The objective facts could not be denied, they boldly and uncomfortably confronted him, while Ignorance balked the progress of his cognitive faculty moving farther onward or rather inward. He was hemmed in on both sides, he did not know how to find his way out, he went first this way and then that way, forever with the same result—the utter inutility of all his mental labour. But he had an indomitable will; he wanted, with the utmost efforts of his will, to get into the very truth of the matter; he knocked and knocked until the doors of Ignorance gave way: and they burst open to a new vista never before presented to his intellectual vision. Thus he was able to exclaim to Upaka, the naked ascetic, whom he happened to meet on his way to Benares after Enlightenment:

'All-conqueror I, knower of all,
From every soil and stain released,
Renouncing all, from craving ceased,
Self-taught; whom should I Master call?

That which I know I learned of none,
My fellow is not on the earth.
Of human or of heavenly birth
To equal me there is not one.

I truly have attained release,
The world's unequalled teacher I,
Alone, enlightened perfectly,
I dwell in everlasting peace.'[1]

---

[1] Translated by Bhikkhu Sīlācara. The original Pāli runs as follows:
Sabbābhibhū sabbavidū 'ham asmi,
Sabbesu dhammesu anūpalitto,
Sabbaṁjaho tanhakkhaye vimutto
Sayaṁ abhiññāya kam uddiseyyaṁ.
Na me ācariyo atthi, sadiso me na vijjati,
Sadevakasmiṁ lokasmiṁ na 'tthi me patipuggalo.
Ahaṁ hi arahā loke, ahaṁ satthā anuttaro,
Eko 'mhi sammasambuddho, sītibhūto 'smi, nibbuto.
Dīgha-Nikāya, XXVI.

When we speak of enlightenment or illumination we are apt to think of its epistemological aspect and to forget the presence of a tremendous will-power behind it—the power in fact making up the entire being of an individual. Especially as in Buddhism the intellect stands forth prominently, perhaps more than it ought to, in the realization of the ideal Buddhist life; scholars are tempted to ignore the significance of the will as the essentially determinate factor in the solution of the ultimate problem. Their attention has thus been directed too much towards the doctrine of the Paticca-samuppāda or the Ariyasacca, which they considered constituted the final teaching of Buddhism. But in this they have been sadly at fault, nor have they been right in taking Buddhism for a sort of ethical culture, declaring that it is no more than a system of moral precepts (*śīla*), without a soul, without a God, and consequently without a promise of immortality. But the true Buddhist ideas of Ignorance, Causation, and Moral Conduct had a far deeper foundation in the soul-life of man Ignorance was not a cognitive ignorance, but meant the darkness of spiritual outlook. If Ignorance were no more than cognitive, the clearing-up of it did not and could not result in enlightenment, in freedom from the Fetters and Defilements, or Intoxicants as some Pāli scholars have them. The Buddha's insight penetrated the depths of his being as the will, and he knew what this was, yathābhūtam, or in its tathābhāva (thatness or suchness), he rose above himself as a Buddha supreme and peerless. The expression 'Anuttara-samyak-sambodhi' was thus used to designate this pre-eminently spiritual knowledge realized by him.

Ignorance, which is the antithesis of Enlightenment, therefore acquires a much deeper sense here than that which has hitherto been ascribed to it. Ignorance is not merely not knowing or not being acquainted with a theory, system or law; it is not directly grasping the ultimate facts of life as expressive of the will. In Ignorance knowing is separated from acting, and the knower from that which is to be known; in Ignorance the world is asserted as distinct from the self; that is, there are always two elements standing in opposition. This is, however, the fundamental condition of cognition, which means that as soon as cognition takes place there is Ignorance clinging to its very act. When we think we know something, there is something we do not know. The unknown is always behind the known, and we fail to get at this unknown knower, who is indeed the inevitable and necessary companion to every act of cognition. We want, however, to know this unknown knower, we cannot let this go unknown, ungrasped without actually seeing what it is; that is, Ignorance is to be enlightened. This involves a great contradiction, at least epistomologically. But until we transcend this condition there is no peace of mind, life grows unbearable.

In his search for the 'builder' (*gahākara*), the Buddha was always accosted by Ignorance, an unknown knower behind knowing. He could not for a long time lay his hands on this one in a black mask until he transcended the dualism of knower and known. This transcending was not an act of cognition, it was self-realization, it was a spiritual awakening and outside the ken of logical reasoning, and therefore not accompanied by Ignorance. The knowledge the knower has of himself, in himself—that is, as he is to himself—is unattainable by any proceedings of the intellect which is not permitted to transcend its own conditions. Ignorance is brought to subjection only by going beyond its own principle. This is an act of the will. Ignorance in itself is no evil, nor is it the source of evil, but when we are ignorant of Ignorance, of what it means in our life, then there takes place an unending concatenation of evils. Taṇhā (craving) regarded as the root of evil can be overcome only when Ignorance is understood in its deeper and proper signification.

The essence of Zen Buddhism consists in acquiring a new viewpoint of looking at life and things generally. By this I mean that if we want to get into the inmost life of Zen, we must forgo all our ordinary habits of thinking which control our everyday life, we must try to see if there is any other way of judging things, or rather if our ordinary way is always sufficient to give us the ultimate satisfaction of our spiritual needs. If we feel dissatisfied somehow with this life, if there is something in our ordinary way of living that deprives us of freedom in its most sanctified sense, we must endeavour to find a way somewhere which gives us a sense of finality and contentment. Zen proposes to do this for us and assures us of the acquirement of a new point of view in which life assumes a fresher, deeper, and more satisfying aspect. This acquirement, however, is really and naturally the greatest mental cataclysm one can go through with in life. It is no easy task, it is a kind of fiery baptism, and one has to go through the storm, the earthquake, the overthrowing of the mountains, and the breaking in pieces of the rocks.

This acquiring of a new point of view in our dealings with life and the world is popularly called by Japanese Zen students 'satori' (*wu* in Chinese). It is really another name for Enlightenment (*annuttara-samyak-saṁbodhi*), which is the word used by the Buddha and his Indian followers ever since his realization under the Bodhi-tree by the River Nairañjanā. There are several other phrases in Chinese designating this spiritual experience, each of which has a special connotation, showing tentatively how this phenomenon is interpreted. At all events there is no Zen without satori, which is indeed the Alpha and Omega of Zen Buddhism. Zen devoid of satori is like a sun without its light and heat. Zen may lose all its literature, all its monasteries, and all its paraphernalia; but as long as there is satori in it it will survive to eternity. I want to emphasize this most fundamental fact concerning the very life of Zen; for there are some even among the students of Zen themselves who are blind to this central fact and are apt to think when Zen has been explained away logically or psychologically, or as one of the Buddhist philosophies which can be summed up by using highly technical and conceptual Buddhist phrases, Zen is exhausted, and there remains nothing in it that makes it what it is. But my contention is, the life of Zen begins with the opening of satori (*kai wu* in Chinese) .

Satori may be defined as an intuitive looking into the nature of things in contradistinction to the analytical or logical understanding of it. Practically, it means the unfolding of a new world hitherto unperceived in the confusion of a dualistically-trained mind. Or we may say that with satori our entire surroundings are viewed from quite an unexpected angle of perception. Whatever this is, the world for those who have gained a satori is no more the old world as it used to be; even with all its flowing streams and burning fires, it is never the same one again. Logically stated, all its opposites and contradictions are united and harmonized into a consistent organic whole. This is a mystery and a miracle, but according to the Zen masters such is being performed every day. Satori can thus be had only through our once personally experiencing it.

Its semblance or analogy in a more or less feeble and fragmentary way is gained when a difficult mathematical problem is solved, or when a great discovery is made, or when a sudden means of escape is realized in the midst of most desperate complications; in short, when one exclaims 'Eureka! Eureka!' But this refers only to the intellectual aspect of satori, which is therefore necessarily partial and incomplete and does not touch the very foundations of life considered one indivisible whole. Satori as the Zen experience must be concerned with the entirety of life. For what Zen proposes to do is the revolution, and the revaluation as well, of oneself as a spiritual unity. The solving of a mathematical problem ends with the solution, it does not affect one's whole life. So with all other particular questions, practical or scientific, they do not enter the basic life-tone of the individual concerned. But the opening of satori is the remaking of life itself. When it is genuine—for there are many simulacra of it—its effects on one's moral and spiritual life are revolutionary, and they are so enhancing, purifying, as well as exacting. When a master was asked what constituted Buddhahood, he answered, 'The bottom of a pail is broken through.' From this we can see what a complete revolution is produced by this spiritual experience. The birth of a new man is really cataclysmic.

In the psychology of religion this spiritual enhancement of one's whole life is called 'conversion'. But as the term is generally used by Christian converts, it cannot be applied in its strict sense to the Buddhist experience, especially to that of the Zen followers; the term has too affective or emotional a shade to take the place of satori, which is above all noetic. The general tendency of Buddhism is, as we know, more intellectual than emotional, and its doctrine of Enlightenment distinguishes it sharply from the Christian view of salvation; Zen as one of the Mahāyāna schools naturally shares a large amount of what we may call transcendental intellectualism, which does not issue in logical dualism. When poetically or figuratively expressed, satori is 'the opening of the mind-flower', or 'the removing of the bar', or 'the brightening up of the mind-works'.

All these tend to mean the clearing up of a passage which has been somehow blocked, preventing the free, unobstructed operation of a machine or a full display of the inner works. With the removal of the obstruction, a new vista opens before one, boundless in expanse and reaching the end of time. As life thus feels quite free in its activity, which was not the case before the awakening, it now enjoys itself to the fullest extent of its possibilities, to attain which is the object of Zen discipline. This is often taken to be equivalent to 'vacuity of interest and poverty of purpose'. But according to the Zen masters the doctrine of nonachievement concerns itself with the subjective attitude of mind which goes beyond the limitations of thought. It does not deny ethical ideals, nor does it transcend them; it is simply an inner state of consciousness without reference to its objective consequences.

I wish to close this Essay by making a few general remarks in the way of recapitulation on the Buddhist experience known as satori.

1. People often imagine that the discipline of Zen is to induce a state of self-suggestion through meditation. This is not quite right. As we can see from the various instances above cited, satori does not consist in producing a certain premeditated condition by intensely thinking of it. It is the growing conscious of a new power in the mind, which enabled it to judge things from a new point of view. Ever since the unfoldment of consciousness we have

been led to respond to the inner and outer conditions in a certain conceptual and analytical manner. The discipline of Zen consists in upsetting this artificially constructed framework once for all and in remodelling it on an entirely new basis. The older frame is called 'Ignorance' (*avidyā*) and the new one 'Enlightenment' (*sambodhi*). It is evident therefore that meditating on a metaphysical or symbolical statement which is a product of our relative consciousness plays no part in Zen, as I have touched on this in the Introduction.

2. Without the attainment of satori no one can enter into the mystery of Zen. It is the sudden flashing of a new truth hitherto altogether undreamed of. It is a sort of mental catastrophe taking place all at once after so much piling of matters intellectual and demonstrative. The piling has reached its limit and the whole edifice has now come to the ground, when behold a new heaven is opened to your full survey. Water freezes suddenly when it reaches a certain point, the liquid has turned into a solidity, and it no more flows. Satori comes upon you unawares when you feel you have exhausted your whole being. Religiously this is a new birth, and, morally, the revaluation of one's relationship to the world. The latter now appears to be dressed in a different garment which covers up all the ugliness of dualism, which is called in Buddhist phraseology delusion (*māyā*) born of reasoning (*tarka*) and error (*vikalpa*).

3. Satori is the *raison d'être* of Zen, and without which Zen is no Zen. Therefore every contrivance (*upāya*), disciplinary or doctrinal, is directed toward the attainment of satori. Zen masters could not remain patient for satori to come by itself; that is, to come sporadically and at its own pleasure. They earnestly seek out some way to make people deliberately or systematically realize the truth of Zen. Their manifestly enigmatical presentations of it were mostly to create a state of mind in their disciples, which would pave the way to the enlightenment of Zen. All the intellectual demonstrations and exhortatory persuasions so far carried out by most religious and philosophical leaders failed to produce the desired effect. The disciples were led further and further astray. Especially when Buddhism was introduced into China with all its Indian equipments, with its highly metaphysical abstractions, and in a most complicated system of moral discipline, the Chinese were at a loss how to grasp the central point of the doctrine of Buddhism. Daruma, Yenō, Baso, and other masters noticed the fact. The natural outcome was the proclamation of Zen; satori was placed above Sūtra-reading and scholarly discussion of the Śastras, and it came to be identified with Zen. Zen therefore without satori is like

pepper without its pungency. But at the same time we must not forget that there is such a thing as too much satori, which is indeed to be detested.

4. This emphasizing in Zen of satori above everything else makes the fact quite significant that Zen is not a system of dhyāna as practised in India and by other schools of Buddhism than the Zen. By dhyāna is understood popularly a kind of meditation or contemplation; that is the fixing of thought, especially in Mahā-yāna Buddhism, on the doctrine of emptiness (śūnyatā). When the mind is so trained as to be able to realize the state of perfect void in which there is not a trace of consciousness left, even the sense of being unconscious having departed—in other words, when all forms of mental activity are swept clean from the field of consciousness, which is now like a sky devoid of every speck of cloud, a mere broad expanse of blue—dhyāna is said to have reached its perfection. This may be called ecstasy or trance, but it is not Zen. In Zen there must be a satori; there must be a general mental upheaval which destroys the old accumulations of intellectuality and lays down a foundation for a new faith; there must be the awakening of a new sense which will review the old things from an angle of perception entirely and most refreshingly new. In dhyāna there are none of these things, for it is merely a quieting exercise of the mind. As such it has doubtless its own merits, but Zen ought not to be identified with such dhyānas. The Buddha therefore got dissatisfied with his two Sankhya teachers, in whose teaching the meditations were so many stages of self-abstraction or thought-annihilation.

5. Satori is not seeing God as he is, as may be contended by some Christian mystics. Zen has from the very beginning made clear its principal thesis, which is to see into the work of creation and not interview the creator himself. The latter may be found then busy moulding his universe, but Zen can go along with its own work even when he is not found there. It is not depending on his support. When it grasps the reason of living a life, it is satisfied. Hōyen, of Gosozan, used to produce his own hand and asked his disciples why it is called a hand. When one knows the reason, there is satori and one has Zen. Whereas with the God of mysticism there is the grasping of a definite object, and when you have God, what is not God is excluded. This is self-limiting. Zen wants absolute freedom, even from God. 'No abiding place' means that; 'Cleanse your mouth even when you utter the word "Buddha"' amounts to the same thing. It is not that Zen wants to be morbidly unholy and godless, but that it knows the incompleteness of a name. Therefore when Yakusan (Yüehshan) was asked to give a lecture, he did not

say a word, but instead came down from the pulpit and went off to his own room. Hyakujo (Pai-chang) merely walked forward a few steps, stood still, and opened his arms—which was his exposition of a great principle of Buddhism.

6. Satori is the most intimate individual experience and therefore cannot be expressed in words or described in any manner. All that one can do in the way of communicating the experience to others is to suggest or indicate, and this only tentatively. The one who has had it understands readily when such indications are given, but when we try to have a glimpse of it through the indices given we utterly fail. We are then like the man who says that he loves the most beautiful woman in the world and yet who knows nothing of her pedigree or social position, of her personal name or family name, knows nothing of her individuality, physical as well as moral. We are again like the man who puts up a staircase in a place where four crossroads meet, to mount up thereby into the upper story of a mansion, and yet who knows not just where that mansion is, in the East or West, in the North or South. The Buddha was quite to the point when he thus derided all those philosophers and vain talkers of his day, who merely dealt in abstractions, empty hearsays, and fruitless indications. Zen therefore wants us to build the staircase right at the front of the very palace into whose upper story we are to mount up. When we can say 'This is the very personality, this is the very house,' we have the satori interviewed face to face and realized by oneself. (*Diṭṭhe va dhamme sayaṁ abhiññā sacchikatvā.*)

7. Satori is not a morbid state of mind, a fit subject for abnormal psychology. If anything it is a perfectly normal state of mind. When I speak of a mental upheaval, one may be led to consider Zen something to be shunned by ordinary people. This is a mistaken view of Zen, unfortunately often held by prejudiced critics. As Nansen (Nan-ch'üan) declared, it is your 'everyday thought'. When later a monk asked a master[1] what was meant by 'everyday thought', he said,

'Drinking tea, eating rice,
I pass my time as it comes;
Looking down at the stream, looking up at the mountains,
How serene and relaxed I feel indeed!'

It all depends upon the adjustment of the hinge whether the door opens in or out. Even in the twinkling of an eye, the whole affair is changed, and you have Zen, and you are as perfect and normal as ever. More than that, you have in the meantime acquired something altogether new. All your mental activities are now

---

[1] Pao-tz'u Wên-ch'in, a disciple of Pao-fu Ts'ung-chan, who died A.D. 928.

working to a different key, which is more satisfying, more peaceful, and fuller of joy than anything you ever had. The tone of your life is altered. There is something rejuvenating in it. The spring flowers look prettier, and the mountain stream runs cooler and more transparent. The subjective revolution that brings out this state of things cannot be called abnormal. When life becomes more enjoyable and its expanse is as broad as the universe itself, there must be something in satori quite healthy and worth one's striving after its attainment.

8. We are supposedly living in the same world, but who can tell the thing we popularly call a stone lying before this window is the same thing to all of us? According to the way we look at it, to some the stone ceases to be a stone, while to others it forever remains a worthless specimen of geological product. And this initial divergence of views calls forth an endless series of divergencies later in our moral and spiritual lives. Just a little twisting, as it were, in our modes of thinking, and yet what a world of difference will grow up eventually between one another! So with Zen, satori is this twisting, or rather screwing, not in the wrong way, but in a deeper and full sense, and the result is the revelation of a world of entirely new values.

Again, you and I sip a cup of tea. The act is apparently alike, but who can tell what a wide gap there is subjectively between you and me? In your drinking there may be no Zen, while mine is brim full of it. The reason is, the one moves in the logical circle and the other is out of it; that is to say, in one case rigid rules of intellection so called are asserting themselves, and the actor even when acting is unable to unfetter himself from these intellectual bonds; while in the other case the subject has struck a new path and is not at all conscious of the duality of his act; in him life is not split into object and subject or into acting and acted. The drinking at the moment to him means the whole fact, the whole world. Zen lives and is therefore free, whereas our 'ordinary' life is in bondage; satori is the first step to freedom.

9. Satori is Enlightenment (*sambodhi*). So long as Buddhism is the doctrine of Enlightenment, as we know it to be, from its earliest as well as from its later literature, and so long as Zen asserts satori to be its culmination, satori must be said to represent the very spirit of the Buddhist teaching.

Additional Readings

ASHVAGHOSA, *The Awakening of Faith in the Mahayana.*

BAILLIE, JOHN, *The Idea of Revelation in Recent Thought.*

————, *Our Knowledge of God.*

BERGSON, HENRI, *Two Sources of Morality and Religion.*

BUBER, MARTIN, *I and Thou.*

BULTMANN, RUDOLF, *Existence and Faith.*

GHOSE, AUROBINDO, *The Life Divine.*

HEPBURN, RONALD, *Christianity and Paradox.*

HOCKING, W. E., *The Meaning of God in Human Experience.*

HUXLEY, JULIAN, *Religion without Revelation.*

JAMES, WILLIAM, *Varieties of Religious Experience.*

MARTIN, C. B., *Religious Belief.*

TERESA, ST., *The Interior Castle.*

THIBAUT, GEORGE (ed.), *The Vedanta Sutras of Badarayana: With the Commentary by Sankara.*

PART IV

RELIGION

AND ETHICS

Well-developed religions have usually been thought to have close relations with ethics. Some of these relations are explored in this section. However, one important topic, that of moral arguments for the existence of God, is not represented here. Selections dealing with that topic are included in Part II ("Arguments for the Divine Reality").

The first five selections in this section deal with the problem of evil. This concerns the difficulty which the existence of evil is thought to raise against any belief that the world is created or ruled by a good and powerful God. Historically, considerations involving evil have been major features in some of the most important objections to religious belief. We should, however, avoid the easy assumption that the phrase, "the problem of evil," refers to a single well-defined issue. It is, rather, a large, loose family of problems that developed in a variety of ways. As a natural consequence of this, solutions to the problem of evil have also developed in a variety of ways.

The student will often encounter attempts to formulate this problem in a series of questions about God and evil (notice the way in which Hume begins his discussion with a series of questions). There is no doubt that these questions are very interesting, and often very difficult (the more specific and detailed the reference to evil, the more difficult the question is likely to be). It is not very clear, however, what further significance these questions are supposed to have. Since we do not know everything about even the simpler features of the world it would not be surprising if we should discover that we did not know everything about God either. A failure to answer such a question about God, then, though it may be disappointing and leave us with considerable perplexity, does not seem to lead to further important consequences.

The essay by J. L. Mackie seems to attempt a much more significant and fruitful development of this problem. He professes to construct an argument (not a question) which has a statement about evil as one of its premises and concludes that some important religious doctrine or belief is false. If Mackie's argument is sound, then something is wrong with the belief of many religious people. This is much more than could be concluded from the fact that such people were unable to answer some question about God.

Alvin Plantinga replies directly to Mackie's argument and others of a similar sort, claiming to show that these arguments are fallacious. He makes a logical point, that a statement to the effect that evil exists is logically compatible with a set of theological doctrines about the existence, goodness and power of God. It may be interesting to consider whether in doing this, Plantinga also provides (or even tries to provide) an answer to the question, "Why does God allow evil in the world?" The student may also apply this question, and the distinction on which it is based, to the discussions of this problem by Augustine and Aurobindo Ghose.

There are, of course, other topics involving both ethics and religion. We may, for example, wonder in what way the moral law depends upon the existence, the character, or the will of God (if it depends upon God at all). Or we may wonder whether it may be possible to justify a moral demand (and, if so, what sort of moral demand) even if we assume that there is no God. Topics of this sort are discussed in the remaining essays printed in this section, as well as in several of the items included in the list of additional readings.

GOOD AND EVIL*

St. Augustine ▓

*Augustine of Hippo (354–430) was per-
haps the most influential of all Christian
philosophical theologians. A native of
North Africa, he became Bishop of Hippo
in 395 and was the author of a very extensive corpus of writings, including:* On
Free Will, On the Trinity, Confessions,
and The City of God.

i. The Supreme Good beyond all others is God. It is thereby
unchangeable good, truly eternal, truly immortal. All other good
things derive their origin from him but are not part of him. That
which is part of him is as he is, but the things he has created are not
as he is. Hence if he alone is unchangeable, all things that he
created are changeable because he made them of nothing. Being
omnipotent he is able to make out of nothing, i.e., out of what has
no existence at all, good things, both great and small, celestial and
terrestrial, spiritual and corporeal. Because he is just, he did not
make the things he made out of nothing to be equal to him whom
he begat of himself. Therefore, all good things throughout all the
ranks of being, whether great or small, can derive their being only
from God. Every natural being, so far as it is such, is good. There
can be no being which does not derive its existence from the most
high and true God. All are not supremely good, but they approxi-
mate to the supreme good, and even the very lowest goods, which
are far distant from the supreme good, can only derive their
existence from the supreme good. Every mutable spirit and every
corporeal thing, that is, the whole of created nature, was made by
God, for everything that exists is either spirit or body. God is
immutable Spirit. Mutable spirit is a created thing, but it is better
than corporeal things. Body is not spirit, though in a different sense
we speak of the wind as spirit because it is invisible to us, and yet
we feel its not inconsiderable force.

ii. There are those who cannot understand that every natural being, that is, every spiritual and corporeal existent, is good by

* From St. Augustine, *De Natura Boni* in John H. S. Burleigh (tr.) , *Augustine:
Earlier Writings,* published 1953. Reprinted by permission of the Westminster
Press.

nature. They are impressed by the wickedness of spirits and the mortality of bodies, and so they endeavour to maintain that there is another nature besides that which God has made, viz., that of malignant spirit and mortal body. On their account we think that what we say can be brought to bear on their understanding, in this way. They admit that there can be no good thing save from the most high and true God. Now this is true and is sufficient to correct them if they will but pay attention.

iii. We, Catholic Christians, worship God, from whom are all good things, great or small, all measure great or small, all form great or small, all order great or small. All things are good; better in proportion as they are better measured, formed and ordered, less good where there is less of measure, form and order. These three things, measure, form and order, not to mention innumerable other things which demonstrably belong to them, are as it were generic good things to be found in all that God has created, whether spirit or body. God transcends all measure, form and order in his creatures, not in spatial locality but by his unique and ineffable power from which come all measure, form and order. Where these three things are present in a high degree there are great goods. Where they are present in a low degree there are small goods. And where they are absent there is no goodness. Moreover, where these three things are present in a high degree there are things great by nature. Where they are present in a low degree there are things small by nature. Where they are absent there is no natural thing at all. Therefore, every natural existent is good.

iv. If we ask whence comes evil, we should first ask what evil is. It is nothing but the corruption of natural measure, form or order. What is called an evil nature is a corrupt nature. If it were not corrupt it would be good. But even when it is corrupted, so far as it remains a natural thing, it is good. It is bad only so far as it is corrupted.

v. Of course it is possible that one nature even when corrupted may still be better than another nature which has remained uncorrupted, because the one has a superior, the other an inferior measure, form and order. According to the estimation of men, judging by what they see before them as they look, corrupted gold is better than uncorrupted silver, and corrupted silver is better than uncorrupted lead. Among spiritual natures of greater potency a rational spirit, even when corrupted by an evil will, is better than an irrational spirit that is uncorrupted; and any spirit, even when corrupted, is better than any body even when uncorrupted. For the thing which when present gives life to a body is better than the body to which it gives life. However corrupt the created spirit of life may become, it can still give life to its body. Hence even when corrupted it is better than its body though the latter be uncorrupted.

vi. If corruption take away from corruptible things all measure, form and order, nothing at all will remain in existence. Similarly any nature which cannot be corrupted will be the supreme good, as God is. Any nature which can be corrupted has some good in it, for corruption could not harm it except by taking away or diminishing what is good in it.

vii. To his most excellent creatures, that is to rational spirits, God has given the power not to be corrupted if they do not will to be; but remain obedient under the Lord their God and cleave to his incorruptible beauty. But if they will not remain obedient and are willingly corrupted by sin, they are unwillingly corrupted by penalties. God is the good, so that it can be well with no one who deserts him; and among his creatures the rational nature is so great a good that no other good save God can make it happy. Sinners are ordained to punishment. This order is contrary to their nature, and is therefore penalty. But it suits their fault and is therefore just.

viii. Other things created out of nothing which are inferior to rational spirit can be neither happy nor miserable. Since they are themselves good, because of the degree of measure and form they possess, and since, though the good in them be small or even minimal, they could not have existed save by the act of the good God most high; they are so ordered that the weaker yield to the stronger, and the feebler to those that have greater might, and the less powerful to the more powerful. So terrestrial things have peace with celestial things, being as it were submissive to things which are more excellent than they are. When things pass away and others succeed them there is a specific beauty in the temporal order, so that those things which die or cease to be what they were, do not defile or disturb the measure, form or order of the created universe. A well-prepared speech is beautiful even though all its syllables and sounds pass in succession as if they are born and die.

ix. The nature and quantity of the penalty due to each fault is determined by the judgment of God, not by that of man. When it is remitted to the converted, that is proof of the great goodness of God. When it is paid as due there is no inequity with God. It is a better order that a thing [natura] should suffer punishment justly than that it should rejoice in sin with impunity. So long as it retains some measure, form and order there is still some good in it no matter into what extremity it may come. If these were all together taken away and destroyed completely there would be no good because there would be nothing left.

x. Corruptible natures would not be natures at all unless they derived being from God. Nor would they be corruptible if they were part of him. They would then be as he is. The fact that they have some measure, form and order is due to their having been created by God. And they are not immutable because they were made out of nothing. It is sacrilegious audacity to equate nothing and God as we do if we want to make that which he created out of nothing equal to that which is born of God.

xi. No hurt whatever can be done to the divine nature, nor can any other nature which is less than divine be hurt unjustly. No doubt some people by sinning do harm unjustly. Their will to harm unjustly is counted against them, but the power by which they are permitted to do the harm comes only from God, who knows, though they do not, what those ought to suffer whom he permits them to harm.

xii. If those who want to introduce a nature other than that which God has made would only pay attention to these clear and certain facts, they would not be filled with such blasphemies as to impute so much good to the supreme evil, and to impute to God so many evils. As I said above, it is sufficient for their correction if they would only pay attention to what truth compels them to confess even against their will, that all good things come from God alone. Good things whether they are great or small all come from one source, that is from the supreme good, which is God.

xiii. Let us, therefore, recall all the good things we can which are worthy to be attributed to God as their author, and let us see whether when they are removed anything will remain in existence. All life, potency, health, memory, virtue, intelligence, tranquillity, plenty, sense, light, sweetness, measure, beauty, peace—all these things whether great or small, and other similar things which may occur to one, and especially those things which are found universally in spiritual or corporeal existence, measure, form and order, come from the Lord God. Whoever willingly makes a bad use of these good things will, by the divine judgment, pay the penalty. But wherever none of them is present at all, absolutely nothing will remain in existence.

xiv. Of these good things, if any of them is present in a small degree it is given a bad name to distinguish that condition from conditions in which it is present in a higher degree. For example, because there is greater beauty in the form of a man, by comparison with it the beauty of an ape is called deformity. And this misleads the unknowing. They think that the one is good and the other bad. They do not notice that the body of the ape has its own proper measure, correspondence of limbs on both sides, concord of all its parts, readiness in self-defence, and other qualities which it would take a long time to pursue.

xv. That what we are saying may be understood and satisfy those whose intelligence is rather slow, or even compel the pertinacious who resist the most patent truth to confess the truth, let us ask whether corruption can harm the body of an ape. If it can, and the ape can become more hideous, what is diminished if not such beauty as it has, which is a good thing? So long as its body continues to exist some beauty will remain. So if the destruction of good implies the destruction of existence nature is good. We say that the slow is the opposite of the swift, but if anyone does not move at all he cannot be said to be slow. We say that a low voice is the opposite of a shrill one, or a harsh voice of a musical one. But if you take away completely every kind of sound there is silence with no sound at all. We are accustomed to contrast silence with sound as contraries for the very reason that silence means the absence of sound. We speak of clear and obscure as contraries, but obscurity may have some light. If it has none at all, the darkness that results from the complete absence of light is like the silence which is the result of the complete absence of sound.

xvi. Qualitative deprivations are so ordered throughout the universe of nature that, for those who consider them wisely, their vicissitudes are not without propriety. By not causing light to shine on certain places and during certain times God made darkness quite as appropriately as day. If by keeping silent we interpose a suitable pause in our speech, how much more does he, the perfect artificer of all things, suitably and appropriately cause these deprivations? Hence, in the *Hymn of the Three Youths,* Light and Darkness alike praise God, that is, cause his praise to arise from the hearts of those who give full and right consideration to them.

xvii. No nature is evil so far as it is naturally existent. Nothing is evil in anything save a diminishing of good. If the good is so far diminished as to be utterly consumed, just as there is no good left so there is no existence left. Not merely no such existence as the Manichees introduce, in which there is so much good that their blindness is wonderfully great, but no such existence as anyone can imagine.

xviii. Not even matter which the ancients called "Hyle" is to be called evil. I do not mean what Manes in his stupid vanity ignorantly calls "Hyle," that is to say the power that forms bodies. He is rightly said to be introducing a second god. None but God can form and create bodies. Nor are bodies created without measure, form and order being created with them. Now I imagine that even the Manichees admit that these things are good and can only come from God. By "Hyle" I mean matter completely without form and quality, out of which are formed the qualities we perceive, as the ancients said. Hence wood is called "Hyle" in Greek, because it is suitable material for workmen, not that it makes anything but that something may be made out of it. That "Hyle" is not to be called evil. It has no form by which we can perceive it. Indeed, it can hardly be conceived because it is so utterly without form. But it has the capacity to receive form. If it could not receive the form imposed on it by the artificer it could not be called material either. Now if form is a good thing, so that those who have a superior form are called beautiful [formosi], doubtless even capacity for form is a good thing. Wisdom is a good thing, and no one doubts that capacity for wisdom is also a good thing. And because every good thing comes from God, no one should doubt that matter, if there is such a thing, derives its existence from God alone.

xix. Gloriously and divinely our God said to his servant: "I am who I am. Say to the children of Israel: He who is hath sent me unto you" (Ex. 3:14). He truly is because he is unchangeable. Every change causes that which was to cease to be. Therefore he truly is who is unchangeable. All other things which he made received existence from him each in its own degree. To him who supremely is there can be no contrary except that which is not. Consequently, just as all that is good comes from him, so from him comes all that has natural existence, since all that has natural existence is good. Every nature is good, and every good thing is from God. Therefore all nature is from God.

xx. Some think that pain whether in mind or body is the chief evil. But there cannot be pain except in things naturally good. For pain means that something that has been is in a sense striving against extinction, because what has been was good. When it is being compelled to become better the pain serves a useful purpose, otherwise it is useless. Mental pain is caused by the will's resisting a greater power. Bodily pain is caused by the senses resisting a more powerful body. But evils that have no accompanying pain are worse. It is worse to rejoice in iniquity than to suffer in corruption. There cannot be no rejoicing except by acquiring inferior good things. Iniquity is the abandonment of the better things. In the body a wound that gives pain is better than a painless festering which is specifically called corruption. The mortal flesh of our Lord did not see, i.e., suffer, corruption, as was foretold in the prophecy: "Thou wilt not give thy Holy One to see corruption" (Ps. 16:10). Who denies that he was wounded by the driving in of the nails and pierced with the spear? Take festering, which men call specifically a corruption of the body. Now if there is still something deep in the wound which it can consume, the corruption grows as good is diminished. But if there is nothing left to consume, there will be no festering since there is no good left. There will be nothing for corruption to corrupt; and there will be no festering, for there will be nothing to fester.

xxi. Tiny little things are in the common usage of speech said to be moderate because some measure remains in them. Without that they would not even be moderate but would not exist at all. Things which have gone too far are called immoderate and are blamed for being over-large. But even these must be kept within bounds under God, who has disposed all things by measure, number and weight.

xxii. We may not say that God has measure, in case that is taken to mean that he has an end. Yet is he not without measure by whom measure is given to all things so that they may in some measure exist. On the other hand we must not say that God has measure, as if it were imposed upon him from elsewhere. If we call him the supreme measure we perhaps say something significant, at any rate if we understand the supreme good by what we call the supreme measure. All measure, so far as it is measure, is good, and we cannot speak of things as moderate, modest or modified without implied praise of them. In another sense we speak of measure as implying end, and we say "measureless" meaning "endless." Sometimes that too implies praise, as in the words: "Of his kingdom there shall be no end" (Luke 1:33). The writer might have said "there shall be no measure [modus]" provided modus was understood to mean end [finis]. For, of course, he who reigns in no measure nullo modo = in no way] simply does not reign at all.

xxiii. Measure, form and order are said to be bad when there is less of them than there ought to be. Or it may be because they are not suited to things as they ought to be. Or they may be called bad because they are alien and incongruous. For example, someone may be said to have acted in a bad manner [modus] because he did less than he ought or more than he ought, or because he acted unsuitably or in a wrong way in the particular situation. The action which is blamed as having been done in a bad manner is justly blamed for no other reason than that it did not preserve modus. We speak of a form or appearance as being bad because it is inferior not in size but in comeliness when it is compared with more comely and beautiful forms. The reason is that it does not suit the things which wear it, and appears alien and unsuitable; as, for example, if a man were to walk naked in the market-place, an action which would give no offence if it took place in the baths. Likewise order is said to be bad when too little order is observed. It is not order but disorder that is bad, where there is less order than there ought to be, or where such order as there is is not as it ought to be. Nevertheless, wherever there is some measure, form and order there is some good and something naturally existing. Where there is no measure, form or order there is neither good nor existence.

2

THE PROBLEM

OF EVIL*

David Hume ▨

David Hume (1711–1776) is one of the most influential philosophers of modern times. He continued and developed the tradition of empiricism initiated in Britain by John Locke and George Berkeley. His major works include A Treatise of Human Nature, Inquiry Concerning the Human Understanding, *and* Dialogues on Natural Religion.

AND is it possible, Cleanthes, said Philo, that after all these reflections, and infinitely more, which might be suggested, you can still persevere in your Anthropomorphism, and assert the moral attributes of the Deity, his justice, benevolence, mercy, and rectitude, to be of the same nature with these virtues in human creatures? His power we allow is infinite: whatever he wills is executed: but neither man or any other animal is happy: therefore he does not will their happiness. His wisdom is infinite: he is never mistaken in choosing the means to any end: but the course of Nature tends not to human or animal felicity: therefore it is not established for that purpose. Through the whole compass of human knowledge, there are no inferences more certain and infallible than these. In what respect, then, do his benevolence and mercy resemble the benevolence and mercy of men?

Epicurus's old questions are yet unanswered.

Is he willing to prevent evil, but not able? then is he impotent. Is he able, but not willing? then is he malevolent. Is he both able and willing? whence then is evil?

You ascribe, Cleanthes (and I believe justly), a purpose and intention to Nature. But what, I beseech you, is the object of that curious artifice and machinery, which she has displayed in all animals? The preservation alone of individuals, and propagation of the species. It seems enough for her purpose, if such a rank be barely upheld in the universe, without any care or concern for the

* From David Hume, *Dialogues Concerning Natural Religion.*

happiness of the members that compose it. No resource for this purpose: no machinery, in order merely to give pleasure or ease: no fund of pure joy and contentment: no indulgence, without some want or necessity accompanying it. At least, the few phenomena of this nature are overbalanced by opposite phenomena of still greater importance.

Our sense of music, harmony, and indeed beauty of all kinds, gives satisfaction, without being absolutely necessary to the preservation and propagation of the species. But what racking pains, on the other hand, arise from gouts, gravels, megrims, toothaches, rheumatisms, where the injury to the animal machinery is either small or incurable? Mirth, laughter, play, frolic, seem gratuitous satisfactions, which have no further tendency: spleen, melancholy, discontent, superstition, are pains of the same nature. How then does the Divine benevolence display itself, in the sense of you Anthropomorphites? None but we Mystics, as you were pleased to call us, can account for this strange mixture of phenomena, by deriving it from attributes, infinitely perfect, but incomprehensible.

And have you at last, said Cleanthes, smiling, betrayed your intentions, Philo? Your long agreement with Demea did indeed a little surprise me; but I find you were all the while erecting a concealed battery against me. And I must confess, that you have now fallen upon a subject worthy of your noble spirit of opposition and controversy. If you can make out the present point, and prove mankind to be unhappy or corrupted, there is an end at once of all religion. For to what purpose establish the natural attributes of the Deity, while the moral are still doubtful and uncertain?

You take umbrage very easily, replied Demea, at opinions the most innocent, and the most generally received, even amongst the religious and devout themselves: and nothing can be more surprising than to find a topic like this, concerning the wickedness and misery of man, charged with no less than Atheism and profaneness. Have not all pious divines and preachers, who have indulged their rhetoric on so fertile a subject; have they not easily, I say, given a solution of any difficulties which may attend it? This world is but a point in comparison of the universe; this life but a moment in comparison of eternity. The present evil phenomena, therefore, are rectified in other regions, and in some future period of existence. And the eyes of men, being then opened to larger views of things, see the whole connection of general laws; and trace with adoration, the benevolence and rectitude of the Deity, through all the mazes and intricacies of his providence.

No! replied Cleanthes, No! These arbitrary suppositions can never be admitted, contrary to matter of fact, visible and uncontroverted. Whence can any cause be known but from its known effects? Whence can any hypothesis be proved but from the apparent phenomena? To establish one hypothesis upon another, is building entirely in the air; and the utmost we ever attain, by these conjectures and fictions, is to ascertain the bare possibility of our opinion; but never can we, upon such terms, establish its reality.

The only method of supporting Divine benevolence, and it is what I willingly embrace, is to deny absolutely the misery and wickedness of man. Your representations are exaggerated; your melancholy views mostly fictitious; your inferences contrary to fact and experience. Health is more common than sickness; pleasure than pain; happiness than misery. And for one vexation which we meet with, we attain, upon computation, a hundred enjoyments.

Admitting your position, replied Philo, which yet is extremely doubtful, you must at the same time allow, that if pain be less frequent than pleasure, it is infinitely more violent and durable. One hour of it is often able to outweigh a day, a week, a month of our common insipid enjoyments; and how many days, weeks, and months, are passed by several in the most acute torments? Pleasure, scarcely in one instance, is ever able to reach ecstasy and rapture; and in no one instance can it continue for any time at its highest pitch and altitude. The spirits evaporate, the nerves relax, the fabric is disordered, and the enjoyment quickly degenerates into fatigue and uneasiness. But pain often, good God, how often! rises to torture and agony; and the longer it continues, it becomes still more genuine agony and torture. Patience is exhausted, courage languishes, melancholy seizes us, and nothing terminates our misery but the removal of its cause, or another event, which is the sole cure of all evil, but which, from our natural folly, we regard with still greater horror and consternation.

But not to insist upon these topics, continued Philo, though most obvious, certain, and important; I must use the freedom to admonish you, Cleathes, that you have put the controversy upon a most dangerous issue, and are unawares introducing a total scepticism into the most essential articles of natural and revealed theology. What! no method of fixing a just foundation for religion, unless we allow the happiness of human life, and maintain a continued existence even in this world, with all our present pains, infirmities, vexations, and follies, to be eligible and desirable! But this is contrary to every one's feeling and experience: it is contrary to an authority so established as nothing can subvert. No decisive proofs can ever be produced against this authority; nor is it possible for you to compute, estimate, and compare, all the pains and all the pleasures in the lives of all men and of all animals: and thus, by your resting the whole system of religion on a point, which, from its very nature, must for ever be uncertain, you tacitly confess, that that system is equally uncertain.

But allowing you what never will be believed, at least what you never possibly can prove, that animal, or at least human happiness, in this life, exceeds its misery, you have yet done nothing: for this is not, by any means, what we expect from infinite power, infinite wisdom, and infinite goodness. Why is there any misery at all in the world? Not by chance surely. From some cause then. Is it from the intention of the Deity? But he is perfectly benevolent. Is it contrary to his intention? But he is almighty. Nothing can shake the solidity of this reasoning, so short, so clear, so decisive; except we assert, that these subjects exceed all human capacity, and that our common measures of truth and falsehood are not applicable to them; a topic which I have all along insisted on, but which you have, from the beginning, rejected with scorn and indignation.

But I will be contented to retire still from this intrenchment, for I deny that you can ever force me in it. I will allow, that pain or misery in man is *compatible* with infinite power and goodness in the Deity, even in your sense of these attributes: what are you advanced by all these concessions? A mere possible compatibility is not sufficient. You must *prove* these pure, unmixed, and uncontrollable attributes from the present mixed and confused phenomena, and from these alone. A hopeful undertaking! Were the phenomena ever so pure and unmixed, yet being finite, they would be insufficient for that purpose. How much more, where they are also so jarring and discordant!

Here, Cleanthes, I find myself at ease in my argument. Here I triumph. Formerly, when we argued concerning the natural attributes of intelligence and design, I needed all my sceptical and metaphysical subtilty to elude your grasp. In many views of the universe and of its parts, particularly the latter, the beauty and fitness of final causes strike us with such irresistible force, that all objections appear (what I believe they really are) mere cavils and sophisms; nor can we then imagine how it was ever possible for us to repose any weight on them. But there is no view of human life, or of the condition of mankind, from which, without the greatest violence, we can infer the moral attributes, or learn that infinite benevolence, conjoined with infinite power and infinite wisdom, which we must discover by the eyes of faith alone. It is your turn now to tug the laboring oar, and to support your philosophical subtilties against the dictates of plain reason and experience.

I scruple not to allow, said Cleanthes, that I have been apt to suspect the frequent repetition of the word *infinite*, which we meet with in all theological writers, to savor more of panegyric than of philosophy; and that any purposes of reasoning, and even of religion, would be better served, were we to rest contented with more accurate and more moderate expressions. The terms, *admirable, excellent, superlatively great, wise,* and *holy;* these sufficiently fill the imaginations of men; and any thing beyond, besides that it leads into absurdities, has no influence on the affections or sentiments. Thus, in the present subject, if we abandon all human analogy, as seems your intention, Demea, I am afraid we abandon all religion, and retain no conception of the great object of our adoration. If we preserve human analogy, we must for ever find it impossible to reconcile any mixture of evil in the universe with infinite attributes; much less can we ever prove the latter from the former. But supposing the Author of Nature to be finitely perfect, though far exceeding mankind, a satisfactory account may then be given of natural and moral evil, and every untoward phenomenon be explained and adjusted. A less evil may then be chosen, in order to avoid a greater; inconveniences be submitted to, in order to reach a desirable end; and in a word, benevolence, regulated by wisdom, and limited by necessity, may produce just such a world as the present. You, Philo, who are so prompt at starting views, and reflections, and analogies, I would gladly hear, at length, without interruption, your opinion of this new theory; and if it deserve our attention, we may afterwards, at more leisure, reduce it into form.

My sentiments, replied Philo, are not worth being made a mystery of; and therefore, without any ceremony, I shall deliver what occurs to me with regard to the present subject. It must, I think, be allowed, that if a very limited intelligence, whom we shall suppose utterly unacquainted with the universe, were assured, that it were the production of a very good, wise, and powerful Being, however finite, he would, from his conjectures, form *beforehand* a different notion of it from what we find it to be by experience; nor would he ever imagine, merely from these attributes of the cause, of which he is informed, that the effect could be so full of vice and misery and disorder, as it appears in this life. Supposing now, that this person were brought into the world, still assured that it was the workmanship of such a sublime and benevolent Being; he might, perhaps, be surprised at the disappointment; but would never retract his former belief, if founded on any very solid argument; since such a limited intelligence must be sensible of his own blindness and ignorance, and must allow, that there may be many solutions of those phenomena, which will for ever escape his comprehension. But supposing, which is the real case with regard to man, that this creature is not antecedently convinced of a supreme intelligence, benevolent and powerful, but is left to gather such a belief from the appearances of things; this entirely alters the case, nor will he ever find any reason for such a conclusion. He may be fully convinced of the narrow limits of his understanding; but this will not help him in forming an inference concerning the goodness of superior powers, since he must form that inference from what he knows, not from what he is ignorant of. The more you exaggerate his weakness and ignorance, the more diffident you render him, and give him the greater suspicion that such subjects are beyond the reach of his faculties. You are obliged, therefore, to reason with him merely from the known phenomena, and to drop every arbitrary supposition or conjecture.

Did I show you a house or palace, where there was not one apartment convenient or agreeable; where the windows, doors, fires, passages, stairs, and the whole economy of the building, were the source of noise, confusion, fatigue, darkness, and the extremes of heat and cold; you would certainly blame the contrivance, without any further examination. The architect would in vain display his subtilty, and prove to you, that if this door or that window were altered, greater ills would ensue. What he says may be strictly true: the alteration of one particular, while the other parts of the building remain, may only augment the inconveniences. But still you would assert in general, that, if the architect had had skill and good intentions, he might have formed such a plan of the whole, and might have adjusted the parts in such a manner, as would have remedied all or most of these inconveniences. His ignorance, or even your own ignorance of such a plan, will never convince you of the impossibility of it. If you find any inconveniences and deformities in the building, you will always, without entering into any detail, condemn the architect.

In short, I repeat the question: Is the world, considered in general, and as it appears to us in this life, different from what a man, or such a limited being, would, *beforehand,* expect from a very powerful, wise, and benevolent Deity? It must be strange prejudice to assert the contrary. And from thence I conclude, that however consistent the world may be, allowing certain suppositions and conjectures, with the idea of such a Deity, it can never afford us an inference concerning his existence. The consistence is not absolutely denied, only the inference. Conjectures, especially where infinity is excluded from the Divine attributes, may perhaps be sufficient to prove a consistence, but can never be foundations for any inference.

There seem to be *four* circumstances, on which depend all, or the greatest part of the ills, that molest sensible creatures; and it is not impossible but all these circumstances may be necessary and unavoidable. We know so little beyond common life, or even of common life, that, with regard to the economy of a universe, there is no conjecture, however wild, which may not be just; nor any one, however plausible, which may not be erroneous. All that belongs to human understanding, in this deep ignorance and obscurity, is to be sceptical, or at least cautious, and not to admit of any hypothesis whatever, much less of any which is supported by no appearance of probability. Now, this I assert to be the case with regard to all the causes of evil, and the circumstances on which it depends. None of them appear to human reason in the least degree necessary or unavoidable; nor can we suppose them such, without the utmost license of imagination.

The *first* circumstance which introduces evil, is that contrivance or economy of the animal creation, by which pains, as well as pleasures, are employed to excite all creatures to action, and make them vigilant in the great work of self-preservation. Now pleasure alone, in its various degrees, seems to human understanding sufficient for this purpose. All animals might be constantly in a state of enjoyment: but when urged by any of the necessities of nature, such as thirst, hunger, weariness; instead of pain, they might feel a diminution of pleasure, by which they might be prompted to seek that object which is necessary to their subsistence. Men pursue pleasure as eagerly as they avoid pain; at least they might have been so constituted. It seems, therefore, plainly possible to carry on the business of life without any pain. Why then is any animal ever rendered susceptible of such a sensation? If animals can be free from it an hour, they might enjoy a perpetual exemption from it; and it required as particular a contrivance of their organs to produce that feeling, as to endow them with sight, hearing, or any of the senses. Shall we conjecture, that such a contrivance was necessary, without any appearance of reason? and shall we build on that conjecture as on the most certain truth?

But a capacity of pain would not alone produce pain, were it not for the *second* circumstance, viz. the conducting of the world by general laws; and this seems nowise necessary to a very perfect Being. It is true, if every thing were conducted by particular volitions, the course of nature would be perpetually broken, and no man could employ his reason in the conduct of life. But might not other particular volitions remedy this inconvenience? In short, might not the Deity exterminate all ill, wherever it were to be found; and produce all good, without any preparation, or long progress of causes and effects?

Besides, we must consider, that, according to the present

economy of the world, the course of nature, though supposed exactly regular, yet to us appears not so, and many events are uncertain, and many disappoint our expectations. Health and sickness, calm and tempest, with an infinite number of other accidents, whose causes are unknown and variable, have a great influence both on the fortunes of particular persons and on the prosperity of public societies; and indeed all human life, in a manner, depends on such accidents. A being, therefore, who knows the secret springs of the universe, might easily, by particular volitions, turn all these accidents to the good of mankind, and render the whole world happy, without discovering himself in any operation. A fleet, whose purposes were salutary to society, might always meet with a fair wind. Good princes enjoy sound health and long life. Persons born to power and authority, be framed with good tempers and virtuous dispositions. A few such events as these, regularly and wisely conducted, would change the face of the world; and yet would no more seem to disturb the course of nature, or confound human conduct, than the present economy of things, where the causes are secret, and variable, and compounded. Some small touches given to Caligula's brain in his infancy, might have converted him into a Trajan. One wave, a little higher than the rest, by burying Cæsar and his fortune in the bottom of the ocean, might have restored liberty to a considerable part of mankind. There may, for aught we know, be good reasons why Providence interposes not in this manner; but they are unknown to us; and though the mere supposition, that such reasons exist, may be sufficient to *save* the conclusion concerning the Divine attributes, yet surely it can never be sufficient to *establish* that conclusion.

If every thing in the universe be conducted by general laws, and if animals be rendered susceptible of pain, it scarcely seems possible but some ill must arise in the various shocks of matter, and the various concurrence and opposition of general laws; but this ill would be very rare, were it not for the *third* circumstance, which I proposed to mention, viz. the great frugality with which all powers and faculties are distributed to every particular being. So well adjusted are the organs and capacities of all animals, and so well fitted to their preservation, that, as far as history or tradition reaches, there appears not to be any single species which has yet been extinguished in the universe. Every animal has the requisite endowments; but these endowments are bestowed with so scrupulous an economy, that any considerable diminution must entirely destroy the creature. Wherever one power is increased, there is a proportional abatement in the others. Animals which excel in swiftness are commonly defective in force. Those which possess both are either imperfect in some of their senses, or are oppressed with the most craving wants. The human species, whose chief excellency is reason and sagacity, is of all others the most necessitous, and the most deficient in bodily advantages; without clothes, without arms, without food, without lodging, without any convenience of life, except what they owe to their own skill and industry. In short, nature seems to have formed an exact calculation of the necessities of her creatures; and, like a *rigid master,* has afforded them little more powers or endowments than what are strictly sufficient to supply those necessities. An *indulgent parent* would have bestowed a large stock, in order to guard against accidents, and secure the happiness and welfare of the creature in the most unfortunate concurrence of circumstances. Every course of life would not have been so surrounded with precipices, that the least departure from the true path, by mistake or necessity, must involve us in misery and ruin. Some reserve, some fund, would have been provided to insure happiness; nor would the powers and the necessities have been adjusted with so rigid an economy. The Author of Nature is inconceivably powerful: his force is supposed great, if not altogether inexhaustible: nor is there any reason, as far as we can judge, to make him observe this strict frugality in his dealings with his creatures. It would have been better, were his power extremely limited, to have created fewer animals, and to have endowed these with more faculties for their happiness and preservation. A builder is never esteemed prudent, who undertakes a plan beyond what his stock will enable him to finish.

In order to cure most of the ills of human life, I require not that man should have the wings of the eagle, the swiftness of the stag, the force of the ox, the arms of the lion, the scales of the crocodile or rhinoceros; much less do I demand the sagacity of an angel or cherubim. I am contented to take an increase in one single power or faculty of his soul. Let him be endowed with a greater propensity to industry and labor; a more vigorous spring and activity of mind; a more constant bent to business and application. Let the whole species possess naturally an equal diligence with that which many individuals are able to attain by habit and reflection; and the most beneficial consequences, without any alloy of ill, is the immediate and necessary result of this endowment. Almost all the moral, as well as natural evils of human life, arise from idleness; and were our species, by the original constitution of their frame, exempt from this vice or infirmity, the perfect cultivation of land, the improvement of arts and manufactures, the exact execution of every office and duty, immediately follow; and men at once may fully reach that state of society, which is so imperfectly attained by the best regulated government. But as industry is a power, and the most valuable of any, Nature seems determined, suitably to her usual maxims, to bestow it on men with a very sparing hand; and rather to punish him severely for his deficiency in it, than to reward him for his attainments. She has so contrived his frame, that nothing but the most violent necessity can oblige him to labor; and she employs all his other wants to overcome, at least in part, the want of diligence, and to endow him with some share of a faculty of which she has thought fit naturally to bereave him. Here our demands may be allowed very humble, and therefore the more reasonable. If we require the endowments of superior penetration and judgment, of a more delicate taste of beauty, of a nicer sensibility to benevolence and friendship; we might be told, that we impiously pretend to break the order of Nature; that we want to exalt ourselves into a higher rank of being; that the presents which we require, not being suitable to our state and condition, would only be pernicious to us. But it is hard; I dare to repeat it, it is hard, that being placed in a world so full of wants and necessities, where almost every being and element is either our foe or refuses its assistance . . . we should also have our own temper to struggle with, and should be deprived of that faculty which can alone fence against these multiplied evils.

The *fourth* circumstance, whence arises the misery and ill of the universe, is the inaccurate workmanship of all the springs and principles of the great machine of nature. It must be acknowledged, that there are few parts of the universe, which seem not to serve some purpose, and whose removal would not produce a visible defect and disorder in the whole. The parts hang all together; nor can one be touched without affecting the rest, in a greater or less degree. But at the same time, it must be observed, that none of these parts or principles, however useful, are so accurately adjusted, as to keep precisely within those bounds in which their utility consists; but they are, all of them, apt, on every occasion, to run into the one extreme or the other. One would imagine, that this grand production had not received the last hand of the maker; so little finished is every part, and so coarse are the strokes with which it is executed. Thus, the winds are requisite to convey the vapors along the surface of the globe, and to assist men in navigation: but how oft, rising up to tempests and hurricanes, do they become pernicious? Rains are necessary to nourish all the plants and animals of the earth: but how often are they defective? how often excessive? Heat is requisite to all life and vegetation; but is not always found in the due proportion. On the mixture and secretion of the humors and juices of the body depend the health and prosperity of the animal: but the parts perform not regularly their proper function. What more useful than all the passions of the mind, ambition, vanity, love, anger? But how oft do they break their bounds, and cause the greatest convulsions in society? There is nothing so advantageous in the universe, but what frequently becomes pernicious, by its excess or defect; nor has Nature guarded, with the requisite accuracy, against all disorder or confusion. The irregularity is never perhaps so great as to destroy any species; but is often sufficient to involve the individuals in ruin and misery.

On the concurrence, then, of these *four* circumstances, does all or the greatest part of natural evil depend. Were all living creatures incapable of pain, or were the world administered by particular volitions, evil never could have found access into the universe: and were animals endowed with a large stock of powers and faculties, beyond what strict necessity requires; or were the several springs and principles of the universe so accurately framed as to preserve always the just temperament and medium; there must have been very little ill in comparison of what we feel at present. What then shall we pronounce on this occasion? Shall we say that these circumstances are not necessary, and that they might easily have been altered in the contrivance of the universe? This decision seems too presumptuous for creatures so blind and ignorant. Let us be more modest in our conclusions. Let us allow, that, if the goodness of the Deity (I mean a goodness like the human) could be established on any tolerable reasons *à priori,* these phenomena, however untoward, would not be sufficient to subvert that principle; but might easily, in some unknown manner, be reconcilable to it. But let us still assert, that as this goodness is not antecedently established, but must be inferred from the phenomena, there can be no grounds for such an inference, while there are so many ills in the universe, and while these ills might so easily have been remedied, as far as human understanding can be allowed to judge on such a subject. I am Sceptic enough to allow, that the bad appearances, notwithstanding all my reasonings, may be compatible with such attributes as you suppose; but surely they can never prove these attributes. Such a conclusion cannot result from Scepticism, but must arise from the phenomena, and from our confidence in the reasonings which we deduce from these phenomena.

Look round this universe. What an immense profusion of beings, animated and organized, sensible and active! You admire this prodigious variety and fecundity. But inspect a little more narrowly these living existences, the only beings worth regarding. How hostile and destructive to each other! How insufficient all of them for their own happiness! How contemptible or odious to the spectator! The whole presents nothing but the idea of a blind

Nature, impregnated by a great vivifying principle, and pouring forth from her lap, without discernment of parental care, her maimed and abortive children!

Here the Manichæan system occurs as a proper hypothesis to solve the difficulty: and no doubt, in some respects, it is very specious, and has more probability than the common hypothesis, by giving a plausible account of the strange mixture of good and ill which appears in life. But if we consider, on the other hand, the perfect uniformity and agreement of the parts of the universe, we shall not discover in it any marks of the combat of a malevolent with a benevolent being. There is indeed an opposition of pains and pleasures in the feelings of sensible creatures: but are not all the operations of Nature carried on by an opposition of principles, of hot and cold, moist and dry, light and heavy? The true conclusion is, that the original Source of all things is entirely indifferent to all these principles; and has no more regard to good above ill, than to heat above cold, or to drought above moisture, or to light above heavy.

There may *four* hypotheses be framed concerning the first causes of the universe: *that* they are endowed with perfect goodness; *that* they have perfect malice; *that* they are opposite, and have both goodness and malice; *that* they have neither goodness nor malice. Mixed phenomena can never prove the two former unmixed principles; and the uniformity and steadiness of general laws seem to oppose the third. The fourth, therefore, seems by far the most probable.

What I have said concerning natural evil will apply to moral, with little or no variation; and we have no more reason to infer, that the rectitude of the Supreme Being resembles human rectitude, than that his benevolence resembles the human. Nay, it will be thought, that we have still greater cause to exclude from him moral sentiments, such as we feel them; since moral evil, in the opinion of many, is much more predominant above moral good than natural evil above natural good.

But even though this should not be allowed, and though the virtue which is in mankind should be acknowledged much superior to the vice, yet so long as there is any vice at all in the universe, it will very much puzzle you Anthropomorphites, how to account for it. You must assign a cause for it, without having recourse to the first cause. But as every effect must have a cause, and that cause another, you must either carry on the progression *in infinitum,* or rest on that original principle, who is the ultimate cause of all things. . . .

3

A VEDANTA SOLUTION OF
THE PROBLEM OF EVIL*

Aurobindo Ghose

Aurobindo Ghose (1872–1950) was perhaps the greatest contemporary exponent of the Vedanta philosophy of Hinduism, although he modified the classical view of Sankara by reinterpreting the latter's cosmic illusionism. Mystic philosopher, early leader of Indian nationalism, and founder of a noted Ashram at Pondicherry, Aurobindo's main works are: The Life Divine, The Synthesis of Yoga, The Ideal of Human Unity, *and* The Human Cycle.

> For who could live or breathe if there were not this delight of existence as the ether in which we dwell?
> From Delight all these beings are born, by Delight they exist and grow, to Delight they return.
>
> *Taittiriya Upanishad.*[1]

BUT even if we accept this pure Existence, this Brahman, this Sat as the absolute beginning, end and continent of things and in Brahman an inherent self-consciousness inseparable from its being and throwing itself out as a force of movement of consciousness which is creative of forces, forms and worlds, we have yet no answer to the question "Why should Brahman, perfect, absolute, infinite, needing nothing, desiring nothing, at all throw out force of consciousness to create in itself these worlds of forms?" For we have put aside the solution that it is compelled by its own nature of Force to create, obliged by its own potentiality of movement and formation to move into forms. It is true that it has this potentiality, but it is not limited, bound or compelled by it; it is free. If, then, being free to move or remain eternally still, to throw itself into forms or retain

---

* From Sri Aurobindo Ghose, *The Life Divine*. Reprinted by permission of Sri Aurobindo Ashram Press.

[1] II. 7; III. 6.

the potentiality of form in itself, it indulges its power of movement and formation, it can be only for one reason, for delight.

This primary, ultimate and eternal Existence, as seen by the Vedantins, is not merely bare existence, or a conscious existence whose consciousness is crude force or power; it is a conscious existence the very term of whose being, the very term of whose consciousness is bliss. As in absolute existence there can be no nothingness, no night of inconscience, no deficiency, that is to say, no failure of Force,—for if there were any of these things, it would not be absolute,—so also there can be no suffering, no negation of delight. Absoluteness of conscious existence is illimitable bliss of conscious existence; the two are only different phrases for the same thing. All illimitableness, all infinity, all absoluteness is pure delight. Even our relative humanity has this experience that all dissatisfaction means a limit, an obstacle,—satisfaction comes by realisation of something withheld, by the surpassing of the limit, the overcoming of the obstacle. This is because our original being is the absolute in full possession of its infinite and illimitable self-consciousness and self-power; a self-possession whose other name is self-delight. And in proportion as the relative touches upon that self-possession, it moves towards satisfaction, touches delight.

The self-delight of Brahman is not limited, however, by the still and motionless possession of its absolute self-being. Just as its force of consciousness is capable of throwing itself into forms infinitely and with an endless variation, so also its self-delight is capable of movement, of variation, of revelling in that infinite flux and mutability of itself represented by numberless teeming universes. To loose forth and enjoy this infinite movement and variation of its self-delight is the object of its extensive or creative play of Force.

In other words, that which has thrown itself out into forms is a triune Existence-Consciousness-Bliss, Sachchidananda, whose consciousness is in its nature a creative or rather a self-expressive Force capable of infinite variation in phenomenon and form of its self-conscious being and endlessly enjoying the delight of that variation. It follows that all things that exist are what they are as terms of that existence, terms of that conscious force, terms of that delight of being. Just as we find all things to be mutable forms of one immutable being, finite results of one infinite force, so we shall find that all things are variable self-expression of one invariable and all-embracing delight of self-existence. In everything that is, dwells the conscious force and it exists and is what it is by virtue of that conscious force; so also in everything that is there is the delight of existence and it exists and is what it is by virtue of that delight.

This ancient Vedantic theory of cosmic origin is immediately confronted in the human mind by two powerful contradictions, the emotional and sensational consciousness of pain and the ethical problem of evil. For if the world be an expression of Sachchidananda, not only of existence that is conscious-force,—for that can easily be admitted,—but of existence that is also infinite self-delight, how are we to account for the universal presence of grief, of suffering, of pain? For this world appears to us rather as a world of suffering than as a world of the delight of existence. Certainly, that view of the world is an exaggeration, an error of perspective. If we regard it dispassionately and with a sole view to accurate and unemotional appreciation, we shall find that the sum of the pleasure of existence far exceeds the sum of the pain of existence,— appearances and individual cases to the contrary notwithstanding, —and that the active or passive, surface or underlying pleasure of existence is the normal state of nature, pain a contrary occurrence temporarily suspending or overlaying that normal state. But for that very reason the lesser sum of pain affects us more intensely and often looms larger than the greater sum of pleasure; precisely because the latter is normal, we do not treasure it, hardly even observe it unless it intensifies into some acuter form of itself, into a wave of happiness, a crest of joy or ecstasy. It is these things that we call delight and seek and the normal satisfaction of existence which is always there regardless of event and particular cause or object, affects us as something neutral which is neither pleasure nor pain. It is there, a great practical fact, for without it there would not be the universal and overpowering instinct of self-preservation, but it is not what we seek and therefore we do not enter it into our balance of emotional and sensational profit and loss. In that balance we enter only positive pleasures on one side and discomfort and pain on the other; pain affects us more intensely because it is abnormal to our being, contrary to our natural tendency and is experienced as an outrage on our existence, an offence and external attack on what we are and seek to be.

Nevertheless the abnormality of pain or its greater or lesser sum does not affect the philosophical issue; greater or less, its mere presence constitutes the whole problem. All being Sachchidananda, how can pain and suffering at all exist? This, the real problem, is often farther confused by a false issue starting from the idea of a personal extra-cosmic God and a partial issue, the ethical difficulty.

Sachchidananda, it may be reasoned, is God, is a conscious Being who is the author of existence; how then can God have created a world in which He inflicts suffering on His creatures, sanctions pain, permits evil? God being All-Good, who created pain and evil? If we say that pain is a trial and an ordeal, we do not solve the moral problem, we arrive at an immoral or non-moral God,—an excellent world-mechanist perhaps, a cunning psychologist, but not a God of Good and of Love whom we can worship, only a God of Might to whose law we must submit or whose caprice we may hope to propitiate. For one who invents torture as a means of test or ordeal, stands convicted either of deliberate cruelty or of moral insensibility and, if a moral being at all, is inferior to the highest instinct of his own creatures. And if to escape this moral difficulty, we say that pain is an inevitable result and natural punishment of moral evil,—an explanation which will not even square with the facts of life unless we admit the theory of Karma and rebirth by which the soul suffers now for antenatal sins in other bodies,—we still do not escape the very root of the ethical problem,—who created or why or whence was created that moral evil which entails the punishment of pain and suffering? And seeing that moral evil is in reality a form of mental disease or ignorance, who or what created this law or inevitable connection which punishes a mental disease or act of ignorance by a recoil so terrible, by tortures often so extreme and monstrous? The inexorable law of Karma is irreconcilable with a supreme moral and personal Deity, and therefore the clear logic of Buddha denied the existence of any free and all-governing personal God; all personality he declared to be a creation of ignorance and subject to Karma.

In truth, the difficulty thus sharply presented arises only if we assume the existence of an extra-cosmic personal God, not Himself the universe, one who has created good and evil, pain and suffering for His creatures, but Himself stands above and unaffected by them, watching, ruling, doing His will with a suffering and struggling world or, if not doing His will, if allowing the world to be driven by an inexorable law, unhelped by Him or inefficiently helped, then not God, not omnipotent, not all-good and all-loving. On no theory of an extra-cosmic moral God, can evil and suffering be explained,—the creation of evil and suffering,—except by an unsatisfactory subterfuge which avoids the question at issue instead of answering it or a plain or implied Manicheanism which practically annuls the Godhead in attempting to justify its ways or excuse its works. But such a God is not the Vedantic Sachchidananda. Sachchidananda of the Vedanta is one existence without a second; all that is, is He. If then evil and suffering exist, it is He that bears the evil and suffering in the creature in whom He has embodied Himself. The problem then changes entirely. The question is no longer how came God to create for His creatures a suffering and evil of which He is Himself incapable and therefore immune, but how came the sole and infinite Existence-Conscious-ness-Bliss to admit into itself that which is not bliss, that which seems to be its positive negation.

Half of the moral difficulty—that difficulty in its one un-answerable form disappears. It no longer arises, can no longer be put. Cruelty to others, I remaining immune or even participating in their sufferings by subsequent repentance or belated pity, is one thing; self-infliction of suffering, I being the sole existence, is quite another. Still the ethical difficulty may be brought back in a modified form; All-Delight being necessarily all-good and all-love, how can evil and suffering exist in Sachchidananda, since he is not mechanical existence, but free and conscious being, free to condemn and reject evil and suffering? We have to recognise that the issue so stated is also a false issue because it applies the terms of a partial statement as if they were applicable to the whole. For the ideas of good and of love which we thus bring into the concept of the All-Delight spring from a dualistic and divisional conception of things; they are based entirely on the relations between creature and creature, yet we persist in applying them to a problem which starts, on the contrary, from the assumption of One who is all. We have to see first how the problem appears or how it can be solved in its original purity, on the basis of unity in difference; only then can we safely deal with its parts and its developments, such as the relations between creature and creature on the basis of division and duality.

We have to recognise, if we thus view the whole, not limiting ourselves to the human difficulty and the human standpoint, that we do not live in an ethical world. The attempt of human thought to force an ethical meaning into the whole of Nature is one of those acts of wilful and obstinate self-confusion, one of those pathetic attempts of the human being to read himself, his limited habitual human self into all things and judge them from the standpoint he has personally evolved, which most effectively prevent him from arriving at real knowledge and complete sight. Material Nature is not ethical; the law which governs it is a coordination of fixed habits which takes no cognisance of good and evil, but only of force that creates, force that arranges and preserves, force that disturbs and destroys impartially, non-ethically, according to the secret Will in it, according to the mute satisfaction of that Will in its own self-formations and self-dissolutions. Animal or vital Nature is also non-ethical, although as it progresses it manifests the crude material out of which the higher animal evolves the ethical impulse. We do not blame the tiger because it slays and devours its prey any more than we blame the storm because it destroys or the fire because it tortures and kills; neither does the conscious-force in the storm, the fire or the tiger blame or condemn itself. Blame and condemnation, or rather self-blame and self-condemnation, are the beginning of true ethics. When we blame others without applying the same law to ourselves, we are not speaking with a true ethical judgment, but only applying the language ethics has evolved for us to an emotional impulse of recoil from or dislike of that which displeases or hurts us.

This recoil or dislike is the primary origin of ethics, but is not itself ethical. The fear of the deer for the tiger, the rage of the strong creature against its assailant is a vital recoil of the individual delight of existence from that which threatens it. In the progress of the mentality it refines itself into repugnance, dislike, disapproval. Disapproval of that which threatens and hurts us, approval of that which flatters and satisfies refine into the conception of good and evil to oneself, to the community, to others than ourselves, to other communities than ours, and finally into the general approval of good, the general disapproval of evil. But, throughout, the fundamental nature of the thing remains the same. Man desires self-expression, self-development, in other words, the progressing play in himself of the conscious-force of existence; that is his fundamental delight. Whatever hurts that self-expression, self-development, satisfaction of his progressing self, is for him evil; whatever helps, confirms, raises, aggrandises, ennobles it is his good. Only, his conception of the self-development changes, becomes higher and wider, begins to exceed his limited personality, to embrace others, to embrace all in its scope.

In other words, ethics is a stage in evolution. That which is common to all stages is the urge of Sachchidananda towards self-expression. This urge is at first non-ethical, then infra-ethical in the animal, then in the intelligent animal even anti-ethical for it permits us to approve hurt done to others which we disapprove when done to ourselves. In this respect man even now is only half-ethical. And just as all below us is infra-ethical, so there may be that above us whither we shall eventually arrive, which is supra-ethical, has no need of ethics. The ethical impulse and attitude, so all-important to humanity, is a means by which it struggles out of the lower harmony and universality based upon inconscience and broken up by Life into individual discords towards a higher harmony and universality based upon conscient oneness with all existences. Arriving at that goal, this means will no longer be necessary or even possible, since the qualities and oppositions on which it depends will naturally dissolve and disappear in the final reconciliation.

If, then, the ethical standpoint applies only to a temporary though all-important passage from one universality to another, we cannot apply it to the total solution of the problem of the universe, but can only admit it as one element in that solution. To do otherwise is to run into the peril of falsifying all the facts of the universe, all the meaning of the evolution behind and beyond us in order to suit a temporary outlook and a half-evolved view of the utility of things. The world has three layers, infra-ethical, ethical and supraethical. We have to find that which is common to all; for only so can we resolve the problem.

That which is common to all is, we have seen, the satisfaction of conscious-force of existence developing itself into forms and seeking in that development its delight. From that satisfaction or delight of self-existence it evidently began; for it is that which is normal to it, to which it clings, which it makes its base; but it seeks new forms of itself and in the passage to higher forms there intervenes the phenomenon of pain and suffering which seems to contradict the fundamental nature of its being. This and this alone is the root-problem.

How shall we solve it? Shall we say that Sachchidananda is not the beginning and end of things, but the beginning and end is Nihil, an impartial void, itself nothing but containing all potentialities of existence or non-existence, consciousness or non-consciousness, delight or undelight? We may accept this answer if we choose; but although we seek thereby to explain everything, we have really explained nothing, we have only included everything. A Nothing which is full of all potentialities is the most complete opposition of terms and things possible and we have therefore only explained a minor contradiction by a major, by driving the self-contradiction of things to their maximum. Nihil is the void, where there can be no potentialities; an impartial indeterminate of all potentialities is Chaos, and all that we have done is to put Chaos into the Void without explaining how it got there. Let us return, then, to our original conception of Sachchidananda and see whether on that foundation a completer solution is not possible.

We must first make it clear to ourselves that just as when we speak of universal consciousness we mean something different from, more essential and wider than the waking mental consciousness of the human being, so also when we speak of universal delight of existence we mean something different from, more essential and wider than the ordinary emotional and sensational pleasure of the individual human creature. Pleasure, joy and delight, as man uses the words, are limited and occasional movements which depend on certain habitual causes and emerge, like their opposites pain and grief which are equally limited and occasional movements, from a background other than themselves. Delight of being is universal, illimitable and self-existent, not dependent on particular causes, the background of all backgrounds, from which pleasure, pain and other more neutral experiences emerge. When delight of being seeks to realise itself as delight of becoming, it moves in the movement of force and itself takes different forms of movement of which pleasure and pain are positive and negative currents. Subconscient in Matter, superconscient beyond Mind this delight seeks in Mind and Life to realise itself by emergence in the becoming, in the increasing self-consciousness of the movement. Its first phenomena are dual and impure, move between the poles of pleasure and pain, but it aims at its self-revelation in the purity of a supreme delight of being which is self-existent and independent of objects and causes. Just as Sachchidananda moves towards the realisation of the universal existence in the individual and of the form-exceeding consciousness in the form of body and mind, so it moves towards the realisation of universal, self-existent and objectless delight in the flux of particular experiences and objects. Those objects we now seek as stimulating causes of a transient pleasure and satisfaction; free, possessed of self, we shall not seek but shall possess them as reflectors rather than causes of a delight which eternally exists.

In the egoistic human being, the mental person emergent out of the dim shell of matter, delight of existence is neutral, semi-latent, still in the shadow of the subconscious, hardly more than a concealed soil of plenty covered by desire with a luxuriant growth of poisonous weeds and hardly less poisonous flowers, the pains and pleasures of our egoistic existence. When the divine conscious-force working secretly in us has devoured these growths of desire, when in the image of the Rig Veda the fire of God has burnt up the shoots of earth, that which is concealed at the roots of these pains and pleasures, their cause and secret being, the sap of delight in them, will emerge in new forms not of desire, but of self-existent satisfaction which will replace mortal pleasure by the Immortal's ecstasy. And this transformation is possible because these growths of sensation and emotion are in their essential being, the pains no less than the pleasures, that delight of existence which they seek but fail to reveal,—fail because of division, ignorance of self and egoism.

The name of That is the Delight; as the Delight we must worship and seek after It.

Kena Upanishad.[1]

IN this conception of an inalienable underlying delight of existence of which all outward or surface sensations are a positive, negative or neutral play, waves and foamings of that infinite deep, we arrive at the true solution of the problem we are examining. The self of things is an infinite indivisible existence; of that existence the essential nature or power is an infinite imperishable force of self-conscious being; and of that self-consciousness the essential nature or knowledge of itself is, again, an infinite inalienable delight of being. In formlessness and in all forms, in the eternal awareness of infinite and indivisible being and in the multiform appearances of finite division this self-existence preserves perpetually its self-delight. As in the apparent inconscience of Matter our soul, growing out of its bondage to its own superficial habit and particular mode of self-conscious existence, discovers that infinite Conscious-Force constant, immobile, brooding, so in the apparent non-sensation of Matter it comes to discover and attune itself to an infinite conscious Delight imperturbable, ecstatic, all-embracing. This delight is its own delight, this self is its own self in all; but to our ordinary view of self and things which awakes and moves only upon surfaces, it remains hidden, profound, subconscious. And as it is within all forms, so it is within all experiences whether pleasant, painful or neutral. There too hidden, profound, subconscious, it is that which enables and compels things to remain in existence. It is the reason of that clinging to existence, that overmastering will-to-be, translated vitally as the instinct of self-preservation, physically as the imperishability of matter, mentally as the sense of immortality which attends the formed existence through all its phases of self-development and of which even the occasional impulse of self-destruction is only a reverse form, an attraction to other state of being and a consequent recoil from present state of being. Delight is existence, Delight is the secret of creation, Delight is the root of birth, Delight is the cause of remaining in existence, Delight is the end of birth and that into which creation ceases. "From Ananda" says the Upanishad "all existences are born, by Ananda they remain in being and increase, to Ananda they depart."

As we look at these three aspects of essential Being, one in reality, triune to our mental view, separable only in appearance, in the phenomena of the divided consciousness, we are able to put in their right place the divergent formulæ of the old philosophies so

[1] IV. 6.

that they unite and become one, ceasing from their agelong controversy. For if we regard world-existence only in its appearances and only in its relation to pure, infinite, indivisible, immutable Existence, we are entitled to regard it, describe it and realise it as Maya. Maya in its original sense meant a comprehending and containing consciousness capable of embracing, measuring and limiting and therefore formative; it is that which outlines, measures out, moulds forms in the formless, psychologises and seems to make knowable the Unknowable, geometrises and seems to make measurable the limitless. Later the word came from its original sense of knowledge, skill, intelligence to acquire a pejorative sense of cunning, fraud or illusion, and it is in the figure of an enchantment or illusion that it is used by the philosophical systems.

World is Maya. World is not unreal in the sense that it has no sort of existence; for even if it were only a dream of the Self, still it would exist in It as a dream, real to It in the present even while ultimately unreal. Nor ought we to say that world is unreal in the sense that it has no kind of eternal existence; for although particular worlds and particular forms may or do dissolve physically and return mentally from the consciousness of manifestation into the non-manifestation, yet Form in itself, World in itself are eternal. From the non-manifestation they return inevitably into manifestation; they have an eternal recurrence if not an eternal persistence, an eternal immutability in sum and foundation along with an eternal mutability in aspect and apparition. Nor have we any surety that there ever was or ever will be a period in Time when no form of universe, no play of being is represented to itself in the eternal Conscious-Being, but only an intuitive perception that the world that we know can and does appear from That and return into It perpetually.

Still world is Maya because it is not the essential truth of infinite existence, but only a creation of self-conscious being,—not a creation in the void, not a creation in nothing and out of nothing, but in the eternal Truth and out of the eternal Truth of that Self-being; its continent, origin and substance are the essential, real Existence, its forms are mutable formations of That to Its own conscious perception, determined by Its own creative conscious-force. They are capable of manifestation, capable of non-manifestation, capable of other-manifestation. We may, if we choose, call them therefore illusions of the infinite consciousness thus audaciously flinging back a shadow of our mental sense of subjection to error and incapacity upon that which, being greater than Mind, is beyond subjection to falsehood and illusion. But seeing that the essence and substance of Existence is not a lie and that all errors and deformations of our divided consciousness represent some truth of the indivisible self-conscious Existence, we can only say that the world is not essential truth of That, but phenomenal truth of Its free multiplicity and infinite superficial mutability and not truth of Its fundamental and immutable Unity.

If, on the other hand, we look at world-existence in relation to consciousness only and to force of consciousness, we may regard, describe and realise it as a movement of Force obeying some secret will or else some necessity imposed on it by the very existence of the Consciousness that possesses or regards it. It is then the play of Prakriti, the executive Force, to satisfy Purusha, the regarding and enjoying Conscious-Being or it is the play of Purusha reflected in the movements of Force and with them identifying himself. World, then, is the play of the Mother of things moved to cast Herself for ever into infinite forms and avid of eternally outpouring experiences.

Again if we look at World-Existence rather in its relation to the self-delight of eternally existent being, we may regard, describe and realise it as Lila, the play, the child's joy, the poet's joy, the actor's joy, the mechanician's joy of the Soul of things eternally young, perpetually inexhaustible, creating and re-creating Himself in Himself for the sheer bliss of that self-creation, of that self-representation,—Himself the play, Himself the player, Himself the playground. These three generalisations of the play of existence in its relation to the eternal and stable, the immutable Sachchidananda, starting from the three conceptions of Maya, Prakriti and Lila and representing themselves in our philosophical systems as mutually contradictory philosophies, are in reality perfectly consistent with each other, complementary and necessary in their totality to an integral view of life and the world. The world of which we are a part is in its most obvious view a movement of Force; but that Force, when we penetrate its appearances, proves to be a constant and yet always mutable rhythm of creative consciousness casting up, projecting in itself phenomenal truths of its own infinite and eternal being; and this rhythm is in its essence, cause and purpose a play of the infinite delight of being ever busy with its own innumerable self-representations. This triple or triune view must be the starting-point for all our understanding of the universe.

Since, then, eternal and immutable delight of being moving out into infinite and variable delight of becoming is the root of the whole matter, we have to conceive one indivisible conscious Being behind all our experiences supporting them by its inalienable delight and effecting by its movement the variations of pleasure, pain and neutral indifference in our sensational existence. That is our real self; the mental being subject to the triple vibration can only be a representation of our real self put in front for the purposes of that sensational experience of things which is the first rhythm of our divided consciousness in its response and reaction to the multiple contacts of the universe. It is an imperfect response, a tangled and discordant rhythm preparing and preluding the full and unified play of the conscious Being in us; it is not the true and perfect symphony that may be ours if we can once enter into sympathy with the One in all variations and attune ourselves to the absolute and universal diapason.

If this view be right, then certain consequences inevitably impose themselves. In the first place, since in our depths we ourselves are that One, since in the reality of our being we are the indivisible All-Consciousness and therefore the inalienable All-Bliss, the disposition of our sensational experience in the three vibrations of pain, pleasure and indifference can only be a superficial arrangement created by that limited part of ourselves which is uppermost in our waking consciousness. Behind there must be something in us,—much vaster, profounder, truer than the superficial consciousness,—which takes delight impartially in all experiences; it is that delight which secretly supports the superficial mental being and enables it to persevere through all labours, sufferings and ordeals in the agitated movement of the Becoming. That which we call ourselves is only a trembling ray on the surface; behind is all the vast subconscient, the vast superconscient profiting by all these surface experiences and imposing them on its external self which it exposes as a sort of sensitive covering to the contacts of the world; itself veiled, it receives these contacts and assimilates them into the values of a truer, a profounder, a mastering and creative experience. Out of its depths it returns them to the surface in forms of strength, character, knowledge, impulsion whose roots are mysterious to us because our mind moves and quivers on the surface and has not learned to concentrate itself and live in the depths.

In our ordinary life this truth is hidden from us or only dimly glimpsed at times or imperfectly held and conceived. But if we learn to live within, we infallibly awaken to this presence within us which is our more real self, a presence profound, calm, joyous and puissant of which the world is not the master—a presence which, if it is not the Lord Himself, is the radiation of the Lord within. We are aware of it within supporting and helping the apparent and superficial self and smiling at its pleasures and pains as at the error and passion of a little child. And if we can go back into ourselves and identify ourselves, not with our superficial experience, but with that radiant penumbra of the Divine, we can live in that attitude towards the contacts of the world and, standing back in our entire consciousness from the pleasures and pains of the body, vital being and mind, possess them as experiences whose nature being superficial does not touch or impose itself on our core and real being. In the entirely expressive Sanskrit terms, there is an *ānandamaya* behind the *manomaya,* a vast Bliss-Self behind the limited mental self, and the latter is only a shadowy image and disturbed reflection of the former. The truth of ourselves lies within and not on the surface.

Again this triple vibration of pleasure, pain, indifference, being superficial, being an arrangement and result of our imperfect evolution, can have in it no absoluteness, no necessity. There is no real obligation on us to return to a particular contact a particular response of pleasure, pain or neutral reaction, there is only an obligation of habit. We feel pleasure or pain in a particular contact because that is the habit our nature has formed because that is the constant relation the receipient has established with the contact. It is within our competence to return quite the opposite response, pleasure where we used to have pain, pain where we used to have pleasure. It is equally within our competence to accustom the superficial being to return instead of the mechanical reactions of pleasure, pain and indifference that free reply of inalienable delight which is the constant experience of the true and vast Bliss-Self within us. And this is a greater conquest, a still deeper and more complete self-possession than a glad and detached reception in the depths of the habitual reactions on the surface. For it is no longer a mere acceptance without subjection, a free acquiescence in imperfect values of experience, but enables us to convert imperfect into perfect, false into true values,—the constant but veritable delight of the Spirit in things taking the place of the dualities experienced by the mental being.

In the things of the mind this pure habitual relativity of the reactions of pleasure and pain is not difficult to perceive. The nervous being in us, indeed, is accustomed to a certain fixedness, a false impression of absoluteness in these things. To it victory, success, honour, good fortune of all kinds are pleasant things in themselves, absolutely, and must produce joy as sugar must taste sweet; defeat, failure, disappointment, disgrace, evil fortune of all kinds are unpleasant things in themselves, absolutely, and must produce grief as wormwood must taste bitter. To vary these responses is to it a departure from fact, abnormal and morbid; for the nervous being is a thing enslaved to habit and in itself the means devised by Nature for fixing constancy of reaction, sameness of experience, the settled scheme of man's relations to life. The mental being on the other hand is free, for it is the means she has devised for flexibility and variation, for change and progress; it is subject only so long as it chooses to remain subject, to dwell in one mental habit rather than in another or so long as it allows itself to be dominated by its nervous instrument. It is not bound to be grieved by defeat, disgrace, loss: it can meet these things and all things with a perfect indifference; it can even meet them with a perfect gladness. Therefore man finds that the more he refuses to be dominated by his nerves and body, the more he draws back from implication of himself in his physical and vital parts, the greater is his freedom. He becomes the master of his own responses to the world's contacts, no longer the slave of external touches.

In regard to physical pleasure and pain, it is more difficult to apply the universal truth; for this is the very domain of the nerves and the body, the centre and seat of that in us whose nature is to be dominated by external contact and external pressure. Even here, however, we have glimpses of the truth. We see it in the fact that according to the habit the same physical contact can be either pleasurable or painful, not only to different individuals, but to the same individual under different conditions or at different stages of his development. We see it in the fact that men in periods of great excitement or high exaltation remain physically indifferent to pain or unconscious of pain under contacts which ordinarily would inflict severe torture or suffering. In many cases it is only when the nerves are able to reassert themselves and remind the mentality of its habitual obligation to suffer that the sense of suffering returns. But this return to the habitual obligation is not inevitable; it is only habitual. We see that in the phenomena of hypnosis not only can the hypnotised subject be successfully forbidden to feel the pain of a wound or puncture when in the abnormal state, but can be prevented with equal success from returning to his habitual reaction of suffering when he is awakened. The reason of this phenomenon is perfectly simple; it is because the hypnotiser suspends the habitual waking consciousness which is the slave of nervous habits and is able to appeal to the subliminal mental being in the depths, the inner mental being who is master, if he wills, of the nerves and the body. But this freedom which is effected by hypnosis abnormally, rapidly, without true possession, by an alien will, may equally be won normally, gradually, with true possession, by one's own will so as to effect partially or completely a victory of the mental being over the habitual nervous reactions of the body.

Pain of mind and body is a device of Nature, that is to say, of Force in her works, meant to subserve a definite transitional end in her upward evolution. The world is from the point of view of the individual a play and complex shock of multitudinous forces. In the midst of this complex play the individual stands as a limited constructed being with a limited amount of force exposed to numberless shocks which may wound, maim, break up or disintegrate the construction which he calls himself. Pain is in the nature of a nervous and physical recoil from a dangerous or harmful contact; it is a part of what the Upanishad calls *jugupsā*, the shrinking of the limited being from that which is not himself and not sympathetic or in harmony with himself, its impulse of self-defence against "others". It is from this point of view, an indication by Nature of that which has to be avoided or, if not successfully avoided, has to be remedied. It does not come into being in the purely physical world so long as life does not enter into it; for till then mechanical methods are sufficient. Its office begins when life with its frailty and imperfect possession of Matter enters on the scene; it grows with the growth of Mind in life. Its office continues so long as Mind is bound in the life and body which it is using, dependent upon them for its knowledge and means of action, subjected to their limitations and to the egoistic impulses and aims which are born of those limitations. But if and when Mind in man becomes capable of being free, unegoistic, in harmony with all other beings and with the play of the universal forces, the use and office of suffering diminishes, its *raison d'être* must finally cease to be and it can only continue as an atavism of Nature, a habit that has survived its use, a persistence of the lower in the as yet imperfect organisation of the higher. Its eventual elimination must be an essential point in the destined conquest of the soul over subjection to Matter and egoistic limitation in Mind.

This elimination is possible because pain and pleasure themselves are currents, one imperfect, the other perverse, but still currents of the delight of existence. The reason for this imperfection and this perversion is the self-division of the being in his consciousness by measuring and limiting Maya and in consequence an egoistic and piecemeal instead of a universal reception of contacts by the individual. For the universal soul of all things and all contacts of things carry in them an essence of delight best described by the Sanskrit aesthetic term, *rasa,* which means at once sap or essence of a thing and its taste. It is because we do not seek the essence of the thing in its contact with us, but look only to the manner in which it affects our desires and fears, our cravings and shrinkings that grief and pain, imperfect and transient pleasure or indifference, that is to say, blank inability to seize the essence, are the forms taken by the Rasa. If we could be entirely disinterested in mind and heart and impose that detachment on the nervous being, the progressive elimination of these imperfect and perverse forms of Rasa would be possible and the true essential taste of the inalienable delight of existence in all its variations would be within our reach. We attain to something of this capacity for variable but universal delight in the aesthetic reception of things as represented by Art and Poetry, so that we enjoy there the Rasa or taste of the sorrowful, the terrible, even the horrible or repellent;[1] and the reason is because we are detached, disinterested, not thinking of ourselves or of self-defence (*jugupsā*), but only of the thing and its essence. Certainly, this aesthetic reception of contacts is not a precise image or reflection of the pure delight which is supramental and supra-aesthetic; for the latter would eliminate sorrow, terror, horror and disgust with their cause while the former admits them: but it represents partially and imperfectly one stage of the progressive delight of the universal Soul in things in its manifestation and it admits us in one part of our nature to that detachment from egoistic sensation and that universal attitude through which the one Soul sees harmony and beauty where we divided beings experience rather chaos and discord. The full liberation can come to us only by a similar liberation in all our parts, the universal aesthesis, the universal standpoint of knowledge, the universal detachment from all things and yet sympathy with all in our nervous and emotional being.

Since the nature of suffering is a failure of the conscious-force in us to meet the shocks of existence and a consequent shrinking and contraction and its root is an inequality of that receptive and possessing force due to our self-limitation by egoism consequent on the ignorance of our true Self, of Sachchidananda, the elimination of suffering must first proceed by the substitution of *titikṣā,* the facing, enduring and conquest of all shocks of existence for *jugupsā,* the shrinking and contraction: by this endurance and conquest we proceed to an equality which may be either an equal indifference to all contacts or an equal gladness in all contacts; and this equality again must find a firm foundation in the substitution of the Sachchidananda consciousness which is All-Bliss for the ego-consciousness which enjoys and suffers. The Sachchidananda consciousness may be transcendent of the universe and aloof from it, and to this state of distant Bliss the path is equal indifference; it is the path of the ascetic. Or the Sachchidananda consciousness may be at once transcendent and universal; and to this state of present and all-embracing Bliss the path is surrender and loss of the ego in

[1] So termed in Sanskrit Rhetoric, the *karuṇa, bhayānaka* and *bībhatsa* Rasas.

the universal and possession of an all-pervading equal delight; it is the path of the ancient Vedic sages. But neutrality to the imperfect touches of pleasure and the perverse touches of pain is the first direct and natural result of the soul's self-discipline and the conversion to equal delight can, usually, come only afterwards. The direct transformation of the triple vibration into Ananda is possible, but less easy to the human being.

Such then is the view of the universe which arises out of the integral Vedantic affirmation. An infinite, indivisible existence all-blissful in its pure self-consciousness moves out of its fundamental purity into the varied play of Force that is consciousness, into the movement of Prakriti which is the play of Maya. The delight of its existence is at first self-gathered, absorbed, subconscious in the basis of the physical universe; then emergent in a great mass of neutral movement which is not yet what we call sensation; then further emergent with the growth of mind and ego in the triple vibration of pain, pleasure and indifference originating from the limitation of the force of consciousness in the form and from its exposure to shocks of the universal Force which it finds alien to it and out of harmony with its own measure and standard; finally, the conscious emergence of the full Sachchidananda in its creations by universality, by equality, by self-possession and conquest of Nature. This is the course and movement of the world.

If it then be asked why the One Existence should take delight in such a movement, the answer lies in the fact that all possibilities are inherent in Its infinity and that the delight of existence—in its mutable becoming, not in its immutable being,— lies precisely in the variable realisation of its possibilities. And the possibility worked out here in the universe of which we are a part, begins from the concealment of Sachchidananda in that which seems to be its own opposite and its self-finding even amid the terms of that opposite. Infinite being loses itself in the appearance of non-being and emerges in the appearance of a finite Soul; infinite consciousness loses itself in the appearance of a vast indeterminate inconscience and emerges in the appearance of a superficial limited consciousness; infinite self-sustaining Force loses itself in the appearance of a chaos of atoms and emerges in the appearance of the insecure balance of a world; infinite Delight loses itself in the appearance of an insensible Matter and emerges in the appearance of a discordant rhythm of varied pain, pleasure and neutral feeling, love, hatred and indifference; infinite unity loses itself in the appearance of a chaos of multiplicity and emerges in a discord of forces and beings which seek to recover unity by possessing, dissolving and devouring each other. In this creation the real Sachchidananda has to emerge. Man, the individual, has to become and to live as a universal being; his limited mental consciousness has to widen to the superconscient unity in which each embraces all; his narrow heart has to learn the infinite embrace and replace its lusts and discords by universal love and his restricted vital being to become equal to the whole shock of the universe upon it and capable of universal delight; his very physical being has to know itself as no separate entity but as one with and sustaining in itself the whole flow of the indivisible Force that is all things; his whole nature has to reproduce in the individual the unity, the harmony, the oneness-in-all of the supreme Existence-Consciousness-Bliss.

Through all this play the secret reality is always one and the same delight of existence,—the same in the delight of the sub-conscious sleep before the emergence of the individual, in the delight of the struggle and all the varieties, vicissitudes, perversions, conversions, reversions of the effort to find itself amid the mazes of the half-conscious dream of which the individual is the centre, and in the delight of the eternal superconscient self-possession into which the individual must wake and there become one with the indivisible Sachchidananda. This is the play of the One, the Lord, the All as it reveals itself to our liberated and enlightened knowledge from the conceptive standpoint of this material universe.

4

EVIL AND OMNIPOTENCE*

J. L. Mackie 🟦

J. L. Mackie is Professor of Philosophy at the University of York. He works primarily within the analytic tradition.

THE traditional arguments for the existence of God have been fairly thoroughly criticized by philosophers. But the theologian can, if he wishes, accept this criticism. He can admit that no rational proof of God's existence is possible. And he can still retain all that is essential to his position, by holding that God's existence is known in some other, nonrational way. I think, however, that a more telling criticism can be made by way of the traditional problem of evil. Here it can be shown, not that religious beliefs lack rational support, but that they are positively irrational, that the several parts of the essential theological doctrine are inconsistent with one another, so that the theologian can maintain his position as a whole only by a much more extreme rejection of reason than in the former case. He must now be prepared to believe, not merely what cannot be proved, but what can be *disproved* from other beliefs that he also holds.

The problem of evil, in the sense in which I shall be using the phrase, is a problem only for someone who believes that there is a God who is both omnipotent and wholly good. And it is a logical problem, the problem of clarifying and reconciling a number of beliefs: it is not a scientific problem that might be solved by further observations, or a practical problem that might be solved by a decision or an action. These points are obvious; I mention them only because they are sometimes ignored by theologians, who sometimes parry a statement of the problem with such remarks as "Well, can you solve the problem yourself?" or "This is a mystery which may be revealed to us later" or "Evil is something to be faced and overcome, not to be merely discussed."

In its simplest form the problem is this: God is omnipotent; God is wholly good; and yet evil exists. There seems to be some contradiction between these three propositions, so that if any two of them were true the third would be false. But at the same time all

* J. L. Mackie, "Evil and Omnipotence" in *Mind*, **LXIV**, No. 254, April 1955. Reprinted by permission of J. L. Mackie and the editor of *Mind*.

three are essential parts of most theological positions: the theologian, it seems, at once *must* adhere and *cannot consistently* adhere to all three. (The problem does not arise only for theists, but I shall discuss it in the form in which it presents itself for ordinary theism.)

However, the contradiction does not arise immediately; to show it we need some additional premises, or perhaps some quasi-logical rules connecting the terms "good," "evil," and "omnipotent." These additional principles are that good is opposed to evil, in such a way that a good thing always eliminates evil as far as it can, and that there are no limits to what an omnipotent thing can do. From these it follows that a good omnipotent thing eliminates evil completely, and then the propositions that a good omnipotent thing exists, and that evil exists, are incompatible.

Adequate Solutions

Now once the problem is fully stated it is clear that it can be solved, in the sense that the problem will not arise if one gives up at least one of the propositions that constitute it. If you are prepared to say that God is not wholly good, or not quite omnipotent, or that evil does not exist, or that good is not opposed to the kind of evil that exists, or that there are limits to what an omnipotent thing can do, then the problem of evil will not arise for you.

There are, then, quite a number of adequate solutions of the problem of evil, and some of these have been adopted, or almost adopted, by various thinkers. For example, a few have been prepared to deny God's omnipotence, and rather more have been prepared to keep the term "omnipotence" but severely to restrict its meaning, recording quite a number of things that an omnipotent being cannot do. Some have said that evil is an illusion, perhaps because they held that the whole world of temporal, changing things is an illusion, and that what we call evil belongs only to this world, or perhaps because they held that although temporal things *are* much as we see them, those that we call evil are not really evil. Some have said that what we call evil is merely the privation of good, that evil in a positive sense, evil that would really be opposed to good, does not exist. Many have agreed with Pope that disorder is harmony not understood, and that partial evil is universal good. Whether any of these views is *true* is, of course, another question. But each of them gives an adequate solution of the problems of evil in the sense that if you accept it this problem does not arise for you, though you may, of course, have *other* problems to face.

But often enough these adequate solutions are only *almost*

adopted. The thinkers who restrict God's power, but keep the term "omnipotence," may reasonably be suspected of thinking, in other contexts, that his power is really unlimited. Those who say that evil is an illusion may also be thinking, inconsistently, that this illusion is itself an evil. Those who say that "evil" is merely privation of good may also be thinking, inconsistently, that privation of good is an evil. (The fallacy here is akin to some forms of the "naturalistic fallacy" in ethics, where some think, for example, that "good" is just what contributes to evolutionary progress, and that evolutionary progress is itself good.) If Pope meant what he said in the first line of his couplet, that "disorder" is only harmony not understood, the "partial evil" of the second line must, for consistency, mean "that which, taken in isolation, falsely appears to be evil," but it would more naturally mean "that which, in isolation, really is evil." The second line, in fact, hesitates between two views, that "partial evil" isn't really evil, since only the universal quality is real, and that "partial evil" is really an evil, but only a little one.

In addition, therefore, to adequate solutions, we must recognize unsatisfactory inconsistent solutions, in which there is only a half-hearted or temporary rejection of one of the propositions which together constitute the problem. In these, one of the constituent propositions is explicitly rejected, but it is covertly reasserted or assumed elsewhere in the system.

Fallacious Solutions

BESIDES these half-hearted solutions, which explicitly reject but implicitly assert one of the constituent propositions, there are definitely fallacious solutions which explicitly maintain all the constituent propositions, but implicitly reject at least one of them in the course of the argument that explains away the problem of evil.

There are, in fact, many so-called solutions which purport to remove the contradiction without abandoning any of its constituent propositions. These must be fallacious, as we can see from the very statement of the problem, but it is not so easy to see in each case precisely where the fallacy lies. I suggest that in all cases the fallacy has the general form suggested above: in order to solve the problem one (or perhaps more) of its constituent propositions is given up, but in such a way that it appears to have been retained, and can therefore be asserted without qualification in other contexts. Sometimes there is a further complication: the supposed solution moves to and fro between, say, two of the constituent propositions, at one point asserting the first of these but covertly abandoning the second, at another point asserting the second but covertly abandoning the first. These fallacious solutions often turn upon some equivocation with the words "good" and "evil," or upon some vagueness about the way in which good and evil are opposed to one another, or about how much is meant by "omnipotence." I propose to examine some of these so-called solutions, and to exhibit their fallacies in detail. Incidentally, I shall also be considering whether an adequate solution could be reached by a minor modification of one or more of the constituent propositions, which would, however, still satisfy all the essential requirements of ordinary theism.

1. "GOOD CANNOT EXIST WITHOUT EVIL" OR "EVIL IS NECESSARY AS A COUNTERPART TO GOOD."

It is sometimes suggested that evil is necessary as a counterpart to good, that if there were no evil there could be no good either, and that this solves the problem of evil. It is true that it points to an answer to the question "Why should there be evil?" But it does so only by qualifying some of the propositions that constitute the problem.

First, it sets a limit to what God can do, saying that God *cannot* create good without simultaneously creating evil, and this means either that God is not omnipotent or that there are *some* limits to what an omnipotent thing can do. It may be replied that these limits are always presupposed, that omnipotence has never meant the power to do what is logically impossible, and on the present view the existence of good without evil would be a logical impossibility. This interpretation of omnipotence may, indeed, be accepted as a modification of our original account which does not reject anything that is essential to theism, and I shall in general assume it in the subsequent discussion. It is, perhaps, the most common theistic view, but I think that some theists at least have maintained that God can do what is logically impossible. Many theists, at any rate, have held that logic itself is created or laid down by God, that logic is the way in which God arbitrarily chooses to think. (This is, of course, parallel to the ethical view that morally right actions are those which God arbitrarily chooses to command, and the two views encounter similar difficulties.) And *this* account of logic is clearly inconsistent with the view that God is bound by logical necessities—unless it is possible for an omnipotent being to bind himself, an issue which we shall consider later, when we come to the Paradox of Omnipotence. This solution of the problem of evil cannot, therefore, be consistently adopted along with the view that logic is itself created by God.

But, secondly, this solution denies that evil is opposed to good in our original sense. If good and evil are counterparts, a good thing will not "eliminate evil as far as it can." Indeed, this view suggests that good and evil are not strictly qualities of things at all. Perhaps the suggestion is that good and evil are related in much the same way as great and small. Certainly, when the term "great" is used relatively as a condensation of "greater than so-and-so," and "small" is used correspondingly, greatness and smallness are counterparts and cannot exist without each other. But in this sense greatness is not a quality, not an intrinsic feature of anything; and it would be absurd to think of a movement in favor of greatness and against smallness in this sense. Such a movement would be self-defeating, since relative greatness can be promoted only by a simultaneous promotion of relative smallness. I feel sure that no theists would be content to regard God's goodness as analogous to this—as if what he supports were not the *good* but the *better,* and as if he had the paradoxical aim that all things should be better than other things.

This point is obscurred by the fact that "great" and "small" seem to have an absolute as well as a relative sense. I cannot discuss here whether there is absolute magnitude or not, but if there is, there could be an absolute sense for "great," it could mean of at least a certain size, and it would make sense to speak of all things getting bigger, of a universe that was expanding all over, and therefore it would make sense to speak of promoting greatness. But in *this* sense great and small are not logically necessary counterparts: either quality could exist without the other. There would be no logical impossibility in everything's being small or in everything's being great.

Neither in the absolute nor in the relative sense, then, of "great" and "small" do these terms provide an analogy of the sort that would be needed to support this solution of the problem of evil. In neither case are greatness and smallness *both* necessary counterparts *and* mutually opposed forces or possible objects for support and attack.

It may be replied that good and evil are necessary counterparts in the same way as any quality and its logical opposite: redness can occur, it is suggested, only if nonredness also occurs. But unless evil is merely the privation of good, they are not logical opposites, and some further argument would be needed to show that they are counterparts in the same way as genuine logical opposites. Let us assume that this could be given. There is still doubt of the correctness of the metaphysical principle that a quality must have a real opposite: I suggest that it is not really impossible that everything should be, say, red, that the truth is merely that if everything were red we should not notice redness, and so we should have no word "red"; we observe and give names to qualities only if they have real opposites. If so, the principle that a term must have an opposite would belong only to our language or to our thought, and would not be an ontological principle, and, correspondingly, the rule that good cannot exist without evil would not state a logical necessity of a sort that God would just have to put up with. God might have made everything good, though *we* should not have noticed it if he had.

But, finally, even if we concede that this *is* an ontological principle, it will provide a solution for the problem of evil only if one is prepared to say, "Evil exists, but only just enough evil to serve as the counterpart of good." I doubt whether any theist will accept this. After all, the *ontological* requirement that nonredness should occur would be satisfied even if all the universe, except for a minute speck, were red, and, if there were a corresponding requirement for evil as a counterpart to good, a minute dose of evil would presumably do. But theists are not usually willing to say, in all contexts, that all the evil that occurs is a minute and necessary dose.

2. "EVIL IS NECESSARY AS A MEANS TO GOOD."

IT is sometimes suggested that evil is necessary for good not as a counterpart but as a means. In its simple form this has little plausibility as a solution of the problem of evil, since it obviously implies a severe restriction of God's power. It would be a *causal* law that you cannot have a certain end without a certain means, so that if God has to introduce evil as a means to good, he must be subject to at least some causal laws. This certainly conflicts with what a theist normally means by omnipotence. This view of God as limited by causal laws also conflicts with the view that causal laws are themselves made by God, which is more widely held than the corresponding view about the laws of logic. This conflict would, indeed, be resolved if it were possible for an omnipotent being to bind himself, and this possibility has still to be considered. Unless a favorable answer can be given to this question, the suggestion that evil is necessary as a means to good solves the problem of evil only by denying one of its constituent propositions, either that God is omnipotent or that "omnipotent" means what it says.

3. "THE UNIVERSE IS BETTER WITH SOME EVIL IN IT
THAN IT COULD BE IF THERE WERE NO EVIL."

MUCH more important is a solution which at first seems to be a mere variant of the previous one, that evil may contribute to the goodness of a whole in which it is found, so that the universe as a whole is better as it is, with some evil in it, than it would be if there were no evil. This solution may be developed in either of two ways. It may be supported by an aesthetic analogy, by the fact that contrasts heighten beauty, that in a musical work, for example, there may occur discords which somehow add to the beauty of the work as a whole. Alternatively, it may be worked out in connection with the notion of progress, that the best possible organization of the universe will not be static, but progressive, that the gradual overcoming of evil by good is really a finer thing than would be the eternal unchallenged supremacy of good.

In either case, this solution usually starts from the assumption that the evil whose existence gives rise to the problem of evil is primarily what is called physical evil, that is to say, pain. In Hume's rather half-hearted presentation of the problem of evil, the evils that he stresses are pain and disease, and those who reply to him argue that the existence of pain and disease makes possible the existence of sympathy, benevolence, heroism, and the gradually successful struggle of doctors and reformers to overcome these evils. In fact, theists often seize the opportunity to accuse those who stress the problem of evil of taking a low, materialistic view of good and evil, equating these with pleasure and pain, and of ignoring the more spiritual goods which can arise in the struggle against evils.

But let us see exactly what is being done here. Let us call pain and misery "first order evil" or "evil (1)." What contrasts with this, namely, pleasure and happiness, will be called "first order good" or "good (1)." Distinct from this is "second order good" or "good (2)" which somehow emerges in a complex situation in which evil (1) is a necessary component—logically, not merely causally, necessary. (Exactly *how* it emerges does not matter: in the crudest version of this solution good [2] is simply the heightening of happiness by the contrast with misery, in other versions it includes sympathy with suffering, heroism in facing danger, and the gradual decrease of first order evil and increase of first order good.) It is also being assumed that second order good is more important than first order good or evil, in particular that it more than outweighs the first order evil it involves.

Now this is a particularly subtle attempt to solve the problem of evil. It defends God's goodness and omnipotence on the ground that (on a sufficiently long view) this is the best of all logically possible worlds, because it includes the important second order goods, and yet it admits that real evils, namely first order evils, exist. But does it still hold that good and evil are opposed? Not, clearly, in the sense that we set out originally: good does not tend to eliminate evil in general. Instead, we have a modified, a more complex pattern. First order good (e.g., happiness) *contrasts with* first order evil (e.g., misery) : these two are opposed in a fairly mechanical way; some second order goods (e.g., benevolence) try to maximize first order good and minimize first order evil; but God's goodness is not this, it is rather the will to maximize *second* order good. We might, therefore, call God's goodness an example of a third order goodness, or good (3). While this account is different from our original one, it might well be held to be an improvement on it, to give a more accurate description of the way in which good is opposed to evil, and to be consistent with the essential theist position.

There might, however, be several objections to this solution.

First, some might argue that such qualities as benevolence—and a fortiori the third order goodness which promotes benevolence—have a merely derivative value, that they are not higher sorts of good, but merely means to good (1), that is, to happiness, so that it would be absurd for God to keep misery in existence in order to make possible the virtues of benevolence, heroism, etc. The theist who adopts the present solution must, of course, deny this, but he can do so with some plausibility, so I should not press this objection.

Secondly, it follows from this solution that God is not in our sense benevolent or sympathetic: he is not concerned to minimize evil (1), but only to promote good (2) ; and this might be a disturbing conclusion for some theists.

But, thirdly, the fatal objection is this. Our analysis shows clearly the possibility of the existence of a *second* order evil, an evil (2) contrasting with good (2) as evil (1) contrasts with good (1). This would include malevolence, cruelty, callousness, cowardice, and states in which good (1) is decreasing and evil (1) increasing. And just as good (2) is held to be the important kind of good, the kind that God is concerned to promote, so evil (2) will, by analogy, be the important kind of evil, the kind which God, if he were wholly good and omnipotent, would eliminate. And yet evil (2) plainly exists, and indeed most theists (in other contexts) stress its existence more than that of evil (1). We should, therefore, state the problem of evil in terms of second order evil, and against this form of the problem the present solution is useless.

An attempt might be made to use this solution again, at a

higher level, to explain the occurrence of evil (2) : indeed the next main solution that we shall examine does just this, with the help of some new notions. Without any fresh notions, such a solution would have little plausibility: for example, we could hardly say that the really important good was a good (3), such as the increase of benevolence in proportion to cruelty, which logically required for its occurrence the occurrence of some second order evil. But even if evil (2) could be explained in this way, it is fairly clear that there would be third order evils contrasting with this third order good: and we should be well on the way to an infinite regress, where the solution of a problem of evil, stated in terms of evil (n), indicated the existence of an evil (n + 1), and a further problem to be solved.

4. "EVIL IS DUE TO HUMAN FREE WILL."

PERHAPS the most important proposed solution of the problem of evil is that evil is not to be ascribed to God at all, but to the independent actions of human beings, supposed to have been endowed by God with freedom of the will. This solution may be combined with the preceding one: first order evil (e.g., pain) may be justified as a logically necessary component in second order good (e.g., sympathy) while second order evil (e.g., cruelty) is not *justified,* but is so ascribed to human beings that God cannot be held responsible for it. This combination evades my third criticism of the preceding solution.

The free-will solution also involves the preceding solution at a higher level. To explain why a wholly good God gave men free will although it would lead to some important evils, it must be argued that it is better on the whole that men should act freely, and sometimes err, than that they should be innocent automata, acting rightly in a wholly determined way. Freedom, that is to say, is now treated as a third order good, and as being more valuable than second order goods (such as sympathy and heroism) would be if they were deterministically produced, and it is being assumed that second order evils, such as cruelty, are logically necessary accompaniments of freedom, just as pain is a logically necessary precondition of sympathy.

I think that this solution is unsatisfactory primarily because of the incoherence of the notion of freedom of the will: but I cannot discuss this topic adequately here, although some of my criticisms will touch upon it.

First I should query the assumption that second order evils are logically necessary accompaniments of freedom. I should ask this: if God has made men such that in their free choices they sometimes prefer what is good and sometimes what is evil, why could he not have made men such that they always freely choose the good? If there is no logical impossibility in a man's freely choosing the good on one, or on several, occasions, there cannot be a logical impossibility in his freely choosing the good on every occasion. God was not, then, faced with a choice between making innocent automata and making beings who, in acting freely, would sometimes go wrong: there was open to him the obviously better possibility of making beings who would act freely but always go right. Clearly, his failure to avail himself of this possibility is inconsistent with his being both omnipotent and wholly good.

If it is replied that this objection is absurd, that the making of some wrong choices is logically necessary for freedom, it would seem that "freedom" must here mean complete randomness or indeterminacy, including randomness with regard to the alternatives good and evil, in other words that men's choices and consequent actions can be "free" only if they are not determined by their characters. Only on this assumption can God escape the responsibility for men's actions; for if he made them as they are, but did not determine their wrong choices, this can only be because the wrong choices are not determined by men as they are. But then if freedom is randomness, how can it be a characteristic of *will*? And, still more, how can it be the most important good? What value or merit would there be in free choices if these were random actions which were not determined by the nature of the agent?

I conclude that to make this solution plausible two different senses of "freedom" must be confused, one sense which will justify the view that freedom is a third order good, more valuable than other goods would be without it, and another sense, sheer randomness, to prevent us from ascribing to God a decision to make men such that they sometimes go wrong when he might have made them such that they would always freely go right.

This criticism is sufficient to dispose of this solution. But besides this there is a fundamental difficulty in the notion of an omnipotent God creating men with free will, for if men's wills are really free this must mean that even God cannot control them, that is, that God is no longer omnipotent. It may be objected that God's gift of freedom to men does not mean that he *cannot* control their wills, but that he always *refrains* from controlling their wills. But why, we may ask, should God refrain from controlling evil wills? Why should he not leave men free to will rightly, but intervene when he sees them beginning to will wrongly? If God could do this, but does not, and if he is wholly good, the only explanation could be that even a wrong free act of will is not really evil, that its freedom is a value which outweighs its wrongness, so that there would be a loss of value if God took away the wrongness and the freedom together. But this is utterly opposed to what theists say about sin in other contexts. The present solution of the problem of evil, then, can be maintained only in the form that God has made men so free that he *cannot* control their wills.

This leads us to what I call the "Paradox of Omnipotence": can an omnipotent being make things which he cannot subsequently control? Or, what is practically equivalent to this, can an omnipotent being make rules which then bind himself? (These are practically equivalent because any such rules could be regarded as setting certain things beyond his control, and vice versa.) The second of these formulations is relevant to the suggestions that we have already met, that an omnipotent God creates the rules of logic or causal laws, and is then bound by them.

It is clear that this is a paradox: the questions cannot be answered satisfactorily either in the affirmative or in the negative. If we answer "Yes," it follows that if God actually makes things which he cannot control, or makes rules which bind himself, he is not omnipotent once he had made them: there are *then* things which he cannot do. But if we answer "No," we are immediately asserting that there are things which he cannot do, that is to say that he is already not omnipotent.

It cannot be replied that the question which sets this paradox is not a proper question. It would make perfectly good sense to say that a human mechanic has made a machine which he cannot control: if there is any difficulty about the question it lies in the notion of omnipotence itself.

This, incidentally, shows that although we have approached this paradox from the free-will theory, it is equally a problem for a theological determinist. No one thinks that machines have free will, yet they may well be beyond the control of their makers. The determinist might reply that anyone who makes anything determines its ways of acting, and so determines its subsequent behavior: even the human mechanic does this by his *choice* of materials and structure for his machine, though he does not know all about either of these: the mechanic thus determines, though he may not foresee, his machine's actions. And since God is omniscient, and since his creation of things is total, he both determines and foresees the ways in which his creatures will act. We may grant this, but it is beside the point. The question is not whether God *originally* determined the future actions of his creatures, but whether he can *subsequently* control their actions, or whether he was able in his original creation to put things beyond his subsequent control. Even on determinist principles the answers "Yes" and "No" are equally irreconcilable with God's omnipotence.

Before suggesting a solution of this paradox, I would point out that there is a parallel Paradox of Sovereignty. Can a legal sovereign make a law restricting its own future legislative power? For example, could the British parliament make a law forbidding any future parliament to socialize banking, and also forbidding the future repeal of this law itself? Or could the British parliament, which was legally sovereign in Australia in, say, 1899, pass a valid law, or series of laws, which made it no longer sovereign in 1933? Again, neither the affirmative nor the negative answer is really satisfactory. If we were to answer "Yes," we should be admitting the validity of a law which, if it were actually made, would mean that parliament was no longer sovereign. If we were to answer "No," we should be admitting that there is a law, not logically absurd, which parliament cannot validly make, that is, that parliament is not now a legal sovereign. This paradox can be solved in the following way. We should distinguish between first order laws, that is laws governing the actions of individuals and bodies other than the legislature, and second order laws, that is laws about laws, laws governing the actions of the legislature itself. Correspondingly, we should distinguish two orders of sovereignty, first order sovereignty (sovereignty [1]) which is unlimited authority to make first order laws, and second order sovereignty (sovereignty [2]) which is unlimited authority to make second order laws. If we say that parliament is sovereign we might mean that any parliament at any time has sovereignty (1), or we might mean that parliament has both sovereignty (1) and sovereignty (2) at present, but we cannot without contradiction mean both that the present parliament has sovereignty (2) and that every parliament at every time has sovereignty (1), for if the present parliament has sovereignty (2) it may use it to take away the sovereignty (1) of later parliaments. What the paradox shows is that we cannot ascribe to any continuing institution legal sovereignty in an inclusive sense.

The analogy between omnipotence and sovereignty shows that the paradox of omnipotence can be solved in a similar way. We must distinguish between first order omnipotence (omnipotence [1]), that is unlimited power to act, and second order omnipotence (omnipotence [2]), that is unlimited power to determine what powers to act things shall have. Then we could consistently say that God all the time has omnipotence (1), but if so no beings at any time have powers to act independently of God. Or we could say that God at one time had omnipotence (2), and used it to assign independent powers to act to certain things, so that God thereafter did not have omnipotence (1). But what the paradox shows is that we cannot consistently ascribe to any continuing being omnipotence in an inclusive sense.

An alternative solution of this paradox would be simply to deny that God is a continuing being, that any times can be assigned to his actions at all. But on this assumption (which also has difficulties of its own) no meaning can be given to the assertion that God made men with wills so free that he could not control them. The paradox of omnipotence can be avoided by putting God outside time, but the free-will solution of the problem of evil cannot be saved in this way, and equally it remains impossible to hold that an omnipotent God *binds himself* by causal or logical laws.

Conclusion

OF the proposed solutions of the problem of evil which we have examined, none has stood up to criticism. There may be other solutions which require examination, but this study strongly suggests that there is no valid solution of the problem which does not modify at least one of the constituent propositions in a way which would seriously affect the essential core of the theistic position.

Quite apart from the problem of evil, the paradox of omnipotence has shown that God's omnipotence must in any case be restricted in one way or another, that unqualified omnipotence cannot be ascribed to any being that continues through time. And if God and his actions are not in time, can omnipotence, or power of any sort, be meaningfully ascribed to him?

5

THE FREE WILL DEFENSE*

Alvin Plantinga (1932–   ) teaches
philosophy at Calvin College. He works
primarily within the analytic tradition,
applying the techniques of logical analysis
to the problems raised by religious con-
ceptions and doctrines.

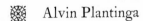 Alvin Plantinga

SINCE the days of Epicurus many philosophers have suggested that the existence of evil constitutes a problem for those who accept theistic belief.[1] Those contemporaries who follow Epicurus here claim, for the most part, to detect logical inconsistency in such belief. So McCloskey:

Evil is a problem for the theist in that a *contradiction* is involved in the fact of evil, on the one hand, and the belief in the omnipotence and perfection of God on the other.[2]

and Mackie:

I think, however, that a more telling criticism can be made by way of the traditional problem of evil. Here it can be shown, not that religious beliefs lack rational support, but that they are positively irrational, that the several parts of the essential theological doctrine are *inconsistent* with one another. . . .[3]

and essentially the same charge is made by Professor Aiken in an article entitled 'God and Evil'.[4]

These philosophers, then, and many others besides, hold that traditional theistic belief is self-contradictory and that the problem

* Alvin Plantinga, "The Free Will Defense" in Max Black (ed.), *Philosophy in America*. Copyright under the Berne convention by George Allen & Unwin, Ltd. Used by permission of Cornell University Press.

[1] David Hume and some of the French encyclopedists, for example, as well as F. H. Bradley, J. McTaggart, and J. S. Mill.

[2] H. J. McCloskey, 'God and Evil', *The Philosophical Quarterly*, Vol. 10 (April 1960), p. 97.

[3] 'Evil and Omnipotence.' J. L. Mackie, *Mind*, Vol. 64, No. 254 (April 1955), p. 200.

[4] *Ethics*, Vol. 48 (1957–58), p. 79.

of evil, for the theist, is that of deciding which of the relevant propositions he is to abandon. But just which propositions are involved? What is the set of theistic beliefs whose conjunction yields a contradiction? The authors referred to above take the following five propositions to be essential to traditional theism: (a) that God exists, (b) that God is omnipotent, (c) that God is omniscient, (d) that God is wholly good, and (e) that evil exists. Here they are certainly right: each of these propositions is indeed an essential feature of orthodox theism. And it is just these five propositions whose conjunction is said, by our atheologians,[1] to be self-contradictory.

Apologists for theism, of course, have been quick to repel the charge. A line of resistance they have often employed is called *The Free Will Defence;* in this paper I shall discuss and develop that idea.

First of all, a distinction must be made between *moral evil* and *physical evil*. The former, roughly, is the evil which results from human choice or volition; the latter is that which does not. Suffering due to an earthquake, for example, would be a case of physical evil; suffering resulting from human cruelty would be a case of moral evil. This distinction, of course, is not very clear and many questions could be raised about it; but perhaps it is not necessary to deal with these questions here. Given this distinction, the Free Will Defence is usually stated in something like the following way. A world containing creatures who freely perform both good and evil actions—and do more good than evil—is more valuable than a world containing quasi-automata who always do what is right because they are unable to do otherwise. Now God can create free creatures, but He cannot causally or otherwise determine them to do only what is right; for if he does so then they do not do what is right *freely*. To create creatures capable of moral good, therefore, he must create creatures capable of moral evil; but he cannot create the possibility of moral evil and at the same time prohibit its actuality. And as it turned out, some of the free creatures God created exercised their freedom to do what is wrong: hence moral evil. The fact that free creatures sometimes err, however, in no way tells against God's omnipotence or against his goodness; for he could forestall the occurrence of moral evil only by removing the possibility of moral good.

In this way some traditional theists have tried to explain or

---

[1] *Natural theology* is the attempt to infer central religious beliefs from premises that are either obvious to common sense (e.g., *that some things are in motion*) or logically necessary. *Natural atheology* is the attempt to infer the falsity of such religious beliefs from premises of the same sort.

justify part of the evil that occurs by ascribing it to the will of man rather than to the will of God. At least three kinds of objections to this idea are to be found both in the tradition and in the current literature. I shall try to develop and clarify the Free Will Defence by restating it in the face of these objections.

I

THE first objection challenges the assumption, implicit in the above statement of the Free Will Defence, that free will and causal determinism are logically incompatible. So Flew:

. . . to say that a person could have helped doing something is not to say that what he did was in principle unpredictable nor that there were no causes anywhere which determined that he would as a matter of fact act in this way. It is to say that if he had chosen to do otherwise he would have been able to do so; that there were alternatives, within the capacities of one of his physical strength, of his I.Q., of his knowledge, open to a person in his situation.
. . . There is no contradiction involved in saying that a particular action or choice was: *both* free, and could have been helped, and so on; *and* predictable, or even foreknown, and explicable in terms of caused causes.
. . . if it is really logically possible for an action to be both freely chosen and yet fully determined by caused causes, then the keystone argument of the Free Will Defense, that there is contradiction in speaking of God so arranging the laws of nature that all men always as a matter of fact freely choose to do the right, cannot hold.[1]

Flew's objection, I think, can be dealt with in a fairly summary fashion. He does not, in the paper in question, explain what he means by 'causal determination' (and of course in that paper this omission is quite proper and justifiable). But presumably he means to use the locution in question in such a way that to say of Jones' action A that it is *causally determined* is to say that the action in question has causes and that given these causes, Jones could not have refrained from doing A. That is to say, Flew's use of 'causally determined', presumably, is such that one or both of the following sentences. or some sentences very much like them, express necessarily true propositions:

(a) If Jones' action A is causally determined, then a set S of events has occurred prior to Jones' doing A such that, given S, it is causally impossible for Jones to refrain from doing A.

1 'Divine Omnipotence and Human Freedom', in *New Essays in Philosophical Theology*, ed. A. Flew and A. MacIntyre, London 1955, pp. 150, 151, 153.

(b) If Jones' action A is causally determined, then there is a set S of propositions describing events occurring before A and a set L of propositions expressing natural laws such that

(1) the conjunction of S's members does not entail that Jones does A, and (2) the conjunction of the members of S with the members of L does entail that Jones does A.

And Flew's thesis, then, is that there is no contradiction in saying of a man, both that all of his actions are causally determined (in the sense just explained) and that some of them are free.

Now it seems to me altogether paradoxical to say of anyone all of whose actions are causally determined, that on some occasions he acts freely. When we say that Jones acts freely on a given occasion, what we say entails, I should think, that either his action on that occasion is not causally determined, or else he has previously performed an undetermined action which is a causal ancestor of the one in question. But this is a difficult and debatable issue; fortunately we need not settle it in order to assess the force of Flew's objection to the Free Will Defence. The Free Will Defender claims that the sentence 'Not all free actions are causally determined' expresses a necessary truth; Flew denies this claim. This strongly suggests that Flew and the Free Will Defender are not using the words 'free' and 'freedom' in the same way. The Free Will Defender, apparently, uses the words in question in such a way that sentences 'Some of Jones' actions are free' and 'Jones did action A freely' express propositions which are inconsistent with the proposition that all of Jones' actions are causally determined. Flew, on the other hand, claims that with respect to the ordinary use of these words, there is no such inconsistency. It is my opinion that Flew is mistaken here; I think it is he who is using these words in a nonstandard, unordinary way. But we need not try to resolve that issue; for the Free Will Defender can simply make Flew a present of the word 'freedom' and state his case using other locutions. He might now hold, for example, not that God made men free and that a world in which men freely do both good and evil is more valuable than a world in which they unfreely do only what is good; but rather that God made men such that some of their actions are *unfettered* (both free in Flew's sense and also causally undetermined) and that a world in which men perform both good and evil unfettered actions is superior to one in which they perform only good, but fettered, actions. By substituting 'unfettered' for 'free' throughout this account, the Free Will Defender can elude Flew's objection altogether.[1] So whether Flew is right or wrong about the

---

[1] And since this is so in what follows I shall continue to use the words 'free' and 'freedom' in the way the Free Will Defender uses them.

ordinary sense of 'freedom' is of no consequence; his objection is in an important sense merely verbal and thus altogether fails to damage the Free Will Defence.

II

FLEW's objection, in essence, is the claim that an omnipotent being could have created men in such a way that although free they would be *causally determined* to perform only right actions. According to a closely allied objection, an omnipotent being could have made men in such a way that although free, and free from any such causal determination, they would nonetheless *freely refrain* from performing any evil actions. Here the contemporary spokesman is Mackie:

. . . if God has made men such that in their free choices they sometimes prefer what is good and sometimes what is evil, why could he not have made men such that they always freely choose the good? If there is no logical impossibility in a man's freely choosing the good on one, or on several occasions, there cannot be a logical impossibility in his freely choosing the good on every occasion. God was not, then, faced with a choice between making innocent automata and making beings who, in acting freely, would sometimes go wrong; there was open to him the obviously better possibility of making beings who would act freely but always go right. Clearly, his failure to avail himself of this possibility is inconsistent with his being both omnipotent and wholly good.[1]

This objection is more serious than Flew's and must be dealt with more fully. Now the Free Will Defence is an argument for the conclusion that (*a*) is not contradictory or necessarily false:[2]

(*a*) God is omnipotent, omniscient, and all-good and God creates free men who sometimes perform morally evil actions.

What Mackie says, I think, may best be construed as an argument for the conclusion that (*a*) *is* necessarily false; in other words, that *God is omnipotent, omniscient and all good* entails *no free men He creates ever perform morally evil actions*. Mackie's argument seems to have the following structure:

(1) God is omnipotent and omniscient and all-good.

(2) If God is omnipotent, He can create any logically possible state of affairs.

---

[1] *Op. cit.,* p. 209.

[2] And of course if (*a*) is consistent, so is the set (*a*) − (*e*) mentioned on page 305, for (*a*) entails each member of that set.

∴ (3) God can create any logically possible state of affairs. (1, 2)

    (4) That all free men do what is right on every occasion is a logically possible state of affairs.

∴ (5) God can create free men such that they always do what is right. (4, 3)

    (6) If God can create free men such that they always do what is right and God is all-good, then any free men created by God always do what is right.

∴ (7) Any free men created by God always do what is right. (1, 5, 6)

∴ (8) No free men created by God ever perform morally evil actions. (7)

Doubtless the Free Will Defender will concede the truth of (4) ; there is a difficulty with (2), however; for

    (a) that there are men who are not created by God is a logically possible state of affairs.

is clearly true. But (2) and (a) entail

    (b) If God is omnipotent, God can create men who are not created by God.

And (b), of course, is false; (2) must be revised. The obvious way to repair it seems to be something like the following:

    (2′) If God is omnipotent, then God can create any state of affairs S such that *God creates S* is consistent.

Similarly, (3) must be revised:

    (3′) God can create any state of affairs S such that *God creates S* is consistent.

(1′) and (3′) do not seem to suffer from the faults besetting (1) and (3) ; but now it is not at all evident that (3′) and (4) entail

    (5) God can create free men such that they always do what is right

as the original argument claims. To see this, we must note that (5) is true only if

    (5a) God creates free men such that they always do what is right

is consistent. But (5a), one might think, is equivalent to:

    (5b) God creates free men and brings it about that they always freely do what is right.

And (5*b*) , of course, is *not* consistent; for if God *brings it about* that the men He creates always do what is right, then they do not do what is right *freely*. So if (5*a*) is taken to express (5*b*) , then (5) is clearly false and clearly not entailed by (3′) and (4) .

On the other hand, (5*a*) could conceivably be used to express:

(5*c*) God creates free men and these free men always do what is right.

(5*c*) is surely consistent; it is indeed logically possible that God creates free men and that the free men created by Him always do what is right. And conceivably the objector is using (5) to express this possibility—i.e., it may be that (5) is meant to express:

(5*d*) the proposition *God creates free men and the free men created by God always do what is right* is consistent.

If (5) is equivalent to (5*d*) , then (5) is true—in fact necessarily true (and hence trivially entailed by (3′) and (4)) . But now the difficulty crops up with respect to (6) which, given the equivalence of (5) and (5*d*) is equivalent to

(6′) If God is all-good and the proposition *God creates free men and the free men He creates always do what is right* is consistent, then any free men created by God always do what is right.

Now Mackie's aim is to show that the proposition *God is omnipotent, omniscient and all-good* entails the proposition *no free men created by God ever perform morally evil actions*. His attempt, as I outlined it, is to show this by constructing a valid argument whose premise is the former and whose conclusion is the latter. But then any additional premise appealed to in the deduction must be necessarily true if Mackie's argument is to succeed. (6′) is one such additional premise; but there seems to be no reason for supposing that (6′) is true at all, let alone necessarily true. Whether the free men created by God would always do what is right would presumably be up to them; for all we know they might sometimes exercise their freedom to do what is wrong. Put in a nutshell the difficulty with the argument is the following. (5*a*) (God creates free men such that they always freely do what is right) is susceptible of two interpretations ((5*b*) and (5*c*)). Under one of these interpretations (5) turns out to be false and the argument therefore fails. Under the other interpretation (6) turns out to be utterly groundless and question begging, and again the argument fails.

So far, then, the Free Will Defence has emerged unscathed

from Mackie's objection. One has the feeling, however, that more can be said here; that there is something to Mackie's argument. What more? Well, perhaps something along the following lines. It is agreed that it is logically possible that all men always do only what is right. Now God is said to be omniscient and hence knows, with respect to any person he proposes to create, whether that person would or would not commit morally evil acts. For every person P who in fact performs morally evil actions, there is, evidently, a possible person P' who is exactly like P in every respect except that P' never performs any evil actions. If God is omnipotent, He could have created these possible persons instead of the persons He in fact did create. And if He is also all-good, He *would*, presumably, have created them, since they differ from the persons He did create only in being morally better than they are.

Can we make coherent sense out of this revised version of Mackie's objection? What, in particular, could the objector mean by 'possible person'? and what are we to make of the suggestion that God could have created possible persons? I think these questions can be answered. Let us consider first the set of all those properties it is logically possible for human beings to have. Examples of properties *not* in this set are the properties of *being over a mile long; being a hippopotamus; being a prime number; being divisible by four;* and the like. Included in the set are such properties as *having red hair; being present at the Battle of Waterloo; being the President of the United States; being born in 1889;* and *being a pipe-smoker.* Also included are such moral properties as *being kind to one's maiden aunt, being a scoundrel, performing at least one morally wrong action,* and so on. Let us call the properties in this set H properties. The complement $\overline{P}$ of an H property P is the property a thing has just in case it does not have P. And a *consistent set of H* properties is a set of H properties such that it is logically possible that there be a human being having every property in the set. Now we can define 'possible person' in the following way:

x is a possible person $= x$ is a consistent set of H properties such that for every H property P, either P or $\overline{P}$ is a member of x.

To *instantiate* a possible person P is to create a human being having every property in P. And a set S of possible persons is a *co-possible set of possible persons* just in case it is logically possible that every member of S is instantiated.[1]

Given this technical terminology, Mackie's objection can be

---

[1] The definiens must not be confused with: For every member M of S, it is logically possible that M is instantiated.

summarily restated. It is granted by everyone that there is no absurdity in the claim that some man who is free to do what is wrong never, in fact, performs any wrong action. It follows that there are many possible persons containing the property *is free to do wrong but always does right*. And since it is logically possible that all men always freely do what is right, there are presumably several co-possible sets of possible persons such that each member of each set contains the property in question. Now God, if he is omnipotent, can instantiate any possible person and any co-possible set of possible persons he chooses. Hence, if He were all-good, He would have instantiated one of the sets of co-possible persons all of whose members freely do only what is right.

In spite of its imposing paraphernalia the argument, thus restated, suffers from substantially the same defect that afflicts Mackie's original version. There are *some* possible persons God obviously cannot instantiate—those, for example, containing the property *is not created by God*. Accordingly it is *false* that God can instantiate just any possible person He chooses. But of course the interesting question is whether

(1) God can instantiate possible persons containing the property of always freely doing what is right.

is true; for perhaps Mackie could substitute (1) for the premise just shown to be false.

Is (1) true? Perhaps we can approach this question in the following way. Let P be any possible person containing the property *always freely does what is right*. Then there must be some action A such that P contains the property of being free with respect to A (i.e., the property of being free to perform A and free to refrain from performing A). The *instantiation* of a possible person S, I shall say, is a person having every property in S; and let us suppose that if P were instantiated, its instantiation would be doing something morally wrong in performing A. And finally, let us suppose that God wishes to instantiate P. Now P contains many properties in addition to the ones already mentioned. Among them, for example, we might find the following: *is born in 1910, has red hair, is born in Stuttgart, has feeble-minded ancestors, is six feet tall at the age of fourteen*, and the like. And there is no difficulty in God's creating a person with these properties. Further, there is no difficulty in God's bringing it about that this person (let's call him Smith) is free with respect to A. But if God *also* brings it about that Smith refrains from performing A (as he must to be the instantiation of P) then Smith is no longer free with respect to A and is hence not the instantiation of P after all. God cannot cause Smith to refrain from performing A, while allowing him to be free with respect to A; and therefore whether or not Smith does A will be entirely up to Smith; it will be a matter of free choice for him. Accordingly, whether God can instantiate P depends upon what Smith would freely decide to do.

This point may be put more accurately as follows: First, we shall say that an H property Q is *indeterminate* if *God creates a person and causes him to have Q* is necessarily false; an H property is *determinate* if it is not indeterminate. Of the properties we ascribed to P, all are determinate except *freely refrains from doing A* and *always freely does what is right*. Now consider P_1, the subset of P containing just the determinate members of P. In order to instantiate P God must instantiate P_1. It is evident that there is at most one instantiation of P_1, for among the members of P_1 will be some such individuating properties as for example, *is the third son of Richard and Lena Dykstra*. P_1 also contains the property of being free with respect to A; and if P_1 is instantiated, its instantiation will either perform A or refrain from performing A. It is, of course, possible that P_1 is such that if it is instantiated its instantiation I will perform A. If so, then if God allows I to remain free with respect to A, I will do A; and if God prevents I from doing A, then I is not free with respect to A and hence not the instantiation of P after all. Hence in neither case does God succeed in instantiating P. And accordingly God can instantiate P only if P_1 is *not* such that if it is instantiated, its instantiation will perform A. Hence it is possible that God cannot instantiate P. And evidently it is also possible, further, that *every* possible person containing the property *always freely does what is right* is such that neither God nor anyone else can instantiate it.

Now we merely suppose that P_1 is such that if it is instantiated, its instantiation will perform A. And this supposition, if true at all, is merely contingently true. It might be suggested, therefore, that God could instantiate P by instantiating P_1 and bringing it about that P_1 is *not* such that if it is instantiated, its instantiation will perform A. But to do this God must instantiate P_1 and bring it about that P_1 is such that if it is instantiated, its instantiation I will *refrain* from performing A. And if God does this then God brings it about that I will not perform A. But then I is not free to perform A and hence once more is not the instantiation of P.

It is possible, then, that God cannot instantiate any possible person containing the property *always freely does what is right*. It is also possible, of course, that He *can* instantiate some such possible persons. But *that* He can, if indeed He can, is a contingent truth.

And since Mackie's project is to prove an entailment, he cannot employ any contingent propositions as added premises. Hence the reconstructed argument fails.

Now the difficulty with the reconstructed argument is the fact that God cannot instantiate just any possible person he chooses, and the possibility that God cannot instantiate any possible persons containing the property of always freely doing what is right. But perhaps the objector can circumvent this difficulty.

The H properties that make trouble for the objector are the indeterminate properties—those which God cannot cause anyone to have. It is because possible persons contain indeterminate properties that God cannot instantiate just any possible person He wishes. And so perhaps the objector can reformulate his definition of 'possible person' in such a way that a possible person is a consistent set S of *determinate* properties such that for any determinate H property P, either P or $\overline{P}$ is a member of S. Unfortunately the following difficulty arises. Where I is any indeterminate H property and D a determinate H property, D or I (the property a person has if he has either D or I) is determinate. And so, of course, is $\overline{D}$. The same difficulty, accordingly, arises all over again—there will be some possible persons God can't instantiate (those containing the properties *is not created by God or has red hair* and *does not have red hair,* for example). We must add, therefore, that no possible person *entails* an indeterminate property.[1]

Even so our difficulties are not at an end. For the definition as now stated entails that there are no *possible free persons,* i.e., possible persons containing the property *on some occasions free to do what is right and free to do what is wrong.*[2] We may see this as follows: Let P be any possible free person. P then contains the property of being free with respect to some action A. Furthermore, P would contain either the property of performing A (since that is a determinate property) or the property of refraining from performing A. But if P contains the property of performing A and the property of being free with respect to A, then P entails the property of freely performing A—which is an indeterminate property. And the same holds in case P contains the property of refraining from performing A. Hence in either case P entails an indeterminate property and accordingly is not a possible person.

Clearly the objector must revise the definition of 'possible person' in such a way that for any action with respect to which a

---

1 Where a set S of properties entails a property P if and only if it is necessarily true that anything having every property in S also has P.

2 This was pointed out to me by Mr. Lewis Creary.

given possible person P is free, P contains neither the property of performing that action nor the property of refraining from performing it. This may be accomplished in the following way. Let us say that a person S is *free with respect to a property* P just in case there is some action A with respect to which S is free and which is such that S has P if and only if he performs A. So, for example, if a person is free to leave town and free to stay, then he is free with respect to the property *leaves town*. And let us say that a set of properties is free with respect to a given property P just in case it contains the property is *free with respect to* P. Now we can restate the definition of 'possible person' as follows:

x is a possible person $= x$ is a consistent set of determinate H properties such that (1) for every determinate H property P with respect to which x is not free, either P or $\overline{P}$ is a member of x, and (2) x does not entail any indeterminate property.

Now let us add the following new definition:

Possibly person P has indeterminate property $I = $ if P were instantiated, P's instantiation would have I.

Under the revised definition of 'possible person' it seems apparent that God, if he is omnipotent, can instantiate any possible person, and any co-possible set of possible persons, he chooses. But, the objector continues, if God is also all-good, He will, presumably, instantiate only those possible persons who have some such indeterminate H property as that of *always freely doing what is right*. And here the Free Will Defender can no longer make the objection which held against the previous versions of Mackie's argument. For if God can instantiate any possible person he chooses, he can instantiate any possible free person he chooses.

The Free Will Defender can, however, raise what is essentially the same difficulty in a new guise: what reason is there for supposing that there are *any* possible persons, in the present sense of 'possible person', having the indeterminate property in question? For it is clear that, given any indeterminate H property I, the proposition *no possible person has I* is a contingent proposition. Further, the proposition *every possible free person freely performs at least one morally wrong action* is possibly true. But if every *possible* free person performs at least one wrong action, then every *actual* free person also freely performs at least one wrong action; hence if every possible free person performs at least one wrong action, God could create a universe without moral evil only by refusing to create any free persons at all. And, the Free Will

Defender adds, a world containing free persons and moral evil (provided that it contained more moral good than moral evil) would be superior to one lacking both free persons and moral good and evil. Once again, then, the objection seems to fail.

The definitions offered during the discussion of Mackie's objection afford the opportunity of stating the Free Will Defence more formally. I said above (p. 209) that the Free Will Defence is in essence an argument for the conclusion that (*a*) is consistent:

(*a*) God is omnipotent, omniscient, and all-good and God creates persons who sometimes perform morally evil actions.

One way of showing (*a*) to be consistent is to show that its first conjunct does not entail the negation of its second conjunct, i.e., that

(*b*) God is omnipotent, omniscient and all-good

does not entail

(*c*) God does not create persons who perform morally evil actions.

Now one can show that a given proposition *p* does not entail another proposition *q* by producing a third proposition *r* which is such that (1) the conjunction of *p* and *r* is consistent and (2) the conjunction of *p* and *r* entails the negation of *q*. What we need here, then, is a proposition whose conjunction with (*b*) is both logically consistent and a logically sufficient condition of the denial of (*c*).

Consider the following argument:

(*b*) God is omnipotent, omniscient and all-good.

(*r*1) God creates some free persons.

(*r*2) Every possible free person performs at least one wrong action.

∴ (*d*) Every actual free person performs at least one wrong action. (*r*2)

∴ (*e*) God creates persons who perform morally evil actions. ((*r*1), (*d*))

This argument is valid (and can easily be expanded so that it is *formally* valid). Furthermore, the conjunction of (*b*), (*r*1) and (*r*2) is evidently consistent. And as the argument shows, (*b*), (*r*1) and (*r*2) jointly entail (*e*). But (*e*) is the denial of (*c*); hence (*b*) and (*r*) jointly entail the denial of (*c*). Accordingly (*b*) does not entail (*c*), and (*a*) (God is omnipotent, omniscient and all-good and God creates persons who perform morally evil acts) is shown to be consistent. So stated, therefore, the Free Will Defence appears to be successful.

At this juncture it might be objected that even if the Free Will Defence, as explained above, shows that there is no contradiction in the supposition that God, who is all-good, omnipotent and omniscient, creates persons who engage in moral evil, it does nothing to show that an all-good, omnipotent and omniscient Being could create a universe containing as *much* moral evil as this one seems to contain. The objection has a point, although the fact that there seems to be no way of measuring or specifying amounts of moral evil makes it exceedingly hard to state the objection in any way which does not leave it vague and merely suggestive. But let us suppose, for purposes of argument, that there is a way of measuring moral evil (and moral good) and that the moral evil present in the universe amounts to ϕ. The problem then is to show that

(b) God is omnipotent, omniscient and all-good

is consistent with

(f) God creates a set of free persons who produce ϕ moral evil.

Here the Free Will Defender can produce an argument to show that (b) is consistent with (f) which exactly parallels the argument for the consistency of (b) with (c) :

(b) God is omnipotent, omniscient and all-good.

(r3) God creates a set S of free persons such that there is a balance of moral good over moral evil with respect to the members of S.

(r4) There is exactly one co-possible set S' of free possible persons such that there is a balance of moral good over moral evil with respect to its members; and the members of S' produce ϕ moral evil.

Set S is evidently the instantiation of S' (i.e. every member of S is an instantiation of some member of S' and every member of S' is instantiated by some member of S) ; hence the members of S produce ϕ moral evil. Accordingly, (b), (r3) and (r4) jointly entail (f) ; but the conjunction of (b), (r3) and (r4) is consistent; hence (b) is consistent with (f) .

III

THE preceding discussion enables us to conclude, I believe, that the Free Will Defence succeeds in showing that there is no inconsistency in the assertion that God creates a universe containing as much moral evil as the universe in fact contains. There remains but one objection to be considered. McCloskey, Flew and others charge that the Free Will Defence, even if it is successful, accounts for only *part* of the evil we find; it accounts only for moral evil, leaving physical evil as intractable as before. The atheologian can therefore restate his position, maintaining that the existence of *physical evil,* evil which cannot be ascribed to the free actions of human beings, is inconsistent with the existence of an omniscient, omnipotent and all-good Deity.

To make this claim, however, is to overlook an important part of traditional theistic belief; it is part of much traditional belief to attribute a good deal of the evil we find to Satan, or to Satan and his cohorts. Satan, so the traditional doctrine goes, is a mighty non-human spirit, who, along with many other angels, was created long before God created men. Unlike most of his colleagues, Satan rebelled against God and has since been creating whatever havoc he could; the result, of course, is physical evil. But now we see that the moves available to the Free Will Defender in the case of moral evil are equally available to him in the case of physical evil. First he provides definitions of 'possible non-human spirit', 'free non-human spirit', etc., which exactly parallel their counterparts where it was moral evil that was at stake. Then he points out that it is logically possible that

(r5) God creates a set S of free non-human spirits such that the members of S do more good than evil,

and

(r6) there is exactly one co-possible set S' of possible free non-human spirits such that the members of S' do more good than evil,

and

(r7) all of the physical evil in the world is due to the actions of the members of S.

He points out further that (r5), (r6), and (r7) are jointly consistent and that their conjunction is consistent with the proposition that God is omnipotent, omniscient and all-good. But (r5) through (r7) jointly entail that God creates a universe containing as much physical evil as the universe in fact contains; it follows then, that the existence of physical evil is not inconsistent with the existence of an omniscient, omnipotent, all-good Deity.

Now it must be conceded that views involving devils and other non-human spirits do not at present enjoy either the extensive popularity or the high esteem of (say) the Theory of Relativity. Flew, for example, has this to say about the view in question:

> To make this more than just another desperate *ad hoc* expedient of apologetic it is necessary to produce independent evidence for launching such an hypothesis (if 'hypothesis' is not too flattering a term for it).[1]

But in the present context this claim is surely incorrect; to rebut the charge of contradiction the theist need not hold that the hypothesis in question is probable or even true. He need hold only that it is not inconsistent with the proposition that God exists. Flew suspects that 'hypothesis' may be too flattering a term for the sort of view in question. Perhaps this suspicion reflects his doubts as to the meaningfulness of the proposed view. But it is hard to see how one could plausibly argue that the views in question are nonsensical (in the requisite sense) without invoking some version of the Verifiability Criterion, a doctrine whose harrowing vicissitudes are well known. Furthermore, it is likely that any premises worth considering which yield the conclusion that hypotheses about devils are nonsensical will yield the same conclusion about the hypothesis that God exists. And if *God exists* is nonsensical, then presumably theism is not self-contradictory after all.

We may therefore conclude that the Free Will Defence successfully rebuts the charge of contradiction brought against the theist. The Problem of Evil (if indeed evil constitutes a problem for the theist) does not lie in any inconsistency in the belief that God, who is omniscient, omnipotent and all-good, has created a world containing moral and physical evil.

[1] *Op. cit.*, p. 17.

6

THE IDEAL OF LOVE*

Wang Yang-Ming (1472–1529) was the last great teacher of the Hsin-Hsueh School (School of Universal Mind) of Neo-Confucianism in China. Emphasizing a philosophy of moral idealism, he expressed his views in numerous writings, the best known of which are Inquiry on the Great Learning *and* Instructions for Practical Living.

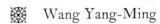 Wang Yang-Ming

Question: The *Great Learning* was considered by a former scholar as the learning of the great man.[1] I venture to ask why the learning of the great man should consist in "manifesting the clear character."[2]

Master Wang said: The great man regards Heaven, Earth, and the myriad things as one body. He regards the world as one family and the country as one person. As to those who make a cleavage between objects and distinguish between the self and others, they are small men. That the great man can regard Heaven, Earth, and the myriad things as one body is not because he deliberately wants to do so, but because it is natural to the humane nature of his mind that he do so. Forming one body with Heaven, Earth, and the myriad things is not only true of the great man. Even the mind of the small man is no different. Only he himself makes it small. Therefore when he sees a child about to fall into a well, he cannot help a feeling of alarm and commiseration.[3] This shows that his humanity forms one body with the child. It may be objected that the child belongs to the same species. Again, when he

---

* Wang Yang-Ming "Inquiry on the *Great Learning*" in *Instructions for Practical Living and Other Neo-Confucian Writings,* tr. by Wing-Tsit Chan (New York and London: Columbia University Press, 1963), pp. 272–280. Reprinted by permission of Columbia University Press.

1 Chu Hsi, *Ta-hsüeh chang-chü,* commentary on the text. Actually, by "great learning" *(ta-hsüeh)* Chu Hsi meant "education for the adult," but the Chinese phrase can also mean the learning of the great man. Wang used the latter interpretation.

2 The text of the *Great Learning.*

3 *Book of Mencius,* 2A:6.

observes the pitiful cries and frightened appearance of birds and animals about to be slaughtered, he cannot help feeling an "inability to bear" their suffering.[1] This shows that his humanity forms one body with birds and animals. It may be objected that birds and animals are sentient beings as he is. But when he sees plants broken and destroyed, he cannot help a feeling of pity. This shows that his humanity forms one body with plants. It may be said that plants are living things as he is. Yet, even when he sees tiles and stones shattered and crushed, he cannot help a feeling of regret. This shows that his humanity forms one body with tiles and stones. This means that even the mind of the small man necessarily has the humanity that forms one body with all. Such a mind is rooted in his Heaven-endowed nature, and is naturally intelligent, clear, and not beclouded. For this reason it is called the "clear character." Although the mind of the small man is divided and narrow, yet his humanity that forms one body can remain free from darkness to this degree. This is due to the fact that his mind has not yet been aroused by desires and obscured by selfishness. When it is aroused by desires and obscured by selfishness, compelled by greed for gain and fear of harm, and stirred by anger, he will destroy things, kill members of his own species, and will do everything. In extreme cases he will even slaughter his own brothers, and the humanity that forms one body will disappear completely. Hence, if it is not obscured by selfish desires, even the mind of the small man has the humanity that forms one body with all as does the mind of the great man. As soon as it is obscured by selfish desires, even the mind of the great man will be divided and narrow like that of the small man. Thus the learning of the great man consists entirely in getting rid of the obscuration of selfish desires in order by his own efforts to make manifest his clear character, so as to restore the condition of forming one body with Heaven, Earth, and the myriad things, a condition that is originally so, that is all. It is not that outside of the original substance something can be added.

Question: Why, then, does the learning of the great man consist in loving the people?

Answer: To manifest the clear character is to bring about the substance of the state of forming one body with Heaven, Earth, and the myriad things, whereas loving the people is to put into universal operation the function of the state of forming one body. Hence manifesting the clear character consists in loving the people, and loving the people is the way to manifest the clear character.

[1] *Ibid.*

Therefore, only when I love my father, the fathers of others, and the fathers of all men can my humanity really form one body with my father, the fathers of others, and the fathers of all men. When it truly forms one body with them, then the clear character of filial piety will be manifested. Only when I love my brother, the brothers of others, and the brothers of all men can my humanity really form one body with my brother, the brothers of others, and the brothers of all men. When it truly forms one body with them, then the clear character of brotherly respect will be manifested. Everything from ruler, minister, husband, wife, and friends to mountains, rivers, spiritual beings, birds, animals, and plants should be truly loved in order to realize my humanity that forms one body with them, and then my clear character will be completely manifested, and I will really form one body with Heaven, Earth, and the myriad things. This is what is meant by "manifesting the clear character throughout the world."[1] This is what is meant by "regulation of the family," "ordering the state," and "bringing peace to the world.[2] This is what is meant by "full development of one's nature."[3]

Question: Then why does the learning of the great man consist in "abiding in the highest good"?[4]

Answer: The highest good is the ultimate principle of manifesting character and loving people. The nature endowed in us by Heaven is pure and perfect. The fact that it is intelligent, clear, and not beclouded is evidence of the emanation and revelation of the highest good. It is the original substance of the clear character which is called innate knowledge of the good. As the highest good emanates and reveals itself, we will consider right as right and wrong as wrong. Things of greater or less importance and situations of grave or light character will be responded to as they act upon us. In all our changes and movements, we will stick to no particular point, but possess in ourselves the mean that is perfectly natural. This is the ultimate of the normal nature of man and the principle of things. There can be no consideration of adding or subtracting anything to or from it. Such a suggestion reveals selfish ideas and shallow cunning, and cannot be said to be the highest good. Naturally, how can anyone who does not watch over himself carefully when alone, and who has no refinement and singleness of mind, attain to such a state of perfection? Later generations fail to

1 The text of the *Great Learning.*

2 *Ibid.*

3 *Doctrine of the Mean,* ch. 22.

4 The text of the *Great Learning.*

realize that the highest good is inherent in their own minds, but exercise their selfish ideas and cunning and grope for it outside their minds, believing that every event and every object has its own peculiar definite principle. For this reason the law of right and wrong is obscured; the mind becomes concerned with fragmentary and isolated details and broken pieces; the selfish desires of man become rampant and the Principle of Nature is at an end. And thus the learning of manifesting character and loving people is everywhere thrown into confusion. In the past there have, of course, been people who wanted to manifest their clear character. But simply because they did not know how to abide in the highest good, but instead drove their own minds toward something too lofty, they thereby lost them in illusions, emptiness, and quietness, having nothing to do with the work of the family, the state, and the world. Such are the followers of Buddhism and Taosim. There have, of course, been those who wanted to love their people. Yet simply because they did not know how to abide in the highest good, but instead sank their own minds in base and trifling things, they thereby lost them in scheming strategy and cunning techniques, having neither the sincerity of humanity nor that of commiseration. Such are the followers of the Five Despots[1] and the pursuers of success and profit. All of these defects are due to a failure to know how to abide in the highest good. Therefore abiding in the highest good is to manifesting character and loving people as the carpenter's square and compass are to the square and the circle, or rule and measure to length, or balances and scales to weight. If the square and the circle do not abide by the compass and the carpenter's square, their standard will be wrong; if length does not abide by the rule and measure, its adjustment will be lost; if weight does not abide by the balances, its exactness will be gone; and if manifesting clear character and loving people do not abide by the highest good, their foundation will disappear. Therefore, abiding in the highest good so as to love people and manifest the clear character is what is meant by the learning of the great man.

Question: "Only after knowing what to abide in can one be calm. Only after having been calm can one be tranquil. Only after having achieved tranquillity can one have peaceful repose. Only after having peaceful repose can one begin to deliberate. Only after deliberation can the end be attained."[2] How do you explain this?

Answer: People fail to realize that the highest good is in their minds and seek it outside. As they believe that everything or every

1 See above, sec. 11, n. 46.   2 The text of the *Great Learning*.

event has its own definite principle, they search for the highest good in individual things. Consequently, the mind becomes fragmentary, isolated, broken into pieces; mixed and confused, it has no definite direction. Once it is realized that the highest good is in the mind and does not depend on any search outside, then the mind will have definite direction and there will be no danger of its becoming fragmentary, isolated, broken into pieces, mixed, or confused. When there is no such danger, the mind will not be erroneously perturbed but will be tranquil. Not being erroneously perturbed but being tranquil, it will be leisurely and at ease in its daily functioning and will attain peaceful repose. Being in peaceful repose, whenever a thought arises or an event acts upon it, the mind with its innate knowledge will thoroughly sift and carefully examine whether or not the thought or event is in accord with the highest good, and thus the mind can deliberate. With deliberation, every decision will be excellent and every act will be proper, and in this way the highest good will be attained.

Question: "Things have their roots and their branches."[1] A former scholar considered manifesting the clear character as the root (or fundamental) and renovating the people as the branch (or secondary), and thought that they are two things opposing each other as internal and external.[2] "Affairs have their beginnings and their ends."[3] The former scholar considered knowing what to abide in as the beginning and the attainment of the highest good as the end, both being one thing in harmonious continuity. According to you, "renovating the people" (*hsin-min*) should be read as "loving the people" (*ch'in-min*). If so, isn't the theory of root and branches in some respect incorrect?

Answer: The theory of beginnings and ends is in general right. Even if we read "renovating the people" as "loving the people" and say that manifesting the character is the root and loving the people is the branches, it is not incorrect. The main thing is that root and branches should not be distinguished as two different things. The trunk of the tree is called the root, and the twigs are called the branches. It is precisely because the tree is one that its parts can be called root and branches. If they are said to be two different things, then since they are two distinct objects, how can we speak of them as root and branches of the same thing? Since the idea of renovating the people is different from that of loving the people, obviously the task of manifesting the character and that of

1 *Ibid.*   2 Chu Hsi, *Ta-hsüeh chang-chü,* commentary on the text.
3 The text of the *Great Learning.*

loving the people are two different things. If it is realized that manifesting the clear character is to love the people and loving the people is to manifest the clear character, how can they be split in two? What the former scholar said is due to his failure to realize that manifesting the character and loving the people are basically one thing. Instead, he believed them to be two different things and consequently, although he knew that root and branches should be one, yet he could not help splitting them in two.

Question: The passage from the phrase, "The ancients who wished to manifest their clear character throughout the world" to the clause, "first [order their state . . . regulate their families . . .] cultivate their personal lives,"[1] can be understood by your theory of manifesting the character and loving the people. May I ask what task, what procedure, and what effort are involved in the passage from "Those who wished to cultivate their personal lives would [first rectify their minds . . . make their will sincere . . . extend their knowledge]" to the clause, "the extension of knowledge consists in the investigation of things"?[2]

Answer: This passage fully explains the task of manifesting the character, loving the people, and abiding in the highest good. The person, the mind, the will, knowledge, and things constitute the order followed in the task. While each of them has its own place, they are really one thing. Investigating, extending, being sincere, rectifying, and cultivating are the task performed in the procedure. Although each has its own name, they are really one affair. What is it that is called the person? It is the physical functioning of the mind. What is it that is called the mind? It is the clear and intelligent master of the person. What is meant by cultivating the personal life? It means to do good and get rid of evil. Can the body by itself do good and get rid of evil? The clear and intelligent master must desire to do good and get rid of evil before the body that functions physically can do so. Therefore he who wishes to cultivate his personal life must first rectify his mind.

Now the original substance of the mind is man's nature. Human nature being universally good, the original substance of the mind is correct. How is it that any effort is required to rectify the mind? The reason is that, while the original substance of the mind is originally correct, incorrectness enters when one's thoughts and will are in operation. Therefore he who wishes to rectify his mind must rectify it in connection with the operation of his thoughts and

1 *Ibid.*   2 *Ibid.*

will. If, whenever a good thought arises, he really loves it as he loves beautiful colors, and whenever an evil thought arises, he really hates it as he hates bad odors, then his will will always be sincere and his mind can be rectified.

However, what arises from the will may be good or evil, and unless there is a way to make clear the distinction between good and evil, there will be a confusion of truth and untruth. In that case, even if one wants to make his will sincere, he cannot do so. Therefore he who wishes to make his will sincere must extend his knowledge. By extension is meant to reach the limit. The word "extension" is the same as that used in the saying, "Mourning is to be carried to the utmost degree of grief."[1] In the *Book of Changes* it is said: "Knowing the utmost, one should reach it."[2] "Knowing the utmost" means knowledge and "reaching it" means extension. The extension of knowledge is not what later scholars understand as enriching and widening knowledge.[3] It is simply extending one's innate knowledge of the good to the utmost. This innate knowledge of the good is what Mencius meant when he said, "The sense of right and wrong is common to all men."[4] The sense of right and wrong requires no deliberation to know, nor does it depend on learning to function.[5] This is why it is called innate knowledge. It is my nature endowed by Heaven, the original substance of my mind, naturally intelligent, shining, clear, and understanding.

Whenever a thought or a wish arises, my mind's faculty of innate knowledge itself is always conscious of it. Whether it is good or evil, my mind's innate knowing faculty itself also knows it. It has nothing to do with others. Therefore, although an inferior man may have done all manner of evil, when he sees a superior man he will surely try to disguise this fact, concealing what is evil and displaying what is good in himself.[6] This shows that innate knowledge of the good does not permit any self-deception. Now the only way to distinguish good and evil in order to make the will sincere is to extend to the utmost the knowledge of the innate faculty. Why is this? When [a good] thought or wish arises, the innate faculty of my mind already knows it to be good. Suppose I do not sincerely love it but instead turn away from it. I would then

1 *Analects,* 19:14.

2 Commentary on hexagram no. 1. Cf. trans. by Legge, *Yi King,* p. 410.

3 Chu-Hsi, *Ta-hsüeh chang-chü,* commentary on the text.

4 *Book of Mencius,* 2A:6, 6A:6.

5 Quoting *Book of Mencius,* 7A:15.

6 Paraphrasing the *Great Learning,* ch. 6.

be regarding good as evil and obscuring my innate faculty which knows the good. When [an evil] thought or wish arises, the innate faculty of my mind already knows it to be evil. If I did not sincerely hate it but instead carried it out, I would be regarding evil as good and obscuring my innate faculty which knows evil. In such cases what is supposed to be knowledge is really ignorance. How then can the will be made sincere? If what the innate faculty knows to be good or evil is sincerely loved or hated, one's innate knowing faculty is not deceived and the will can be made sincere.

Now, when one sets out to extend his innate knowledge to the utmost, does this mean something illusory, hazy, in a vacuum, and unreal? No, it means something real. Therefore, the extension of knowledge must consist in the investigation of things. A thing is an event. For every emanation of the will there must be an event corresponding to it. The event to which the will is directed is a thing. To investigate is to rectify. It is to rectify that which is incorrect so it can return to its original correctness. To rectify that which is not correct is to get rid of evil, and to return to correctness is to do good. This is what is meant by investigation. The *Book of History* says, "He [Emperor Yao] investigated (*ko*) heaven above and earth below";[1] "[Emperor Shun] investigated (*ko*) in the temple of illustrious ancestors";[2] and "[The ruler] rectifies (*ko*) the evil of his heart."[3] The word "investigation" (*ko*) in the phrase "the investigation of things" combines the two meanings.

If one sincerely loves the good known by the innate faculty but does not in reality do the good as he comes into contact with the thing to which the will is directed, it means that the thing has not been investigated and that the will to love the good is not yet sincere. If one sincerely hates the evil known by the innate faculty but does not in reality get rid of the evil as he comes into contact with the thing to which the will is directed, it means that the thing has not been investigated and that the will to hate evil is not sincere. If as we come into contact with the thing to which the will is directed, we really do the good and get rid of the evil to the utmost which is known by the innate faculty, then everything will be investigated and what is known by our innate faculty will not be deficient or obscured but will be extended to the utmost. Then the mind will be joyous in itself, happy and without regret, the functioning of the will will carry with it no self-deception, and sincerity may be said to have been attained. Therefore it is said, "When

---

1 *Book of History*, "Canon of Yao." Cf. trans. by Legge, *Shoo King*, p. 15.

2 *Ibid.*, "Canon of Shun." Cf. Legge, *Shoo King*, p. 41.

3 *Ibid.*, "The Charge to Ch'iung." Cf. Legge, *Shoo King*, p. 585.

things are investigated, knowledge is extended; when knowledge is extended, the will becomes sincere; when the will is sincere, the mind is rectified; and when the mind is rectified, the personal life is cultivated."[1] While the order of the tasks involves a sequence of first and last, in substance they are one and cannot be so separated. At the same time, while the order and the tasks cannot be separated into first and last, their function must be so refined as not to be wanting in the slightest degree. This is why the doctrine of investigation, extension, being sincere, and rectification is a correct exposition of the true heritage of Sage-Emperors Yao and Shun and why it coincides with Confucius' own ideas.

[1] The text of the *Great Learning*.

7

MORAL CONSCIENCE
AND DIVINE LAW*

Joseph Butler ▓

Joseph Butler (1692–1752) was a Bishop of the Church of England. His best-known works are Fifteen Sermons *and* The Analogy of Religion.

"For when the Gentiles, which have not the law, do by nature the things contained in the law, these, having not the law, are a law unto themselves."
                                                                        —Rom. ii. 14.

As speculative truth admits of different kinds of proof, so likewise moral obligations may be shown by different methods. If the real nature of any creature leads him and is adapted to such and such purposes only, or more than to any other; this is a reason to believe the Author of that nature intended it for those purposes. Thus there is no doubt the eye was intended for us to see with. And the more complex any constitution is, and the greater variety of parts there are which thus tend to some one end, the stronger is the proof that such end was designed. However, when the inward frame of man is considered as any guide in morals, the utmost caution must be used that none make peculiarities in their own temper, or anything which is the effect of particular-customs, though observable in several, the standard of what is common to the species; and above all, that the highest principle be not forgot or excluded, that to which belongs the adjustment and correction of all other inward movements and affections: which principle will of course have some influence, but which being in nature supreme, as shall now be shown, ought to preside over and govern all the rest. The difficulty of rightly observing the two former cautions; the appearance there is of some small diversity amongst mankind with respect to this faculty, with respect to their natural sense of moral good and evil; and the attention necessary to survey with any exactness what passes within, have occasioned that it is not so much agreed what is the standard of the internal nature of man, as of his external form.

* From Joseph Butler, *The Analogy of Religion*. Reprinted by permission of G. Bell & Sons, Ltd.

Neither is this last exactly settled. Yet we understand one another when we speak of the shape of a human body: so likewise we do when we speak of the heart and inward principles, how far soever the standard is from being exact or precisely fixed. There is therefore ground for an attempt of showing men to themselves, of showing them what course of life and behaviour their real nature points out and would lead them to. Now obligations of virtue shown, and motives to the practice of it enforced, from a review of the nature of man, are to be considered as an appeal to each particular person's heart and natural conscience: as the external senses are appealed to for the proof of things cognizable by them. Since, then, our inward feelings, and the perceptions we receive from our external senses, are equally real; to argue from the former to life and conduct is as little liable to exception, as to argue from the latter to absolute speculative truth. A man can as little doubt whether his eyes were given him to see with, as he can doubt of the truth of the science of *optics* deduced from ocular experiments. And allowing the inward feeling, shame; a man can as little doubt whether it wɛs given him to prevent his doing shameful actions, as he can doubt whether his eyes were given him to guide his steps. And as to these inward feelings themselves; that they are real, that man has in his nature passions and affections, can no more be questioned, than that he has external senses. Neither can the former be wholly mistaken; though to a certain degree liable to greater mistakes than the latter.

There can be no doubt but that several propensions or instincts, several principles in the heart of man, carry him to society, and to contribute to the happiness of it, in a sense and a manner in which no inward principle leads him to evil. These principles, propensions, or instincts which lead him to do good, are approved of by a certain faculty within, quite distinct from these propensions themselves. All this hath been fully made out in the foregoing discourse.

But it may be said, "What is all this, though true, to the purpose of virtue and religion? these require, not only that we do good to others when we are led this way, by benevolence or reflection, happening to be stronger than other principles, passions, or appetites; but likewise that the *whole* character be formed upon thought and reflection that *every* action be directed by some determinate rule, some other rule than the strength and prevalency of any principle or passion. What sign is there in our nature (for the inquiry is only about what is to be collected from thence) that this was intended by its Author? Or how does so various and fickle a temper as that of man appear adapted thereto? It may indeed be absurd and unnatural for men to act without any reflection; nay, without regard to that particular kind of reflection which you call conscience; because this does belong to our nature. For as there never was a man but who approved one place, prospect, building, before another: so it does not appear that there ever was a man who would not have approved an action of humanity rather than of cruelty; interest and passion being quite out of the case. But interest and passion do come in, and are often too strong for and prevail over reflection and conscience. Now as brutes have various instincts, by which they are carried on to the end the Author of their nature intended them for: is not man in the same condition; with this difference only, that to his instincts (*i.e.,* appetites and passions) is added the principle of reflection or conscience? And as brutes act agreeably to their nature, in following that principle or particular instinct which for the present is strongest in them: does not man likewise act agreeably to his nature, or obey the law of his creation, by following that principle, be it passion or conscience, which for the present happens to be strongest in him? Thus different men are by their particular nature hurried on to pursue honour, or riches, or pleasure: there are also persons whose temper leads them in an uncommon degree to kindness, compassion, doing good to their fellow-creatures: as there are others who are given to suspend their judgment, to weigh and consider things, and to act upon thought and reflection. Let every one, then, quietly follow his nature; as passion, reflection, appetite, the several parts of it, happen to be strongest: but let not the man of virtue take upon him to blame the ambitious, the covetous, the dissolate; since these equally with him obey and follow their nature. Thus, as in some cases we follow our nature in doing the works *contained in the law,* so in other cases we follow nature in doing contrary."

Now all this licentious talk entirely goes upon a supposition, that men follow their nature in the same sense, in violating the known rules of justice and honesty for the sake of a present gratification, as they do in following those rules when they have no temptation to the contrary. And if this were true, that could not be so which St. Paul asserts, that men are *by nature a law to themselves.* If by following nature were meant only acting as we please, it would indeed be ridiculous to speak of nature as any guide in morals: nay, the very mention of deviating from nature would be absurd; and the mention of following it, when spoken by way of distinction, would absolutely have no meaning. For did ever any one act otherwise than as he pleased? And yet the ancients speak of deviating from nature as vice; and of following nature so much as a distinction, that according to them the perfection of virtue consists therein. So that language itself should teach people another sense to the words *following nature,* than barely acting as we please. Let it however be observed, that though the words *human nature* are to be explained, yet the real question of this discourse is not concerning the meaning of words, any other than as the explanation of them may be needful to make out and explain the assertion, that *every man is naturally a law to himself,* that *every one may find within himself the rule of right, and obligations to follow it.* This St. Paul affirms in the words of the text, and this the foregoing objection really denies by seeming to allow it. And the objection will be fully answered, and the text before us explained, by observing that *nature* is considered in different views, and the word used in different senses; and by showing in what view it is considered, and in what sense the word is used, when intended to express and signify that which is the guide of life, that by which men are a law to themselves I say, the explanation of the term will be sufficient, because from thence it will appear, that in some senses of the word *nature* cannot be, but that in another sense it manifestly is, a law to us.

I. By nature is often meant no more than some principle in man, without regard either to the kind or degree of it. Thus the passion of anger, and the affection of parents to their children, would be called equally *natural.* And as the same person hath often contrary principles, which at the same time draw contrary ways, he may by the same action both follow and contradict his nature in this sense of the word; he may follow one passion and contradict another.

II. *Nature* is frequently spoken of as consisting in those passions which are strongest, and most influence the actions; which being vicious ones, mankind is in this sense naturally vicious, or vicious by nature. Thus St. Paul says of the Gentiles, *who were dead in trespasses and sins, and walked according to the spirit of disobedience, that they were by nature the children of wrath*[1]. They could be no otherwise *children of wrath* by nature, than they were vicious by nature.

Here, then, are two different senses of the word *nature,* in neither of which men can at all be said to be a law to themselves. They are mentioned only to be excluded; to prevent their being confounded, as the latter is in the objection, with another sense of it, which is now to be inquired after and explained.

III. The apostle asserts, that the Gentiles *do by nature the things contained in the law.* Nature is indeed here put by way of distinction from revelation, but yet it is not a mere negative. He

[1] Ephes. ii. 3.

intends to express more than that by which they *did not,* that by which they *did* the works of the law; namely, by *nature.* It is plain the meaning of the word is not the same in this passage as in the former, where it is spoken of as evil; for in this latter it is spoken of as good; as that by which they acted, or might have acted virtuously. What that is in man by which he is *naturally a law to himself,* is explained in the following words: *Which shew the work of the law written in their hearts, their consciences also bearing witness, and their thoughts the mean while accusing or else excusing one another.* If there be a distinction to be made between the *works written in their hearts* and the *witness of conscience;* by the former must be meant the natural disposition to kindness and compassion, to do what is of good report, to which this apostle often refers; that part of the nature of man, treated of in the foregoing discourse, which with very little reflection and of course leads him to society, and by means of which he naturally acts a just and good part in it, unless other passions or interests lead him astray. Yet since other passions, and regards to private interest, which lead us (though indirectly, yet they lead us) astray, are themselves in a degree equally natural, and often most prevalent; and since we have no method of seeing the particular degrees in which one or the other is placed in us by nature; it is plain the former, considered merely as natural, good and right as they are, can no more be a law to us than the latter. But there is a superior principle of reflection or conscience in every man, which distinguishes between the internal principles of his heart, as well as his external actions which passes judgment upon himself and them; pronounces determinately some actions to be in themselves just, right, good; others to be in themselves evil, wrong, unjust: which, without being consulted, without being advised with, magisterially exerts itself, and approves or condemns him the doer of them accordingly: and which, if not forcibly stopped, naturally and always of course goes on to anticipate a higher and more effectual sentence, which shall hereafter second and affirm its own. But this part of the office of conscience is beyond my present design explicitly to consider. It is by this faculty, natural to man, that he is a moral agent, that he is a law to himself: but this faculty, I say, not to be considered merely as a principle in his heart, which is to have some influence as well as others; but considered as a faculty in kind and in nature supreme over all others, and which bears its own authority of being so.

This *prerogative,* this *natural supremacy,* of the faculty which surveys, approves or disapproves the several affections of our mind and actions of our lives, being that by which men *are a law to themselves,* their conformity or disobedience to which law of our nature renders their actions, in the highest and most proper sense, natural or unnatural; it is fit it be further explained to you: and I hope it will be so, if you will attend to the following reflections.

Man may act according to that principle or inclination which for the present happens to be strongest, and yet act in a way disproportionate to, and violate his real proper nature. Suppose a brute creature by any bait to be allured into a snare, by which he is destroyed. He plainly followed the bent of his nature, leading him to gratify his appetite: there is an entire correspondence between his whole nature and such an action: such action therefore is natural. But suppose a man, foreseeing the same danger of certain ruin, should rush into it for the sake of a present gratification; he in this instance would follow his strongest desire, as did the brute creature: but there would be as manifest a disproportion, between the nature of a man and such an action, as between the meanest work of art and the skill of the greatest master in that art: which disproportion arises, not from considering the action singly in *itself* or in its *consequences,* but from *comparison* of it with the nature of the agent. And since such an action is utterly disproportionate to the nature of man, it is in the strictest and most proper sense un-natural; this word expressing that disproportion. Therefore instead of the words *disproportionate to his nature,* the word *unnatural* may now be put; this being more familiar to us; but let it be observed, that it stands for the same thing precisely.

Now what is it which renders such a rash action unnatural? Is it that he went against the principle of reasonable and cool self-love, considered *merely* as a part of his nature? No: for if he had acted the contrary way, he would equally have gone against a principle, or part of his nature, namely, passion or appetite. But to deny a present appetite, from foresight that the gratification of it would end in immediate ruin or extreme misery, is by no means an unnatural action; whereas to contradict or go against cool self-love for the sake of such gratification, is so in the instance before us. Such an action then being unnatural; and its being so not arising from a man's going against a principle or desire barely, nor in going against that principle or desire which happens for the present to be strongest; it necessarily follows, that there must be some other difference or distinction to be made between these two principles, passion and cool self-love, than what I have yet taken notice of. And this difference, not being a difference in strength or degree, I call a difference in *nature* and in *kind.* And since, in the instance still before us, if passion prevails over self-love, the consequent action is unnatural; but if self-love prevails over passion, the action is natural: it is manifest that self-love is in human nature a superior principle to passion. This may be contradicted without violating that nature; but the former cannot. So that, if we will act conformably to the economy of man's nature, reasonable self-love must govern. Thus, without particular consideration of conscience, we may have a clear conception of the *superior nature* of one inward principle to another; and see that there really is this natural superiority, quite distinct from degrees of strength and prevalency.

Let us now take a view of the nature of man, as consisting partly of various appetites, passions, affections, and partly of the principle of reflection or conscience; leaving quite out all consideration of the different degrees of strength, in which either of them prevail, and it will further appear that there is this natural superiority of one inward principle to another, and that it is even part of the idea of reflection or conscience.

Passion or appetite implies a direct simple tendency towards such and such objects, without distinction of the means by which they are to be obtained. Consequently it will often happen there will be a desire of particular objects, in cases where they cannot be obtained without manifest injury to others. Reflection or conscience comes in, and disapproves the pursuit of them in these circumstances; but the desire remains. Which is to be obeyed, appetite or reflection? Cannot this question be answered, from the economy and constitution of human nature merely, without saying which is strongest? Or need this at all come into consideration? Would not the question be *intelligibly* and fully answered by saying, that the principle of reflection or conscience being compared with the various appetites, passions, and affections in men, the former is manifestly superior and chief, without regard to strength? And how often soever the latter happens to prevail, it is mere *usurpation:* the former remains in nature and in kind its superior; and every instance of such prevalence of the latter is an instance of breaking in upon and violation of the constitution of man.

All this is no more than the distinction, which everybody is acquainted with, between *mere power* and *authority:* only instead of being intended to express the difference between what is possible, and what is lawful in civil government; here it has been shown applicable to the several principles in the mind of man. Thus that principle, by which we survey, and either approve or disapprove our own heart, temper, and actions, is not only to be considered as what is in its turn to have some influence; which may be said of every passion, of the lowest appetites: but likewise as being superior; as from its very nature manifestly claiming superiority over all others; insomuch that you cannot form a notion of this faculty, conscience, without taking in judgment, direction, superintendency. This is a constituent part of the idea, that is, of the faculty itself: and to preside and govern, from the very economy and constitution of man, belongs to it. Had it strength, as it had right: had it power, as it had manifest authority, it would absolutely govern the world.

This gives us a further view of the nature of man shows us what course of life we were made for: not only that our real nature leads us to be influenced in some degree by reflection and conscience; but likewise in what degree we are to be influenced by it, if we will fall in with, and act agreeably to, the constitution of our nature: that this faculty was placed within to be our proper governor; to direct and regulate all under principles, passions, and motives of action. This is its right and office: thus sacred is its authority. And how often soever men violate and rebelliously refuse to submit to it, for supposed interest which they cannot otherwise obtain, or for the sake of passion which they cannot otherwise gratify; this makes no alteration as to the *natural right* and *office* of conscience.

Let us now turn this whole matter another way, and suppose there was no such thing at all as this natural supremacy of conscience; that there was no distinction to be made between one inward principle and another, but only that of strength; and see what would be the consequence.

Consider, then, what is the latitude and compass of the actions of man with regard to himself, his fellow-creatures, and the Supreme Being? What are their bounds, besides that of our natural power? With respect to the two first, they are plainly no other than these: no man seeks misery as such for himself; and no one unprovoked does mischief to another for its own sake. For in every degree within these bounds, mankind knowingly, from passion or wantonness, bring ruin and misery upon themselves and others. And impiety and profaneness, I mean, what every one would call so who believes the being of God, have absolutely no bounds at all. Men blaspheme the Author of Nature, formally and in words renounce their allegiance to their Creator. Put an instance, then, with respect to any one of these three. Though we should suppose profane swearing, and in general that kind of impiety now mentioned, to mean nothing, yet it implies wanton disregard and irreverence towards an infinite Being, our Creator: and is this as suitable to the nature of man, as reverence and dutiful submission of heart towards that Almighty Being? Or suppose a man guilty of parricide, with all the circumstances of cruelty which such an action can admit of. This action is done in consequence of its principle being for the present strongest: and if there be no difference between inward principles, but only that of strength; the strength being given, you have the whole nature of the man given, so far as it relates to this matter. The action plainly corresponds to the principle, the principle being in that degree of strength it was: it therefore corresponds to the whole nature of the man. Upon comparing the action and the whole nature, there arises no disproportion, there appears no unsuitableness between them. Thus the *murder of a father* and the *nature of man* correspond to each other, as the same nature and an act of filial duty. If there be no difference between inward principles, but only that of strength; we can make no distinction between these two actions, considered as the actions of such a creature; but in our coolest hours must approve or disapprove them equally: than which nothing can be reduced to a greater absurdity.

. . .

THE natural supremacy of reflection or conscience being thus established; we may from it form a distinct notion of what is meant by *human nature,* when virtue is said to consist in following it, and vice in deviating from it.

As the idea of a civil constitution implies in it united strength, various subordinations, under one direction, that of the supreme authority; the different strength of each particular member of the society not coming into the idea: whereas, if you leave out the subordination, the union, and the one direction, you destroy and lose it: so reason, several appetites, passions, and affections, prevailing in different degrees of strength, is not *that* idea or notion of *human nature;* but *that nature* consists in these several principles considered as having a natural respect to each other, in the several passions being naturally subordinate to the one superior principle of reflection or conscience. Every bias, instinct, propension within, is a natural part of our nature, but not the whole: add to these the superior faculty, whose office it is to adjust, manage, and preside over them, and take in this its natural superiority, and you complete the idea of human nature. And as in civil government the constitution is broken in upon, and violated by power and strength prevailing over authority; so the constitution of man is broken in upon and violated by the lower faculties or principles within prevailing over that which is in its nature supreme over them all. Thus, when it is said by ancient writers, that tortures and death are not so contrary to human nature as injustice; by this to be sure is not meant, that the aversion to the former in mankind is less strong and prevalent than their aversion to the latter: but that the former is only contrary to our nature considered in a partial view, and which takes in only the lowest part of it, that which we have in common with the brutes; whereas the latter is contrary to our nature, considered in a higher sense, as a system and constitution contrary to the whole economy of man.[1]

And from all these things put together, nothing can be more evident, than that, exclusive of revelation, man cannot be considered as a creature left by his Maker to act at random, and live at large up to the extent of his natural power, as passion, humour, wilfulness, happen to carry him; which is the condition brute creatures are in: but that *from his make, constitution, or nature, he is in the strictest and most proper sense a law to himself.* He hath the rule of right within: what is wanting is only that he honestly attend to it.

The inquiries which have been made by men of leisure after some general rule, the conformity to, or disagreement from which, should denominate our actions good or evil, are in many respects of great service. Yet let any plain honest man, before he engages in any

[1] Every man in his physical nature is one individual single agent. He has likewise properties and principles, each of which may be considered separately, and without regard to the respects which they have to each other. Neither of these are the nature we are taking a view of. But it is the inward frame of man considered as a *system* or *constitution:* whose several parts are united, not by a physical principle of individuation, but by the respects they have to each other; the chief of which is the subjection which the appetites, passions, and particular affections have to the one supreme principle of reflection or conscience. The system or constitution is formed by and consists in these respects and this subjection. Thus the body is a *system* or *constitution:* so is a tree: so is every machine. Consider all the several parts of a tree without the natural respects they have to each other, and you have not at all the idea of a tree; but add these respects, and this gives you the idea. The body may be impaired by sickness, a tree may decay, a machine be out of order, and yet the system and constitution of them not totally dissolved. There is plainly somewhat which answers to all this in the moral constitution of man. Whoever will consider his own nature, will see that the several appetites, passions, and particular affections, have different respects amongst themselves. They are restraints upon, and are in a proportion to each other. This proportion is just and perfect, when all those under principles are perfectly coincident with conscience, so far as their nature permits, and in all cases under its absolute and entire direction. The least excess or defect, the least alteration of the due proportions amongst themselves, or of their coincidence with conscience, though not proceeding into action, is some degree of disorder in the moral constitution. But perfection, though plainly intelligible and unsupposable, was never attained by any man. If the higher principle of reflection maintains its place, and as much as it can corrects that disorder, and hinders it from breaking out into action, this is all that can be expected from such a creature as man. And though the appetites and passions have not their exact due proportion to each other; though they often strive for mastery with judgment or reflection: yet, since the superiority of this principle to all others is the chief respect which forms the constitution, so far as this superiority is maintained, the character, the man, is good, worthy, virtuous.

course of action, ask himself, Is this I am going about right, or is it wrong? Is it good, or is it evil? I do not in the least doubt but that this question would be answered agreeably to truth and virtue, by almost any fair man in almost any circumstance. Neither do there appear any cases which look like exceptions to this; but those of superstition, and of partiality to ourselves. Superstition may perhaps be somewhat of an exception: but partiality to ourselves is not; this being itself dishonesty. For a man to judge that to be the equitable, the moderate, the right part for him to act, which he would see to be hard, unjust, oppressive in another; this is plain vice, and can proceed only from great unfairness of mind.

But allowing that mankind hath the rule of right within himself, yet it may be asked, "What obligations are we under to attend to and follow it?" I answer: it has been proved that man by his nature is a law to himself, without the particular distinct consideration of the positive sanctions of that law; the rewards and punishments which we feel, and those which from the light of reason we have ground to believe, are annexed to it. The question then carries its own answer along with it. Your obligation to obey this law, is its being the law of your nature. That your conscience approves of and attests to such a course of action, is itself alone an obligation. Conscience does not only offer itself to show us the way we should walk in, but it likewise carries its own authority with it, that it is our natural guide; the guide assigned us by the Author of our nature: it therefore belongs to our condition of being, it is our duty to walk in that path, and follow this guide, without looking about to see whether we may not possibly forsake them with impunity.

However, let us hear what is to be said against obeying this law of our nature. And the sum is no more than this "Why should we be concerned about anything out of and beyond ourselves? If we do find within ourselves regards to others, and restraints of we know not how many different kinds; yet these being embarrassments, and hindering us from going the nearest way to our own good, why should we not endeavour to suppress and get over them?"

Thus people go on with words, which, when applied to human nature, and the condition in which it is placed in this world, have really no meaning. For does not all this kind of talk go upon supposition, that our happiness in this world consists in somewhat quite distinct from regard to others; and that it is the privilege of vice to be without restraint or confinement? Whereas, on the contrary, the enjoyments, in a manner all the common enjoyments of life, even the pleasures of vice, depend upon these regards of one kind or another to our fellow-creatures. Throw off all regards to others, and we should be quite indifferent to infamy and to honour; there could be no such thing at all as ambition; and scarce any such thing as covetousness; for we should likewise be equally indifferent to the disgrace of poverty, the several neglects and kinds of contempt which accompany this state; and to the reputation of riches, the regard and respect they usually procure. Neither is restraint by any means peculiar to one course of life: but our very nature, exclusive of conscience and our condition, lays us under an absolute necessity of it. We cannot gain any end whatever without being confined to the proper means, which is often the most painful and uneasy confinement. And in numberless instances a present appetite cannot be gratified without such apparent and immediate ruin and misery, that the most dissolute man in the world chooses to forego the pleasure, rather than endure the pain.

Is the meaning then, to indulge those regards to our fellow-creatures, and submit to those restraints, which upon the whole are attended with more satisfaction than uneasiness, and get over only those which bring more uneasiness and inconvenience than satisfaction? "Doubtless this was our meaning." You have changed sides then. Keep to this; be consistent with yourselves; and you and the men of virtue are *in general* perfectly agreed. But let us take care and avoid mistakes. Let it not be taken for granted that the temper of envy, rage, resentment, yields greater delight than meekness, forgiveness, compassion, and goodwill: especially when it is acknowledged that rage, envy, resentment, are in themselves mere misery; and the satisfaction arising from the indulgence of them is little more than relief from that misery; whereas the temper of compassion and benevolence is itself delightful; and the indulgence of it, by doing good, affords new positive delight and enjoyment. Let it not be taken for granted, that the satisfaction arising from the reputation of riches and power, however obtained, and from the respect paid to them, is greater than the satisfaction arising from the reputation of justice, honesty, charity, and the esteem which is universally acknowledged to be their due. And if it be doubtful which of these satisfactions is the greatest, as there are persons who think neither of them very considerable, yet there can be no doubt concerning ambition and covetousness, virtue and a good mind, considered in themselves, and as leading to different courses of life; there can, I say, be no doubt, which temper and which course is attended with most peace and tranquillity of mind, which with most perplexity, vexation, and inconvenience. And both the virtues and vices which have been now mentioned do, in a manner, equally imply in them regards of one kind or another to our fellow-creatures. And with respect to restraint and confinement: whoever will consider the restraints from fear and shame, the dissimulation, mean arts of concealment, servile compliances, one or other of which belong to almost every course of vice, will soon be convinced that the man of virtue is by no means upon a disadvantage in this respect. How many instances are there in which men feel and own and cry aloud under the chains of vice with which they are enthralled, and which yet they will not shake off! How many instances, in which persons manifestly go through more pains and self-denial to gratify a vicious passion, than would have been necessary to the conquest of it! To this is to be added, that when virtue is become habitual, when the temper of it is acquired, what was before confinement ceases to be so, by becoming choice and delight. Whatever restraint and guard upon ourselves may be needful to unlearn any unnatural distortion or odd gesture; yet, in all propriety of speech, natural behaviour must be the most easy and unrestrained. It is manifest that, in the common course of life, there is seldom any inconsistency between our duty and what is *called* interest: it is much seldomer that there is any inconsistency between duty and what is really our present interest; meaning by interest, happiness and satisfaction. Self-love, then, though confined to the interest of the present world, does in general perfectly coincide with virtue; and leads us to one and the same course of life. But, whatever exceptions there are to this, which are much fewer than they are commonly thought, all shall be set right at the final distribution of things. It is a manifest absurdity to suppose evil prevailing finally over good, under the conduct and administration of a perfect mind.

The whole argument, which I have been now insisting upon, may be thus summed up, and given you in one view. The nature of man is adapted to some course of action or other. Upon comparing some actions with this nature, they appear suitable and correspondent to it: from comparison of other actions with the same nature, there arises to our view some unsuitableness or disproportion. The correspondence of actions to the nature of the agent renders them natural: their disproportion to it, unnatural. That an action is correspondent to the nature of the agent, does not arise from its being agreeable to the principle which happens to be the strongest: for it may be so, and yet be quite disproportionate to the nature of the agent. The correspondence, therefore, or disproportion, arises from somewhat else. This can be nothing but a difference in nature and kind, altogether distinct from strength, between the inward principles. Some, then, are in nature and kind superior to others. And the correspondence arises from the action being conformable to the higher principle; and the unsuitableness from its being contrary to it. Reasonable self-love and conscience are the chief or superior principles in the nature of man: because an action may be suitable to this nature, though all other principles be violated; but becomes unsuitable, if either of those are. Conscience and self-love, if we understand our true happiness, always lead us the same way. Duty and interest are perfectly coincident, for the most part in this world, but entirely and in every instance if we take in the future, and the whole; this being implied in the notion of a good and perfect administration of things. Thus they who have been so wise in their generation as to regard only their own supposed interest, at the expense and to the injury of others, shall at last find, that he who has given up all the advantages of the present world, rather than violate his conscience and the relations of life, has infinitely better provided for himself, and secured his own interest and happiness.

8

THE RELIGIOUS DIMENSION
OF THE MORAL IMPERATIVE*

Paul Tillich ▨

Paul Tillich (1886–1965) was a German philosophical theologian who spent most of his academic years at Union Theological Seminary in New York, and later taught at both Harvard and Chicago. Widely known as an interpreter of Christianity through the categories of both Hegelian idealism and Existentialism, Tillich wrote: Systematic Theology, The Courage to Be, *and* Dynamics of Faith.

To understand the meaning of the phrase "moral imperative," we must distinguish the three basic functions of the human spirit: morality, culture, and religion. When we call them functions of man's "spirit," we point to the dynamic unity of body and mind, of vitality and rationality, of the conscious and the unconscious, of the emotional and the intellectual. In every function of the human spirit the whole person is involved, and not merely one part or one element. As I have often insisted, we must revive the term "spirit" as designating a natural quality of man. It cannot be replaced by "mind" because "mind" is overweighted by its intellectual aspect.

None of the three functions of the spirit ever appears in isolation from the other two. They must be distinguished, nonetheless, because they are able to relate to each other in many different ways. Most concisely, we might say: morality is the constitution of the bearer of the spirit, the centered person; culture points to the creativity of the spirit and also to the totality of its creations; and religion is the self-transcendence of the spirit toward what is ultimate and unconditioned in being and meaning.

The first of these functions is our direct and primary subject. But in order to deal with it adequately we must continually refer to the other two. This presents a difficulty hardly to be resolved in an essay such as this, and only overcome within a system that comprises

* From *Morality and Beyond* by Paul Tillich. Copyright, 1963. Used by permission of Harper & Row.

the whole of man's interpretation of himself and the meaning of his life (which I undertook to develop in my *Systematic Theology*). The present study must presuppose but cannot develop such an interpretation; however, we must refer to it, and derive from it a possible solution of the problem at hand—"the religious principles of moral action."

The moral act establishes man as a person, and as a bearer of the spirit. It is the unconditional character of the moral imperative that gives ultimate seriousness both to culture and to religion. Without it culture would deteriorate into an aesthetic or utilitarian enterprise, and religion into an emotional distortion of mysticism. It was the prophetic message, as recorded in the Old Testament, that contrasted the moral imperative, in terms of the demand for justice, with both the culture and the religion of its time. The message is one of ultimate seriousness and has no equivalent in any other religion. The seriousness of Christianity depends upon it, as does also any ultimate seriousness in Western culture. Science and the arts, politics, education—all become empty and self-destructive if, in their creation, the moral imperative is disregarded. The imperative exhibits itself in scientific and artistic honesty to the extent of self-sacrifice; in one's commitment to humanity and justice in social relations and political actions; and in the love of one toward the other, as a consequence of experiencing the divine love. These are examples which demonstrate that, without the immanence of the moral imperative, both culture and religion disintegrate because of lack of ultimate seriousness.

The moral imperative is the command to become what one potentially is, a *person* within a community of persons. Only man, in the limit of our experience, can become a person, because only man is a completely centered self, having himself as a self in the face of a world to which he belongs and from which he is, at the same time, separated. This dual relation to his world, belongingness and separation, makes it possible for him to ask questions and find answers, to receive and make demands. As a centered self and individual, man can respond in knowledge and action to the stimuli that reach him from the world to which he belongs; but because he also *confronts* his world, and in this sense is free from it, he can respond "responsibly," namely, after deliberation and decision rather than through a determined compulsion. This is his greatness, but also his danger: it enables him to act *against* the moral demand. He can surrender to the disintegrating forces which tend to control the personal center and to destroy its unity. But before we pursue this line of thought, we must consider more thoroughly some of our concepts up to this point.

Man has a world, namely, a structured whole of innumerable parts, a *cosmos*, as the Greeks called it, because of its structured character which makes it accessible to man through acts of creative receiving and transforming. Having a world is more than having environment. Of course, man, like any other being, has environment; but in contrast to the higher animals, for example, he is not bound to it. He can transcend it in any direction, in imagination, thought and action (e.g., social utopias or ontological concepts or space exploration). Man has "world" through every part of his environment. His encounter with any of the objects surrounding him is always an encounter with the universe manifest in a particular object. Man never encounters *this* tree only as *this* tree, but also as *tree*, one of many trees, as an example of the species tree (in itself a special manifestation of the universal power of being).

Such an encounter presupposes freedom from the particular, and the ability to see the universal within the particular. The manifestation of this freedom is language. Language lives in universals. It is one and the same thing to have world, to transcend environment, and to speak in concepts and meaningful propositions. All this constitutes man's essential freedom and is the presupposition of man's experience of the moral imperative.

The moral imperative is the demand to become actually what one is essentially and therefore potentially. It is the power of man's being, given to him by nature, which he shall actualize in time and space. His true being shall become his actual being—this is the moral imperative. And since his true being is the being of a person in a community of persons, the moral imperative has this content: to become a person. Every moral act is an act in which an individual self establishes itself as a person.

Therefore, a moral act is not an act in obedience to an external law, human or divine. It is the inner law of our true being, of our essential or created nature, which demands that we actualize what follows from it. And an antimoral act is not the transgression of one or several precisely circumscribed commands, but an act that contradicts the self-realization of the person as a person and drives toward disintegration. It disrupts the centeredness of the person by giving predominance to partial trends, passions, desires, fears, and anxieties. The central control is weakened, often almost removed. And when this happens, and other partial trends also aspire to predominance, the self is split, and the conflicting trends make it their battlefield. The "will," in the sense of a self that acts from the centered totality of its being, is enslaved. Freedom is replaced by compulsion. Deliberation and decision, the hallmarks of freedom, become mere façades for overwhelming drives that predetermine the decision. The voice of man's essential being is silenced, step by step; and his disintegrating self, his depersonalization, shows the nature of the antimoral act and, by contrast, the nature of the moral act.

The moral act as the self-actualization of the centered self or the constitution of the person as a person, has analogies in the realm of all living beings, including man from the biological point of view. The analogy to the diminution or loss of centeredness in man is the psychosomatic phenomenon of disease. In disease, some processes that are necessary elements in the whole of a life process take an independent course and endanger the functioning of the whole. The cancerous growth of parts of the body is the most illuminating analogy to what happens in the centered self when particular trends conquer the center and destroy the unity of balanced trends. The analogy between the antimoral act and bodily disease is in many (somehow in all) cases more than an analogy. Both are expressions of the universal ambiguity of life, according to which the processes of self-integration are continuously combated by movements toward disintegration. For the ethical problem this means that the moral act is always a victory over disintegrating forces and that its aim is the actualization of man as a centered and therefore free person.

At this point a short semantic remark seems necessary. In this study, I use the terms "morality," "morals," and "moral" throughout most of the text. And sometimes the term "ethical" appears. There would be no confusion if, as I now suggest, we defined ethics as the "science of the moral." But this is not a generally accepted definition, the chief reason being that the word "moral," through historical accidents, has received several distorting connotations. Since the eighteenth century, at least in Europe, it has carried the implication of "moralism" in the sense of graceless legalistic ethics. And in the United States, it has, under the influence of Puritanism, taken on a sexual signification: to be "amoral" means to be sexually lawless, or at least to deny conventional sex ethics. Because of these two connotations, one has tried to replace "moral" by "ethical." Were this generally accepted, however, the term "ethical" would soon acquire the connotation of "moral," and there would be no change. Therefore, I recommend that "ethical" be reserved for the *theory* of morals, and that the term "moral" and its derivatives be purged of those associations, and used to describe the moral act itself in its fundamental significance.

We have discussed the nature of the moral act, its all-permeating character, and its immanence in the other two chief functions of man's spirit—the cultural and the religious. We must now ask: what is the religious dimension of the moral imperative, and (in Chapter II) what is the relation of cultural creativity to morality?

In answer to the first question, we can say: the religious dimension of the moral imperative is its unconditional character. This, of course, leads to a subsequent question: why is the moral imperative unconditional, and in which respects can one call it so, and in which not? In our daily life we use innumerable imperatives; but most of them are conditional: "you ought to leave *now,* if you wish to catch your plane." But perhaps you prefer to stay, even though you miss the plane. This obviously is a conditional imperative. However, if getting to the plane should be a matter of life and death, as, for example, in the case of a physician who must immediately operate upon a patient, the conditional imperative becomes unconditional. To miss the plane through negligence would then be an antimoral act, and would affect the person of the physician in a disintegrating manner. We might compare the disintegrating effect that the failure to save a drowning woman has on the main character in Camus' *The Fall.*

There are many cases in which conditional imperatives have some bearing on an unconditional imperative. The missing of the plane might also arouse anxiety in those who expect the arrival of a friend. And there are cases in which several imperatives compete for supreme validity, and in which the decision is a moral risk. But despite these "mixed" cases, the moral imperative in itself is, as Immanuel Kant called it, "categorical" rather than "hypothetical," or as I would say, unconditional as opposed to conditional.

We may ask, however, whether a moral decision can stand under an unconditional imperative if the decision is a moral risk—the "risk" implying that it might prove to be the wrong decision. The answer to this question is that the unconditional character does not refer to the content, but to the form of the moral decision. Whichever side of a moral alternative might be chosen, however great the risk in a bold decision may be, if it be a *moral* decision it is dependent only on the pure "ought to be" of the moral imperative. And should anyone be in doubt as to which of several possible acts conforms to the moral imperative, he should be reminded that each of them might be justified in a particular situation, but that whatever he chooses must be done with the consciousness of standing under an unconditional imperative. The doubt concerning the justice of a moral act does not contradict the certainty of its ultimate seriousness.

The assertion of the intrinsically religious character of the moral imperative can be criticized from different points of view.

Theology can strongly affirm the unconditioned character of the moral imperative, but deny that this character makes it religious. Moral commands, one argues then, are religious because they are divine commandments. They are ultimately serious because they express the "Will of God." This alone makes them unconditional. God could have willed differently, and we must open our eyes to His revelation in order to know what His Will actually is. Such an argument, of course, would exclude any kind of secular ethics. Not only the content but also the unconditional character of the moral imperative would have to be sanctioned by a divine command, and conserved in holy traditions or sacred books.

I maintain, however, that the term "Will of God" can and must be understood differently. It is not an external will imposed upon us, an arbitrary law laid down by a heavenly tyrant, who is strange to our essential nature and therefore whom we resist justifiably from the point of view of our nature. The "Will of God" for us is precisely our essential being with all its potentialities, our created nature declared as "very good" by God, as, in terms of the Creation myth, He "saw everything that he made." For us the "Will of God" is manifest in our essential being; and only because of this can we accept the moral imperative as valid. It is not a strange law that demands our obedience, but the "silent voice" of our own nature as man, and as man with an individual character.

But we must go one further step. We can say: to fulfill one's own nature is certainly a moral demand intrinsic in one's being. But why is it an unconditional imperative? Do I not have the right to leave my potentialities unfulfilled, to remain less than a person, to contradict my essential goodness, and thus to destroy myself? As a being that has the freedom of self-contradiction, I should have the right to this possibility, and to waste myself! The moral imperative is unconditional only if I choose to affirm my own essential nature, and *this is* a condition! The answer to this argument is the experience that has been expressed in the doctrine of the infinite value of every human soul in the view of the Eternal. It is not an external prohibition against self-destruction—bodily, psychologically, or morally—that we experience in states of despair, but the silent voice of our own being which denies us the right to self-destruction. It is the awareness of our belonging to a dimension that transcends our own finite freedom and our ability to affirm or to negate ourselves. So I maintain my basic assertion that the unconditional character of the moral imperative is its religious quality. No religious heteronomy, subjection to external commands, is implied if we maintain the immanence of religion in the moral command.

The intrinsically religious character of the moral imperative is indirectly denied by the philosophy of values. Its representatives think in terms of a hierarchy of values, in which the value of the holy may or may not find a place; when it does, it is often on the top of this pyramid, above the moral, legal, social, political, and economic values. For our problem, this means first of all that values lie above and below each other and that there can be no immanence of one within another. The value of the holy, for example, cannot be immanent in the value of the good, and conversely. The relationship is external and may lead to the elimination of one or the other—most frequently, in this case, the value of the holy.

A second character of the value theory has a considerable bearing on our problem. The establishment of values and their relationships presupposes a valuating subject, and the question arises: how can values that are relative to a valuating individual or group (e.g., pleasure values) be separated from values that are valid by their very nature regardless of personal or social attitudes? If there are such "absolute values" (absolute in the sense of being independent of a valuating subject, what is the source of their absoluteness, how can they be discovered, how are they related to reality, and what is their ontological standing? These questions lead unavoidably to a situation that the value theory by its very nature tries to avoid—namely, a doctrine of being, an ontology. For values have reality only if they are rooted in reality. Their validity is an expression of their ontological foundation. *Being precedes value,* but value fulfills being. Therefore, the value theory, in its search for absolute values, is thrown back upon the ontological question of the source of values in being.

A third way in which the religious dimension of the moral imperative is questioned can be described as the attempt, with the help of psychological and sociological explanations, to deny the unconditional character of the moral altogether. The psychological impact of realities like the demanding and threatening parents, or of doctrines like that of the commanding and punishing God, evokes the feeling of something unconditionally serious from which there is no escape and with which there can be no compromise.

The same argument can be strengthened by sociological considerations. For example, one can derive, like Nietzsche, the shaping of the conscience of the masses from centuries of pressure exercised by the ruling groups, who did not hesitate to employ all, even the most cruel, tools of suppression—military, legal, educational, psychological. From generation to generation this pressure produced an increasing internalization of commands, namely, the sense of standing under an inner unconditional command, an absolute moral imperative.

This type of argument seems convincing. But it is circular because it presupposes what it tries to prove—the identity of two qualitatively different structures. In the one case, persons and groups are bound by traditions, conventions, and authorities, subjection to which is demanded by the conscience, which may be weak or strong, compromising or insistent, healthy or compulsory, reasonable or fanatic. Psychological or sociological explanations of such states of mind are fully justified. Nothing that happens in the mind should be exempt from psychological or sociological exploration and explanation. But within this structure of causation, another is manifest—what we might call the "structure of meaning" or, to use a famous medieval term revived by modern phenomenology, the structure of "intentionality" or the *noetic* structure (from *nous,* "mind"). This structure would be evident, for example, should a mathematicisn, psychologically and sociologically conditioned like everyone else, discover a new mathematical proposition. The validity of this proposition is independent of the series of conditions which made the discovery possible. In a similar way, the meaning of the unconditional in being and in what ought-to-be appears within the psychological and sociological processes which make its appearance possible. But its validity is not dependent on the structure in which it appears. Psychological and sociological pressures may provide occasion for the appearance of such structures; but they cannot produce the meaning of the unconditional. However strong the pressures be, they are themselves conditioned, and it is possible to contradict them and to be liberated from them, as, for example, from the father-image or from the socially produced conscience. This is not possible with regard to the unconditional character of the moral imperative. One can, of course, discard every particular content for the sake of another, but one cannot discard the moral imperative itself without the self-destruction of one's essential nature and one's eternal relationship. For these reasons, the attempts to undercut the unconditional character of the moral imperative by psychological and sociological arguments must fail.

There is, however, a more fundamental question, raised and thoroughly discussed by the ancient ethical philosophers, namely, the question of the moral aim. We have called it "becoming a person within a community of persons," and we have indicated that the centered person is the bearer of the spirit, its creativity, and its self-transcendence. Insofar as it is the moral aim to constitute and preserve the person with these potentialities, we can say that the moral imperative demands the actualization of man's created potentiality. But now the question arises: is this an unconditional demand? The answer depends on the idea of man's intrinsic aim, of the *telos* for which he is created. If the aim implies something above finitude and transitoriness, the fulfillment of this aim is infinitely significant, or unconditional in its seriousness. When Plato said that the *telos* of man is "to become as much as possible similar to the God," such a *telos* gives unconditional character to the moral imperative. If, however, the *telos* is, as in the hedonistic school, the greatest possible amount of pleasure to be derived from life, no unconditional imperative is at work, but merely the very much conditioned advice to calculate well what amount of pain must be suffered in order to attain to the greatest possible amount of pleasure. Between these two extremes of the definition of man's inner *telos* are several definitions which set a finite aim according to the formulation, but in which something unconditional with respect to the moral imperative shines through. This is true of utilitarianism, in which the moral imperative demands work for "the greatest happiness of the greatest number." Here pleasure is replaced by "happiness," and above all, it is not the individual happiness, but that of the many, which is the aim. And the happiness of the many is not possible without self-restraint in the individual's search for happiness. Therefore, a demand appears that cannot be drived from the merely natural trends of the individual, a demand that implies the acceptance of the other person as a person, and an unconditional element besides, whether acknowledged or not.

The Epicureans deal with the problems of the *telos* and the moral imperative from another angle. They also use the term "happiness," but for them happiness consists in the life of the spirit in community with friends, and in the creative participation in the cognitive and aesthetic values of their culture. The relationship to friends as well as to cultural creativity demands unconditional subjection to the norms and structures of friendship, knowledge, and beauty.

Nearest to Plato's definition of the human *telos* is Aristotle's thought that man's highest aim is participation in the eternal divine self-intuition. This state can be fully reached only by entering the eternal life above finite life. This does not mean that the individual has immortality but that, within time, he can participate in eternity through the "theoretical" life, the life of intuition. Wherever this state of participation is reached, there is *eudaimonia,* fulfillment under the guidance of a "good daimon," a half-divine power. To reach this goal is an unconditional imperative. And since the practical virtues are the precondition for fulfillment through participation in the divine, they also have unconditional validity.

We have used the Greek word *eudaimonia* (badly translated

as "happiness") in order to point out the moral aim as described in several ethical schools. *Eudaimonia* belongs to those words that have suffered a marked deterioration in meaning. Most responsible for this process were the Stoic and Christian polemics against Epicureanism, which often unjustly confused Epicureanism with hedonism. The word in itself means fulfillment with divine help, and consequent happiness. This happiness does not exclude pleasure, but the pleasure is not the aim, nor is happiness itself the aim. It is the companion of fulfillment, reached together with it. If we derogate this concept of *eudaimonia,* we must also derogate the Christian hope for eternal blessedness. For, even though the Calvinist names the glory of God as the aim of his life, he experiences blessedness in fulfilling this aim and serving the glory of God. The same, of course, is true of *theosis* ("becoming Godlike") , *fruitio Dei* ("enjoying the intuition of the divine life") , or working for and participating in the "Kingdom of God" described as the aim of the individual man, of mankind, and the universe.

Happiness or blessedness as the emotional awareness of fulfillment is not in conflict with the unconditional, and therefore religious, character of the moral imperative. A conflict exists only when the function of self-transcendence in man's spirit is denied, and man is seen as totally imprisoned in his finitude. But this diminution of man to a finite process has rather rarely occurred in the history of thought. Even highly secularized philosophers were conscious of the function of self-transcendence in man's spirit, and consequently of the dimension of the unconditional for the religious dimension.

There are two concepts in the preceding discussion that have been frequently used without having been thoroughly discussed. The one is "conscience," the channel through which the unconditional character of the moral imperative is experienced, and the other is the term "religious" (in the title and in many other parts of this chapter) . The concept of conscience will be fully discussed in Chapter IV. Regarding the concept of religion (which I have developed in much of my work) , I can restrict myself to the following summary: the fundamental concept of religion is the state of being grasped by an ultimate concern, by an infinite interest, by something one takes unconditionally seriously. It is in view of this concept that we have formulated the main proposition of this chapter, namely, that there is a religious dimension in the moral imperative itself. Derived from the fundamental concept of religion is the traditional concept that religion is a particular expression, in symbols of thought and action, of such ultimate concern within a social group as, for example, a church. If the moral imperative were derived from religion in the traditional sense of the word, secular ethics would have to sever any ties with religion, for it rejects direct dependence on any particular religion. If, however, the religious element is intrinsic to the moral imperative, no conflict is necessary.

Additional Readings

BRADLEY, F. H., *Ethical Studies.*

FLEW, ANTONY, "Divine Omnipotence and Human Freedom," in Flew, A. and McIntyre, A., *New Essays in Philosophical Theology.*

HICK, JOHN, *Evil and the God of Love.*

JOAD, C. E. M., *God and Evil.*

KANT, I., *Religion within the Limits of Reason Alone.*

KIERKEGAARD, S. K., *Fear and Trembling.*

LEWIS, C. S., *The Problem of Pain.*

LEIBNIZ, G. W. F., *Theodicy.*

NYGREN, ANDERS, *Agape and Eros.*

PIKE, NELSON (ed.), *God and Evil* (an anthology of recent and contemporary discussions).

ROYCE, JOSIAH, *The World and The Individual,* Volume 2, Chap. 9.

SARTRE, J. P., *Existentialism and Humanism.*

SORLEY, W. R., *Moral Values and the Idea of God.*

Amoghapasa Mandala (1863). Buddhist, Nepal.
(Courtesy, Museum of Fine Arts, Boston)
Bigelow collection

PART V

MEANING and

MEANINGFULNESS

This section deals with the questions of whether, and how, it is possible to speak meaningfully about God in human language. While these questions received some attention in earlier times, they have come into special prominence in the twentieth century, and a large amount of current work in the philosophy of religion is devoted to them.

Like many other philosophical questions, however, these are not entirely clear. It is not immediately obvious what the "How" means in "How can one speak of God in human language?" In certain moods a person might indeed wonder how it is possible to talk about such diverse things as mountains, prepositions, emotions, and historical trends in a single human language. But the thing is actually done, and it is not easy to explain further just what we may want to know about "how" it is possible.

A. J. Ayer, a representative of the philosophical movement known as Logical Positivism, attemps to formulate the difficulty in a precise way. He holds that there is a certain logical requirement for cognitively meaningful statements, statements which may be true or false, and that the most important and unique religious statements do not meet this requirement. Therefore, they have no cognitive meaning.

Ayer's requirement was meant to refer to "verifiability." As he explains in the selection printed here, a number of earlier attempts to specify this requirement (including an attempt of his own), failed. They either excluded many important scientific statements as meaningless or else they included every indicative sentence, including all those of religion, as meaningful. It is interesting to note that the much more complex attempt which Ayer makes here also fails. Contrary to his expectation, it also allows every indicative sentence to be meaningful. Surprisingly, no positivist seems to have been able to discover any criterion at all which would distinguish religious statements from scientific statements. Students who wish to pursue this aspect of the problem may refer to the articles by Carl Hempel and Alonzo Church cited in the additional readings and to the further references given in Hempel's article.

The selections from St. Thomas and E. L. Mascall utilize the notion of analogy. They argue that while God is different from all the other possible objects of discourse, there are nevertheless *analogies* between Him and other things. Therefore, a language adapted to discourse about those other things may be understood analogically when it is applied to God.

The essays by Frederick Copleston and Ian Ramsey printed here provide other sorts of replies to Ayer's challenge, and attempt constructive defenses of the possibility of theological discourse.

I

_____

ANALOGY*

St. Thomas Aquinas

Thomas Aquinas (1226–1274) was a scholar and university teacher of the Dominican Order whose Christianized version of Aristotelianism has become virtually the official philosophy of the Roman Catholic Church and the classical expression of the philosophic tradition which bears his name. His principal works are: Summa Theologica *and* Summa Contra Gentiles *in which he expounds and defends his philosophical theology.*

Now although things that exist and live are more perfect than those which only exist, yet God Who is not distinct from His own existence, is universally perfect being.[1] And by universally perfect I mean that He lacks not the excellence of any genus.

For every excellence of any being whatsoever is ascribed to a thing in respect of its being, since no excellence would accrue to man from his wisdom, unless thereby he *were* wise, and so on. Wherefore, according as a thing has being, so is its mode of excellence: since a thing, according as its being is contracted to some special mode of excellence more or less great, is said to be more or less excellent. Hence if there be a thing to which the whole possibility of being belongs, no excellence that belongs to any thing can be lacking thereto. Now to a thing which is its own being, being belongs according to the whole possibility of being: thus if there were a separate whiteness, nothing of the whole possibility of whiteness could be wanting to it: because something of the possibility of whiteness is lacking to a particular white thing through a defect in the recipient of whiteness, which receives it according to its mode and, maybe, not according to the whole possibility of whiteness. Therefore God, Who is His own being, as shown above,[2]

* From St. Thomas Aquinas, *Summa Contra Gentiles,* tr. by *The English Dominican Fathers.* Reprinted by permission of the English Dominicans and Burns, Oates, & Washbourne, Ltd.

[1] *Sum. Th.* P. I., Q. iv., A. 2.   [2] Ch. xxii.

has being according to the whole possibility of being itself: and consequently He cannot lack any excellence that belongs to any thing.

And just as every excellence and perfection is in a thing according as that thing is, so every defect is in a thing according as that thing in some sense is not. Now just as God has being wholly, so is not-being wholly absent from Him, since according as a thing has being it fails in not-being. Therefore all defect is removed from God, and consequently He is universally perfect.

But those things which only exist are imperfect, not on account of an imperfection in absolute being itself, for they have not being according to its whole possibility, but because they participate being in a particular and most imperfect way.

Again. Every imperfect thing must needs be preceded by some perfect thing: for seed is from some animal or plant. Wherefore the first being must be supremely perfect. Now it has been shown[1] that God is the first being. Therefore He is supremely perfect.

Moreover. A thing is perfect in so far as it is in act, and imperfect in so far as it is in potentiality and void of act. Wherefore that which is nowise in potentiality but is pure act, must needs be most perfect. Now such is God.[2] Therefore He is most perfect.

Further. Nothing acts except according as it is in act: wherefore action follows upon the mode of actuality in the agent; and consequently it is impossible for the effect that results from an action to have a more excellent actuality than that of the agent, although it is possible for the actuality of the effect to be more imperfect than that of the active cause, since action may be weakened on the part of that in which it terminates. Now in the genus of efficient cause we come at length to the one cause which is called God, as explained above,[3] from Whom all things proceed, as we shall show in the sequel.[4] Wherefore it follows that whatever is actual in any other thing, is found in God much more eminently than in that thing, and not conversely. Therefore God is most perfect.

Again. In every genus there is some thing most perfect relatively to that genus, by which every thing in that genus is measured: since every thing is shown to be more or less perfect according as it approaches more or less to the measure of that genus: thus white is said to be the measure in all colours, and the virtuous among all men.[5] Now the measure of all beings can be

---

[1] Ch. xiii.   [2] Ch. xvi.   [3] Ch. xiii.   [4] Bk. II., ch. xv.
[5] *Ethic.* iv. 5; v. 10.

none other than God Who is His own being. Therefore no perfection that belongs to any thing is lacking to Him, otherwise He would not be the universal measure of all.

Hence it is that when Moses sought to see the face of God, the Lord answered him: *I will show thee all good* (Exod. xxxii. 18, 19), giving thus to understand that the fulness of all good is in Him. And Dionysius says (*Div. Nom.* v.): *God exists not in any single mode, but embraces and prepossesses all being within Himself, absolutely and without limit.*

It must however be observed that perfection cannot fittingly be ascribed to God if we consider the meaning of the word in respect of its derivation: since what is not *made,* cannot seemingly be described as *perfect.* Yet since whatever is made has been brought from potentiality to act, and from not-being to being, when it was made; it is rightly described as perfect, i.e., *completely made,* when its potentiality is completely reduced to act, so that it retains nothing of not-being, and has complete being. Accordingly by a kind of extension of the term, *perfect* is applied not only to that which has arrived at complete act through being made, but also to that which is in complete act without being made at all. It is thus that we say that God is perfect, according to Matt. v. 48: *Be ye perfect as also your heavenly Father is perfect.*

.   .   .

IN sequence to the above we may consider in what way it is possible to find in things a likeness to God, and in what way it is impossible.[1]

For effects that fall short of their causes do not agree with them in name and ratio, and yet there must needs be some likeness between them, because it is of the nature of action that a like agent should produce a like action, since every thing acts according as it is in act. Wherefore the form of the effect is found in its transcendent cause somewhat, but in another way and another ratio, for which reason that cause is called *equivocal.* For the sun causes heat in lower bodies by acting according as it is in act; wherefore the heat generated by the sun must needs bear some likeness to the sun's active power by which heat is caused in those lower bodies and by reason of which the sun is said to be hot, albeit in a different ratio. And thus it is said to be somewhat like all those things on which it efficaciously produces its effects, and yet again it is unlike them all in so far as these effects do not possess heat and so forth in the same way as they are found in the sun. Thus also God bestows all perfec-

[1] *Sum. Th.* P. I., Q. iv., A. 3.

tions on things, and in consequence He is both like and unlike all.

Hence it is that Holy Writ sometimes recalls the likeness between Him and His creatures, as when it is said (Gen. i. 26) : *Let Us make man to Our image and likeness:* while sometimes this likeness is denied, according to the words of Isa. xl. 18: *To whom then have you likened God; or what image will you make for Him?* and of the psalm:[1] *O God, who shall be like to Thee?*

Dionysius is in agreement with this argument, for he says (*Div. Nom.* ix.) : *The same things are like and unlike to God; like, according as they imitate Him, as far as they can, Who is not perfectly imitable; unlike, according as effects fall short of their causes.*

However,[2] according to this likeness, it is more fitting to say that the creature is like God than vice versa. For one thing is like another when it possesses a quality or form thereof. Since then what is in God perfectly is found in other things by way of an imperfect participation, that in which likeness is observed is God's simply but not the creature's. And thus the creature has what is God's, and therefore is rightly said to be like God. But it cannot be said in this way that God has what belongs to His creature: wherefore neither is it fitting to say that God is like His creature; as neither do we say that a man is like his portrait, although we declare that his portrait is like him.

And much less properly can it be said that God is assimilated to the creature. For assimilation denotes movements towards similarity, and consequently applies to one that receives its similarity from another. But the creature receives from God its similarity to Him, and not vice versa. Therefore God is not assimilated to His creature, but rather vice versa.

.   .   .

AGAIN in sequel to the above we may consider what can and what cannot be said of God; also what is said of Him alone, and what is said of Him together with other beings.

For since every perfection of creatures is to be found in God, albeit in another and more eminent way, whatever terms denote perfection absolutely and without any defect whatever, are predicated of God and of other things; for instance, goodness, wisdom, and so forth. But any term that denotes suchlike perfections together with a mode proper to creatures, cannot be said of God

---

[1] Ps. lxxxii. 1.   [2] *Sum. Th., l.c., ad* 4.

except by similitude and metaphor, whereby that which belongs to one thing is applied to another, as when a man is said to be a stone on account of the denseness of his intelligence. Such are all those terms employed to denote the species of a created thing, as *man* and *stone:* for its proper mode of perfection and being is due to each species: likewise whatever terms signify those properties of things that are caused by the proper principles of the species, therefore they cannot be said of God otherwise than metaphorically. But those which express these perfections together with the mode of supereminence in which they belong to God, are said of God alone, for instance *the sovereign good,* the *first being,* and the like.

Now, I say that some of the aforesaid terms denote perfection without defect, as regards that which the term is employed to signify: for as regards the mode of signification every term is defective. For we express things by a term as we conceive them by the intellect: and our intellect, since its knowledge originates from the senses, does not surpass the mode which we find in sensible objects, wherein the form is distinct from the subject of the form, on account of the composition of form and matter. Now in those things the form is found to be simple indeed, but imperfect, as being non-subsistent: whereas the subject of the form is found to be subsistent, but not simple, nay more, with concretion. Wherefore whatever our intellect signifies as subsistent, it signifies it with concretion, and whatever it signifies as simple, it signifies it not as subsisting but as qualifying. Accordingly in every term employed by us, there is imperfection as regards the mode of signification, and imperfection is unbecoming to God, although the thing signified is becoming to God in some eminent way: as instanced in the term *goodness* or *the good:* for goodness signifies by way of non-subsistence, and the good signifies by way of concretion. In this respect no term is becomingly applied to God, but only in respect of that which the term is employed to signify. Wherefore, as Dionysius teaches,[1] such terms can be either affirmed or denied of God: affirmed, on account of the signification of the term; denied, on account of the mode of signification. Now the mode of supereminence in which the aforesaid perfections are found in God, cannot be expressed in terms employed by us, except either by negation, as when we say God is *eternal* or *infinite,* or by referring Him to other things, as when we say that He is the *first cause* or the *sovereign good.* For we are able to grasp, not what God is, but what He is not, and the relations of other things to Him, as explained above.[2]

[1] *Cæl. Hier.* ii. 3.   [2] Ch. xiv.

. . .

FROM what has been said we are also able to see that the divine perfection and the various names applied to God are not inconsistent with His simplicity.

For we asserted that all the perfections to be found in other things are to be ascribed to God in the same way as effects are found in their equivocal causes:[1] which causes are in their effects virtually, as heat is in the sun. Now this virtue unless it were in some way of the genus of heat, the sun acting thereby would not generate its like. Wherefore by reason of this virtue the sun is said to be hot, not only because it causes heat, but because the virtue whereby it does this, is something in conformity with heat. Now by this same virtue by which the sun causes heat, it causes also many other effects in lower bodies, such as dryness. And so heat and dryness, which are distinct qualities in fire, are ascribed to the sun in respect of the one virtue. And so too, the perfections of all things, which are becoming to other things in respect of various forms, must needs be ascribed to God in respect of His one virtue. And this virtue is not distinct from His essence, since nothing can be accidental to Him, as we have proved.[2] Accordingly God is said to be *wise* not only because He causes wisdom, but because in so far as we are wise, we imitate somewhat the virtue whereby He makes us wise. He is not however called a *stone,* although He made the stones, because by the term stone we understand a definite mode of being, in respect of which a stone differs from God.[3] But a stone imitates God as its cause, in respect of being, goodness and so forth, even as other creatures do.

The like of this may be found in human cognitive powers and operative virtues. For the intellect by its one virtue knows all that the sensitive faculty apprehends by various powers, and many other things besides. Again, the intellect, the higher it is, the more things is it able to know by means of one, while an inferior intellect can arrive at the knowledge of those things only by means of many. Again the royal power extends to all those things to which the various subordinate powers are directed. And so too, God by His one simple being possesses all manner of perfections, which in a much lower degree other things attain by certain various means. Whence it is clear how it is necessary to give several names to God. For since we cannot know Him naturally except by reaching Him from His effect,[4] it follows that the terms by which we denote His perfection must be diverse, as also are the perfections which we find in things. If however we were able to understand His very essence as

---

[1] Ch. xxix.   [2] Ch. xxiii.   [3] *Cf.* ch. xxx.   [4] *Cf.* ch. xi.

it is, and to give Him a proper name, we should express Him by one name only: and this is promised in the last chapter of Zacharias[1] to those who will see Him in His essence: *In that day there shall be one Lord, and His name shall be one.*

. . .

FROM the above it is clear that nothing can be predicated univocally of God and other things. For an effect which does not receive the same form specifically as that whereby the agent acts, cannot receive in a univocal sense the name derived from that form: for the sun and the heat generated from the sun are not called hot univocally. Now the forms of things whereof God is cause do not attain to the species of the divine virtue, since they receive severally and particularly that which is in God simply and universally.[2] It is evident therefore that nothing can be said univocally of God and other things.

Further. If an effect attain to the species of its cause, the name of the latter will not be predicated of it univocally unless it receive the same specific form according to the same mode of being: for *house* in art is not univocally the same as *house* in matter, since the form of house has an unlike being in the one case and in the other. Now other things, even though they should receive entirely the same form, do not receive it according to the same mode of being: because there is nothing in God that is not the divine being itself, as shown above,[3] which does not apply to other things. Therefore it is impossible for anything to be predicated univocally of God and other things.

Moreover. Whatever is predicated of several things univocally is either genus, or species, or difference, or proper accident. Now nothing is predicated of God as genus or as difference, as we have proved above,[4] and consequently neither as definition nor as species, which consists of genus and difference. Nor can anything be accidental to Him, as was shown above,[5] and consequently nothing is predicated of God, either as accidental or as proper, for the proper is a kind of accident. It follows therefore that nothing is predicated of God and other things univocally.

Again. That which is predicated univocally of several things is more simple than either of them, at least in our way of understanding. Now nothing can be more simple than God, either in reality or in our way of understanding. Therefore nothing is predicated univocally of God and other things.

[1] xiv. 9.   [2] Chs. xxviii, xxix.   [3] Ch. xxiii.   [4] Chs. xxiv., xxv.
[5] Ch. xxiii.

Further. Whatever is predicated univocally of several things belongs by participation to each of the things of which it is predicated: for the species is said to participate the genus, and the individual the species. But nothing is said of God by participation, since whatever is participated is confined to the mode of a participated thing, and thus is possessed partially and not according to every mode of perfection. It follows therefore that nothing is predicated univocally of God and other things.

Again. That which is predicated of several things according to priority and posteriority is certainly not predicated of them univocally, since that which comes first is included in the definition of what follows, for instance substance in the definition of accident considered as a being. If therefore we were to say *being* univocally of substance and accident, it would follow that substance also should enter into the definition of being as predicated of substance: which is clearly impossible. Now nothing is predicated in the same order of God and other things, but according to priority and posteriority: since all predicates of God are essential, for He is called being because He is very essence, and good because He is goodness itself: whereas predicates are applied to others by participation; thus Socrates is said to be a man, not as though he were humanity itself, but as a subject of humanity. Therefore it is impossible for any thing to be predicated univocally of God and other things.

．　　．　　．

It is also clear from what has been said that things predicated of God and other things are not all pure equivocations, as are the effects of an equivocal cause. For in the effects of an equivocal cause we find no mutual order or relationship, and it is altogether accidental that the same name is applied to various things; since the name applied to one does not signify that thing to have any relationship to another. Whereas it is not so with the terms applied to God and creatures: for in employing these common terms we consider the order of cause and effect, as is clear from what we have said.[1] Therefore certain things predicated of God and other things are not pure equivocations.

Moreover. Where there is pure equivocation, we observe no likeness of things, but merely sameness of name. Now there is some kind of likeness of things to God, as shown above.[2] Therefore it follows that they are not said of God by pure equivocation.

Again. When one thing is predicated of several by pure

[1] Ch. xxxii.　　　[2] Ch. xxix.

equivocation, we cannot be led from one to the knowledge of the other, for the knowledge of things depends not on words but on the meaning of names. Now we come to the knowledge of things divine from our observation of other things, as shown above.[1] Therefore the like are not pure equivocations when said of God and other things.

Further. The use of equivocal terms breaks the continuity of an argument. Therefore if nothing were said of God and creatures except by pure equivocation, no argument could be made by proceeding to God from creatures, whereas the contrary is evidenced by all who speak of divine things.

Moreover. It is useless to predicate a name of a thing unless by that name we understand something about that thing. Now if names are predicated altogether equivocally of God and creatures, we understand nothing of God by those names: since the meanings of those names are known to us only as applied to creatures. It would therefore be to no purpose to prove about God that God is being, good, or any thing else of the kind.

If, however, it be asserted that by suchlike terms we only know of God what He is not, so that, to wit, He be called *living* because He is not in the genus of inanimate beings, and so forth. it follows at least that *living* when said of God and creatures agrees in the negation of inanimate being: and thus it will not be a pure equivocation.

· · ·

It follows, then, from what has been said[2] that those things which are said of God and other things are predicated neither univocally nor equivocally, but analogically, that is according to an order or relation to some one thing.

This happens in two ways. First, according as many things have a relation to some one thing: thus in relation to the one health, an animal is said to be *healthy* as its subject, medicine as effective thereof, food as preserving it, and urine as its sign. Secondly, according as order or relation of two things may be observed, not to some other thing, but to one of them: thus being is said of substance and accident, in so far as accident bears a relation to substance, and not as though substance and accident were referred to a third thing.

Accordingly such names are not said of God and other things analogically in the first way, for it would be necessary to suppose something previous to God; but in the second way.

[1] In various places.　　　[2] Chs. xxxii., xxxiii.

Now in this analogical predication the relationship is sometimes found to be the same both as to the name and as to the thing, and sometimes it is not the same. For the relationship of the name is consequent upon the relationship of knowledge, since the name is the sign of intellectual conception. Accordingly when that which comes first in reality is found to be first also in knowledge, the same thing is found to be first both as to the meaning of the name and as to the nature of the thing: thus substance is prior to accident both in nature, in as much as substance is the cause of accident, and in knowledge, in as much as substance is placed in the definition of accident. Wherefore *being* is said of substance previously to being said of accident, both in reality and according to the meaning of the word. On the other hand, when that which comes first according to nature, comes afterwards according to knowledge, then, in analogical terms, there is not the same order according to the reality and according to the meaning of the name: thus the healing power in health-giving (medicines) is naturally prior to health in the animal, as cause is prior to effect; yet as we know this power through its effect, we name it from that effect. Hence it is that *health-giving* is first in the order of reality, and yet *healthy* is predicated of animal first according to the meaning of the term.

Accordingly, since we arrive at the knowledge of God from other things, the reality of the names predicated of God and other things is first in God according to His mode, but the meaning of the name is in Him afterwards. Wherefore He is said to be named from His effects.

2

ANALOGY*

E. L. Mascall ■

*Eric L. Mascall (1905–   ), Professor of
Historical Theology at King's College,
The University of London, since 1962,
has made some of the most important
recent attempts to develop and restate a
Thomistic point of view. He has written
a large number of works, including:* He
Who Is, Existence and Analogy, *and*
Words and Images.

ONE preliminary remark may be made before the discussion is
opened, namely that the function of the doctrine of analogy is not
to make it possible for us to talk about God in the future but to
explain how it is that we have been able to talk about him all
along. In spite of all that has been said by positivists, logical and
other, we do in fact find ourselves talking about God, and talking
about him in a way that is significant. It is, I would maintain,
transparently clear to anyone whose judgment is not shackled by a
predetermined dogma that, if two men respectively affirm and deny
that God exists, they are in fact disagreeing about the nature of
reality, and not merely expressing different emotional or aesthetic
attitudes. There is, unfortunately, a recurrent tendency among
philosophers, in analysing the mental activities of human beings in
general, to assume that until their analysis and criticism have been
satisfactorily completed, nobody has the right to make any affirmations at all; so deeply has Cartesianism entered into our heritage.
The consequence is that the plain man laughs at the philosophers
and goes on his own way without them. Against this tendency we
are, as I see it, bound to assert that the task of any philosophical
critique is to account for, to render precise and, if necessary, to
correct the body of doctrine that the human mind has acquired by
the natural exercise of its own powers, but not, except in a purely
relative and *ex post facto* way, to provide a justification for the
activity of thought itself. To forget this is to doom oneself to a kind
of intellectual suicide. For the critical philosopher is himself the
heir of his past; before he was a philosopher at all he was a man,

* From E. L. Mascall, *Existence and Analogy*. Reprinted by permission of Long-
mans, Green & Co., Limited, publishers.

and before he was a man he was a child. To enter a second time into the womb and to be born again equipped with a fully developed critique of knowledge is a sheer impossibility. The fact is that, however fallible it may be, the human mind does acquire knowledge by the exercise of the powers which it possesses, and a sane philosophy will recognize this fact. To return, then, to the subject of our present discussion, the doctrine of analogy is not concerned to discover whether discourse about God is antecedently possible, or to endow it with a possibility that was originally absent, but to account for the fact that discourse about God has, as matter of experience, been taking place in spite of various considerations that might seem at first sight to rule its possibility out of court.

I would further add that the question of analogy does not arise at all in the mere proof of the existence of God; it arises only when, having satisfied ourselves that the existence of finite being declares its dependence upon self-existent being, we then apprehend that no predicate can be attributed to finite and to self-existence being univocally. Penido's remarks seem to me to be of the first importance here. "Formally," he writes, "the problem of analogy is a problem of nature, not of existence. We can arrive at the existence of God without *explicit* recourse to analogy, while it is impossible to think about the divine nature without conceiving it as equivocal, univocal or analogous to our own." And again: "It is quite true that the proofs of God are analogical *realities,* otherwise they would prove nothing. But they do not fall under the jurisdiction of the *method* of analogy, as theology employs it. Let us distinguish carefully—without separating them and still more without opposing them—the problem of analogical knowledge and the metaphysical problem of analogy. The former belongs in full right to the treatise on God, while it is only after the treatise on creation that we can approach the latter in its fullness. . . . Does this mean that analogy in no way depends on the *quinque viae?* By no means. Analogy begins at the precise point where the rational demonstration ends."[1] We had no need of any doctrine of analogy in the last chapter, in arguing from the existence of finite beings to the existence of God. When, however, the argument was complete, we saw that the God whose existence we were now asserting was a being

---

[1] *Rôle de l'Analogie,* pp. 85–7. The point, as I see it, of the assertion that, while the proofs of God are analogical realities, they do not fall under the jurisdiction of analogy is that, while any *mode of existing* can only be predicated analogically of God and creatures (since mode of existence is essence and falls under the concept), the act of existing, which is not conceptualizable, can be affirmed without any analogical reservation. There is thus no concession to the doctrine of univocity of being.

of so radically different an order from everything else in our experience that it became a real question whether the word "God" in that context meant anything at all. There can be little satisfaction in demonstrating the existence of a being whom the very demonstration shows to be altogether inapprehensible. God would seem to have slipped from between our hands at the very moment when we had at last laid hold on him. It is at this point that the doctrine of analogy becomes altogether necessary, and it is for this reason that its full investigation only began among Christian philosophers who gave primacy of place to the existential approach to God.

The doctrine, as we find it in the Thomist tradition, appears in at least three distinct departments of philosophy, namely the metaphysical or ontological, the epistemological or psychological, and the logical or linguistic. This is only what we might expect in a fundamentally realist philosophy, which holds that words are not merely noises and that thought is not merely about ideas, but that speech with its words and thought with its ideas are ultimately about things.[1] It is well to make this point clear at the start or we shall find ourselves puzzled to know what precisely is the question with which analogy is concerned. Is it "How can we talk about God?" or "How can we think about God?" or "How are things related to God?"? In fact it is about all three, and we need not be worried by the way in which it slips from one to the other, so long as our attitude is confidently realist.[2] I shall, however, take the first question as my starting-point and consider the problem of analogical predication.

Is it possible, we therefore ask, for statements expressed in human language to mean anything when made about God—that is to say, are theological statements meaningful or meaningless? (The relevance of this discussion to the questions raised by the logical positivists will be immediately clear to those who have any acquaintance with their works. Starting from a famous distinction made by Aristotle,[3] we remark that, even within the realm of discourse about

---

[1] "I am not yet so lost in lexicography," wrote Dr. Johnson in the Preface to his Dictionary, "as to forget that words are the daughters of earth, and that things are the sons of heaven."

[2] "Tripliciter quaelibet res, ad nos quantum attinet, considerari potest: ut est nempe *in se*, ut est *in intellectu nostro*, ut est *in nostro ore*, 'vox*, a postremo nunc incipiendo, *conceptus in anima*, et *res extra* seu conceptus objectivus,' uti ad rem Cajetanus docet (*De Nom. Anal.*, cap. iv, no. 31). Triplex hinc exsurgit ordo: ordo videlicet *essendi*, ordo *cognoscendi*, ordo *significandi*" (S. Alvarez-Menendez, Introduction to Cajetan, *De Nominum Analogia* (1934), p. viii).

[3] *Categories*, I. It is true that in this text Aristotle mentions only univocity and equivocity, though elsewhere he makes considerable use of the notion of analogy. Cajetan remarks *à propos* of this text that logicians (in contrast to philosophers) call analogy of attribution equivocation (*De Nom. Anal.*, cap. ii, no. 19).

finite beings, one and the same word, when applied to two things, sometimes bears the same sense in both applications and sometimes different ones. In the former case it is used *univocally* (συνωνύμως) ; as when Carlo and Fido are both called dogs. Even if Carlo is a great Dane and Fido a Pomeranian, we mean the same thing about each of them when we call them both *dogs;* the characteristics in each that distinguish Carlo as a Dane from Fido as a Pomeranian, while they cannot be found in their totality except in dogs, are additional to caninity as such. But sometimes we use words purely equivocally (ὁμωνύμως) , as when we apply the word "mug" both to a drinking utensil and to the victim of a fraud. (The neglect of this distinction can lead to unfortunate consequences, as the choirboys found who were starting a cricket team, when they asked the vicar for one of the bats which the verger had led them to believe were in the belfry.) But in addition to these two uses, it is alleged, a word is sometimes applied to two objects in senses that are neither wholly different nor yet wholly the same, as when we say that Mr. Jones and Skegness are both healthy, the former because he *enjoys,* and the latter because it *induces,* health; in this case we are said to use the term "healthy" *analogically* (ἀνάλογως) .

At first sight the introduction of this mode of predication might seem to be unnecessary and trivial, and certainly Aristotle did not accord to it anything like as much attention as the scholastics do. We might be tempted to suppose that analogy is only a dignified kind of univocity, and that it is quite sufficient to say that the healthiness of Mr. Jones and the healthiness of Skegness are merely two ways of being healthy, just as the Danishness of Carlo and the Pomeranianity of Fido are merely two ways of being canine. Or, alternatively, we might go to the other extreme and say that analogy is only equivocity in sheep's clothing, that to enjoy health and to induce health are two altogether different activities and that only for the sake of economy in words can there be any justification for using the same term "healthy" *tout court* to denote them both. Furthermore, it might be asked, even if we admit this *tertium quid* of analogy, can we ever be quite sure when it applies? When we say that Mr. Jones is alive and that an oyster is alive, is the difference between the life of Mr. Jones and the life of the oyster something additional to a quality, namely life, which is found univocally in both, as the Danishness of Carlo and the Pomeranianity of Fido are additional to their common caninity? Or, on the other hand, is the life which is attributed to Mr. Jones and to the oyster, as the scholastics would say, an analogical perfection, contracted to each subject not by external *differentiae* but by different internal modes of participation? Can one possibly settle this kind of question? Can we even give the distinction any real meaning?

Now, so long as we are merely considering qualities and properties of finite beings, the introduction of analogical discourse, in addition to univocal and equivocal, might well appear to be an unnecessary and artificial complication. There are, however, two instances in which it—or something like it—seems to be unavoidable, namely when we are discussing transcendentals and when we are discussing God. And it is worth noting that, in Christian thought, it is precisely the necessity of talking about God that has given rise to the great development which the doctrine of analogy has undergone. Let us consider these instances in order.

The transcendentals, in scholastic thought, are those six primary notions—*ens, res, unum, aliquid, verum* and *bonum*—which, because of their very universality, refuse to fall in any of the Aristotelian categories, but cut across them all.[1] The last five ultimately reduce to the first, so it will be sufficient to consider that. What, then, is meant by the analogy of being? Why is it denied that being is univocal? Simply because there is nothing outside being by which it could be differentiated. When we say that Carlo and Fido are both dogs, the word "dog" means precisely the same when applied to each of them; the differences that distinguish them as dogs are, as we have seen, extrinsic to caninity as such. But when we say that Carlo and Fido are both *beings*, the differences that distinguish them as beings cannot be extrinsic to being as such, for being, in its altogether universal reference, must embrace everything, including differences; if differences were not instances of being, they would be non-existent, and then no two things could be distinct from each other. So the scholastics tell us, being is not a genus,[2] since there is nothing outside it which could act as a differentia to it, to subdivide it into species; nevertheless everything is an instance of being, and being is differentiated by its own inherent analogical variety. To be is to be in a certain way, and the way is the very heart of the being. So the whole order of beings, of

[1] It should be noted that they are called transcendentals because they transcend the categories. This is not the meaning which the word "transcendent" has when applied to God to indicate that he transcends the realm of finite being. Nor is it the meaning that "transcendental" has for Kant: "I apply," he says, "the term *transcendental* to all knowledge which is not so much occupied with objects as with the mode of our cognition of these objects, so far as this mode of cognition is possible *a priori*" (*Critique of Pure Reason,* Introduction, ch. vii, trans. Meiklejohn). Cf. Garrigou-Lagrange, *Dieu,* p. 200, *n.* 1.

[2] R. G. Collingwood surprisingly asserts that for the traditional metaphysics being is the *summum genus* of which the ten Categories are species; in consequence he has little difficulty in arguing that there cannot be a science of pure being (*Essay in Metaphysics,* pp. 9, 10 f). What Aristotle actually thought will be found in *Met.* B., 998b.

entia, from the triune Deity down to the speck of dust and the electron, consists of nothing more and nothing less than analogical instances of being: self-existent being and dependent being, actual being and possible being, substantial being and accidental being, real being and notional being, not in any pantheistic or monistic sense, as if being were some kind of cosmic material, a metaphysical modelling-clay appearing now in this shape and now in that, but in the far more profound sense that every being must *be,* and must be in some determinate way, and—the theist will add—in the sense that the way in which it has being depends in the last resort upon its relation to the self-existent Being which is the prime analogate of all.

Now what is true about beings as such in their relation to one another must be true *a fortiori* about finite beings in their relation to the God who is self-existent Being. If being is not a genus, then the supreme Being transcends all genera, and the principle of analogy, which we have seen applies even between creatures when they are considered as they participate in the transcendentals, will apply with even greater force when creatures are brought into comparison with the altogether transcendent God and when God is spoken about in words whose meaning is derived from their application to finite things. Here, if anywhere, the distinction between the *perfectio significata* and the *modus significandi* will hold; here, if anywhere, will the classical definition of analogy apply, namely that it is the application of a concept to different beings in ways that are simply diverse from each other and are only the same in a certain respect, *simpliciter diversa et eadem secundum quid.*[1] It is noticeable that St. Thomas does not deny that analogues are equivocal but only that they are purely so.[2]

Let us now proceed to consider in more detail this classical

---

[1] This is the Thomist definition of analogical discourse. For the Suarezians, however, with their conceptualist bias and the consequent sharp line drawn between thought and the extra-mental thing, an analogical concept applies to different beings in ways *simpliciter eadem et diversa secundum quid.*

[2] *Hoc modo aliqua dicuntur de Deo et creaturis analogice, et non aequivoce pure neque univoce* (S. Theol., I, xiii, 5c). We may compare the well-known statement of the Fourth Lateran Council that "between the creator and the creature no likeness can be discerned without a greater unlikeness having to be discerned as well" (*inter creatorem et creaturam non potest tanta similitudo notari quin inter eos major sit dissimilitudo notanda,* cap. ii; Denzinger-Bannwart, *Enchiridion,* 11th ed., no. 432). It is easy to see what this means, but it would be difficult to defend it as a precise philosophical statement, as it appears to assume that likeness and unlikeness are two different species of a measurable genus. One can validly say that two objects are less alike in one respect than they are in another, but to say that they are less alike in one respect than they are *unlike* in another does not seem to be strictly intelligible.

doctrine of analogy. The precise classification of the various types of analogy that can be distinguished is to this day a matter of considerable controversy; the method that I shall adopt will, however, bring out the salient points.

. . .

IN the first place, we may distinguish between analogy *duorum ad tertium* and analogy *unius ad alterum;* this is the fundamental distinction made by St. Thomas in both the *Summa Theologica* and the *Summa contra Gentiles*.[1] Analogy *duorum ad tertium* is the analogy that holds between two beings in consequence of the relation that each of them bears to a third (the analogy considered is, it must be noticed, between the *two;* the *tertium* only comes in as something in the background to which they are both related). For example, if the adjective "healthy" is applied both to Skegness and to the complexion of Mr. Jones who lives there, this double attribution of the adjective can only be seen to be legitimate if it is grasped that in its strict and primary application the adjective applies neither to Skegness nor to the complexion but to Mr. Jones. It is he who is (in the scholastic sense) *formally* healthy and is the *prime analogate*. His complexion is healthy only in the sense that it is a *sign* of health in him, Skegness is healthy only in the sense that it *induces* health in him (or in others like him) ; we cannot rationally justify the attribution of the same predicate "healthy" to things as diverse as a complexion and a seaside town except by referring them both to human beings to whom the predicate formally and properly belongs.

This type of analogy can, however, have little or no application to the case where we are attributing the same predicate to God and to a creature, for there is no being antecedent to God to whom the predicate can apply more formally and properly than it applies to him. We therefore pass to the other type of analogy, analogy *unius ad alterum,* which is founded not upon diverse relations which each of the analogates bears to a third, but upon a relation which one of them bears to the other. And this type of analogy itself subdivides into two.

The former of these sub-types is that which is known as analogy of *attribution* or of *proportion,* analogy *unius ad alterum* in the strict sense. In this case the predicate belongs formally and properly to one of the analogates (which is thus not merely *an* analogate but is the *prime* analogate), and only relatively and derivatively to the other. Thus it is by an analogy of attribution or

[1] *S. Theol.,* I, xiii, 5c; *S.c.G.* I xxxiv.

proportion that Mr. Jones and his complexion are both described as healthy; health is found formally and properly in Mr. Jones, and his complexion is described as healthy only because it bears a certain relation to his health, namely the relation of being a sign of it. In its theological application, where the analogates concerned are God and a creature, the relation upon which the analogy is based will be that of creative causality; creatures are related to God as his effects, by all those modes of participation by the creature in the perfection of its creator which are indicated, for example, by the Thomist Five Ways. Thus when we say that God and Mr. Jones are both good or that they are both beings, remembering that the content which the word "good" or "being" has for us is derived from our experience of the goodness and the being of creatures, we are, so far as analogy of attribution is concerned, saying no more than that God has goodness or being in whatever way is necessary if he is to be able to produce goodness and being in his creatures. This would not seem necessarily to indicate anything more than that the perfections which are found formally in various finite modes in creatures exist *virtually* in God, that is to say, that he is able to produce them in the creatures; it does not seem to necessitate that God possesses them formally himself. (In the case of Mr. Jones, of course, his complexion did indicate his formal possession of health, but there is, literally, all the difference in the world between the relation between two analogates in the finite realm and that between God and a creature.) Analogy of attribution certainly does not exclude the formal possession of the perfections by God, but it does not itself ascribe it to him. The mode in which the perfection which exists in the secondary analogate also exists in the prime analogate will depend on the relation between them; and if this relation is merely that the latter analogate is the *cause* of the former, the possession by the latter of a perfection that exists formally in the former will not, so far as the present mode of analogy is concerned, be necessarily anything more than a virtual one. Creatures are good (formally but finitely), God is the cause of them and of all that they have, therefore the word "good" applied to God need not mean any more than that he is able to produce goodness.[1] It is at this point that the second sub-type of analogy comes to the rescue.

[1] It is important to observe that we are not arguing that the formal possession of goodness by creatures does not *prove* that goodness is formally in God; the argument is not here on the metaphysical but merely on the linguistic and logical plane. All that is asserted is that if the only analogy between God and creatures was analogy of attribution then the word "good" applied to God would not necessarily mean any more than that goodness was in God virtually. *In fact* the

This is analogy of proportionality, also called analogy *plurium ad plura.* In it there is a direct relation of the mode in which a perfection is participated to the being by which it is participated, independently of any relation to a prime analogate. (There may be a prime analogate, and indeed some would maintain that there must be,[1] but it does not come in at this stage.) A spurious, though sometimes useful, form of this type of analogy is *metaphor,* in which there is not a formal participation of the same characteristic in the different analogates but only a similarity of effects. Thus, to take a classic example, the lion is called the king of the beasts because he bears to savage animals a relation similar to that which a king bears to his subjects, but no one would assert that kingship is to be found formally in the lion. Again, God is described as being angry, because his relation to the punishments which he imposes is similar to that which an angry man has to the injuries which he inflicts, but no one (at least, no scholastic philosopher) would say that anger was to be found formally in God.[2] In the strict sense, an analogy of proportionality implies that the analogue under discussion is found formally in each of the analogates but in a mode that is determined by the nature of the analogate itself. Thus, assuming that life is an analogous and not a univocal concept, it is asserted that cabbages, elephants, men and God each possess life formally (that is each of them is, quite

---

metaphysical relation of the world to God implies analogy of proportionality as well, and it is at this latter stage that the formal attribution of goodness to God becomes clear.

[1] Thus Garrigou-Lagrang writes: "It is not necessary here to mention the principal analogate in the definition of the others, but there nevertheless always is a prime analogate. In metaphorical analogy of proportionality, it is the one to which the name of analogue belongs in the strict sense. In strict analogy of proportionality, the principal analogate is that which is the higher cause of the others: the analogical similitude that exists in this latter case is always based on causality; it exists either between the cause and the effect or between the effects of the same cause" (*Dieu,* p. 532, *n.* 3). This last remark seems to imply the assertion that will be made later on: that in its theological application analogy of proportionality needs to be reinforced by analogy of attribution; Garrigou-Lagrange does not, however, explicitly make the assertion. We may add here, as a point of terminology, that the word "analogue" (*analogum*) refers to the common predicate (or common quality or transcendental signified by it), while the word "analogate" (*analogatum*) refers to the various subjects to which it is attributed, or to its diverse modes in them. An alternative nomenclature refers to the analogue as *analogum analogans* and the analogate as *analogum analogatum.*

[2] A further example of purely metaphorical proportionality is provided by Canning's celebrated epigram:
> "Pitt is to Addington
> As London is to Paddington."

literally and unmetaphorically, *alive*), but that the cabbage possesses life in the mode proper to a cabbage, the elephant in that proper to an elephant, the man in that proper to a man, and finally God in that supreme, and by us unimaginable, mode proper to self-existent Being itself. This is commonly expressed in the following quasi-mathematical form, from which, in fact, the name "analogy of proportionality" is derived:[1]

$$\frac{\text{life of cabbage}}{\text{essence of cabbage}} = \frac{\text{life of elephant}}{\text{essence of elephant}}$$

$$= \frac{\text{life of man}}{\text{essence of man}} = \frac{\text{life of God}}{\text{essence of God}}$$

We must, however, beware of interpreting the equal sign too literally. For the point is not that the life of the cabbage is determined by the essence of the cabbage in the *same* way as that in which the life of the man is determined by the essence of the man, but that the way in which cabbage essence determines cabbage life is proper to cabbagehood, while the way in which the human essence determines human life is proper to manhood. But at this point various objections rapidly spring to the mind.

In the first place, it may be asked, has not the remark just made landed us in an infinite regress? We began by denying the univocity of the identity,

$$\text{life of cabbage} = \text{life of man,}$$

and substituted for it the proportionality:

$$\frac{\text{life of cabbage}}{\text{essence of cabbage}} = \frac{\text{life of man}}{\text{essence of man}}$$

But we now have denied that the equal sign in this latter equation really signifies equality and have substituted for it a proposition which, in quasi-mathematical form, can be written as follows:

[1] "Let magnitudes which have the same proportion (λόγος) be called proportional (ἀνάλογον)" (Euclid V, Def. 6). For the sake of clarity it may be useful to indicate by a diagram the classification of analogy which I have adopted:

    I. Analogy *duorum ad tertium*.
    II. Analogy *unius ad alterum*.
        (i) Analogy of attribution or proportion, strictly *unius ad alterum*.
        (ii) Analogy of proportionality, *plurium ad plura*.
            (*a*) in loose sense (metaphor)
            (*b*) in strict sense.
Slightly different classifications may be found in Garrigou-Lagrange, *Dieu*, p. 351; Maquart, *Elem. Phil.*, III, ii, p. 36.

$$\frac{\text{way in which life of cabbage is determined by essence of cabbage}}{\text{essence of cabbage}}$$

$$= \frac{\text{way in which life of man is determined by essence of man}}{\text{essence of man}}$$

And again we shall have to remember that the equal sign means not identity but similarity, and shall now have to write:

$$\frac{\text{way in which way-in-which-life-of-cabbage-is-determined-by-essence-of-cabbage is determined by essence of cabbage}}{\text{essence of cabbage}}$$

$$= \frac{\text{way in which way-in-which-life-of-man-is-determined-by-essence-of-man is determined by essence of man}}{\text{essence of man}}$$

and so *ad infinitum.*

To put this more briefly, if we write L for "life of" and E for "essence of," c for "cabbage" and m for "man," and use A/B to signify "determination of A by B," we began by denying $Lc = Lm$, and put in its place

$$Lc/Ec = Lm/Em;$$

then we said that what we really meant was

$$(Lc/Ec)/Ec = (Lm/Em)/Em;$$

then we found that for this we should have to substitute

$$[(Lc/Ec)/Ec]/Ec = [(Lm/Em)/Em]/Em.$$

The next stage will be

$$\{[(Lc/Ec)/Ec]/Ec\}/Ec = \{[(Lm/Em)/Em]/Em\}/Em,$$

and so we shall go on for ever, at each successive stage denying progressively more complicated relationships between cabbages and men, and never managing to assert a relationship which we shall not immediately have to deny. And at the end of it we shall have nothing but a series of negations:

$$Lc \neq Lm,$$
$$Lc/Ec \neq Lm/Em,$$
$$(Lc/Ec)/Ec \neq (Lm/Em)/Em,$$
$$[(Lc/Ec)/Ec]/Ec \neq [(Lm/Em)/Em]/Em,$$

etc.

Our proportionality has completely collapsed, and all we are left with is the fact that cabbages have nothing in common with men except the fact that, for no valid reason, men have described them both as being alive. In fact, the introduction of analogy as a *via media* between univocity and equivocity has turned out to be nothing more than an imposing piece of mystification. This is the first objection of which we must take account; it is obviously a serious one. It strikes, not in particular at the analogical application of terms to God, but to analogical predication as such. I shall not attempt a full reply until I have stated another objection which is concerned with the specifically theological case, but I shall offer a few observations in passing.

First, then, we may remark that the objection, while on the surface plausible, has something of the appearance of a conjuring trick. It brings to mind two somewhat similar feats of philosophical legerdemain. The first is Lewis Carroll's *What the Tortoise said to Achilles*.[1] In this problem, which its originator did not perhaps intend to be taken as seriously as it really demands, Achilles maintained that, if two premisses A and B logically implied a conclusion Z, then anybody who saw this and also accepted A and B as true would have to accept Z as true also. The tortoise objected that this would only be the case if he accepted a further proposition C, namely that if A and B are true then Z must be true. Achilles was thus forced to modify his original assertion, so that it now took the form "Anyone who accepts A, B and C as true must accept Z as true also." But again the tortoise objected that this involved the acceptance of another proposition D, which was that, if A and B and C are all true, Z must be true as well. And so on for ever! This corresponds, of course, to the well-known fact that the principle of inference is incapable of formal symbolic statement within the logical calculus to which it applies.[2] A logical system cannot, as it were, operate under its own steam, without help from outside; we shall derive from this fact a pointer towards the solution of our present problem. The other puzzle to which I wish to refer is one which its originator took much more seriously: I mean Mr. F. H. Bradley's famous argument that relations are illusions.[3] It is, he urged, of the essence of a relation to unite terms, but how is each term united to the relation? It can only be by another relation, but if so, what unites the term to this? To make the first relation intelligible we have to presuppose an infinite sequence of relations

[1] *The Complete Works of Lewis Carroll*, pp. 1104 f.

[2] Cf. B. Russell, *The Principles of Mathematics*, pp. 16, 35, where explicit reference is made to Lewis Carroll's puzzle.

[3] *Appearance and Reality*, I, ch. iii.

antecedent to it, and none of these is yet intelligible. Hence, Mr. Bradley concluded, relations are mere illusion. Lord Russell has caustically remarked that if Bradley's argument were valid it would prove that chains are impossible—and yet they exist.[1] Dr. C. D. Broad has dealt with Bradley's problem in some detail. He takes as an instance of it the fact that A is father of B. "Here," he writes, "we have a perfectly intelligible statement, involving the non-formal[2] relation of *fatherhood*. At the next stage we get the fact that A is referent to *fatherhood,* and the fact that B is relatum to *fatherhood.* The 'relations' introduced at this stage are purely formal. At the next stage we get the fact that A is referent to *referent to,* that *fatherhood* is relatum to *referent to,* that *fatherhood* is referent to *referent to,* and that B is relatum to *referent to.* Thus no new 'relations' are introduced at this or any subsequent stage. The fact that at every stage after the first the relating relations are purely formal and are merely repeated shows that we are now embarked on the self-evidently impossible task of explaining, by means of particular relational judgments, that general relational form which is presupposed by all relational judgments whatever."[3] We might, in fact, say that, while it is of the essence of relations to unite terms, they are not themselves terms in this context (though, of course, in another context they may become terms, as when we pick out two relations, or a relation and a term, and ask what is the relation between them) . Similarly, in the case of analogy of proper proportionality, we might reply to our objector that we are simply concerned with the fact that essences determine their qualities, and that the truth of this is not in the least affected by the fact that they can only do this if they also determine the way in which they determine their qualities, and the way in which they determine the way in which they determine their qualities, and so on to the crack of doom. *Ce n'est que le premier pas qui coûte.*

Such a reply would, I think, go a very long way, though I am doubtful whether it is altogether sufficient. For the fact remains that we have denied that our equal signs really stand for equality and we have not indicated anything definite that they do stand for. Can we in some way re-establish this bond that we have broken? Clearly we cannot by analogy of proportionality, but I shall suggest

---

1 *Outline of Philosophy,* p. 263.

2 "Formal," for Broad and all the modern logicians, means "purely logical," "having no reference to particular concrete individual entities." This is very different from the scholastic use of the word.

3 *Examination of McTaggart's Philosophy,* I, p. 86.

that we can by analogy of attribution, and that the two types of analogy, while either in separation is insufficient, can in combination do what is required.[1] But this is an anticipation. I will pass on now to consider the second objection, which is specially concerned with analogical discourse about God.

[1] It may be interesting to see how Dr. A. M. Farrer deals with this difficulty. For him "this proportionality claims to hold between four terms, and not two relations. We are not saying," he continues, " 'The way in which the divine intelligence is related to the divine existence resembles the way in which the creaturely intelligence is related to the creaturely existence' for that is exactly what we have to deny. The way in which the several aspects of the divine being (e.g. intelligence) have their synthesis into one, itself differs from the way in which the several aspects of the creaturely being have their synthesis into one, *as* the divine being itself differs from the creaturely. What we are saying is completely different, viz. 'Divine intelligence is appropriate to divine existence as creaturely to creaturely' " (*Finite and Infinite*, p. 53, italics in original) .

Dr. Farrer's first point seems to me to be valuable, at least as denying *equality* of relations; in this respect the older mathematical notation for proportionality, $a : b :: c : d$, might be less misleading than the more modern $\frac{a}{b} = \frac{c}{d}$ But I do not think any scholastic would deny that proportionality was *some* sort of relation between two relations or would reduce it simply to a polyadic relation uniting four terms. Dr. Farrer himself in the quotation above seems, by italicizing the word "*as*," to admit the equal sign at a subsequent stage and, while denying

$$\frac{\text{divine intelligence}}{\text{divine existence}} = \frac{\text{human intelligence}}{\text{human existence}},$$

to be asserting

$$\frac{\text{synthesis of aspects in God}}{\text{being of God}} = \frac{\text{synthesis of aspects in creature}}{\text{being of creature}},$$

but I cannot think that this was his intention. He has previously said that the formula "presupposes that intelligence can be attributed to God, and declares how it is to be understood when it is attributed to him and not to the creature, viz. as differing from its creaturely mode with a difference analogous to that by which the divine existence differs from the creaturely. And so it presupposes also the 'proportion' between the two 'existences.' " He goes on to say: "Proportion logically underlies proportionality, but this need not mean that we originally entertain the notion of the proportion 'divine existence/creaturely existence except as the foundation for a proportionality; the two are distinguished by philosophical analysis only." The proportion now mentioned is, it will be noticed, not either of the proportions that form the two sides of the proportionality, but the proportion between a term on one side and a term on the other. This seems to be in line with my assertion that, in the relation of God to creatures, analogy of proportionality and of attribution (proportion) are interlocked. Dr. Farrer continues: "The natural use of the proportion is inseparable from that of the proportionality, as the apprehension of the very fact of the divine being is inseparable from some apprehension of its mode."

. . .

LET us therefore see what happens when we attribute life both to a creature and to God; any other perfection which can be formally predicated of God would, of course, do as well. Analogy of proportionality asserts:

$$\frac{\text{life of man}}{\text{essence of man}} = \frac{\text{life of God}}{\text{essence of God}}$$

Now, the objector urges, even if the first objection has been successfully overcome, so that we have no longer to bother about the fact that the equal sign does not indicate an exact identity of relationship, our formula will not in fact tell us in what sense life is to be predicated of God. For the essence of God is as little known to us as is his life; indeed his life is, formally considered, identical with it. Our equation has therefore two unknowns and cannot be solved. Nor can we get out of our difficulty by comparing essence with existence and saying that the essence of a being will correspond to, and be determined by, the act in virtue of which it exists:

$$\frac{\text{essence of man}}{\text{existential act of man}} = \frac{\text{essence of God}}{\text{existential act of God}}$$

Once again, both the terms on the right-hand side are unknown. Sheer agnosticism seems to be the outcome. What reply can we make?

Some scholastic philosophers, of whom Garrigou-Lagrange is one, claim to answer this objection, while remaining in the realm of analogy of proportionality, by denying that there are two unknown terms on the right-hand side. This last-mentioned writer, for example, taking the analogy

$$\frac{\text{creature}}{\text{its being}} = \frac{\text{first cause}}{\text{its being}}$$

asserts that only the fourth term is in fact unknown. "We have," he says, " (1) *the very confused concept of being in general,* which a child possesses from the moment of its first intellectual knowledge, (2) *the concept of finite being,* of which we know positively the finite mode and which is nothing else than the essence of the things that we see, stones, plants, animals, etc., (3) *the concept of analogous being,* imperfectly abstracted from the finite mode . . . ; it is a precision of the first very confused concept possessed by the child, and the metaphysician acquires it by recognizing that the formal notion of being does not in itself include the finite mode which accompanies it in the creature, (4) *the concept of the divine being,* the cause of created beings. These latter," he continues, "not having in their essence the reason of their existence, require a cause which exists of itself. In the concept of the divine being, the divine mode is expressed only in a negative and relative way, e.g. as non-finite or as supreme being. What is positive in this analogical knowledge of God is what God has that is proportionally common to him and the creature."[1] Again, he writes, *"being* designates *that which* has relation to existence; this relation is implied in the very nature of that which exists and it is essentially varied according as it is necessary or contingent. The created essence in its inmost entity is altogether relative to its contingent existence, which it can lose; the uncreated essence is conceived only relatively to that necessary existence with which it is identified. . . . Analogous perfections are thus not pure relations. They are perfections which imply in the creature a composition of two correlative elements, potentiality and act, but which in God are pure act. Our intelligence conceives that they are realized more fully according as they are purified of all potentiality; in God they exist therefore in the pure state. We thus see that there are not two unknowns in the proportionalities set up by theology."[2]

For this distinguished French Dominican, therefore, the third term in the formula is given us as that in which essence and existence are identical, and this gives us a limited and analogical, but nevertheless genuine, knowledge of the fourth term, while remaining within the realm of analogy of proportionality.[3] We can transfer the notion of any perfection from a finite being to God,

[1] *Dieu,* p. 541. [2] Ibid., p. 542.

[3] Penido's answer to the objection (*Rôle de l'Analogie,* pp. 136 f.) rests upon his assertion previously noticed (p. 96, *n.* 1, *supra*) that no use of analogy is necessary in the mere demonstration of the *existence* of God. Thus, in the proportionality,

$$\frac{\text{essence of creature}}{\text{existential act of creature}} = \frac{\text{essence of God}}{\text{existential act of God}},$$

the fourth term is not unknown; it is already given to us as self-existence, *ipsum esse subsistens,* existence not really distinct from essence. Thus, whereas for Garrigou-Lagrange the *third* term is given to us *in* and *through* the analogy, for Penido the *fourth* term is given to us *prior to* the analogy; thus he writes, "L'analogie . . . n'apparait pas *explicitement* au début de notre marche vers Dieu, elle ne s'occupe pas de la question 'an sit,' elle n'entre en jeu que lorsqu'il s'agit du 'quomodo sit'" (*Rôle,* p. 138). I cannot help feeling that at this point Penido is nearer the truth.

remembering that the difference of mode is that which corresponds to the difference between a being whose essence involves merely a possibility of existence and one whose essence involves existence of necessity. Of course, we do not know positively what the mode of the perfection in God is; to demand that would be to demand a quidditative knowledge of the divine essence and to abolish analogy altogether in favour of univocity. We are given all that we have a right to ask for; the comparison of the finite and the infinite modes of perfection is based on a comparison of the relations to existence which are proper to finite essence and to the divine essence respectively.

Now all this seems very satisfactory so far as it goes, but does it go far enough? Is it sufficient simply to base the comparison of the finite and infinite modes of a perfection upon a comparison of the finite and infinite modes of the essence-existence relation, without bringing in an explicit reference to the concrete relation which the creature has to God? There are indeed traces in Garrigou-Lagrange's own discussion of an awareness of the need of this further step; the very form in which he writes the formula last quoted suggests this. For he does not describe the finite being as a being in whom essence does not necessarily involve existence, but as a "creature"; and he does not describe God as a being whose essence necessarily involves existence, but as the "first cause." "In these equations," he writes, "two created terms are known directly, one uncreated term is known indirectly *by way of causality* and we infer the fourth term which is known indirectly in a *positive* manner as regards what is analogically common with creatures and in a *negative* and relative manner as regards its proper divine mode."[1] And the first cause and the creature are directly related by the relation of creation, which thus, as it were, cuts horizontally across the analogy of proportionality with an analogy of attribution.[2] The equal sign does not, as we have seen earlier, express a mathematical identity, but, on the other hand, the two sides of the formula are not left in complete separation. They are bound together by an analogy of attribution *unius ad alterum,* of the creature to God in the case which we have just been considering. In the cases con-

[1] *Dieu,* p. 543 (first set of italics mine).

[2] Garrigou-Lagrange himself writes: "If the analogy of being is formally an analogy of proportionality it is virtually an analogy of attribution, in the sense that if, *per impossibile,* being did not belong intrinsically to the creature it could still be extrinsically attributed to it, in so far as the creature is an effect of the prime Being" (*Dieu,* p. 541, note). It is the word "virtually" in this passage from which I am disposed to dissent. Penido lays great stress upon the "mixed" nature of the analogy between God and the world (*Rôle de l'Analogie,* p. 134 *et al.*).

sidered earlier, where the two sides of the formula both refer to finite beings, the linking analogy is an analogy *duorum ad tertium,* which holds in view of the fact that each of the analogates is in an analogy of attribution *unius ad alterum,* of itself to God. The figure below may help to make this plain.[1]

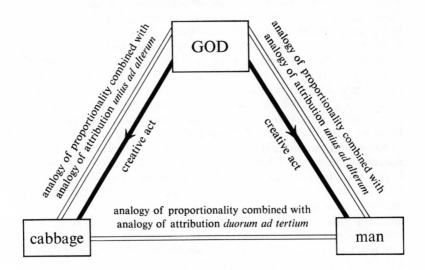

analogy of proportionality combined with analogy of attribution *duorum ad tertium*

The conclusion would thus seem to be that, in order to make the doctrine of analogy really satisfactory, we must see the analogical relation between God and the world as combining in a tightly interlocked union both analogy of attribution and analogy of proportionality. Without analogy of proportionality it is very doubtful whether the attributes which we predicate of God can be ascribed to him in more than a merely virtual sense; without analogy of attribution it hardly seems possible to avoid agnosticism. Which of the two forms of analogy is prior to the other has been, and still is, a hotly debated question among scholastic philosophers.

.   .   .

So long as we are talking about finite beings we can make statements about their natures or essences without any assertion

[1] It should here be noted that analogy *duorum ad tertium* is itself an instance of analogy of attribution.

about their existence. I can say that a unicorn has a horn on its nose and that a rhinoceros has a horn on its nose without suggesting that any animals with horns on their noses exist; that rhinoceroses do exist and that unicorns do not is a purely empirical fact. But I cannot say that God is good without asserting the existence of a good being; for since God is by definition self-existent being, to affirm that God is good is to speak of self-existent goodness, that is to say of goodness that cannot but exist.[1] Again, in talking about finite beings, we can ascribe to them properties not necessarily included in their essences. If I say that the Cambridge buses are red, I am not asserting that redness is necessarily inherent in the nature of a Cambridge bus; in fact there was a time when the Cambridge buses were green. When, however, I say that God is good or wise or just, I am inevitably asserting that goodness, wisdom and justice are inherent in the nature of God, for in God there are no accidents, no qualities that are not included in his essence.[2] It follows that all our statements about God have a directly existential reference, such as is possessed by none of our statements about finite beings except those in which existence is explicitly asserted. The only way in which I can assert that beings with horns on their noses exist is by affirming existence either of such beings in general or of some such being (for example, a unicorn or a rhinoceros) in particular; but I can assert that a good being exists simply by affirming that God is good. Since in God essence and existence are identical, any assertion about God's essence is at the same time an assertion about existence; anything which is affirmed to be included in God's nature is at the same time affirmed to exist, and indeed to be self-existent.

It is then, I suggest, in virtue of this inherently existential element in all our affirmations about God that the possibility of analogical knowledge of God and of analogical discourse about him can be maintained. If it were possible to make a statement about God that bore exclusively on the essential or conceptual order, that statement would collapse into sheer equivocity and agnosticism, for no concept of the essence of God can be formed by a finite mind.[3] Since, however, God's essence necessarily involves his existence, no

---

[1] I am assuming here, of course, that God has been already shown to exist. Until that has been done, to assert that God is good does not ascribe to goodness existence *ut exercita*, but only *ut signata*; to hold otherwise would be to accept the ontological argument.

[2] The apparent exceptions to this statement, arising from God's action in the finite realm, are discussed elsewhere in this book. (Ch. vi *infra*.)

[3] On this ground one can, I think, justify Sertillanges' description of Thomism as "an agnosticism of definition" (*Le Christianisme et les Philosophies*, I, p. 270), for definition is concerned with the essence and the concept. One could not

statement about him can remain in the essential or conceptual order; it passes over immediately into the order of existence and the judgment. What begins as an attempt to conceive God's goodness— an attempt which is doomed to failure—issues in an affirmation that self-existent goodness exists; but even this last statement needs careful interpretation if it is not to be taken as implying that we form a concept of "self-existent goodness."[1] It would perhaps be better to say that goodness exists self-existingly, for then the fundamental dependence of analogical predication upon the metaphysical analogy of being is made clear. We can then see how we must interpret the formula

$$\frac{\text{goodness of finite being}}{\text{finite being}} = \frac{\text{goodness of God}}{\text{God}}$$

as holding not merely in the order of essence but in that of existence, as expressing not a comparison of concepts but an existential judgment. The second term on the left-hand side of our formula ("finite being") expresses precisely that contingency of existence which arises from the fact that in finite beings essence and existence are really distinct; the second term on the right-hand side ("God") expresses that necessity of existence which arises from the fact that in God essence and existence are really identical. And the two sides of the formula are held together by that analogy of attribution which asserts, not merely in the conceptual but in the existential order, that finite being can exist only in dependence upon God. The goodness of God is thus declared to be self-existent goodness, and, as such, identical not merely with God's essence but with the act by which God exists. Analogy does not enable us to *conceive* God's goodness as identical with his essence but to *affirm* it as identical with his existence. Hence all our assertions about God are grossly inadequate in so far as they apply concepts to him, but they are thoroughly adequate in so far as they affirm perfections of him. Here the relevance of the distinction between the *perfectio*

---

validly describe Thomism as "an agnosticism of the judgment." It is important to grasp that, whereas in the case of analogy between finite beings, the doctrine of analogy has merely to grapple with the distinction between the *perfectio significate* and the *modus significandi*, in the case of analogy between a finite being and God it has to grapple with the far greater difficulty of the gulf that separates the finite creature from the infinite Creator.

[1] The tendency of the human mind to take refuge in concepts is as ineradicable as its tendency to turn to sensible images: *convertit se ad phantasmata,* indeed, but also *ad conceptus!* It is always trying to conceptualize existence instead of affirming it.

significata and the *modus significandi* can be seen at the full, as can also the reconciliation of the apparent contradiction between St. Thomas's "agnosticism" and his conviction that we can make genuine assertions about God. The names which we apply to God, he says, "designate the divine substance and are predicated of God substantially, but they fall short of representing him."[1] We cannot, in short, know God's essence by forming a concept of it, but we can know it analogically in our concepts of finite beings. I shall conclude at this point this already over-long discussion of the scholastic doctrine of analogy, and in doing so I will remind the reader again that its purpose has been, not to discover whether it is possible intelligibly to talk about God, but to explain how it is that we have been able to do so and to analyse what it is that we have in fact been doing.

[1] *Nomina significant substantiam divinam et praedicantur de Deo substantialiter sed deficiunt a repraesentatione ipsius (S. Theol., I., xiii, 2c).*

3

RELIGION AS NONSENSE*

*Alfred J. Ayer (1910–   ) is Wykeham
Professor of Logic at Oxford University.
An early and influential exponent of
logical positivism, he has recently modified
his views somewhat. His* major works
include Language, Truth and Logic, The
Problem of Knowledge, *and* The Concept
of a Person and Other Essays.

A. J. Ayer

IT will be seen that, in this book, I begin by suggesting that a statement is "weakly" verifiable, and therefore meaningful, according to my criterion, if "some possible sense-experience would be relevant to the determination of its truth or falsehood." But, as I recognize, this itself requires interpretation; for the word "relevant" is uncomfortably vague. Accordingly, I put forward a second version of my principle, which I shall restate here in slightly different terms, using the phrase "observation-statement," in place of "experiential proposition," to designate a statement "which records an actual or possible observation." In this version, then, the principle is that a statement is verifiable, and consequently meaningful, if some observation-statement can be deduced from it in conjunction with certain other premises, without being deducible from those other premises alone.

I say of this criterion that it "seems liberal enough," but in fact it is far too liberal, since it allows meaning to any statement whatsoever. For, given any statement *"S"* and an observation-statement *"O," "O"* follows from *"S"* and "if *S* then *O*" without following from "if *S* then *O*" alone. Thus, the statements, "the Absolute is lazy" and "if the Absolute is lazy, this is white" jointly entail the observation-statement "this is white," and since "this is white" does not follow from either of these premises, taken by itself, both of them satisfy my criterion of meaning. Furthermore, this would hold good for any other piece of nonsense that one cared to put, as an example, in place of "the Absolute is lazy," provided only that it had the grammatical form of an indicative sentence. But a

* From *Language, Truth and Logic* by Alfred Jules Ayer. Published by Dover Publications, Inc., New York 14, N.Y. Reprinted by permission of the publisher.

criterion of meaning that allows such latitude as this is evidently unacceptable.[1]

It may be remarked that the same objection applies to the proposal that we should take the possibility of falsification as our criterion. For, given any statement "S" and any observation-statement "O," "O" will be incompatible with the conjunction of "S" and "if S then not O." We could indeed avoid the difficulty, in either case, by leaving out the stipulation about the other premises. But as this would involve the exclusion of all hypotheticals from the class of empirical propositions, we should escape from making our criteria too liberal only at the cost of making them too stringent.

Another difficulty which I overlooked in my original attempt to formulate the principle of verification is that most empirical propositions are in some degree vague. Thus, as I have remarked elsewhere,[2] what is required to verify a statement about a material thing is never the occurrence of precisely this or precisely that sense-content, but only the occurrence of one or other of the sense-contents that fall within a fairly indefinite range. We do indeed test any such statement by making observations which consist in the occurrence of particular sense-contents; but, for any test that we actually carry out, there is always an indefinite number of other tests, differing to some extent in respect either of their conditions or their results, that would have served the same purpose. And this means that there is never any set of observation-statements of which it can truly be said that precisely they are entailed by any given statement about a material thing.

Nevertheless, it is only by the occurrence of some sense-content, and consequently by the truth of some observation-statement, that any statement about a material thing is actually verified; and from this it follows that every significant statement about a material thing can be represented as entailing a disjunction of observation-statements, although the terms of this disjunction, being infinite, can not be enumerated in detail. Consequently, I do not think that we need be troubled by the difficulty about vague-ness, so long as it is understood that when we speak of the "entail-ment" of observation-statements, what we are considering to be deducible from the premises in question is not any particular observation-statement, but only one or other of a set of such statements, where the defining characteristic of the set is that all its members refer to sense-contents that fall within a certain specifiable range.

---

[1] Vide I. Berlin, "Verifiability in Principle," *Proceedings of the Aristotelian Society*, Vol. XXXIX.

[2] *The Foundations of Empirical Knowledge*, pp. 240–1.

There remains the more serious objection that my criterion, as it stands, allows meaning to any indicative statement whatsoever. To meet this, I shall emend it as follows. I propose to say that a statement is directly verifiable if it is either itself an observation-statement, or is such that in conjunction with one or more observation-statements it entails at least one observation-statement which is not deducible from these other premises alone; and I propose to say that a statement is indirectly verifiable if it satisfies the following conditions: first, that in conjunction with certain other premises it entails one or more directly verifiable statements which are not deducible from these other premises alone; and secondly, that these other premises do not include any statement that is not either analytic, or directly verifiable, or capable of being independently established as indirectly verifiable. And I can now reformulate the principle of verification as requiring of a literally meaningful statement, which is not analytic, that it should be either directly or indirectly verifiable, in the foregoing sense.

.   .   .

THIS mention of God brings us to the question of the possibility of religious knowledge. We shall see that this possibility has already been ruled out by our treatment of metaphysics. But, as this is a point of considerable interest, we may be permitted to discuss it at some length.

It is now generally admitted, at any rate by philosophers, that the existence of a being having the attributes which define the god of any non-animistic religion cannot be demonstratively proved. To see that this is so, we have only to ask ourselves what are the premises from which the existence of such a god could be deduced. If the conclusion that a god exists is to be demonstratively certain, then these premises must be certain; for, as the conclusion of a deductive argument is already contained in the premises, any uncertainty there may be about the truth of the premises is necessarily shared by it. But we know that no empirical proposition can ever be anything more than probable. It is only *a priori* propositions that are logically certain. But we cannot deduce the existence of a god from an *a priori* proposition. For we know that the reason why *a priori* propositions are certain is that they are tautologies. And from a set of tautologies nothing but a further tautology can be validly deduced. It follows that there is no possibility of demonstrating the existence of a god.

What is not so generally recognised is that there can be no

way of proving that the existence of a god, such as the God of Christianity, is even probable. Yet this also is easily shown. For if the existence of such a god were probable, then the proposition that he existed would be an empirical hypothesis. And in that case it would be possible to deduce from it, and other empirical hypotheses, certain experiential propositions which were not deducible from those other hypotheses alone. But in fact this is not possible. It is sometimes claimed, indeed, that the existence of a certain sort of regularity in nature constitutes sufficient evidence for the existence of a god. But if the sentence "God exists" entails no more than that certain types of phenomena occur in certain sequences, then to assert the existence of a god will be simply equivalent to asserting that there is the requisite regularity in nature; and no religious man would admit that this was all he intended to assert in asserting the existence of a god. He would say that in talking about God, he was talking about a transcendent being who might be known through certain empirical manifestations, but certainly could not be defined in terms of those manifestations. But in that case the term "god" is a metaphysical term. And if "god" is a metaphysical term, then it cannot be even probable that a god exists. For to say that "God exists" is to make a metaphysical utterance which cannot be either true or false. And by the same criterion, no sentence which purports to describe the nature of a transcendent god can possess any literal significance.

It is important not to confuse this view of religious assertions with the view that is adopted by atheists, or agnostics.[1] For it is characteristic of an agnostic to hold that the existence of a god is a possibility in which there is no good reason either to believe or disbelieve; and it is characteristic of an atheist to hold that it is at least probable that no god exists. And our view that all utterances about the nature of God are nonsensical, so far from being identical with, or even lending any support to, either of these familiar contentions, is actually incompatible with them. For if the assertion that there is a god is nonsensical, then the atheist's assertion that there is no god is equally nonsensical, since it is only a significant proposition that can be significantly contradicted. As for the agnostic, although he refrains from saying either that there is or that there is not a god, he does not deny that the question whether a transcendent god exists is a genuine question. He does not deny that the two sentences "There is a transcendent god" and "There is no transcendent god" express propositions one of which is actually true and the other false. All he says is that we have no means of

[1] This point was suggested to me by Professor H. H. Price.

telling which of them is true, and therefore ought not to commit ourselves to either. But we have seen that the sentences in question do not express propositions at all. And this means that agnosticism also is ruled out.

Thus we offer the theist the same comfort as we gave to the moralist. His assertions cannot possibly be valid, but they cannot be invalid either. As he says nothing at all about the world, he cannot justly be accused of saying anything false, or anything for which he has insufficient grounds. It is only when the theist claims that in asserting the existence of a transcendent god he is expressing a genuine proposition that we are entitled to disagree with him.

It is to be remarked that in cases where deities are identified with natural objects, assertions concerning them may be allowed to be significant. If, for example, a man tells me that the occurrence of thunder is alone both necessary and sufficient to establish the truth of the proposition that Jehovah is angry, I may conclude that, in his usage of words, the sentence "Jehovah is angry" is equivalent to "It is thundering." But in sophisticated religions, though they may be to some extent based on men's awe of natural process which they cannot sufficiently understand, the "person" who is supposed to control the empirical world is not himself located in it; he is held to be superior to the empirical world, and so outside it; and he is endowed with super-empirical attributes. But the notion of a person whose essential attributes are non-empirical is not an intelligible notion at all. We may have a word which is used as if it named this "person," but, unless the sentences in which it occurs express propositions which are empirically verifiable, it cannot be said to symbolize anything. And this is the case with regard to the word "god," in the usage in which it is intended to refer to a transcendent object. The mere existence of the noun is enough to foster the illusion that there is a real, or at any rate a possible entity corresponding to it. It is only when we enquire what God's attributes are that we discover that "God," in this usage, is not a genuine name.

It is common to find belief in a transcendent god conjoined with belief in an after-life. But, in the form which it usually takes, the content of this belief is not a genuine hypothesis. To say that men do not ever die, or that the state of death is merely a state of prolonged insensibility, is indeed to express a significant proposition, though all the available evidence goes to show that it is false. But to say that there is something imperceptible inside a man, which is his soul or his real self, and that it goes on living after he is dead, is to make a metaphysical assertion which has no more factual content than the assertion that there is a transcendent god.

It is worth mentioning that, according to the account which we have given of religious assertions, there is no logical ground for antagonism between religion and natural science. As far as the question of truth or falsehood is concerned, there is no opposition between the natural scientist and the theist who believes in a transcendent god. For since the religious utterances of the theist are not genuine propositions at all, they cannot stand in any logical relation to the propositions of science. Such antagonism as there is between religion and science appears to consist in the fact that science takes away one of the motives which make men religious. For it is acknowedged that one of the ultimate sources of religious feeling lies in the inability of men to determine their own destiny; and science tends to destroy the feeling of awe with which men regard an alien world, by making them believe that they can understand and anticipate the course of natural phenomena, and even to some extent control it. The fact that it has recently become fashionable for physicists themselves to be sympathetic towards religion is a point in favour of this hypothesis. For this sympathy towards religion marks the physicists' own lack of confidence in the validity of their hypotheses, which is a reaction on their part from the anti-religious dogmatism of nineteenth-century scientists, and a natural outcome of the crisis through which physics has just passed.

It is not within the scope of this enquiry to enter more deeply into the causes of religious feeling, or to discuss the probability of the continuance of religious belief. We are concerned only to answer those questions which arise out of our discussion of the possibility of religious knowledge. The point which we wish to establish is that there cannot be any transcendent truths of religion. For the sentences which the theist uses to express such "truths" are not literally significant.

An interesting feature of this conclusion is that it accords with what many theists are accustomed to say themselves. For we are often told that the nature of God is a mystery which transcends the human understanding. But to say that something transcends the human understanding is to say that it is unintelligible. And what is unintelligible cannot significantly be described. Again, we are told that God is not an object of reason but an object of faith. This may be nothing more than an admission that the existence of God must be taken on trust, since it cannot be proved. But it may also be an assertion that God is the object of a purely mystical intuition, and cannot therefore be defined in terms which are intelligible to the reason. And I think there are many theists who would assert this. But if one allows that it is impossible to define God in intelligible terms, then one is allowing that it is impossible for a sentence both to be significant and to be about God. If a mystic admits that the object of his vision is something which cannot be described, then he must also admit that he is bound to talk nonsense when he describes it.

For his part, the mystic may protest that his intuition does reveal truths to him, even though he cannot explain to others what these truths are; and that we who do not possess this faculty of intuition can have no ground for denying that it is a cognitive faculty. For we can hardly maintain *a priori* that there are no ways of discovering true propositions except those which we ourselves employ. The answer is that we set no limit to the number of ways in which one may come to formulate a true proposition. We do not in any way deny that a synthetic truth may be discovered by purely intuitive methods as well as by the rational method of induction. But we do say that every synthetic proposition, however it may have been arrived at, must be subject to the test of actual experience. We do not deny *a priori* that the mystic is able to discover truths by his own special methods. We wait to hear what are the propositions which embody his discoveries, in order to see whether they are verified or confuted by our empirical observations. But the mystic, so far from producing propositions which are empirically verified, is unable to produce any intelligible propositions at all. And therefore we say that his intuition has not revealed to him any facts. It is no use his saying that he has apprehended facts but is unable to express them. For we know that if he really had acquired any information, he would be able to express it. He would be able to indicate in some way or other how the genuineness of his discovery might be empirically determined. The fact that he cannot reveal what he "knows," or even himself devise an empirical test to validate his "knowledge," shows that his state of mystical intuition is not a genuinely cognitive state. So that in describing his vision the mystic does not give us any information about the external world; he merely gives us indirect information about the condition of his own mind.

These considerations dispose of the argument from religious experience, which many philosophers still regard as a valid argument in favour of the existence of a god. They say that it is logically possible for men to be immediately acquainted with God, as they are immediately acquainted with a sense-content, and that there is no reason why one should be prepared to believe a man when he says that he is seeing a yellow patch, and refuse to believe him when he says that he is seeing God. The answer to this is that if the man who asserts that he is seeing God is merely asserting that he is experiencing a peculiar kind of sense-content, then we do not for a moment deny that his assertion may be true. But, ordinarily, the man who says that he is seeing God is saying not merely that he is experiencing a religious emotion, but also that there exists a transcendent being who is the object of this emotion; just as the man who says that he sees a yellow patch is ordinarily saying not merely that his visual sense-field contains a yellow sense-content, but also that there exists a yellow object to which the sense-content belongs. And it is not irrational to be prepared to believe a man when he asserts the existence of a yellow object, and to refuse to believe him when he asserts the existence of a transcendent god. For whereas the sentence "There exists here a yellow-coloured material thing" expresses a genuine synthetic proposition which could be empirically verified, the sentence "There exists a transcendent god" has, as we have seen, no literal significance.

We conclude, therefore, that the argument from religious experience is altogether fallacious. The fact that people have religious experiences is interesting from the psychological point of view, but it does not in any way imply that there is such a thing as religious knowledge, any more than our having moral experiences implies that there is such a thing as moral knowledge. The theist, like the moralist, may believe that his experiences are cognitive experiences, but, unless he can formulate his "knowledge" in propositions that are empirically verifiable, we may be sure that he is deceiving himself. It follows that those philosophers who fill their books with assertions that they intuitively "know" this or that moral or religious "truth" are merely providing material for the psycho-analyst. For no act of intuition can be said to reveal a truth about any matter of fact unless it issues in verifiable propositions. And all such propositions are to be incorporated in the system of empirical propositions which constitutes science.

4

POSITIVISM AND RELIGION*

Frederick C. Copleston (1907–   ),
Professor of History of Philosophy at
Heythrop College (Oxford) and at the
Gregorian University of Rome, is a leading
contemporary Catholic philosopher. He
is probably best known for his seven-
volume History of Philosophy, *though he*
is the author of several other books and
articles.

Frederick Copleston

It is now generally recognized, I think, that the procedure whereby one first analyzes the meaning of a particular type of statement (in the present context an empirical hypothesis) and then forms on this basis a general criterion of meaning, should be reckoned as a purely methodological procedure, useful perhaps for elucidating an important difference between statements of one particular class and statements which do not belong to that class but inadequate for establishing what statements are meaningful in a more general sense. But I should like to illustrate the point by utilizing some examples which I once cited in an (unpublished) broadcast talk on *Meaning.*

Suppose that a friend who is stopping in my house says to me: "I am looking for the evening paper. Do you know where it is?" And suppose that I reply: "It is on the table in the far corner of the room." As I was aware that my friend was looking for the paper, and as I wished to help him to find it, it is at least not unreasonable to say that the intended meaning of my reply was: "If you look on the table in the far corner of the room, you will see the paper." In other words, it is not unreasonable to analyze my reply as being equivalent to a prediction. Again, take the statement that the chemical formula for water is H_2O. It is not unreasonable to say that the statement is a prediction and that it means: "If anyone were to burn oxygen and hydrogen in the proportions mentioned, he would obtain water, and conversely, if anyone were to institute a

* From Frederick Copleston, S.J., *Contemporary Philosophy.* Reprinted by permission of Burns and Oates.

chemical analysis of water he would obtain oxygen and hydrogen in the proportions mentioned."

But is there not perhaps some confusion here? If I tell my friend that the paper is on the table in the far corner of the room, my statement can be said to "mean" that if he looks on the table in question he will see the paper, in the sense that the first statement implies the second statement in a loose sense of the word "imply." But the meaning of the first statement cannot be identical with the meaning of the second statement. In view of my practical purpose in telling my friend that the paper is on the table, it is natural, if one wishes to analyze my statement as a prediction, to say that it means that if my friend looks on the table he will see the paper. But it requires no great ingenuity to see that it also means other things. In other words, that my friend on looking at the surface of the table will see the paper is not the only verifying statement which is implied by the statement that the paper is on the table. The latter statement can be verified in a number of other ways. Thus a number of other predictions could be "derived" from it. And it would certainly be a strange and paradoxical position if one were to maintain that the meaning of the statement that the paper is on the table cannot be understood until one knows all the possible ways of verifying it. Further, if this position is to be rejected, it can hardly be maintained that the meaning of my reply to my friend is identical with the meaning of the statement which enunciates one particular mode of verifying it.

I have spoken above of implying "in a loose sense of the word 'imply'." If the ordinary man were asked whether the statement that the paper is on the table implies that anyone who is not blind and who looks on the table will see the paper, provided that there is sufficient light in the room, he would doubtless answer "yes." But it is clear that the second statement introduces fresh ideas which are not contained in the original statement. And this is, of course, one reason why positivists have said, not that an empirical statement must be accounted meaningless unless an observation-statement can be derived from it alone, but rather that it must be accounted meaningless unless an observation-statement can be derived from it plus other statements. But how could we set about this process of deriving unless we first knew the meaning of the original statement? And if we must first know the meaning of the original statement, this meaning cannot be identical with the meaning of any observation-statement derived from it plus other statements. The most that we could legitimately say would be that it does not qualify for inclusion in the rank of empirical hypotheses unless it is possible to derive from it, together with other statements, an observation-statement. This would follow from the meaning given to the term "empirical hypothesis." But in this case nothing would immediately follow with regard to the meaningfulness of statements which do not fulfil this condition. Except that they are not "empirical hypotheses." To call a statement meaningless would be no more than to say that it is not an empirical hypothesis.

It may be said that I have been flogging a dead horse. And I am, indeed, well aware that those who make explicit use of the principle of verifiability acknowledge that they use it as a methodological principle. I am also aware that they admit that when they use this principle as a criterion of meaning they do not intend to assert that statements which fail to satisfy the criterion are devoid of meaning in every sense. They would not wish to say that ethical statements, for example, are "nonsensical," unless, indeed, the word "nonsensical" is given a technical significance which renders the assertion innocuous. Hence I am not under the illusion that I have been waging a victorious campaign against Professor X or Professor Y. None the less, I wished to indicate one or two of the reasons why the old positivist approach to the problem of meaning seems to me to be inadequate.

.   .   .

AT the same time it is, I think, possible to free the principle of verifiability from its association with the analysis of scientific statements as predictions and to state it in such a way that it becomes acceptable as a general criterion of the meaningfulness of factual and descriptive statements.

Let us take the statement that the car is in the garage. I cannot be said to know the meaning of this statement unless I can understand what state of affairs is asserted. This is obvious. And I cannot understand what state of affairs is asserted unless I am in a position to understand what state of affairs is excluded. For if I thought that the statement that the car is in the garage was compatible with the statement that the car is in some other place than the garage, I could not be said to know the meaning of the statement that the car is in the garage. And if the statement that the car is in the garage was really compatible with the statement that the car is not in the garage but in some other place, we could not say that the statement possessed any definite meaning. This is not an arbitrary criterion of meaning. Reflection on the nature of descriptive language will show that a statement which asserts a certain state of affairs excludes a contradictory state of affairs. If it does not do so, it cannot be said to have any definite meaning. And if I am not capable of understanding what is excluded (even though I do not here and now advert to what is excluded), I cannot be said to understand the meaning of a descriptive statement.

Now, the statement is true if the state of affairs which is asserted actually obtains. It is thus true to say that we do not understand the meaning of the statement, unless we understand what would verify the statement. In order to understand the meaning of the statement it is not, of course, necessary that we should know whether the statement is in fact true. But we cannot be said to understand its meaning unless we understand what would make it true, if it were true. It follows that there is a sense in which we can legitimately claim that we do not understand the meaning of a factual or descriptive statement unless we know "the mode of its verification." But here there is no question of "deriving" observation-statements, with the consequent difficulty that we could not derive any further statement unless we first knew the meaning of the original statement. It is merely a question of understanding the state of affairs asserted.

. . .

IF these considerations provide us with a general criterion or test of meaning, it must, of course, apply to metaphysical statements. But we obviously cannot apply it to "the metaphysical statement" in the abstract. It is generally recognized now that metaphysical statements have to be examined separately. To claim that such statements can be meaningful is not the same thing as claiming that all the statements ever made by metaphysicians are meaningful. Metaphysicians are probably much like other people, and they may sometimes make statements to which it is difficult to attach any clear meaning. After all, it is not entirely unknown for one metaphysician to question the meaningful character of a statement made by another metaphysician.

I should not, however, wish to press the term "clear meaning." The minimum requirement for the understanding of a factual or descriptive statement is that we should understand the state of affairs asserted to the extent of being capable of understanding at least something which is excluded. It is not required that we should have a perfect understanding of the state of affairs asserted before the statement can be recognized as meaningful. This is a point of some importance. Further mention of it in a particular context is made in the essay on *The Meaning of the Terms Predicated of God*.

A final point. Let us suppose that we do not understand the

meaning of a factual or descriptive statement unless we understand the state of affairs which would verify it, if it were in fact true, to the extent at least of being able to distinguish between the state of affairs which is asserted and the contradictory state of affairs, which is excluded. By the word "understand" I do not necessarily mean "imagine." The examples of the paper on the table and of the car in the garage may suggest that I do mean this. But the conclusion would be incorrect. If by "understand" I simply meant "imagine," I should have to exclude from the rank of meaningful statements all metaphysical statements, for example, which concerned spiritual entities. Some would doubtless wish to do this, following in the footsteps of Hobbes. But I have been trying to free the "principle of verifiability" not only from a too close association with a particular analysis of scientific propositions but also from dependence on any particular philosophical presuppositions. If stated on the lines indicated above, it has, in itself, nothing to do with dogmatic materialism. One may add perhaps that if we substitute "imagine" for "understand" in all cases, we may very well find ourselves in considerable difficulty with regard to a number of the propositions of physical science, quite apart from the bearing of this substitution on metaphysics.

5

THE POSSIBILITY
OF THEOLOGY*

Ian Ramsey ▩

*Ian T. Ramsey (1915–   ) is Nolloth
Professor of the Philosophy of the Christian Religion in the University of Oxford.
He has attempted to apply the analytic
techniques of modern philosophy to
problems of religious language. His writings include* Religious Language *and*
Models and Mystery.

I

Here a Mill and there a river
Each a glimpse and gone forever.

So in *A Child's Garden of Verses* Robert Louis Stevenson epito-
mizes the transitoriness which characterizes the landscape seen on a
railway journey, when we are presented with new scenes and new
objects passing before our eyes in rapid succession. It is in such
situations that people consult their guide books; love to have landmarks pointed out to them; like to know their bearings. It is in such
situations that people display, I would suggest, their metaphysical
tendencies. For metaphysics arises from man's desire to know, in a
world of change and transitoriness, just where he is journeying; it
arises whenever man seeks to map the Universe and to plot his
position within it. Kant provides a ready illustration. The three
questions by which he expresses his interests:[1] What can I know?
What ought I to do? What may I hope? are easily seen as a particular expression of man's metaphysical desire to plot his cosmic
position.

---

* Ian Ramsey, "On the Possibility and Purpose of a Metaphysical Theology" in
Ian Ramsey (ed.), *Prospect for Metaphysics*. Reprinted by permission of the
Philosophical Library.

[1] 'All the interests of my reason . . . combine in the three following questions. . . .' I. Kant, *Critique of Pure Reason*, Transcendental Doctrine of Method,
II. The Canon of Pure Reason, Section 2, trans. N. Kemp Smith, p. 635.

Whatever their different starting points and methods, metaphysians have all shared in the desire to have an outline map of the Universe, some over-all scheme capable of placing whatever transitoriness brought with it.[1] It is such an outline map that Descartes essays to construct in his *Meditations* and develops somewhat in his *Principles of Philosophy* and *Passions of the Soul*. Alternatively, if we feel helpless against the manifold powers of a threatening world, Spinoza's hope is that his metaphysics will enable us to see our due place in the Universe, replacing bewilderment by a beatific vision, fear by an intellectual love of God, confusion by the Third Kind of Knowledge. Nor do these outline maps exclude the most commonplace and ordinary events. On the contrary, if we feel a pain by eating lobster, Leibniz would show us how these two events occurred together according to a pre-established harmony which resulted from God actualizing what he judged to be the best of all the different worlds that were logically possible. Our lobster-pain takes on a cosmic significance.

So it is that Whitehead can rightly say that 'the true method of philosophical construction is to frame a scheme of ideas, the best that one can, and unflinchingly to explore the interpretation of experience in terms of that scheme. The importance of philosophy lies in its sustained effort to make such schemes explicit and thereby capable of criticism and improvement.'[2] Here is the broad purpose of metaphysics: to elaborate some explicit interpretative scheme, critically suited as far as may be to the whole of experience.

Metaphysicians, then, seek for some kind of language-map by which, in some way, to understand the whole Universe. Now what is the relation of such a map to ordinary language? To answer that question let us first give three examples of maps which while not being in themselves metaphysical, can yet afford clues as to what metaphysics does.

(1) We see a field of cows, and say 'five'. Here is a highly generalized concept associated with the language of arithmetic; a language which can link talk about cows with talk of fingers and toes, talk of balls on a counting-frame, and much else. We may generalize even further. If we see a billiard ball and talk of $x^2 + y^2 + z^2 = C^2$, we link talk about the billiard ball with talk about oranges, about the earth, about an Association (but not a Rugby) football, about tennis balls, squash balls, raindrops and suet dum-

---

1 Such a scheme, as P. F. Strawson notes in his *Individuals*, p. 9, may be either 'descriptive' or 'revisionary', but we may agree that 'perhaps no actual metaphysician has ever been, both in intention and effect, wholly the one thing or the other'.

2 *Process and Reality* (Preface).

plings. Again, we look on the waves rising and falling at sea, and when we talk of them in terms such as sin θ, we use language linking our talk of the sea with talk about wireless and television programmes, about the vibration of bridges and so on. Mathematics in this way provides languages such as arithmetic, algebraical geometry and trigonometrical analysis, which, brought alongside common-sense language, can help to unite what is apparently diverse, can help us to attain wide sweeps of generalization. The same is true, and more so, of such mathematical theory as is used in the sciences, as well as of scientific theory itself which can relate what is, for common sense, utterly diverse. For example, the chemistry of carbon unites soot and diamonds; gravitational theory unites falling apples, the stars and the tides. Some have been so impressed by this generalizing power possessed by mathematics and scientific theory that they have asserted that what could not be talked about in terms of the precision languages of mathematics and science 'is not really there'; that, for instance, the redness of the sunset is no more than the vibrations of certain colourless point particles. But this is plainly a blunder if it means that what falls outside express treatment by mathematics or the sciences 'does not exist'; that there is no 'redness' of the sunset. Mathematics, like the exact sciences, is as such only an ancillary scheme. We shall see that despite many differences metaphysics, too, must be likewise regarded as an ancillary scheme.

(2) Similarly, logic—whether traditional or modern—is a scheme, less or more complex, less or more unified, whose purpose is to illuminate, as and where it can, the connexions between assertions which occur in ordinary discourse. At this point we may usefully quote an illustration which Strawson gives in his *Introduction to Logical Theory*:[1]

'The formal logician now aims at an exact and highly systematic logic, comparable in these respects with mathematics. But he cannot give the exact and systematic logic of expressions of everyday speech; for these expressions have no exact and systematic logic. What he can and does do, is to devise a set of rules which satisfies his requirements and, at the same time, while not doing full justice to the complexities of ordinary usage, and diverging from it in many ways, does touch ordinary usage at some vital points. The formal logician, in relation to ordinary language, might be compared with a man ostensibly mapping a piece of country of which the main contours are highly irregular and shifting. But the man is passionately addicted to geometry, and insists on using in his drawings only geometrical figures for which rules of construction can be given; and on using as few of such rules as he can. Naturally his maps will never

[1] *loc. cit.*, pp. 57–8.

quite fit. But a good many landmarks are identifiable on his drawing, and there is a rough correspondence between some of the main features of the country and some of the main lines of the map. The logician, we may say, manufactures the elements of a language of his own, which, unlike ordinary language, is subject to rigid and systematically connected rules, and some of the symbols of which exhibit logical analogies to familiar expressions of ordinary speech, as those expressions are commonly, though not always, used. And in the process of system-construction he may, and does—if only by contrast—teach us a good deal about the logic of ordinary discourse.'

What the logician does, then, is 'to devise a set of rules which satisfies his [formal] requirements and, at the same time, while not doing full justice to the complexities of ordinary usage, and diverging from it in many ways, does touch ordinary usage at some vital points'. The metaphysician is guided by other 'requirements', but he likewise is concerned to devise a system which touches ordinary usage at vital points.

(3) Thirdly, we take an example from elementary physics. Crossing a footbridge over a stream, we put our stick in the water, and say 'It looks bent'. We then kneel on the bridge, run our finger along the stick, and say 'Yet, it's straight'. So far we are using ordinary language: but ordinary language is now puzzling. For how can we talk of this stick being bent and straight *at the same time?*

And now along comes the physicist with his Theory of Refraction. We hear talk of light being some kind of wave motion; with its speed different in different media; that therefore light 'rays' are bent in passing from air to water. Geometrical diagrams are now produced to show why sticks look bent in water, ponds look shallower than they are, and so on.

Now what exactly does this Theory of Refraction do? Has the physicist got some super-microscopic insight which sees light actually changing its speed in the water, as a ship or a swimmer might do? Nothing as simple and straightforward as that. Rather has the physicist resolved our perplexity, and released our tongues (and done much else with which we need not now concern ourselves) by bringing alongside the puzzle a rather complex map—the Theory of Refraction. Look at it like this, he says: and then he entertains us with talk of light rays, their speed in different media, refraction at the boundary between two media, and so on. If we are willing to buy his wares, then our tongues become loosed. His 'theory' makes it possible for us with justification to use 'bent' and 'straight' of the stick at one and the same time by saying 'The stick is *really* straight: it only appears (or seems) bent'.

In this way, the physicist, by bringing his theory alongside ordinary language, provides us with language links of such a kind that the problematical character of our original assertion disappears. The theory enables us to make logical connexions which hitherto we found impossible to forge; and we declare our acceptance of the theory, we acknowledge its illumination in using the word 'really'. This is the option we are taking seriously, in what the preacher calls 'a very real sense'.

With these examples in mind, what suggestions can we make already about the character of metaphysics and its relation to ordinary language? Our reflections suggest that, like logical theory, mathematics or the sciences, metaphysics is an ancillary scheme. That it is a distinctive kind of ancillary scheme we need not for a moment deny. Indeed it will be essential for us to formulate in due course the character of this distinctiveness. But already there arise one or two points about metaphysics that are worth making.

First, we may already understand the better part at least of what might be meant by saying that metaphysics is concerned with 'Reality'. For we have seen that an option for some particular ancillary scheme is often expressed in terms of the 'really—seem' distinction. Words such as these—'really', 'seem'—are (as in the case of the 'bent stick' example) hints that we have brought a supplementary language map alongside ordinary language to illuminate it. Now those metaphysicians who have been traditionally concerned with Reality and Appearance have been concerned, at least in part, with opting for some large-scale map by which to illuminate and organize the diverse assertions of ordinary language. For instance when a metaphysician says 'Evil is really only good misperceived', he need not deny any common-sense talk about good and evil. He certainly need not deny that for us all there is a perfectly proper use of the word 'evil'. At the same time, by his metaphysical assertion he is expressing his option for some map which while allowing all that, believes talk about good and evil to be most reliably structured, and its logical relations best shown, by a large-scale map which includes no talk about evil at all. Again, if some metaphysician says 'When you look at a daffodil it's *really* the Absolute of which you are aware', he is, at least in part, opting for a map which, allowing ordinary language about daffodils, believes this to be most reliably structured, its connexion with all our other talking best shown, on a scheme which talks of no 'objects' but only of the 'Absolute'. We might make the same kind of point about Bertrand Russell's one-time claim (and I would say near-metaphysical claim) that tables are *really* only groups of sense-data, sensibilia, or what you will. Here is the claim that all talk about tables is most reliably and most illuminatingly mapped in terms of statements about nothing but sense-data. Similar remarks are true of the mathematical metaphysician's claim that physical objects are 'not really red' at all.

As I have said, this is by no means the whole story of what is involved in metaphysics, and not even the whole story about the metaphysical use of 'Reality', but it is a very proper part of it. We can also see the point, as well as the misunderstanding, behind G. E. Moore's remark that when anyone says X is really Y, the one thing of which you can be sure is that it is not. In one sense Moore was right: X is always X. 'Everything is what it is, and not another thing.'[1] But when someone, and it is most often a metaphysician, says X is *really* Y, he need not be denying that X is X. What he is doing by this remark is rather to commend to us his own option for a large-scale map dominated by Y, as that which not only gives a suitable place to talk about X but also, he would claim, gives the best and most illuminating view of the Universe. Moore's remark blinds us to the character of metaphysics, and confuses metaphysics and ordinary language.

Which leads us to three other interim points:

(1) Metaphysics is no mere extension of ordinary language —a kind of Honours Course in the use of words. It has a different logical character altogether—consistent with being an ancillary scheme illuminative of common-sense assertions as a whole.

(2) Yet, we can, I hope, see the great truth behind the view of philosophy as clarification, the view associated especially with Bertrand Russell and G. E. Moore. In constructing metaphysics in the way we have visualized we would in fact be performing an exercise which brought clarification, because illumination, to the utterances of common-sense. There is also a sense in which we could speak of metaphysics as being, in C. D. Broad's phrase, 'critical common sense'; for it would be concerned, in a critical fashion, to organize common-sense assertions in accordance with some perspective or other. But, on the interpretation given above, there would be no suggestion of *replacing* ordinary language by another sort of language; common sense would still remain as ever it was. Or nearly so. For there is an important qualification to be made here.

(3) While metaphysics, like the precision languages of the sciences, is from a logical standpoint an ancillary language, we must recognize that psychologically there is (as always with ancillary languages) likely to be a mixing of words. Yet, if that mixing is done without an awareness of the additional logical complexity which is thereby brought to ordinary language, we shall only be in

[1] Joseph Butler, *Fifteen Sermons Preached at the Rolls Chapel*, Preface, § 39. Quoted by Moore on the title-page to *Principia Ethica*.

even greater muddles at the second move. The remark is relevant to many discussions, e.g. about the 'nature' of so and so, which are frequently at cross-purposes simply because 'nature', in its metaphysical use, is not distinguished from 'nature' and 'natural' in common-sense talk.

While there may be, then, and for a variety of reasons, as a matter of *psychological* fact, some transfers of words between a metaphysical scheme and ordinary language, this does not at all deny what we have insisted to be the special *logical* status of metaphysics, consistent with its being an ancillary scheme.

Now at this point it may be said that the character of metaphysics, as I have given it, compromises the possibility of any metaphysics distinctive and worthy of the name, and this brings us to the essential and important question we postponed a little while ago. For in arguing that its logical status is importantly similar to that of mathematics and scientific theories, do we not imply (it might be said) that a metaphysics is only some sort of high-grade scientific theory after all? In trying to become clearer about the purpose of metaphysics, have we not made the logical status of metaphysics too close to that of a scientific scheme?

The point may be put like this. We have seen that it is the function of the sciences to provide precision languages by means of which puzzles, discrepancies or problematical phrases can be resolved, and logical links provided where none existed before. We have said that metaphysics is pre-eminently a venture after unity: an endeavour to provide a scheme of maximum interpretative power. Where then does metaphysics differ from a high-grade scientific scheme? Why should not the sciences provide us with the over-all scheme and supply us with such integrator words as we need?

The short answer is that there can be no genuine union of two logically diverse scientific languages[1] by means of words native to either. For any such uniting words would commit type-trespass in the language to which they were not native. For the same reason, no third brand of scientific discourse could unite the two diverse languages: otherwise the same difficulty would be twice repeated. So we look in vain for genuine integration by scientific words: we look in vain for what might be called a scientific metaphysics, where even the high-grade integrations are in the last resort cashed in terms of observables.

The consequent cost of a total over-all map, of the kind the metaphysicians seek, is integrator words not native to any of the diverse observational languages of the sciences, yet able to combine

---

[1] I take it as agreed that such logical diversity characterizes what is talked of misleadingly by the one word 'science'.

with and supplement them: words which, while able in this way to secure a reference to observables by associating with scientific discourse, are not confined within its logical patterns.

We need not deny that a certain amount of integration apparently can be and is done by the sciences. What were traditionally such logically diverse areas as light, heat and magnetism and electricity, for example, have been integrated by concepts such as mass, velocity, energy. But we must recognize that the new integrated language is an alternative to, and does *not* incorporate, the former disintegrated and separate languages. Rather it talks in another kind of way altogether about what hitherto needed two different languages for discussion, and what that was is never given except in terms of the ordinary language from which we started. Indeed, in science, any gain in comprehensiveness seems to be at the expense of particularity. The more generalized the scientific scheme, the further distant does it seem to be logically from the assertions of ordinary language. Every new-born child produced by scientific generalization belongs to yet another logical generation. We need do no more than recall the following kind of sequence: 'red sunset', 'light waves', 'electrons', 'fundamental particles', to see the widening logical gap which such scientific sequences present. At any rate, such increased integration as is provided by scientific generalization leaves many diverse, and in some ways still indispensable, languages strewn about the path of progress. Integration done by the sciences is not at all a matter of integrating diverse languages; rather does it consist of *replacing* diversity by more generalized and less diverse schemes.

It may, however, be that large areas of scientific discourse, and even diverse areas of such discourse, suggest some common highly generalized concept. As illustrations we might mention Matter or Evolution; and the way some phenomena, especially in physics, are co-ordinated has led to their being talked of in terms of something like personal qualities, e.g. the 'attraction' of unlike magnetic poles for each other, the 'repulsion' of similar magnetic poles, the 'cussedness' of Lenz's Law.

Further, such concepts have sometimes become the cornerstone of 'metaphysical' maps—matter and evolution being easily recognized as bold aspirants of a century ago. In this way it might again seem that science could, in principle, provide the integrative concepts that metaphysics needs.

To such a suggestion our reply must be twofold:

(1) There is no reason why, *as a matter of psychological fact,* our metaphysical key-words should not be thrown up and suggested by scientific discourse. It may be, e.g., that the metaphysical concept of substance has been derived by extrapolating from the

scientific concept of matter or a particle; it may be that a meta-physical concept such as Process (for Whitehead) or Activity (for Berkeley) could be suggested by reflecting on the scientific concepts of change or interaction, and so on. But if these concepts have no other grounding, and no other anchorage than in scientific phenomena, they will provide us with but pseudometaphysics; they will be at best useful jingles which, mnemonic-like, associate diverse scientific languages. They will at best have the curiously uncertain status of Kant's Regulative Ideas.

(2) Contrariwise, even though these concepts are suggested by scientific discourse, and even though they are rightly detected as structuring such discourse, they will only be metaphysical if they are not native to scientific language at all, but have their ground and logical origin elsewhere. They will only be metaphysical if, in that origin, they are to be anchored in situations not limited to the spatio-temporal observables with which scientific discourse is wholly concerned.

By this rather circuitous route we have now reached a point to which we might have passed much earlier, viz.: the view that metaphysics, to be genuine metaphysics, must have reference to more than observables, i.e. to the unseen. If our reasoning is reliable, this is in fact our conclusion. For metaphysical integrators, being not native to any scientific language, must have their grounding in what is more than spatio-temporal, i.e. they must be 'meta-physical' in a more obviously traditional sense. For metaphysics is not merely (what I suggested much earlier) the construction of some kind of ancillary map—it is (as we now begin to see) the construction of a map in accordance with a vision of the unseen.

From what we have said, then, about the purpose of metaphysics, whose aim is to construct as complete a map of the Universe as possible, which in particular will link together the various precision languages of the sciences, it follows that the possibility of metaphysics depends on there being words which, not being native to any of the languages of science:

(a) are able to unify these logically diverse languages; and

(b) are given by reference to what is more than spatio-temporal.

If then we are to justify the possibility of metaphysics, we are left with two questions on our hands:

(a) How do distinctively metaphysical words unify?

(b) What empirical grounding or foundation can such integrator words be given?

To answer these questions we may well ask others: Where will such integrator words be found—words which, not being themselves descriptive in their use, can nevertheless be united with words which are descriptive? What indeed is the fact which justifies metaphysics? If it is given in a vision of the unseen, what sort of empirical circumstance does that phrase describe? I propose to answer these questions by taking a specific example of a metaphysics, viz. theism.

The suggestion which I propose to outline in the second part of this paper is that the situation which justifies metaphysics is very like what justifies for each of us our own use of 'I', and that in this word 'I' we have a paradigm for all metaphysical intergrators.[1] But we may readily recall one or two other examples whose relation to this one I will not further discuss. 'Being'[2] is sometimes claimed as an integrator word which unifies assertions about all particular existents, and is given by reference to an 'intuition'. Again, 'Absolute' is sometimes offered as an integrator word belonging to a unified over-all scheme, and is then given by reference to what F. H. Bradley called 'immediate experience', something which breaks in on us when we 'see' the unsatisfactoriness of stories about terms and relations.

I only mention these other examples to show that our concept of metaphysics is by no means restricted to theism, though it is by theism that I shall exemplify it, and it is 'God' which I believe (for reasons which lie outside the present essay) to be the integrator word which provides the most simple, far-reaching and coherent metaphysical map.

II

WE left our first section with two questions:

(1) Where can we find words which, not being themselves descriptive (and so native to scientific language), can nevertheless be united with words which are used descriptively? We shall have answered that question when we have provided actual specimens of metaphysical integrators.

(2) How can such words be given by reference to what is more than spatio-temporal? We shall have answered this question when we have shown the kind of situation which justifies any and all systems of metaphysics.

[1] C. B. Daly approaches a similar point from another direction in Ch. XI.
[2] See Ch. VII.

To succeed in answering either question I suggest that we first consider yet another question:

Can human behaviour in principle, and on all occasions, be adequately and satisfactorily treated in terms of observables, in terms of what can be perceptually verified?

Let us admit at the outset that human behaviour would be no more than the observables which characterize it if A's saying 'I did X' *always* meant in principle no more than B's saying of A, 'He did X'. Further, let us readily admit that *sometimes* this is the case. Sometimes I *do* speak of myself as others speak of me, i.e. wholly in terms of observables. Let us take two examples to illustrate this contention. An undergraduate rushes in for some kind of decanal permission. But the Dean is immersed in administration, so he says, to make it clear that he is saying something of official necessity which does not at all harmonize with his personal wishes to be helpful and kind: *'The Dean is busy; come back in an hour.'* Meanwhile, we may note that, if I am the Dean, this assertion does not entail 'I am busy,' for 'I' may have what is called 'deep contentment' or 'inward peace' below the rigours of decanal administration.

Again, someone might ask the Bishop 'Who preached the sermon last week?' And he might answer, *'The Bishop preached'.* Very true, because it had been a very official, prelatical, impersonal sermon, so that people said, 'Just like the Bishop's purple self'.

Now the very oddness of the two italicized remarks shows that the circumstances they describe do not normally cover the case, that normally more might and must be said. Sometimes it *may* suffice, but normally it will *not* be enough to talk of my behaviour in terms of the Dean (if I'm the Dean), or the Bishop (if I'm the Bishop). So while we may readily allow that 'I' sometimes functions· like 'he', yet we may also argue that this is not the whole account of the logic of 'I'. At this point we are both echoing and rejecting something which Wittgenstein once said.

As Professor J. R. Jones reminded us in a recent paper to the Aristotelian Society,[1] Wittgenstein, according to Moore, 'was quite definite that the word "I" or "any other word which denotes a subject" is used in "two utterly different ways", one in which it is "on a level with other people" and one in which it is not. This difference, he said, was a difference in the grammar of our ordinary language'.[2]

[1] 'The two contexts of mental concepts', *P.A.S.* 1958–9, VI, pp. 105–24.
[2] 'Wittgenstein's Lectures in 1930–33', G. E. Moore, *Mind,* January 1953, p. 14. Quoted by J. R. Jones *loc. cit.,* p. 116.

There are thus two uses of 'I'. But Wittgenstein said, let us notice, that this difference is just a difference of 'grammar', and by this I suppose he meant not only that the distinctive use of 'I' is not one which is perceptually verifiable (with which we would agree), but more positively (with which we would not agree) that the difference arises merely and simply because we need somehow to distinguish the speaker from the hearer. I do not deny that we need to make the distinction. *My point is that more needs saying as well.* But what 'more'?

To answer that question consider the three assertions:

(a) 'The Dean shuts the door', said by the Dean or someone else, say *B*, of the Dean.

(b) 'I shut the door', said by the Dean of the Dean.

(c) 'He shut the door', said by *B* of the Dean.

There is no difficulty with (a); everything can be verified equally well by everybody; speaker and hearer are on the same footing. But in (b) does 'I' just 'indicate' the speaker? Certainly it does that; but it surely does more than peg the assertion to this point, this speaker, this chap talking. For it asserts that particular existence which I know to be definitely mine. Now I agree that this 'extra' in (b) is not a perceptually verifiable 'more'. It is not like the 'more' we tell about Tom's uncle by speaking of 'Tom's *rich* uncle'. The 'more' in this assertion (b) is something which can never be enumerated in observational terms. How then can it be secured?

If *per impossibile* we could give our identity descriptively, our individuality would have disappeared. The subject would have been objectified. We would have become, as I have implied elsewhere,[1] so public as to be lost in the crowd. This same reflection occurs at the end of Professor Jones's paper. 'If, through suppression of the sense in which "I" is not replaceable by "he" I am placed in a relation [for instance] to my anger such that, when I make an avowal of anger, *it is as if I were actually saying,* "He is angry", and implying no more by this than *you* mean by it, then, although what is being *said,* namely, that I am angry, is unaffected, my sentence now lies for me in a surrounding in language which is radically decomposed—the surrounding of the grammar of what I am saying. And the consequence is a straining of what I would call my deep sense of the grammar. Something is disturbed which involves my

[1] *Philosophical Quarterly,* Vol. 5 No. 20. July 1955 'The Systematic Elusiveness of "I" '. See esp. pp. 197, 199, 203.

whole ability to use language. This is why, I suggest, the cumulative impression is one of *deep* paradox.'

'The ghosts of occult contents, and processes "stowed away in some peculiar medium", proved exorcizable. But a "ghost" is built into grammar. And it will not be laid.'[1]

But if there is 'more', where the 'more' cannot be perceptually verified, we return to our question above: what is its empirical basis? How do we come to recognize this 'more'? The answer is: In a disclosure, a disclosure in which I come to myself and realize myself as more than the observable behaviour I display. The stock example of such a disclosure is that of David and Nathan, when at Nathan's 'Thou art the man!' David comes to himself, the 'penny drops' and the disclosure occurs. What 'I' distinctively stands for, what I am to myself more than I as he is to you, is something which *a fortiori cannot be described*. It can only be evoked in and for each of us, and that means given (as we have said) in a disclosure that justifies our use of 'I' in the extended sense, the sense which belongs to a situation not restricted to the observables in terms of which other people (as well as I) can talk of it.

Here is a word—'I' for each of us—which is, then, not descriptive, and yet it can be united with any number of descriptive words. We may say 'I'm angry' or 'I'm a neurotic' or 'I'm a malaria case', or 'I'm a wage-earner' or 'I'm busy', and so on.[2] 'I exist' is entailed by assertions such as 'He's a wage-earner'; 'He's a neurotic' in the languages of economics, medicine, psychology; and in so doing it becomes an integrator of these logically diverse areas.[3] Further, what is, in spatio-temporal terms, non-descriptive about 'I exist', is given in a disclosure situation. Here, then, is a paradigm for metaphysics. Here is a metaphysical integrator, given by reference to a disclosure which transcends the spatio-temporal. Here is solipsism as the primitive metaphysics,[4] though I am not pretending

---

[1] *loc cit.*, p. 124.

[2] That some of these may be assertions in ordinary language I neither doubt nor deny; but as such they would not interest us for our present purpose. Further, the possibility of words moving between metaphysics, science and common sense has been explicitly allowed for above.

[3] Or if it be held that supposing my temperature is 98.4°, then 'I exist' *and* 'His temperature is not 98.4°' are not together self-contradictory, it might be said not so much that 'His temperature is 98.4°' entails 'I exist' as that 'I exist' is a *presupposition* of making this or any other scientific assertion about me; that the scientist in making his assertions *commits* himself to the existential claim. See P. F. Strawson, *Introduction to Logical Theory*, p. 175, for this same point. It is also one which accords with the general thesis of M. Polanyi's *Personal Knowledge:* that scientific understanding presupposes 'personal knowledge'.

[4] Wittgenstein, *Tractatus Logico-philosophicus*, 5.641, cp. 5.64 and 5.62.

that Wittgenstein would have agreed with my present interpretation of that remark.

(ii) Let us now continue our argument by recalling assertion (c) which we enumerated above, where B says of the Dean 'He shut the door'. This *may* imply for B something of an objective disclosure around that pattern of observable behaviour known as 'The Dean', revealing something corresponding to what we know subjectively in the case of ourselves. In any case we must not suppose that a 'disclosure', a penny dropping, is something utterly and wholly subjective. I become aware of myself as I become aware of an environment transcending observables. Look at it like this, and here I take up again the two uses of 'I'. Can we not all recall a primitive state where we talk of ourselves in terms of proper names such as 'Neeny', where these are wholly restricted to our public behaviour. Even at this stage we are of course aware of ourselves. My point is that at this stage we have no language to fit. We use of ourselves a word 'Neeny' which others can use in precisely the same kind of way. But when we later use 'I' significantly of ourselves, it is because we recognize it as being used as an indicator word by others for themselves, relating to their public behaviour and more, and we recognize that we ourselves want to talk precisely of that, of 'Neeny' and more, and so of 'I'. In short, the use of the word 'I' commits us also to pluralism of persons. It is not likely that we should use 'I' for ourselves, if there were nothing else but ourselves. So we become aware of ourselves as we become aware of an environment transcending observables. But this 'objective' awareness has many recognizable differences. Already we have seen that [part] of the awareness may be *prima facie of* other persons. Now let us see how else it can be characterized. Let us begin with an example which makes another point as well.

I am absent-minded, so before I start on my journey my wife ties string round my finger to remind me to get petrol. I have been travelling oblivious of it for some hours; being bored, relieving the boredom by inventing problems to solve or giving lifts to hitch-hikers and so on. Then, on chancing to feel the string, the 'penny drops', there is a disclosure. I recall my need; look out actively for the next pump, and stop. What has happened? On seeing the string I have ceased to be the bored traveller, the problem-solver, the conversation-maker, and become 'myself'. It is in such cases, in such self-awareness, that I have suggested that there occurs a situation which is more than the observables it contains, but even here we get a little of an objective element. I come to myself on remembering the circumstances in which I left my wife, her words, her directions, and so forth. It is true that my keeping a look out for the petrol station may be no more than a quasi-reflex action, in which case there would be no disclosure at all. Here is the first and extra point which this example makes, and it warns us that there may be cases of alert, integrated behaviour which may be deceptively like that which accompanies what we call disclosures. We may be psychologically alert and integrated without 'coming to ourselves'—we then lack what the extentialists call 'authenticity'. The same point arises again in the second example which follows.

But leaving that on one side let us notice the possible presence even in remembering of an objective element, and let us notice that there would be rather more of such an objective element in a detective novel, where, when the penny drops we suddenly 'see' the culprit, when the solution forces itself on us. There would be even more of this objective element in a situation of moral challenge.

This last and very important point can be illustrated by two more examples. We may remember the story of Robin Hood and the Tinker who searches for him with a warrant from the Sheriff of Nottingham. The Tinker unexpectedly meets Robin Hood and the conversation proceeds like this:

Q. Do you know Robin Hood?
A. Oh, very well indeed, I have the closest knowledge of him.
Q. Where is he now, I wonder?
A. I am sure he cannot be very far away.
Q. Is he strong?
A. Fairly so. He had a successful bout with a very skilled wrestler the other day.
Q. How tall is he?
A. Just about my height.
Q. Colour of hair?
A. Brown.
Q. Is he clever?
A. He has misled a lot of folk.

Now supposing Robin Hood had concluded such question-and-answering like this: 'And I'm the man.' What would be added by this claim that 'It is I'? There are two possible answers. Some might say, as I have admitted, that 'I' is purely indicative. It just says: What you see now, this body, this chap talking with you, is of a part with all we have been describing. Nor can this be denied. The leading question is: Is that all? For another answer is possible. When Robin makes his confession, there might be a disclosure. The sequence to date, plus the pattern before the Tinker, then becomes part of a disclosure situation where the Tinker discerns around

'Robin Hood' an objective challenge. We may recall some remarks by Berkeley about 'seeing Alciphron'.[1] If what we mean by 'seeing' is to 'see' the visible surface, the hair, face, skin, etc., then in this sense we never 'see' Alciphron. To see Alciphron is to 'see' more than this. For Berkeley such a disclosure—of what is visible and more—occurred when Alciphron moved or acted. For the Tinker, a similar disclosure occurred as a moral challenge.

This same point can be made by a second example where we might consider someone sweeping up the litter on Hampstead Heath on the day after a Bank Holiday. The brush goes backwards and forwards making always an equal angle with the vertical, and the sweeper proceeds with leisurely tread. Hardly a person, we might be tempted to say. A mechanical sweeper might do the same. Descriptive language would be quite adequate for the situation. Then there appears among the litter a pound note, and the sweeper is (we might say) 'touched off'. Already there is the prospect of another drink or two; already the mouth waters like Pavlov's dog. Still, there need be no disclosure as we have been using the word, though criteria such as surprise and heart-throbbing would be there, and might deceive us. It might be (as we noted above) hardly different from a reflex action. Once again we must be on our guard at supposing that disclosures have occurred when they have not, when the visible circumstances may be deceptively similar. But then among the litter occurs a letter marked 'Confidential', and the writing is that of the sweeper's son to a girl friend, or the sweeper's daughter to a boy friend. Now, without any doubt, the sweeper comes to himself. He is presented with a moral challenge, indeed with what may be a moral conflict: should he or should he not read this letter? He has ceased to be a mere sweeper, or even a sweeper throbbing for a drink. He has become 'himself' when confronted by a moral challenge. Generalizing the example, we may say that 'I' come to myself most characteristically in relation to a moral challenge which equally—but 'objectively'—goes beyond observables.

So we can see how, besides 'I', there arise other metaphysical words which are grounded in what is 'objectively' revealed in a disclosure. Amongst such words are (as we saw earlier) those which we use of 'other persons'. We have now seen how other metaphysical words or phrases may be grounded in that objective challenge which is talked of in terms of obligation and duty. We see how, e.g., 'Duty' may arise as a metaphysical category.

It may be useful to develop this particular example a little further. We recognize something as an obligation or duty, or more

[1] *Alciphron,* Dialogue IV, § 5.

strictly as a *prima facie* obligation and duty, when (as we have said) it presents itself to us within a disclosure situation. But it is notorious that there can be 'conflicts' of duty—the Hampstead Heath sweeper may think he has a duty to exert a protective providence over his son or his daughter; equally well a duty to respect his or her privacy. We then have the prospect of a disclosure presenting us with two challenges which generate conflicting responses. The only way to resolve the difficulty is to develop the empirical details in each case until there arises within the one disclosure a single challenge and response. When men have spoken of Absolute Duty, Absolute Goodness, or Absolute Perfection, they have been searching for an appropriate label to a disclosure situation in which there was no possibility of any other than a single unambiguous, unmistakable response. But it would not seem that this is ever the case with *formulations* of duty. In short (as we shall see presently) a disclosure labelled 'Absolute Duty' or 'Absolute Perfection' is one which closely resembles in its character the disclosure to which theists appeal when they speak of 'God'—for here again it is claimed that we have some kind of guarantee linked with descriptive corrigibility.

Meanwhile, let us notice how contemporary developments in ethics can be related to this discussion of disclosures. It is pointed out in another paper[1] how it is being increasingly recognized that in the language of ethics the descriptive and the evaluative elements are intertwined. This accords well with what we have said about disclosures, though I am not pretending that all of those who recognize the intertwining would agree with my account of the matter. What I suggest is that those who have attempted, in whatever diverse ways, to make ethics wholly descriptive are those who would ignore or deny the kind of transcendence which what we have called a disclosure demands and provides. Next, to recognize ethics as being at one and the same time descriptive and evaluative is, I suggest, to allow for a disclosure which is *both* spatio-temporal and *more* than spatio-temporal. The language of ethics which speaks of such a disclosure is, in virtue of the spatio-temporal elements, *descriptive;* it becomes *evaluative* in so far as it concerns something which is distinctively my active, personal response. But to speak of 'response' means that I would now go further than even an evaluatory theory, and see the language of ethics as not only descriptive and evaluative, but also responsive, i.e. responsive to a transcendent challenge whose description demands metaphysical words like 'Duty'.

But now we return to our concept of metaphysics as a single

[1] Ch. I, pp. 16–20.

all-embracing map of the Universe. Does this not mean that the various metaphysical words already cast up need themselves to be organized? The claim of the theist is that they are all of them organized in relation to the word God.[1] Which brings us to our third and last sub-section.

(iii) God. Taking up our last point we may say that all the traditional proofs of God's existence can be regarded, in principle, as techniques to evoke disclosures, to commend the word 'God' diversely in relation to what is objectively disclosed, and so to approach the one concept 'God' from diverse directions. In short, the traditional proofs may be regarded as a somewhat crude exercise to carry out the programme indicated in the concluding paragraph of (ii).

If there were no other disclosures but those around persons, we might be content with a pluralistic map; if there were no other disclosures but those reached by ethical techniques we might be believers in 'Absolute Values'—ethical humanists like Russell at the present time. But disclosures are more diverse than this, and in outline the justification for theism arises because the word 'God' is such an admirable integrator. Disclosures can occur which do not arise around personal nor moral behaviour but around cosmic events or microscopic phenomena. These can occur when we reflect on causal sequences, when we look at daffodils in a particular way, or penetrate into the secrets of the ocean-bed. In all such disclosures we are aware of some 'other', which cannot be thought to be another 'I'. Such situations as these are *pre-eminently* those which afford the empirical basis for theism. For they connect 'God' with all those features of the world that a metaphysics confined to persons or values would have to ignore. 'God' can now integrate not only talk about persons and values but talk about science and perception.

But how do we then talk about this integrator word 'God'? Despite all we have just said, our *first* move towards an answer must

---

1 Incidentally, this is also why, if we are asked what a disclosure discloses, several answers are possible. A first answer might be, in relation to the examples we have given: 'my wife's warning', 'Robin Hood', 'his son's letter'. But for the theist all these phrases would be brought in relation to the answer which supplements them all, without replacing any, viz. 'God'. So the theist would speak (for example) of seeing God in a friend, finding God in literature, family relations and so on. If the theist sponsors any doctrine of creation, he need not apologize for ultimately relating every disclosure to God, especially when he recalls that there are many who associate the disclosures evoked by the salt in their stew, the cream in their coffee, the sugar in their tea and so on with the disclosure which occurs when they speak of their girl-friend: 'You'—'You are the salt in my stew', etc.

be: model 'God' on 'I'. This means, more broadly, that we shall speak about God by qualifying any and all descriptive language—whether of people, human behaviour, or the Universe—in such a way that it tells a more than descriptive story, in such a way that it evokes a disclosure, and this I suggest is most generally done either by qualifying descriptive language infinitely, or qualifying descriptive language negatively. I have developed this suggestion at great length elsewhere.[1] All I need remark now is that talk about God is certainly *never* apt if it is in terms of plain descriptions alone. To be more positively helpful and reverting to our earlier remark, we might say that the logical behaviour of 'I', being grounded in a disclosure and ultimately different from all descriptive language, while nevertheless being associated with it, is always a good first clue to the logical behaviour of 'God'. Further, with reference to the unifying character of metaphysical language, just as 'I' acts (as we saw) as an integrator word for all kinds of scientific and other descriptive assertions about myself, 'I exist' being a sort of contextual presupposition for them all, so also may 'God' be regarded as a contextual presupposition for the Universe. 'I am active' is entailed by all kinds of scientific descriptions and links them together. Likewise, we might say, and certainly as a first move, 'God is active' links any and all descriptive assertions about the Universe, such as science in particular specializes in.

So to a brief recapitulation. The possibility of metaphysics arises (i) because there is at least one integrator word 'I'—hence solipsism is the logical primitive metaphysics; and (ii) because this word 'I' is given in relation to a vision of the unseen, a disclosure situation. The possibility of a metaphysical theology arises when, to talk of the objective constituent of all disclosure situations which go beyond what is seen, to unite the various metaphysical words that are cast up in this way, we use the word 'God'. This word 'God' is modelled on, though it has necessarily important differences from, 'I'.[2] These differences are in fact grounded in the observable features of those various disclosure situations which more aptly lead us to God rather than to ourselves or other people.

Let me now conclude by mentioning three implications.

(1) The language we use about God will always have to be so constructed that it is potentially generative of, evocative of, a disclosure. It must have within it the potentiality to make pennies drop, to evoke a disclosure which contains observables and more, a disclosure of the kind we know when each of us comes to himself.

[1] See, e.g., my *Religious Language*, especially Ch. II, and *Freedom and Immortality*, especially pp. 113–14.

[2] The reader will find this same point approached from different directions, and discussed further in Chs. XI and XII.

We can therefore deny the possibility of a metaphysical theology for two reasons. We may do it on *philosophical* grounds when we believe that observables are all that there is. But can we believe that at least of ourselves? What I am saying is that a true estimate of personality and a true estimate of religion stand or fall together; there can be devilish parodies of both. Alternatively, we may deny the possibility of a metaphysical theology because as a matter of *psychological* fact we have never known what a disclosure was. That reflection reminds us how much of our culture today is inhibitive of disclosures, and atrophies vision. It is not easy to have vision when there is growing uniformity about our environment and greater standardization of life, when personal relations tend to be overlaid and screened by a rigorous efficiency and so on. Such uniformity, standardization and efficiency may be both inevitable and representative of genuine progress. But we need all the more, and all the more is it difficult to provide for, 'pennies dropping'.

(2) Our reflections can help, I believe, in a question which various papers have raised:[1] the matter of intuitions and what is guaranteed in an intuition. For the same questions of incorrigibility and misdescription arise about myself. We may go back to Professor J. R. Jones's paper. On page 121 he says: ' "He is angry" . . . is an interpretation and, for that reason, corrigible. It is an interpretation of the user's emotion in the light of his behaviour and of his behaviour in the light of the situation in which he is placed. I do not mean that an onlooker can never arrive at the recognition that someone is angry without conscious inference or even some research. Sometimes he has to look for the explanation of the other person's behaviour, sometimes not. My point is simply that logically "He is angry" has the status of an interpretation and is, therefore, always, in principle, corrigible.' With this we cannot disagree. But Professor J. R. Jones has said earlier: 'The avowal "I'm angry" as spoken from within my involvement, is intrinsically "hall-marked" and, therefore, incorrigible.'[2] But is it? Is not all that is incorrigible my existence in relation to some other? What happens in the case of

---

1 See e.g. pp. 78, 81, 141–52 and Ch. XII, especially §§ X, XI, XII.

2 *loc. cit.* pp. 120–21. On this point Dom Illtyd Trethowan would agree with Professor Jones as against me, and consider that (at least in some cases) 'I'm angry' or 'I'm in pain' was incorrigible—that here were some incorrigible descriptions. While I am naturally very willing (as I indicate in the next paragraph) to allow degrees of corrigibility for descriptions, I cannot see that it will ever reach zero, without a word changing its logical character from a descriptive to a proper name. But Dom Illtyd would no doubt reject this antithesis precisely at this point. At any rate, while our positions are broadly similar, he would plainly give a rather simpler answer than I do to the basic question of what an intuition 'delivers', and so take a less complex view of assertions about God than I do in the paragraphs which follow.

ourselves is that we know something incorrigibly, to which corrigible descriptions are inevitably applied.

We might perhaps then say that we are as certain of God as we are of ourselves. But any and all description, no matter how attenuated, in both cases is more or less problematical. The furthest we could go might be to say that there would be nothing puzzling about (say) 'I am active' if it were clearly seen that this was on a different logical level from all other phrases, being merely meant to bear witness to that part of a self-disclosure which is an invariant. Even so, the very use of the word 'active' may be going too far, and would go too far if it had any 'descriptive' element. All the same 'I've a pain', for example, affords a better clue to 'I exist' or 'I'm active' than some more complex descriptive phrase such as 'I've fibrositis in my shoulder'.

Thus God is guaranteed to us very much as we are to ourselves. But no description is guaranteed. The basic assertion about God does not stand or fall on one or many particular verifiable assertions. Yet as with ourselves, so with God, intuition and description come together.

What we are claiming indeed is that there is in fact a basic assertion both about ourselves and about God which can neither be rightly regarded as 'absolutely certain' or 'wholly corrigible'. For neither of these phrases is appropriate to the unique status it has. For it combines in one and the same assertion incorrigibility and corrigibility, and if we wish to devise any apt label for it at all (though here again there could be grave misunderstanding) it might be 'probable'. For it would be 'probable' in Butler's sense, a sense which makes a 'probable' utterance completely determinative of one's total behaviour. In our own case, we might display the matter as follows:

I have a headache
= There's a headache .... which is mine.
   (descriptive, corrigible; relating to 'objects')   (incorrigible)
= I exist .... with a headache.
   (incorrigible)   (corrigible)
   |_____'probable'_____|

But if we do so display the argument, we must notice that 'probable' relates to the peculiar logical status of the *total* assertion. It *does not* imply (for example) that the assertion about my own existence is 'probable'. In a similar way, we might wish to regard 'God exists' as formally indicative of the 'incorrigible' element in any total theistic assertion.

(3) A more general conclusion: all and every brand of metaphysics will, as we have seen, plead integrator words with respect to disclosure situations in which we are aware of what is more than observables. We might then judge between different brands of metaphysics as to how successful their integrator concepts were in effecting a unified scheme. That such a task brings immense difficulties is obvious. But one reflection may be permitted at the outset. So far as I can see, no integrator concept will be in principle justifiable which does not begin by being modelled on 'I'. In short, there cannot be a justifiable sub-personal metaphysics. But that is not to say that a metaphysics which was no more than personally structured would be adequate. Theism needs to be much more subtle than that.

Additional Readings

BRAITHWAITE, R. B., *An Empiricist's View of the Nature of Religious Belief.*

CASSIRER, E., *The Philosophy of Symbolic Forms.*

CHURCH, A., Review of A. J. Ayer's *Language, Truth, and Logic. The Journal of Symbolic Logic,* Vol. 14 (1949) , pp. 52–53.

FERRÉ, F., *Language, Logic and God.*

FLEW, A. and MCINTYRE, A. (eds.) , *New Essays in Philosophical Theology.*

HEMPEL, CARL, "Problems and Changes in the Empiricist Criterion of Meaning" in Leonard Linsky, *Semantics and the Philosophy of Language.*

MASCALL, E. L., *Words and Images.*

RAMSEY, IAN, *Religious Language.*

URBAN, W. M., *Language and Reality.*

PART VI

GOD, MAN

AND THE WORLD

A final set of problems concerns the nature of the Divine Reality and its relation both to the natural universe generally and to human destiny particularly. Many perspectives on these very questions have emerged in the previous selections, but the particular emphases that appear here are basically concerned with two issues. The first is the general nature of the relation between the Divine Reality and the universe. The second is the problem of human immortality.

Four basic positions on the relationship between God and the universe are presented.

The first of these is the theistic perspective which is exemplified here by A. N. Whitehead's philosophy of organism. Theism in general is the view that the total natural universe depends for its existence upon an ultimate personal mind whose reality is not itself dependent upon that universe, and whose purposive aim is progressively expressed within it. For Whitehead the world consists basically of actual entities and actual occasions which are so related to each other that every one is what it is because of its complex dependence on all the others. His view is called the philosophy of organism precisely because the parts of an organic body provide an example of this kind of relationship. However, since the world of actual occasions must first of all be logically possible, Whitehead holds that it depends for its existence both on a realm of eternal objects, which is the sphere of all logical possibilities for existence, and upon a principle of selection or concretion, which explains why, of all possible worlds in the realm of eternal objects, precisely the present actual universe exists. This principle of selectivity is God; and in explaining how God, as himself the highest actual entity, fulfills this metaphysical role, Whitehead finds it necessary to ascribe to God the characteristics of personality, creativity and purposive aim which are definitive of a theistic view in the broad sense.

In contrast to such a view, with its genuine distinctions among actual entities in the world and between the world, on the one hand, and the realm of eternal objects and God, on the other, absolute idealism, exemplified by Vasubandhu and Hsuan-Tsang in the Vijnanavada (Pure Consciousness) school of Mahayana Buddhism, argues that the distinctions which characterize the world of our experience are merely a phenomenal appearance of a single ultimate reality whose sole nature is that of pure and undifferentiated consciousness. For this view, even the separate individual minds of finite knowers are not ultimately distinct from each other but are themselves phenomenal manifestations of the one all-inclusive consciousness. All distinctions fall within that absolute consciousness and thus possess only a relative status in comparison to it. Thus it follows that for the highest knowledge only the pure consciousness itself exists: all else is comparatively illusory.

The formalism of the contemporary Neo-Confucian thinker Fung Yu-Lan holds, with Whitehead and against the Vijnanavadins, that the order of particular things has actual existence and cannot be explained as a phenomenal illusion; and it further agrees with Whitehead that these particular things become actual only as instances of eternal ideas or formal principles which represent the essential natures of the various classes of particulars. In emphasizing such a realm of eternal objects or principles both Fung and Whitehead are reminiscent of the world-view of Plato, for whom such forms constitute the highest order of reality. But unlike either Whitehead or Plato, Fung argues that only the realm of particular things has actual existence, while the transcendent realm of essences has only formal reality as a series of explanatory concepts which are metaphysically empty. Hence these formal principles have a merely logical priority to the world of actual experience.

Finally, the materialistic empiricism of Ludwig Feuerbach contrasts with all three of the previous perspectives in at least two important respects.

First, Feuerbach argues that the natural universe is the only realm there is and that it is completely explicable in terms of the chance inter-action of ultimately physical elements without any dependence whatever on a transcendent realm, irrespective of how that realm is conceived. In the second place, while the three previous views all accept the genuineness of necessary principles of reason that are in some sense independent of material conditions of existence, Feuerbach rejects all such principles and holds that physical sensation is as ultimate in knowing as material substance is in being. Setting out with such assumptions, Feuerbach goes on to argue that ideas of God, or of any transcendent reality, are to be explained as projections of the human imagination to which no genuine reality corresponds. Such concepts are, in short, merely the fanciful dreams of the human spirit unrestrained by the discipline of material, empirically discerned fact.

The second main topic presented under this heading is the problem of immortality. Basically the discussion of this problem rests on a view of human nature which makes the survival of physical death at least a possibility for man. In this context, A. E. Taylor argues for a literally true concept of human survival, while Nicolas Berdyaev regards the notion of immortality—interpreted through the idea of resurrection—as essentially symbolic of the quality of spiritual life in present experience.

GOD AND THE WORLD*

*Alfred North Whitehead (1861–1947)
began his academic career as a mathematical logician at Cambridge University,
where he began his collaboration with
Bertrand Russell as co-author of* Principia
Mathematica, *but he culminated his
career at Harvard University by developing one of the most impressive
speculative metaphysical philosophies of
the twentieth century. The best known
writings of this last period are:* Science
and the Modern World, Process and
Reality, *and* Adventures of Ideas.

 Alfred N. Whitehead

ARISTOTLE found it necessary to complete his metaphysics by the introduction of a Prime Mover—God. This, for two reasons, is an important fact in the history of metaphysics. In the first place if we are to accord to anyone the position of the greatest metaphysician, having regard to genius of insight, to general equipment in knowledge, and to the stimulus of his metaphysical ancestry, we must choose Aristotle. Secondly, in his consideration of this metaphysical question he was entirely dispassionate; and he is the last European metaphysician of first rate importance for whom this claim can be made. After Aristotle, ethical and religious interests began to influence metaphysical conclusions. The Jews dispersed, first willingly and then forcibly, and the Judaic-Alexandrian school arose. Then Christianity closely followed by Mahometanism, intervened. The Greek gods who surrounded Aristotle were subordinate metaphysical entities, well within nature. Accordingly on the subject of his Prime Mover, he would have no motive, except to follow his metaphysical train of thought whithersoever it led him. It did not lead him very far towards the production of a God available for religious purposes. It may be doubted whether any properly general metaphysics can ever, without the illicit introduction of other

---

considerations, get much further than Aristotle. But his conclusion does represent a first step without which no evidence on a narrower experiential basis can be of much avail in shaping the conception. For nothing, within any limited type of experience, can give intelligence to shape our ideas of any entity at the base of all actual things, unless the general character of things requires that there be such an entity.

The phrase, Prime Mover, warns us that Aristotle's thought was enmeshed in the details of an erroneous physics and an erroneous cosmology. In Aristotle's physics special causes were required to sustain the motions of material things. These could easily be fitted into his system, provided that the general cosmic motions could be sustained. For then in relation to the general working system, each thing could be provided with its true end. Hence the necessity for a Prime Mover who sustains the motions of the spheres on which depend the adjustment of things. To-day we repudiate the Aristotelian physics and the Aristotelian cosmology, so that the exact form of the above argument manifestly fails. But if our general metaphysics is in any way similar to that outlined in the previous chapter, an analogous metaphysical problem arises which can be solved only in an analogous fashion. In the place of Aristotle's God as Prime Mover, we require God as the Principle of Concretion. This position can be substantiated only by the discussion of the general implication of the course of actual occasions,—that is to say, of the process of realisation.

We conceive actuality as in essential relation to an unfathomable possibility. Eternal objects inform actual occasions with hierarchic patterns, included and excluded in every variety of discrimination. Another view of the same truth is that every actual occasion is a limitation imposed on possibility, and that by virtue of this limitation the particular value of that shaped togetherness of things emerges. In this way we express how a single occasion is to be viewed in terms of possibility, and how possibility is to be viewed in terms of a single actual occasion. But there are no single occasions, in the sense of isolated occasions. Actuality is through and through togetherness—togetherness of otherwise isolated eternal objects, and togetherness of all actual occasions. It is my task in this chapter to describe the unity of actual occasions. The previous chapter centered its interest in the abstract: the present chapter deals with the concrete, *i.e.,* that which has grown together.

Consider an occasion *a*—we have to enumerate how other actual occasions are in *a*, in the sense that their relationships with *a* are constitutive of the essence of *a*. What *a* is in itself, is that it is a unit of realised experience; accordingly we ask how other occasions are in the experience which is a. Also for the present I am excluding cognitive experience. The complete answer to this question is, that the relationships among actual occasions are as unfathomable in their variety of type as are those among eternal objects in the realm of abstraction. But there are fundamental types of such relationships in terms of which the whole complex variety can find its description.

A preliminary for the understanding of these types of entry (of one occasion into the essence of another) is to note that they are involved in the modes of realisation of abstractive hierarchies, discussed in the previous chapter. The spatio-temporal relationships, involved in those hierarchies as realised in a, have all a definition in terms of a and of the occasions entrant in a. Thus the entrant occasions lend their aspects to the hierarchies, and thereby convert spatio-temporal modalities into categorical determinations; and the hierarchies lend their forms to the occasions and thereby limit the entrant occasions to being entrant only under those forms. Thus in the same way (as seen in the previous chapter) that every occasion is a synthesis of all eternal objects under the limitation of gradations of actuality, so every occasion is a synthesis of all occasions under the limitation of gradations of types of entry. Each occasion synthesises the totality of content under its own limitations of mode.

In respect to these types of internal relationship between a and other occasions, these other occasions (as constitutive of a) can be classified in many alternative ways. These are all concerned with different definitions of past, present, and future. It has been usual in philosophy to assume that these various definitions must necessarily be equivalent. The present state of opinion in physical science conclusively shows that this assumption is without metaphysical justification, even although any such discrimination may be found to be unnecessary for physical science. This question has already been dealt with in the chapter on Relativity. But the physical theory of relativity touches only the fringe of the various theories which are metaphysically tenable. It is important for my argument to insist upon the unbounded freedom within which the actual is a unique categorical determination.

Every actual occasion exhibits itself as a process: it is a becomingness. In so disclosing itself, it places itself as one among a multiplicity of other occasions, without which it could not be itself. It also defines itself as a particular individual achievement, focussing in its limited way an unbounded realm of eternal objects.

Any one occasion a issues from other occasions which collectively form its *past*. It displays for itself other occasions which collectively form its *present*. It is in respect to its associated hierarchy, as displayed in this immediate present, that an occasion finds its own originality. It is that display which is its own contribution to the output of actuality. It may be conditioned, and even completely determined by the past from which it issues. But its display in the present under those conditions is what directly emerges from its prehensive activity. The occasion a also holds within itself an indetermination in the form of a future, which has partial determination by reason of its inclusion in a and also has determinate spatio-temporal relatedness to a and to actual occasions of the past from a and of the present for a.

This future is a synthesis in a of eternal objects as not-being and as requiring the passage from a to other individualisations (with determinate spatio-temporal relations to a) in which not-being becomes being.

There is also in a what, in the previous chapter, I have termed the 'abrupt' realisation of finite eternal objects. This abrupt realisation requires *either* a reference of the basic objects of the finite hierarchy to determinate occasions other than a (as their situations), in past, present, future; *or* requires a realisation of these eternal objects in determinate relationships, but under the aspect of exemption from inclusion in the spatio-temporal scheme of relatedness between actual occasions. This abrupt synthesis of eternal objects in each occasion is the inclusion in actuality of the analytical character of the realm of eternality. This inclusion has those limited gradations of actuality which characterise every occasion by reason of its essential limitation. It is this realised extension of eternal relatedness beyond the mutual relatedness of the actual occasions, which prehends into each occasion the full sweep of eternal relatedness. I term this abrupt realisation the 'graded envisagement' which each occasion prehends into its synthesis. This graded envisagement is how the actual includes what (in one sense) is not-being as a positive factor in its own achievement. It is the source of error, of truth, of art, of ethics, and of religion. By it, fact is confronted with alternatives.

This general concept, of an event as a process whose outcome is a unit of experience, points to the analysis of an event into (i) substantial activity, (ii) conditioned potentialities which are there for synthesis, and (iii) the achieved outcome of the synthesis. The unity of all actual occasions forbids the analysis of substantial activities into independent entities. Each individual activity is nothing but the mode in which the general activity is individualised by the imposed conditions. The envisagement which enters into the synthesis is also a character which conditions the synthesising activity.

The general activity is not an entity in the sense in which occasions or eternal objects are entities. It is a general metaphysical character which underlies all occasions, in a particular mode for each occasion. There is nothing with which to compare it: it is Spinoza's one infinite substance. Its attributes are its character of individualisation into a multiplicity of modes, and the realm of eternal objects which are variously synthesised in these modes. Thus eternal possibility and modal differentiation into individual multiplicity are the attributes of the one substance. In fact each general element of the metaphysical situation is an attribute of the substantial activity.

Yet another element in the metaphysical situation is disclosed by the consideration that the general attribute of modality is limited. This element must rank as an attribute of the substantial activity. In its nature each mode is limited, so as not to be other modes. But, beyond these limitations of particulars, the general modal individualisation is limited in two ways: In the first place it is an actual course of events, which might be otherwise so far as concerns eternal possibility, but *is* that course. This limitation takes three forms, (i) the special logical relations which all events must conform to, (ii) the selection of relationships to which the events do conform, and (iii) the particularity which infects the course even within those general relationships of logic and causation. Thus this first limitation is a limitation of antecedent selection. So far as the general metaphysical situation is concerned, there might have been an indiscriminate modal pluralism apart from logical or other limitation. But there could not then have been these modes, for each mode represents a synthesis of actualities which are limited to conform to a standard. We here come to the second way of limitation. Restriction is the price of value. There cannot be value without antecedent standards of value, to discriminate the acceptance or rejection of what is before the envisaging mode of activity. Thus there is an antecedent limitation among values, introducing contraries, grades, and oppositions.

According to this argument the fact that there is a process of actual occasions, and the fact that the occasions are the emergence of values which require such limitation, both require that the course of events should have developed amid an antecedent limitation composed of conditions, particularisation, and standards of value.

Thus as a further element in the metaphysical situation, there is required a principle of limitation. Some particular *how* is necessary, and some particularisation in the *what* of matter of fact is necessary. The only alternative to this admission, is to deny the reality of actual occasions. Their apparent irrational limitation must be taken as a proof of illusion and we must look for reality behind the scene. If we reject this alternative behind the scene, we must provide a ground for limitation which stands among the attributes of the substantial activity. This attribute provides the limitation for which no reason can be given: for all reason flows from it. God is the ultimate limitation, and His existence is the ultimate irrationality. For no reason can be given for just that limitation which it stands in His nature to impose. God is not concrete, but He is the ground for concrete actuality. No reason can be given for the nature of God, because that nature is the ground of rationality.

In this argument the point to notice is, that what is metaphysically indeterminate has nevertheless to be categorically determinate. We have come to the limit of rationality. For there is a categorical limitation which does not spring from any metaphysical reason. There is a metaphysical need for a principle of determination, but there can be no metaphysical reason for what is determined. If there were such a reason, there would be no need for any further principle: for metaphysics would already have provided the determination. The general principle of empiricism depends upon the doctrine that there is a principle of concretion which is not discoverable by abstract reason. What further can be known about God must be sought in the region of particular experiences, and therefore rests on an empirical basis. In respect to the interpretation of these experiences, mankind have differed profoundly. He has been named respectively, Jehovah, Allah, Brahma, Father in Heaven, Order of Heaven, First Cause, Supreme Being, Chance. Each name corresponds to a system of thought derived from the experiences of those who have used it.

Among medieval and modern philosophers, anxious to establish the religious significance of God, an unfortunate habit has prevailed of paying to Him metaphysical compliments. He has been conceived as the foundation of the metaphysical situation with its ultimate activity. If this conception be adhered to, there can be no alternative except to discern in Him the origin of all evil as well as of all good. He is then the supreme author of the play, and to Him must therefore be ascribed its shortcomings as well as its success. If He be conceived as the supreme ground for limitation, it stands in His very nature to divide the Good from the Evil, and to establish Reason 'within her dominions supreme.'

2

THE ENCOMPASSING*

Karl Jaspers (1883–) was Professor of Philosophy at the University of Basel until 1961. He is one of the leading contemporary exponents of existentialism. Some of his major works include: Reason and Existence, The Origin and Goal of History, *and* Myth and Christianity.

 Karl Jaspers

Introduction: The Meaning of Philosophical Logic

ONE possible way of philosophizing is the movement of philosophical logic in those acts of thought which formally represent the various modes of Being. Since we shall make an initial investigation of this possibility in the three middle lectures, here we shall ignore all concrete philosophizing, that is, the development of particular physical, existential, or metaphysical subjects. Rather we shall be concerned with the horizons and forms within which philosophical contents can be established without deception—horizons which became visible when our humanity was pushed to its very limits by Kierkegaard and Nietzsche.

A. 1. THE QUESTION OF THE ENCOMPASSING.

IN order to see most clearly into what is true and real, into what is no longer fastened to any particular thing or colored by any particular atmosphere, we must push into the widest range of the possible. And then we experience the following: everything that is an object for us, even though it be the greatest, is still always within another, is not yet all. Wherever we arrive, the horizon which includes the attained itself goes further and forces us to give up any final rest. We can secure no standpoint from which a closed whole of Being would be surveyable, nor any sequence of standpoints through whose totality Being would be given even indirectly.

We always live and think within a horizon. But the very fact

* Reprinted from *Reason and Existence* by Karl Jaspers, by permission of Farrar, Straus & Giroux, Inc. Copyright 1955 by The Noonday Press.

that it is a horizon indicates something further which again surrounds the given horizon. From this situation arises the question about the Encompassing. The Encompassing is not a horizon within which every determinate mode of Being and truth emerges for us, but rather that within which every particular horizon is enclosed as in something absolutely comprehensive which is no longer visible as a horizon at all.

2. THE TWO MODES OF THE ENCOMPASSING.

THE Encompassing appears and disappears for us in two opposed perspectives: either as Being itself, in and through which we are—or else as the Encompassing which we ourselves are, and in which every mode of Being appears to us. The latter would be as the medium or condition under which all Being appears as Being for us. In neither case is the Encompassing the sum of some provisional kinds of being, a part of whose contents we know, but rather it is the whole as the most extreme, self-supporting ground of Being, whether it is Being in itself, or Being as it is for us.

All of our natural knowledge and dealings with things lies between these final and no longer conditioned bases of encompassing Being. The Encompassing never appears as an object in experience, nor as an explicit theme of thinking, and therefore might seem to be empty. But precisely here is where the possibility for our deepest insight into Being arises, whereas all other knowledge about Being is merely knowledge of particular, individual being.

Knowledge of the many always leads to distraction. One runs into the infinite unless one arbitrarily sets a limit by some unquestioned purpose or contingent interest. And in that case, precisely at these limits, one always runs into bewildering difficulties. Knowledge about the Encompassing would put all the knowable as a whole under such conditions.

B. HISTORICAL REFLECTIONS ON THIS BASIC PHILOSOPHICAL QUESTION.

To seek this Being itself beyond the endlessness of the particular and partial was the first, and is always the new way, of philosophizing. This is what Aristotle meant when he said, "And indeed the question which was raised of old and is raised now and always, and is ever the subject of doubt is, what is Being" (*Metaphysics*, 1028 b). Schelling, too, held it to be "the oldest and most correct explanation of what philosophy is . . . that it is the science of Being. But to find what Being is, that is, true Being—that is the difficulty: *hoc opus, hic labor est"* (II, 3, 76). That from the beginning of philosophy up to the present this question continually recurs might arouse confidence in the abiding, fundamental meaning of philosophy throughout its almost endless multiplicities of appearance.

The first difficulty is to understand the question correctly. And the correct understanding of the question shows itself in the answer, shows itself in the degree to which we can appropriate the truth and reject the falsity of historically given questions and answers in their basic and connected meaning. But such a task, in the light of the enormous projects and catastrophes of philosophy, can be accomplished neither through a collection of ideas, nor through forcibly limiting it to some supposedly basic feature to which everything is to be added. We must presuppose a philosophic attitude whose passion for the truth, in a continuing attempt to grasp one's own Existenz, achieves awareness of an unlimited range by continued questioning. In such an unlimited range, the simplicity of the origin may finally be given truly.

Of the two approaches to Being as the Encompassing, the most usual and most natural way for every beginning philosophy is toward Being in itself, conceived as Nature, World, or God. However, we shall approach it from the other, and since Kant unavoidable, way; we shall search into the Encompassing which we are. Although we know, or at least take into account, the fact that the Encompassing which we are is in no wise Being itself, still this can be seen in critical purity only after we have gone to the end of the path opened up by Kant.

I. THE ENCOMPASSING WHICH WE ARE: EMPIRICAL EXISTENCE, CONSCIOUSNESS AS SUCH, SPIRIT.

WHETHER we call the Encompassing which we are our empirical existence, consciousness as such, or spirit, in no case can it be grasped as though it were something in the world which appeared before us. Rather it is that in which all other things appear to us. In general, we do not appropriately cognize it as an object; rather we become aware of it as a limit. This is confirmed when we abandon the determinate, clear—because objective—knowledge which is directed to particular things distinguishable from other things. We should like, so to speak, to stand outside ourselves in order to look and see what we are; but in this supposed looking we are and always remain enclosed within that at which we are looking.

Let us consider for a moment some beginnings from which,

by repeated questioning, the Encompassing can be conceived. I am, first of all, an empirical existent. Empirical existence means the actual taken comprehensively, which immediately shows itself to empirical consciousness in the particularities of matter, living body, and soul, but which, as such particularities, is no longer the Encompassing of empirical existence. Everything which is empirically actual for me must in some sense be actual as a part of my being, as, for example, in the continually perceptible presence of my body as it is touched, altered, or as it is perceiving.

Empirical existence, as the overpowering Other which determines me, is the world. The Encompassing of empirical existence which I am when made into an object also becomes something alien like the world. As soon as our empirical existence becomes an object for investigation, we become absorbed into the being of the world which is that incomprehensible Other, Nature. In this fashion we are apprehended only as one sort of being among others, not yet as properly human. Knowledge of the Encompassing of empirical existence with which we are united removes from particular sciences the claim of grasping us as a whole.

Although I can never comprehend my empirical existence as an Encompassing, but only particular empirical forms like matter, life, and soul which I can never reduce back to a single principle, still I stand in the continuous presence of this embracing empirical reality. But even if we know the body, life, the soul, and consciousness merely as they become objectively accessible to us, even here we can, so to speak, see through them all back to that Encompassing of empirical existence with which we are one and which becomes only particularized in every physical, biological, and psychological object, but which, as such, is no longer the Encompassing. Thus the empirical awareness which I have as a living actuality is, as such, not constitutive by itself of that Encompassing which I am as an empirical existent.

The second mode of the Encompassing which I am is consciousness as such. Only what appears to our consciousness as experienceable, as an object, has being for us. What does not appear to consciousness, what can in no wise touch our cognition, is as good as nothing for us. Hence, everything which exists for us must take on that form in which it can be thought or experienced by consciousness. It must in some fashion appear in the form of an object; it must become present through some temporal act of consciousness; it must become articulated and thereby communicable through its thinkability. That all being for us must appear in those forms under which it can enter into consciousness is what imprisons us in the Encompassing of thinkability. But we can make clear its limits and, with this consciousness of limits, become open to the possibility of the Other which we do not know. Consciousness has two meanings however: (i) we are conscious as living existents and, as such, are not yet or no longer encompassing. This consciousness is carried by life itself, the unconscious ground of what we consciously experience. As living existents which we are *in* an absolute Encompassing of empirical existence, we become possible objects of empirical investigation for ourselves. We find ourselves divided into groups of races and into those always particular individualities into which this form of reality divides itself. However, we are not only countless single consciousnesses, which are more or less similar to one another; we are also therein (ii) consciousness as such. Through such consciousness we think we can refer to Being, not only in similar ways of perception and feeling, but in an identical way. Contrasting with empirical consciousness, this is the other sense of consciousness which we are as Encompassing. There is a leap between the multiplicity of subjective consciousnesses and the universal validity of that true consciousness which can only be *one*. As the consciousness of living beings, we are split into the multiplicity of endless particular realities, imprisoned in the narrowness of the individual and not encompassing. As consciousness in general, we participate in an inactuality, the universally valid truth, and, as such consciousness, are an infinite Encompassing. As a conscious living actuality, we are always a mere kind, even a unique individual enclosed within its own individuality. But we participate in the Encompassing through the possibility of knowledge and through the possibility of common knowledge of Being in every form in which it appears to consciousness. And, indeed, we participate, not only in the validity of the knowable, but also in a universally recognized, formal lawfulness in willing, action, and feeling. So defined, truth is timeless, and our temporal actuality is a more or less complete actualization of this timeless permanence.

This sharp separation, however, between the actuality of living consciousness in its temporal process and the inactuality of consciousness in general, as the site of the timeless meaning of the one common truth, is not absolute. Rather it is an abstraction which can be transcended through the clarification of the Encompassing. The actual existence of this timeless meaning insofar as it is something produced, something temporal, which grasps and moves itself, is a new sense of the Encompassing, and this is called spirit.

Spirit is the third mode of the Encompassing which we are. Out of the origins of its being, spirit is the totality of intelligible thought, action, and feeling—a totality which is not a closed object for knowledge but remains Idea. Although spirit is necessarily oriented to the truth of consciousness as such, as well as to the actuality of its Other (Nature as known and used), yet in both directions it is moved by Ideas which bring everything into clarity and connection. Spirit is the comprehensive reality of activity which is actualized by itself and by what it encounters in a world which is always given yet always being changed. It is the process of fusing and reconstructing all totalities in a present which is never finished yet always fulfilled. It is always on its way toward a possible completion of empirical existence where universality, the whole, and every particular would all be members of a totality. Out of a continuously actual and continuously fragmenting whole, it pushes forward, creating again and again out of its contemporary origins its own possible reality. Since it pushes toward the whole, spirit would preserve, enhance, and relate everything to everything else, exclude nothing, and give to everything its place and limits.

Spirit, in contrast to the abstraction of timeless consciousness as such, is again a temporal process, and as such it is comparable to empirical existence. But, as distinguished from this latter, it moves by a reflexivity of knowledge instead of by some merely biologico-psychological process. Understood from within and not capable of being investigated as a natural object, spirit is always directed toward the universality of consciousness as such. Thus it is a grasping of itself, a working upon itself through denial and approval. It produces itself by struggling with itself.

As mere empirical existence and as spirit, we are an encompassing reality. But as empirical existence, we are unconsciously bound to our ultimate bases in matter, life, and the psyche. When we understand ourselves as objects in this horizon, we see ourselves in an infinite, and only from the outside. We become split from one another, and only as thus split are we objects of scientific investigation (as matter, living beings, psyches). But as spirit we are consciously related to everything which is comprehensible to us. We transform the world and ourselves into the intelligible, which encloses totalities. As objects in this mode of the Encompassing, we know ourselves from within as the one, unique, all-embracing reality which is wholly spirit and only spirit.

The distinctions of empirical existence, consciousness as such, and spirit do not imply separable facts. Rather they represent three starting points through which we can come to feel that comprehensive Being which we are and in which all Being and everything scientifically investigable appears.

These three modes taken individually are not yet the Encompassing as we represent it. Consciousness as such, the location of universally valid truth, is in itself nothing independent. On one side, it points to its basis in empirical existence. On the other it points to spirit, the power it must let itself be dominated by if it would attain meaning and totality. In itself, consciousness as such is an unreal articulation of the Encompassing. Through it, the Encompassing is differentiated into those modes according to one of which the Encompassing can become individuated and knowable as empirical natural processes, and, according to the other of which it is understandable, a self-transparent, totalizing reality or Freedom. Empirical existence and spirit produce forms of reality; consciousness as such is the form in which we envisage the Encompassing as the condition of the universally valid and communicable.

II. THE ENCOMPASSING AS BEING ITSELF; WORLD AND TRANSCENDENCE.

WE pass beyond the Encompassing which we are (empirical existence, consciousness as such, and spirit) when we ask whether this whole is Being itself.

If Being itself is that in which everything that is for us must become present, then it might be thought that this appearance-for-us is in fact all Being. Thus Nietzsche, who conceived all Being as interpretation and our being as interpretative, wanted to reject any further being as an illusory otherworld. But the question does not stop with the limits of our knowledge of things, nor in the inwardness of the limiting consciousness of the Encompassing which we are. Rather this Encompassing which I am and know as empirical existence, consciousness as such, and spirit, is not conceivable in itself but refers beyond itself. The Encompassing which we are is not Being itself, but rather the genuine appearance in the Encompassing of Being itself.

This Being itself which we feel as indicated at the limits, and which therefore is the last thing we reach through questioning from our situation, is in itself the first. It is not made by us, is not interpretation, and is not an object. Rather it itself brings forth our questioning and permits it no rest.

The Encompassing which we are has one of its limits in fact. Even though we create the form of everything that we know, since it must appear to us in those modes according to which it can become an object, yet knowledge can not create the least particle of dust in its empirical existence. In the same way, Being itself is that which shows an immeasurable number of appearances to inquiry, but it itself always recedes and only manifests itself indirectly as that determinate empirical existence we encounter in the progress of our experiences and in the regularity of processes in all their particularity. We call it the World.

The Encompassing which we are has its other limit in the question through which it is. Being itself is the Transcendence which shows itself to no investigative experience, not even indirectly. It is that which as the absolute Encompassing just as certainly "is" as it remains unseen and unknown.

III. EXISTENZ, ANIMATION AND GROUND OF ALL MODES OF THE ENCOMPASSING.

ANY philosopher who is not lost in the perspective of the conceptual but wishes to push toward genuine Being feels a deep dissatisfaction looking at all the hitherto mentioned modes of the Encompassing. He knows too little in the vast superfluity of apparently immeasurable multiplicities toward which he is directed. He can not find Being itself in all the dimensions of an Encompassing so conceived. He is liberated into a vastness where Being becomes void. The Transcendent seems to be merely an unknowable which makes no difference, and the spirit comes to seem like a sublime whole, but one in which each individual in his deepest inwardness almost seems to have disappeared.

The central point of philosophizing is first reached in the awareness of potential Existenz.

Existenz is the Encompassing, not in the sense of the vastness of a horizon of all horizons, but rather in the sense of a fundamental origin, the condition of selfhood without which all the vastness of Being becomes a desert. Existenz, although never itself becoming an object or form, carries the meaning of every mode of the Encompassing.

While mere empirical existence, consciousness as such, and spirit all appear in the world and become scientifically investigable realities, Existenz is the object of no science. In spite of which, we find here the very axis about which everything in the world turns if it is to have any genuine meaning for us.

At first Existenz seems to be a new narrowing, for it is always merely one among others. It might appear as though the spaciousness of the Encompassing had been contracted into the uniqueness of the individual self which, in contrast to the reality of encompassing spirit, looks like the emptiness of a point. But this contracted point lodged, so to speak, in the body of empirical existence, in this particular consciousness, and in this spirit, is, in fact, the sole possible revelation of the depths of Being as historicity. In all modes of the Encompassing, the self can become genuinely certain of itself only as Existenz.

If we first contrast Existenz with consciousness as such, it becomes the hidden ground in me to which Transcendence is first revealed. The Encompassing which we are exists only in relation to something other than itself. Thus, as I am conscious only insofar as I have something else as an objective being before me by which I then am determined and with which I am concerned, so also I am Existenz only as I know Transcendence as the power through which I genuinely am myself. The Other is either the being which is in the world for consciousness as such, or it is Transcendence for Existenz. This twofold Other first becomes clear through the inwardness of Existenz. Without Existenz the meaning of Transcendence is lost. It remains only something indifferent and not to be known, something supposed to be at the bottom of things, something excogitated, or, perhaps for our animal consciousness, something weird or terrifying plunging it into superstition and anxiety, a subject to be investigated psychologically and removed through a rational insight into the factual by consciousness as such. Only through Existenz can Transcendence become present without superstition, as the genuine reality which to itself never disappears.

Further, Existenz is like the counterpart to spirit. Spirit is the will to become *whole;* potential Existenz is the will to be authentic. Spirit is intelligible throughout, coming to itself in the whole; but Existenz is the unintelligible, standing by and against other Existenzen, breaking up every whole and never reaching any real totality. For spirit, a final transparency would be the origin of Being; Existenz on the other hand remains in all clarity of spirit as the irremediably dark origin. Spirit lets everything disappear and vanish into universality and totality. The individual as spirit is not himself but, so to speak, the unity of contingent individuals and of the necessary universal. Existenz however is irreducibly in another; it is the absolutely firm, the irreplaceable, and therefore, as against all mere empirical existence, consciousness as such, and spirit, it is authentic being before Transcendence to which alone it surrenders itself without reservation.

Spirit wants to grasp the individual either as an example of a universal or as a part of a whole. On the other hand, Existenz, as the possibility of decision derivable from no universal validity, is an origin in time, is the individual as historicity. It is the apprehension of timelessness through temporality, not through universal concepts.

Spirit is historical by representing itself in retrospect as a transparent totality. Existenz is historical as eternity in time, as the absolute historicity of its concrete empirical existence in a spiritual opacity which is never removed. But Existenz is not merely this incompletion and perversity in all temporal existence, which, as such, must always expand and change into some spiritual totality, but rather temporal existence thoroughly and authentically penetrated: the paradox of the unity of temporality and eternity.

Spirit in its immediacy is the *potential Idea,* whose universality unfolds into full clarity. Existenz in its immediacy, on the other hand, is its historicity in relation to Transcendence, i.e., the irremovable immediacy of its faith.

The faith of spirit is the life of the universal Idea, where *Thought is Being* ultimately is valid. The faith of Existenz, however, is the Absolute in Existenz itself on which everything for it rests, in which spirit, consciousness as such, and empirical existence are all bound together and decided, where for the first time there is both impulse and goal; here Kierkegaard's proposition, "Faith is Being," applies.

When Existenz understands itself, it is not like my understanding of another, nor the sort of understanding whose contents can be abstracted from the person understanding, nor a sort of looking at; rather it is an origin which itself first arises in its own self-clarification. It is not like sharing in something else, but is at once the understanding and the being of what is understood. It is not understanding through universals, but moves above such understanding in the medium of spirit to become an understanding without any generalization in the absolute present, in deed, in love, and in every form of absolute consciousness. It is the difference between the love of another, which I understand but yet never really understand, and my own love, which I understand because I am that love. Or, in other words, the difference between understanding other things by empathy as process or experience, and understanding myself as unique since I know myself before Transcendence.

When we compare Existenz with consciousness as such, spirit, or any other mode of the Encompassing, the same thing appears: without Existenz everything seems empty, hollowed out, without ground, fake, because everything has turned into endless masks, mere possibilities, or mere empirical existence.

IV. REASON: THE BOND BETWEEN THE VARIOUS MODES OF THE ENCOMPASSING.

WE have seen as modes of the Encompassing:

a) Being as the Other, which was either World (empirical existence which can be investigated in a universally valid way) or Transcendence (as Being in itself).

b) The Being of the Encompassing which we are, which was either our empirical existence (the still indeterminate, comprehensive actuality), or consciousness as such (the site of all objective and intelligible validities for us), or spirit (the single whole of coherent movement of consciousness as it is activated by Ideas).

But for the source from which all these modes of the Encompassing receive animation and for which they speak, we touched upon Existenz, the dark ground of selfhood, the concealment out of which I come to encounter myself and for which Transcendence first becomes real.

Inextricably bound to Existenz is something else which concerns the connection of all these modes of the Encompassing. This is no new whole, but rather a continuing demand and movement. It is not a mode through which the Encompassing appears, but rather the *bond* which unites all modes of the Encompassing; it is called reason.

There is a question as to what "reason" means in the history of philosophy, how it comprehended itself, what it meant for Kierkegaard and Nietzsche, what they meant when they both trusted and mistrusted it. The clarification of the modes of the Encompassing must go into the ambiguity of what has passed for reason.

If reason means clear, objective thinking, the transformation of the opaque into the transparent, then it is nothing more than the Encompassing of consciousness as such. So considered, it would be better to call it, in accordance with the tradition of German idealism, understanding [Verstand].

If reason means the way to *totalities,* the life of the Idea, then it is the Encompassing of *spirit.*

But if reason means the pre-eminence of thought in all modes of the Encompassing, then more is included than mere thinking. It is then what goes beyond all limits, the omnipresent demand of thought, that not only grasps what is universally valid and is an *ens rationis* in the sense of being a law or principle of order of some process, but also brings to light the Other, stands before the absolutely counter-rational, touching it and bringing it, too, into being. Reason, through the pre-eminence of thought, can bring all the modes of the Encompassing to light by continually transcending limits, without itself being an Encompassing like them. It is, so to speak, like the final authentic Encompassing which continually must withdraw and remain inconceivable except in those modes of the Encompassing in which it moves.

Reason of itself is no source; but, as it is an encompassing bond, it is like a source in which all sources first come to light. It is the unrest which permits acquiescence in nothing; it forces a break with the immediacy of the unconscious in every mode of the Encompassing which we are. It pushes on continually. But it is also that which can effect the great peace, not the peace of a self-confident rational whole, but that of Being itself opened up to us through reason.

Reason is the inextinguishable impulse to philosophize with whose destruction reason itself is destroyed. This impulse is to achieve reason, to restore reason; it is that reason which always rises clearer from all the deviations and narrowings of so-called "reason" and which can acknowledge the justice of objections to reason and set their limits.

Reason should not get caught within any mode of the Encompassing: not in empirical existence to favor a will-to-exist which in its very narrowness asserts itself purposively yet blindly; nor in consciousness as such in favor of endless validities which are indifferent to us; nor in spirit in favor of a self-enclosed, harmonious totality which can be contemplated but not lived.

Reason is always too little when it is enclosed within final and determinate forms, and it is always too much when it appears as a self-sufficient substitute.

With the rational attitude I desire unlimited clarity; I try to know scientifically, to grasp the empirically real and the compelling validities of the thinkable; but at the same time, I live with an awareness of the limits of scientific penetrability and of clarity in general; however, I push forward from all sources in all modes of the Encompassing toward a universal unfolding of them in thought and reject above all thoughtlessness.

But reason itself is no timeless permanence; it is neither a quiet realm of truth (such as the contents of scientific cognition whose validity does not change although their attainment is an endless and restless movement) ; nor is it Being itself. Neither is it the mere moment of some chance thought. Rather it is the binding, recollecting, and progressive power whose contents are always derived from its own limits and which passes beyond every one of these limits, expressing perpetual dissatisfaction. It appears in all forms of the modes of the Encompassing yet seems to be nothing itself, a bond which does not rest upon itself but always on something else out of which reason produces both what it itself is and what it can be.

Reason drives toward unity, but it is not satisfied either with the one level of knowable accuracies for consciousness as such, or with the great effective unities of spirit. It goes along just as well with Existenz where the latter breaks through these unities, and so reason is again present in order to bring Existenzen separated by an abyss of absolute distance together into communication.

Its essence seems to be the universal, that which pushes toward law and order or is identical with it. But it remains a possibility in Existenz even when these fail. Reason is itself still the only thing by and for which the chaos of the negative in its passion for Night preserves its mode of potential Existenz, a reason which otherwise would be surrendered to what is absolutely alien at these extreme limits.

V. REASON AND EXISTENZ.

THE great poles of our being, which encounter one another in every mode of the Encompassing, are thus reason and Existenz. They are inseparable. Each disappears with the disappearance of the other. Reason should not surrender to Existenz to produce an isolating defiance which resists communication in despair. Existenz should not surrender to reason in favor of a transparency which is substituted for substantial reality.

Existenz only becomes clear through reason; reason only has content through Existenz.

There is an impulse in reason to move out of the immobility and endless triviality of the merely correct into a living bond through the totality of the ideas of the spirit, and out of these toward Existenz as that which supports and first gives authentic being to the spirit.

Reason is oriented toward its Other, toward the content of the Existenz which supports it, which clarifies itself in reason, and which gives decisive impulses to reason. Reason without content would be mere understanding, without any basis as reason. And, as the concepts of the understanding are empty without intuition, so reason is hollow without Existenz. Reason is not itself as mere understanding, but only in the acts of potential Existenz.

But Existenz is also oriented toward an Other. It is related to Transcendence through which it first becomes an independent cause in the world; for Existenz did not create itself. Without Transcendence, Existenz becomes a sterile, loveless, and demonic defiance. Existenz, oriented to reason through whose clarity it first experiences unrest and the appeal of Transcendence, under the needling questioning of reason first comes into its own authentic movement. Without reason, Existenz is inactive, sleeping, and as though not there.

Thus reason and Existenz are not two opposed powers which struggle with one another for victory. Each exists only through the other. They mutually develop one another and find through one another clarity and reality.

Although they never combine into an ultimate whole, every genuine accomplishment is whole only through them.

Reason without Existenz even in the richest possible field finally passes into an indifferent thinking, a merely intellectual movement of consciousness as such, or into a dialectic of the spirit. And as it slips away into intellectual universality without the binding root of its historicity, it ceases to be reason.

Irrational Existenz which rests upon feeling, experiencing, unquestioned impulse, instinct, or whim, ends up as blind violence, and therewith falls under the empirical laws which govern these actual forces. Without historicity, lost in the mere particularities of contingent empirical existence in a self-assertion unrelated to Transcendence, it ceases to be Existenz.

Each without the other loses the genuine continuity of Being and, therefore, the reliability which, although it can not be calculated, is nevertheless appropriate to genuine reason and Existenz. They separate themselves from one another only to become violent powers lacking any communication. In isolation they no longer mean what they should; only formulas without either basis or purpose remain, in a narrowing sphere of empirical existence. There, through a veil of justifications which are no longer true and no longer believed, they are simply the means of expression for mutually destructive empirical existents.

But there is rest nowhere in temporal existence. Rather there is always movement issuing forth from the ultimate substantial ground—movement in the tension between the individual and the universal, between the actual and the total range of the possible, between the unquestionable immediacy of existential faith and the infinite movement of reason.

3

THE MIND-ONLY DOCTRINE*

Vasubandhu (c. 420–c. 500) was an Indian Mahayana Buddhist whose writings explain and defend dialectically a system of absolute idealism according to which Pure Consciousness is the only reality. This view, called Vijnanavada or Yogacara, is especially developed in his chief writings: the Vimshatika *and the* Trimshika.

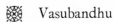 Vasubandhu

    I.   Because our ideation gives rise to the false ideas of the ego and *dharmas* (elements of existence),
There are various revulsions of appearances.
This ideation, depending on the mind, goes through certain transformations.
These transformations are of three kinds.

    II.   They are the consciousness of "ripening in a different life,"
The consciousness of intellection, and the consciousness of the discrimination of the objective world.
First of all, the *ālaya* (ideation-store) consciousness,
Which brings into fruition all seeds [or effects of good and evil deeds].

    III.   [In its state of pure consciousness], it is not conscious of its clingings and impressions.
In both its objective and subjective functions, it is always associated with touch,
Volition, feeling, thought, and cognition.
But it is always indifferent to its associations.

    IV.   It is not affected by the darkness of ignorance or by the memory [of the distinction of good and evil].
The same is true in the case of touch, etc.
It is always flowing like torrent,
And is abandoned in the state of the *arhat*.

---

* Reprinted from *A Source Book in Indian Philosophy* by S. Radhakrishnan and C. A. Moore (eds.), by permission of Princeton University Press. Copyright, 1957, Princeton University Press.

V.   The second transformation
     Is called the mind-consciousness,
     Which, while it depends on the ideation-store conscious-
       ness, in turn conditions it.
     Its nature and characteristic consists of intellection.

VI. It is always accompanied by the four evil desires,
     Namely, ignorance of the self, view of the self [as being
       real and permanent],
     Self-pride, and self-love,
     And by touch, etc. [volition, feeling, thought, and cog-
       nition].

VII. It is free from the memory [of the distinction of good and
       evil] but not from the darkness of ignorance.
     It follows its objects in their emergence and dependence.
     It is abandoned by the *arhat* when he arrives at the state
       of complete extinction of sensation and thought,
     And transcends this mundane world.

VIII. Next comes the third transformation,
      Which consists of the last six categories of discrimination
        [the consciousness of touch, sight, hearing, smell, taste,
        and the sense-center consciousness].
      Its nature and characteristic consists of the discrimina-
        tion of objects.
      It is neither good nor evil.

IX. Mental functions consist of general mental functions,
     Particular mental functions, good functions, evil func-
       tions,
     Minor evil functions, and indeterminate mental func-
       tions.
     They all impress the mind in three ways [of joy, of
       suffering, and of indifference].

X.   General mental functions are touch, etc. [volition, feel-
       ing, thought, cognition].
     Particular mental functions are desire,
     Resolve, remembrance, concentration, and wisdom,
     Each depending on different conditions.

XI. Good mental functions are belief, sense of shame, bash-
       fulness,
     The three roots of the absence of covetousness, etc. [the
       absence of hatred and the absence of attachment],

Energy, repose of mind, vigilance,
Equanimity, and non-injury.

XII.   Evil mental functions are covetousness, hatreds,
Attachment, arrogance, doubt, and false view.
Minor evil mental functions are anger,
Enmity, concealment, affliction, envy, parsimony,

XIII.   Deception, fraudulence, injury, pride,
Absence of the sense of shame, absence of bashfulness,
High-mindedness, low-mindedness,
Unbelief, indolence,

XIV.   Idleness, forgetfulness,
Distraction, and non-discernment.
Indeterminate mental functions are repentance, drowsiness,
Reflection, and investigation, the former two composing
a different class from the latter.

XV.   Based on the mind-consciousness
The five consciousnesses [of the senses] manifest themselves in concomitance with the objective world.
Sometimes the senses manifest themselves together, and sometimes not,
Just as waves are dependent on the water.

XVI.   The sense-center consciousness always arises and manifests itself,
Except when born in the realm of the absence of thought,
In the state of unconsciousness, in the two forms of concentration,
In sleep, and in that state where the spirit is depressed or absent.

XVII.   Thus the various consciousnesses are but transformations.
That which discriminates and that which is discriminated
Are, because of this, both unreal.
For this reason, everything is mind only.

XVIII.   As the result of various ideations which serve as seeds,
Different transformations take place.
The revulsion-energy of these ideations
Gives rise to all sorts of discrimination.

XIX.   Due to the habit-energy of various *karmas*
The habit-energy of both the six organs and their objects
is influenced.

As the previous "ripening in a different life" is completed,
Succeeding "ripenings in a different life" are produced.

XX. Because of false discriminations,
Various things are falsely discriminated.
What is grasped by such false discrimination
Has no self-nature whatsoever.

XXI. The self-nature which results from dependence on others
Is produced by the condition of discrimination.
The difference between the Absolute (perfect wisdom) and the dependent
Is that the former is eternally free from what is grasped by false discrimination.

XXII. Thus the Absolute and the dependent
Are neither the same nor different;
As in the case of impermanence and permanence,
The one can be seen only in the other.

XXIII. From the three aspects of entity,
The three aspects of non-entity are established.
Therefore the Enlightened One abstrusely preached
That all *dharmas* have no entity.

XXIV. The first is the non-entity of phenomenon.
The second is the non-entity of self-existence.
The last is the non-entity of the ultimate existence
Of the falsely discriminative ego and *dharmas* now to be eliminated.

XXV. The supreme truth of all *dharmas*
Is nothing other than the True Norm [suchness].
It is forever true to its nature,
Which is the true nature of mind-only.

XXVI. Inasmuch as consciousness in its unawakened state
Is not in the abode of the reality of mind-only,
The six sense-organs, their objects, and the seeds of evil desires
Cannot be controlled and extirpated.

XXVII. To hold something before oneself,
And to say that it is the reality of mind-only,
Is not the state of mind-only,
Because it is the result of grasping.

XXVIII. But when [the objective world which is] the basis of
conditioning as well as the wisdom [which does the
conditioning]
Are both eliminated,
The state of mind-only is realized,
Since the six sense-organs and their objects are no longer
present.

XXIX. Without any grasping and beyond thought
Is the supra-mundane wisdom [of *bodhisattva*hood].
Because of the abandonment of the habit-energy of various *karmas* and the six sense-organs as well as their
objects,
The revulsion from relative knowledge to perfect wisdom
is attained.

XXX. This is the realm of passionlessness or purity,
Which is beyond description, is good, and is eternal,
Where one is in the state of emancipation, peace, and joy.
This is the law of the Great Buddha.

4

ANSWERS TO OBJECTIONS*

Hsuan-Tsang   ▨

Hsuan-Tsang (596–664), Chinese exponent of Vasubandhu's Yogacara or Vijnanavada Buddhism, spent many years in India and brought back to China in 645 a large collection of Buddhist philosophical treatises which he proceeded to summarize and systematize in what is perhaps the clearest classical presentation of this position: Treatises on the Establishment of the Doctrine of Consciousness Only.

(1) *Objection:* On the basis of what doctrines is the principle of Consciousness-Only established?

Answer: Have we not already explained? However, the explanations are not sufficient. One's own principle cannot be established by demolishing those of others. One should definitely present his own doctrine in order to establish it.

The true scriptures[1] declare that "in the Three Worlds there is nothing but mind,"[2] that objects are but manifestations of consciousness-only,[3] that all dharmas are not separated from the mind,[4] that sentient beings become pure or impure in accordance with the mind,[5] that bodhisattvas[6] (saints of the Mahāyāna) who

---

* Reprinted from *A Source Book in Chinese Philosophy* by Wing-Tsit Chan (tr. and ed.), by permission of Princeton University Press. Copyright © 1963 by Princeton University Press.

[1] Literally, the scriptures that teach correct principles.

[2] *Shih-ti ching (Daśabhūmi sūtra* or Ten-Stage Scripture), ch. 4, sec. 6, TSD, 10:533. See K'uei-chi, 42:7b.

[3] *Chieh shen-mi ching (Sandhinirmocana sūtra* or Scripture Explaining the Deep and the Secret), ch. 2, sec. 4–5, TSD, 16:693; see K'uei-chi, 42:8a.

[4] *Ju Leng-chia ching (Laṅkāvatāra sūtra* or Scripture about [the Buddha] Entering into Lanka), ch. 5, TSD, 16:543. See translation by Suzuki, *Laṅkāvatāra sūtra,* pp. 171–175. See K'uei-chi, 42:8b.

[5] *Shuo Wu-kou-ch'eng ching (Vimalakīrtinirdeśa sūtra* or Scripture Spoken by Vimalakīrti), ch. 1, TSD, 14:559. See K'uei-chi, 42:8b.

[6] A bodhisattva is one who has a strong determination to seek enlightenment and salvation for all.

440 |

perfected the Four Wisdoms will, following their awakening, penetrate the truth of consciousness-only and the absence of spheres of
objects.[1]

The Four Wisdoms are: first, the wisdom that contradictory
consciousnesses are but characters. This means that the same thing
perceived by ghosts, human beings, and deities appear differently to
them in accordance with their past deeds. If there is really an
external sphere, how can this be possible? Second, the wisdom that
consciousness takes non-being as its object. This means that the
past, the future, images in dreams, and things imagined have no
real, objective basis. They are possible because they are manifestations of consciousness. If these objective bases are nonexistent, the
rest is also nonexistent. The third is the wisdom that naturally
there should be no perversion of truth. This means that if the
intelligence of ordinary people is able to perceive the real spheres
of objects, they should naturally achieve freedom from perversion
and should be able to achieve emancipation without any effort.
[Since they are not emancipated, it shows that the objective spheres
they perceive are not real at all.][2] The fourth is the wisdom
changing with three wisdoms:

a) Changing with the wisdom of the one who is free and at
ease. This means that he who has realized the freedom and the ease
of mind can change and transform earth [into gold] and so forth
without fail according to his desires. If there was really an external
sphere, how can these transformations be possible?

b) Changing with the wisdom of the one who meditates and
sees clearly. This means that when one who has achieved supreme
calmness and has practiced the meditation on the Law meditates on
one sphere of objects, its various characters appear in front of him.
If the sphere is real, why does it change according to his mind?

c) Changing with the wisdom of no discrimination. This
means that as the non-discriminating wisdom which realizes truth
arises, all spheres of objects and their characters will cease to
appear. If there are real spheres of objects, why should they do so?
The bodhisattva who achieves the Four Wisdoms will definitely
understand and penetrate the principle of consciousness-only.

Furthermore, the hymn says:

> The objects of mind, thought-center consciousness, and [the other
> six] consciousnesses
> Are not distinct from their own nature.

---

[1] The name of this scripture is uncertain. See de la Vallée Poussin, *la siddhe de
Hiuan-tsang*, p. 421, n.l. K'uei-chi was not sure (42:9a).

[2] According to K'uei-chi, 42:10a.

Therefore I declare that all things
Are consciousness only and there is nothing else [which is external
to the mind]. . . .[1]

(2) *Objection:* If what seem to be external spheres are
simply the products of the inner consciousness, why is it that what
we see in the world, whether sentient beings or non-sentient objects,
are definite with respect to space [for example, a certain mountain
is always seen in a certain place] and time but indefinite with
respect to people [for example, when many people see the same
mountain at the same time, their consciousness of it is not determined by any one of them] and function [for example, food has
real function in waking life but not in a dream]?

Answer: Your doubt may be dispelled with reference to the
world of dreams.

(3) *Objection:* Why did the World-Honored One (Bhagavat, the Buddha) teach the Twelve Bases (the five senses, the mind,
and their organs)?

Answer: These are transformations based on consciousness.
They are not real things separated from consciousness. In order to
introduce [his disciples] to the truth of the emptiness of the self,
He spoke to the six internal bases and six external bases, just as He
spoke of the continuity of sentient beings in order to deny the [false]
view that things come to an end. And in order to introduce them
to the truth of the emptiness of dharmas, He also spoke of consciousness-only, so they know that external dharmas are also non-
existent.

(4) *Objection:* Is the nature of consciousness-only not also
empty?

Answer: No. Why? Because it is not a matter of clinging? We
say dharmas are empty because the [so-called] real dharmas erroneously conceived on the basis of transformations of consciousness
are contrary to reason. We do not say dharmas are empty because
there is no nature of consciousness-only realized by correct and

1 *Hou-yen ching (Ghanavyūha sūtra* or Rich and Splendid (Scripture), according to K'uei-chi, 42:11b. The title *Hou-yen ching* is that of the Tibetan translation. The two Chinese translations of the scripture are both entitled *Ta-ch'eng
mi-yen ching* (Secret and Splendid Scripture of the Mahāyāna), but I cannot
find the passage in them. The general idea, however, runs through the scripture,
especially in sec. 8 of the first version, TSD, 16:740.

indescribable wisdom. If there were no such consciousness, there would be no worldly (relative) truth, and if there were no worldly truth, there would be no absolute truth, for the Two Levels of Truth are established on the basis of each other. To reject the Two Levels of Truth is to have evil ideas of Emptiness, a disease the Buddhas consider to be incurable. We should realize that some dharmas [which are imagined] are empty and some [which depend on something else, i.e., cause, to be complete][1] are not, and that is why Maitreya[2] recited the two verses above [to the effect that some dharmas are empty and some are not].

Comment. It is interesting to note that the position of this school with reference to the Two Levels of Truth is somewhere between that of the Three-Treatise School, which subordinates worldly truth to absolute truth, and the Hua-yen School, which identifies them. Although this school represents the doctrine of being, actually it aims at a synthesis of both being and non-being. Consequently both character and nature of dharmas are emphasized and both inner and external spheres are stressed.

(5) *Objection:* If the bases of the various forms of matter are consciousness in substance, why do the various consciousnesses of matter appear and manifest themselves in the semblance of characters of matter—homogeneous, unchangeable—and transform continuously?

Answer: Because [these manifestations] arise through the force of the influence of names and words [residing in the body from time immemorial], and are based on pure and impure dharmas. If there were none [of these characters], there would be no perversion of truth, and thus there would be neither dharmas of defilement nor pure dharmas. This is why the various consciousnesses appear in the semblance of matter. . . .

Comment. Like any idealistic philosophy, Consciousness-Only faces the most difficult task of explaining the regularity, consistency, and continuity of ideas. Instead of resorting to a belief in God, as Berkeley did, who assumes that God is the giver of them, this school treats regularity and so forth as simply characters of dharmas and as such, to be explained in terms of cause and effect. In this process of mutual cause and effect, certain seeds regularly perfume in a certain way, and therefore people with similar seeds in them are perfumed in the same way. The answer to the second objection above is no evasion, for dreams, like ideas in waking life, are governed by the law of cause and effect. By the use of

1 According to K'uei-chi, 43:7a.
2 The next Buddha, who is to come in the future to save the world.

this law, idealistic Buddhism has avoided the necessity of a belief in God as it has avoided the necessity of a belief in an ego.[1]

(6) *Objection:* The external spheres of color and so forth are clearly and immediately realized. How can what is perceived through immediate apprehension be rejected as nonexistent?

Answer: At the time the external spheres are realized through immediate apprehension, they are not taken as external. It is later that the sense-center consciousness discriminates and erroneously creates the notion of externality. Thus the objective spheres immediately apprehended are the perceived portion of the consciousnesses themselves. Since they are transformations of consciousness, we say they exist. But since color and so forth, which the sense-center consciousness conceives as external and real, are erroneously imagined to be existent, we say they are nonexistent. Furthermore, objective spheres of color and so forth are not colors but appear to be color, and are not external but appear to be external. They are like objects in a dream, and should not be taken as real, external color.

(7) *Objection:* If color and so forth perceived when we are awake are all like objects in a dream and inseparable from consciousness, then as we awake from a dream, we know that they are only mental. Why is it that when we are awake we do not know that the objective sphere of color perceived by ourselves is not consciousness only?

Answer: We do not realize ourselves [that objects in a dream are unreal] as long as we have not awakened from the dream. It is only after we have awakened that we, in retrospect, come to realize it. We should know that the same is true of our knowledge of the objective sphere of color in our waking life. Before we reach the state of true awakening, we do not ourselves know it, but when we reach the state of true awakening, we can also, in retrospect, come to realize it. Before we achieve true awakening, we are perpetually in the midst of a dream. This is why the Buddha spoke of the long night of transmigration, because of our failure to understand that the objective spheres of color [and so forth] are consciousness only.

(8) *Objection:* If external matter is really nonexistent, it may be granted that it is not a sphere of objects for one's inner

[1] For a fuller answer to these objections, see Vasubandhu's *Viṁśatikā,* trans. by Hamilton, *Wei Shih Er Shih Lun.*

consciousness. But the mind of another person really exists. Why is it not an object of one's own consciousness?

Answer: Who says that another person's mind is not a sphere of objects for one's own consciousness? We only say that it is not its immediate and direct object. This means that when the consciousness [of another person's mind] arises, it has no real function. The case is different from that of the hands and so forth which grasp an external thing immediately and directly, or that of the sun and so forth, which spread their light and by direct contact shine on external spheres immediately and directly. The consciousness is merely like a mirror, in which what seems to be an external sphere appears. It is in this sense that it is called the mind that discriminates another. But it cannot discriminate [another mind] immediately and directly. What it discriminates immediately and directly are its own transformations. Therefore the true scripture[1] says that not the least dharma [one's own mind] can grasp other dharmas [other minds].[2] It is only when consciousness is produced that it manifests a character similar to that of another thing. This is called grasping another thing. It seems like taking another person's mind as an object. The same is true of matter and so forth.

(9) *Objection:* Since there is [another mind] distinct from [one's own] sphere of objects,[3] how can you say there is consciousness only?

Answer: How extraordinarily obstinate! You raise doubts at every point. Does the doctrine of Consciousness-Only assert that there is only one individual consciousness? No, it does not. Why? Please listen carefully.

If there were only one individual consciousness, how is it that there is a variety of ordinary people, saints, the honored ones and lowly ones, and causes and effects in the ten cardinal directions? Who would then expound teachings to whom? What dharmas would there be? And what goal is there to seek? Therefore there is a deep purpose in saying there is consciousness only.

The word "consciousness" generally expresses the idea that all human beings each possess eight consciousnesses, six categories of mental qualities,[4] the perceiving portion and perceived portion

1 Interpretation according to K'uei-chi, 43:15a.
2 *Chieh shen-mi ching,* ch. 3, sec. 6, TSD, 16:698.
3 These interpretations are K'uei-chi's, 43:15b.
4 These six categories are mentioned in verses 9–14, above.

which are products of transformation, the different categories of [dharmas of consciousness, dharmas of matter and mind, and dharmas not associated with the mind], and True Thusness (True Reality) [1] revealed by the principle of the emptiness [of the self and dharmas].

Because consciousnesses are their own characters, because consciousnesses are associated with mental qualities, because of the transformations of the perceiving portion and perceived portion, because of the three categories of dharmas, and because of these four true realities, all dharmas are inseparable from consciousness and the general term "consciousness" has been set up. The word "only" is employed merely to deny what ordinary people take to be real matter definitely separated from the various consciousnesses. . . .

If there is consciousness only and no external causes, how did the various discriminations arise? The verse says:

> 18. Because consciousness involves all kinds of seeds,
>   Different transformations take place.
>   Because of their power to turn on and on,
>   All sorts of discriminations are produced.

The Treatise says:

By consciousness evolving all kinds of seeds is meant that functions and differentiations in the root consciousness spontaneously produce their own fruition. . . . (ch. 7, TSD, 31:38–40)

Comment. The Consciousness-Only philosophy is permeated with the concepts of change and transformation like the Book of Changes. However, certain fundamental differences should not be overlooked. The change in this philosophy takes place in consciousness, whereas that of Change operates in the objective world. In both philosophies change operates in the pattern of opposition—in perfuming by pure or impure seeds in the one and in the alteration of yin and yang (passive and active cosmic forces) in the other. But while the direction of perfuming is circular, that of yin yang is progressive—from yin yang to the Four Forms (major and minor yin and yang) and the myriad things. Most important, change in Buddhism leads finally to quietness and silence in Nirvana, but transformation in Confucianism is an eternal process of "production and reproduction."

---

[1] See below, ch. 24, n. 19.

5

HUMAN LIFE AND
THE TRANSCENDENT*

*Fung Yu-Lan (1895–   ), professor of
philosophy at Peking University, is an
outstanding historian of Chinese philosophy and reinterpreter of the* **Li-Hsueh**
*or Rationalistic School of Neo-Con-
fucianism. Among his writings are:*
History of Chinese Philosophy, The
New Rational Philosophy, *and* The
Spirit of Chinese Philosophy.

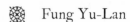 Fung Yu-Lan

IN the West the last fifty years has seen the most remarkable
progress in the study of logic. Yet among Western philosophers
there would seem to be few who have been able to utilize this
advance in logic as a means for building up the new study of
metaphysics, whilst there have been quite a number of logicians
who have used this advance as a means for eliminating metaphysics
altogether. Whilst they think they have thus eliminated metaphysics, really all that they have eliminated is the time-honoured
metaphysics of Western philosophy, not metaphysics itself. It is
impossible to eliminate metaphysics itself. Nevertheless after these
present criticisms have got home, there are bound to be new
metaphysical systems which will be very different from the old. The
need here is for something not bound to the actual, for affirmations
which are not bound by shapes and features but transcend them.
Any new metaphysic must avoid assertions about the actual. In
what it does have to say, it will say nothing positive. Now, in the
history of Western philosophy there would seem to have been no
such tradition in metaphysics, and Western philosophers apparently
have not found it easy to comprehend how the nonsense which says
something but really says nothing can constitute a metaphysic. In

* From Fung Yu-Lan, *The Spirit of Chinese Philosophy,* tr. by E. R. Hughes.
(First Chinese edition published in 1947 under the title *Hsin Yuan Tao.* First
English edition published in 1947 by Kegan Paul, Trench, Trubner & Co., Ltd.,
England. First published as a Beacon paperback in 1962 by arrangement with
E. R. Hughes.) Reprinted by permission of Harold Ober Associates Incorporated.

the history of Chinese philosophy, fortunately, such a tradition has been created, one built up by the pre-Ch'in Taoists, the Wei-Chin Mystics, and the T'ang Inner-light thinkers. The philosophy which I have called a new *Li Hsüeh* derives its inspiration from this tradition. With the help of the criticisms of metaphysics made by modern logic it sets up a metaphysic which is entirely divorced from the actual.

The new *Li Hsüeh* also derives from the *Li Hsüeh* of the Sung and Ming eras. Thus, in regard to its practical application it bears a resemblance to the Confucianists' concern for the common. In so far as it speaks of *li* it bears a resemblance to what the pre-Ch'in Logicians designated as "universals" (*chih*). At the same time it discovers a suitable position for what in Chinese philosophical language is known as the nameable. In its use of *"ch'i"* the meaning bears a resemblance to the early Taoists' Tao. As for the "unnameable", as it is called in Chinese philosophy, it also has its proper place. In so far as it is the nonsense which appears to say something and really says nothing, it bears a resemblance to the Taoist, Mystic, and Inner-light Schools. Hence, in its devotion to the sublime it goes beyond the pre-Ch'in and Sung and Ming Confucianist philosophers. Thus it is the inheritor from every point of view of the best traditions in Chinese philosophy. At the same time it passes the test of the criticisms of metaphysics made by modern logic. Being entirely divorced from the actual, it may be described as "empty" (*k'ung*). Its emptiness, however, is only in the sense of the metaphysic having no positive content, not in the sense in which people speak of man's life or the world as empty. In this respect the meaning is different from that given to it by the Taoist, Mystic, and Inner-light thinkers. And finally, if I may be allowed to say so, although it is a continuation of the Neo-Confucianists, it is, if not an entirely new metaphysic, at the least an opening of a new road in metaphysical thinking.

In this metaphysical system there are four main concepts, namely *li* (principle or ideal form), *ch'i* (matter), *Tao Ti* (the Evolution of the Tao), and *Ta Ch'üan* (the Great Whole). These all come in the category of formal concepts and have no positive content. They are empty (*k'ung*) concepts. Also, in this new *Li Hsüeh* metaphysic there are four sets of main propositions which also are formal propositions. The four main concepts are derived from these four sets of propositions.

The first set is this: any and every thing (lit. event and thing, or event-thing) cannot but be a certain thing, and being such cannot but belong to a certain class of thing. If a certain class of thing is, then there is that by which that class of thing is that class of thing. To borrow an old expression in Chinese philosophy, "If there are things, there must be *tsê* (principles or laws) ."

Let us illustrate this proposition that everything is a certain thing. Thus a mountain is a mountain, a river is a river. It is obviously all right to say "a mountain is a mountain", or "a river is a river". Being a certain thing, it follows directly that the thing in question belongs to a certain class of thing, for instance a mountain to the class "mountain", a river to the class "river". A metaphysic is not in a position to say in point of fact what classes there are in the actual world, but it is in a position to say that all things cannot but belong to one class or another.

A mountain is a mountain, and a river is a river. A mountain is not a not-mountain, nor a river a not-river. The reason why a mountain is a mountain and not a not-mountain is that a mountain possesses that by which a mountain is a mountain. The same applies to a river: the reason why a river is a river and not a not-river is that a river possesses that by which a river is a river. Here is the formal explanation of a mountain being a mountain or a river being a river. That by which a mountain is a mountain or a river a river is not possessed by this or that upstanding mass of mountain alone, or by this or that length of river alone. There can be no question that other mountains have that by which a mountain is a mountain, and other rivers that by which a river is a river. Other mountains are different from this particular upstanding mass of mountain, but they all equally possess that by which mountains are mountains. The same also applies to other rivers and this or that particular length of river. That which all mountains have in common is that by which mountains are mountains. That which all rivers have in common is that by which rivers are rivers. This is what the new *Li Hsüeh* designates as the *li* of mountains and the *li* of rivers. If there be a mountain, then there is a *li* to it; and if there be a river, then there is a *li* to it. If there be a certain class of thing, then there is a certain *li* to that class. The *li* of any class of thing is nameable, and the things which belong to any class are things for which it is possible to have a name.

Let us look further into the statement that given there is a certain class of thing, there must be that by which that class of thing is that class of thing. We state it in the form of a proposition: "that there is a certain class of thing implies that there is that by which that class of thing is that class of thing." In this proposition what is implied cannot say more than that which affords the implication. Here, "there is a certain class of thing", is that which implies, and "there is that by which that class of thing is that class of thing", is that which is implied. The word "is" in the second part of this proposition cannot mean more than the word "is" in the first part. The word "is" in the first part connotes what my new *Li Hsüeh* calls the actual be-ing, which means the existence in time and space. The word "is" in the second part connotes what the new *Li Hsüeh* calls the real be-ing, which means not existing in time and space, and yet not to be spoken of as being nothing. Actual "be-ing" is what Western philosophy has denoted as "existence": "real be-ing" is what Western philosophy has denoted as "subsistence".

From this proposition we can infer two other propositions. The one proposition is: "it is possible there is that by which a certain class of thing is that class of thing without there being that class of thing." The other proposition is: "there being that by which a certain class of thing is that class of thing is logically prior to the be-ing of the things in that class." Let us illustrate. "There is a mountain implies there is that by which mountains are mountains." In this proposition, if "there is a mountain" be true, then "there is that by which mountains are mountains" is also true. But if "there is that by which mountains are mountains" be true, it does not necessarily follow that "there is a mountain" is true. This is to say, given the existence of a mountain, then there must be that by which mountains are mountains, but given the subsistence of that by which mountains are mountains, it does not necessarily follow that there is a mountain in existence. That being so, that by which mountains are mountains can subsist without there being any mountains in existence.

I take a second illustration. "That there is a mountain implies there is that by which mountains are mountains." According to this proposition, if there are mountains, then there must first be that by which mountains are mountains. This is just like saying "that Mr. A. is a man implies that Mr. A. is an animal", then his being a man must be preceded by his being an animal. In these two sentences, "first" and "preceded" refer to logical priority and not priority in time. That by which mountains are mountains is not in time, nor is it actual.

Speaking, then, from the point of view of knowledge, if there be no class of a certain kind of thing, we cannot know that there is that by which this class of thing is this class of thing. On the other hand, speaking from the point of view of logic, without there being that by which this class of thing is this class of thing, it is impossible that there should be this class of thing. Thus, we can infer from the non-subsistence of a certain *li* (principle or ideal form) that no such thing exists, but we cannot infer from the non-existence of the thing the non-substance of the *li*. For this reason we are warranted in saying there are more *li* than there are classes of things: that is, assuming that we can properly speak of the *li* (plural) as having a definite number, the number of the *li* is greater than the number of the classes of things.

The *li* taken as a whole are designated in the new *Li Hsüeh* as the *T'ai Chi,* or alternatively as the world of *li.* This world of *li,* logically speaking, has precedence of the actual world. As has been said, "it is empty, silent, without a sign and yet with all forms there"; and, to use pictorial language, we may say that the variegation among them can be greater than is the case in the actual world. Thus, from a formal explanation of the actual we discover a new world, "a world which is pure and empty of actual content."

In the new *Li Hsüeh* metaphysic, the second set of main propositions is as follows. Things cannot but exist. Those things which exist cannot but be able to exist. Those things which are able to exist cannot but have that by which they are able to exist. To borrow an old expression in Chinese philosophy, "if there is *li,* there must be *ch'i* (matter) ."

In the first set of these main propositions the subject of consideration is classes of things. In the second set the subject of consideration is the individual thing. In the first set we saw that given there be a certain class of thing, then there must be that by which that class of thing is that class of thing, but it does not necessarily follow that if there be that by which a class of thing is that class of thing, there must be that class of thing in existence. We cannot infer the actual from the *li.* All the more we cannot derive the actual from the *li.* Neither can we from the *li* of existence infer existence. The *li* of existence is that by which existence is existence. Given that there is that by which existence is existence, it does not necessarily follow that there is existence. On the other hand, each individual thing is in existence. Starting with the individual thing as the subject of consideration, we make a formal explanation in relation to its existence. Thus, we get the propositions we have set forth above. Those things which can exist must have that by which they can exist, and this, according to the new *Li Hsüeh,* is what is called *ch'i.* Actual things in all cases belong to classes of things: that is to say, actual things actualize their *li.* A *li* cannot actualize itself. There must be a thing in existence before the *li* of it is actualized. Since things must have that by which they can exist before they do exist, therefore we maintain that "if there is *li* there must be *ch'i*", by which we mean that if there be actualization of a *li* there must be the *ch'i* which actualizes the *li.*

The term *ch'i* may have a relative meaning and also an absolute meaning. Speaking of the relative meaning, it is possible for *ch'i* to be in reference to a certain class. For instance, we ask the question: what is that in an individual man by which he can exist? The answer may be given that his blood and flesh and sinews and bones are that by which he is able to exist, and these constituent parts may be summed up in one word, *ch'i* in the relative sense. Blood and flesh and sinews and bones are things of certain classes, and they too must have that by which they can exist. We may say that a certain kind of organic element is that by which a man's blood and flesh and sinews and bones can exist. But this element is itself things of a certain class, and must have that by which it can exist. Thus, we can extend the inquiry until we arrive at something about which we cannot say what it is. This something is after all that by which all things can exist, and in itself is only a potentiality of existence. Because it is only a potentiality of existence, therefore we cannot ask what is that by which it can exist. This is what in the new *Li Hsüeh* is called the true, primordial *ch'i*. In thus speaking of *ch'i* as true and primordial the aim is to express an abstract meaning for the term *ch'i*. In my own terminology the term *ch'i* always has an absolute meaning.

The *ch'i* is the something about which we cannot say what it is. There are two reasons for this. One is that if we say what *ch'i* is, we are bound to say that the things which exist are the product of this whatever-it-is, and to say this is to make an assertion about the actual, and this whatever-it-is is *ipso facto* in the sphere of shapes and features. The second reason is that if we say that *ch'i* is anything definite, then what is called *ch'i, ipso facto,* becomes something which can exist and ceases to be that by which all things are able to exist. *Ch'i* is not a "what". It is the unnameable, or to use the term used so often in this book, "non-being."

In the new *Li Hsüeh* metaphysic the third set of main propositions is as follows. Existence is a continuous process. All existences are existences of things. The existence of a thing is the process of actualization of a certain *li* by means of its *ch'i*. Existence viewed as a whole is the process of actualization of the *T'ai Chi* (the Supreme Point of Perfection) by means of the true primordial *ch'i*. All continuous processes taken as a whole are to be called "the Evolution of the Tao". All processes imply change and movement, and the change and movement implied in all processes is to be called *Ch'ien Yüan* (the First Mover). To borrow an old expression in Chinese philosophy, "there is non-being, yet there is the *T'ai Chi"*; and again, "the *Ch'ien Tao* transforms, and everything is true to its nature and destiny."

This set of propositions comes from a formal explanation of the actuality of things. Therefore we may draw the conclusion that these propositions are necessarily true in regard to everything.

Existence is a continuous process, because to exist is itself a move-ment, is to do something. A movement must continue to move, otherwise it ceases to be a movement. Existence must continue to exist, otherwise it ceases to be existence. Continuation is the con-tinuation of process. In actual fact, there is no such thing as just bare existence as such, and this is why all existences are existences of things. Whatever exists is a thing; and since things being things must belong to one or more classes of things, it follows that they are the actualization of one or more *li*. That being so, that which actualizes one or more *li* is *ch'i*. Since the *ch'i* which actualizes a certain *li* becomes the things which are in that class, and since there is no thing which does not exist, and no existence which is not the existence of a thing, and since there is no thing which is a thing and yet does not belong to a certain class, it follows that the existence of a thing is the process of actualizing a certain *li* by means of *ch'i*.

The actual is then the whole of things, whilst the *T'ai Chi* is the whole of the *li*. From this it follows that the existence of the actual is the process by which the primordial *ch'i* actualizes the *T'ai Chi* (Supreme Point of Perfection). Since all the processes taken together as a whole equal the Evolution of the Tao, this evolution is the process of this actualization.

Since all processes imply change and movement, and process is itself change and movement, then actualization of the *li* of change and movement by means of *ch'i* is prior in the logical sense to the actualization of the rest of the *li*. As a matter of fact, there is no bare process as such. All processes are processes of the actualization of the *li* of certain classes of things. For example, all the animals there are belong to one class of animal or another. Being an animal of a certain class implies being an animal. Speaking logically, in order to be an animal of a certain class, an animal must first be an animal. On the other hand, as a matter of fact, there is no animal which is not an animal of a certain class, that is to say, a mere animal as such does not exist. Although a mere animal as such does not exist, it is implied in an animal "being an animal of a certain class". So the mere animal as such is logically prior to any class of animal. In pictorial thought when mention is made of priority, the reference is always to time. From this angle then, an animal which is prior to any class of animal is ancestor of all animals. But in our statements above we are not referring to priority in the sense of time, and when we speak of animals generally we are not thinking of the ancestor of the animals but only of "animal".

Actually there is no such thing as bare process as such, but the bare process as such is implied in any sort of process. Logically speaking, it is prior to any sort of process. It is "the First Mover". In pictorial thought "the First Mover" was the creator of all things, namely the being spoken of as God. But this First Mover is not God, nor is it a creator. It is only the change and movement implied in all sorts of process. Since this change and movement is change and movement, it follows that it is the actualization of the *li* of change and movement by means of *ch'i*. In my *Hsin Li Hsüeh* book, this is called "the changing and moving *ch'i*", and later on it is spoken of as "*Ch'ien Yüan*" (the First Mover). This name of *Ch'ien Yüan* may appear to mean what in pictorial thought is thought of as the Creator, but in my thought it may be described as the pure activity of *ch'i*. By that is meant that what is actualized is no more than the *li* of change and movement and not yet the *li* of anything else. This "not yet" has only a logical significance, not an actual or temporal one. To speak of a *Ch'ien Yüan* is only to make a formal explanation of the actual. Hence, to speak of there being a *Ch'ien Yüan* does not entail any assertion about the actual. To speak of God or a Creator is in the nature of an assertion about the actual.

In the new *Li Hsüeh* metaphysic, the fourth set of main propositions is as follows. The sum total of beings is the Great Whole. The Great Whole is then the sum total of beings. To borrow an old expression in Chinese philosophy, "the One is the all, and the all is the One."

Since the Great Whole is another name for all that is, to say that the Great Whole is the sum total of beings is a tautological proposition. To this I reply that all things equally belong to the Great Whole, but what belongs to the Great Whole is not only things. The task of metaphysics is to make a formal explanation of everything actual. Once this grade of explanation is made, there is in addition the discovery of the world of *li*. The subject matter of metaphysics is all that is and at the beginning of its task the all is seen to be the all in the realm of the actual. When metaphysics is near to completing its task, the all is seen to be not only the all in the realm of the actual but also the all in the realm of the real.[1] There is that which has actual be-ing: there is that which only has real be-ing; and all these taken together are what is called the Great Whole. Because all that is is included in it, therefore it is called the whole. This whole is not a sectional whole, not like China as a whole or mankind as a whole. Hence it is the Great Whole.

The Great Whole may also be called the universe. This which I call the universe is not the universe of physics or astronomy. That is the physical universe. The physical universe may be said to

---

[1] The real includes the actual. (F. Y. L.)

be a whole but it is only a sectional whole, it is not the supreme whole beyond which there is no other. What I mean by the universe is not the physical universe but the supreme whole.

The Great Whole may be named the One. The pre-Ch'in philosophers, as also the Buddhists and Western philosophers, constantly spoke of the One. What they wished to express was not what was usually meant by oneness. Thus the term "Supreme Oneness" or "Great Oneness" was constantly on the lips of the pre-Ch'in philosophers, whilst the Buddhists spoke of the "Mysterious Oneness". Western philosophers have constantly trusted to the first letter of the word for "one" being written with a capital. The new *Li Hsüeh* borrows the Buddhist saying, "the One is the all and the all is the One."

Although I borrow the Buddhists' words to express my meaning, yet my meaning is not the same as the Buddhists' meaning. The new *Li Hsüeh,* in speaking of the One as the all and the all as the One, makes no assertion that there are inner connections or internal relations[1] between things. What the new *Li Hsüeh* is asserting is merely a formal oneness. The One is only the general name for the all, so that although we speak of the One being the all and the all being the One, there is no assertion about the actual.

The four sets of propositions above are all analytical propositions, or, as we may say, formal propositions, and from these we get four formal concepts, one of *li,* one of *ch'i,* one of the Evolution of the Tao, and one of the Great Whole. From the new *Li Hsüeh* point of view the true task of metaphysics consists in proposing and expounding these four concepts.

Li and *ch'i* are concepts gained from speculative analysis in regard to things. The Evolution of the Tao and the Great Whole are concepts gained from speculative synthesis in regard to things. In Chapter V the statement was made that what the *Yi Amplifications* called the Tao was an unclear idea in relation to what we mean by *li,* and what the Taoists called the Tao was an unclear idea in relation to what we mean by *ch'i.* These ideas are open to criticism as unclear because what they call the Tao is in both cases capable of being analysed further. The "Tao" of the *Amplifications* and the "Tao" of the Taoists were both able to produce. Thus we are in a position to say that where there is something which is able to produce there must be that by which a producer is a producer, namely the *li* of a producer. The actual producer is an existent

---

[1] Internal relations are those relations which idealist philosophers such as Bradley have emphasized. The inner connections are such connections as the Buddhists have emphasized. (F. Y. L.)

something, and it must have that by which it is able to exist. This is the *ch'i* of those things which can produce. The Tao in the *Yi Amplifications* is akin to what we call *li*, but it is not purely *li*. What the Taoists called Tao is akin to *ch'i*, but it is not purely *ch'i*. This is why I say that these concepts are not pure concepts. What they represent is not "that which is prior to things".[1] This priority is not in connection with time: it is a logical priority. *Li and ch'i* are both prior to things. Because *li* and *ch'i* represent the final result of speculative analysis in regard to things, it is impossible to go any further in regard to analysis. Therefore *li* and *ch'i* are prior to all things: nothing can be logically prior to them.

The concept of *li* bears a resemblance to the concept of "being" in Greek philosophy, notably in Plato and Aristotle, and in modern philosophy, notably in Hegel. The concept of *ch'i* also bears a resemblance to the concept of "non-being" in these philosophers. The concept of the Evolution of the Tao bears a resemblance to their concept of "becoming" or "change". The concept of the Great Whole bears a resemblance to their concept of "the Absolute". According to the theories of the Western tradition the task of metaphysics is also to propose and to expound these concepts. From my point of view the four concepts which I set up only bear a resemblance to Western traditional metaphysics with its four concepts. This is because the four concepts in the new *Li Hsüeh* are derived by the formal method, and therefore are entirely formal concepts. In them there is no positive element. In the Western tradition the four concepts are not necessarily derived by the formal method and do contain some positive elements; and being so make assertions about the actual. That, however, which has no positive element contains no assertion about the actual.

Speaking strictly, the concept of the Great Whole and that which it attempts to represent do not correspond to each other. The concept of the Great Whole is a concept, and all concepts are in the realm of thought. But what this concept attempts to represent cannot be made an object of thought. Since the Great Whole equals all being, there can be nothing outside it; as Hui Shih said: "the greatest has nothing beyond itself and is to be called the Great One." The Great Whole is just this Great One. If it were not and there were something outside, then the Great Whole is not a whole, and the one is a duality, in other words not one. If we take the Great Whole as an object of thought, then the Great Whole as an object of thought does not include the thought of it. That being so, then this Great Whole has something outside itself and is not the

[1] An expression found in the *Chuang Tzŭ* Book. (E. R. H.)

Great Whole. The conclusion is that the Great Whole cannot be thought. That being so, it cannot be expressed in words, because the Great Whole which is expressed in words does not include that expression. That being so, this Great Whole has something outside itself and is not the Great Whole. What cannot be the object of thought or put into words is something which cannot be comprehended. That does not necessarily mean that it is a "chaos". All we say is that it is impossible for it to be the object of comprehension.

Continuing from this angle, the Evolution of the Tao also is something which cannot be thought or expressed because it is the whole of all forms of process. Thought and speech are themselves processes. The Evolution of Tao as an object of thought and expression does not include these processes. Any total of all forms of process which does not include these two processes is not the whole of all the forms of process and accordingly is not the Evolution of the Tao.

Ch'i also cannot be thought or expressed, but the reason why it is inexpressible is different from the reason why the Great Whole and the Evolution of the Tao are so. The reason for their being so is that it is impossible for them to be the objects of thought and speech, for if they are, then they are not the Great Whole and Evolution of the Tao. The reason why *ch'i* is not thinkable or expressible is that it is impossible for it to have a name. If we give it a general name, then we *ipso facto* make it some sort of thing and in accordance with its *li*. But it is not any sort of thing nor is it in accord with any *li*. This is why in my *Hsin Li Hsüeh* book it is maintained that though a name is given it, namely *ch'i,* this is to be taken as a proper name. Since metaphysics is not history, how can it have proper names? This is a very real difficulty. Hence our naming *ch'i* is done because we cannot help doing so, as was the case with Lao Tzǔ in naming his Tao.

It may be some one will say that the reason for the Ch'ing era scholars criticizing Neo-Confucianism was because it was an "empty kind of knowledge". (*Vide* Ku Ting-ling's *Sayings.*) That was to say, it was not practical. Yen Hsi-chai said: "The sage man in coming forth undoubtedly would build up a work of peace in the cause of Heaven and Earth." The northern and southern Sung Neo-Confucianists at their most flourishing period "on the one hand did not achieve anything to help in the danger the country was in, and on the other hand did not produce any one who had the calibre of a prime minister or a general. Should an age of many sages and worthies be like that?" (*Ts'un Hsüeh Pien, Criticism of Hsing and Li.*) By parity of reasoning, if the new *Li Hsüeh's* main concepts are all formal, then it is empty and not practical, and all the less can it give men positive knowledge about the actual. The Neo-Confucianists denied that they came near to mysticism or the Inner-light position. The new *Li Hsüeh* publicly confesses that it is near to mysticism and the Inner-light position. How can it fail then to be more impractical?

All we then need to say is that what we are discussing is philosophy. We can only take philosophy as philosophy, and philosophy of its very nature is an "empty branch of knowledge". It is a form of study which enables men to achieve entry into the highest sphere of living. It is not concerned with increasing man's knowledge or ability concerning the actual. Lao Tzŭ made a distinction between the Tao and ordinary knowledge. A philosophical discussion or the study of philosophy belongs to the branch of the Tao, not to that of ordinary learning.

The mistakes in the former Chinese philosophers for the most part do not arise from their attention to the "empty branch of knowledge", but from their failure to know themselves or from their failure to express clearly that what they studied was the "empty branch of knowledge". Some of them were wrong in regarding the sage man as one who merely by virtue of his being a sage had the very highest form of knowledge with regard to the actual, or the ability of controlling practical affairs. Some of them may not have had this wrong idea, but the words they used to describe the sage gave people this wrong impression. For instance, the *Yi Amplifications* say: "The sage man makes an accord between Heaven and Earth and his virtue, between the sun and the moon and his intelligence, between the four seasons and his sense of order, between the manes and the spirits and his good and bad fortune." Or, as the *Chung Yung* put it: "The sage man is in a position to aid the transforming, nourishing processes of Heaven and Earth." Or, as the *Hsiang-Kuo Commentary* on the *Chuang Tzŭ Book* (*Sao Yao Yu Chapter*), says: "The minds of sage men explored the possibilities of the Yin and the Yang to their furthest point, exhausted the mysterious destinies of all things." Sheng Chao in his *Essays* said about the sage man: "His knowledge has an exhaustive and mysterious purview, his divine powers have the utility of meeting all occasions." He also said: "The sage men's achievements are as sublime as Heaven and Earth and yet are not *jen*, they shine with the splendour of the sun and the moon and yet are obscure to view." Chu Hsi, in speaking of the effort entailed in the examination of things and the extension of knowledge, said: "With regard to the long expenditure of strength and then one day, in a flash, everything becoming linked up together, this is a revelation of the outside and the inside, of the refined and the coarse in all things,

and my mind in its essence and its prime function becomes enlightened in every way." These words are apt to make the deep impression that the sage man is one who merely in virtue of his being a
sage has nothing which he cannot know, has nothing which he
cannot do. To learn to be a sage man is like what amongst Buddhists and Taoists was spoken of as learning to be a Buddha,
learning to be an immortal. To learn up to a certain standard
naturally entails having a certain numinous power. Ordinary people regard a sage man as bound to have the very greatest knowledge, the very greatest practical ability; and amongst the Neo-
Confucianists there were a number who thought so. Thus, amongst
these scholars there were a number who regarded themselves as
having expended the necessary effort "in dwelling in reverence and
maintaining sincerity", and so, in knowledge of the actual and in
practical ability, as being themselves fully capable without any need
of further learning. Thus they did not work for any further
knowledge or ability. To be in that state of mind is inevitably to be
without knowledge and without ability. "These men used such
loose words in setting up a standard for the people, establishing a
mind for Heaven and Earth, setting forth the achievement of peace
for ten thousand generations, to intimidate and silence all men.
When suddenly the country was in danger and the time came for
them to pay their debt to their country, then their jaws dropped,
and they were like men sitting in a mist." (Huang Li-chou's (A.D.
1610–95) Sayings, *Nang Lei Wen Ting, Later Collection,* ch. 3.)
These men were quite useless, and this for the reason that they did
not know that they had learnt an empty learning. If they had
known that their learning was such, they might have taken early
measures to learn something else which was of some use, and so have
avoided becoming useless.

In the new *Li Hsüeh* it is realized that it is concerned with
philosophy and that philosophy of its very nature can do nothing
more than exalt man's sphere of living, that philosophy is not
qualified to give men positive knowledge in regard to the actual.
Because this is so, it is also not qualified to give men the ability of
controlling practical affairs. Philosophy has the power to enable
men, in the midst of answering to the claims of humdrum affairs, to
make the most of their inherent nature and achieve their highest
destiny. It has this power also whilst an airman is engaged in taking
a plane up into the air or a gunner is engaged in firing his gun. But
it has no knowledge to give on how to discharge the humdrum
duties, on how to control a plane or fire a gun. Thus, from this
point of view philosophy is useless.

This being the position affirmed by the new *Li Hsüeh,* it is to be noted that of all the schools of thought mentioned in the foregoing chapters only two agree with it, namely the Inner-light School and the school of Wang Yang-ming. The former of the two understood and acknowledged that the sage man, in virtue only of his being a sage man, was not necessarily endowed with knowledge and ability. They said that what the sage man could do was to wear clothes and eat food, to relieve his bowels and make water. As they said, the Inner-light method is the gold-and-ordure method; namely, when you do not understand it, it is like gold, when you do understand it, it is like ordure. Nevertheless, most people had the idea that the Inner-light School, in saying this, meant something deliberately paradoxical. Also, because this school had not entirely lost its religious quality therefore ordinary people also made the legend that the great teachers of this school had every kind of miraculous power. This is the reason why later generations have not understood or paid attention to the fact that this school had this philosophical position.

Wang Yang-ming had his "theory of eradicating the root and blocking the source". As he said, "If theories of eradicating the root and blocking the source be not understood anywhere in the country, then for all those everywhere who are learning the way of sagehood, the longer they do it, the more difficult they find it. These men are sunk in animality and barbarism and yet thinking they are learning to be sages." Further: "To learn to be a sage consists in something extremely simple and extremely easy, something easy to know and easy to carry out, easy to learn and easy to be competent in. The reason for this is that, generally speaking, the way to become a sage is nothing more than restoring the original essence of the mind, which is common to all men, and leaving knowledge and skill out of account. (*Reply to Ku Tung-ch'iao, Recorded Sayings for Exercising,* ch. 2.) Wang Yang-ming also said: "That by which pure gold is pure gold is the purity and not the weight: that by which a sage is a sage is his being perfect in the *li* (ideal pattern) of Heaven and not in his having any skill. The result is that all men can take on this learning by which their minds can become perfect in the *li* of Heaven, and thus they can become sages, just as with an ounce of gold in comparison with ten thousand pounds of it, although the weight is different, the purity is the same. That is why all men can become a Yao or a Shun." (*Op. cit.,* ch. 1.)

Although this statement is true, yet in one respect it does not go far enough. Practical ability and sphere of living are two entirely different matters, nor do they necessarily have any connection with each other. To speak of a sage with great ability as ten thousand pounds of gold, of a sage without this ability as an ounce of gold, is as if ability and sphere were connected with each other to some extent. In this respect, we may say that Wang Yang-ming did not wean himself entirely from the ordinary attitude of mind.

Positive knowledge and practical ability, this, as has been emphasized, is outside the purview of the new *Li Hsüeh*. Yet the concepts of *li* and *ch'i* can enable men's minds to wander in that which is prior *(ch'u)* to things and the concepts of the Evolution of the Tao and the Great Whole enable men's minds to wander in the wholeness of being. With the aid of these concepts, men can know Heaven, can serve Heaven, and can rejoice in Heaven to the point where they become identified with Heaven. With the help of these concepts the sphere in which men live can become different from the unselfconsciously natural, the utilitarian and the moral.

These four concepts are also "empty". What they represent is what transcends shapes and features. Therefore the sphere we attain to with their aid is the sphere of the empty beyond. The men who are in this sphere are absorbed in the abstract and ferried over into the beyond.

Although these men have become thus ferried over into the beyond, yet the business in which they are engaged may be the discharge of the daily duties in human relations. They are mysteriously remote and yet not divorced from actual utility. They are in the beyond, and yet they are still engaged in "carrying water and chopping wood", "in serving their fathers and serving their sovereign." And this does not merely mean that these humble offices are no barrier to their being in the beyond, but that in regard to their selves these offices are an absorption in the abstract, are a ferrying over into the beyond. The sphere in which they live is that of the sublime, but this sublime is one and the same as the common.

The men of this sphere are sage men. If philosophy can enable men to become sage men, then this is the usefulness of philosophy's uselessness. And should this coming to be a sage man be the reaching to the height of what it means to be a man, this is the usefulness of philosophy's uselessness. This kind of uselessness may rightly be called the highest form of usefulness.

As Shao Yung said in the Sung era: "The sage man is the perfection of humanity." Humanity's highest point is what Chuang Chou called "the perfect man". A certain branch of knowledge or kind of ability may make a man an expert in a certain profession, for instance as a physician or an engineer. Philosophy cannot do that. It can only make a man a perfect man. The perfect man is not limited to any particular profession. Any man whose avocation is of use to society can become a perfect man. But nobody can devote himself to the profession of being a perfect man. Should he attempt to do that, he would at once become like a monk devoting himself to the profession of becoming a Buddha. Immediately he would fall between the two stools of the sublime and the common.

A sage man cannot merely by virtue of being a sage become a competent man of affairs. But he can by virtue alone of being a sage become a king. What is more, and speaking strictly, it is only a sage who is supremely suited to be a king. When I say "king", I am thinking of the man who has the highest quality of leadership in a society. There is no need for such a leader to do anything very much himself. Indeed, he ought not to do anything much himself, in other words he should be *wu wei* (inactive), as the Taoists maintained. As the *Chuang Tzŭ Book* put it: "The man at the top must certainly be *wu wei* and so employ all men in society: the man below must certainly be *yu wei* (active) and so be employed for the whole of society." This does not mean that the supreme leader in his *wu wei* just does nothing, but that he gets all the talents in the country to do their best. And since the supreme leader does not do anything himself, there is no need for him to have any special professional knowledge and ability. And, should he have any such knowledge and ability, he ought not to exercise it; and this because, if he does something, he *ipso facto* becomes inoperative in other ways. He should not be operative but set all the talents in the country to do their best. Let him do that, and he will do nothing, but everything will get done.

What the man who is the supreme leader needs is a mind which is open and impartial and all-embracive. It is only the man who lives in the transcendent sphere who can really be like this. He identifies himself with the Great Whole and can see things from the standpoint of the Great Whole. His mind is like the Great Whole in which all things follow their own course and do not conflict with each other. Thus his mind is all-embracing. In his sphere of living he is not on the same level with things, but is above them. Therefore he is the most suitable to be the supreme leader in society.

Hence the sage man, by virtue alone of his being a sage man, is best suited to be king. If then what philosophy deals with is the Tao by which men can become sage men, then the result is what early in this book was spoken of as sageness within and kingliness without. In spite of the highly mystical and "empty" nature of the new *Li Hsüeh,* yet it retains this feature, that it upholds sageness within and kingliness without, and, further, attempts to probe into the essential elements in this Tao.

6

GOD AS A PROJECTION*

Ludwig A. Feuerbach (1804–1872), a leading religious philosopher of nineteenth century Germany, began his philosophical career under the influence of Hegelian idealism, but gravitated increasingly toward materialism and empiricism in reaction against his heritage. His principal work, The Essence of Christianity *(1840), was a systematic attempt to interpret religious concepts as imaginative projections of the human spirit.*

🕸Ludwig Feuerbach

WHAT we have hitherto been maintaining generally, even with regard to sensational impressions, of the relation between subject and object, applies especially to the relation between the subject and the religious object.

In the perceptions of the senses consciousness of the object is distinguishable from consciousness of self; but in religion, consciousness of the object and self-consciousness coincide. The object of the senses is out of man, the religious object is within him, and therefore as little forsakes him as his self-consciousness or his conscience; it is the intimate, the closest object. "God," says Augustine, for example, "is nearer, more related to us, and therefore more easily known by us, than sensible, corporeal things."[1] The object of the senses is in itself indifferent—independent of the disposition or of the judgment; but the object of religion is a selected object; the most excellent, the first, the supreme being; it essentially presupposes a critical judgment, a discrimination between the divine and the non-divine, between that which is worthy of adoration and that which is not worthy.[2] And here may be applied, without any limitation, the proposition: the object of any subject is nothing else than the subject's own nature taken objectively. (Such as are a

---

* From Ludwig Feuerbach, *The Essence of Christianity*, tr. by Marian Evans.

[1] De Genesi ad litteram, 1. v. c. 16.

[2] Unusquisque vestrum non cogitat, *prius* se debere Deum *noose*, quam *colere.*— M. Minucii Felicis Octavianus, c. 24.

man's thoughts and dispositions, such is his God;) so much worth as a man has, so much and no more has his God. Consciousness of God is self-consciousness, knowledge of God is self-knowledge. By his God thou knowest the man, and by the man his God; the two are identical. Whatever is God to a man, that is his heart and soul; and conversely, God is the manifested inward nature, the expressed self of a man,—religion the solemn unveiling of a man's hidden treasures, the revelation of his intimate thoughts, the open confession of his love-secrets.

But when religion—consciousness of God—is designated as the self-consciousness of man, this is not to be understood as affirming that the religious man is directly aware of this identity; for, on the contrary, ignorance of it is fundamental to the peculiar nature of religion. To preclude this misconception, it is better to say, religion is man's earliest and also indirect form of self-knowledge. Hence, religion everywhere precedes philosophy, as in the history of the race, so also in that of the individual. Man first of all sees his nature as if *out of* himself, before he finds it in himself. His own nature is in the first instance contemplated by him as that of another being. Religion is the childlike condition of humanity; but the child sees his nature—man—out of himself; in childhood a man is an object to himself, under the form of another man. Hence the historical progress of religion consists in this: that what by an earlier religion was regarded as objective, is now recognised as subjective; that is, what was formerly contemplated and worshipped as God is now perceived to be something *human*. What was at first religion becomes at a later period idolatry; man is seen to have adored his own nature. Man has given objectivity to himself, but has not recognised the object as his own nature: a later religion takes this forward step; every advance in religion is therefore a deeper self-knowledge. But every particular religion, while it pronounces its predecessors idolatrous, excepts itself—and necessarily so, otherwise it would no longer be religion—from the fate, the common nature of all religions: it imputes only to other religions what is the fault, if fault it be, of religion in general. Because it has a different object, a different tenour, because it has transcended the ideas of preceding religions, it erroneously supposes itself exalted above the necessary eternal laws which constitute the essence of religion—it fancies its object, its ideas, to be superhuman. But the essence of religion, thus hidden from the religious, is evident to the thinker, by whom religion is viewed objectively, which it cannot be by its votaries. And it is our task to show that the antithesis of divine and human is altogether illusory, that it is nothing else than the antithesis between the human nature in general, and the human individual: that, consequently, the object and contents of the Christian religion are altogether human.

Religion, at least the Christian, is the relation of man to himself, or more correctly to his own nature (*i.e.,* his subjective nature) ;[1] but a relation to it, viewed as a nature apart from his own. The divine being is nothing else than the human being, or, rather the human nature purified, freed from the limits of the individual man, made objective—*i.e.,* contemplated and revered as another, a distinct being. All the attributes of the divine nature are, therefore, attributes of the human nature.[2]

In relation to the attributes, the predicates, of the Divine Being, this is admitted without hesitation, but by no means in relation to the subject of these predicates. The negation of the subject is held to be irreligion, nay, atheism; though not so the negation of the predicates. But that which has no predicates or qualities, has no effect upon me; that which has no effect upon me, has no existence for me. To deny all the qualities of a being is equivalent to denying the being himself. A being without qualities is one which cannot become an object to the mind; and such a being is virtually non-existent. Where man deprives God of all qualities, God is no longer anything more to him than a negative being. To the truly religious man, God is not a being without qualities, because to him he is a positive, real being. The theory that God cannot be defined, and consequently cannot be known by man, is therefore the offspring of recent times, a product of modern unbelief.

As reason is and can be pronounced finite only where man regards sensual enjoyment, or religious emotion, or æsthetic contemplation, or moral sentiment, as the absolute, the true; so the proposition that God is unknowable or undefinable can only be enunciated and become fixed as a dogma, where this object has no longer any interest for the intellect; where the real, the positive, alone has any hold on man, where the real alone has for him the significance of the essential, of the absolute, divine object, but where at the same time, in contradiction with this purely worldly tendency, there yet exist some old remains of religiousness. On the

---

1 The meaning of this parenthetic limitation will be clear in the sequel.

2 Les perfections de Dieu sont celles de nos âmes, mais il les possède sans bornes —il y a en nous quelque puissance, quelque connaissance, quelque bonté, mais elles sont toutes entières en Dieu.—Leibnitz, (Theod. Preface.) Nihil in anima esse putemus eximium, quod non etiam divinae naturae proprium sit—Quidquid a Deo alienum definitionem animae.—S. Gregorius Nyss. Est ergo, ut videtur, disciplinarum omniuf pulcherrima et maxima se ipsum nosse; si quis enim se ipsum norit, Deum cognoscet.—Clemens Alex. (Psed. l. iii. c. l.)

ground that God is unknowable, man excuses himself to what is yet remaining of his religious conscience for his forgetfulness of God, his absorption in the world: he denies God practically by his conduct,—the world has possession of all his thoughts and inclinations,—but he does not deny him theoretically, he does not attack his existence; he lets that rest. But this existence does not affect or incommode him; it is a merely negative existence, an existence without existence, a self-contradictory existence,—a state of being, which, as to its effects, is not distinguishable from non-being. The denial of determinate, positive predicates concerning the divine nature, is nothing else than a denial of religion, with, however, an appearance of religion in its favour, so that it is not recognised as a denial; it is simply a subtle, disguised atheism. The alleged religious horror of limiting God by positive predicates, is only the irreligious wish to know nothing more of God, to banish God from the mind. Dread of limitation is dread of existence. All real existence, *i.e.,* all existence which is truly such, is qualitative, determinate existence. He who earnestly believes in the Divine existence, is not shocked at the attributing even of gross sensuous qualities to God. He who dreads an existence that may give offence, who shrinks from the grossness of a positive predicate, may as well renounce existence altogether. A God who is injured by determinate qualities has not the courage and the strength to exist. Qualities are the fire, the vital breath, the oxygen, the salt of existence. An existence in general, an existence without qualities, is an insipidity, an absurdity. But there can be no more in God, than is supplied by religion. Only where man loses his taste for religion, and thus religion itself becomes insipid, does the existence of God become an insipid existence—an existence without qualities.

There is, however, a still milder way of denying the Divine predicates than the direct one just described. It is admitted that the predicates of the divine nature are finite, and, more particularly, human qualities, but their rejection is rejected; they are even taken under protection, because it is necessary to man to have a definite conception of God, and since he is man, he can form no other than a human conception of him. In relation to God, it is said, these predicates are certainly without any objective validity; but to me, if he is to exist for me, he cannot appear otherwise than as he does appear to me, namely, as a being with attributes analogous to the human. But this distinction between what God is in himself, and what he is for me, destroys the peace of religion, and is besides in itself an unfounded and untenable distinction. I cannot know whether God is something else in himself or for himself, than he is for me; what he is to me, is to me all that he is. For me, there lies in these predicates under which he exists for me, what he is in himself, his very nature; he is for me what he can alone ever be for me. The religious man finds perfect satisfaction in that which God is in relation to himself; of any other relation he knows nothing, for God is to him what he can alone be to man. In the distinction above stated, man takes a point of view above himself, *i.e.* above his nature, the absolute measure of his being; but this transcendentalism is only an illusion; for I can make the distinction between the object as it is in itself, and the object as it is for me, only where an object can really appear otherwise to me, not where it appears to me such as the absolute measure of my nature determines it to appear—such as it must appear to me. It is true that I may have a merely subjective conception, *i.e.* one which does not arise out of the general constitution of my species; but if my conception is determined by the constitution of my species, the distinction between what an object is in itself, and what it is for me ceases; for this conception is itself an absolute one. The measure of the species is the absolute measure, law, and criterion of man. And, indeed, religion has the conviction that its conceptions, its predicates of God, are such as every man ought to have, and must have, if he would have the true ones—that they are the conceptions necessary to human nature; nay, further, that they are objectively true, representing God as he is. To every religion the gods of *other* religions are only notions concerning God, but its own conception of God is to it God himself, the true God—God such as he is in himself. Religion is satisfied only with a complete Deity, a God without reservation; it will not have a mere phantasm of God; it demands God himself. Religion gives up its own existence when it gives up the nature of God; it is no longer a truth, when it renounces the possession of the true God. Scepticism is the archenemy of religion; but the distinction between object and conception—between God as he is in himself, and God as he is for me, is a sceptical distinction, and therefore an irreligious one.

That which is to man the self-existent, the highest being, to which he can conceive nothing higher—that is to him the Divine being. How then should he inquire concerning this being, what He is in himself? If God were an object to the bird, he would be a winged being: the bird knows nothing higher, nothing more blissful, than the winged condition. How ludicrous would it be if this bird pronounced: to me God appears as a bird, but what he is in himself I know not. To the bird the highest nature is the bird-nature; take from him the conception of this, and you take from him the conception of the highest being. How, then, could he ask whether God in himself were winged? To ask whether God is in himself what he is for me, is to ask whether God is God, is to lift oneself above one's God, to rise up against him.

Wherever, therefore, this idea, that the religious predicates are only anthropomorphisms, has taken possession of a man, there has doubt, has unbelief obtained the mastery of faith. And it is only the inconsequence of faint-heartedness and intellectual imbecility which does not proceed from this idea to the formal negation of the predicates, and from thence to the negation of the subject to which they relate. If thou doubtest the objective truth of the predicates, thou must also doubt the objective truth of the subject whose predicates they are. If thy predicates are anthropomorphisms, the subject of them is an anthropomorphism too. If love, goodness, personality, &c., are human attributes, so also is the subject which thou pre-supposest, the existence of God, the belief that there is a God, an anthropormorphism—a pre-supposition purely human. Whence knowest thou that the belief in a God at all is not a limitation of man's mode of conception? Higher beings—and thou supposest such—are perhaps so blest in themselves, so at unity with themselves, that they are not hung in suspense between themselves and a yet higher being. To know God and not oneself to be God, to know blessedness, and not oneself to enjoy it, is a state of disunity, of unhappiness. Higher beings know nothing of this unhappiness; they have no conception of that which they are not.

Thou believest in love as a divine attribute because thou thyself lovest; thou believest that God is a wise, benevolent being, because thou knowest nothing better in thyself than benevolence and wisdom; and thou believest that God exists, that therefore he is a subject—whatever exists is a subject, whether it be defined as substance, person, essence, or otherwise—because thou thyself existest, art thyself a subject. Thou knowest no higher human good, than to love, than to be good and wise; and even so thou knowest no higher happiness than to exist, to be a subject; for the consciousness of all reality, of all bliss, is for thee bound up in the consciousness of being a subject, of existing. God is an existence, a subject to thee, for the same reason that he is to thee a wise, a blessed, a personal being. The distinction between the divine predicates and the divine subject is only this, that to thee the subject, the existence, does not appear an anthropomorphism, because the conception of it is necessarily involved in thy own existence as a subject, whereas the predicates do appear anthropomorphisms, because their necessity— the necessity that God should be conscious, wise, good, &c.—is not an immediate necessity, identical with the being of man, but is evolved by his self-consciousness, by the activity of his thought. I am a subject, I exist, whether I be wise or unwise, good or bad. To exist is to man the first datum; it constitutes the very idea of the subject; it is presupposed by the predicates. Hence, man relinquishes the predicates, but the existence of God is to him a settled, irrefragable, absolutely certain, objective truth. But, nevertheless, this distinction is merely an apparent one. The necessity of the subject lies only in the necessity of the predicate. Thou art a subject only in so far as thou art a human subject; the certainty and reality of thy existence lie only in the certainty and reality of thy human attributes. What the subject is, lies only in the predicate; the predicate is the *truth* of the subject—the subject only the personified, existing predicate, the predicate conceived as existing. Subject and predicate are distinguished only as existence and essence. The negation of the predicates is therefore the negation of the subject. What remains of the human subject when abstracted from the human attributes? Even in the language of common life the divine predicates—Providence, Omniscience, Omnipotence—are put for the divine subject.

The certainty of the existence of God, of which it has been said that it is as certain, nay, more certain to man than his own existence, depends only on the certainty of the qualities of God—it is in itself no immediate certainty. To the Christian the existence of the Christian God only is a certainty; to the heathen that of the heathen God only. The heathen did not doubt the existence of Jupiter, because he took no offense at the nature of Jupiter, because he could conceive of God under no other qualities, because to him these qualities were a certainty, a divine reality. The reality of the predicate is the sole guarantee of existence.

Whatever man conceives to be true, he immediately conceives to be real (that is, to have an objective existence), because, originally, only the real is true to him—true in opposition to what is merely conceived, dreamed, imagined. The idea of being, of existence, is the original idea of truth; or, originally, man makes truth dependent on existence, subsequently, existence dependent on truth. Now God is the nature of man regarded as absolute truth,—the truth of man; but God, or, what is the same thing, religion, is as various as are the conditions under which man conceives this his nature, regards it as the highest being. These conditions, then, under which man conceives God, are to him the truth, and for that reason they are also the highest existence, or rather they are existence itself; for only the emphatic, the highest existence, is existence, and deserves this name. Therefore, God is an existent, real being, on the very same ground that he is a particular, definite being; for the qualities of God are nothing else than the essential qualities of man himself, and a particular man is what he is, has his existence, his reality, only in his particular conditions.

Take away from the Greek the quality of being Greek, and you take away his existence. On this ground, it is true that for a definite positive religion—that is, relatively—the certainty of the existence of God is *immediate;* for just as involuntarily, as necessarily, as the Greek was a Greek, so necessarily were his gods Greek beings, so necessarily were they real, existent beings. Religion is that conception of the nature of the world and of man which is essential to, *i.e.,* identical with, a man's nature. But man does not stand above this his necessary conception; on the contrary, it stands above him; it animates, determines, governs him. The necessity of a proof, of a middle term to unite qualities with existence, the possibility of a doubt, is abolished. Only that which is apart from my own being is capable of being doubted by me. How then can I doubt of God, who is my being? To doubt of God is to doubt of myself. Only when God is thought of abstractly, when his predicates are the result of philosophic abstraction, arises the distinction or separation between subject and predicate, existence and nature—arises the fiction that the existence or the subject is something else than the predicate, something immediate, indubitable, in distinction from the predicate, which is held to be doubtful. But this is only a fiction. A God who has abstract predicates has also an abstract existence. Existence, being, varies with varying qualities.

The identity of the subject and predicate is clearly evidenced by the progressive development of religion, which is identical with the progressive development of human culture. So long as man is in a mere state of nature, so long is his god a mere nature-god—a personification of some natural force. Where man inhabits houses, he also encloses his gods in temples. The temple is only a manifestation of the value which man attaches to beautiful buildings. Temples in honour of religion are in truth temples in honour of architecture. With the emerging of man from a state of savagery and wildness to one of culture, with the distinction between what is fitting for man and what is not fitting, arises simultaneously the distinction between that which is fitting and that which is not fitting for God. God is the idea of majesty, of the highest dignity: the religious sentiment is the sentiment of supreme fitness. The later more cultured artists of Greece were the first to embody in the statues of the gods the ideas of dignity, of spiritual grandeur, of imperturbable response and serenity. But why were these qualities in their view attributes, predicates of God? Because they were in themselves regarded by the Greeks as divinities. Why did those artists exclude all disgusting and low passions? Because they perceived them to be unbecoming, unworthy, unhuman, and consequently ungodlike. The Homeric gods eat and drink;—that implies: eating and drinking is a divine pleasure. Physical strength is an attribute of the Homeric gods: Zeus is the strongest of the gods. Why? Because physical strength, in and by itself, was regarded as something glorious, divine. To the ancient Germans the highest virtues were those of the warrior; therefore, their supreme god was the god of war, Odin,—war, "the original or oldest law." Not the attribute of the divinity, but the divineness or deity of the attribute, is the first true Divine Being. Thus what theology and philosophy have held to be God, the Absolute, the Infinite, is not God; but that which they have held not to be God, is God: namely, the attribute, the quality, whatever has reality. Hence, he alone is the true atheist to whom the predicates of the Divine Being,—for example, love, wisdom, justice, are nothing; not he to whom merely the subject of these predicates is nothing. And in no wise is the negation of the subject necessarily also a negation of the predicates considered in themselves. These have an intrinsic, independent reality; they force their recognition upon man by their very nature; they are self-evident truths to him; they prove, they attest themselves. It does not follow that goodness, justice, wisdom, are chimæras, because the existence of God is a chimæra, nor truths because this is a truth. The idea of God is dependent on the idea of justice, of benevolence; a God who is not benevolent, not just, not wise, is no God; but the converse does not hold. The fact is not that a quality is divine because God has it, but that God has it because it is in itself divine: because without it God would be a defective being. Justice, wisdom, in general every quality which constitutes the divinity of God, is determined and known by itself, independently, but the idea of God is determined by the qualities which have thus been previously judged to be worthy of the divine nature; only in the case in which I identify God and justice, in which I think of God immediately as the reality of the idea of justice, is the idea of God self-determined. But if God as a subject is the determined, while the quality, the predicate is the determining, then in truth the rank of the god-head is due not to the subject, but to the predicate.

Not until several, and those contradictory, attributes are united in one being, and this being is conceived as personal—the personality being thus brought into especial prominence—not until then is the origin of religion lost sight of, is it forgotten that what the activity of the reflective power has converted into a predicate distinguishable or separable from the subject, was originally the true subject. Thus the Greeks and Romans deified accidents as substances: virtues, states of mind, passions, as independent beings. Man, especially the religious man, is to himself the measure of all things, of all reality. Whatever strongly impresses a man, whatever produces an unusual effect on his mind, if it be only a peculiar, inexplicable sound or note, he personifies as a divine being. Religion embraces all the objects of the world; everything existing has been an object of religious reverence; in the nature and consciousness of religion there is nothing else than what lies in the nature of man and in his consciousness of himself and of the world. Religion has no material exclusively its own. In Rome even the passions of fear and terror had their temples. The Christians also made mental phenomena into independent beings, their own feelings into qualities of things, the passions which governed them into powers which governed the world, in short, predicates of their own nature, whether recognized as such or not, into independent subjective existences. Devils, cobolds, witches, ghosts, angels, were sacred truths as long as the religious spirit held undivided sway over mankind.

7

IMMORTALITY*

Alfred E. Taylor (1869–1945), was Professor of Moral Philosophy in Edinburgh University from 1924 to 1941. He was a well-known Platonic scholar whose own philosophical leanings were toward idealism. His major writings include several works on Plato and Aristotle as well as The Faith of a Moralist, Does God Exist? *and* The Christian Hope of Immortality.

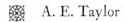 A. E. Taylor

Our preliminary results, so far, have been in the main negative. We have urged that even the bare fact of survival of death (to say nothing of the hope of a new quality of life) cannot be unambiguously established by the methods of experimental science; that arguments based on the assumed intrinsic nature of personality are inconclusive when taken by themselves; that the attempt to reach assurance by consideration of what is implied in the upright man's sense of the supreme reverence due to the moral law is equally indecisive unless we can also presuppose a "metaphysical" doctrine about the structure of the universe which clearly contains as an integral part of itself the very result we are trying to reach. We are thus driven to make a new beginning in our inquiry. We shall try, as impartially as we can, to ask ourselves what it means to be alive, and alive as a person who is capable of response both to the command of duty and to the solicitation to worship. It may be that when we take all the facts of our human situation fairly into account we shall find reason to entertain anticipations for ourselves and our fellows which are met adequately only by the specifically Christian conception of eternal life. If so, we shall have done all that can be expected of us, we shall have vindicated the reasonableness of faith in a "revelation", a disclosure which, now that it has been made, is seen to satisfy the demands of the intelligence, though it was not reached, and could not have been reached, by any process of formal and abstract reasoning.

* From A. E. Taylor, *The Christian Hope of Immortality*. Reprinted by permission of Geoffrey Bles, Ltd.

What, then, does it mean to be alive as a self at all? (I do not yet say, to be alive as a person, a reflective and thinking self.) As we have already said, to *exist* as a self does not mean simply to be there as one among a multitude of things which an observer must take account of in his attempt to describe what he finds before his notice and to shape his own actions accordingly. Existence in that sense must be ascribed to an indefinite multiplicity of things which cannot intelligibly be said to be living selves. The stone in my path exists as an object presented to my notice, for I shall trip, or stumble, or hurt myself, if I do not walk round it, or lift my foot to step over it. I exist, and my dog, if I have one, exists in that sense no less than the stone. You have to shape your path so as to avoid running into the dog, or into me, as you have to avoid running against stocks or stones. But in the case of the stone, it is enough for you to avoid colliding with it; you may come to trouble with the dog, or with me, without any physical collision, if you "hurt our feelings", or "arouse our hostility". We, in a word, can *feel,* as the stone apparently cannot. That I can feel is a fact of which I need no evidence, an immediate fact of "consciousness" in the old Scottish sense of the word, and that my dog can feel is so certain that it has never been doubted except by Cartesian philosophers wedded to a theory for which the fact was a disconcerting one.

Now when I say that it is an immediately certain fact that I feel, I do not mean that I observe among the multitude of things presented to my notice one thing of a certain size, shape, and colour which exhibits certain eccentricities of behaviour; "reacting", for example, to one "stimulus" by a tear or a frown, and to another by a caressing movement or a smile. All this is only as much as I might learn about you by observing you, but it never occurs to me to suppose that you are myself, or that I feel your experiences. I can, to a certain extent, observe my own behaviour, much as I do that of other selves and things, though it is hard to learn to do this accurately, and the attitude cannot be consistently maintained for long together. But the whole point of the statement that what is being thus observed is *myself* lies in something which is added to the observations, the *identification* of the particular "object" now under notice with that which is experiencing the observing, the "subject" which *has* the feelings, and this "subject" is precisely just the one thing in the universe which is not a "presented object" among others. It is not one of the things "found there", but that which finds them, exactly as the eye is that which sees other things but does not see itself. (Or if you object that indirectly, by the use of a mirror, the eye can be made to see itself, the real point is left untouched; I may see my eye in the mirror, but I do not see its *seeing* in the mirror any more than I see your seeing when I look into your eyes). The very possibility of the simplest experience is thus dependent on a mysterious act of identification, an identification of one of the "things observed" as in some way the same thing with that which "finds" all these things there without being one of them. Without this act of identification, no feeling and no selves.

Naturally and unavoidably in the last paragraph the appeal has been made to the reader's experience of *himself* as a "subject", the only experience, in the strictest sense of the word, which he can have, and the reader's experience is that of one who is not merely a self but a person, a *thinking* self. We have no grounds to believe that the subhuman animals think or reflect, except in the most inchoate way and in exceptional moments; most of them, perhaps, never genuinely think at all. Yet it is plainly true that each of them feels, and so is something more than an object among others; each is an *experiencer* in its degree, not merely an object to be experienced. Each of them is a self, though a self of a lowly order, at once the feeler and the felt. Each, like ourselves, though in its own particular way, *possesses* the contents of its experience. The creature which can, in however rudimentary a way, "learn by experience" does not merely behave differently for the outside observer when it has so learned, it is different for itself, it *feels* differently. This means that the distinction between what a thing *appears* to be and what it *is* comes to have, in the case of all such creatures, a significance it has not in reference to anything inanimate. In reference to an inanimate thing this distinction between what it appears to be and what it is is only a distinction between what is observed by an inaccurate or hasty onlooker, and what is observed, or observable, by one who is more accurate and careful. In the case of the self which feels there is the much more important distinction between the creature as it can be observed and described from without by the most careful and thorough of observers, and the same creature as it is directly for itself, as the centre of a unique and incommunicable experiencing. Every self has this strictly incommunicable and hidden existence of its own as the *subject* of its experiences, that which *has* them all, but is itself none of them. This was why we remarked in an earlier paragraph that the vital question about what happens at death is not what dying looks like to the outside observer—a question easy enough to answer in principle—but what the experience of dying is to the self who is experiencing it. What is it to experience dying?

Now this question at once raises a grave difficulty. Can dying ever be experienced at all? If to die means not merely to cease to be among the objects which make up the field of some other self's observation, but to cease to be a subject experiencing anything, to experience dying should mean to experience the transition from having experiences to having none, from feeling to feeling nothing. But to experience the total absence of experience, to feel that one is feeling nothing, is surely a contradiction in set terms, and unless both conditions are experienced, there can be no experience of the passage from the one to the other. It should seem then that dying, if it means the cessation of existence as an experiencing subject, must be an event which no creature can ever experience, just as none can experience the event of coming into being, in the sense of transition from being nothing at all to being something. Both, if they occur, are events in their own nature of such a kind that they can never be experienced by anyone, but at most, observed by those who are not experiencing them. And *their* observations, as we said, cannot be conclusive. The observer can satisfy himself that something is now perceptible which was formerly imperceptible, or something formerly perceptible now imperceptible; he cannot actually observe non-existence passing into existence, or existence into non-existence. Both transitions, if they occur, are as incapable of being observed as they are of being experienced. And the reason why they are incapable of being observed is not simply that, like physical events which are asserted to take place in the submicroscopic world, they are on too small a scale for us to detect them, or that, in some further way, the physical conditions necessary for the stimulation of our sense-organs are not fulfilled; it is that it is a formal logical absurdity to think of a condition of non-existence at all; there is no such condition, and therefore there can be no transition from it to anything else, or from anything else to it. The coming to be of something before wholly non-existent would be no transformation or transition, but absolute *origination,* and the sheer ceasing of anything existent to be would be *annihilation.*

Men of science, who concern themselves exclusively with "nature", the field of "things presented to our observation", simply presupposing (as for their purpose they are fully entitled to do) the observer of the field as a datum with which they are not concerned, are, of course, quite alive to the fact. They never, as students of science, deal with absolute beginnings or absolute endings. Even when they talk, as they are doing to some extent to-day, of a "creation" of the world, or of an end of the world, their language shows clearly enough that they do not mean an absolute beginning or ending. "Creation" with them, unless they supplement their science by an appeal to their personal theological convictions, means no more than the transition of something already in existence into a new form in which it becomes amenable to their scientific formulae, and annihilation no more than transition to a state in which the formulae are no longer applicable. Hence Sir James Jeans, for example, can talk freely of the *annihilation* of "matter" when he means simply the conversion of mass into "energy of radiation" (whatever that may be), and is so far from believing in any real annihilation that he can assume that, in this conversion, a definite amount of the one is replaced by a definite amount of the other.

It is still more difficult to think of an absolute beginning or cessation of selfhood, or subjecthood. We may try to imagine experiencing, consciousness, as somehow arising, at a certain stage, in history in a world from which it had been wholly absent. But this would be the same thing as to imagine that what had hitherto existed only as a thing possibly to be noticed by an outside observer had suddenly become itself the observer of itself and other things; that transition seems as unthinkable as it is unthinkable that reflections in a mirror should turn into beings who might see themselves, and us. A field of presented objects *presupposes* an actual or possible observer, who is not one of them; it does not account for him. We must therefore dismiss all attempts to think of the "emergence" of consciousness in a universe from which it was originally absent. *Experiencing,* awareness, of some sort must be at least coeval with the world of objects. (It may, indeed, be more than merely coeval with the world, since, as we have said, there seem to be some experiences—like those in which consciousness is filled with the sense of pleasure or pain—which are not awareness of objects but simply the experiencer's possession of his *own* being.)

As for particular owners of experience, like you and me, this leaves it still an open question whether or not we must think of ourselves as having a first origination or final annihilation. If we have, we can, of course, experience neither, since no one can experience being without experience, nor yet can the observations of others tells us anything conclusive on such a matter. But supposing what we have just been saying to be sound, it will follow that our first beginning and our final ending, if we have any, cannot be the effects of mere change in the "natural" world of presented objects. Either we must sit down content with the assertion that selves begin to be and cease to be without any reason at all, or we must look for the reasons for this beginning and ending (assuming them to be really facts) in creative or annihilating activity on the part of a being which is itself a primary self (or subject), standing outside and above all the vicissitudes of birth and death. It was thus not without reason that "early man" seems universally to have taken it for granted that the dead have not passed from existence to non-entity, but from one state of existence to another. And we can understand how Leibniz, the most extraordinary man of genius of modern times, could insist in his philosophy on asserting the immortality, not merely of "the soul", but of "the animal".

BUT a human self is not merely a self like that of a dog or cat; it is something more, a *personal* self; we cannot, if we are to think reasonably about its origin and destiny, omit to consider what this personality may imply. What, then, are we asserting when we say that a man has personality, or is a person? We shall not do amiss in discussing the question to start from the famous definition given by Boethius, more than fourteen hundred years ago, in a sentence which sums up the results of more than a millennium of Græco-Roman philosophical thinking, and becomes a starting-point for the whole development of subsequent Christian theology and philosophy: *A person is an individual substance of rational nature.* A person, that is, is on the one hand unitary, is *a* self, or *one* self—unlike, for example, a swarm of bees, a flock of sheep, or a concourse, or tribe, or nation of men. The swarm or flock is made up of selves, the tribe or nation is made up of persons, but the swarm or flock is not actually a self, or the nation or tribe a person, and when we speak of them as though the one were a self, or the other a person, as we often enough do, we are using a metaphor which may easily mislead us if we once forget that it is only a metaphor. The flock or the nation may be said to have experiences, but it only has them because the individual sheep or men of which it is composed have them, and it has no experiences which are not those of some or other of its component sheep or men; it is not itself a centre of further experiences. Or, to put it another way, the experiences we ascribe to it only belong to it because they belong of first right to this or that constituent of it. But *this* sheep, or *this* man, owns its or his experiences of first right; they are not *its* possession on the strength of being first the possession of sub-constituents of it. When, for example, a whole flock or herd is said to see or hear something, or to feel hunger or thirst, this can only be said because all, or most, of the members of it see or hear, or feel hungry or thirsty; but a man is not said to see because his eyes see, or to hear because his ears hear, or to feel thirst because his throat and palate feel it. As Plato long ago remarked, it is not the eye which sees or the ear which hears, but the *man* who sees with his eyes and hears with his ears. Scatter the flock or disperse the tribe, and there will be still as much seeing and hearing and feeling as before; resolve the individual animal or man into constitutents of any kind, and seeing, hearing and all the characteristic experiences of sheep or man are abolished. The man or the animal is one in a special way in which no group or combination of men or animals is one.

But on the other hand, a person is an individual of a *rational* nature, not a mere self, but a reasonable or intelligent self. The person can not merely feel, but think and reflect; he not only owns his experiences, but is aware that he owns them. To be a person, or reasonable self, is not merely to possess one's own being, but to know that one possesses it; only when we have reached that knowledge are we capable of saying *I,* and he who cannot say to himself *"I am"* is not yet a person. We see this interestingly illustrated in the utterances of young children. A very young child will often speak of himself "in the third person", by the name he hears applied to him by those around him, before he has learned to say *I;* he will say, "Jacky (or Tommy) wants this or that" before he says *"I* want it." Here we have a being who already is an experiencing subject or self—if he were not, he could feel no wants—and is also interested in an object in the field of his observation which he will one day discover to be in a unique way identical with the experiencer observing it, but he has not yet made the identification; when it has been made, he will no longer talk of what Jacky (or Tommy) wants, but of what "I want". I have known the still more interesting case of a child who, as far as could be discovered (and I watched him carefully) never thus spoke of himself "in the third person"; until he learned to say *I,* he always spoke of himself as *you.* He had apparently discovered, by the time he began to speak at all, that the particular object which stood out so prominently in the field of his interests and observations was more than a "presented object", was, in fact, a *self,* but not that it was his self. He had learned the difference between a person and a thing before he had come to knowledge of his *own* personality.

This discovery of our own personality has a double significance: it is the source of what Kant calls the *practical* and what he calls the *speculative* use of reason; the possibility both of morality and of science depends upon it. On the one hand, the being who has come to know himself as a person and by the same process to recognize those around him as persons like himself, is now in a position to think of himself as having reasonable and rightful expectations in respect of the treatment he receives from the other persons, and of them similarly as having rightful and reasonable claims in respect of the treatment they get from him, and here we have the simple beginnings of all that will subsequently expand into a whole code of moral rights and duties. Kant's famous attempt to reduce the whole content of morality to the principle that every man's personality is always to be treated by every man with unqualified reverence may not be entirely successful, since there are some duties (like that of humanity to the lower animals) which it cannot perhaps fairly be made to cover. But it is at least true that genuine morality only becomes possible in principle when we recognize that a person is always to be treated as a person, never as a mere animal self, and still less as a thing with no selfhood at all. And our morality is still implicit rather than explicit until we understand that this right of a person to be treated as personal belongs to him *as* a person, not as one connected with ourselves by the further bond of kindred, or race, or nationality, or friendship. There are *no* "lesser breeds without the law", if that means "breeds" towards which we are discharged from its obligations. In this way the discovery of our own personality is the beginning of morality (the *practical* use of reason) .

Again, it is when he has discovered his own personality that man ceases to take events as they happen to come and go, with the incurious acquiescence of the animals. He now feels that he has a right to ask *why* they come and go thus and not otherwise, the right of an intelligent being to an intelligible answer to his demand for the why and wherefore of things; and it is here that the speculative employment of reason from which the sciences are born takes its rise. Men are not merely intrigued and inquisitive, as some of the higher animals also are, about the novel and unfamiliar: with these animals curiosity often enough ends in the pulling of the unfamil- iar thing to pieces, but it does not lead even to the rudiments of science. A man's curiosity has the further characteristic of being *intelligent* curiosity which will be contented with nothing short of what he can accept as a coherent and *reasonable* account of the "why and wherefore". He goes on the tacit assumption that there is an intrinsic reasonableness of pattern in the world of "objects", answering to the intelligence he finds in himself as the experiencing "subject". (Of course at a stage at which his own intelligence is still undeveloped, what appears to him an intelligible connection is very often one which our more developed intelligence pronounces un- intelligible, but that is another matter.) He expects of the course of events that it shall be an intelligible pattern, as he expects intelli- gible pattern in the connection of his own actions, or those of other men, and science is born from this expectation—its success, so far as it goes, is the justification of the expectation—or else it is a mere inexplicable "lucky accident".

And there is still a further point to note. Rational selfhood, intelligent personality, in ourselves is something which has to be gradually won, and that not without difficulty; we inherit it only in part and with many fluctuations of degree, and *prima facie* it goes as it comes. In what we see of the life of children, or remember of our own childhood, we seem to see a self which at first cannot be discriminated by observation from that of a mere *feeling* being growing by degrees into that of the *thinking* person, as we gradually bring more and more of steady conscious purpose into the control of our own actions, and discover more and more of coherent pattern in the sequence of events round us. The process is never finally completed; there are tracts of our experience (notably, for example, our dreams) in which moral principle and "patternedness" of sequence seem to be alike in abeyance; even in waking life, the man who has, in his prime, apparently attained high success in the moral ordering of his own life and the coherent understanding of the pattern of events often seems to relapse into moral and intellectual "childishness" if his days are sufficiently prolonged. Complete personality, then—the self's full and conscious possession of itself and its "environment"—would seem, in the world of our experience, to be always an unattained ideal; all science and all morality consist in the approach to it, but not in the possession of it. To *be* a full and complete person would be at once to have a plan and purpose in one's own life subject to no anterior vacillation and disturbance and to understand the whole world in a way which left nothing in it baffling and unintelligible. To such a being defeat and death would have lost all its meaning; his life would be strictly *eternal* life.

This train of reflection at once suggests to us several things. In the first place, it is no more possible to think of personality, rational selfhood, as "emerging on the scene as a product of evolution" than it is to think in the same way of selfhood itself. If we found it incredible that mere "experienced objects" should, of themselves, turn into "subjects of experience", beings who can feel it is equally unthinkable that beings who can merely feel should, of themselves, turn into beings who can think and know. Personality, thinking and reasonable selfhood, must be no less irreducible to mere selfhood than selfhood is irreducible to thinghood. That is, there must be primitive and unoriginated personality, as well as primitive selfhood, at the very foundation of things. Our own imperfectly attained personality, always exposed to the dangers of lapse from its highest level, must be communicated from the unoriginated personality which knows "no variableness, neither shadow of turning". Even if we had reason to think that our personal existence had no beginning in time, we should still have to regard it, because of its "variableness", as a *created* personality, depending for its being on the supreme uncreated personality. And this is not all. If uncreated complete personality is an irreducible fact, to such a personality there can be nothing in the universe which is unintelligible or not understood. All that is, or was, or will be must be transparent to the "eyes of Him with whom we have to do". But if this is so, then the whole world of being and all that it contains can have no source but Himself. If there could be anything which had its source elsewhere, there would be at once the possibility that "here is a thing which is unintelligible, not only to me, but to Him." The world itself must be His creation, an expression of His intelligence, intelligible through and through *because* its Author is pure and perfect intelligence.

Now to say as much as this implies more than might appear at first sight. A creation which is intelligible through and through because its Creator is pure and perfect intelligence must be intelligible not merely in the sense that some sort of pattern can be detected running through it—that much is true even of the mere play of a child—but in the deeper sense that the pattern so embodied is one which approves itself to a perfect intelligence as wholly and absolutely "worth while". There must be "meaning" in its structure and history in the same sense in which there is meaning in the great works of art which are the crowning glory of our human intelligence; whereas the artistically crude and bad is "unmeaning". The history of such a world must embody a purpose, and a purpose which, in the eyes of the perfectly intelligent Creator, is wholly and utterly good. In simpler words, a completely intelligible universe must also be a *moral* system, an embodiment of the great principles of *moral* value. There must be a moral purpose in the world's history, and the moral purpose must be universally good, if the world is really intelligible. This does not mean, of course, that we, with our imperfect insight and limited acquaintance with the course of history, must be able to see that the purpose is there, or how it is attained. To us, with our very imperfect knowledge of the facts of the past and the present, and our all but total ignorance of the future, the world may look to be a scene of moral confusion. Still less is it meant, as is too often assumed, that if there is a moral purpose in history, that purpose can only be to "make us all happy". Even in our condition of imperfect knowledge of the course of fact, we can at least see for ourselves that the mere purpose of making all of us happy, irrespective of our conduct and characters, would hardly be one to commend itself to the perfect intelligence. We cannot, if we are serious men, well dispute Kant's dictum that the purpose to train us into making ourselves persons who *deserve* to be happy by the steady exercise of an intelligent and moral will is much more "worthy of" a perfectly intelligent and good Creator than the mere purpose to make us happy at all costs. It is true that we cannot directly *see* in the little we actually know of the world's history that this purpose is in fact attained, but at least we must *believe*, if we really believe that the world is intelligible, that if we could see the whole history of ourselves and our world "as God sees it", we *should* find that, in spite of appearances, this purpose is attained. If it is not, the universe is in the end more or less irrational and unintelligible, and to make that admission is as fatal to science as it can be to morality.

Granted then that the history of the universe has a purpose, and an intelligent moral purpose, it fairly follows that the course of that history treats a *person* as having the intrinsic and absolute right to respect, the moral value which morality declares to be inherent in him. A world in which beings have the conscious ideal of intelligent and moral personality before them, and so capable of being educated into such personality, only made their appearance to vanish again into impersonality would be as truly an irrational and unintelligible world as one in which the law of contradiction or the laws of arithmetic did not hold good. Either would be, quite literally, a "mad world". But if the real world which is "the home of all of us" is intelligible, because the creature of an intelligent Creator, it is not a mad world but a sane one. We may reasonably believe, then, that it is what Keats called it, a "vale of soul-making", and that it really provides for each of us the opportunity, if we will avail ourselves of it, of achieving the ideal which morality sets before us, growth into a full and complete personality in conscious possession of itself and all that ministers to it, no longer subject to disruptive influences from its own unexplored "consciousness", or from a hostile "environment". The real world, that is, provides for all of us the opportunity of attaining "eternal" life. So much, though no more, seems to me clearly implied in principle when we commit ourselves to the primary act of faith in rationality which is made by the simplest distinctions between *true* and *false, right* and *wrong*. If we are unwilling to make this act of faith, we should in consistency abstain from so much as asking a single question about the course of events or the path either of duty or of prudence, since we no longer have the right to regard one answer to such a question as more or less true than any other.

(It is not, of course, meant by speaking thus of faith in reason to encourage any spirit of hasty and superficial dogmatism. A sane man knows well enough that there are an infinity of questions which he cannot expect to decide confidently by a simple appeal to "his reason". The facts which are needed as a basis for decision may be unascertainable to him; even when they are ascertainable, he knows only too well how unreasonable what he calls "his own reason" can be, how often he overlooks some fundamental link in the "chain of reasoning", or takes for granted as "evident" something which is not evident, and is perhaps actually false. What he is really putting his faith in is not "his" reason, but the "reasonableness of things", which, we have argued, implies the reality of a perfect reason which is not his own. His confidence is simply that the whole universe, natural and moral, is such that to a definite and intelligible question there is a definite and intelligible answer, though it may often enough be an answer which it is not, and never may be, in his power to give.)

So far we have been concerned with an attempt to indicate the state of mind in which a thoughtful and dispassionate inquirer, with an intelligent eye for all the relevant facts and no *parti pris,* would approach the specifically Christian teaching about the hope which "remains for the people of God". He could come to the examination, if we are not mistaken, with a hope of his own for a life to come of a certain quality, a hope based ultimately on certain convictions (call them philosophical, or religious, or both, as you please) about the existence and nature of the Creator. The question for him would be whether the more specific anticipations of Christianity harmonize or conflict with these "anticipations of reason". That issue we are now to consider, always, of course, remembering that the specific assertions of Christianity are made as matter of faith, and that there is no question of *demonstrating* their truth.

8

HUMAN DESTINY*

*Nicolas Berdyaev (1874–1948), though
a Marxist for a time, eventually returned
to the Russian Orthodox Church. Exiled
from Russia in 1922, he became widely
known as an existentialist interpreter
of Christian theology, and founder of a
school called the Academy of Religious
Philosophy. His writings include:* The
Meaning of History, The Destiny of
Man, Spirit and Reality, *and* The
Beginning and The End.

Nicolas Berdyaev

ORDINARY systems of philosophical ethics do not deal with the problems of eschatology. If they treat of immortality, they do so without going deep into the question of death but discuss it chiefly in connection with man's moral responsibility, rewards and punishments, or, at best, with the need of satisfying his longing for infinity. The conception of immortality has been defended on the ground of naturalistic metaphysics and the idea of the soul as a substance. It left completely untouched the problem of death, so fundamental for the religious and especially for the Christian consciousness. Death is a problem not only for metaphysics but also for ontological ethics. Thinkers like Kierkegaard and Heidegger recognize this. It also acquires a central significance in Freud. It is the problem of death, inseverably connected with that of time, that has a primary significance; the problem of immortality is secondary, and as a rule it has been wrongly formulated. The very word "immortality" is inexact and implies a rejection of the mysterious fact of death. The question of the immortality of the soul forms part of a metaphysic that is utterly out of date. Death is the most profound and significant fact of life, raising the least of mortals above the mean commonplaces of life. The fact of death alone gives true depth to the question as to the meaning of life. Life in this world has meaning just because there is death; if there were no death in our world, life would be meaningless. The meaning is

* From Nicolas Berdyaev, *The Destiny of Man*, tr. by Natalie Duddington. Reprinted by permission of Geoffrey Bles, Ltd.

bound up with the end. If there were no end, i.e. if life in our world continued for ever, there would be no meaning in it. Meaning lies beyond the confines of this limited world, and the discovery of meaning presupposes an end here. It is remarkable that although men rightly feel the horror of death and rightly regard it as the supreme evil, they are bound to connect with it the final discovery of meaning. Death—the supreme horror and evil—proves to be the only way out of the "bad time" into eternity; immortal and eternal life prove to be only attainable through death. Man's last hope is connected with death, which manifests so clearly the power of evil in the world. This is the greatest paradox of death. According to the Christian religion death is the result of sin and is the last enemy, the supreme evil which must be conquered. And at the same time in our sinful world death is a blessing and a value. It inspires us with terror not merely because it is an evil, but because the depth and the greatness of it shatter our everyday world and exceed the powers accumulated by us in this life to meet this world's requirements. Spiritual enlightenment and an extraordinary intensity of spiritual life are needed to give us a right attitude towards death. Plato was right in teaching that philosophy was the practice of death. The only trouble is that philosophy as such does not know how one ought to die and how to conquer death. The philosophic doctrine of immortality does not show the way.

It might be said that ethics at its highest is concerned with death rather than with life, for death manifests the depth of life and reveals the end, which alone gives meaning to life. Life is noble only because it contains death, an end which testifies that man is destined to another and a higher life. Life would be low and meaningless if there were no death and no end.

Meaning is never revealed in an endless time; it is to be found in eternity. But there is an abyss between life in time and life in eternity, and it can only be bridged by death and the horror of final severance. When this world is apprehended as self-sufficient, completed and closed in, everything in it appears meaningless because everything is transitory and corruptible—i.e. death and mortality in this world is just what makes it meaningless. This is one-half of the truth seen from a narrow and limited point of view. Heidegger is right in saying that the herd-mentality (*das Man*) is insensitive to the anguish of death.[1] It feels merely a low fear of death as of that which makes life meaningless. But there is another half of the truth, concealed from the ordinary point of view. Death

[1] See *Sein und Zeit*, chapter *Das mögliche Ganzsein des Daseins und das Sein zum Tode.*

not merely makes life senseless and corruptible: it is also a sign, coming from the depths, of there being a higher meaning in life. Not base fear but horror and anguish which death inspires in us prove that we belong not only to the surface but to the depths as well, not only to temporal life but also to eternity. While we are in time, eternity both attracts and horrifies us. We feel horror and anguish not only because all that we hold dear dies and comes to an end, but still more because we are conscious of a yawning abyss between time and eternity. Horror and anguish at having to cross the abyss contain at the same time a hope that the final meaning shall be revealed and realized. Death holds hope as well as horror for man, though he does not always recognize this or call it by an appropriate name. The meaning that comes from the other world is like a scorching flame to us and demands that we should pass through death. Death is not only a biological and psychological fact but a spiritual fact as well. *The meaning of death is that there can be no eternity in time and that an endless temporal series would be meaningless.*

But death is a manifestation of life, it is found on this side of life and is life's reaction to its own demand for an end in time. Death cannot be understood merely as the last moment of life followed either by non-being or by existence in the world beyond. Death is an event embracing the whole of life. Our existence is full of death and dying. Life is perpetual dying, experiencing the end in everything, a continual judgment passed by eternity upon time. Life is a constant struggle against death and a partial dying of the human body and the human soul. Death within life is due to the impossibility of embracing the fullness of being, either in time or in space. Time and space are death-dealing, they give rise to disruptions which are a partial experience of death. When, in time, human feelings die and disappear, this is an experience of death. When, in space, we part with a person, a house, a town, a garden, an animal, and have the feeling that we may never see them again, this is an experience of death. The anguish of every parting, of every severance in time and space, is the experience of death. I remember what anguish I felt as a boy at every parting. It was so all-embracing that I lived through mortal anguish at the thought of never seeing again the face of a stranger I met, the town I happened to pass through, the room in which I spent a few days, a tree or a dog I saw. This was, of course, an experience of death within life.

Space and time cannot enfold the wholeness of being but condemn us to severances and separations, and death always triumphs in life; it testifies that meaning is to be found in eternity and in fullness of being, that in the life in which meaning will triumph there shall be no parting, no dying, no corruption of human thoughts and feelings. We die not only in our own death but in the death of those we love. We have in life the experience of death, though not the final experience of it. And we cannot be reconciled to death—to the death neither of human beings nor of animals, plants, things or houses. The striving for eternity of all that exists is the essence of life. And yet eternity is reached only by passing through death, and death is the destiny of everything that exists in this world. The higher and more complex a being is, the more it is threatened with death. Mountains live longer than men, although their life is less complex and lower in quality; Mont Blanc appears to be more immortal than a saint or a genius. Things are comparatively more stable than living beings.

Death has a positive significance, but at the same time it is the most terrible and the only evil. Every kind of evil in the last resort means death. Murder, hatred, malice, depravity, envy, vengeance are death and seeds of death. Death is at the bottom of every evil passion. Pride, greed, ambition are deadly in their results. There is no other evil in the world except death and killing. Death is the evil result of sin. A sinless life would be immortal and eternal. Death is a denial of eternity and therein lies its ontological evil, its hostility to existence, its striving to reduce creation to non-being. Death resists God's creation of the world and is a return to the original non-being. Death wants to free the creature by bringing it back to primeval freedom that preceded the creation of the world. There is but one way out for the creature which in its sin resists God's conception of it—death. Death is a negative testimony to God's power and to the Divine meaning manifested in the meaningless world. It might be said that the world would carry out its godless plan of an endless (but not eternal) life if there were no God; but since God exists, that plan is not realizable and ends in death. The Son of God, the Redeemer and Saviour, absolutely sinless and holy, had to accept death, and thereby He sanctified death. Hence the double attitude of Christianity to death. Christ has destroyed death by His death. His voluntary death, due to the evil of the world, is a blessing and a supreme value. In worshipping the cross we worship death which gives us freedom and victory. In order to rise again we must die. Through the cross death is transfigured and leads us to resurrection and to life. The whole of this world must be made to pass through death and crucifixion, else it cannot attain resurrection and eternity.

If death is accepted as a part of the mystery of life, it is not final and has not the last word. Rebellion against death in our world is rebellion against God. But at the same time we must wage a heroic struggle against death, conquer it as the last evil and pluck out its sting. The work of Christ in the world is in the first instance victory over death and preparation for resurrection and eternity. The good is life, power, fullness and eternity of life. Death proves to be the greatest paradox in the world, which cannot be understood rationally. Death is folly that has become commonplace. The consciousness that death is an ordinary everyday occurrence has dulled our sense of its being irrational and paradoxical. The last achievement of the rationalized herd-mind is to try to forget about death altogether, to conceal it, to bury the dead as unobtrusively as possible. It is the very opposite of the spirit expressed in the Christian prayer "ever to remember death". In this respect modern civilized people are incomparably inferior to the ancient Egyptians.

The paradox of death takes an aesthetic as well as a moral form. Death is hideous, the acme of hideousness, it is dissolution, the loss of all image and form, the triumph of the lower elements of the material world. But at the same time death is beautiful, it ennobles the least of mortals and raises him to the level of the greatest, it overcomes the ugliness of the mean and the commonplace. There is a moment when the face of the dead is more beautiful and harmonious than it had been in life. Ugly, evil feelings pass away and disappear in the presence of death. Death, the greatest of evils, is more noble than life in this world. The beauty and charm of the past depends upon the ennobling influence of death. It is death that purifies the past and puts upon it the seal of eternity. Death brings with it not only dissolution but purification as well. Nothing perishable, spoiled and corruptible can stand the test of death—only the eternal can. Terrible as it is to admit it, the significance of life is bound up with death and is only revealed in the face of death. Man's moral worth is manifested in the test of death, which abounds in life itself.

But at the same time struggle with death in the name of eternal life is man's main task. The fundamental principle of ethics may be formulated as follows: act so as to conquer death and affirm everywhere, in everything and in relation to all, eternal and immortal life. It is base to forget the death of a single living being and to be reconciled to it. The death of the least and most miserable creature is unendurable, and if it is irremediable, the world cannot be accepted and justified. All and everything must be raised to eternal life. This means that the principle of eternal being must be affirmed in relation to human beings, animals, plants and even inanimate things. Man must always and in everything be a giver of life and radiate creative vital energy. Love for all that lives, for every creature, rising above the love for abstract ideas, means struggle against death in the name of eternal life. Christ's love for the world and for man is victory over the powers of death and the gift of abundant life.

Asceticism means struggle with death and with the mortal elements within oneself. Struggle with death in the name of eternal life demands such an attitude to oneself and to other people as though both I and they were on the point of death. Such is the moral significance of death in the world. Conquer the low animal fear of death, but always have a spiritual fear of it, a holy terror before its mystery. It was death that first gave man the idea of the supernatural. Enemies of religion such as Epicurus thought they disproved it by showing that it originated in the fear of death. But they will never succeed in disproving the truth that in the fear of death, in the holy terror of it, man comes into touch with the deepest mystery of being and that death contains a revelation. The moral paradox of life and of death can be expressed by a moral imperative: treat the living as though they were dying and the dead as though they were alive, i.e. always remember death as the mystery of life and always affirm eternal life both in life and in death.

.　　.　　.

ETHICS must be eschatological. The question of death and immortality is fundamental to a personalistic ethics and confronts us in every act and every expression of life. Insensitiveness to death and forgetfulness of it, so characteristic of the nineteenth and twentieth century ethics, mean insensitiveness to personality and to its eternal destiny, as well as insensitiveness to the destiny of the world as a whole. Strictly speaking, a system of ethics which does not make death its central problem has no value and is lacking in depth and earnestness. Although it deals with judgments and valuations, it forgets about the final judgment and valuation, i.e. about the Last Judgment. Ethics must be framed not with a prospect to happiness in an unending life here, but in view of an inevitable death and victory over death, of resurrection and eternal life. Creative ethics calls us not to the creation of temporary, transitory and corruptible goods and values which help us to forget death, the end, and the Last Judgment, but to the creation of eternal, permanent, immortal goods and values which further the victory of eternity and prepare man for the end.

Eschatological ethics does not by any means imply a passive renunciation of creative activity. Passive apocalyptic moods are a thing of the past, they are a sign of decadence and an escape from life. On the contrary, eschatological ethics based upon apocalyptic experience demands an unprecedented intensity of human creativeness and activity. We must not passively await in horror and anguish the impending end and the death of human personality and the world. Man is called actively to struggle with the deadly forces of evil and creatively to prepare for the coming of the Kingdom of God. Christ's second coming presupposes intense creative activity on our part, preparing both mankind and the world for the end. The end itself depends upon man's creative activity and is determined by the positive results of the cosmic process. We must not passively wait for the Kingdom of Christ, any more than for that of antichrist, but must actively and creatively struggle against the latter and prepare for the Kingdom of God which is taken by force.

To regard apocalyptic prophecies with passive resignation means to interpret them in a naturalistic sense, to rationalize them and deny the mysterious combination of Divine Providence and human freedom. It is equally wrong to take up a passive and fatalistic attitude to one's own death, to the death of personality, and regard it as a predetermined natural fact. We must accept death freely and with an enlightened mind, and not rebel against it; but this free and enlightened acceptance of death is a creative activity of the spirit. There is a false activity which rebels against death and refuses to accept it. It leads to unendurable suffering. But there is also the true activity which is the victory of eternity over death. An active spirit does not really fear death—only a passive spirit does. An active spirit experiences an infinitely greater fear and terror than that of death—the fear of hell and eternal torments. It lives through its own eternity; death exists for it not inwardly but merely as an external fact. It experiences terror at the thought of its eternal destiny and of the judgment which is in eternity.

We come here upon a psychological paradox which to many people is unknown and incomprehensible. An active spirit which has a direct inward experience of being eternal and indestructible may, so far from fearing death, actually desire it and envy those who do not believe in immortality and are convinced that death is the end. It is a mistake to imagine that the so-called faith in immortality is always comforting and that those who have it are in a privileged and enviable position. Faith in immortality is a comfort and makes life less hard, but it is also a source of terror and of an overwhelming responsibility. Those who are convinced that there is no immortality know nothing of this responsibility. It would be more correct to say that the unbelievers rather than the believers make life easy for themselves. Unbelief in immortality is suspicious just because it is so easy and comforting; the unbelievers comfort themselves with the thought that in eternity there will be no judgment of meaning over their meaningless lives. The extreme, unendurable terror is not the terror of death but of judgment and of hell. It does not exist for the unbelievers, only the believers know it. A passive spirit seldom experiences it, but an active one experiences it with particular intensity, because it is apt to connect its destiny, and consequently judgment and the possibility of hell, with its own creative efforts. The problem of death inevitably leads to that of hell. Victory over death is not the last and final victory. Victory over death is too much concerned with time. The last, final and ultimate victory is victory over hell. It is wholly concerned with eternity. Still more fundamental than the task of raising the dead, preached by Feodorov, is the task of conquering hell and freeing from it all who are suffering "eternal" torments. The final task, which ethics is bound to set us in the end, is creative liberation of all beings from the temporal and "eternal" torments of hell. If this task is not realized, the Kingdom of God cannot be realized either.

Additional Readings

A. On Immortality

HOCKING, W. E., *The Meaning of God in Human Experience.*

MARITAIN, J., *The Range of Reason.*

PRINGLE-PATTISON, SETH, *The Idea of Immortality.*

B. On Miracles

HUME, DAVID, *An Enquiry Concerning Human Understanding,* Section X.

LEWIS, C. S., *Miracles.*

TENNANT, F. R., *Miracle and Its Philosophical Presuppositions.*

C. General views on the relations of God and the world.

ALEXANDER, S., *Space, Time and Deity.*

BRIGHTMAN, E. S., *The Problem of God.*

GHOSE, AUROBINDO, *The Life Divine.*

HEGEL, G. W. F., *Lectures on the Philosophy of Religion.*

HEIM, KARL, *God Transcendent.*

MARCEL, G., *Homo Viator.*

NIEBUHR, REINHOLD, *The Nature and Destiny of Man.*

RADHAKRISHNAN, S., and C. A. MOORE (eds.), *A Source Book in Indian Philosophy.*

SCHELER, MAX, *On the Eternal in Man.*

TEILHARD DE CHARDIN, PIERRE, *The Phenomenon of Man.*

TEMPLE, WM., *Nature, Man and God.*

URBAN, W. M., *Humanity and Deity.*

Absolute, 56, 150
Absolute dependence, and
    religion, 167-179
Absolute values, 407
Absolutely necessary being,
    97
Absolutism, 34-35, 45
Actions, and beliefs, 20-23
Activity, and piety, 174
Adultery, 113
Advaita, doctrine of, 221
Agnostics, 4, 28
Agreement, 9
Aiken, Professor, and evil,
    293
All-bliss, 273, 277
All-consciousness, 273
Analogy, 346-355, 356-376
    of attribution, 373
    of proportionality, 364-376
    subtypes, 362
Analysis, 5-7
Animation, 428-430
Anthropomorphism, 134,135,
    138, 468
Anti-Christ, 89
Argument, and intellect, 18
    moral, 113-120
    and reason, 65
    religious experience,180-
    191
    teleological, 128-142
Aristotle, 107, 110, 111, 340,
    422, 456, 473
    Prime Mover, 415-416
Aristotelianism, 10, 103
    and Hegelianism, 36
Atheism, 5
Atonement, 213
Attribution, analogy of, 373
Avoidable option, 28
Ayer, A.J., 344-345
    "Religion and Nonsense,"
    377-384

Being, absolutely necessary,
    97
    encompassing of, 422-423

infinite of, 150
not a real predicate, 100
omnipotence, 147
supreme, 102
Vedanta concept of, 270
Belief(s), and actions, 20-23
    and divine truth, 12-14
    effects of, on will, 23-24
    ethics of, 20-26
    false, 25
    not private matter, 23
    physical sciences and,
    30-31
    religion and, 48
Believing, will to, 27-46
Berdyaev, Nicholas, 5
    "Human Destiny," 485-492
Berkeley, George, 128, 250,
    398, 405
Bible, as revelation, 203-214
    and theology, 77
Blasphemy, 49
Blessedness, 341
Bradley, F.H., 367-368
Brahman, 262, 263
Broad, C.D., 368, 395
    "The Argument for Religi-
    ous Experience,"180-192
Brunner, Emil, 5
    "The Bible and Revela-
    tion," 203-204
    "Philosophy and Theolo-
    gy," 73-79
Buddha, 220, 226
Buddhism, 220
    Mayhayana, 423, 435
    mind-only doctrine, 435-439
    Theravada, 220
    Vijnanavada, 413, 440
    See also Zen Buddhism
Butler, Joseph, 117-118
    "Moral Conscience and
    Divine Law," 318-331

Campbell, Charles A., 39
    "Reason and Revelation,"
    61-72
Causality, 86

Cause, and God's existence, 104

Chance, 146
and evidence, 121-123
necessity and, 147

Character, 309
Confucian concept, 314-316

Chinese philosophy, 467-462

Christ, concept of, and scientific knowledge, 70
God's reincarnation in, 76-77
as Reedemer, 213

Christian philosophy, 89-90

Christian piety, 169

Christian theology, and the Bible, 77

Christianity, 415, 465
and God's existence, 469
monotheistic, 218
Pascal's wager, 29-30
Protestant philosophy, 74-75
psychiatric perspective, 166
Roman Catholic philosophy, 10, 103, 346

Chu Hsi, 458

Chuang Chou, 461

Chung Yung, 458

Church, Alonzo, 345

Clifford, W.K., 4, 8, 31, 32, 35, 37-38, 40
"The Ethics of Belief," 20-26

Cognitive approach to reality, 80-81

Cognitivism, 6-7

Comfort, in truth, 60

Competence, and religion, 61-62

Conceptions, network of, and systems, 1-2

Conditional imperative, 336

Conflict, theology/philosophy, 88-90

Confucianism, 309-317, 413, 448, 457-458
See also Neo-Confucianism

Conscience, concept of, 341
moral, and divine law, 318-331

Conscious-Being, 272

Conscious-Force, 270

Consciousness, 144, 147-149, 423-427
of God, 464
of object and self, 463

Consciousness-Force, 149

Consciousness-Only principle, 440

Convergence, 88

Conversion, Buddhist concept, 234

Conviction(s), influence on, 33
nonintellectual influence, 33
sincerity in, 20-21

Copleston, Frederick, 345
"Positivism and Religion," 385-389

Creation, and Book of Genesis, 68

Credulity, harm in, 25

Criteria, of reason, 65-67

Criticism, right of, 54

Cruelty, Vedanta concept of, 266

Culture, and moral imperative, 332

Curiosity, 480

●

Dead option, 28

Death, 485-492
and immortality, 473
paradox of, 486, 489
significance of, 488

Deity, identified with objects, 381
and soul, 138

Delight, Vedanta concept of, 269, 270

Delusions, 185

Dependence, 175
and religion, 167-179

Descartes, René, 36, 391

Destiny, 485-492

Detachment, 85

Dionysius, 349

Discovery, and revelation, 192

Discursive intellect, 3

Dishonesty, 25

Divergence, 88

Divine law, and moral, conscience, 318-331

Divine life, devotion to, 57
worth of, 54-55
Divine reality, 92-94
Divine thought, 57
Divine truth, 10
and beliefs, 12-14
Divinity, 147
Dogmatism, 171
Double-truth hypothesis, 72
Doubt, and philosophic truth,
54
and religious experience,
188-189
Doubting, fear of, 24, 26

●

Eckhart, Meister, 229
Ego, 174
Electric energy, 145
Emerson, Ralph Waldo, 41
Empirical existence, 423-427
Empiricism, 3-4, 34-35
Encompassing, modes of,
422-427, 428-430
Energy, 144, 145
inconscient, 147
material, 148
and matter, 149
of Nature, 146
Enlightenment, and Buddhism,
227-231
Epicureans, 340
Error, avoidance of, 37-38
and truth, 43
Ethics, 20-26, 335
eschatological, 490
language of, 406
and religion, 240-241
Vedanta concept of, 266-267
Evidence, chances and
121-123
insufficient, 23, 26
objective, 35
and sensation, 123-127
Evil, 58-59, 240
death and, 488
fallacious solution, 283-292
and good(ness), 242-249,
282-292
moral, 294
and omnipotence, 280-292
physical, 294
problem of, 250-261

solution to, 281-282
Vedanta solution to, 262-
279
Excellence, 346-347
Existence, in Chinese
philosophy, 452
concept of, 100
explanation of, 2
qualitative, 466
Vedanta concept of, 262-
263, 271-272
Existence-Consciousness-
Bliss, 263, 279
Existentialism, 4-5, 80, 87,
151-156, 332, 358, 485
Existenz, 428-430
and reason, 433-434
Experience, 134
vulgar, 138
See also Religious exper-
ience

●

Fact, faith creating, 42
Faith, 8-9, 171
adopted, 27
and creating fact, 42
investigation by reason,
14-15
presence of God, 201
and revelation, 213-214
and truth, 17-18
Farmer, Herbert H., 4
"Revelation," 192-202
Feeling, philosophy and, 49
and piety, 167-173
Feuerbach, Ludwig, 413-414
"God as a Projection,"
463-472
Flew, A., 308
on free will, 295-296, 297
Force, Vedanta concept of,
263, 279
Forced option, 28
religion as, 43
Forgiveness, 211
Four Wisdoms, 441
Fox, George, vision of cre-
ation, 68, 70
Free will, defense of, 293-308
Freedom, feeling of, 175,
176-177
Freethinking, 27

Freud, Sigmund, 485
Fung Yu-lan, 3, 413
  "Human Life and the Tran-
    scendent," 447-462

●

Gandhi, Mahatma, 222
Genesis, and creation, 68
Generation, 140-141
Gentiles, 321
Genuine option, 28
Ghose, Aurobindo, 3, 94
  "Difficulties of Both
    Naturalism and Theism,"
    143-150
  "The Vedanta Solution to
    the Problem of Evil,"
    262-279
God, assurance of presence,
    180
  consciousness of, 464
  dependence upon, 177-179
  and evil, 240-241
  existence of, 154-155, 380,
    407, 469
  existence, proofs of, 103-
    112
  existential approach to, 358
  and faith, 201
  and good and evil, 183
  image of, man as, 349
  incarnation of, in Christ,
    76-77
  knowledge of, 198
  language about, 408
  and man, 412-414
  man's relation to, 466
  names for, 420
  nature of, 3
  object of reason, 62-63
  omnipotence of, 100, 280,
    297-206
  Pascal's wager, 29-30
  as person, 206
  personal, 36
  primacy of, 36
  as a projection, 463-472
  and reason, 151
  reincarnation of, 76-77
  rejection of, 12
  revelation of, 197, 199-
    200, 204-205, 206
  self-revelation, 64
  and the senses, 121-127
  as truth, 57
  and the universe, 412-414
  Vedanta concept of, 264
  Will of, 337
  and the world, 412-414,
    415-420
Godhead, 221, 224
Gods, Homeric, 470-471
Good(ness), Confucian con-
    cept, 311-313
  and evil, 242-249, 283-292
  personal, 112-120
Great Whole, in Chinese
    philosophy, 454-455
Guilt, 211

●

Happiness, 120, 341
Hartmann, Nicolai, 82
Hegel, George Wilhelm
    Friedrich, 81, 458
Hegelianism, 62, 80, 332, 463
  and Aristotelianism, 36
Heidegger, Martin, 5, 485
Hempel, Carl, 345
Hilary, St., 19
Hinduism, Vedanta philoso-
    phy of, 143, 262
Hinton, Charles H., 36
History, biblicists and, 83
Hodgson, S.H., 32
Homeric gods, 470-471
Honesty, 25
Hsuan-Tsang, 413
  "Answer to Objections,"
    440-446
Huang Li-chou, 459
Human behavior, 400
Human consciousness, and
    revelation, 78-79
Human life, 447-462
Human nature, 326
Human spirit, basic func-
    tions, 332
Humanity, worship of, 50
Hume, David, 4, 93, 215
  "Difficulties of the Teleo-
    logical Argument," 128-
    142
  "The Problem of Evil,"
    250-261
Huxley, 31, 33

Hypothesis, 28-29
  double truth, 72
  religious, 42-46

●

Idealism, 2-3
Ignorance, Buddha and,
    226-227
  Buddhist concept, 231-232
Immoral religion, 48
Immortality, 473-485
Impersonalism, 3
Incarnation, doctrine of, 222
Inconscience, 147
Infinite, 55-56, 59, 143
  of Being/Power, 150
  perfection in, 58
Infinite life, 56
Infinite mind, 59
Infinite reason, 56
Infinite spirit, 57
Infinite thought, 55
Infinite truth, 55
Infinite worth, 51
Inquiry, 20-26
  method and spirit of, 52
Insight, intellectual, 31-33
  religious, 63
Instinct, 141
Intellect, and contrary ar-
    gument, 18
  degree of, 11
  rational/discursive, 3
Intellectual concepts, 3
Intellectual insight, 31-33
Intelligence, 147
  abstractions of, 143
Intolerance, 114
Irrationality, 106, 122, 215

●

James, William, 4, 8
  "The Will to Believe,"
    27-46
Jaspers, Karl, 85n
  "The Encompassing,"
    421-434
Jeans, Sir James, 477
Jews, dispersal of, 415
Jones, John R., 400, 409
Judaic-Alexandrian philoso-
    phy, 415
Judgment, 98-99

Kant, Immanuel, 3, 49, 93,
    215, 336, 390, 398,
    479
  "The Impossibility of an
    Ontological Proof," 97-
    102
Karma, 265
Kierkegaard, Soren, 4, 5, 93-
    94, 431, 485
  "The Uselessness of
    Proofs," 151-152
Knowledge, and concept of
    Christ, 70
  Confucian concept, 316-
    317
  deficiency in, 12
  religion, 379
  and revelation, 69, 196,
    208-210
  spectator theory of, 15
Ku Ting-ling, 457

●

La Place, Pierre, 47
Language, religious, 390-411
Lao-tzu, 4, 160
  "Mystical Union," 161-164
Last Judgment, 490
Law of right, validity of, 119
Learning, Confucian con-
    cept, 309n, 310-311
Levity, and reason, 16-17
Leibnitz, Gottfried Wilhelm,
    81, 102
Life, 144
  and death, 487
Li-Hsüeh See Neo-
    Confucianism
Lila, 272
Living option, 28
Locke, John, 128, 250
Logic, 447
  Hegelian, 81
  philosophical, 421-435
  and religious hypothesis,
    44
Logical criteria, of reason,
    65, 66-67, 68-72
Logical positivism, 344
Logical predicate, 100
Love, Confucian concept,
    309-317
  divine attribute, 468

Mackie, J.L., 241
"Evil and Omnipotence,"
280-292
and free will, 293, 297,
299, 300, 301
McCloskey, H.J., 293, 307
Mahayana Buddhism, 413, 435
Man, God and, 412-414
and God's image, 349
natural power, 327
rationality of, 478-479
relationship to God,
466-467
relationship to himself, 465
self-existent, 467
and the world, 412-414
Manicheans, rejection of
God, 12
Mascall, E.L., 345
"Analogy," 356-376
Material nature, Vedanta
concept, 466
Matter, 114
energy and, 149
inconscience in, 269, 470
involution in, 149
Maya, 270-271, 272
Meaning, and meaningful-
ness, 344-345
revelation of, 486
Meaningfulness, 344-345
Mechanical necessity, 147-149
Mephistophelian skepticism,
41
Metaphysical concepts, 398
Metaphysical theology, de-
nial of, 409
Metaphysics, 224-225
concept of, 406-407
Mind, 146-147
doctrine of, 435-439
and inconscience, 149
Vedanta concept of, 269
Miracles, 222
Mohammed, 17
Mohammedanism, 415
Momentous option, 28, 42
Monism, 219
Monistic explanation, 2
Monotheism, 218-219, 223
Mood, and reverence, 53
Moore, G.E., 395, 400

Moral act, 333, 335
Moral argument, 113-120
Moral code, religion and, 48,
50-51
Moral commands, 337
Moral conscience, divine
law, 318-331
Moral, evil, 294, 299
Moral imperative, religious
dimension of, 332-342
Moral insight, 57
Moral philosophy, and re-
ligion, 71
Moral questions, 40
Morality, 113-120
and moral imperative, 332
Morals, theory of, 335
Motion, and God's existence,
103-104, 105-106
Mysticism, 4, 160, 382, 383
Mystics, 183
Mystery, God as, 206-207

Natural law, worship of, 50
Natural science, and religi-
on, 382
Natural supremacy, 321
Natural theology, 4, 215
Naturalism, difficulties of,
143-150
Naturalists, 137
Nature, 141, 144, 321
energy of, 147
explanation of, 149
Vedanta concept of, 266
worship of, 50
Nature-process, 144-145
Necessary truth, 6
Necessity, 146
and chance, 147
and God's existence, 104
Neo-Confucianism, 309-317,
413, 447-462
Neo-Hegelian idealism, 47
Neo-Kantian school, 82
Neo-orthodoxy, 203-214
Nescience, 147
New Testament, and revela-
tion, 203-204
Newman, Cardinal, 33
Nietzsche, Friedrich Wilhelm,
89, 338, 431

Nirvana, 47, 220
Noncognitivism, 6-7
Nonexistence, 143
Nonsensory empiricism, 4

●

Occult, 136
Old Testament, and revelation, 203, 204
Omnipotence, 100, 147-148
  evil and, 280-292
  paradox of, 284, 290
  and sovereignty, 291-292
One-Existence, 278
Ontological argument, 95-96
Ontological proof, 97-102
Opinions, empiricist tendency, 34
  passional nature and, 38-40
  psychology of, 29-31
Option, kinds of, 28
Orthodoxy, scholastic, 34-35
Otto, Rudolf, 217, 218

●

Panlogism, 62
Pantheism, 219
Paradox of omnipotence, 284, 290
Pascal, Blaise, 29-30, 33, 40
Pascal's wager, 29-30
Passion, 21
Passional nature, 33
  and opinion, 38-40
Penido, 357, 371n
Perception, 123
Perfection, 347-348, 349-351
Peripatetics, 136
Person, defined, 478
Personal being, 3
Personalism, 3
Personality, 479-480
Phenomenology, 217
Philosopher, and theologian, 85-90
  and truth of religion, 74
Philosophical analysis, 216
Philosophical faith, 85n
Philosophical logic, 421-434
Philosophical truth, and doubt, 54

Philosophy, 8-9
  and feeling, 49
  indefinable, 80-81
  Judaic-Alexandrian, 415
  moral, and religion, 71
  Protestant, 74-75
  and reality, 82-83
  and religion, 47-60, 80-90
  religious, 51
  Roman Catholic church, 10, 103, 146
  and theology, 73-79, 89-90
  theoretic, 51
  understanding, 81-82
Physical evil, 294
Physical sciences, and belief, 30-31
Piety, Christian, 169
  expressions of, 173-179
  and feeling, 167-173
  and self-consciousness, 167-173, 173-179
Plantinga, Alvin, 241
  "The Free Will Defense," 293-308
Plato, 82, 107, 109, 340, 413, 456, 473, 478
  and Infinite Truth, 55
Pleasure, vedanta concept, 174-177
Polytheism, 218-219
Pope, Alexander, 282
Positivism, and religion, 385-389
Possibility, and God's existence, 104
Power, and beliefs, 24
  infinite of, 150
Pragmatism, 4, 27
Prakriti, 272
Predicate, logical, 100
Prejudice, 21, 49
  and inquiry, 52
  systematical, 138
  vulgar, 138
Prestige, and opinions, 32
Prime Mover, Aristotle and, 415-416
Processes, in Chinese philosophy, 452
Projection, God as a, 463-472

Proofs, uselessness of, 151–156
Proportionality, analogy of, 364–376
Protestant liberalism, 167
Protestant philosophy, 74–75
Psychiatry, Christian perspective, 165–166
Psychological fact, 397
Psychological criteria, of reason, 65–66
Psychology, 338–339
Pure consciousness, 413, 435
Purusha, 272

Ramsey, Ian T., 7, 345
  "The Possibility of Theology," 390–411
Rasa, 277–278
Rational intellect, 3
Rational objectivity, 5
Rationalism, 2–3, 62
Rationalist epistemology, 2
Rationality, 136, 478–479
  and thought, 57–58
Rationalizing, 20
Reality, 394–395
  cognitive approach, 40, 81
  concept of, 100
  and idealism, 2
  and philosophy, 82–83
  and theology, 83
Reason, 8–9, 134, 140–141
  argument and, 65
  competence of, 61
  criteria of, 65–67
  defined, 61–62
  encompassing, 430–433
  and existenz, 433–434
  finiteness of, 465
  and God, 62–63, 151
  infinite, 56
  investigation of, 14–15
  and levity, 16–17
  and religions, 215–225
  and revelation, 61–72, 199, 215–225
  truth and, 17–18, 18–19
  and unknown, 155
Receptivity, 175
Reciprocity, 175

Redemption, 213
Reid, Thomas, 36
Religion, and action, 48
  and belief, 48
  consciousness of God, 464
  defines duty, 50
  and dependence, 167–179
  differences in, 42–46
  ethics in, 21, 240–241
  immoral, 48
  makeup of, 48
  and moral code, 48, 50–51
  and moral imperative, 332
  and moral philosophy, 71
  as nonsense, 377–384
  and philosophy, 47–60, 80–90
  positivism and, 385–389
  primary concern, 69–70
  and reason, 215–225
  and revelation, 215–225
  truth of, 74
Religious beliefs, evaluating, 8
Religious experience, 63, 158–160, 165–166, 383
  argument from, 180–191
  doubts, 188–189
  existence of, 182
  genetic and causal conditions, 181
  interpretation of, 184
  psychological analysis, 181
  and revelation, 196
  validity, 189–191
Religious hypothesis, 42–46
Religious insight, 63
Religious knowledge, 379
Religious language, 390–411
Religious philosophy, 51
Revelation, 158–160, 192–202
  Bible and, 203–214
  concept of, 200
  and death, 473
  defined, 205
  and faith, 213–214
  and human consciousness, 78–79
  meaning of, 208, 211, 212
  negative presupposition, 207

Revelation (cont.)
  and reason, 61-72, 199
  and religions, 215-225
  religious usage, 195-197
  and scientific knowledge,
    69
  theological idea of, 203
Reverence, 53
Rig Veda, 269
Right, law of, 119
Roman Catholics, 33
  concept of good and evil,
    242-249
  philosophy of, 10, 103, 346
  St. Thomas Aquinas, 90
Royce, Josiah, 3
  "Religion and Philosophy,"
    47-60
Russell, Lord, 368, 395, 407,
    415

●

Sacerdotalism, 33
St. Anselm, 3
  "The Ontological Argu-
    ment," 95-96
St. Augustine, 3, 463
  "Good and Evil," 242-249
  infinite faith, 55
St. Paul, 320, 321
St. Theresa, 183
St. Thomas Aquinas, 3, 4, 9,
    90, 93, 183, 345, 362-363
  "Analogy," 346-355
  "Five Proofs of God's Ex-
    istence," 103-112
  "Reason and Faith," 10-19
Sankara, 262
Sarte, Jean-Paul, 5
Satan, 307
Satori, 160, 226-238
  defined, 233
Schelling, Friedrich Wilhelm,
    422
Schleiermacher, Friedrich, 4
  "Religion as the Feeling of
    Absolute Dependence,"
    167-179
Science, theology and, 80
Secrétan, Charles, 42
Sects, errors in, 17
Self-consciousness, and piety,
    167-173, 173-179

Self-revelation, by God, 64
Semantics, 390-411
Sensation, and evidence,
    123-127
Senses, and God, 121-127
Serenity, Confucian con-
    cept, 312-313
Shao Yung, 461
Sheng Chao, 458
Simonides, 15
Skepticism, 43, 52
  mephistophelian, 41
  pyrrhonistic, 35
Smart, Ninian, 7
  "Revelation, Reason and
    Religions," 215-225
Sociology, 338-339
Socrates, 72, 109, 155
Soul, of world, Deity as, 138
  Vedanta concept, 272
Sovereignty, and omnipotence,
    291-292
Space, 143
Space-time, 143
"Spectator" theory of knowl-
    edge, 5
Spencer, Herbert, 39
Spinoza, Baruch, 47, 152-153,
    391, 419
Spirit, 423-427
  and existenz, 429-430
Spititual orientation, 66
Stephen, Fitz-James, 45
Stevenson, Robert Louis, 115
Strawson, P.F., 391-392
Substance, creation, 149
Supermind, 150
Supreme being, 102
Suzuki, D.T., "Satori," 226-
    239
System, defined, 1-2
Systematic classification, ar-
    bitrary, 2
Systematical prejudices, 138

●

Taoism, 161, 448, 455-457
  and Confucianism, 312
Taylor, A.E., 3, 93, 414
  "Immortality," 473-
    485
  "The Moral Argument,"
    113-120

Taylor, Richard, "From the Senses to God," 121-127
Teleological argument, 128-142
Theism, 138, 221-222
  difficulties of, 143-150
  and evil, 294
Theologian, and philosopher, 85-90
Theology, 390-411
  abstract nature of, 78
  aim, 75-76
  Bible and, 77
  Christian, 74-75
  metaphysics, 409
  and philosophy, 73-79, 89-90
  and reality, 93
  and science, 80
Theoretic philosophy, 51
Theravada Buddhism, 220
Things, in Chinese philosophy, 451
  graduation of, in God's existence, 105
Thinking, 49
Thought, 146
  rationality and, 57-58
Tillich, Paul, 5
  "Philosophy and Religion," 80-90
  "The Religious Dimension of the Moral Imperative," 332-342
Time, 143
Time-eternity, 150
Tournier, Paul, 160
  "A Religious Experience," 165-166
Transcendence, 427-428
  and existenz, 429
Transcendent, 447-472
Transcendentalism, 360, 413-414
Trinity, doctrine of, 224
Trivial option, 28
Truth, 146
  comfort in, 60
  and error, 43
  and faith, 17-18
  God as, 57
  infinite, 55

  knowledge of, 37-38
  and personal actions, 42
  philosophic, and doubt, 54
  and reason, 17-18, 18-19
  of religion, 74
  revelation of, 10
  revelation of, and discovery, 192
  reverence for, 25
  reverence obscures, 53
  Vedanta concept of, 273-274
  verification of, 39-40
Truth-consciousness, 150
Twelvefold Change of Causation, 227

•

Ultimate arbiter, 64
Understanding, Buddhist concept, 228
Universal will, 57
Universe, God and, 412-414
Unknown, reason and, 155

•

Vaisnavism, 222
Values, relationship of, 338
Vasubandhu, 3, 413, 440
  "The Mind-Only Doctrine," 435-439
Vedanta, 143
  and evil, solution to, 262-279
Vegetation, 141
Verification, of truth, 39-40
Vijnanavada Buddhism, 413, 440
Virtue, 351-352
Vulgar experience, 138
Vulgar prejudice, 138

•

Want Yang-ming, 460
  "The Ideal of Love," 309-317
Ward, Wilfrid, 39
Weismann, 39
Whitehead, Alfred North, 3, 391, 398, 412-413
  "God and the World," 415-420
Will, 146-147
  Vedanta concept of, 266
Will of God, 337

Wittgenstein, Ludwig, 400–401, 403
World, God and, 412–414, 415–420
  governance of, and God's existence, 105, 112
  man's, 334
  men and, 412–414
  and transcendence, 427–428
World-Existence, Vedanta concept of, 272

Worship, types of, 50
Worth, comparison of, 40
  infinite, 51

●

Yogis, Eastern, 186

●

Zen Buddhism, 160, 226–238
  essence of, 232–233
  and Satori, 235–238
Zöllner, Hohann Karl, 36